780.922 B/600S

THE
Goossens

A Musical Century

THE
Goossens

A Musical Century

CAROLE ROSEN

ANDRE DEUTSCH

First published in 1993 by
André Deutsch Ltd
106 Great Russell Street
London WC1B 3LJ

ISBN 0 233 98833 5

Cataloguing-in-Publication data available for this title
from the British Library

Typeset by Falcon Graphic Art Ltd
Wallington, Surrey
Printed by WSOY, Finland

In memory of my parents,
Sadie and Albert,
with love and gratitude.

CONTENTS

LIST OF ILLUSTRATIONS

33. Bumps, Léon and Eugene, Wetherby Gardens, 1935.

63. Sidonie's official retirement from the BBC Symphony Orchestra, 1981.
64. Sidonie, Léon and Marie, New South Wales House, London, 1983.
65. Marie with Tony and Jean, Buckingham Palace, March 1984.
66. Marie, Sidonie and Dame Eva Turner, Wigmore Hall, June, 1987.

We would like to express our gratitude to the following for allowing us to reproduce the above photographs:

Sidonie Goossens, Goossens Archives, Mrs Benedicta Cooksey, Mrs Anne Goossens Obermer, Jennie Goossens, Tony Laurence, James Brown, Thorne Printing & Publishing, the Royal Opera House, Covent Garden, The British Library and The Britten-Pears Library.

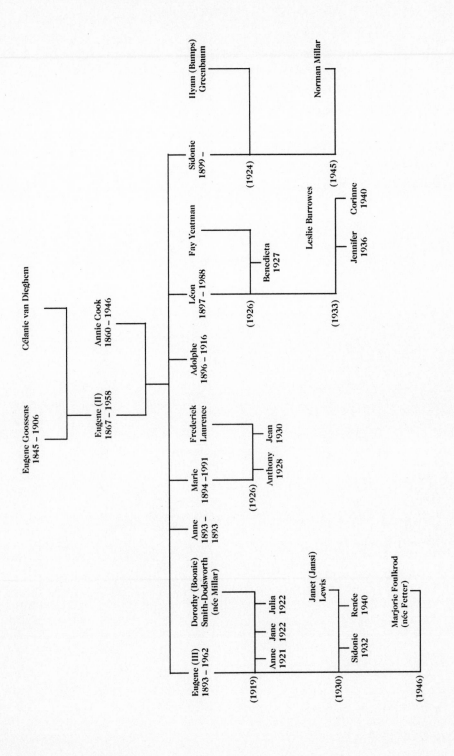

Eugene Goossens
1845 – 1906

Célanie van Dieghem

Eugène (II)
1867 – 1958

Annie Cook
1860 – 1946

Eugène (III)
1893 – 1962

Dorothy (Boonie)
Smith-Dodsworth
(née Millar)

Anne
1893 –
1893

Marie
1894 –1991

Frederick
Laurence

Adolphe
1896 – 1916

Léon
1897 – 1988

Fay Yeatman

Sidonie
1899 –

Ilyann (Bumps)
Greenbaum

(1919)

Anne
1921

Jane
1922

Julia
1922

Janet (Jansi)
Lewis

(1926)

Anthony
1928

Jean
1930

(1926)

Benedicta
1927

Leslie Burrowes

(1924)

Norman Millar

(1930)

Sidonie
1932

Renée
1940

Marjorie Foulkrod
(née Fetter)

(1933)

Jennifer
1936

Corinne
1940

(1945)

(1946)

ACKNOWLEDGEMENTS

I first fell under the spell of the Goossens family on 24th February 1987 when I went with Piers Plowright to meet Marie Goossens, intensified by our visit to Sidonie Goossens the following day. We were preparing a Radio 4 feature programme, 'Playing from the Heart' which was broadcast on Christmas Day, 1988. I was then commissioned by George Darby to write an article on Marie and Sidonie for the *Telegraph* weekend magazine of 19th August 1989. Four days later I received a letter from T G Rosenthal, Managing Director of André Deutsch Ltd.: 'I greatly enjoyed your piece in the *Telegraph* . . . and I have a feeling that there might be a book in all this.'

Writing the book has been a pleasure and a privilege; it would not have been possible without the trust and co-operation of three generations of the Goossens family, their colleagues and their friends. In the first instance I would like to thank Sidonie for the many hours in which she has entranced me with her total recall of British musical life over the last ninety years and for allowing me access to her father's diaries, meticulously kept from 1916. In these he recorded not only his own professional conducting engagements but the careers of his children Eugene, Marie, Léon and Sidonie and the letters that they wrote home.

I must also thank Pamela Main for her generosity in allowing me the freedom of Sir Eugene Goossens' Archives and the use of copyright material which they contain. She has provided a catalogue of his compositions and Raymond Cooke (Léon's son-in-law) has compiled a unique and comprehensive discography of the family.

I would like to thank the following members of the Goossens family for their interviews:

The late Marie Goossens;
Anne Goossens Obermer, Sidonie Goossens Scott, Renée Goossens, (three of Sir Eugene's daughters);
Anthony Laurence (Marie's son);

Christopher Laurence, Andrew Laurence, Patrick Laurence (three of Marie's grandsons);
Benedicta Cooksey, Jennie Goossens, Corinne Lopez (Léon's daughters);
The late Major Norman Millar, Pamela Laurence, Raymond Cooke and Brian Spink (related by marriage).

Much to my regret I was not able to meet Lady Marjorie Goossens (Sir Eugene's widow) because of her ill health but appreciated her letter wishing me 'good luck with your book'.
My thanks to Jean Meek for allowing me to use extracts from her mother Marie Goossens' book *Life on a Harp String*.

I would also like to thank the following friends and colleagues of members of the family for their personal reminiscences:

Lady Aberdeen, Denis ApIvor, Felix Aprahamian, Malcolm Arnold, Norah Barnaby, Dene Barnett, Richard Bonynge, Pierre Boulez, Dallas Bower, Gwydion Brooke, James Brown, Jack Brymer, Natalie Caine, Tana Constable, Kenneth Corden, David Cox, Donald Davison, Dame Ninette de Valois, Bela Dekany, John Dennison, Vivien Dixon, Roy Douglas, The late the Hon. Mrs Earle, Margaret Eliot, Sir Keith Falkner, the late Norman Feasey, Raymond Fisher (Fischer), Helen Gaskill, Bernard Greenbaum, Kyla Greenbaum, Lord and Lady Harewood, Margaret Harrison, Cecil James, Maureen Jones, Wilfrid Josephs, the late Brenton Langbein, Mabel Lovering, Sir Charles and Lady Mackerras, David McKenna, Yehudi Menuhin, Lady Olivier, Geoffrey Parsons, Monica Pudney, Denby Richards, Robin Richards (The Colonnade Hotel), Tessa Robbins, Evelyn Rothwell (Lady Barbirolli), Edwin Roxburgh, Lionel Salter, Richard Temple Savage, Hans Hubert Schönzler, Malcolm Smith, Paul Strang, Dame Joan Sutherland, Barry Tuckwell, Ursula Vaughan Williams, Lady Walton, Elizabeth Welch, Howard Williams, Malcolm Williamson, Irene Wilson.

Rochester

My thanks to William L Cahn, Vincent A Lenti (Eastman School of Music), Milan Yanich, Philip West and Mordecai Lurie for their help with my research into Eugene Goossens' tenure in Rochester (1923 – 31).

Acknowledgements

Cincinnati

I am indebted to Judith Smith for allowing me access to her research for her doctoral thesis: *The Instrumental Chamber Music of Sir Eugene Goossens*, University of Cincinnati, 1987. I would also like to thank Donald Gibson and Tom Martin for their help and Mrs Stephen F Dana, Philip Dreyfuss and Siegfried Humphreys for their memories of Eugene Goossens' years in Cincinnati (1931 – 47).

Australia

I would like to thank the following people for the information they gave me during my visit to Australia in January – February 1992 concerning Sir Eugene Goossens' tenure there (1947 – 56):

Ron Best, Geoffrey Chard, Valerie Collins-Varga, Roger Covell, Kaye and George Dreyfus, Ken Ellis, George Fleischer, Rosemary Florrimell (Grainger Museum), Howard Gellman, Clifford Goodchild, Stephen Hall, Dame Joan Hammond, Geoffrey Harris (ABC Archives), Donald Hazlewood, John Hopkins, Gerald Krug, Ruth Llewellyn, Donald MacDonald, David Malouf, Lloyd Martin, Tom Mead, Ann Menzies, Helen Mills, Thérèse Radic, Stephen Ramsay, Stuart Revill, Mrs Ritchie, Phillip Sametz, Ronald Smart, Mollie Stuart, Ken Tribe, Mary Valentine, Eva Wagner, Albert and Betty Wargren, Phyllis Williams.

My greatest debt in Australia was to Ruth and Warren Jones for their kindness and hospitality during my three weeks as their house guest in Sydney.

I am also indebted for the help I received in my Australian research from:

Suzanne Altman, Overseas Information Branch Office, Department of Foreign Affairs and Trade, Sydney; Barry O Jones MP, Federal Member for Labor (Australian House of Representatives); Russell B Nash; Jim Payne, Counsellor Public Affairs, Australian High Commission (London) and David Salter (ABC TV).

I flew to Sydney via Hong Kong as the guest of Cathay Pacific Airways; Leading Hotels of the World enabled me to enjoy the hospitality of the Peninsula Hotel, Hong Kong, the Regent, Sydney and Rockman's Regency, Melbourne.

Many professional friends and colleagues have most generously given of their time and expertise to help me in writing this book. I would like to thank in the first instance:

John Ward for his invaluable research on the careers of Aynsley, Harriet, Alice and Annie Cook, the Payne Family and the early history of the Carl Rosa Opera Company; Colin Osman for information on George Davison; Malcolm Rudland for correspondence relating to the friendship between Eugene Goossens and Philip Heseltine; Margaret Campbell, Nick McCarty and Paul Mitchell for convincing me that light did exist at the end of the tunnel.
  My gratitude is also due to:

Stephen Banfield, John Bird, William Blezard, Alan Brazier, Lionel Carley, Stewart Craggs, Oliver Davies, Lewis Foreman, the late Andrew Guyatt, Rhonda Hammond, Alan Jefferson, Lyndon Jenkins, Michael Kennedy, Beresford King-Smith, Mark Le Fanu (The Society of Authors), Stephen Lloyd, Sheila Macrindle, Oliver Neighbour, Anthony Payne, Tom Peel (Carl Rosa Trust), Christine Shuttleworth, Lionel Simmonds and Peter Todd.

I would like to express my thanks to the following organisations for help in my archival research:

The Australian Broadcasting Corporation; Boosey & Hawkes Ltd.; The British Library; National Sound Archive; Newspaper Library, Colindale; BBC Research Library; BBC Written Archives Centre, Caversham; The Britten – Pears Library; Chesters Music; The Grainger Museum, Melbourne; The Mitchell Library, Sydney; The Royal College of Music; The Royal Opera House, Covent Garden.

My thanks to Zoë Ross for her painstaking editing and long-suffering resilience.

In conclusion this history of the Goossens family would not have been possible without the patience and support of my family, in particular my late mother Sadie Rosen, my children Matthew and Katy and my husband Peter Marsh.

Carole Rosen, July 1993.

Heritage

The Goossens family are renowned for their musical genius, their generosity of spirit and their longevity. Shortly before her ninety-fifth birthday in August 1989, Marie Goossens formulated a new explanation for the extraordinary flowering of musical gifts in the five children of Eugene Goossens II, conductor of the Carl Rosa Opera Company, and contralto Annie Cook.[1] Generations of their father's family in Bruges had absorbed the reverberation of Gothic church bells, ringing every quarter. In London, parallel generations of their mother's family had lived under the benign influence of Bow Bells. As the unborn child absorbs the rhythms of its mother's body, so Marie felt that those bells ringing on either side of the English Channel had nurtured the innate musicality of the Goossens and the Cooks and blended together in a unique harmony.

Goossens or Hoossens is a common Flemish Catholic name in Belgium and Southern Holland. The family house of Jean-Baptiste Maria Goossens, born on 30th May 1793, still stands in the medieval centre of Bruges in the shadow of Notre Dame at the corner of Rue du Vieux Bourg. Starting as a jeweller's apprentice, Jean-Baptiste eventually became a master silversmith and married a couturière. They had three children, Adolphe (1841), Eugene (1845) and Julia. To supplement the family income, the Choir Master of Notre Dame became their lodger and discovered that the two little boys had beautiful voices. They graduated from Bruges to the Brussels Conservatoire, founded after Belgian Independence with the celebrated Belgian musicologist François-Joseph Fétis as Director from 1833. He was still Director in 1870 when he presented Eugene with a Certificate of Excellence for harmony, counterpoint and composition together with First Prize for violin playing. As Fétis was by then eighty-five and within a few months of his death, the brilliant young musician only briefly benefited from his personal tuition.

Eugene quickly fell in love and married a pretty young dancer, Célanie van Dieghem, with whom he toured France and Belgium. On one of these tours their only child Eugene II was born, on 28th January 1867, in Bordeaux. Most ambitious artists graduated from the provincial backwater of Belgium to the wider horizons of Paris but to Eugene I, London seemed to offer more possibilities for a solo violin career.

Throughout the winter of 1873 he looked in vain for concert engagements at St James's Hall or the Portman Rooms and was lucky to eke out an existence playing at the Cremorne Pleasure Gardens in Chelsea. Many times the young couple must have condemned London as an inhospitable Philistine city and questioned their decision to turn their backs on the family home in Bruges, leaving their small son there at the College of St Louis. One day the miracle happened. Singer and manager, Kate Santley, found herself without a conductor for her London operetta season and was recommended by the Management of Covent Garden Opera House to an ambitious Belgian violinist playing in their orchestra. Eugene found himself for the first time baton in hand, conducting Offenbach's *La Périchole* and *Orpheus in the Underworld*, together with forgotten Victorian favourites like *La Marjolaine* and *Olivette*. He received the princely salary of £20 a week.

Despite his inexperience, he knew that the secret of a conductor's success is a thorough knowledge of the scores and the London critics were soon praising the expertise of the boyish foreigner. By 1878 Rupert D'Oyly Carte was engaging him at the Opéra Comique in the Strand where, on 25th May, he conducted a gala performance of *H.M.S. Pinafore* in the presence of Her Majesty Queen Victoria. So much for Gilbert and Sullivan's conviction that only an Englishman could handle the subtleties of the Savoy Operas!

The pretty little ballerina, now known as Madame Sidonie, appeared at the Alhambra Theatre in 1882 as leading dancer in *La Belle Hélène* and *Geneviève de Brabant*. In August 1882 her husband made his debut as second conductor with the Carl

2

Rosa Opera Company, sharing the baton with John Pew. After performances in Blackpool and Dublin, in September he conducted *Lady in White* (Boïeldieu's *La Dame Blanche*), Gounod's *Faust* and Donizetti's *Lucrezia Borgia* in Manchester. Madame Sidonie choreographed ballets for their new productions including *Nordisa*, a three act opera commissioned from Frederick Corder. *Nordisa* was a great box office success, thanks not so much to its musical merit as to the introduction of an avalanche in the last act, one of Rosa's most sensational stage achievements. The *Liverpool Daily Post* commented after its premiere on 16th January 1887: 'To Mr Goossens, who has been mainly instrumental in creating the delightful exposition of the work the thanks of all concerned are due. Also to Mme Goossens (better known as Mme Sidonie) to whose artistic invention the charming and characteristic ballets are attributable.'

Both her husband and son were devastated by her premature death in Liverpool in the early spring of 1889 at the age of forty-two but her name and her legend live on in the family. According to her granddaughter Marie, 'she was so tiny that her wedding ring wouldn't go on my finger and I'm small enough!'

The Carl Rosa Opera Company was to play a leading role in the careers of all three generations of conductors bearing the name Eugene Goossens. Carl Rosa was a German violinist, a gifted combination of musician and businessman, who married a leading operatic soprano, Euphrosyne Parepa in 1867.[2] He started his first touring English opera company in 1872 with a season at the Prince's Theatre in Manchester and later moved his headquarters to the Royal Court Theatre in Liverpool. Three main elements contributed to Rosa's success as an operatic impresario: his ability to spot embryonic operatic stars, often from his own chorus; his inspired programme-building, mixing the old with the new, the classical with the popular; and his introduction of subscription tickets at all prices in the house. This system, the mainstay of provincial opera houses in Germany and Eastern Europe, has never found general favour with English managements.

In 1889, when Rosa died, Eugene I became principal conductor. During his ten years with the company he conducted

3

over forty operas including the first English performances of *Tannhäuser* (14th February 1882 at Her Majesty's Theatre) and Massenet's *Manon*. Sir Henry Wood was later to tell Marie Goossens that he had learnt *Carmen* from her grandfather. Eugene I was a strict disciplinarian, respected for his absolute musical integrity but feared as an irascible martinet. He would often rehearse the orchestra all day until a couple of hours before the evening performance and his players condemned him as tyrannical and unfeeling.

There are many anecdotes of his lack of patience with temperamental opera singers. On one occasion a Russian bass engaged to sing Mephistopheles in Gounod's *Faust* failed to attend rehearsals. He sang so inaccurately in performance that Goossens called him for a solo rehearsal the following day. The singer lost his temper at being corrected so many times and informed Goossens that he had sung the role in all the great capitals of the world, under many famous conductors, 'whose boots, *you* Mr Goossens are not fit to brush'. As a final comment he added that he knew the part upside down. 'Ah,' replied Goossens, with unruffled equanimity, 'that is quite evident, but we don't play it that way in this company!'

In May 1892 an Edinburgh journalist, reviewing the Carl Rosa season at the Lyceum Theatre, profiled their Director of Music:

> Mr Goossens' chief characteristics as a conductor are a fine discernment of a composer's meaning and intention, a keen sense of musical proportion, skill in controlling the forces under his baton and unfaltering decision. No one who has listened to a performance of, say Mascagni's *Cavalleria Rusticana*, can have failed to observe that it is the reading of a musician who is not only exceptionally gifted in grasping the dramatic contents of the work he has in hand, but who can induce those under his leadership to convey his interpretation with fidelity and sympathy. Personally Mr Goossens is the most modest and unassuming of men, and he commands the respect and esteem of all connected with the company.

By the time young Eugene II had completed his education in Bruges it was evident that he was destined to follow his father as a professional musician. At the age of sixteen he was enrolled for the obligatory five-year course at the Brussels Conservatoire, studying the violin with Cornelis and composition with Gevaert.[3] (François Auguste Gevaert, had been Musical Director of the Paris Opera and his prolific operatic output included a version of Sir Walter Scott's *Quentin Durward*.) Despite his French birth and later long residence in England, he was to retain his Belgian nationality with great pride throughout his life.

After he graduated in 1889, his father appointed him leader of the second violins in the Carl Rosa Orchestra and tested him out for the post of assistant conductor with a performance of *The Marriage of Figaro*. Even his newly acquired beard could not disguise the young man's nervousness and lack of authority over stage and orchestra. A more imaginative parent and musical director might have given him the opportunity to learn the conductor's craft by working within the company, but Eugene I decided that the 22-year-old needed a further course of theoretical study. He tried to enrol him in Massenet's composition class at the Paris Conservatoire through the good offices of the Company's leading soprano, Madame Marie Roze. Massenet explained that a foreign student had to spend at least one year as an observer and even after that would not be eligible to compete for the Prix de Rome. Instead he was sent to the Royal Academy of Music in London, for a two-year course in Harmony, Counterpoint and Composition under Frederick Corder.

As a dutiful Victorian son, Eugene II accepted his father's decision but, after working with a professional opera company, he found it very difficult to resume his studies. A further complication was that he had fallen in love with a young contralto in the Carl Rosa. He tried to drown his sorrows in the composition of a *De Profundis*, but halfway through he became seriously ill and never completed the work. His father relented and re-engaged him with the Carl Rosa Orchestra. On 18th January 1892 Eugene Goossens married Annie Cook, daughter of Aynsley Cook, the Company's leading bass baritone. Her name features on Carl Rosa programmes singing supporting contralto roles, including the Nurse in *Romeo and Juliet*, Mercedes in *Carmen*, Marcellina in *The Marriage of Figaro* and Martha in *Faust*.

The voice was not of star quality but she was a very competent musician, able to cope with operatic emergencies. One such occasion was when Marion Burton, principal contralto playing the travesti role of Lazarillo in *Maritana*, was suddenly taken ill just as the curtain was going up for the second act. Eugene II recalled the incident fifty years later among family reminiscences he was collecting for his son's autobiography *Overture and Beginners*. 'Mum was in the wings. She was almost pushed on the stage, and a score of the opera placed in her hands. She sang the opening song, "Alas those chimes" and the whole of that scene in her day walking out costume. She had a great success!'[4]

The marriage was destined to be a long and happy one, although the relationship between father of the groom and father of the bride continued to be stormy. Cook was an irrepressible extrovert and Goossens, a dictatorial conductor, objected to the liberties he took in some of the most popular roles of his repertoire. Singing in *Zampa* (Hérold), *Fra Diavolo* (Auber) or *Peter the Shipwright* (Lortzing's *Zar und Zimmermann*), he would accuse him of sacrificing musical exactitude for comic effect. The contrasting temperaments of the two were prominent at a Royal Command Performance of Donizetti's *Daughter of the Regiment* at Balmoral on 8th November 1892. Goossens took exception to the interfering theatre manager who insisted that the orchestra must play in a window recess at the side of the State Rooms to avoid having their backs to or sitting in front of the Queen. Only the timely arrival of Her Majesty saved Goossens from physical attack by the irate and inebriated flunkey.

During the performance Queen Victoria was much taken with Cook's hilarious portrayal of Sergeant Sulpice and afterwards asked him whether he had sung in Balfe's opera *Satanella* at Covent Garden in 1858. When Cook confirmed the accuracy of the Royal memory, the Queen rewarded him with her special scarf pin. A sidelight on Royal protocol comes from a contemporary newspaper account which mentions that the Queen rose with the rest of the assemblage when the National Anthem was sung!

The Cook family originally hailed from Yorkshire and claimed descent from the famous explorer. With a tradition of silver-beating rather than music, there are interesting parallels with the Goossens family. Aynsley's father was a City silversmith with a family business established on Cornhill at the beginning of the nineteenth century. The boy made his name as a gifted soprano engaged as 'Chamber Singer' to the Marquis of Anglesey, a hero of Waterloo, and sang solos in concerts conducted by Mendelssohn and Spohr. At the age of fourteen, Anglesey sent him to Würzburg to study with Professor Lutz, laying the foundation for further ramifications of kinship. Lutz's son Meyer, who later found fame as a composer and conductor at the Gaiety Theatre, emigrated to England and married Aynsley's sister, Elizabeth. The youngest sister, Alice, sang soubrette roles with the D'Oyly Carte Company before joining the Gaiety Theatre. A full page illustration in the *Lancashire Figaro and Northern Charivari* of February 1881 shows her as Prince Plenteous in *Cinderella* at the Prince's Theatre, Manchester, a very early example of the Principal Boy in pantomime. Her opulent curves and excellent legs are shown to surprisingly modern advantage in a fringed thigh-length tunic over fleshings and high-heeled boots. She lived to a ripe old age until 7th April 1938, revered by the Goossens children as 'Sporty Aunty Al'.

Aynsley made his bass debut, somewhat incongruously for a teenager, as the Commendatore in *Don Giovanni*. He sang for five years in provincial Bavarian opera houses and then returned to England where he created his most famous role of Devilshoof in Balfe's *Bohemian Girl*. In *The Golden Age of Opera*, the critic Hermann Klein describes his performance in Norwich in the 1870s. 'Could the finest operatic ballet ever yield a more exciting climax than the breathless dance of Devilshoof as executed by Aynsley . . . twisting, twirling, gyrating around the stage a dozen times or more, until everyone grew giddy save the leaping gipsy himself?' Devilshoof abducts a child and Annie Cook made her operatic debut at the age of five in her father's arms. One night the escape scene nearly ended in tragedy as the operatic villain tripped on the high bridge and narrowly missed plummeting to the stage with his small daughter.

Annie had been born on 28th June 1860, when Aynsley and his young wife Harriet were on tour in the United States with a company run by Lucy Escott, and she often used to tell her children and grandchildren how her parents were forced to flee back to England by the outbreak of the American Civil War.

Before the advent of Carl Rosa and the foundation of an efficiently managed and financially viable touring opera company with reasonable standards of performance, life for an English opera singer was a precarious hand to mouth affair. Aynsley and Harriet survived the rapid turnover of English opera companies at Covent Garden and in the provinces such as J H Tully's National Opera Company, the Pyne and Harrison English Opera Company and Loveday's Grand English Opera. The companies had different names but the same singers. Aynsley was also engaged with international artists including the great Italian prima donna Guilia Grisi; he sang her father, the Archdruid Oroveso in *Norma* at the Theatre Royal, Liverpool. His real forte however was in buffo parts. He made the role of General Boom his own, in the English premiere of Offenbach's *The Grand Duchess of Gerolstein* at Covent Garden in 1867 and brought the house down every night with his bravura display of bombast and swagger.

Harriet came from a famous theatrical dynasty of comics and clowns, the Paynes. They were renowned for their Harlequinade in the Christmas Pantomime: 'the best panto-mimists I ever saw,' wrote Albert Douglass, recalling them in *Dick Whittington* at the Standard Theatre, Shoreditch. 'The father, W H Payne, was Pantaloon; Madame Esta, the mother Columbine; Harry, the Clown; and Fred the most versatile of all, the Harlequin.'[5] Harry Payne became the highlight of the annual Drury Lane pantomime, crawling round the edge of the Dress Circle on all fours, distributing buns to his young audience who were reduced to hysterical laughter.

The Paynes often appeared on the same bill as the Cooks, providing a ballet after the opera as well as taking comic roles in opéra bouffe like Offenbach's *Bluebeard*. This was another great success at the Standard. Harriet inherited her family's comic gifts and her portrayal of Queen Clementina amused the show's leading soprano, Emily Soldene. 'She was so funny and when the King was naughty carried him off, kicking in her arms like a baby.'[6]

Later she mainly sang supporting contralto roles such as

Martha in *Faust* or Inez in *Il Trovatore*. Surprisingly for the rest of her repertoire, she is credited with the highly dramatic and vocally taxing soprano role of Donna Elvira in *Don Giovanni*, as performed by John Russell's Covent Garden Company at the Theatre Royal, Manchester in June 1865.

Both singers were members of Madame Parepa Rosa's Grand English Opera Company touring the USA in 1871. 'As for Aynsley Cook,' the diva reported from Washington DC (writing to her friend and mentor Wilhelm Ganz on 15th November), 'he is excellent and sings the Duke in *Lucrezia Borgia* splendidly and as Leporello is immense. He is also one of the clever English artistes who for *bread* has had to adapt himself to do anything to earn for his family!'[7] Despite the great Chicago fire and the near loss of all their possessions, the tour continued successfully into the New Year. Cook was credited with 'an earnest and conscientious performance' as the Count in *Il Trovatore* in Boston on 25th January 1872. Their last performance was a 'Farewell Gala Night' at the Academy of Music in New York on 30th April 1872. Harriet sang the Gypsy Queen from Act II of *The Bohemian Girl* with Aynsley as Devilshoof.

Aynsley built up a large and varied repertoire. He sang nineteen roles in the 1876 – 7 Carl Rosa season, ranging from Daland in *The Flying Dutchman* and Rocco in *Fidelio*, to Rosembourg in Balfe's *Siege of Rochelle* and Don Japhet in Adam's *Giralda*. One of his most popular successes was as Falstaff in Nicolai's *The Merry Wives of Windsor*. The *Illustrated Sporting and Dramatic News* of 23rd February 1878 devoted a double page illustration to the brilliant final scene of the Fat Knight's discomfiture in Windsor Forest playing every night for two weeks at the Adelphi Theatre, although he was criticised for being unrealistically obese.

Tiring of the vagaries of operatic life, for a time Harriet and Aynsley ran the historic Jack Straw's Castle on Hampstead Heath, which Charles Dickens had earlier praised as a hostelry where he might obtain 'a red hot chop for dinner and a glass of good wine.'[8] They were too generous to charge their friends for food and drink, lost all their profits and were forced back to touring. Harriet was still a beautiful woman and in 1879

9

made an undying impression on one Liverpool opera buff as the Marble Image of Alice de Manfredi in *Zampa*. 'It was absolutely thrilling and no one in the vast audience was more stirred than I when the Image raised a denunciatory hand!'[9]

She died suddenly in 1880 at the age of forty-eight when Aynsley was on tour in America.

Aynsley returned to the Rosa after Harriet's death. By the time he was interviewed by the *Liverpool Review* in January 1889, he was regarded as the doyen of English opera singers. The profession would appear to have changed little in the last hundred years; journalists still ask the same questions and singers give the same replies!

'Nowadays when anyone can do nothing else they try if they have a voice. You'd be astonished if you knew how many people imagine they can sing. Years ago it was considered a great privilege to be allowed a chance of trying one's voice before an impresario, but now we have people coming to the Rosa company to try their voices nearly every day by Mr Goossens, and as a rule these aspirants are not fit even for the chorus, much less for leading parts.'

To the interviewer's question as to prospects, Cook comments on improved conditions in the profession. 'Many of our leading artists are receiving the most handsome pay and as I use the word artist just let me say that the voice alone does not make a fine singer. A fine singer must have the ear, the brain, the soul of an artist.'

'I have spoken with singers very often about the question of diet. Have you any ideas on that subject, Mr Cook?' prompts the interviewer.

'My idea is that a singer must keep his brain clear. If his brain is out of order it throws his stomach out of gear, and that upsets his voice. A singer should dine at three in the afternoon and take simply a cup of tea about six. He should never use stimulants during singing. After his business is over then let him take what stimulants he likes, but never during the day.'

Cook astonishes the interviewer with his repertoire of ninety-two operas. 'But how on earth do you manage to remember so many parts?' he asks.

'It is a special kind of memory, I suppose. Use and experience have a great deal to do with it. The other day, I sang in *Maritana* and *Faust* and had not looked at the scores since first studying the parts nearly twenty years ago, but I managed them perfectly well.'

Despite his affability Mr Cook has to prepare for his evening performance and is anxious to bring the interview to a close, but the interviewer insists on one last question. 'Now before I go just tell me if you have any hobbies. I suppose singers are like other mortals in that respect?'

'Riding and driving are my hobby, but I am too heavy for riding and can't afford to drive. Still I have a hobby in my music. My ambition is to die in harness, which I hope will not happen until I am a centenarian.'

Alas this was an ambition he did not fulfil. He died on 16th February 1894, aged sixty-two. Zélie de Lussan, the French Canadian soprano, equally delectable as Carmen and the Daughter of the Regiment, placed on his grave a massive harp-shaped wreath of white and blue lilies with the inscription 'Farewell Sergeant Sulpice', the role he had so often sung with her. The large crowd of mourners, both Company members and Liverpool opera-lovers alike, found their eyes filled with tears.

Aynsley and Harriet Cook passed on their musical and theatrical heritage to their six children. Tom and Jim were choristers of the Chapel Royal Windsor and Queen Victoria is reputed to have described the singing of young Master Thomas Cook as the most beautiful she had ever heard in the Chapel. Later they both had successful careers as theatrical managers. Tom worked for the Kendals and Madge Kendal confided to young Eugene Goossens III at one of her tea parties in Portland Place before the First World War: 'I remember your uncle. Too good looking for a manager. My husband couldn't stand him. I liked him!'[10] Katie sang small roles with the Rosa and she and her sister Annie appeared together as two of the Pages in *Lohengrin*.

Annie Cook began her singing career at the age of fifteen in the chorus of the Italian Opera at Covent Garden. She never forgot the music or the words, which she learnt parrot fashion in phonetic sounds without meaning. She graduated to the Carl Rosa Company as a principal and fell in love with the conductor's handsome young son. She was seven years his senior and she was to remain the imperturbable bedrock of a remarkably stable marriage.

Liverpool

Opera companies frequently suffer from chronic financial instability and in the first seven years of his marriage, Eugene Goossens II was, in rapid succession, conductor of the Burns-Crotty Company, the Arthur Rousbey Company and the Moody-Manners Company. In 1899 he returned as Principal Conductor to the Carl Rosa Company, where he was to remain until the First World War. Part of his job was to train local musicians, selected to reinforce the skeleton touring orchestra. He recalled one small town where business was so bad that he was reduced to conducting *Cavalleria Rusticana* with five players: harmonium, cornet, horn and two violins. The next evening, for *Tannhäuser*, there was only enough money left to pay the harmonium and violins!

When in London, Eugene and Annie favoured 'professional apartments', as theatrical boarding houses preferred to be known, in the Camden Town area. On 26th May 1893, their twins were born in one such establishment in Rochester Square; the boy was christened Eugene to carry on the family tradition and the girl Sidonie Anne in memory of her grandmother. Both children were delicate; the girl died when she was six months old and the boy was later found to have a damaged heart valve (Mitral stenosis). The following year Marie was born on 11th August 1894 and, two years later, another boy Adolphe, on 28th April 1896.

From their infancy the Goossens children were surrounded by music and inured to the hardships of a wandering minstrel's existence. Every Sunday during the touring opera season, Eugene, Marie and Adolphe would be waiting on the platform with their mother for the train that would take them to the coming week's venue. They would be surrounded by thirteen packages including two large skips, a pram, a tin bath and a sewing machine. As much as Eugene enjoyed the company of his wife and children on tour, he was beginning to realise that the family needed a settled home and persuaded his father to let them live with him in Liverpool. Marie's earliest memories were of the three-storeyed Victorian house at No 2, Oxford Street and Grandpa's beautiful Bechstein grand piano, out of bounds to little fingers, in the drawing room.

Grandpa Goossens had decided to retire from the operatic world to try to establish a permanent symphony orchestra in Liverpool. The *Liverpool Mercury* commented on the first of four subscription concerts in the Philharmonic Hall, an all Wagner programme, on 1st November 1893: 'It is gratifying to note that, with the exception of about eight, all the instrumentalists are residents of Liverpool, and the quality of the performance, under Mr Goossens' direction, was such as to afford hope that the dream of a permanent orchestra in this city would sooner or later resolve itself into an accomplished fact.'

Alas for the critic's hope. The audience for the second concert was disappointingly small and Goossens decided to cancel the remaining two concerts and return the subscriptions. His grandson was to experience a similar disillusionment in London thirty years later.

He then devoted himself to choral conducting and teaching the violin and voice production. One of his pupils, Roland Foster, who later became a leading vocal expert in Australia, gives an insight into his method: 'The first principles of good singing as expounded by Monsieur Goossens – freedom, ease, mental instead of physical control and preference for quality rather than quantity – cannot immediately be comprehended and applied. Bearded, benign and dignified, he inspired me with confidence from the very start.'[1]

Victorian Liverpool prided itself on providing the most appreciative audiences for good singing; in 1894 Goossens founded his own Male Voice Choir in the Belgian style. He had been encouraged by the success of his brother Adolphe when he visited England in August 1892 with the *a cappella* Belgian Artisans' Choir. The Goossens Male Voice Choir was run as a co-operative with an entrance fee of half a crown and a small weekly subscription. Profits from concerts were invested and eventually divided amongst the members. Their 'Open Rehearsal' at the Picton Lecture Hall on 9th May 1895 received high praise: 'Precision of attack, fullness of tone, delicacy of *pianos*, and an amount of phrasing and expression almost too marked, testified what can be done by voices directed by patience, enthusiasm and musical ability.'[2]

They were soon filling the Philharmonic Hall for performances of virtuoso 'Vocal Symphonies' of a style unknown to British audiences such as *The Tomb of the Janissaries* by Limnander and *The Survivors of Tydal* by Hegar. In 1902 Goossens received further popular and critical acclaim when he conducted Elgar's *Te Deum and Benedictus*. The composer wrote to him: 'Have such excellent accounts of your Men's Chorus that I feel sure your choral society will be a great success. I wish all good things.'[3]

For his eldest grandson Eugene, choir rehearsals were a frightening occurrence. Twice a week he would be woken up in bed as the house shook with the combined voices of thirty tenors and basses massed in the long drawing room. During the day Annie Goossens was finding it increasingly difficult to keep her three small children quiet in the basement kitchen while singing lessons were in progress upstairs. The situation worsened on 12th June 1897 when Léon was born; his brother described him as 'the noisiest and worst-tempered baby I've ever heard'. A few months later Eugene II managed to move his wife and children into a home of their own, across the Mersey in Liscard, where he rented 78, Sea View Road. There, on 19th October 1899, the family was completed by the birth of Annie Sidonie, thereafter known by her second name.

Returning to Liscard in 1990, the only vestige of her childhood Sidonie could find was the tunnel to the firm white sands where the children used to play and have their lunch of meat pies peppered with sand. Marie remembered Liscard as a village still served by horse-drawn buses, with an open top where the driver sat, wrapped in a thick coat and blanket with a tarpaulin fastened down on either side of the bus to protect him from the rain. There was a similar tarpaulin to cover the passengers travelling outside, while inside the floor was covered with straw to soak up the water. Once a week Grandpa Goossens would arrive on the bus from the ferry to keep an eye on the children's progress while their father was away on tour. He sweetened his catechism with cakes for their tea. Sidonie would offer up her face for a farewell kiss; she still remembers the embarrassment of her grandfather fastidiously wiping her runny nose with his handkerchief before he would bestow it.

On Sunday the children would parade to church in white felt hats with white ribbons, white gloves and white broderie anglaise collars. These had to be specially starched and goffered before they could be attached to their navy coats of Sicilian cloth, thought to be far superior to alpaca. They sat on the front bench of St Alban's Catholic Church. 'Father would spread a clean white handkerchief so that when we knelt down our knees would not get dirty. He would open our prayer books at the correct page to follow the Mass closely; we had pictures too, which helped.'[4]

One of Marie's earliest musical memories was lying in bed in the darkness when the thick curtains of art serge were cosily drawn and the fire had burnt down in the grate, listening to her parents playing Grieg's Norwegian Dance no. 2 as a piano duet in the room below. The children's life revolved around the upstairs nursery, complete with rocking horse on which all five of them used to ride – one in the saddle, one on the tail, one at each end and one hanging on underneath.

In later life Eugene, Marie and Léon were all to publish memoirs, recalling their childhood with great vividness and affection. They remembered the fireworks to celebrate the Relief of Mafeking, the bells tolling for Queen Victoria's funeral, the monkeys stealing their mother's parasol at New Brighton Zoo, their father taking them on a Sunday to their first concerts in the Tower Ballroom and above all, the love and emotional security with which their parents surrounded them. The children always retained the French pronunciation of their names but within the family circle they were affectionately referred to as Zenny, Mor, Addie, Lee and Sid.

Being so close in age, five surviving children born within six years, the bonds between the exuberant brood were very strong. Marie had an especial affinity with Adolphe and assumed the role of little mother towards Léon and Sidonie. When she was seven, for a treat, the family joined their father in Manchester where the Carl Rosa was on tour. They stayed in the best professional apartments costing £3 a week and ate prunes for breakfast. 'Four each was the ration,' Marie recalled. 'I was so worried in case "the children" should swallow the stones. I could not concentrate on my own ration until I counted four stones on each plate.' Despite Marie's sobering influence, Adolphe and Léon disgraced themselves by breaking both the lid of the china soap dish of the washstand set and a window in the dining room.

Young Eugene was not one of the sparring partners. At the age of eight, despite his delicate health, he had been sent to Bruges to board at St Francis Xavier's School. His budding artist's eye was captivated by the beauty of the city and the Flemish landscape in winter, like a Brueghel painting come to life. But he never forgot the bitter cold of those mornings, of having to wake at five and break the ice on the water to wash before Mass at 5.30am.

There was an inexplicable hostility between the hundred English boarders and the Flemish boys which flared up during the Russo-Japanese War. 'One day we fought it out in the playground and, armed with slings made of thick paper wads weighted with lead and tied to long pieces of string, we tried to crack each other's skulls, to the tune of numerous casualties.' The whole school was gated for three days.

The Brothers were kindly towards their young charges but scholastic standards were not very high and musical tuition even more disappointing. For his third year in Bruges his father enrolled him in the Conservatorium where he attended twice a week for violin, piano, harmony and solfège. His violin teacher, Léon Queekers, had superb technique and could play the twenty-four caprices of Paganini without missing a note. He had a low opinion of his pupil's talent, one which Eugene feared the Great Composers shared. When he stumbled through Viotti's twenty-third concerto, a plaster bust of Schumann tumbled to the floor and shattered.

In June 1904, after a bout of scarlet fever, much to his relief, his father relented and decided that he could return home to continue his education in Liverpool, although he was to retain fluent French and an affinity for French music throughout his career. On the strength of that one year at the Bruges Muziek-Conservatorium, some musicologists persist

17

in classifying him as a Belgian composer. He had developed an independence and self-reliance far in advance of his years; but the emotional legacy of his exile was to prove far more damaging when it came to establishing lasting relationships as an adult. Always more intellectual and withdrawn than his brothers and sisters, he never enjoyed the same extrovert friendliness and their ability to establish immediate contact with people from all walks of life.

The family had moved back across the Mersey, to a terraced house round the corner from Grandfather, in Chatham Street, off Abercromby Square. From here the boys could walk to the Christian Brothers Institute in Hope Street and the girls to the Convent of Notre Dame. They continued their musical studies at the Liverpool College of Music. A photograph from 1904 shows Eugene conducting a family quartet of four violinists, his brothers in Norfolk suits and Eton collars, his sisters in their best dresses with bows in their hair. All three boys now sang in Grandfather's choir at St Anne's Benedictine Church, Edgehill. He continued to take a close interest in the children's musical education, advising their father to select more unusual instruments for them in addition to their piano and violin studies. Adolphe started the horn with Otto Paersch, first horn with the Hallé Orchestra, and Léon the oboe with Charles Reynolds, the same orchestra's first oboe and outstanding player of his generation. Marie and Sidonie took up the harp.

Eugene I did not live to see his gifted grandchildren fulfil their promise. In October 1906 he made his annual pilgrimage to Lourdes, hoping for a cure for his rheumatism. He caught a severe chill on the return journey and died of a seizure at the age of sixty-one on 30th December. A year later, Annie and the children attended a ceremony at Anfield Cemetery to unveil a Celtic cross of Irish limestone, a memorial to him initiated by members of his Male Voice Choir. 'On the basement a scroll of music, with the master's baton, is carved as if reverently laid there by loving hands,' described the *Liverpool Daily Post*. One notable absentee was Eugene II. He was conducting the Carl Rosa Company in his first appearance at Covent Garden, in a two week season of *Cavalleria Rusticana*, *Pagliacci*, *Esmeralda* (Goring Thomas), *Tannhäuser* and *Trovatore*.

Annie Goossens was now in sole charge while her husband was away on tour. She arranged a complex timetable for the five children to fit in piano and instrumental practice as well as their school homework. 'Mother had to be fairly strict with us,' recalled Marie, 'but we didn't resent having to practise. We were supposed to be musicians and musicians we were. Mother would listen to us from the kitchen below. She had perfect pitch and would bang on the ceiling with a broom and call out, "Wrong note, dear". She wrote Dad a daily report of our progress. She gave up her own career when we were born but she always sang to us while she was doing the washing up and we were drying the dishes. I remember her beautiful golden hair hanging down her back in a long plait.'[5] One of Marie's favourite pieces of music was to remain Debussy's 'La fille aux cheveux de lin' because it reminded her of her mother's hair.

Christmas was always the crown of the year with the excitement of Father coming home and hurrying to complete the Nativity Crib, the house full of light and laughter, Christmas music and presents. Their mother's brother, Tom Aynsley Cook, was the Manager of the Empire Theatre (for Moss Empires) and arranged for them to have a box at the Shakespeare or the Court Theatre, wherever the best pantomime was. He would be standing Front of House to greet them, a tall imposing figure with a moustache and immaculate evening dress, his opera hat at an angle. He always presented them with a box of chocolates and looked in at the interval to see how they were enjoying 'Little Tich' or the Chinese magician Chung-ling-Soo, who, disappointingly, turned out to be a Yorkshireman.

It was a warm and loving childhood but not an affluent one. Every week for the housekeeping, Eugene would send his wife a £5 note, cut in half and posted in two separate envelopes. On Friday morning when the post arrived she would stick the two halves together and ask one of the boys to go with her to Parr's Bank, which the children interpreted as 'Pa's' and decided their father must be very rich to own his own bank. But they soon learned the principles of home economics and how little money there was to spare for luxuries. Eugene recalled their regular down-town jaunts on a Saturday afternoon, when the three inseparable brothers would

19

press their noses longingly against the glass of 'shop windows filled with the things we loved: steam engines, model ships, electric motors and all the things we coveted but could never afford.'[6] Even Sidonie, as youngest of the family, appreciated that their parents had to live very carefully. 'We lived simply but well, Mother bought really good clothes for us that would last, good nourishing food, roast beef on Sundays, cold meat on Mondays, mince on Tuesdays, always fish on Fridays and a little drink of wine at Christmas, even as tiny children. It was a very comfortable, homely atmosphere and we loved it.'[7]

Léon never forgot the Northern high teas with cold beef, omelette, or fried eggs to start; mounds of Mother's own freshly baked bread with plenty of butter, jam and Golden Syrup, their favourite; a large fruit cake, Queen cakes, rock cakes and pots of steaming tea.[8] After a meal they would sit round the dining table playing Mahjong or Crazy Patience, enjoying all the fun of a boisterous large family.

When their father was at home, Sunday evenings were devoted to musical soirées. Sidonie described the trepidation they caused:

> We knew he was a perfectionist. We had to play our solo pieces and we were all a bit humble and terrified of the mistakes we had made. 'Wasn't it awful?' we'd say to each other. Léon would always try to make excuses not to play, saying he had a broken reed or his lips were sore. Daddy used to transpose string trios for horn, oboe and piano, the horn playing the viola part. We would stand round the piano singing bits of opera or part songs. He liked to hear us sight read and we all learnt to read music very quickly which he knew would be invaluable in our professional lives.
>
> He was very serious and he would never joke. 'You do that right and do it again,' he would say. If he wasn't in the room with us when we were practising but he was in the house, we knew perfectly well he was listening. He would suddenly appear and say we didn't have the expression quite right or our tempi were wrong. He was always in the background.[9]

They never questioned their father's authority and accepted that he knew best, however harsh his actions might seem. On one occasion Marie spent her pocket money on some sheet music of two current popular songs, 'The Honeysuckle and the Bee' and 'I Wouldn't Leave My Little Wooden Hut For You'. 'I'd heard them at the pantomime and thought they were lovely. I left both copies on the piano for safety. Father tore them up in front of me. Léon had a mouth-organ once and kept it under his pillow, but Father thought he might get a sore mouth and spirited it away.'[10]

During the eight-week summer break, the children would hear their father coaching opera singers in their roles and giving singing lessons. He was renowned for his meticulousness and his superb phrasing. His eldest son was inspired from a very early age to follow his example as a conductor. 'Musically speaking I was happiest when listening to Father preparing new operas at the piano. Not only did he memorise each bar of the music, but as he went along marked in pencil in the score every nuance and inflection of the vocal line. No wonder singers used to say, "Once you've coached a role with Eugene Goossens, you don't forget it till you die." '[11] According to Sidonie, they also used to comment 'Have you ever seen Goossens smile?' 'He was always very nervous when he conducted and looked extremely serious. So did my brother Eugene.'[12]

When the company was in Liverpool he used to take the little boy with him to daily rehearsals. 'Sometimes I'd just sit right behind him in the front row of the stalls, peering over the orchestra rail and watching the singers on stage. I loved everything about those rehearsals. I lived in a conflicting world of romanticism and reality. Even the sight of Lohengrin in a fedora and overcoat or Amneris in a tippet and muff didn't disillusion me.'[13]

The Carl Rosa Opera Company came to the Shakespeare Theatre in Liverpool twice a year and as soon as they were old enough to stay awake, all the young Goossens would go with their mother to hear their father conduct. Afterwards they would be taken backstage and the singers would enthuse over their conductor's attractive and talented children. Sidonie's memories of those exciting occasions go back to 1906. 'I fell in love with the tenor when I was six. We would go off in a four wheeler cab across the cobblestones and as soon as we got inside the theatre I could smell the dressing-rooms and the powder and I used to think "I wonder if he's singing tonight."

When he came on stage I used to feel almost ill. You see what love is like at that age! When I came home I would start doing the ballet with mother's shawls or start singing. I wanted to go on the stage but Daddy put his foot down.'14

The tenor she fell in love with was Walter Wheatley, singing Don José in *Carmen*. Sidonie had the chance of making her operatic debut as her mother had done as the little girl in *The Bohemian Girl*; to her great disappointment, at the last minute her father said no.

Both girls had inherited the vocal talent of the Cook family and wanted to sing, but their father gave them neither encouragement nor singing lessons. 'He had decided that we should both play the harp as in those days there were no women orchestral players except for the harp. If we had become singers we would have lost our voices by the time we were sixty, but as harpists our careers would be much longer.'15 As usual, 'Daddy knew best', Marie reluctantly retired from playing when she was eighty-nine. Sidonie was a member of the BBC Symphony Orchestra until the age of eighty-one and continued playing with them until she was ninety. She won the hearts of worldwide TV audiences playing at the Last Night of the Proms a few weeks before her ninety-second birthday.

Despite his authoritarianism, their father showed great psychological insight in preparing the children to take up the instruments he had chosen for them. 'Adolphe had thick lips for the horn, Léon thin lips for the oboe,' Marie recalled.16 Léon's first visit to the opera was to *Lohengrin*. His father's assistant, Mr Van Noorden, was deputed to sit in the box behind him and point out the oboe every time it had a solo passage. 'I got so accustomed to the sound that whenever the oboe came in, I used to say: "There's the oboe again". After a while I naturally concluded that this was the most attractive instrument in the world and when my father took me on his knee and asked me if I would like to learn the oboe, I leapt at the opportunity.'

It was not until the summer of 1908, when he was ten years old, that Léon was old enough for two trial lessons with the redoubtable Charles Reynolds, Principal Oboe with the Hallé Orchestra. 'I found him a very sharp boy who shaped very well indeed,' Reynolds reported back to his father. 'I think he will make a good player if he keeps up his practice. He seems very fond of it which goes a long way in learning an instrument. His fingers however are not quite long enough yet, for he had to make great exertions in stretching them to cover the holes. He also found the Oboe very heavy, for he had to have very frequent rests for his arms.'[17] Reynolds recommended a sharp pitch oboe from the French firm of Lorée. Eventually Léon would need three instruments: a Cor Anglais and two further oboes for flat pitch. It seemed an unnecessary expense to Eugene until Reynolds explained. 'As the flat pitch is only used in the very best orchestras in this country, it will be years before he is able to get into these orchestras. Should he play at a theatre or ordinary Concert work to gain experience he will require a sharp pitch Oboe and Cor Anglais.'[18]

As soon as he had obtained an instrument, Reynolds offered to teach him at the cost of £2 for ten lessons, half his normal fee. There was also the question of cane to consider. 'If you intend Léon to go on with the Oboe I would advise you to send for 4 kilogrammes of Oboe cane (Roseau). It takes 3 years to Season, that is it requires 3 years to dry sufficiently before using. I'll send you the address of the man who grows it. He will send it to you in a small sack. It must be put away in a *dry place* and let it *remain in the dark*.'[18]

Léon made rapid progress and soon found that the enforced hours of practice need not interfere with other pastimes; the oboe was excellent for disguising the noise of his clockwork train set. Adolphe, rapidly becoming an accomplished horn player, found that he could combine horn arpeggios with reading his favourite books. The practice routine was not relaxed even when they spent a week's holiday with their mother's wealthy Aunt Annie who had a beautiful house in Beaumaris in Anglesey. The boys had 'to keep their lips in'; the girls were more fortunate as the harp was too heavy to take with them. The room with the piano where they practised overlooked the Menai Straits and here they played for hours at a time. When Marie went in she found

23

both her brothers sustaining long notes automatically with one hand while Addie watched the ships through a telescope and Lee through binoculars.

Liverpool was an ideal city to develop their passion for boats and the lure of distant harbours. 'Our chief amusement,' recalled Marie, 'was the bi-weekly visit to the Landing Stage where we travelled the world whilst sitting on the chains, rocking ourselves to and fro, imagining we were on our bicycles which we were never allowed to possess. A P & O liner, gleaming white, would hoist its Blue Peter flag and we were off to India; the *Lusitania* was next and we were off to the USA and so we spent our Wednesday and Saturday afternoons.'[19] As adults, Léon was to become a passionate yachtsman while Eugene, when he lived in New York and Sydney, maintained an encyclopaedic knowledge of the schedules of all ocean-going liners.

The musical environment that Liverpool provided was an even more valuable influence, particularly the regular visits of the Hallé Orchestra under Hans Richter. Richter was a martinet but the players loved him and he had made the Hallé one of the best orchestras in Europe. The eleven-year-old Eugene got parental permission to attend all the concerts at the Philharmonic Hall. He found a seat by the organ, on the top tier of the orchestra from where he had a bird's eye view of conductor and players. Henry Wood, travelling with his Queen's Hall Orchestra, appealed to him as a more sympathetic personality than Richter: he was 'handsome, dynamic and indefatigably energetic'.[20] Marie used to sit in the stalls with Eugene for what were called the 'Ladies' and the Gentlemen's Concerts'; Sidonie's memories were of 'going to all the concerts as tiny people, of hearing Pachmann and Backhaus play.'

Meanwhile, at grass roots level, the three brothers were battling through Haydn and Mozart symphonies with the Music College Orchestra. Eugene was also playing in the Società Armonica, an amateur orchestra made up of socialites, shipping magnates and professional men and women who gave public concerts in the plush Victorian décor of St George's Hall, under the energetic baton of Vasco Ackroyd, also leader of the Liverpool Philharmonic Orchestra. By the time he was thirteen, he was leading the second violins. The contact led to the three Goossens brothers' first professional engagement, in 1909, playing light music at the Kursaal on the Pier at New Brighton. Their fee was one guinea a week each for a concert every evening, with an additional matinée on Sundays. Léon made his solo debut at the age of ten on the Cor Anglais, playing the notoriously difficult 'ranz des vaches' from *William Tell*.

The mountain pastures of Switzerland were a long way from Abercromby Square. The family survived the milk bought from a so-called dairy in Vine Street, an unsalubrious neighbourhood at the back of the house. Marie recalled: 'A small girl sometimes delivered the milk and one day she heard Adolphe practising long notes on the French Horn. She looked up in astonishment and said to Mother, "Is that a cow?" '[21]

Despite their intelligence, none of the children shone in their scholastic careers which were always of secondary importance to their music studies. In 1907 Eugene completed his education by passing the Oxford Local Examination in all subjects except Music! 'A boy of thirteen could hardly have been expected to cope with what was practically an examination for the degree of Doctor of Music,' he commented retrospectively.[22] As an executant, he won the Liverpool Scholarship to the Royal College of Music in London to study the violin, with piano as his second subject. The scholarship was a prestigious and valuable one, worth £52.10 shillings a year. As tuition fees at the RCM were twelve guineas a year, Eugene would be provided with an adequate living allowance from the remainder.

He wrote to his 'Darling Dad' away on tour telling him he had found the ideal fiddle for his new status in George Byrom's violin shop: a 'Nicolas aîné' *signed*.

It is a fine toned instrument, has a handsome appearance, and would be the ideal fiddle for leading a quartett [*sic*] or playing a solo on, anywhere! The tone is very rich and of full volume, in fact I don't think there is a dull tone on the instrument. Byrom wanted £15 for it. I think it is quite worth it, but as he is willing to exchange it for some of your fiddles, thus eliminating the money question altogether, I think you will agree with me that it is worth doing. I have subjected the instrument to a good test and so you have it from me that it *is* worth the exchange.

Needless to say, I shall not consider the transaction made till it has your sanction, which I conjecture it already has – however to make sure, let me have a note at the very earliest, please Dad, to say you approve of the bargain. Mr Ross [his violin teacher] pronounces the fiddle to be a genuine Nicolas, although owing to his having been laid up for a fortnight with rheumatism, he was unable to play on it.

Best love from your ever loving Eugene.

The letter reveals a literary style, mature judgement and reliance on a musical and business acumen far in advance of the average thirteen-year-old. Yet he remains the affectionate and respectful son, dependent on his father's approval and superior judgement. The relationship was to continue unchanged for more than fifty years.

Three days later he wrote again to his father, telling him the exchange was completed but that Byrom had driven a hard bargain and he had had to part with two family fiddles. 'I am sorry about the Maggini in so far as it was Grandpa's fiddle (the same with the David as it used to be yours!) but I think it was better to dispose of it in order to get me a better fiddle, than to have it lying on the shelf getting dusty!'[23] (Both instruments were, of course, copies.)

Once the pattern was established, it was only a matter of time before the other children joined Eugene in London at the RCM. Meanwhile they graduated via the Società Armonica to professional orchestral engagements. Marie made her debut at the Philharmonic Hall in the overture to *The Flying Dutchman*, looking demure in a grey dress made by her mother and her hair in two plaits. When the Liverpool Symphony Orchestra required a third oboe for *Till Eulenspiegel*, Reynolds recommended his pupil Léon, aged twelve. The guest conductor looked up, pointed to Léon in his Eton collar and asked 'Who is that little boy playing third oboe?' Reynolds, playing first, replied, 'That's Master Goossens, Mr Beecham.' 'Oh really! And has he a licence?' (Child actors had to be licenced to appear on stage.) Beecham was to play a significant role in the careers of all the Goossens. Léon was to become one of his favourite instrumentalists, his beautiful phrasing and distinctive tone unmistakable in any performance of Beecham's London Philharmonic Orchestra between the wars.

Adolphe seemed destined for an equally brilliant career as a horn player. It was a unique phenomenon for five siblings to be equally talented and equally successful. Usually in a musical family one child's talent overshadows the rest, as was the case with the Barbirollis (also a family of immigrant orchestral musicians) and the Menuhins, where Yaltah and Hephzibah could never compete with Yehudi for their mother's devotion. In contrast the Goossens showed no discrimination between their sons and their daughters, a remarkable example of sexual equality.

Sometimes ambitious and unscrupulous parents exploit their children as child prodigies. In the early years of the century, many poor Jewish immigrants in the East End of London or New York's East Side deluded themselves that their precocious offspring might emulate the success of a Heifetz or a Rubinstein. It was usually the more affluent social classes who were able to foster their children's musical talent, as with the Harrison sisters. Colonel Harrison gave up his army career so that he and his wife could accompany their gifted daughters to study with Becker in Berlin and Auer in St Petersburg.[24] Eugene was to find that many of his contemporaries as conductors or composers, like Boult and Bliss, had the advantage of an Oxford or Cambridge education and a private income.

Eugene and Annie Goossens came from a tradition of musicians as artisans rather than artists. Music for them had no connection with the dream world of the amateur or the concert enthusiast. They knew what was required to make a successful career in the profession: well taught talent, exemplary musicianship, unrelenting discipline and hard work. They had no illusions as to its excitement or glamour. Eugene II and his father decided that all five children had the necessary musicality to earn their living as competent orchestral musicians and chose their instruments accordingly. They were not destined for solo careers, they were never treated as prodigies and never regarded themselves as such. They did not consider themselves in any way out of the ordinary and because they loved and respected their parents, did not question the training regime which was enforced or the decisions that were made to ensure their future. 'We were supposed to be musicians and musicians we were,' reiterated Marie.[25]

On the vexed question as to whether musicians were born or made, Sidonie's verdict is that talent is first inherited and then improved on. Léon passed on to his daughter Jennie a more negative view of the 'improving' process: 'Those children were brought up with a rod of iron. My father was made to practise until his lips bled.'[26]

3

London

In September 1907 Eugene found himself once more exiled from the bosom of the family, this time to the bustle and excitement of Edwardian London. His father had entrusted him to an elderly Irish spinster, Miss Lynch, who ran a small boarding house in Cromwell Crescent, Earl's Court, conveniently situated for the Royal College of Music behind the Albert Hall. 'Fanny Lynch, in her way quite a *grande dame* among landladies, taught me chess, manners and good reading, and tolerated no nonsense in the manner of late hours.'[1]

When the Carl Rosa came to Covent Garden, Eugene looked forward to the additional pleasure of sharing theatrical lodgings in Brixton with his father. The latter received particular praise in the London press when he conducted the opening night of *Tannhäuser* in December 1908 and for a new production of *Tristan* in the autumn of 1909. (The company's season was from 18th October to 13th November.) The most cherished tribute, however, came from his five children in an illuminated manuscript, executed by the artistically gifted Eugene. It was dedicated as a 'Souvenir of our loving appreciation of your finished production and masterly conducting of *Tristan and Isolde* at Covent Garden Theatre, London, October 1909 and to add our note of praise to the well-won approbation of the public. In your children's hearts your music shall "give momentary feeling permanence, so that thy capture hold, a century hence truth's very heart of truth".'

It was not easy for an English touring company to follow the star artists and lavish productions of an epoch-making international opera season. In the summer of 1909, young Eugene had deserted his violin practice for a perch high in the gallery to hear the British stage premieres of *Samson and*

29

Delilah, Charpentier's *Louise* and *Pelléas and Mélisande*, Debussy himself having supervised the final rehearsals.

Eugene studied at the RCM for five years, winning a year's extension to his scholarship. His violin professor was Achille Rivarde, a fiery Latin American who had led the Lamoureux Orchestra in Paris for six years. The relationship was a stormy one.

> His personality intimidated me so much at the outset that it was some time before I was able to hold my bow steady in his presence. He started by ruthlessly tearing my playing to pieces, making me unlearn everything I knew and re-learn exclusively his own system of style and technique. He judged me lazy and with no real talent for the violin (in both of which he was right), and I looked upon him as a surly, venomous, completely unsympathetic martinet. But in later years we became firm friends. There has probably never been a violinist who could impart to a student such fastidious elegance of playing as he did. It was his fierce obsession for a flawless, stylized virtuosity which in the end resulted in his concentrating almost exclusively on technique rather than interpretation.[2]

Despite the initial misgivings of both pupil and teacher, by the autumn of 1910 Eugene had progressed to the leadership of the second violins in the College orchestra. Camille Saint-Saëns was visiting London and Sir Hubert Parry, Director of the RCM, invited the French composer to conduct a rehearsal of his Third Symphony. In the Finale the second violins bungled a lead and the irate composer demanded that they play it by themselves. Finally, in desperation, he called on Eugene to show the others how it should be performed. His comment on the boy's tremulous and ineffective rendering was '*Gentil garçon, mais quel sacre violiniste!*' (Nice boy, but what a terrible violinist!) Eugene was totally crushed but at the end of the rehearsal, as he left the rostrum, the great man caught his eye and winked.

Students were not allowed to accept professional engagements without the permission of the Director. Parry kind-heartedly allowed him to supplement his scholarship by joining the ensemble in a few select hotels. The repertoire, played in an alcove of the hotel restaurant, extended from Grand Opera to the latest 'Cakewalk'. On one occasion, a well-known member of the peerage drunkenly pressed a five pound note into Eugene's hand and requested in nonsensical French: '*Jouez-moi quelque chose de très moutarde.*'

Eugene graduated to West End theatre orchestras, which offered better pay and shorter hours, and even fulfilled his ambition to play at Covent Garden. Beecham was conducting *Don Giovanni* and in the ballroom scene used two orchestras on stage on balconies and wooden towers. Eugene began to feel a little nervous when, uncomfortably dressed in a heavy brocade costume and perched precariously with his violin, his tower got stuck during the blackout. Panic ensued and the performance was unable to continue until, the frantic pushing and shoving from extra stage-hands, the tower finally trundled into place on stage. The lights, the heat and the swaying made him feel sea-sick but he battled on to play the right notes until the end of the scene, when he scrambled down and made an undignified exit to throw up in the wings.

In 1910 Eugene had been accepted for composition classes by Sir Charles Villiers Stanford, now unjustly neglected both as a composer and a teacher. He held the Chair of Music at Cambridge as well as being Professor of Composition at the RCM and there were very few composers of significance between 1887 and 1924 who did not come under his influence. His pupils included Vaughan Williams, Arthur Bliss, Arthur Benjamin, Gustav Holst, John Ireland, E J Moeran and Constant Lambert. Eugene was much influenced by the French Impressionists following a Christmas gift of Debussy's piano pieces, *Estampes*. He had been bowled over by Debussy's London debut with the Queen's Hall Orchestra on 1st February 1908, when he had heard him conduct *L'Après-midi d'un faune* and *La Mer*.

Stanford started him off on a theme and 32 variations for piano, claiming that the supreme test for creative ingenuity lay in extracting the utmost variety from a good tune. 'Some of the more "modern" variations he erased on the ground of "cacophony", a subject which made him foam at the mouth,' Eugene recalled. ' "Damned ugly, me bhoy! Take it out," he would say in his inimitable Irish brogue.' He laid the blame for the wildness of his radical young pupils on the

31

pernicious influence of Debussy and Strauss. When Eugene told him that he had been thrilled by the London premiere of *Elektra* at Covent Garden, conducted by Beecham, Stanford threatened to give him up as a lost soul if he heard any more of that 'pornographic rubbish'.[3]

Arthur Bliss, Eugene's friend and fellow student, was similarly subjected to Stanford's wholesale condemnation of consecutive fifths, the whole tone scale and excessive modulation. 'How well I remember the savage delight with which our master would rend us as imitators of Debussy, if we innocently placed three major thirds in succession. No matter what the mood, what the context, those little thirds, did the trick; we were thereafter followers of Debussy.'[4]

The Coronation year of 1911 provided another seminal influence when Diaghilev brought his Ballet Russe to Covent Garden. Night after night Eugene sat intoxicated by the sumptuous, spectacular productions and the legendary dancing of Nijinsky, Pavlova and Karsavina. The musical climax came with Stravinsky's *Firebird*. Eugene and his closest friends, all Stanford students from the RCM, Bliss, Herbert Howells and Arthur Benjamin, were enthralled, swept along by the dynamic force and creative inspiration, of music totally unlike anything they had ever heard. Eugene felt he could never emulate such a model but it did provide the impetus for his Opus I: 'Variations for Orchestra on a Chinese Theme', completed in February 1912. 'At first Stanford expressed many misgivings and blue pencilled the opus freely. Many of his blue pencillings I secretly erased, so convinced was I that the "ugly" sounds I had written were vital to the colour of the work.'[5]

Stanford decided that the work merited a performance and asked him to 'take the stick' at a College orchestral rehearsal and then at the final public concert of the spring term. Eugene's debut as conductor and composer was reviewed by the *Times*, who judged that the nineteen-year-old, 'not only knows what to do with his orchestra when he is writing for it, but is well able to get it done when it is written. He took command with complete assurance, and yet without ostentation, and his clear beat and simple indications to the players secured an admirable performance. The work too has the qualities of clearness and simplicity, and there is a quantity of certain melody, a vein of

32

sentiment which is not afraid of being obvious, and sufficient harmonic variety to suggest that plenty of it will come from him in the future.'[6] Here was a critic who knew how to spot a winner!

By 1912, when Marie, Adolphe and Léon were sent to join their brother in London, Miss Lynch had moved her boarding house to Berkeley Gardens, Notting Hill Gate. Their fellow lodger, Miss Fletcher, was studying singing, and as soon as she found out that Adolphe was an excellent pianist, she co-opted him to accompany her exercises for half a crown an hour. She tried to persuade him to play the 'Women's March' for a Suffragette meeting in the drawing room, which was decorated with the purple and green flags of the movement. She was disappointed when he refused but she managed to recruit Marie. Miss Lynch, also a keen suffragette, had fallen on hard times and unbeknown to the Goossens was trying daily to placate the bailiffs in a small room off the hall with trays of food and drink. Fortunately she held them at bay until the young musicians were reunited with Sid and their parents at 70, Edith Road, West Kensington.

Father rented the house for £60 a year and it was to be the family home until 1927. Their neighbours were another French-speaking family with a musical daughter, Yvonne Arnaud, who later made a dual reputation as a pianist and as an actress in light comedy.

Eugene had proudly escorted his sister and two brothers to the RCM for their entrance examination, which they all passed with flying colours. Despite some superficial modernisation, the main building of the RCM has changed little in eighty years but student life has altered considerably. The central foyer is still dominated by a staircase on either side; when the Goossens were students, young ladies were restricted to the stairs on the right and young gentlemen to those on the left. The formidable Mrs Bindon was on duty to chaperone the female students and make sure that no fraternisation occurred except for strictly musical purposes. She reprimanded Marie for talking to a male student in the entrance hall and was very sceptical of the explanation that the guilty party was her brother and that he existed in triplicate.

Parry was delighted by the new influx of Goossens talent

but could not offer any reduction in fees. Marie won an Exhibition for her second year, but Wind Scholarships were given only to students aged seventeen and over. By the time they reached the requisite age, both Adolphe and Léon were playing in professional orchestras. (According to the records of the RCM, Eugene was a student from September 1907 until July 1912, Adolphe and Léon only from May 1912 to December 1913, Marie from May 1912 to April 1914 and Sidonie for one year from the autumn of 1915.)

The foundations of Léon's oboe technique had been excellently laid by Charles Reynolds. He wrote to Eugene II when the family left Liverpool. 'It has been a great pleasure for me to teach Léon the Oboe. He is a very intelligent, sharp boy with a very loveable disposition and has given me little or no trouble with his lessons. However he has one slight fault which is easily remedied, he has a tendency to play *too loud*. I have told him of it and for the time he has altered but boylike soon forgets. Mr Malsch, his new teacher, I am afraid does the same, therefore you must remind Léon from time to time. Conductors nowadays have a tendency to keep the *tone* of *the Oboe down* and Léon must do the same.'[7] Malsch, who taught at the RCM, was Principal Oboe with the London Symphony Orchestra and according to the youngest Eugene, his playing ruined the tone quality of the orchestra for years!

Marie studied with Miriam Timothy who was Principal Harp with the LSO. To begin with she did not find the relationship an easy one: 'She was renowned as a harpist and a beautiful woman. Unfortunately she did not like the harp; the piano was her favourite instrument. This had a bad effect on me. On the way to my lesson I used to tremble in the bus, worrying over the bars I had not mastered in case I was wasting her time.'[8] On the days when she came dressed in white, Marie used to feel even more nervous as it meant Miss Timothy was impatient to get away and play tennis. But she soon realised she had a very talented pupil and asked Marie to play in a concert with her at the rival establishment, the Royal Academy of Music. They had no sufficiently good harpists to play Chabrier's flamboyant *España*.

In February 1914, Parry engaged Marie and Léon to play

in Oxford in the incidental music which he had composed for an OUDS production of Aristophanes' comedy *The Acharnians*. There were nine performances and Parry and Hugh Allen, then organist of New College, shared the conducting. Adrian Boult played the celeste in the orchestra; on 24th February when Allen had to go down to London to take a Bach Choir rehearsal, the baton was handed over to him.[9]

Marie studied piano with the same teacher as Eugene, a former pupil of Clara Schumann, who rejoiced in the name of 'J St O Dykes'. 'I never found out what the "St O" stood for! He was a dapper little man with a small moustache which he twirled round his fingers as he walked diagonally across the room, between the two grand pianos, occasionally "shooting his cuffs" if they were not showing the obligatory two and a half inches below the sleeves of his jacket.' Despite the fact that he also sang during this procedure, Marie found him an excellent teacher. To her amazement she progressed through works of Chopin and Brahms to Beethoven's 1st piano concerto. One day he sat down at the second piano and played the orchestral part to her solo. His only comment on her performance was 'Why do all harpists play their chords arpeggiated?'[10]

Sidonie also started private harp lessons with Miss Timothy while she was a pupil at the Sacred Heart Convent in Hammersmith. She used to take her weekly Disciplinary Certificates home for Eugene to sign 'EG' like her father. 'I didn't dare show them to Daddy unless they were "Very Good". Léon was always sweet on the girls and he and his friends from the RCM, Frank Probyn (horn) and Cedric Sharpe (cello) used to come and meet me and my friends after school and we'd go for a walk along the towpath.'[11]

The girls took their harp studies very seriously and it did not enter their heads that the instrument could have a humorous side.

When Sidonie and I were students we saw in large letters outside the Coliseum Theatre: 'Roxy de la Rocco, Wizard of the Harp'. I can't imagine how we managed to find the 3/6d for the seats, but we made up our minds that we must hear this harpist. So having previously booked front seats in the stalls for a matinée, we found ourselves in a wonderful position to see and hear the harp at its best.

The full-sized American harp was carried on (we had only a small one between us so we're envious), followed by the player in evening dress. Presently the orchestra struck up with the noisiest part of the *William Tell* overture. Roxy joined in the mêlée and rushed up and down the strings trying to outdo the noise that was coming from the pit. I never heard such a battle either before or since. They all finished together – three *fortissimos* – and Roxy pulled the bottom string and proved it to be elastic! To show our indignation, we both rose from our seats and walked out. Such sacrilege could not be tolerated.[12]

Adolphe and Léon had been quickly recognised as the most gifted horn and oboe players that the RCM had produced for many years. Léon was frustrated by the lack of solo pieces available for the oboe. Most conductors still regarded it as a loud, crude instrument, little advanced since the massed oboe bands of the eighteenth century and without all the refinements of the instrument today. One of his first London engagements was *Messiah* at the Handel Festival at Crystal Palace, conducted by Dr Henry Coward. 'My Professor, William Malsch, was playing first oboe and I was playing sixteenth. There were almost as many oboes as violins! It was still mostly played with a crude and heavy tone. Even Reynolds who played first oboe at Covent Garden as well as with the Hallé had to spread a handkerchief over his music-stand and play into that for Wagner operas, otherwise he couldn't get quiet enough for accompanying and all the lovely little solos in *Parsifal* and *Tristan*.'[13]

Léon heard the sound he wanted to make from Henri du Busscher in the Queen's Hall Orchestra, mellow and beautifully disciplined, able to do full justice to the Good Friday music from *Parsifal* and Strauss' *Don Juan*. Night after night he sat in the audience learning to emulate his idol.

In July 1912, Eugene had joined the first violins of Sir Henry Wood's Queen's Hall Orchestra while continuing to nurse his ambitions as conductor and composer. Léon and Sidonie had differing memories of the first composition he wrote for his brothers and sisters, an arrangement of Christmas Carols. Léon recalled it being for violin, oboe, horn and harp. 'We went to all the smart places in the centre of Liverpool we could think of but no one wanted to know. It was a bitterly cold night. We rang all the door bells but they didn't even open, except one who gave us half a crown to go away.'[14]

Sidonie agreed on the weather but not on the other details. 'It was in 1912, after we had come to London. It was for violin, oboe and horn as we couldn't take the harp with us. The boys stood under a lamp-post to play and I did the collecting. We went all the way down Queen's Gate but everyone in those big houses was away. I had to go down to the basements as the only place I could get an answer was from the kitchen staff. Nobody gave us half a crown. All we got was fourpence! We ended up in May Mukle's flat in Porchester Terrace.'[15]

Eugene had been playing for a year as second violinist with the Langley-Mukle Quartet, joining Beatrice Langley as leader, James Lockyer viola and May Mukle cello. They were much in demand among music-loving patrons at fashionable society soirées in London and houseparties in the country. By the time he was twenty, Eugene, with his unaffected charm, intelligence, talent and good looks, had become an established favourite with hostesses and guests alike. His friends and acquaintances now included the writers Yeats, Galsworthy and Arnold Bennett, the painters Sargent, Glyn Philpot and Harold Speed and two composers whom he was to value as his closest friends throughout their lives, Cyril Scott and Percy Grainger.

Typical of the unique mixture of wealth, culture and Bohemianism in those golden autumnal days before the First World War were the weekends at Sir Samuel Boulton's country house in Totteridge, which Eugene recalled in his autobiography, *Overture and Beginners*:

They were fantastic affairs for his elderly daughter rarely invited fewer than twenty or thirty house guests and the amount of food consumed at the interminable breakfasts, lunches and dinners would have fed an army. Grace Lovat-Fraser, Vladimir Rosing and Bertram Binyon usually supplied the vocal relief alternating with contributions by our own quartet. Sometimes the Sunday night supper was an elaborate fancy-dress affair. Once I appeared at dinner as the Masque of the Red Death, creating a macabre sensation. It was all inconceivably and remotely Babylonian – and at times slightly vapid.[16]

When the Langley-Mukle Quartet disbanded, Eugene was invited by friends from the RCM to be a founder member of the Philharmonic Quartet. For them he wrote his C major Quartet and Two Sketches: 'By the Tarn' and 'Jack o' Lantern'. In May 1912 he was presented with the Silver Medal of the Worshipful Company of Musicians and shortly afterwards introduced into the most Olympian of London's musical circles. He received a message from Claude Aveling, Parry's secretary at the RCM, asking him to go that evening to the far reaches of Chelsea where some Americans named Draper were short of a viola player for some chamber music. He arrived at 19, Edith Grove at ten o'clock, steeling himself to smile politely through a session with well-meaning amateurs. Instead he found himself playing a Brahms two-viola quintet with some of the greatest virtuosi in the world: Jacques Thibaud, Paul Kochanski and Pablo Casals, together with the English viola player, Rebecca Clarke.

The Drapers had converted 19a into a sumptuous studio, furnished with Gothic tapestries, a magnificent Kien Lung screen, a huge sofa and large floor cushions around the Bechstein piano. Through the flickering light of candelabra, the haze of cigar smoke and of wood burning in the Tudor fireplace, Eugene glimpsed the faces of Arthur Rubinstein, Felix Salmond, Alfred Cortot, Louis Persinger who was later to teach Yehudi Menuhin, the Spanish violinist Fernandez Arbos and the cellist Rubio. As the night proceeded, Eugene played with them all in turn while between quartets Henry James discoursed on the virtues and beauties of great music.

After a short pause for supper at 1am, the music continued until the blue-grey of dawn showed through the skylight. Then Rubinstein gave a magisterial performance of an unknown fugue by his friend and countryman Karol Szymanowski and Thibaud played a Bach Chaconne on Kochanski's Stradivarius. Even the gods of music need physical sustenance and Eugene followed them to the dining room where a breakfast of coffee, scrambled eggs and great bowls of raspberries and strawberries had miraculously appeared. At last he stumbled from this enchanted realm out into the prosaic light of Edith Grove. Round the corner at 31a, King's Road lived his friend Percy Grainger, eager to hear of the night's adventures. Eugene and the Langley-Mukle

Quartet used to rehearse in Percy's rooms above a tobacconist's shop and on 21st May 1912 took part in the first all Grainger concert at the Aeolian Hall.

Paul and Muriel Draper, blessed with youth, beauty, wealth and an insatiable love of music had come to London in 1911 for Paul to study singing with Raimund von Zur Mühlen, reputed to be the greatest teacher of German *Lieder*. They were soon on friendly terms with the impresario Montague Vert Chester, depicted by Muriel Draper as 'astute, asthmatic, benevolent, bald-headed and immaculately white-gloved.'[17] He brought Rubinstein, Thibaud and Casals to dinner. They stayed to play chamber music and a legendary era was born. Any international artist performing in London would be invited back to their studio. They rarely refused the opportunity of playing chamber music purely for pleasure in such ideal circumstances throughout the night. When Casals and Suggia played in turn, hidden behind the Chinese screen, like the rest of the audience Eugene found it impossible to tell which cellist was which.

Another vivid memory was playing in the Schumann piano quintet with Cortot when suddenly in the doorway appeared the giant figure of Chaliapin towering over the wraith-like, little Nijinsky. Eugene lost his way in the second violin part, much to Cortot's annoyance. Chaliapin had just made a sensational London debut at Covent Garden singing Boris Godunov. He was the only person allowed to sit beside the pianist in a chamber music ensemble and hum the themes as he read them. Normally the sound of the human voice has too subjective a quality to be absorbed in an instrumental ensemble but Muriel Draper described how the Russian bass, 'with unerring pitch could follow the thematic development through every movement with a sound that was like a new and hitherto unused instrument, a cunning combination of vibrations and percussion.'[18]

Eugene had become a great favourite at Edith Grove. Muriel Draper, habitually resplendent in a jewelled and feathered turban and daring harem skirt, recalled him as a 'curly headed, gallant young Belgian, brought up in a monastery. He conducted Wagner's [*Siegfried*] *Idyll* for us, a work scored for seventeen instruments, from the perilous vantage of a soap box that threatened at every moment to overturn him, though it never threatened his calm. His fluency, sensitiveness and rhythmic subtlety were marked. His power and control increased from season to season.'[19] He had introduced Adolphe and Léon who were valued performers in the Wagner, and a repertory including the Schubert Octet, Beethoven Septet and Mozart Oboe Quartet.

One evening Eugene was invited to try out his 'Chinese Variations' in a reduced form at Edith Grove. Muriel Draper found it 'an exceptionally mature work for so young a composer. It was listened to with high pleasure by as discriminating a musical audience as he could ask for. Harold Bauer, Arbos, Rubinstein, Kochanski, Lionel Tertis, Thibaud, and Cortot.' There was one dissenting voice to the chorus of praise: Baroness von Hutten, an American renowned for her striking good looks, her friendship with the matinée idol Henry Ainley and her propensity for uttering arrogant nonsense in the guise of musical criticism.

'All very nice, my dear boy, but the theme is not Chinese.'

'I am very sorry, dear madame,' answered Eugene, with composure, 'but it is Chinese.'

'Dear boy, don't be foolish, because I *know* it's not.'

'Baroness von Hutten, you are wrong,' replied a slightly less composed Eugene. 'It is one of the historical musical themes of China, taken from the one unquestionably authoritative work on the subject, which has been the source of all we know of Chinese music for the last thousand years.'

'Well, my child, you may think so, but I assure you it is not. You see I have been there and I know.'[20]

According to their hostess, Eugene adopted the only course open in face of such an attitude and with a dignity and maturity far in excess of his nineteen years, walked away.

Sir Henry Wood had no such reservations about the work's authenticity and invited Eugene to conduct it at a Promenade Concert in the Queen's Hall on 6th September 1913. After acknowledging the applause, he returned to his seat in the first violins for the remainder of the programme. Wood predicted that Eugene would make a great name for himself; they were to remain life-long friends. Among the other novelties scoring a success that season were Vaughan Williams' incidental music to *The Wasps* and Grainger's *Irish Tune* and *Shepherd's Hey*.

For nine weeks in the spring and summer of 1914, London's musical life was transformed by a Grand Season of Russian Opera and Ballet at the Theatre Royal, Drury Lane, organised and financed by Thomas Beecham. Eugene played in the first violins and relished a worm's eye view of the British premieres of Borodin's *Prince Igor* and three operas by Rimsky-Korsakov, *Nuit de Mai*, *Ivan the Terrible* and *The Golden Cockerel*, as well as three ballets commissioned from Diaghilev including *Daphnis and Chloe*. Diaghilev antagonised Ravel by liquidating the off-stage chorus (an integral part of the ballet's tonal scheme), saying the singers took up too much room and got in the way of the scene shifters.

The controversial American writer Gertrude Stein came to London for the Russian season. Muriel Draper describes her sitting in Buddhistic calm at Edith Grove until some topic of conversation arose which stimulated her interest, 'and then she would talk for hours.' Eugene, like most of the musicians, found Paul's cousin Ruth Draper's witty monologues far more to his taste. Suspicions were aroused amongst the neighbours that the Drapers were running a gambling den as no one could stay up all night just to play music. One night they staged a demonstration, blowing policemen's whistles, shooting off torpedoes and filling the night air with hootings and rattles. 'They were answered by John Warner and Arthur Rubinstein playing a Bach Prelude and Fugue for four hands on the piano. Bach is stirring enough played by two hands: by four, it is not conducive to sleep.'[21]

Eugene was to look back with nostalgia on the summer of 1914 and the enchanted world of music at midnight, but the lamps were going out in Edith Grove as well as all over Europe.[22] Unknown to their guests the Drapers were on the verge of bankruptcy. Eugene's enjoyment of a golfing holiday outside Edinburgh before the Promenade Concert Season began was shattered by the announcement of the outbreak of war. The three Goossens brothers tried to enlist in the Officers' Training Corps; they were told that as they had not attended a public school they could not be considered as officer material. Other minor details were that Adolphe and Léon were under age and Eugene was medically unfit because of his heart condition.

4

The Great War

At the outbreak of war, to the delight of many British artists, all German professional musicians in Britain were sent back to 'the Fatherland'. Eugene and his friends in the Philharmonic Quartet found that their engagements substantially increased. Like all young men, they wore khaki armbands over their dress clothes at concerts to signify that they were in the process of joining, or had been rejected by, the Army.

Ranks of chorus and orchestra were gradually depleted as more and more young men enlisted but musical life survived. Eugene II continued his provincial tours with the Carl Rosa Opera Company. At the beginning of 1915 he was responsible for the debut of a singer destined to take her place amongst the great dramatic sopranos of the twentieth century, Eva Turner. He gave her her first solo role as a Page in *Tannhäuser* with six words to sing. Dame Eva explained that it was known as a 'one and six and tights role. We got threepence a word extra and had to wear tights with four pennies stitched into the tops to keep them up!'[1]

Shortly after this there was a falling out between conductor and management ending an association of more than thirty years between the Goossens family and the Carl Rosa Opera Company. Both father and son were to return to the company in 1921, at Covent Garden, when the roster included Eva Turner as Madame Butterfly conducted by Goossens senior.

Despite her excellent results at college, Marie was finding it much more difficult to establish a professional career than Eugene. She stayed at home in Edith Road, helping her mother with the housework. She learnt the major repertoire of solo works for harp with which both Goossens sisters were to become associated as incomparable interpreters, including the Mozart Concerto for Flute and Harp, the Debussy Sonata for Flute, Viola and Harp and the Ravel Introduction and Allegro.

Meanwhile, she waited for the telephone to ring. Eventually it did, inviting her to tour Ireland with Miss Muriel Jack's Ladies Orchestra. Although the orchestra was small, their concerts were of high standard; she found it excellent experience, improvising from piano parts in lieu of harp parts and taking her turn to perform solos.

They sailed back from Rosslare to Fishguard for a short tour of South Wales and were forced to travel two hours off course as they were being pursued by a German submarine. 'The cook came up from below with his telescope and let me have a look through it. I actually saw the periscope, but he told me to keep quiet in case any of the passengers fainted.'[2] Marie had already developed the down-to-earth unflappability which enabled her to cope with all the personal and professional crises that life was to bring.

Their next engagement was the Shakespeare Season of 1916 at Stratford-upon-Avon with Ben Greet as leading actor. Eugene had already made the acquaintance of Marie Corelli who invited his sister to tea. 'There sat the famous authoress in all her frills and furbelows which made her look like a little doll. On a side-table lay a copy of *The Sorrows of Satan* (her most famous novel), by way of self-advertisement. She instructed her companion to have her gondolier ready with her gondola to take the evening air on the River Avon.'[3]

Then came a summer season at Llandrindod Wells, playing outside the Pump Room where visitors came to take the waters. One lady insisted that Marie was a Belgian refugee because of her name, and when one of her wire strings broke, gave her half a crown to buy a new one. She did not refuse. Because of the extra expense of her strings, her weekly fee was £2.10 shillings, the same as the leader. She shared rooms and food with three other girls at a cost of fifteen shillings each, sent £1 home to her parents and kept the remaining fifteen shillings for herself.

As the war continued, money and food became progressively more scarce and Marie and Sidonie felt that they must find more regular employment to earn their keep. They applied to Somerset House to become Female Clerical Substitutes and after successfully completing an addition sum were immediately engaged. Sidonie was posted to the Salaries Office and Marie to the Land Tax Department. Marie, who always enjoyed working with pens, pencils and writing paper, was in her element.

Food was a major preoccupation in the office. The word would go round that a queue was forming at Hale's Stores in Drury Lane, although nobody knew what for. They joined it in the lunch-hour and joyfully arrived home with Blue Band margarine or Cocoa Butter. On one occasion Marie managed to buy a few herrings which made a tasty Sunday lunch.

Their harp teacher Miriam Timothy was playing in *Chu Chin Chow* at His Majesty's Theatre; the composer Frederic Norton had written a taxing part for the harp and she felt that she needed some evenings off. She asked Marie and Sidonie to take turns deputising for her. 'One night,' Marie recalled, 'there was an air-raid and the electricity went off. Even though most of the players knew their parts from memory the show could not continue in the dark, and we had to stand on the stairs until the "all clear" was sounded by a Boy Scout on a bugle.'[4]

Oscar Asche's Oriental fantasy, premiered in 1916, created a record by running for 2,238 performances without a break. At the mature age of forty-eight, Miriam Timothy decided to get married, and Sidonie took over for the last two years of the run.

Oscar Asche who played Abu Hassan weighed over twenty stone and his wife, the actress Lily Brayton who was also in the show, nearly as much. She was very beautiful though. The show made a great impact on London audiences with the lavishness of its sets and the daring costumes of the harem girls, with their little beaded tops and chiffon trousers. In those days nobody ever showed their navel!

I remember one night Prince George [later to be the Duke of Kent] sat in the front row of the stalls in his midshipman's uniform. I had a terrible temptation to tickle his ankles![5]

The next royal visitor was the Shah of Persia, complete with his harem of veiled ladies. He was captivated by the beautiful young harpist and asked Oscar Asche how much he wanted for her, complete with harp. He was most disappointed to hear that neither Sidonie nor the harp was for sale . . .

There was a growing demand for music as the war progressed as distraction from the carnage in the mud of the Somme and on the beaches of Gallipoli. Marie and Sidonie found themselves playing every night and in danger of falling asleep at their desks the next morning. After two years as temporary Civil Servants they gave in their notice and became full-time musicians.

Eugene's reputation as a composer was growing. Sir John Barbirolli, recalling his success as a cellist at the age of sixteen in a series of recitals with the pianist Ethel Bartlett, mentioned that they 'were among the earliest interpreters of the then new works of Goossens, Debussy, Delius, Ireland, Bax and others'.[6] The Goossens works included his arrangement of 'Variations of a Chinese Theme' for violin (or cello) and piano, published by Curwen as 'Old Chinese Folk Song'.

Eugene's social circle was continually growing. Early in 1915 he made two new friends, Cecil Gray and Philip Heseltine, both budding critics and would-be composers. Thanks to the influence of Lady Cunard, at the age of twenty Philip was engaged as music critic for the *Daily Mail* from February to June 1915. He and Eugene racketed around the Cotswolds on a decrepit motorcycle, dividing their attention between the aesthetic attractions of the churches which Eugene sketched and the pubs where they consumed large quantities of the local beer. They descended in some disarray on one of Eugene's influential lady patrons: Mrs Connie Rose at Bourton-on-the-Water and made an incongruous appearance at a tea-party of Marie Corelli's in Stratford.

Eugene returned to London for the Proms and wrote to Philip nostalgically from Edith Road:

I envy you your solitary fastness on Crickley Hill, with Puma, Indians, Primus Stove etc. etc. and would heartily give up next week's salary to be once more basking in the sun on that verandah, dividing my attentions between the light of your elegance and the shadow on the Cathedral. However the Fates have it otherwise, and nine weeks of hard work at Queen's Hall is no consoling prospect. Thanks, my dear chap, for your solicitude. I hope to have something better than *Perseus* for next year's Proms, something less Straussian!

As for that opera, I haven't as yet heard from Beecham, and rely solely upon Lady C's empty promises. In fact I've almost reconciled myself to being out of it altogether, as I hear that Pitt, McCunn and Ronald have been deputed to conduct. Moral. Put not your faith in T.B. – I shall certainly *not* play second fiddle to any of the above.

I miss you muchly – on your return we must have many evenings at the Savoyard – or elsewhere. There's lots I really want to talk about – as you're quite the most 'understanding' person where I'm concerned. The depression of London, with its war, its music *and* its domestic troubles is occasionally over-powering.[7]

In the autumn of 1915, the London String Quartet gave the first performance of Eugene's 'Phantasy Quartet'. Philip tried to help him by interesting his idol and mentor Delius in his new friend's compositions, and sent him the score. Delius wrote from Grez-sur-Loing on 22nd January 1916. 'Just a few words to tell you how much I like the Goossens quartet; it is the best thing I have seen coming from an English pen and full of emotion. Tell Goossens that I will get it published for him as soon as the war is over.'[8] According to Philip, Delius' enthusiasm for the new work 'may have served to break down his apparent aversion to quartet writing, since his latest work has been cast in this form.'

Philip wrote to Delius on 22nd April 1916 describing with great enthusiasm the first concert Eugene had organised of his own chamber works, on 14th April.

The Aeolian Hall was fuller and more enthusiastic than I have seen it since the war began. To hear a representative selection of Goossens' work in one concert was indeed an artistic revelation. Most heartily do I endorse your verdict that his is the finest music that England has yet produced and although he will no doubt be submerged for years as you were beneath the tide of mediocrity, yet one day, the tide will ebb and leave at least two figures standing firm amidst the wrack. He had the Phantasy Quartet I sent you, a delicious Suite for the difficult combination of Flute, Violin and Harp, two groups of songs, the longer Quartet in which his three colleagues of the Philharmonic Quartet are mirrored and his two most exquisite sketches for String Quartet which are the most perfect and wholly satisfying pieces I have ever heard for that combination [*By the Tarn* and *Jack O' Lantern*].

Not the least amazing thing about Goossens is the careless rapidity with which he can produce perfectly finished works. These two pieces, for example were thrown off in a week and the Phantasy Quartet in little more time than it would take the average composer to make a fair copy of his work. All his music seems to come so straight through – there is never any sign of technical limitation which I think is marvellous seeing that Goossens is only twenty-two.

Delius completed only three movements of his quartet in 1916 and the work was premiered on 17th November; he added a scherzo the following year. In his opinion 'there is only one quality for great music and that is "emotion".'[9] By the following year he had developed reservations about the emotional content of Eugene's music, bracketing him with Debussy and Ravel: 'The French composers are all far too clever – Debussy wrote his best things before 30 and got gradually more superficial and uninteresting. The same with Ravel who is even cleverer than Debussy but even more flimsy and superficial. But their chief idea is to startle and be brilliant. Eugene Goossens is also far too clever altho' he is gifted and will I hope do something.'[10]

Meanwhile Philip had written an article on Eugene published in November 1916 in a Chamber Music Supplement to *The Music Student*, the first time he had written under the pseudonym Peter Warlock.[11] He had sent Eugene a copy of the article for his comments two months beforehand on 12th September 1916, deprecating his efforts. 'It is not good, but limitation of space and the utter putrescence of the paper for which it is intended prevent it from being anything but a few staccato, sforzato notes. For various important reasons please conceal the authorship from Cobbett and Co. It is by your dear friend Peter Warlock.'

Walter Willson Cobbett was a wealthy businessman and musical amateur who edited the *Cobbett Cyclopedia of Chamber Music*. In this he described the 'Phantasy Quartet' as 'a work in which one discerns the quality of genius.' Eugene had won first prize in a competition Cobbett organised to revive the one movement phantasy form.

Philip went on to give Eugene details of the opera season he and Cecil Gray planned to mount including 'a new work (by Goossens?) . . . No "stars" but everyone efficient in an unostentatious way. *No vibrato singers!* You *must* help us. *Will you write a new work?*' he reiterates, but like so many of his schemes it came to naught.[12]

In the article he repeats the effusive praise he had written to Delius of the 'Phantasy Quartet' and the two sketches. 'The technique is masterly, so right that it does not seem to exist at all. For Goossens there are no barriers, he has only to recollect an experience, and at once it takes on a musical form he can recollect in terms of pure sound.'

Eugene continually tried to bolster Philip's confidence in his ability as a composer and to help him discipline his talent by offering him lessons in composition . . . 'In December,' announced Philip, to Colin Taylor who had taught him music at Eton, 'I am going to begin a long and strenuous course of lessons with Goossens in the hope that I may be relieved of the fear which is hounding me that I have no musical bowels at all!'[13]

Successive Decembers passed without him taking the decisive step but the friendship continued. Marie remembers answering a knock on the door in Edith Road to a tall man with a neat beard, large brimmed hat and black cloak. 'I said "Hello Phil" and he nearly fell backwards down the steps – he was now disguised and his name was Peter Warlock, the well-known composer – he could not make out how I had recognised him.'[14]

Despite his growing success as a composer, Eugene could not yet afford to leave the Queen's Hall Orchestra. In the spring of 1915, he heard that Léon's inspiration, Henri de Busscher, was quitting London to go to the Los Angeles Philharmonic. Although Léon was only seventeen, he had received such glowing reports from Stanford for his outstanding performances with the RCM orchestra, that Sir Henry Wood agreed to audition him for the post of Principal Oboe. Léon presented himself with beating heart after a Sunday afternoon concert and Eugene listened to his brother's ordeal behind a curtain at the side of the platform. He made a great impression with his technical skill, beauty of tone and virtuosity in a florid piece by Colin. Then came exhaustive sight-reading tests in which he acquitted himself with amazing accuracy. He only betrayed a momentary nervousness when he suddenly caught sight of his father in the gallery, a far more daunting figure than Sir Henry.

Before his appointment was confirmed for the Promenade Season, he was asked to go with the Orchestra on a ten-week tour of Wales. Léon recalled:

> I made more mistakes than ever before or since, but Sir Henry seemed quite satisfied. He warned me that there would be no time to rehearse the Prom repertory and I would be performing two thirds of the works without ever having played them before. 'Goossens, you must be very brave. I can't run through everything just for one person. You must rely on me implicitly. I will give you your leads; come straight in.' Sometimes I didn't quite trust him and came in on my own. I was always wrong but he was very charming about it! It was a very frightening experience, not knowing the works and having to rely on the conductor.[15]

Even Eugene could not detect his nervousness.

> Sitting in the same orchestra as Léon, I remember marvelling at his sangfroid and musicianship when, confronted by a succession of new works (many unrehearsed) he would give an immaculate account of them. I always anticipated with some trepidation his first encounter with the oboistic high spots in the orchestral literature, like the slow movement from the Brahms violin concerto, the cadenza at the opening of Beethoven's Fifth Symphony, *obligati* from the Bach arias, not to mention the difficult passages of Strauss, Debussy and Sibelius. In those first three months of the season, Léon laid the solid foundation of a great career.[16]

The war did little to interfere with seaside holiday makers and the traditional entertainment of brass band music on the promenade. Adolphe spent a season at Torquay conducted by Basil Hindenberg, before the latter was advised to change his German name to Cameron. He then joined the Scottish Orchestra in Glasgow under Emil Mlynarski, the distinguished Polish conductor. He was making his mark as a gifted horn player and had also started to compose. One day the Gordon

Highlanders marched down the street past the rehearsal hall, bagpipes at full drone. On an impulse, Adolphe fell into step behind them, still with his horn case in his hand. He joined the Artists' Rifles and was rapidly posted to France at the beginning of the Somme offensive. Casualties were so heavy that arrangements were made for private soldiers who were recognised as being of exceptionally high calibre to be commissioned in the field. Adolphe fixed his new badges of rank on his epaulettes and took command of a platoon.

The next morning, with a sergeant who boasted that he had never brought back an officer alive, the twenty-year-old led his men 'over the top'. He was the first to reach the German trenches and was immediately mown down by enemy fire while his men pushed on. He was shot through the thigh and lay all night on the battlefield unable to drag himself back to British lines. He was discovered the next day when Australian troops moved in and taken to a Casualty Clearing Station where a priest administered the Last Rites. He died of his wounds and gas gangrene poisoning the following morning, 17th August 1916, and was buried in the Military Cemetery at Puichvillers.

The family was devastated by the news of his death. Sidonie remembers a desperate need to escape from the house and be by herself; of travelling on a bus all day, oblivious of where it was going. Marie, who had been particularly close to Adolphe, her nearest in age, had to continue with that evening's concert despite her grief as there was no one to take her place. Léon, who had enlisted with the Middlesex Yeomanry, was in Dublin, schooling horses for the Western Front. He was on guard when a telegram was handed to him: Tragic news, poor Addie died of wounds yesterday. Dad. He was relieved of his duties and broke down when he reached the guardroom.

Eugene's grief was intensified by the thought that Léon was also shortly due to leave for France. He tried for the third time to enlist and for the third time was rejected on medical grounds. Leaving the recruiting office, he bumped into a Canadian baritone friend, Edmund Burke, who was O.C. Divisional Bands for the Canadian Army. He persuaded Eugene to accept the rank of honorary lieutenant and conduct 275 bandsmen on a goodwill tour of France.

Despite the atrocities of war or perhaps because of people's desire to be diverted from them, there was a growing demand for concerts in London. The brothers Isidore and Frederick de Lara started promoting the works of contemporary British composers in a series of 'War Emergency Concerts' at the Steinway Hall where many of Eugene's early chamber works were performed. They then engaged the Queen's Hall Orchestra for three concerts of contemporary British orchestral works. Six weeks before the second of these, scheduled for mid-November 1915, Isidore de Lara asked Eugene if he had anything ready for performance. Not wishing to let the opportunity slip by, Eugene told him he 'was on the verge of completing a symphonic poem', and rapidly cast around for a suitable subject. His 'Symphonic Poem' based on a fragment by Ossian, was completed in a month. 'It employed a very large orchestra, an organ, and the enormous mushroom bells of Queen's Hall up in the organ-gallery, likewise a thunder machine. I used such a big orchestra that de Lara remarked, "Are you *quite* sure you haven't forgotten something?" The din of the climax created a great effect and while the musical content of the piece didn't bear too close scrutiny, the public seemed enraptured.'[17]

Also appearing on the programme was Debussy's first Mélisande, the Scottish soprano Mary Garden. They next met in the USA in Rochester and she agreed to sing Carmen for him in February 1927 with students from the Opera Department of the Eastman School of Music. 'There are only two things I remember about that concert in London,' she told him. 'One was a damnably noisy piece of yours and the other was a simply awful hat I wore which cost me fifteen guineas!'

After conducting his composition, Eugene returned to his accustomed place in the first violins and caught sight of Thomas Beecham in the audience. At the end of the concert he received a message saying that TB wanted to see him at the stage door. After offering his congratulations, he asked him to come to his house in Cavendish Square the following morning. 'Shall I bring my violin, Mr Beecham?' 'Heaven forbid!' was the acerbic reply.

Beecham greeted him the next day in a mauve silk dressing-gown and pink pyjamas. He had promised to conduct two new English operas, *The Critic* by Stanford based on the Sheridan comedy and *The Boatswain's Mate* by Ethel Smyth. As he was

51

feeling somewhat jaded he had decided to take a holiday in Italy instead. Would Eugene care to take over the two works? Beecham handed him the two scores and told him there was a piano rehearsal of *The Critic* at the Shaftesbury Theatre the following morning. 'Just tell the producer and the singers you're taking my place, and go ahead!' Eugene's violin playing days were over.

Many of the distinguished cast of singers, which included Frederick Ranalow, Frank Mullings and Percy Heming, had sung with Eugene I and II. They realised from that first rehearsal that Eugene III was a worthy inheritor of the family's operatic baton. He knew exactly what he was doing and they entrusted themselves to his professional competence. Stanford, after he had recovered from his surprise at finding his erstwhile pupil in charge, persuaded him to conduct all the performances of his opera disguised as Mr Linley of Bath, involving full stage make-up, costume and wig. It is doubtful whether TB would have acquiesced.

Beecham's confidence in his 22-year-old protégé was fully justified. He had previously offered Grainger the post of assistant conductor but he had turned it down with the excuse that his heart lay in composing rather than performing. The real reason lay in his racial prejudice and theories of Aryan supremacy: Beecham was not racially acceptable because he had brown eyes!

Fortunately Eugene did not share his friend's prejudices and recognised the opportunity as an unparalleled launch into the realm of opera; he even managed to cope with Ethel Smyth. 'At the last minute she took over the baton, thinking herself the heaven-sent conductor she was not. This necessitated last-minute rehearsals, which she directed with a maximum of fuss, pomposity and ineptitude. The men had the utmost difficulty in following her beat (she always rolled the sleeves of her blouse well beyond her elbow, so that "the gentlemen of the orchestra could see the beat plainly!") and the ensemble at the premiere suffered severely from her inability to convey accurate indications to orchestra and stage.'[18] Eugene conducted the subsequent performance and as a token of her appreciation, the composer presented him with a large silver cigarette case.

The Beecham company went to Manchester for a six week season at the New Queen's Theatre, opening with *Boris Godunov*. Beecham conducted the first performance and then handed the baton to Eugene. He also had to conduct *The Magic Flute*, *Phoebus and Pan*, *Madame Butterfly*, *Aida* and *Pagliacci*, all without orchestral rehearsal. Eugene recalled: 'Out of the sixty or seventy operas I conducted during my English operatic years, forty or more were without orchestral rehearsal. You can dispense with the latter only if you have a good knowledge of the score and a strong nerve, both of which I had; but it was a grilling test of apprenticeship.'[19] 'Oh Mr Goossens,' Marie used to relate, imitating Beecham's distinctive tones, 'would you go and conduct *Aida* tonight?'[20]

When the company returned to London to the Aldwych theatre (owned by Sir Joseph Beecham), Eugene found himself conducting Verdi's *Otello* from the same score that his grandfather and father had used with the Carl Rosa Company. 'It always gave me a strange emotion to encounter their two familiar pencil markings; often I was constrained to add my own to keep the three-generation record straight.'[21]

At the end of the season, Beecham reminded the audience: 'Thirty weeks of opera in English so far, with a war going on, and more to come before the year ends.' Before the war, London audiences had turned up their noses at opera in English, and touring companies like the Carl Rosa found their popular support in the provinces. By 1916 Londoners had no choice. It was the enforced absence of foreign singers rather than an upsurge of patriotism that led to the increased popularity of opera in English.

No sooner had the opera season opened in the autumn of 1916 than Eugene received a call from Beecham in the early hours of the morning. He was to pack a bag and come by taxi immediately to Beecham senior's house in Hampstead. 'My father died two hours ago,' TB told him on arrival. 'Take these scores, catch the 8.30 from Euston to Liverpool and conduct the concert there for me tonight. The rehearsal is this afternoon at two. Then go to Manchester tomorrow and take over my concert with the Hallé orchestra in the evening, rehearsal in the afternoon. There's a third concert in Bradford with the Orchestral Society the day after tomorrow. Forsyth [the Manager of the Hallé] will meet you at Liverpool. Good luck!'[22]

Eugene needed it. He had four hours on the train to absorb more than half a dozen unfamiliar works. The Directors of the Liverpool Philharmonic had received the news of the substitution with some misgivings. They remembered the talented young lad who had played the fiddle at the Kursaal in New Brighton only six years earlier but, apart from his own works with the Queen's Hall Orchestra, Eugene had never conducted a symphony orchestra.

His recent experience with the opera company stood him in good stead; he knew how to master a score in record speed, to organise his limited rehearsal time and concentrate on the salient points of the evening's performance. 'Orchestra and chorus, most of whom at the outset appeared sceptical about my being able to tackle the job efficiently in one rehearsal, had shown themselves increasingly co-operative as the afternoon wore on. The concert passed off without a hitch and with the greatest enthusiasm.'[23] Afterwards in the Green Room, Riley, the Secretary, who remembered Eugene as a schoolboy, paid him the greatest compliment he knew and opened the bottle of vintage claret which had stood since time immemorial on the Green Room mantelpiece of the Liverpool Philharmonic Hall; Eugene does not record whether or not it was drinkable. The Manchester and Bradford concerts were equally successful.

Although Beecham claims in his autobiography to have engaged the 22-year-old Eugene initially as his 'general secretary', he does give him generous praise as a conductor: 'His coolness and facility were phenomenal, and he had good need of both, as I do not think any man of his age was ever subjected to such ordeals as I imposed on him.'[24]

The family rejoiced in Eugene's growing success, although they could not forget Adolphe's tragic loss and Léon at risk, fighting in the trenches in France. In 1917 when the Beecham Opera Company performed in Birmingham, the names of both Eugene senior and junior appeared on the billboards. Eugene recalls in *Overture and Beginners*: 'My father had been suddenly engaged to reinforce the conductorial staff, with the result that standard works like *Aida*, *Trovatore*, *Pagliacci* and *Faust* felt the grip of his experienced hand and singers who had lapsed into

complacent ways were rudely shaken out of them every time
Father appeared in the orchestra pit. It can't be said that this
added to his popularity; for in the Carl Rosa days his severity
had been a byword.'[25]

Eugene found his father's example beneficial to his own
conducting. 'The facility I had acquired in the ways of opera –
I think I was born with it – hadn't really been accompanied by
a proportionate depth of interpretative powers. The example of
my father's conscientious approach to his work finally brought
this about, plus a growing realisation of the competitive professionalism which surrounded me.'

The relationship between father and son deepened into
a mutual respect for each other's qualities of musicianship.
The older man's experience and discipline contrasted with the
younger's intuitive flair. Throughout his professional career,
Eugene valued the critical opinion of his father more than
any other person. An added bonus of touring with Father was
that he could abandon the impersonality of second-class hotels
for the welcome of theatrical lodgings. The landladies greeted
his father as a familiar friend and piled both their plates with
substantial breakfasts and delicious high teas.

Beecham asked Goossens senior to open the autumn season
of 1917 at Drury Lane with Rimsky-Korsakov's *Ivan the Terrible*.
Goossens junior was handed a 'newly furbished production' of
Tannhäuser in English, which he conducted on the same day,
21st March 1918, as the Germans launched their last major
offensive of the war. At no time was there any protest at the
continuation of Wagner's operas, although during one performance of *Tannhäuser* a bomb fell on an air-raid shelter near
the theatre killing a hundred people. A piece of shrapnel came
through the glass roof onto the stage, just missing Mullings as
the eponymous hero, on his return to the Wartburg.

Such occasions were a stabbing reminder of the horrors that
Léon was undergoing in France. He had survived the Battle of
Arras, during which he had gone over the top of the trenches
three times in one day and survived unscathed. He agreed,
under pressure, to return to England to take up a commission as
a Second Lieutenant with the Sherwood Foresters. His mother
was distraught at the possibility of a second son risking his life

as he led his men forward with reckless impetuosity. At the end of his embarkation leave, on an impulse Eugene handed his brother the silver cigarette case from Ethel Smyth. He put it in the left-hand breast pocket of his tunic, together with his steel shaving mirror.

On the evening of 3rd November 1918 he reached the front line at Landrecies on the Somme. His company commander informed him that he would be taking out a patrol the next morning and introduced him to his platoon sergeant: 'This is Mr Goossens.' There was a faint shock of recognition and then the chilling statement: 'I was your brother's platoon sergeant. I was with him on the day he died.' This was the man who had boasted to Adolphe that he had never brought an officer back alive.

Léon broke the grim record and returned safely to base after his first day on active service as an officer. He had captured a platoon of German infantrymen who had thrown down their weapons and surrendered. He snatched a few hours sleep before his batman woke him with a mug of tea at 4am. It was essential that his men should not see him shivering in the grey freezing air before the dawn as he led them into battle so he put on a warm yellow cardigan underneath his tunic, carefully placing the cigarette case and shaving mirror in his breast pocket.

At the height of the battle, Léon determined to link up with a reinforcement of machine-gunners to his right. As soon as he reached them, he was struck by a high velocity bullet at forty yards range. It hit him just above the heart but he was more fortunate than his brother. Within minutes the stretcher bearers arrived and he was taken to a casualty post. The surgeon extracted the cigarette case and the shaving mirror from Léon's tunic. The bullet had passed straight through the steel mirror and been deflected downward from the heart by the cigarette case.[26]

Marie recalled 9th November, two days before Armistice Day, the ring on the doorbell that they had all been dreading and a second telegram arriving from the War Office. With relief they read that Léon was alive and was *en route* for the Epsom War Hospital. Mother, Father and Marie went to visit him there the next day. 'When we arrived there were screens up round his bed and we feared the worst. Then we heard his voice saying "It's all right Mum. I'm only having my feet washed!" He had to stay in hospital for two months and when he went back to the Queen's Hall Orchestra all Sir Henry Wood said, in his lovely Cockney voice, was " 'Ad a good toim?" '[27]

5

My Heart Loosens When I Listen to Goossens

The original version of Noel Coward's song in praise of Eugene was 'My heart just loosens when I'm listening to Mr Goossens'. Coward wrote 'Russian Blues', sung to the tune of the 'Maiden's Dance' from *Prince Igor*, during a Sunday afternoon concert at the Albert Hall in November 1921. Those were the days when London was still obliterated by pea-soupers; the sound of the orchestra wafted over to his box, but the fog was so dense in the auditorium that Noel could not see his friend Gene on the podium.

Coward's witticism epitomised the fame that Eugene enjoyed in London in the 'Roaring Twenties'; the brilliant young conductor and composer, friend of titled hostesses, of Stravinsky, Ravel, Epstein and Arnold Bennett, conducting opera for Beecham or ballet for Diaghilev, fêted alike for his championship of contemporary composers or conducting his own works. An early tribute to his status among contemporary composers had been an invitation from the writer and critic Edwin Evans to join three older and more established of his friends, all published by J & W Chester, Frank Bridge, Arnold Bax and John Ireland, in composing variations on the French folk song 'Cadet Rousselle'.[1] These were first performed at the Aeolian Hall on 6th June 1919 by the French light soprano Raymonde Collignon and London's most beautiful young pianist, Harriet Cohen, the protégées of Evans and Arnold Bax respectively.

Eugene had been too busy conducting for Beecham to complete his variation. Evans accompanied him to Manchester and in desperation followed the example of Mozart's friends in Prague, when they forced him to complete the overture to *Don Giovanni*. 'Early next morning before he was up,' recalled

Evans, 'I went to his hotel bedroom armed with a supply of music paper, perched myself on his bed and firmly refused to let him have his bath until he had produced the missing variation. Without more ado he made a desk of his knees, wrote a very clever final variation on "Cadet Rousselle" as a climax to the whole set, and within a quarter of an hour he was having his bath.'*

The effect of 'listening to Goossens' was equally apt for the burgeoning careers of the other members of the family. For Léon it had been in the balance whether he would return to the career of a professional musician after the war. In the trenches he had struck up a friendship with Rex Workman who was emigrating to the Argentine to train as a ranch manager. Léon, who had always loved horses and life in the open air, decided to go with him. The only problem was raising the money for the fare and the necessary capital of £100. Rex was invited home to Edith Road for one of Annie's famous high teas and promptly fell in love with Léon's beautiful young sister, Sidonie. They became engaged; ranch managers were not allowed to marry until they had completed a four year training so they reconciled themselves to the long separation before she could travel out to join him.

Instead of advancing Léon the amount he needed, his father persuaded him to collect his oboe from the vaults of the Midland Bank in Piccadilly, where it had been in safe keeping during his war service, and earn the money from professional engagements. Within a few months he had returned to the Queen's Hall Orchestra for the 1919 Promenade Season. Rex sailed without him while Léon continued to delay his departure as more and more solo engagements built up. He never reached the Argentine. Once again his father had been proved right in determining his children's musical careers. Within five years Léon had achieved an unrivalled position as the best oboe player in the country, while Marie and Sidonie were recognised as the most gifted, decorative and reliable young harpists. Eugene II and Annie could be

---

*Twenty-five years later, on 1st November 1944, Evans was to recall the incident and Eugene's speed and fluency as a composer in a BBC Interval Talk for the British premiere of Eugene's Phantasy Concerto for Piano.

justifiably proud of their offspring.

Sir Thomas Beecham was determined to continue his career as the Maecenas of English music despite the financial complications caused by his father's death. Both Eugene Goossens senior and junior were employed by the Beecham Opera Company. On one Saturday in March 1919, at Drury Lane, Eugene junior conducted a matinée of *La Bohème*, handing over the baton to his father in the evening for *Aida*. The *Telegraph* commented that the son 'conducted with a keen sense of climax', whereas the father 'turned his opportunities and his long experience to the best account'.[2]

Eugene senior had always been admired for his efficiency, musicality and meticulousness in preparing a score but he was not always an inspired or inspiring operatic conductor. 'Always careful if never exactly stimulating,' was the verdict of the *Globe* on his *Ivan the Terrible*.[3] His natural caution and musical conventionality were becoming intensified by middle age. Although he continued to conduct opera on tour until 1930, as Eugene Goossens senior, his reputation was rapidly outdistanced by the vigour and vitality of his son. The relationship between them remained an ideal one of love and respect, no jealousy on the father's part, only enormous pride and satisfaction in his son's success, which was indeed shared by both parents in the achievements of all their children. As far as Eugene III was concerned, his father was enshrined as his sternest critic, the one person whose opinion and judgement he valued most throughout his career.

Annie Goossens had resumed going on tour with her husband. She remained the powerhouse of the family, a kindly but redoubtable figure, adored by her children in their adult years. 'Quite stout but with nice legs,' recalled Sidonie affectionately. 'I used to take her to Harrods to buy her hats. She always chose a toque that made her look like Queen Mary.'[4]

London's musical life had gradually returned to normal after the war although when the Grand Opera Season was resumed at Covent Garden in the Spring of 1919, Dame Nellie Melba complained that she saw men sitting in the stalls in shabby tweed overcoats instead of evening dress. Eugene was on tour with the Beecham Opera Company when he was suddenly called to replace an indisposed Albert Coates and conduct Melba in *Faust*. Melba had just celebrated her sixtieth birthday, a trifle old for Gounod's Marguerite but she was still 'a heavenly woman, jocund, gleaming, wicked'.[5]

Goossens presented himself at the diva's dressing-room as requested fifteen minutes before the performance. 'Have you ever conducted *Faust* before?' she demanded imperiously. 'Frequently,' he replied. 'But in French?' 'No, but I speak French fluently,' he reassured her. He asked whether she made any changes in the traditional tempi. 'None whatsoever. I sing it exactly as Gounod wrote it. And I hope,' she added suspiciously, 'you conduct it the same way!'

Much to his surprise, Eugene was bowled over by her performance. 'Her singing of the role turned out to be a most refreshing musical experience. With none of the kittenish tricks and simperings elderly prime donne usually indulge in when they're playing a youthful role, the incomparable singer realised Gounod's Marguerite to perfection, and made our task in the orchestra pit easeful and unapprehensive. The purity of vocal style which was her great characteristic remained unimpaired. At our final curtain call together, she plucked a rose from her bouquet and thrust it in my shirt front with a spontaneous gesture which carried as pleasant a tribute as I shall ever know.'[6]

Ten years later Melba was to be on the other side of the footlights at Covent Garden, for the first night of Eugene's opera, *Judith*.

Beecham continued in his gratitude to Eugene for being 'an indispensable standby, as well as a loyal and devoted colleague' throughout the five years of their association, but the younger man was tiring of his 'always the bridesmaid, never the bride' status. He tried unsuccessfully to rebel when he was forced to take over the very difficult score of Stravinsky's opera *Le Rossignol* at three days' notice.

Edwin Evans, one of Eugene's most outspoken champions, castigated the event in *New Witness*:

Considering the scanty preparation, the orchestra did wonders and Mr Eugene Goossens who conducted it, and who really understands Stravinsky, laboured heroically in a lost cause. The Beecham Company has done a great deal of excellent work, for which it has received due credit. It cannot complain if it is judged by the standards which it has contributed to raise. That it should deliberately disfigure its record with this caricature is one of those things which defy explanation. The only wise course now would be to remove the production as quickly as possible and then set seriously to work with the preparation of a performance which would afford some compensation to the injury inflicted upon his name.[7]

Because of the opera Eugene had to postpone his honeymoon. The day of the second performance coincided with his 'first excursion into matrimony' on 18th November 1919.[8] His bride was Dorothy Millar, a talented painter, known as 'Boonie'. She was a beautiful and imposing woman, somewhat Bohemian in lifestyle. Born Dorothy Smith-Dodsworth in 1891, she came from a wealthy aristocratic family in Yorkshire, related to the Lascelles. Her first ambition was to be a cellist; she had studied in Brussels in her teens but been forced into an early marriage with the son of a neighbouring landowner. The marriage was unhappy and after the birth of a son she had left her husband, making her a social outcast in the eyes of provincial society. When she met the handsome and fascinating Eugene at a society lunch party there was an immediate mutual attraction. They made a striking couple and were quickly established in the socially acceptable, fast living, artistic circles of London in the 'Gay Twenties'. After they were married, Boonie studied painting with J D Fergusson[9] and was commissioned by Chesters to design the covers for three of Eugene's works: 'Four Conceits', op. 20, 'Nature Poems', op. 25 and the opera *Judith*.

Eugene was finding it increasingly difficult to devote as much time as he wanted to composition. The solution was to develop a dual musical personality. 'When I was conducting a thirty-week operatic season, I found that if I was to write the music for which my conscience insisted it was essential I should write, I must of necessity so school my mind that I could use what free hours came my way each day. Instead of leaving the opera house after rehearsals with the idea that I was tired and needed relaxation from everything musical, the minute I closed the door behind me I began plotting music in my head. I went home and forced myself to write.'[10]

The policy was successful: he gave a joint concert of chamber works in Brussels with the Italian composer Casella and the French violinist André Mangeot, and the first performance of his 'Lyric poem' in Paris for the Société Musicale Independante in the Salle Gavreau. The Paris programme included works by Ravel and Milhaud; a riot broke out in the audience between their supporters and a Vorticist claque including Erik Satie and Florent Schmitt who gave their vociferous support to a recherché composer called Obukhof.

Passion for contemporary music never rose as high in London. Commenting on a performance at the Wigmore Hall of Eugene's Violin and Piano Sonata given by Albert Sammons and William Murdoch, his old friend Arthur Bliss wrote: 'This sonata is enlivened with a wealth of ideas, and permeated with that characteristic elegance of thought that distinguishes Goossens from many of his English contemporaries.'[11]

Philip Heseltine indulged in irreverent comments on the contemporary music scene for the amusement of his friend Elizabeth Poston:

> Said a critic, 'It all comes to this:
> British music is nothing but piss . . .
> So we'll charge Eugene Goossens
> With committing a nuisance
> And puncture the bladder of Bliss.'*[12]

The precariousness of London's musical life engendered not by the passions of Paris but by lack of public interest and financial support was underlined in 1920 when Beecham was forced into bankruptcy. The out of work members of his opera company found appropriate employment in *The Beggar's Opera*. Nigel Playfair's delightful production of Gay's ballad opera opened at the Lyric, Hammersmith, with music rearranged by Frederic Austin and costumes and sets designed by Claud Lovat Fraser. It proved an unexpected popular success and ran for two and a half years. Eugene conducted the first four weeks and his father took out the provincial tour.

Unlike Beecham, Boult or Bliss, Eugene did not start with

*'From the toilet rolls in the hands of the executors of the late Elizabeth Poston.'

the advantage of a wealthy father to finance his musical career but he did have influential friends. One of the most colourful of these was George Davison. GD, as he liked to be known, was a wealthy English eccentric, a self-made man, son of a ship's carpenter, who had become an accomplished landscape photographer. In 1898 George Eastman had appointed him Managing Director of foreign business for the Eastman Kodak Company. He held somewhat unorthodox political views as a socialist anarchist and marched in a demonstration past the Kodak headquarters in High Holborn waving a banner aloft. Eastman objected, not because Davison's banner had denounced capitalism but because he had appeared in public without wearing a hat! In 1912 Eastman finally asked him to resign from the board of Kodak Limited as Davison was financing a publication called *The Anarchist*.[13]

He had acquired considerable wealth by the judicious buying of Kodak shares and in 1908 he built a large neo-medieval house, Plas Wernfawr in Harlech. The small resort on the North Wales coast attracted a growing colony of writers, artists and musicians; the summer concerts of the United Temperance Choral Society within the castle and its grounds eventually developed into the Harlech Music Festival with massed choirs of 16,000 voices under the batons of Walford Davies and Edward Elgar.

When he went to Wernfawr for the first time in 1918, Eugene found his friends Cyril Scott, Granville Bantock and Joseph Holbrooke all living and busily composing nearby. Eugene had introduced GD to Margaret Morris and John Fergusson. Meg's summer school of modern dance imparted what Eugene described as, 'an Attic flavour to Harlech that surprised – and occasionally shocked – the elders of the town. John Fergusson, eminent Scottish painter, came along as usual to supervise the rather Cézanne-ish efforts of the School in its afternoon painting work. The rhythmic improvisations of the dance – in which Meg and her pupils excelled – he translated into terms of colour and brush stroke, so that, at Harlech, the two arts were synonymous in theory and practice.'[14] Eugene helped to add a smattering of music to the curriculum by lectures on rhythm and form.

Meg vividly recalled the atmosphere of one amusing evening

when they all took part in a cod opera: 'I was the prima donna, Boonie, tall and handsome (but very well covered!) was the prima ballerina. A Spaniard, a musician but not a singer, called Pedro de Morales, was the hero and Goossens and Bax improvised the music.'[15] (Morales was a poet and friend from the Muriel Draper days, later to advise Eugene on Spanish authenticity for his opera, *Don Juan de Mañara*.)

The Great Hall at Wernfawr seated two hundred and was equipped with a large Aeolian pipe-organ. GD enjoyed playing excerpts from Holbrooke's Welsh operas. 'GD, having little musical capacity and being slightly hard of hearing, would play at fantastic speed, producing unheard of effects from the organ. This bewildered everyone,' recalled Eugene, 'including the composer, who would rush to the organ and pull the control lever hard over to decelerate the headlong pace of his opus.'[16]

GD had installed a similar organ in his London home at 32, Holland Park and turned the whole ground floor into a music room. This had provided the venue for performances by the Plough Club, dedicated in 1918 to the collaboration between writers, painters and musicians and 'stimulating interest in good art of an unconventional kind'. Eugene wrote incidental music for a Plough Club production of *Philip the Second*, a melodrama of the Inquisition by Emile Verhaeren. Other distinguished members included Jacob Epstein, Lady Lavery and Charles Rennie Mackintosh.[17]

Early in 1921 Eugene rented the studio apartment over the mews at the end of the garden for himself and Boonie and it was here that their daughter Anne was born, on 31st March. The baby and her nurse were installed in the basement of the main house so that she did not interfere with her parents' busy lives.

GD gave Eugene the key to the music room which was to be the scene of many memorable musical evenings. When Ravel was in London, Eugene invited a few friends to meet him and then had the greatest difficulty in tearing him away from the Aeolian organ. He was fascinated by its celesta, chimes, harp and 'echo-organ' effects and even the eruption of Adrian Boult pushing his bicycle in through the front door failed to shift his concentration. Eventually when Manuel de Falla (in London for the first performance of his *Nights in the*

Garden of Spain) and Malipiero arrived, Ravel was persuaded to leave his experiments with its sonorities.

Eugene had decided that the only way to launch himself as a conductor of contemporary music was to organise his own orchestra and promote his own concert at the Queen's Hall. 7th June 1921 was to prove an epoch-making event in his career. The hand-picked orchestra was made up of 105 of the best instrumentalists, including Marie, Sidonie and Léon. The programme promoted two English works: Lord Berners' *Spanish Fantasy* and John Ireland's prelude *The Forgotten Rite*, followed by Ravel's *La Valse*. After the interval there was to be the first concert performance of Stravinsky's *Le Sacre du Printemps*. Eugene was determined that Stravinsky's masterpiece should at last be given the performance it deserved; British audiences had previously only heard it played as an indifferent ballet accompaniment.

Two days before the concert, disaster threatened. Eugene's main financial backer withdrew but the enterprise was saved by a cheque for £500 from Lord Howard de Walden, patron of his friend, Joseph Holbrooke. A brilliant audience assembled in the Queen's Hall including Mrs Asquith, George Bernard Shaw, Sir Alfred Mond and Arnold Bennett. Eugene prolonged the interval as long as he dared, waiting for the arrival of Stravinsky from Paris. 'Just as I raised my stick to give the bassoon player his cue for the opening phrase, a movement in the dress circle caught my eye, and a trio of weary travellers – Stravinsky, Diaghilev and Massine – crept into their seats. The suspense was broken, and the orchestra settled down to give Londoners twenty-five minutes of ensemble-cum-virtuoso fireworks, more dazzling, I venture to think, than anything so far heard in Queen's Hall.'[18]

The next morning Robin Legge in the *Daily Telegraph* led the critics' unanimous praise, bowled over by Eugene's brilliance: 'Since *Ein Heldenleben* first shocked a London audience many years ago, no such first performance as this has been heard in Queen's Hall. Apparently the young conductor is one of the coolest musical brains in England, and his control of this epic dance, his building up of his climaxes, surely, inexorably to the climax that is the climax of all – this in a score of stupendous difficulty and complexity, this alone marks Goossens out as a conductor, *pur sang*. Belgium has given us precious hostages in this young Londoner and his kin.'

The *Observer* asked George Bernard Shaw, 'our oldest music critic', to give his view of the Stravinsky: 'Mind I'm not to be understood as condemning it, but if it had been by Rossini people would have said that it had too much *rum-tum* in it.'

A week later, Robin Legge reported: 'Nothing succeeds like success. It is pleasant to hear that in response to urgent requests Mr Goossens will repeat the programme in the Queen's Hall on the evening of 23rd June. How Goossens' ears must have been tingling since that memorable night. Stravinsky himself acknowledges that it was the finest performance of his *Sacre du Printemps* he has heard.'

For this repeat performance, Eugene included his own symphonic poem *The Eternal Rhythm*, which he had conducted at a Promenade Concert the previous September. Thanks to the generosity of the Earl of Lathom, Eugene was able to announce four further Goossens Orchestral Concerts of contemporary music most imaginatively planned. An extra bonus was to be a series of fanfares, composed by contemporary musicians for publication in a short lived periodical called *Fanfare*, edited by Philip Heseltine and Leigh Henry.

The programmes were as follows:

27th October 1921
Fanfares – de Falla, Satie, Prokofiev, Harty, Goossens, Milhaud, Roussel, Felix White.
Fugue in C minor – Bach-Elgar
Tone Poem: The Garden of Fand – Arnold Bax
Pastorale – Arthur Honegger
Suite: Beni Mora – Gustav Holst
Symphony no. 1 in C minor – Brahms
(substituted for Stravinsky's *The Song of the Nightingale*)

9th November 1921
Overture: The Siege of Corinth – Rossini
Mêlée Fantasque – Arthur Bliss
Symphonic Poem: The Builders of Joy – J R Heath
Alborada del Gracioso – Ravel

Five Orchestral Pieces – Schoenberg
Tone Poem: Thus spake Zarathustra – Strauss

23rd November 1921
Fugue in C minor – Bach-Elgar
Fantasie: The Wild Sea-Fowl (from *Dylan*) – Holbrooke
Symphonic Poem: Prometheus – Liszt
Aubade – Cyril Scott
Suite: El Amor Brujo – de Falla
Rondes de Printemps – Debussy
Symphony: Antar – Rimsky-Korsakov

12th December 1921
Further selection of Fanfares – Bax, Julius Harrison, Milhaud, Malipiero, Poulenc and Wellesz
Suite in G for Organ, Oboe and Strings (with Léon as oboe soloist) – Bach-Wood
Symphonic Rhapsody: Mai Dun – Ireland
Suite: Oriente Immaginario – Malipiero
Symphony for Wind Instruments – Stravinsky
Le Sacre du Printemps – Stravinsky (by general request)

After the first concert, Richard Capell commented: 'Mr Goossens and his picked orchestra gave us a wonderful concert, the first of a series, the rest of which ought to be overcrowded, else Londoners indeed will prove themselves slow to know a good thing.' He praised both 'the superb performances and the cunning arrangement of the programme.'

Edwin Evans was equally enthusiastic: 'Mr Goossens conducted splendidly, with insight and with youthful energy. Considering the amount that has been thrust upon him of late, his temperamental buoyancy is out of the common.' (He was also conducting for the Carl Rosa season at Covent Garden and Diaghilev's Russian Ballet at the Alhambra.)

The concerts were an outstanding critical and artistic success and Eugene was encouraged by the growth of public interest in stimulating programmes of new music. But although the cheap seats in the pit and gallery had been full, Eugene and Boonie's fashionable friends, on whom he was relying for financial support, had stayed away. Two years later he embarked on a more modest series of contemporary chamber music concerts at the Aeolian Hall on Wednesday evenings at 5.25pm. The composer, Herbert Bedford, agreed to share the expenses as long as each concert included one of his 'unaccompanied songs'. Bedford was a monocled and likeable man but unfortunately did not share his late wife Liza Lehmann's gift for popular melody.

The five imaginative programmes included Vaughan Williams' Phantasy Quintet, Holst's Four songs for voice and violin performed by Dora Labbette and Isolde Menges and Eugene's Phantasy Quartet. The audiences were disappointing and Eugene sadly concluded, 'a steady diet of novelty without a leavening of classics was insufficient to hold a regular clientele.'

In January 1922 it was announced that the old Beecham Opera Company was reforming, to work on independent and co-operative lines as the British National Opera Company. While they started out on tour with Eugene senior, Covent Garden was experimentally turned into a Picture Palace, albeit a superior one. Eugene junior was engaged by Walter Wanger, head of United Artists in Hollywood, to arrange and conduct the music for their first season of films. He was to have an orchestra of sixty-five players drawn from the London Symphony Orchestra, for matinées and evening performances.

The programme grandiloquently proclaimed: 'The Royal Opera House, Covent Garden, because of its historical associations, prestige, dignity of interior construction and decoration and great size, has been chosen for the presentation of the world's choicest example of screen craft commencing with Douglas Fairbanks' production of *The Three Musketeers*. Only film masterpieces will be shown during the present season and always with the finest of orchestral music.' Aeons away from the ubiquitous little old lady pounding the piano in the local flea pit!

With the help of Frederick Laurence (soon to become Marie's husband), who was in charge of the Goodwin & Tabb music hire library, Eugene put together eighty minutes of stirring accompaniment for Fairbanks' dashing adventures. He found the symphonies of August Enna an invaluable source of musical clichés. The second film was *Atlantide*, a superb

69

French film directed by Jacques Feyder from the novel by Pierre Benoit. That also failed to draw an audience to Covent Garden, so inconveniently situated amongst the cabbage stalks and rotten oranges. It was replaced by a romantic American thriller called *Love. The Glorious Adventure*, an epic of the Great Fire of London starring the beautiful Lady Diana Manners, had more success, but that was an English film made by the Stoll Film Company with which Eugene was not involved.

From 1916 onwards Eugene Goossens senior had been keeping a comprehensive diary, not only a record of his and Annie's private commitments and his conducting engagements but also a record of his children's professional careers. He notes down and comments on their performances often adding programmes and press reviews, an invaluable treasury of source material for a future historian or biographer. He kept up a voluminous correspondence with family, friends and colleagues and, wherever possible, carefully preserved the letters he received in his large 'page a day' annual volumes. In February 1922, he was delighted to receive a letter from Aurelie Révy-Chapman, a German soprano who had made her pre-war debut with the Carl Rosa, describing how she had resumed her English career with a concert in Bournemouth:

> Yesterday I sang with your son and it has touched me up so much – I was so exited [*sic*] that I couldn't help it – I always had to think what I always have said to everybody how much I owe to you, my first conductor in all those operas which I sang under your baton! Today I can confess it to you that those I never had done before, so your influence and your education made me to become so conscious and punctual to every little semiquaver!
>
> As your son I was quite certain about him and never troubled him or me about a rehearsal for the old *Traviata* aria and off it went splendidly! Are you not proud of him? Such a big artist and such a fine looking young man! My heartiest congratulations!
>
> I have not been in England since about ten years – meanwhile having been the Manager of the Opera Comique at Berlin. I had to give it up during the war, being the wife of an English Officer, but now I want to stay on here to freshen up entirely my old reputation. I would so much like to see you once more!'[19]

Eugene senior's reputation as a repetiteur and vocal coach continued to grow. The actress Viola Tree wrote to say how much she benefited from her lessons; amongst the people who approached him for advice was an undergraduate from St John's College, Oxford who signed himself W Tyrone Guthrie: 'It has been suggested to me that I should study with a view to becoming an operatic singer. Before taking any steps in the matter I am anxious to get an expert opinion about my voice. Will you hear me sing and be good enough to give me your advice?' he wrote.[20] After the audition at Edith Road, Eugene senior commented in his diary on 23rd March 1923: 'Very fair voice. No training.'

The junior household had been further augmented on 28th August 1922 when Boonie gave birth to daughters, Julia and Jane. 'Brilliant conductor baffled by his twins,' was the press comment. 'Though he can read the most difficult score at sight, Mr Eugene Goossens cannot tell his twin daughters apart!'

Eugene returned to Harlech for a final summer, without Boonie. Bernard Shaw was staying nearby and visited the Davisons every day for intellectual debate and piano duets with the beautiful Harriet Cohen.

Another pleasure was the Pageant of Harlech against the backdrop of the castle ruins. Eugene recalls 'Cyril Scott's quavering performance as Old Father Time. Foster the herbalist disguised as a medieval bowman and my impersonation of Edward II, with Mr Parry the chemist as Simon de Montfort were highlights of an impressive performance – that is when we didn't forget our lines!'[21] The 1922 pageant was written under the aegis of another distinguished English resident A P Graves, father of Robert.

Despite these amusements, Eugene found the atmosphere of Harlech conducive to composition. He rapidly completed two totally disparate commissions both due to be performed in September 1922. The first was incidental music for *East of Suez*, a new play by Somerset Maugham produced by Basil Dean at His Majesty's Theatre starring Basil Rathbone and Meggie Albanesi. One afternoon wandering through Limehouse in search of inspiration, Eugene had discovered an old Chinese grocer with a side-line in one string fiddles. Behind the shop, he was taken down a sinister flight of stairs and a long dark corridor to discover not an opium den but Chang Tim's band of Chinese seamen. They played Chinese fiddles, flutes, wooden blocks, gongs and cymbalum and he adapted their themes for Western notation and instruments.

The second work was for the Three Choirs Festival in Gloucester Cathedral, a setting for chorus and orchestra of Walter de la Mare's poem 'Silence'. The morning concert opened with Skriabin's *Poem of Ecstasy*, which Elgar, as a Catholic, found unsuitably erotic.

'To think that Gloucester Cathedral should ever echo to such music!' he complained to Eugene. 'Write a festival mass and atone for this outrage.'

'All right, Sir Edward, but Mother Church won't approve of my modernism.'

'Never mind, I'll be in Heaven by then; I'll make it all right for you! Don't forget, plenty of percussion in the *Sanctus*!'[22]

It was to be thirty years before Eugene fulfilled Sir Edward's instructions with his soul stirring choral magnum opus *The Apocalypse*.

The concert ended with the premiere of Bliss' *Colour Symphony*. Elgar's admitted preference for this did not mar the friendship between the two young composers nor the enormous roast beef lunch they enjoyed with Elgar followed by an afternoon walking with him along the banks of the Severn.

As a mark of Eugene's position as a leader of Britain's musical avant-garde, he was invited by the newly formed International Society for Contemporary Music to conduct the Berlin Philharmonic Orchestra in an all British programme, in December 1922. He quickly overcame the orchestra's hostility (he was, after all, the first Englishman to conduct them since the war), and received rhapsodical praise from press and public. The most popular item in the programme, which included Elgar's *Cockaigne* overture and Holst's *The Planets*, was his own symphonic poem, *The Eternal Rhythm*. Eugene also conducted the premiere of a British opera to open the BNOC's 1923 summer season at Covent Garden, *The Perfect Fool* by his friend Gustav Holst. Despite a strong cast including Maggie Teyte as the Princess and Walter Hyde as The Troubadour it was too whimsical for contemporary taste.

His own new composition 'Sinfonietta' proved to have more staying power. It had been inspired when, returning through the deserted London streets around 4am with the night fading and birds stirring, he had heard the sound of a milkman whistling a careless, lively tune.

The *Musical Times* called it his Quarter-of-an-Hour Symphony. 'The whole work flies in the face of some of the theories and principles of its own composer, as laid down in numerous lectures and articles. Nothing has been lost by this frank adoption of the old-fashioned "development" system and by the representation of "extra musical emotion"! The fact is, of course, that none of these young men bite half as hard as they bark.'[23] Eugene had conducted the premiere with the London Symphony Orchestra on 18th February. It was to become one of his most popular works and a favourite with Toscanini who conducted it both in New York and London.

In August 1923 Eugene and Boonie holidayed with George Davison in the South of France. GD had moved there because of the delicate health of his little daughter. Margaret Morris and John Fergusson worked with him to convert a half-built mansion at Cap d'Antibes into 'le Chateau des Enfants'. Here he could house the orphans he had adopted, provide a base for the Morris Summer School and lavishly entertain all his friends. They helped to launch Antibes as a fashionable summer resort together with a few chosen guests at the Hotel du Cap, including Picasso and F Scott Fitzgerald. Eugene retained happy memories of those hot carefree days. 'One day Meg Morris, Picasso and I were at Eden-Roc, and a small octopus half crawled out of the sea on to a nearby rock and posed for us. This delighted Picasso but he didn't draw it. I got sunstroke on the way back to the hotel, and Picasso insisted on my wearing his black felt hat, with a wet handkerchief tucked into it.'[24]

He wrote a glowing description to his parents in Edith Road. 'We're just back from the best holiday that ever was – and if "circs" permit, it's clearly indicated that the place for you all next year is Antibes. Besides writing a sextet – a good work which is now in America, Boonie and I wallowed in heat and blue clear sea in which you can't sink and pine woods with a nasty habit of spontaneously combusting and merry parties at the local estaminet.'*

He asked his father for a chapter of family history to include in the book he was writing. *Overture and Beginners* would not be published for another twenty-eight years. 'It is high time people realised the role that our family and its connections played in the history of music during the past fifty years in this country.

'Now, I'm preparing for the first night of Dean's production at His Majesty's of *Hassan* with Delius' music – on the 20th – which I've promised to conduct, after which, on the 22nd, Boonie and I leave for the States on the *Aquitania* – returning to England at the end of November for a rather animated concert season.'[25]

Eugene had conducted the British premiere of Delius' cello concerto at the Queen's Hall on 3rd July 1923. Beatrice Harrison, the soloist, thought that he had conducted it 'most beautifully', but Delius had not been satisfied by the reports. Jelka subsequently complained: 'It always breaks my heart that this beautiful work had such an unfortunate first performance in London – so slow that it took nine minutes too long. (Goossens)'[26]

Hassan, James Elroy Flecker's poetic drama, was an instant and fashionable success, thanks to the lavishness of Basil Dean's production and the excellence of cast and orchestra. Delius, accompanied by his long-suffering wife Jelka, had travelled to London from his home at Grez-sur-Loing for the final rehearsals. Eugene was shocked by his physical condition and found him peevish about tempi and dynamics.

The final dress rehearsal made an indelible impression on Basil Dean: 'Delius, carefully tended by his wife, sitting wrapped up in the stalls, hearing the music played for the first time by a special orchestra conducted by Eugene Goossens, with brother Léon playing the oboe and Sidonie the harp. So well I remember Delius' high-pitched expostulations when, because we were a little slow in changing the scenery, Eugene,

---

*The sextet for three violins, viola and two cellos, had been commissioned by Mrs Elizabeth Sprague Coolidge for the 1923 Berkshire Festival at a fee of $1,000, an astronomical figure for those days.

obeying the instinct of an experienced theatre conductor, filled in the vacant time by repeating one of the interludes. There was about the theatre a sense of great occasion.'[27]

Even Delius was pleased: 'The whole thing was splendidly staged and the press marvellously favourable. The music is *very* good, orchestra as well as choruses. It was the event of the season.'[28]

The cast was led by Henry Ainley in the title role and Basil Rathbone. Fay Compton and Cathleen Nesbit were two of the actresses to play the part of the slave girl, Yasmin during the long run. The girls in the chorus were exceptionally attractive. One soprano in particular, Fay Yeatman caught Léon's fancy. Sidonie remembers them making a striking couple at the Hassan Ball at the Hyde Park Hotel where everyone wore oriental robes.

Later that year Eugene was to conduct one of the first commercial recordings of Delius' music, *Brigg Fair* and *On Hearing the First Cuckoo in Spring* with the Royal Albert Hall Orchestra.

Sidonie found the music for *Hassan* very difficult. 'Delius never learnt to write for the harp. His pedalling was awful and I had to spend hours rewriting the parts. We recorded a selection of the music for HMV at Hayes, the first recording I ever made. They liked the sound of the Erard harp and asked me to make my first solo recordings of *Woodland Sketches* by MacDowell and *Spring Fancies* by Hamilton Harty.'[29]

Eugene was not available for the *Hassan* recording. He was involved in a much more exciting adventure: conducting George Eastman's new orchestra in Rochester, USA.

6

Sisters

'We should be performing a small service to a good many people by introducing Miss Marie and Miss Sidonie Goossens separately,' announced the *Musical News and Herald* on 31st January 1925. 'Both are so completely efficient as harpists that most people who engage orchestras are quite satisfied to say that "Miss Goossens" will be a member of the orchestra and trouble themselves not at all which of the two actually appears. The result is, most people do not know which is which.'

Marie was the small, dark, jolly one, Sidonie the tall, elegant, fascinating beauty with Titian hair. Their father's training combined with their innate gifts had ensured that both were superb musicians, utterly reliable and capable of playing the most difficult score at sight without turning a hair.

Marie made her orchestral debut with the Diaghilev Ballet conducted by Ansermet at the Alhambra Theatre on 30th April 1919. She was originally engaged as Second Harp but her colleague took fright when she saw the parts for *Les Sylphides* and Marie was asked to take over as First Harp. After the first night, she anxiously awaited the verdict of her teacher, the formidable Miss Timothy. 'Very nice dear, but you must have a larger harp!' She hired a Gothic model Erard to replace her small Grecian harp but could not afford to buy her own instrument until 1925.

The season included the first British performances of *La Boutique Fantasque* and *The Three Cornered Hat*. De Falla arrived from Spain to supervise his composition and asked her to read a passage from the harp part which was written in manuscript. It proved to be as complex as it looked. He was so impressed with her sight-reading ability that he extolled to the press the excellence of British musicians in general and Marie Goossens in particular.

At the next crisis, she was called to take over from an indisposed Jeanne Chevreau in Rutland Boughton's *The Immortal Hour* at the Old Vic. Her beautiful rendering of the 'Faery Song' led to her first solo recording at EMI of Hasselmans' *Prière*, followed by another vintage favourite, *Chant sans Paroles* by Dubez. Her first experience of the pioneering days of recording had been with a small ensemble at Edison Bell when the cylinder method was still in use. At Vocalion in the early twenties, violin, cello and harp had to huddle precariously round the huge horn which could not register the harp playing any notes below middle C. There was no possibility of editing as the sound was cut directly onto a matrix of hot wax; to ensure the right studio atmosphere, the walls were hung with mattresses filled with seaweed.

Life was becoming exciting at Edith Road. 'The phone was always ringing with a request for me to take over because the harpist engaged had taken fright when she saw the music she had to play. That was how I came to play for the Queen's Hall Orchestra under Sir Henry Wood in the premiere of Holst's *The Planets*. They told me the second harp had run away when she saw the music for "Mercury"! Soon after this, another harpist fled and I was engaged overnight to play Wagner's *Song of the Rhine Maidens*, which was played behind a curtain at the side of the stage.'[1]

Sidonie had made her orchestral debut in the Promenade Concerts of 1921, joining Marie and Léon for the first concert they played together under Sir Henry Wood. 'We wore knee-length dresses for concerts then,' Sidonie recalled, 'and Sir Henry insisted that we wore dark stockings because if he saw our legs in fashionable gun metal stockings, it distracted him!'[2]

Léon and the two girls were involved in most of the musical events Eugene conducted. As well as orchestral and chamber concerts, Sidonie's vivid memories *East of Suez*, the BNOC's season at His Majesty's, the premieres of Vaughan Williams' *Hugh the Drover*, Holst's *The Perfect Fool*, *Hassan* and the Diaghilev Russian Ballet Seasons. 'I always felt more nervous when Léon was playing a solo or Eugene was conducting. I would have liked a cue sometimes but he never looked at me!'[3] Eugene was so confident of his siblings' reliability that he felt they needed no help.

Although they were to retain a family solidarity all their lives, once they were established in their careers and particularly after they married, the lives of the talented young Goossens were very different. It is difficult to realise how much social life has changed since the end of the First World War, particularly for women. Apart from the West End theatres and restaurants, London's night life depended on private entertaining and went on behind the closed doors of wealthy private houses. Eugene and Boonie moved in these circles.

There was no equivalent of the free and easy café society of Paris, Berlin or Vienna. After the tea shops closed there was nowhere that a respectable young woman could go on her own for refreshment. To fill this gap Margaret Morris had started a club in 1915 in her Chelsea dance studio at the corner of Flood Street and the King's Road which became a meeting place for painters, writers and musicians. Augustus John, Epstein, Katherine Mansfield and Ezra Pound were all regulars there; Eugene, Cyril Scott and Constant Lambert would sit down and improvise at the piano.

For Marie it became a real haven. 'We used to sit on the floor talking whilst shows were being planned for the club. Some of the members we met were very young but afterwards became famous – amongst them Angela and Hermione Baddeley in their Greek tunics, bare feet and sandals. Here we had tea, coffee and lemonade.'[4] Marie cherished the memory of the summer evening in the garden of the Chelsea Arts Club when she played Debussy's First Arabesque for Penelope Spencer, one of Margaret Morris' principal dancers.

Sidonie had a completely different impression of Margaret Morris' Club. 'Léon and I used to go and dance in the evenings. There would be some exhibition dancing and we would all recline on mattresses round the floor. That was the first time I saw a topless woman [Margaret]. She did one dance where she was naked to the waist. Her breasts were exposed and beautifully made up. I thought it was terrific. I used to dance madly. It was wonderful free dancing. We used to leap across the floor!'[5]

By 1922, Marie was playing regularly for the London Symphony Orchestra as second harp to Jeanne Chevreau, which prompted one journalist to enquire, 'Why are there so few men harpists?' The obvious answer was that a man did look a little clumsy behind the instrument and his physical outline and features did not harmonise with the graceful lines and curves of a beautifully modelled harp. Miss Chevreau explained that the partiality members of the 'gentler sex' showed towards the harp and their marked proficiency over the men was that suppleness of finger and delicacy of touch were required rather than strength.[6]

The best known male harpist was John Cockerill and Marie played second to him in the Queen's Hall Orchestra until the day he announced he was giving up the harp in favour of conducting. She was left with parts she had never seen including Rimsky-Korsakov's *Capriccio Espagnol* with its virtuoso cadenza. 'It is no exaggeration for me to say that I did not even know how to divide it between the hands – but I took it home and worked on it and played it that evening. The pressure was so great – we had a stack of music on the stand and only three hours rehearsal for that evening's concert. When I arrived for the concert, I found a huge piece of manuscript from Sir Henry – his own arrangement of a Paganini Violin Concerto. I had to read it, there was no way out.'[7]

This was her test piece to determine whether she should be offered the contract as Principal Harp in the Queen's Hall Orchestra. As usual she acquitted herself with flying colours and the job was hers.

Marie's elevation was noted at the First Night of the Proms in 1923. 'All the important people who matter so much to regular Promenaders were in their place; the only considerable change was that Miss Marie Goossens stroked the harp, Mr Cockerill having resigned.'[8] She made her solo debut in the series two years later on 4th September 1925. The *Times* was impressed: 'After the interval we were rewarded by a delicious work of Mozart's, which is quite unfamiliar, a concerto for flute, harp and orchestra in C major. The solo parts were superbly played by Miss Marie Goossens (harp) and Mr Robert Murchie (flute), and the orchestra backed them up neatly.' Murchie was First Flute in the Orchestra. Charles Woodhouse, who led the orchestra, composed two cadenzas for the occasion.

Marie had found her father of invaluable help in preparing the concerto. 'He was such a wonderful teacher. It was he who taught me to make a crescendo as I played the scale passages so that I could keep up the tone.' She had little spare time to find a suitable dress for the occasion. As a relief from the habitual black of orchestral ladies, she chose a pretty pale lilac, with silver shoes and the luxury of real silk stockings. The mistake was that the dress had flowers all the way round the skirt about six inches from the hem. 'Half the battle is to feel good but I would advise any harpist not to have flowers round the hem, they get in the way.' She was to have a similar experience with a black dress trimmed with ostrich feathers. 'When I got up to take my bow, I found all the feathers had come off and were on the floor round my feet!'9

Like all other instrumentalists at that time, both girls combined orchestral engagements with theatrical touring. In April 1923 her parents saw Marie off from Liverpool Street Station bound for Ipswich and a tour of *The Little Dutch Girl*. She reported home: 'The show is too funny for words. Mr B the conductor uses a copper stick such as we used to stir the clothes with but the fun is that during every ten minutes or a quarter of an hour's rest we slip out under the stage where lovely armchairs are arranged on carpets, and tea is served ad lib with cakes and sandwiches. It looks just like Heals' basement down there. You must just drop the hint at the Winter Garden, Sid. It's so nice to slip into a soft chair.'10

There were certainly no soft chairs at Covent Garden or any time to slip into them when the three Goossens were engaged in 1924 for the controversial first German Opera Season since the war. Despite a campaign of protest led by Sir Alexander Mackenzie of the Royal Academy and Sir Hugh Allen of the Royal College of Music, the Covent Garden Syndicate had engaged continental artists for *Rosenkavalier* and *The Ring*, conducted by Bruno Walter. They included Lotte Lehmann, Elisabeth Schumann, Friedrich Schorr and Lauritz Melchior, protégé of Hugh Walpole, making his Wagner debut as a Heldentenor in London. The first few moments of *Das Rheingold*, after the lights have dimmed and the wonderful sound of the horns rises from the orchestra pit, were to remain for Marie the most thrilling experience in the operatic repertoire.

By the mid-twenties, the Goossens family was well established on the musical map. Under the heading 'Musical Children', Marie, Principal Harpist in the Royal Philharmonic Society and Queen's Hall Orchestra, was described as 'yet another example of the musical genius of the family. Eugene Goossens the father had two sons and two daughters. One of the sons is Eugene the conductor and composer. The other is Léon, Principal Oboe in the Royal Opera orchestra, the first Englishman to give oboe recitals and one of the few to decline invitations to settle in America. Both the daughters are famous as harpists.'

Marie and Sidonie rapidly rose to the top of the profession because they were outstanding executants and musicians and because good harpists were rare. The fact that they were the female exception in a male dominated orchestral world did not seem to cause them or their male colleagues any problems. Marie usually found herself without a separate dressing-room and so devised a method of changing into her concert clothes behind the harp.

When Sidonie first toured with Beecham and the LSO in February 1924, she was the only girl amongst seventy to eighty men and had no difficulty in coping with the fuss that everyone made of her. 'I always stayed at the best hotel where Beecham usually stayed and I would be invited to join the conductor's party for supper after the concert. TB was in terrific form. He sometimes arrived late for a concert and the leader would have to carry on until the car arrived from Manchester where he had been visiting a lady described as his "niece". I can't say I regretted the other girls coming in though.'

To the layman, the composition of London orchestras in the 1920s was somewhat confusing. 'There is a popular idea, founded upon fact, yet somewhat misleading, that there is one London orchestra, and that it possesses various labels. Miss Sidonie lends colour to this notion by announcing, somewhat apologetically, that she is a member of the Royal Philharmonic, Queen's Hall, Royal Albert Hall and Eugene Goossens' Orchestras.'[11]

Sidonie was already becoming known to a wider audience through the infant British Broadcasting Company and its station 2LO at Savoy Hill. She first broadcast in 1923 with the 2LO Wireless Quartette of violin, flute, harp and organ. They also recorded commercially as the Kneale Kelley Quartet; Kelley was the violinist, Frank Almgill the flautist and the organist is named as E Malkin. 'We made a few records for Columbia including "Killarney" and "Sing me to sleep". We arranged most of the stuff as we played it,' she recalled in a BBC interview in November 1949. 'We also took part in the first broadcast to America from Savoy Hill at about 1am.' She was a founder member of the 2LO Wireless Orchestra at a salary of £10 a week and in 1924 was able to buy herself an Erard harp for £130. 'We only had verbal contracts and the bassoon player came and paid us cash every Friday afternoon. We played concerts, opera, musical comedy, lots of Edward German and light music. One of the first things I played was "Casse Noisette". Our first conductors were Stanton Jefferies, Dan Godfrey Junior, then Percy Pitt and Stanford Robinson. There was a very friendly atmosphere; we knew all the announcers who always greeted us in evening dress: Rex Palmer chief announcer. Stewart Hibberd, Cecil Lewis, they all had lovely speaking voices.'[12]

Initially there was much professional opposition to concerts and opera being broadcast by the BBC. On 1st June 1923 it was announced that Nellie Melba had declined, on the advice of her agents, to permit her singing to be broadcast the previous night. 'Dame Nellie Melba probably realised that enabling 100,000 people to hear her for nothing might lessen her value in the concert room.'[13] By the following year listeners could hear the augmented Wireless Symphony Orchestra in a short series of concerts broadcast from Covent Garden, with Sidonie still its only female player.

Sidonie was often engaged to provide music at private houses. She has vivid memories of playing at Cherkley Court, Lord Beaverbrook's country home near Leatherhead. Gwen Frangcon-Davies, the star of *The Immortal Hour*, was a fellow artist and the guest of honour was Lloyd George. 'Beaverbrook discovered I was interested in books and showed me round his library. The next day we were sitting down to high tea in the kitchen at Edith Road when a uniformed chauffeur arrived with a pile of books. Beaverbrook had lent me a complete first edition set of D H Lawrence to read. He had great charm and behaved perfectly properly towards me. I only played for him once but he engaged Léon to play one evening while he was romancing one of his ladies and he commissioned Eugene to write a series of articles on music for the *Daily Express*.'[14]

Although Sidonie never played in an opera orchestra conducted by her father, she did take part in some of his recording sessions for Columbia. She remembers particularly four records made in July 1924: 'My father was very tense and nervous as we were recording Edward German's "Nell Gwyn Dances" and the players weren't used to light music.'[15]

Eugene II's greatest contribution to the development of the gramophone came in 1927 when he conducted the first complete recording of an opera on stage: Leoncavallo's *I Pagliacci*, recorded in the Scala Theatre by the Principals, Chorus and Orchestra of the British National Opera Company. Hermann Klein, in his review for *The Gramophone* was ecstatic:

> It is not a reproduction but the thing itself. Perfect in every detail; the last word so to speak, in gramophonic achievement . . . The singing of Miss Miriam Licette as Nedda, of Frank Mullings as Canio, of Mr Harold Williams as Tonio, of Mr Denis Noble as Silvio and of Mr Heddle Nash as Harlequin touches and maintains the high level associated with their art at its best. Yet I would fain reserve my warmest tribute for a quarter where I am as a rule least able to bestow it – I mean the orchestra. Mr Goossens must have taken enormous pains to secure such a clear, vivid and crisp yet refined rendering of Leoncavallo's clever instrumentation. Exquisitely balanced and always sufficiently audible, it imparts the requisite solidity of tonal foundation to the whole performance.[16]

Eugene II also distinguished himself in the field of film music. In January 1924, he had devised the musical accompaniment for the *Epic of Everest*, Captain Noel's film of Mallory and Irvine's heroic attempt to conquer the Roof of the World, shown at the (New) Scala Theatre. The film was preceded by a prologue featuring seven Tibetan lamas clad in embroidered silk robes who had been brought over by Captain Noel from the monastery of Gyantse. A trumpet player with an instrument fifteen feet long, decorated in brass and silver, stood on either side of the Chief Lama, who played a pair of brass cymbals – a difficult act for Eugene senior to follow!

'No film in London today has had more care taken in securing good and appropriate music,' commented the *Morning Post*.[17] 'Amid the general low level of cinema music in London, the New Scala at the moment stands out most honourably.' Eugene's score became a controversial issue and H Gordon in the *Musical News and Herald* took up the cudgels in his defence: 'The Showman (of "The Passing Show") has been lifting up his voice in protest "against the raucous and utterly inappropriate music that was played" for the Mount Everest film.' He continues, 'Either music should be specially written for the films by first-rate composers or a first-rate musician should have the choosing of the music to be played.' After listing the music which included Mussorgsky's 'A Night on the Bare Mountain', Eugene's 'Old Chinese Folk Song' and numerous Tibetan folk tunes, Gordon concludes: 'Musicians would be no more likely to class Mr Eugene Goossens senior and Mr Frederick Laurence as second-rate craftsmen than journalists would be likely to classify the Showman as a second-rate gossip writer.'[18]

The partnership between Noel and Goossens, with the invaluable help of Laurence, continued with two films from Soviet Russia advertised for the Polytechnic Cinema in Regent Street in October 1925. *Red Russia* made by Noel and a young German-American photographer, Hermann Basler, ran into trouble with the censor. He banned scenes of street crowds gripped with revolutionary fervour, glimpses of Lenin and Trotsky and the burning of an effigy of Lord Curzon. The second film was *Morosko*, a folk film by players from the Moscow Art Theatre with music specially composed by Laurence and conducted by Goossens. Laurence was cruelly disappointed when the short run was abandoned and wrote to his future father-in-law: 'I can never thank you enough for your enthusiastic assistance and above all I do so much appreciate that insight into my work which revealed far more than I ever realised the score contained. The termination of our enterprise after such a short run is very darkening – indeed I have taken the matter very much to heart. But there – further opportunities must arise and we shall make the people come yet.'[19]

Laurence, a widower with two young children, found Marie's sympathy a great solace. Marie was much less sophisticated than Sidonie. 'We've always been as different as chalk and cheese but we've never had a quarrel. I always felt shabby next to my tall, slender sister,' Marie explained. 'One day we strolled up Shaftesbury Avenue and looking in a very smart dress shop I suddenly saw a black shiny coat, like a lovely soft satin. I said "I want that coat" so we went inside and I tried it on. The lining was of grey crêpe-de-chine; it fitted me and without even asking the price I said I would have it. It lasted me for years – the price was £7, which was a week's wages at the theatre. When we played together we used to make our dresses to match. My favourite was in Liberty's satin, a lovely apricot colour with old lace sleeves and a little bunch of fruit in my hair; Sidonie's was in midnight blue.'[20]

One of her more unusual engagements was to play at a dress show of Norman Hartnell's at his Salon in Bruton Street. Hartnell requested Puccini and the Wedding March for the Grand Finale of the Bride's Dress. She was fascinated by a hat in a smoky blue satiny material and spent her fee of £3 on it to wear at Léon's wedding to Fay Yeatman, on 26th July 1926.

Marie retained a delightful innocence that appealed to the avuncular instinct of older men. She had first met Sir Edward Elgar in the Green Room when she was playing with the Queen's Hall Orchestra. 'I thought I was looking the bees knees in my little white fur cape but he put his arm around me and said "Didn't your mother tell you never to wear white?" It was because I had a sallow complexion and white didn't really suit me!'[21]

In June 1924 Elgar conducted the London Symphony Orchestra in Paris in two concerts, including *The Dream of Gerontius* and his Second Symphony. Much to her delight Marie was asked to go with the orchestra as second harp. After Paris, they played in Dieppe where they rehearsed in the Casino. 'We had a little flutter on the gaming tables. Elgar was there so he helped me as I knew nothing of the art. It was good fun. I learnt "Faites vos jeux" and "Le jeu est fait" [*sic*] and lost my money. But owing to his guidance I played again and came out having laid down seventy francs in all and won them back.'[22] It was the first and last time she ever gambled!

Sidonie has a prized photograph of Elgar inscribed 'To Sidonie, with thanks and devoted admiration. Edward Elgar, 1927.' 'During the Three Choirs Festival he invited the two harpists and Willie Reed the leader of the LSO to breakfast, the only time he could entertain us. There was an enormous table and a Victorian spread of cold pheasants and whole hams.' She thought him a great conductor of his own music with 'a wonderful big spreading beat that was with the music. You felt freedom with him when he conducted. He conveyed the music so much more than some conductors who would make an effort with a certain passage, such as that climactic pause towards the end of the first movement of the Second Symphony. But Elgar just let it go and it went alright.'[23]

His great sense of fun remained with him to the end. After his last appearance at a Promenade Concert, conducting *Gerontius*, he wrote an identical letter to Sidonie and her fellow harpist Jeanne Chevreau: 'Langham Hotel, midnight, 17th August 1933. My evening was completely spoilt as I could not say "thanks" and farewell to the loveliest/lovelier Harpist. E.E.

Now which is which?'

Considering the professional status and success of his sisters, one would have expected Eugene to speak out in favour of sexual equality among musicians. During the Diaghilev season of 1926 he expressed surprisingly chauvinistic views in an article headed 'Should women conduct large orchestras?':

> To conduct a very large orchestra entails endurance and nerve strain for which a woman is not physically fitted. A conductor must have a forceful personality also. I have met few women musicians with a personality sufficiently forceful to ensure the control of a very large orchestra either of men only, or men and women, or of women.
>
> I do not believe in mixed orchestras. There are two women harpists in my orchestra at His Majesty's, it is true, for women

play the harp with extraordinary sympathy and feeling; but what I really mean by 'mixed orchestras' are orchestras in which there are about as many men as women.

Perhaps I am old-fashioned, but I never care to see a woman put through the severe task of real hard, strenuous work, which playing in an orchestra, which has to go through nightly performances of music of the type of Russian Ballet music and opera music, involves.

For the woman who plays the violin, the cello or any other musical instrument really well I think there is much more scope in solo work, on the concert platform, or even on the variety stage. But to conduct or be first violin in an orchestra which has to perform every night is a very different thing!

Marie and Sidonie were career musicians but they were also dutiful daughters; as well brought up, Convent educated young ladies, they hoped to find Catholic husbands of whom their parents would approve. Marie was the last of the Goossens children to leave the parental nest. In 1926 when she was thirty-two, she married Frederick Laurence, who was ten years her senior. He was one of those indispensable figures behind the scenes of the musical world. As a composer his orchestral legend *The Spirit's Wayfaring* had been played by Sir Henry Wood at a Promenade Concert in 1918 and *The Dance of the Witch Girl* in 1920. His most popular work was *Tristis* for string orchestra. He was Librarian of the Proms from 1916 to 1924 and engaged the players for the Royal Philharmonic Society Concerts and the Goossens Orchestra. He was also musical adviser at EMI. When Sir Thomas Beecham and Malcolm Sargent wanted to set up the London Philharmonic Orchestra in 1931 they asked Laurence to select the players as he had a comprehensive knowledge of the capabilities and availabilities of every orchestral player in London.

They moved into a new semi-detached house in North London, 'Crewkerne' at 562, Finchley High Road. When their two children were born, Anthony in 1928 and Jean in 1930, Marie relied on the help of her mother-in-law who lived with them to enable her to carry on with her busy orchestral schedule. She also had the support of her own parents just up the road at Number 576. They had bought 'Durban', a similar house for £800 in 1927, more comfortable and compact than their home in West Kensington, although North Finchley was a far longer trek home after Covent Garden or the Queen's Hall. Dad was to spend long happy hours in the garden complete with greenhouse, tending his prize vegetables and chrysanthemums.

Marie had found the partner she needed, not someone who would add glamour or luxury to her life, but a steady and loving musical companion for an unpretentious life in the suburbs, although Fred remains a somewhat shadowy figure in the Goossens saga.

Sidonie opted for a completely different partnership. Through Léon she had met his friend Hyam Greenbaum, who led the second violins in the Queen's Hall Orchestra. He had been known as 'Bumps' ever since a phrenologist had expressed amazement at the configurations of his cranium. Born in Brighton on 12th May 1901, the son of a Polish Jewish tailor and a Scottish mother who converted to Judaism, he made his musical debut as a child prodigy of seven, in velvet suit and lace collar, playing the Beethoven Violin Concerto. The Mayor rewarded him with a free season ticket to the Aquarium. At the age of eleven, he won an open scholarship to the Royal College of Music. When war broke out he falsified his date of birth and at fifteen was in France fighting in the trenches. Much to his chagrin his parents made representations to the War Office so that he was sent home and discharged.

By the time Sidonie met him, he was recognised as a brilliant string player and a gifted composer with ambitions to conduct; a young man of boundless energy, vivacity and enthusiasm. His name begins to figure in the band for the Goossens concerts and in the family diary at Edith Road in 1922: 10th January 'Went with Bumps to Olympia Circus'; 28th March 'Bumps' champagne uncorked'. On St George's Day 1922 he arranged the music for a Shakespeare recital at the Royal Colonial Institute which he and Sidonie played, with the unusual combination of viola and harp.

Sidonie recalled: 'Bumps took rooms with a cellist friend Ben Levy on the first floor of a house at the end of Edith Road. I could see his light from my window. He was very serious and was always buying books. We would have fascinating discussions not only about music but about philosophy, theosophy and spiritualism and he'd produce a loaf of bread, salami and a bottle of wine for our supper.'[24]

Sidonie was still officially engaged to Rex Workman, both of them patiently waiting until he had established himself in a sufficiently good position for her to join him in the Argentine. He confided in his future father-in-law: 'I certainly could not pursue that patience were it not for the wonderful example that Sidonie sets me in her letters, always cheerful, full of hope and never drifting for a moment from the ambitions that decided us in going through with this separation.'[25]

But by June of the following year Rex was writing to express his doubts as to whether he was justified in expecting Sidonie to continue waiting for him. On 25th August 1922 comes the diary entry: 'Sid informed us her engagement broken off with Rex'. 'My parents were very upset and my father told me that if I broke off my engagement to Rex I couldn't go on seeing Bumps! He liked him as a man and respected him as a musician but he was very concerned about our marrying because of the difference in religion. Léon said "I'd rather you married a Chinaman" which hurt me very much.'[26]

Sid and Bumps were both leading busy professional lives. Entertaining the public left few evenings free for their private enjoyment of the Gay Twenties, but there were highlights like the Three Arts Ball at Covent Garden. 'Bumps and I had supper first at the Eiffel Tower Restaurant in Charlotte Street. We had a private room, the Vorticist Room where the walls were covered with Cubist Paintings. We were both dressed in harlequin costume. I had green hair and by the end of the Ball the colour was running down into my face. I was very tired after working all day and got a bit tiddly which was a pity because by the end I felt quite ill. Bumps had hired a Daimler to take us home. I don't know how he paid for everything; he must have saved up for weeks!'[27]

The Eiffel Tower, run by a genial Austrian Rudolph Stulik, was a favourite haunt of writers, painters and socialites where Mayfair rubbed shoulders with Chelsea and Bloomsbury. Pagani's, round the corner from the Queen's Hall in Portland Street, was the more conventional musicians' restaurant, offering substantial fare and Edwardian red plush comfort to famous soloists before and after their concerts. Eugene recalled a luncheon party there in honour of Sibelius who consumed liberal quantities of schnapps, even with the specialité de la maison 'Pêche Melba'.[28]

Eugene was not at his sister's wedding. She became Mrs Greenbaum at 10am on Saturday 26th April 1924 at Kensington Registry Office.

> It was a pouring wet morning and our neighbour called a taxi for me. None of the family was there. My parents sent me a telegram wishing me every happiness. They were on tour and everyone else was working. I had to rush off to the Albert Hall where I was playing in a trade show for a new film *Siegfried and the Niebelung*. I apologised to the conductor for being late which I never was in normal circumstances; he forgave me when I said I had just got married! Bumps and I met at the Haymarket Restaurant for lunch, just up the road from His Majesty's where I was playing in a matinée of *Hassan*. Marie took over for the second half and we caught the train down to Seaford for a very short honeymoon. The next day Bumps took me to meet his parents in Brighton.[29]

They set up home in a first floor flat in the Fulham Road, opposite the Michelin building. Sidonie indulged her excellent eye for décor with a black carpet, and apple green curtains lined with sunshine yellow for the living room.

Sidonie was able to give full rein to her vocal and dramatic talents as leading lady in the Reviews staged by the BBC's Amateur Dramatic Society. Described as the BBC's 'strangest and merriest production', Sidonie won all hearts in May 1928 with her exuberant charleston and a torch song called 'Those Hypnotising Eyes'. 'Nigel Playfair wanted to make me into a stage star. I was very tempted but decided I had a better future as a harpist. Admiral Carpendale, who was Deputy Director General, took a fancy to me and was always waving to me through the glass window of studio doors. There were all sorts of rumours going around that we were having an affair – Harp and Carp. Someone even complained to Reith – totally ridiculous!'[30]

Bumps had ambitions as a composer. Following the pattern of his brother-in-law Eugene, he twice left his seat as leader of the second violins to conduct in a Queen's Hall Promenade

Concert: *Parfum de la Nuit*, three miniatures for oboe and small orchestra which he had written for Léon in 1922 and *A Sea Poem* for full orchestra the following year. Sir Henry Wood was very kind to young composers and Spike Hughes suspected that Bumps composed largely to have the opportunity of conducting the orchestra.

In 1925 Bumps left the Queen's Hall Orchestra to concentrate on chamber music as second violin in the Brosa Quartet; it was led by Antonio (Tony) Brosa, with Leonard Rubens viola and Anthony (Charlie) Pini cello. In addition to her own professional schedule and housekeeping duties, Sidonie found time to manage the quartet. She got them their initial dates writing to all the music clubs in the country and only made one mistake when she sent them to Bangor a week too early. Lord Beaverbrook was delighted to engage them to play at his new residence of Stornaway House, off St James's; the quartet found it difficult to gauge which item he most enjoyed as he talked incessantly throughout their performance. She also used her influence to get them into the excellent small orchestra, which included Léon and Aubrey Brain, for *No, No, Nanette*, starring Binnie Hale at the Palace Theatre.

The Brosa Quartet quickly became acknowledged as the leading quartet in England and one of the finest in Europe, touring with great success in France, Germany and Italy. They continued to lead the string sections for the Diaghilev Ballet in London, conducted by Eugene. In September 1928 Sidonie went with them to Sienna for the sixth ISCM Festival, where they participated in a riotous performance of Walton's *Façade* and an unforgettable dinner at Montegufoni, the parental seat of the Sitwells.

Despite their reservations on religion, once he married their youngest child, Eugene and Annie welcomed Bumps as one of the family. 'Sid and Bumps came to lunch,' Dad recorded in the diary on Christmas Day 1928. The children had clubbed together to buy them a 'Wireless Set'; then Zenny had cabled from Rochester for the delivery of an HMV gramophone, complete with his records that had just been issued. 'Lee and Fay joined us in the evening for supper and *dance* 'à la Russe' to the tune of Zenny's records *Boutique Fantasque*. Fred too called in – we did miss dear "Marnie" so! [It was only

three weeks since Anthony, the first grandson, had been born.]
Sid and Bumps stayed the night.'

At the beginning of 1929 they moved to a larger flat, the top
floor of 5, Wetherby Gardens, SW5. It became the favourite
meeting place for a brilliant group of young composers who
clustered around Bumps: William Walton, Constant Lambert,
Alan Rawsthorne and Patrick Hadley together with Spike
Hughes and Cecil Gray. They all adored Sidonie and fancied
themselves a little in love with her. 'They all just sat down at
the piano and improvised. Sometimes we had a cod opera and
I always sang the heroine. Willie Walton used to say to me:
"Why did your father make you play the harp? You should have
been an opera singer!" Philip Heseltine was always there
making Bumps drink too much. I had the greatest difficulty
in persuading everyone to go home but the landlady used to
complain if we made a noise after 11pm. We used to end our
parties with Heseltine's beautiful arrangement of the Corpus
Christi carol which we could sing very quietly.'[31]

The family were overjoyed by the news that Sid was expecting a baby. The details remain etched indelibly in her memory,
even after sixty years: 'I had no intimation that there was
anything wrong beforehand but it was an impacted breach
birth. The midwife and the doctor fought as long as they
could, then they tried to reach the surgeon to give me a
Caesarean on the kitchen table. The phone was out of order,
there was no way of contacting anybody. I had been in labour
for twenty-four hours but it seemed to be forever and the
landlady complained about the noise I was making. The baby
was born dead; they couldn't revive him with brandy. He was
a beautiful baby, a little boy, but it was not to be. When they
told Bumps what had happened, he threw every clock out of
the window.'[32]

If the child had lived, their lives might have been very
different.

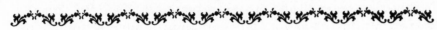

7

Rochester

T he city of Rochester, up-state New York, enjoyed the benevolent despotism of George Eastman, founder of the Kodak Eastman photographic empire. Eastman, a dedicated bachelor, had come up the hard way to become a multi-millionaire. He gave three million dollars to the Massachusetts Institute of Technology and endowed the Eastman Dental Hospital in London as well as numerous philanthropic projects for the benefit of the citizens of Rochester.

His first musical recognition came from Gilbert and Sullivan in 1893: 'You only need a button press/And we do all the rest' sang the Royal Princesses in *Utopia Limited*.[1] (Eastman's advertising slogan was: 'Kodak cameras. You press the button. We do the rest.')

'I am interested in music personally and I want to share my pleasure with others,' he explained in a *New York Times* interview entitled 'Philanthropy Under a Bushel'. 'Without the presence of a large body of people who understand music and who get joy out of it, any attempt to develop the musical resources of any city is doomed to failure.'[2]

To start his project he endowed the Eastman School of Music as part of the University of Rochester. He planned to encourage the appreciation of music through the popularity of motion-pictures and built a magnificent 3,500 seat theatre, complete with a sixty-piece orchestra. The next step in making his city a true home of musical art was to raise the musicians' status to that of a Philharmonic Orchestra. In 1923 he engaged two leading British conductors, Eugene Goossens and Albert Coates for an inaugural concert series.

On his first morning in Rochester, Eugene was summoned to breakfast with the 'Kodak King' and warned to arrive punctually at 7.30am. The meal was accompanied by a recital on the Aeolian organ. Eastman, described as 'a modest, direct man in his sixty-ninth year – a person without any frills', briefed Eugene on his plans for the community's musical future, his ambitions for the orchestra and Eugene's role in them. The monologue gave his latest protégé 'a useful insight into the mental processes which govern the business mind when it toys with things musical. He relied implicitly on the opinion of the experts he hired, like all other ruthless business heads, he judged them finally and implacably by results.'[3]

After breakfast, Eugene and Boonie were shown over the lavishly equipped Eastman Theatre and adjacent School of Music. He told Jack Warner, writing for the *Rochester Times Star* that 'such a building in London would settle the whole question of the financial problems of chamber and orchestral concerts. They would be bound to succeed.' A rueful comment in the light of his own difficulties as an entrepreneur.

His opening concert with the orchestra on Wednesday, 17th October 1923 was considered of sufficient importance to be reported in the *New York Times*. The guest critic was H C Colles who normally wrote for the *Times* in London. His review of Eugene's American debut was a perspicacious one: 'What fits him peculiarly to fill such a post as this is that he has turned the worst defect of English orchestral performances, its paucity of rehearsal to artistic profit. Though he only arrived in this country a fortnight ago and since then has had only sixteen hours' rehearsal with a more or less unformed orchestra, he was able to give a performance which showed the orchestra to be already something more than a collection of good players – an interpretative body which should within a short time under such leadership as his become a first-rate organization.'[4]

Eugene's brief was to provide a programme which would appeal to the best in popular taste. He chose the *Tannhäuser* overture, Dvořák's cello concerto, two 'lollipops' by his friend Percy Grainger, Debussy's *L'Après-midi d'un Faune*, ending with Brahms' Second Symphony. The top seat price was fifty cents and the large audience gave the orchestra and its conductor an enthusiastic ovation. By the last of the three matinée concerts that followed, the auditorium was filled to capacity and the audience's enthusiasm for the glamorous young conductor, overwhelming. A concert of his songs and chamber music, in which he featured as accompanist and solo pianist, underlined his outstanding talents.

'Mr and Mrs Goossens have been tendered an unusual amount of hospitality in the city,' gushed a society columnist, 'and the last few weeks of their stay were crowded with delightful gatherings at which their many friends and acquaintances expressed regret at the departure of the interesting young conductor and his charming wife. Mr Eastman's announcement at the dinner which he gave Monday evening in their honour to the effect that Mr Goossens will return next year and will resume his leadership of the Philharmonic Orchestra, was greeted with flattering exclamations of delight and continued and enthusiastic applause.'

In a rare moment when he allowed the public behind his guard, Eugene confided: 'The hospitable people of the new country in which I found myself frightened me a little by the disarming warmth of their welcome. So utterly unlike was it to anything I had known, so foreign to the insular reserve to which I was accustomed, that for a long time my shyness seemed intensified, and hampered early friendships which should have spontaneously generated.'[5]

His first taste of American hospitality had been on his way to Rochester at Mrs Coolidge's Berkshire Festival of Chamber Music. He had miscalculated the journey time from New York to Pittsfield, Massachusetts and missed the premiere of his sextet. Richard Aldrich, reviewing the work for the *New York Times*, found that 'his music has an aerial flight of imagination, a shifting scheme of harmony. It is high spirited and touches boisterousness at times, but his adventurous harmonies somehow seduce the ear.' It had been excellently performed by an ensemble including Lionel Tertis and May Mukle.

The English contingent at the Festival included the London String Quartet, Myra Hess, Arthur Bliss and Frank Bridge. The latter's wife, Ethel wrote a somewhat indiscreet description of their mistress of ceremonies and Eugene's debacle, to her friend Marjorie Fass in England: 'Well, well, well, Goosie *didn't* arrive in time for his sextet this morning – he reached Pittsfield at a quarter to one so turned up for the last concert this afternoon. Before the sho' started tho', old Susie [Mrs Coolidge] hauled him onto the platform and altogether made an occasion for him and he looking most uncomfortable all the time . . . Of course the only thing she wants is *publicity*, it's not artistry. Eugh! the way the whole hall *stands up* to attention if ever she appears to say a word or to play the piano.'6

In Rochester Eugene suggested that Frank Bridge should be offered a post as a string teacher at the Eastman but he declined it. Eugene himself was delighted when his contract was renewed for the next season and for the following two years continued to share the engagement with Albert Coates. There had been other candidates under consideration. Adrian Boult had visited Rochester in October 1923 and met the Goossens at dinner at the home of the Warners. The Warners were influential friends of George Eastman and Michael Kennedy, Boult's biographer, suggests that they 'wanted Boult to become conductor of the Rochester Philharmonic Orchestra and his eventual refusal led to Goossens holding the post from 1923 to 1931. Back in London Boult pondered the Rochester offer. It is probable he would have accepted it – he later told Gwen Becket [his secretary] he had his bags packed – had not Sir Henry Wood resigned in November as conductor of the Birmingham Festival Choral Society and nominated Boult as his successor.'7

This might have been wishful thinking on Boult's part. No doubt the Warners suggested him to Eastman but Eugene had already been engaged to open the inaugural season in 1923 and following his success with the orchestra, Eastman announced on 12th November that he had been re-engaged for the following season.

Boult omits any reference to Rochester in his version of events in his autobiography, engagingly entitled *My Own Trumpet*: 'I finally decided that if nothing appeared by the summer of 1924, I should go to Canada and/or the USA. Thanks to Sir Henry Wood, a glimmer of light appeared on the horizon. In the summer of 1923, he resigned from the Birmingham Festival Choral Society and proposed me as his successor. I cheerfully accepted . . . for 1923 – 4.'8

Boult did however benefit from a further round of musical chairs the following year. Eugene was offered the conductorship of the City of Birmingham Orchestra when Appleby Matthews resigned. Because of his commitments in Rochester he declined the solo post as well as a suggestion that he should share it with Boult. The latter was then officially appointed in October 1924.

Eugene had decided that America offered him a more promising future than England. He had been disheartened by the financial failure of a second series of Goossens Concerts in the Aeolian Hall early in 1924. The challenging programmes included Stravinsky's *Histoire du Soldat*, Milhaud's *Catalogue des Fleurs*, Schoenberg's Second String Quartet and Eugene's String Sextet with André Mangeot, G. Barbirolli cello and Eugene himself playing viola amongst the performers. Edwin Evans found it a work 'which steadily improves on acquaintance'.

Eugene was still shackled to Herbert Bedford; as joint concert promoter the latter's insistence on unaccompanied song resulted in a disconcerting variety of standards of composition and performance. The third concert, according to Edwin Evans in the *Musical Times* 'almost baffles description. Miss Dorothea Webb sang unaccompanied songs and others to eight different forms of accompaniment, from harpsichord plain and harpsichord coloured with violin and cello, to Zulu marimba and various instruments the names of which, for aught I know, may have been culled from the menu of a Chinese restaurant . . . By far the most fascinating feature was Mozart's Quartet for oboe and strings, in which Léon Goossens once more distinguished himself.'[9]

Plus ça change! One might be reading a disparaging review of avant-garde vocal compositions in the 1990s.

At the other end of the scale, Eugene was involved in a project which was to become one of London's most popular annual musical events. He conducted the opening season of *Hiawatha* at the Albert Hall where one thousand sedate members of the Royal Choral Society endeavoured to transform themselves into Red Indian Braves and Squaws. Unfortunately no one had told them to remove their spectacles and watches. Samuel Coleridge Taylor's invigorating setting of Longfellow had been converted into a dramatic pageant by T C Fairbairn. It continued to fill the Albert Hall every year until 1940, under the baton of another talented young conductor, Malcolm Sargent.

The financial losses of Eugene's concert ventures led to litigation which had been widely reported in the press. America seemed to offer a far more fertile and appreciative environment for creative endeavour than England. He sailed for New York at the end of September 1924 on the *Majestic*, on the same crossing as his friends Somerset Maugham, Noel Coward and Basil Dean. In those distant days before air travel, luxury transatlantic liners provided a cocoon of sybaritic high living suspended between London and New York. Often the mixture of personalities on board reads like a random round of Consequences: on one voyage Eugene enjoyed the company of Rachmaninov, Harry Lauder and the beautiful film idol, Mae Murray. The one predictable factor was the bugler who summoned the passengers to meals; he always turned out to have been a member of the Carl Rosa Opera Company.

Before he sailed, the *Musical News and Herald* published an article headed 'Eugene Goossens – an SOS', analysing the significance of his potential loss to British music.

> Eugene Goossens is the most outstanding figure in the younger musical generation. He's been lionised by the press, almost canonised by the musical public, and subsidised – by himself. He has earned the interest of the press and the praise of the public by his musical genius and his fearless enterprise in the cause of musical progress.
>
> If he is wondering mildly what, say, New York might be able to offer an energetic, versatile and brilliant young composer and conductor, nobody could decently express either surprise or disapproval.
>
> Let it not be forgotten that the path trodden by Eugene Goossens is quite the British normal. Our complete lack of a sense of responsibility implies that if a musical genius arises in our midst, we may be called upon to give support tomorrow which we owe today, and to pay our debt of lip service and of anything else the said genius may choose – except cash. And if he packs up – well, after all, they do these things differently in America, don't they? Besides, it is the thing now in the New World for millionaires to patronise the arts. [10]

From 1925 Eugene's status in Rochester changed. Eastman appointed him sole Musical Director of the Rochester Philharmonic Orchestra. He now had the security of a permanent post for a full season's activities and regular conducting classes at the Eastman School of Music. He always stressed the importance of thorough grounding in musicianship, meticulous preparation of any work to be performed and acquiring a clear stick technique. The best preparation for a conductor was to play in an orchestra under great exponents as he had done. But he was convinced that conductors were born not made, as he explained in an interview for *Musical America*.

A true flair for conducting depends first on something which cannot be taught. This is the capacity to inspire players with personal thought and feeling, something which we call magnetism and assertion of personality – this must precede technique.

A conductor must be more than a technician; he must be capable of drawing the best from his players. The orchestra is a very sensitive and human machine, and the orchestral players of today are intelligent and highly sensitive musicians. If the orchestra does not give the conductor what he wants at first, he must exercise all his patience and skill at his command to obtain it. Often a little time spent in finding new ways of making himself understood secures what a conductor wants, and at the same time strengthens the co-operative attitude of his players.[11]

Throughout his career he believed that the conductor had to control the orchestra with an iron hand. The secret was to conceal it within a velvet glove!

Eugene also became musical director of the new Opera Department of the Eastman School with the Russian tenor Vladimir Rosing as head of productions. Eastman had a flair for discovering talent; Martha Graham, the doyenne of American modern dance, started her career teaching ballet at Eastman and Rouben Mamoulian, later to become famous as a film director and producer, taught drama. The writer Paul Horgan was also on the staff. The department developed into the American Opera Company; Eugene conducted them at the Guild Theatre in New York in 1927 in highly praised productions of *Figaro*, *Faust* and *Butterfly*.

Throughout his career in America, Eugene wrote regular letters home to his parents. These provide an invaluable chronicle of his achievements, his personal and professional relationships with his contemporaries and are a unique assessment of American musical life between 1923 and 1947. His father remained his closest musical confidant and critic. As far as the complexities of his emotional life were concerned, Eugene always kept his own counsel.

He describes his first opera students in a letter to his parents in October 1925:

> I have under me about fifty or sixty people, all with fine voices and also – most important – young and good looking, quite a change from the starchy prime donne of the BNOC. Next week we produce *Martha* with three different casts. This we follow by *Tales of Hoffmann* and later *Tosca* and *Carmen* . . . America seems so far away from Europe and yet when one is here one realises how truly it is the hub of the musical world.
>
> I was in New York last weekend and had a long chat with Damrosch. We saw lots of new plays, including some of Noel Coward's, who afterwards gave an enormous party at his flat (which formerly belonged to Mae Murray, the film actress and is all imitation Gothic). My New York concerts will be the most important event hitherto in my career.[12]

He wanted his father to join him as Head Operatic Coach which would have fulfilled his dream of bringing his parents to America and also given his father professional and financial security. The scheme did not materialise; the following season when the BNOC regained its financial feet, Eugene senior and Annie returned to the familiar pattern of provincial touring.

Walter Damrosch had invited Eugene junior to conduct two weeks of concerts with the New York Symphony Orchestra at the beginning of January 1926. The programme for the first pair included Brahms' Second Symphony, the Haydn cello concerto with Casals and the work with which his success was most closely associated, *Sacre du Printemps*. After the concert the President of the orchestra described Stravinsky's masterpiece as 'obscene music'.

Eugene reported back to Edith Road:

> It seems to have been a good stunt to kick off with the *Sacre*, as at any rate, all the critics agreed that it was the finest per-

formance ever heard in New York. On the subject of Brahms
they did not enthuse quite so much, probably because I gave
a reading of it in direct contrast to the high colour perver-
sions which New York audiences are accustomed to of poor old
Brahms.

The orchestra was marvellously sympathetic and we were great
friends in the first five minutes. The orchestra is a revelation
in the classics, though less elastic in new works, but its tone
and quality are better than anything we have in Europe today.
There is no doubt that I shall be re-engaged for a longer period
next season. Between ourselves also, I hear that Klemperer, my
German successor, is not making good owing to his drill sergeant
methods and lack of variety in his programmes.

Toscanini was also in town with the rival New York Philharmonic and Eugene seized the opportunity to meet a conductor
he greatly admired. 'I had a long talk with him and found him
very interesting and sympathetic. I learned a lot from him as a
conductor, which is a great deal for me to say. He is certainly
the world's greatest because, although an oldish man, he infuses
so much vitality into his work that the result is stunning. His
beat is free from affectations and his interpretations sincere and
straightforward (exactly like my Brahms!). We drank coffee together in a little restaurant and I also talked to him about
you, Dad.'

After his three concerts in Boston with an orchestra which
he found 'second to none in the world', he telegraphed his
parents on 6th February 1926: 'Boston was colossal triumph.
Please deny rumour am succeeding Koussevitzky next season.'

His triumphal tour concluded with a Composers' Guild
concert in New York on 23rd January in which Respighi,
Casella, Tailleferre and Salzedo also took part. The highlight of
the evening was Eugene conducting half a dozen futuristic jazz
songs, sung by Florence Mills, the celebrated black singer from
'The Plantation Review', a black show which, like the Cotton
Club, had become popular with white audiences. Toscanini,
Eugene's guest, was entranced by her performance and came
backstage to congratulate her.

Eugene had been provided with an entourage of two sec-
retaries and a special correspondent from the Press Associa-

tion to record his daily activities. He found the return to Rochester 'rather a slump' after conquering New York and Boston, where 'the glut of conductors is appalling and the standard of criticism and accomplishment the highest in the world.'

At the beginning of the season, Eugene and Boonie had hoped that his permanent position in Rochester would enable them to establish a family home there. 'My greatest longing is to have the children out here, where they'd be in beautiful surroundings and among lots of friends. I don't see why I should be separated from them for seven or eight months in the year, and Boonie, although she rightly feels that her place is here with me, can't become reconciled to being without them.'[13]

Finally they gave up their London flat in Wetherby Gardens; Anne, Jane and Julia sailed on the *Majestic* with their nurse and were installed in an adjacent apartment in Rochester at the end of December 1925. By March, Eugene was writing to his parents with a change of plan. 'I have strong hopes of coming home very soon and bringing the children with me. Our idea was of asking you whether you would care to act as "pension" for the children and a new nurse during the next few months. I don't want to bury myself in this country for a whole year round and it seems to me that the feasible plan would be to spend six months and a half here and five and a half in England, in which case I should be happier to have the children in England for the whole time than over here. These things never work out until one has tried them.'[14]

In the event, Boonie decided to stay in England and Eugene returned to America at the end of July alone. It was a tragic irony that a man for whom home and family were so important should make the mistake of marrying a woman who failed to provide him with domestic or emotional stability. It was a mistake he was to repeat three times. Boonie came from a milieu of nannies and governesses, a world away from the love and warmth of Annie Goossens' high teas. Mum and Dad never interfered but they were disconcerted by Boonie's lack of concern for her children.

Anne Goossens' earliest memories are of her father and music:

He was the most important person in my life, the background to everything that was going on. There was a big piano in the music room but that was sacred forbidden territory. He didn't spend much time being interested in what the children were doing. Our place was to keep well in the background and not to be heard. He was a very serious, quiet person, not a temperamental artist. I didn't realise until I was much older how important his contribution to musical life was. He would walk around and people would call him 'God' as a nickname!

He was tremendously admired from the time he was a young man and he was very attractive to women. He had a valet called Billham who had to protect him from women admirers. They would rush into the dressing-room and try to cut pieces from his tie like a film star!

My parents never had a permanent home, always hotels and rented apartments but wherever they were, they were the centre of a glamorous and exciting life. They loved jazz and I remember listening at the keyhole in my nightdress when American jazz singers, the Blackbirds, were at their London parties. They had little time for us. They were away a great deal, travelling and working.[15]

Eugene returned to the USA on 24th July 1926. Two days before he sailed, Basil Dean asked him to write the incidental music for Margaret Kennedy's play *The Constant Nymph*, due to go into production in three weeks with Edna Best and Noel Coward. He later recalled that it was written 'in the smoke room of the SS *Carmania* and took exactly ten days to write away from a piano and the composer fortified merely by dry Martinis supplied by the steward at appropriate intervals. I wrote the last note as we passed Quarantine, New York and on landing posted it back to Basil Dean.'

The score included his solitary attempt to write a pot-boiler 'When Thou Art Dead', which might have made his fortune if he had found the right publisher to promote it. When the film version of *The Constant Nymph* was shown at the Marble Arch Pavilion in February 1928, the incidental music had to be padded out with excerpts from his other compositions. Eugene had had double pneumonia and was not able to complete the assignment for an extended score.

He had already encountered the American film world. At the beginning of August 1925 he had made his debut at the

103

Hollywood Bowl in the Fifth Great Gala Season of 'Symphonies under the Stars'. 'Hollywood Bowl Summer Concerts are the triumph of an ideal to bring GREAT music to GREAT masses at SMALL cost' proclaimed the ecstatic programme. Eugene was welcomed with similar hyperbole in 'Sips from the Bowl'. 'Known from Petrograd to Buenos Aires, Stockholm in Sweden to Cape Town as the young lion among British conductors, Eugene Goossens, after casting a spell with his wand over New York City and Boston with his "stick" will next week be "heard and seen" for four gala concerts at the Hollywood Bowl.'

Not everyone could cope with the brashness of Hollywood. The week before Eugene's appearance, Sir Henry Wood, bowing to the applause after conducting Elgar's Symphony no. 1, had found himself upstaged by a large papier-mâché lion complete with wagging tail and an explosion of fireworks. He laid down his baton and refused to complete the concert.

Eugene was twenty-five years younger and enjoyed both the razzmatazz and the opportunity of enlivening the programmes with 'modern' novelties by Debussy, Stravinsky, Berners and Bantock. He became a favourite conductor at the Bowl to which he was to return annually. He found three old colleagues from the Queen's Hall Orchestra in the Los Angeles Philharmonic: Léon's hero, Henri de Busscher, horn player Alfred Brain and Alfred Kastner harp. He relished the round of after-concert suppers and parties with Mary Pickford, Gloria Swanson, Marion Davies, Pola Negri and Charlie Chaplin. The elite of the silent screen made him realise that 'the movie colony was not the pleasure-loving congregation of numbskulls they are usually painted, but a group of intelligent people of culture who could discuss music as well as the best.'[16]

He sent a progress report to his parents at the beginning of 1927 telling them of his success in building up the Rochester Philharmonic. 'Rochester is finally on the map as one of the most important musical centres of America.' One of his guest soloists that season had been a twelve-year-old violin prodigy called Yehudi Menuhin. Eugene was still young enough to enjoy making gigantic snowballs with him.

He had been concerned to hear reports of his father's poor health on the BNOC tour.

I hope the strain hasn't been too great, as I remember you were always apt to be, if anything, over conscientious on the matter of operatic scores and details! But it's good to think that instead of masterly inactivity at Edith Road, you're having the opportunity of showing the world that the 'old dog' still retains his old animation and prowess! The Liverpool paper rightly called you the 'doyen' of English opera conductors, and it's time that you attracted a certain amount of rightful appreciation from the public you've served so well . . .

Christmas here was as jovial as possible, I mean under the rather trying circumstances that this was the first Christmas that I'd spent with no family at all to cheer me up, but my friends make life very pleasant. I spent New Year's Eve in New York finishing up at 4am with Heifetz. But on the whole I have too much to do to spare much time in dissipation and I'm not too keen on too much of that sort of thing anyway! I miss the children very much and of course Boonie most of all.

I think of you all the time, darlings and my only hate against life is the fact that I'm fated to spend so much time away from those I love dearly. I often philosophise that in spite of the fact that I owe all my musical accomplishments to you, you get very little 'kick' out of the results. Some day soon perhaps I'll be able to show you that my youthful efforts weren't exactly a waste of time.

The writer Paul Horgan describes Eugene of the Rochester days: 'Tall and as famously tailored for his concerts as Toscanini and Stravinsky, and he moved with the languid gait of an officer off duty. Stylishly abrupt in speech, wittily amused at most matters which he noticed, he had the air of being tuned out much of the time – he talked freely and fondly to me when I would ask to know about Stravinsky.'[17]

Horgan later fictionalised his experiences at the 'Ganson School of Music' in 'Dorchester' in a prize-winning novel entitled *The Fault of Angels*. Eugene took exception to what he considered 'acid digs' against himself. 'Ah but you cause me pain, mon cher,' Horgan replied on the defensive. 'You do not grant me latitude? I mean in the necessity of salting my characters, so that there will be not a dull monotone of either virtue or villainy. But it is idle to explain to you, of all people, the nature of an artistic problem. Your creative sensitiveness is so rare and so marvellously intuitive.'[18] Their friendship survived unimpaired.

Eugene made international headlines in April 1927, after conducting a concert of music by the American composer George Antheil at Carnegie Hall, including his *Ballet Mécanique* for fourteen grand pianos, eight xylophones, two aeroplane propellers and a riveting machine. The *Liverpool Daily Post* reported: 'Music seems to be taken very seriously in New York, judging by the enthusiastic reception there the other night of an "ultra-modern" ballet by a young American composer. Unfortunately the enthusiasm was not very flattering either to the composer or to the conductor – who incidentally was Mr Eugene Goossens – as it consisted of booing, cat calling, whistling and rattle play. Nevertheless it was enthusiasm, for the true enemy of art is not opposition but indifference.' Eugene dismissed the work as 'a rather Dada-esque fiasco'.

The following year established him as the most successful and sought after young conductor in America. The St Louis Orchestra season was divided between Arbos, the fiery Spaniard whom Eugene had not seen since Muriel Draper's Salon, Emil Oberhoffer and himself. He reported to his parents in March 1928:

My four concerts in St Louis (a fine orchestra) have knocked that community cold and the press has been trying to get me away from Rochester permanently next season. They finally compromised by re-engaging me for sixteen concerts (representing £1,000 in salary).

Detroit is being vacated this next season by Gabrilowitsch (for a holiday) and I have been asked to conduct six concerts there in December. Detroit is the best provincial orchestra outside of Boston. In addition to eight concerts at the Bowl, two in Pittsburgh, two in Baltimore, there are also rumoured appearances with the Philadelphia and New York Philharmonic.

Recently I had the experience of conducting five concerts with the fine New York Symphony, owing to Walter Damrosch's sudden illness. Altogether reviewing this season, it's the best I've had so far, and I'm very satisfied and peaceful about everything.

I recently conducted a performance in Washington of *Hugh the Drover* in an international week by invitation of the British Embassy, which gave a party in honour of Mr and Mrs Goossens. Next Tuesday, 27th March I conduct a grand gala concert in New York, by the Philharmonic Orchestra, in which five different conductors

(Toscanini, Damrosch, Bodanzky, Arbos and Goossens) take part, each doing a work of their own country. [Eugene's choice had been Delius' *Brigg Fair*.]

Toscanini still rules the world of conductors and is the idol of New York. It is the day of sensational conductors, and we are the only people who really count in the concert world today. Certainly we are the highest paid and act more like prima donnas (except yours truly) than the prima donnas themselves. There is a tremendous shifting about among the orchestras and fresh sensational rumours crop up every day. I am the twenty-fifth guest conductor in New York, this season!!!

TB [Thomas Beecham] was here, making quite a hit in a way, though I think due as much to his sensational methods as anything. We had lunches together, and he was in great form, save that he hurt his leg in Philadelphia and conducted in a pair of carpet slippers. What an eye for effect he has . . . ! He seems very hopeful of his scheme going through, and wanted me to go back as his chief conductor when it starts! Nothing doing! He asked 'tenderly' after you and was very cordial about you.

Beecham was about to relaunch the financially troubled BNOC as the National League of Opera but his hopes for a secure financial basis for the company were to prove shortlived. Much though he would have welcomed the right opportunity for a permanent base in England, Eugene had long grown out of Beecham's shadow.

The following year however Eugene owed one more triumphal debut to Beecham. Stokowski had engaged him as guest conductor with the Philadelphia Orchestra and when Beecham was taken ill, Eugene was asked to replace him in seven concerts culminating in New York at Carnegie Hall, on 5th March 1929. Olin Downes, the doyen of American critics, awarded him the palm of praise for his 'vigorous, warm, youthfully spirited performance of Brahms' Fourth Symphony. It may be said that the symphony has seldom been heard of late when it sounded so characteristic of the mature, but virile, noble and bearish Brahms. It was apparent that the symphony stirred Mr Goossens, heated his blood, quickened his pulse, and he saw to it that the audience felt likewise. The Fourth Symphony last night was not the expression of an autumn mood, but an affirmation of splendid strength and beauty communicated with the contagious spirit of a young man.'[19]

He had also received a rapturous reception in Detroit where he established a lasting friendship with Ossip Gabrilowitsch, the Russian pianist and conductor whose idiosyncrasies recalled the vanished world of St Petersburg. His wife was Clara Clemens, daughter of Mark Twain. Ralph Holmes of the *Detroit Evening Times* described Eugene as 'an electric personality who succeeded in thrilling some of us musically as we haven't been musically thrilled for quite a while. Never have the men played at such sustained speed as under his urgent baton; seldom have they found themselves lashed to such frantic frenzies. And they acted as though they liked it. The high moment was easily the Ravel (no. 2 Suite from *Daphnis and Chloe*) which Mr Goossens poured from the orchestra like molten gold at the beginning and then ignited into as gorgeous a display of orchestral fireworks as ever took the breath. Swift, sudden, languorous, hesitant, headlong, glowing, flashing – it made us understand why Mr Goossens is ranked so high as an interpreter of modern music.'[20]

At the end of January 1929 Eugene added another orchestral first to his list. Fritz Reiner, the conductor of the Cincinnati Orchestra, was called to the New York Philharmonic when Toscanini suddenly developed a crippling neuritis in his right arm. Eugene's manager, Arthur Judson, asked him to fill the gap. He found 105 players of one of America's oldest orchestras 'packed like sardines on the stage of Emery Auditorium. They produced a torrential sound of great technical accuracy, but string phrasing which lacked sweep and spaciousness. It was largely a matter of faulty acoustics and cramped stage.'[21]

By the end of 1928 Eugene and Boonie had reached the reluctant conclusion that their marriage had ground to a halt. According to their daughter, Anne: 'they remained on good terms. She always adored him and kept his photo up all the time. She agreed to divorce him thinking that Bettie Holmes meant to marry him. Many years later Boonie admitted that both Bettie Holmes and she had been surprised by his marriage to Janet Lewis.'[22]

The gossip columnists had a field day; a prime example was in the *New York Evening Journal* of 16th January 1929:

Friends of Mrs Christian R Holmes, one of the wealthiest widows in the United States and well known in Gotham's social and musical circles, are interested in the report that she will again take unto herself a husband. The gentleman is said to be Eugene Goossens, conductor of the Rochester Philharmonic Orchestra, who has recently obtained a divorce from his wife.

Mrs Holmes possesses claims to fame other than her enormous wealth which is said to approximate one hundred million dollars and her patronage of music and musicians which has been lavish. Prior to marrying her late husband, Mrs Holmes was Miss Bettie F Fleischmann of Cincinnati, and a member of the family which owes its tremendous fortune to the manufacture of yeast. Mr Goossens is considerably younger than Mrs Holmes.

She financed an orchestral concert for Eugene 'assisted by Igor Stravinsky and full orchestra of 110 players', in the Queen's Hall on 13th June 1929. It was the social and musical event of the season despite being held at three o'clock on a Thursday afternoon. It brought home to London audiences what they had been missing by his absence from the orchestral podium for nearly seven years.

'A most astonishing sight was the Queen's Hall yesterday afternoon,' commented Robin Legge in the *Daily Telegraph*, 'when a very large and, musically very representative audience, gave Eugene Goossens a warmer welcome than surely he ever enjoyed over here before. And well deserved was the enthusiasm, for Eugene Goossens now holds a position so lofty that one is justified in honouring him by omitting his forename! He is among the great. Alert to a degree and with a finely developed authority, he can now look to music of all colours, all atmospheres, all shapes and sizes!'

Richard Capell greeted him in the *Daily Mail* as 'one of the finest conductors our country has ever produced', but had reservations about the 'eminent if problematic Mr Stravinsky' giving the British premiere of his Concerto for Piano and Wind Orchestra: 'The audience of *cognoscenti* showed a distinct liking for this curious work – a parody and rather a grim one, but interesting in its way.'

Nora Barr-Adams, a young music critic forced to disguise her identity under a male pseudonym, listened to the Stravinsky with less prejudiced ears and noted in her programme: 'musically funny in parts – but you laugh *with* it not at it. And can't help *listening* and taking notice. Very striking. Would like to hear it again *soon*.'

Eugene particularly cherished a personal letter that Robin Legge, now describing himself as a *very* old man, had sent him immediately after the concert. 'I can recall nothing quite like it since Arthur Nikisch's debut in Queen's Hall about 1895. Your newly (to me) acquired authority, your definitiveness and clarity and sanity and musicianship were a joy, so ripe have they become, and my article in the *Daily Telegraph* tomorrow would have been at least three times as long if they – the authorities – had allowed me a couple of columns.'

Thanks to Mrs Holmes, Eugene was able to conduct a second concert the following year on 20th May 1930 when he gave the British premiere of Arnold Bax's Second Symphony and his own concertino in a new version for double string orchestra (the original version of 1926 had been written for String Octet). It was a critical success but the lack of a star attraction like Stravinsky resulted in a disappointingly small audience.

Bettie Holmes was an accomplished poet and Eugene set some of her work to music. Much though he appreciated her poetry and her generosity, he informed his sister Sidonie that he had no intention of marrying his grandmother! Instead, he married a piano graduate from the Eastman School of Music, a stunningly pretty girl with auburn hair and sapphire-coloured eyes, called Janet Lewis. They married very quietly while he was guest conductor in Detroit, early on Sunday morning 5th January 1930 at the Northwood Congregational Church. 'Please don't tell the orchestra about it,' he told a journalist at the afternoon rehearsal. 'I don't want the concert to end with a wedding march.' The bride was twenty-two and the groom thirty-six.

Boonie remarried a month after Eugene, again at Kensington Registry Office, this time to Daniel J Reagan, Commercial Attaché to the United States Embassy in Paris. In the years to follow, Anne, Julia and Jane remained mostly with their mother and step-father in Paris.

Eugene's new bride, Jansi as she was affectionately known,

won over the family's hearts when he brought her to England in the summer of 1930. A delightful personality, a trained musician, intelligent, warm and affectionate, his parents hoped that Eugene had now found a partner with whom he could enjoy a happy and stable marriage. On their return to Rochester she started writing affectionate letters back to 'Mum and Dad' at Durban.

Eugene had already been appointed conductor of the prestigious Cincinnati May Festival for 1931 before which he had his usual full season of guest engagements to complete. 'Goossens' conducting superb' was the verdict on his return for three Autumn productions with the Philadelphia Grand Opera Company.[23] Mary Garden defied the years singing the title role in Massenet's *Le Jongleur de Notre Dame*; tenor Richard Crooks made his American operatic debut in *Tosca* with Bianca Saroya and even *Thaïs*, a somewhat jaded offering, was inspired with new life by Eugene's baton.

When he conducted in Minneapolis for the first time, he found three members of the orchestra who had toured in England under his father. One of them, Syd Cunnington had played the bassoon in the Carl Rosa Orchestra when Eugene I had conducted before Queen Victoria in 1892.

This was to be Eugene's last season in Rochester. In December it was announced that he had accepted a two year contract to succeed Fritz Reiner as Chief Conductor of the Cincinnati Symphony Orchestra.

He left Rochester with genuine regret and much appreciated George Eastman's generously worded tribute. 'I do not think it could reasonably have been expected that Rochester would keep Mr Goossens permanently. I feel it is fortunate that we have had him here to accomplish so much that is important to the success of our project with orchestral music in this city. It would perhaps have been better for us orchestrally if we might have had Mr Goossens for a time longer, but I believe his work has been so well done, that firm foundations are laid upon which it may stand in permanence.'

Eugene had raised the orchestra from 'swaddling clothes to impressive, robust musical stature'. At the age of thirty-seven Eugene had also reached maturity as a conductor and it was time for him to move into the premier orchestral league.

8

Diaghilev, Chaliapin and Arnold Bennett

Eugene's admiration for Diaghilev dated from the legendary pre-war seasons of the Ballet Russe at Covent Garden and his modest involvement as a deputy violinist in *Petrushka* in May 1913. Diaghilev was always on the look out for up and coming young conductors. He noted Eugene's phenomenal success with *Le Sacre du Printemps* and in October 1921 asked him to conduct Tchaikovsky's *Sleeping Princess*, opening at the Alhambra Theatre on 2nd November. Eugene was already committed to a full schedule of opera and concert engagements but agreed to share the run with the Polish conductor Gregor Fitelberg whose work he admired.

The spectacular staging of Petipa's choreography was more lavish than the original production in St Petersburg in 1890. Additional dances were devised by Nijinska, Léon Bakst designed the scenery and costumes and the cast included some of the greatest Russian ballerinas – Trefilova, Spessivtseva and Lopokova. Vera Soudekeina, later to marry Stravinsky, played the Queen in a robe of gold and silver embroidery resplendent enough for a real coronation. But London audiences were not accustomed to sitting through a full-length ballet and despite critical acclaim, attendance began to dwindle after three weeks. At the beginning of February Eugene conducted the last performance and Sir Oswald Stoll, who owned the theatre, sequestrated the scenery and costumes against the huge debts Diaghilev had incurred.

The impresario was back in Paris trying to prevent the disintegration of his company. He even had to sell his black pearl stud, a treasured gift from Lady Ripon. The Princesse de Polignac came to his financial rescue and thanks to her influence the company was able to continue as 'Les Ballets Russes de Monte Carlo', under the patronage of Prince Pierre and Princesse Charlotte. By the time he could afford to reclaim the sets and costumes of *The Sleeping Princess*, stored beneath the Coliseum stage, Diaghilev found that many of them had been ruined by a leaking swimming pool installed for a music hall act, but at least half of Bakst's 300 costumes were eventually saved.[1]

Eugene renewed his engagement with Diaghilev at the beginning of May 1925 for a two week season in Barcelona and an exhausting schedule of four ballets a night. A typical programme was composed of *Petrushka*, *Les Sylphides*, *Carnaval* and *La Boutique Fantasque*, starting at 10pm and ending at 1.30am. He described the Liceo as the best opera house in Europe. Every day he took a morning rehearsal with the ballet and after lunch, a rehearsal with Pablo Casals' orchestra. The schedule proved so tiring that he hired a motor boat every afternoon and told the captain to cruise around the harbour while he slept.

Nevertheless he liked Barcelona, processing down the Calle de los Ramblas with Diaghilev and his inseparable companions, Boris Kochno, his secretary-librettist and Serge Lifar, his favourite young dancer. They would dine at the Master's favourite restaurant and then watch the best flamenco dancing in Spain at 'Villa Rosa'. Memories of the child dancer Carmen Amaya would remain with him for more than thirty years and become the inspiration for 'Ballet Flamenco' in his last orchestral work, *Divertissement* op. 66.[2]

On 18th May they opened at the Coliseum with ballet twice daily, sandwiched in between variety acts. The ballets included 'Aurora's Wedding' (dances from the last act of *The Sleeping Princess*), the British premiere of Poulenc's *Les Biches* (*The House Party*) and Balanchine's adaptation of Stravinsky's *Le Chant du Rossignol*. Eugene preferred this to the operatic version. It provided a starring role for Diaghilev's newest protégée: fourteen-year-old Alice Marks, whom he had renamed Alicia Markova. Marie, who had played with the Diaghilev Company in London since 1919, was fascinated to watch her in rehearsal: 'She appeared in a large wicker cage, and attired in black leotard and tights she danced so gracefully that it seemed she had not a bone in her body.'[3]

Another company member dancing small solo roles was Ninette de Valois. She had previously met Eugene in September 1918 when he was conducting *Phoebus and Pan* for Beecham at the Palladium. She had been engaged as a guest artist and had to dance one solo variation in an important dance suite.

> The ballet mistress whose choreography terrified me, allowed me to take my variation home and write it myself. After the opera Eugene asked who I was and said he'd like to meet me. I was brought up to him and he said 'You're very musical. I like the way you arranged your dance!'
>
> I found him a very sympathetic conductor for dance but he found the Russians difficult to deal with. They're very spoilt when it comes to music; they're used to the conductor following them meticulously. After each performance there would be a queue of dancers asking him to do this or that for them. He was absolutely horrified; he would say to me 'You weren't in the queue but everybody else was!' I explained to him that I wasn't brought up to think you treated conductors like that.

Dame Ninette considered he was totally justified in his criticism of the musical sloppiness of the Diaghilev Company.

> The dancers weren't very rhythmical; they had a strange sense of tempi which would vary from one performance to the next. He found that the whole mood of a movement would be changed by a dancer's unexpected alteration of tempo. This was not true of the choreographers: Nijinska and Massine were marvellous and very rhythmical.
>
> He rather despised dancers. 'Don't they ever listen?' he asked me. He would hear them counting but at the slightest change of tempi they all got very excited and unreliable especially the Russians! On one occasion I was so irritated by their lack of musicality that I gave the line of girls a push to get on stage on the right beat. Unfortunately the one in front fell down!
>
> Goossens was charming, a very attractive man, very amusing, very quick on the uptake. He was very unaffected and natural, unlike Diaghilev's parties which were very stiff and formal in full evening dress. He stood up to Diaghilev and spoke out if he thought he was being too demanding, unlike all the other conductors who crawled to him.

I remember watching a scene between them once and Goossens going off roaring with laughter. Diaghilev was struck dumb. Eugene had had enough of dancers' complaints and he just waved them all to one side. Diaghilev's face was a study![4]

Diaghilev realised his value as a competent and reliable conductor. Eugene, a heterosexual with a burgeoning career as a conductor in America, was not beholden to the omnipotent impresario and the hothouse intrigues of his entourage. Conducting for Diaghilev was a useful summer engagement in Europe between Rochester and the Hollywood Bowl.

In June 1926 he was engaged for a season of Russian ballet at His Majesty's Theatre, including eight newly commissioned works. As an experiment, the programmes also featured 'symphonic interludes' between the ballets of new or unfamiliar works, mainly by Russian and French composers. The exceptions were Walton's overture *Portsmouth Point*, Berners' *Fugue* and Eugene's *Nonet*. He warmed particularly to Honegger's *Pacific 231*, reflecting his own passion for the mighty kings of the silver rail developed during his long train tours across the USA.

The opening night included the British premiere of Stravinsky's *Les Noces*, with composers Auric, Poulenc, Rieti and Dukelsky playing four grand pianos on stage. Eugene complained that he had more trouble obtaining a satisfactory ensemble from them than from the Russian chorus imported from Paris or the English percussion players. The critics' abuse of the work brought H G Wells to its defence with a letter to the *Times*: 'Writing as an old-fashioned popular writer, not at all of the high-brow set, I do not know of any other ballet so interesting, so amusing, so fresh, or nearly so exciting as *Les Noces*. I want to see it again and again, and because I want to do so, I protest against this wilful stupidity that may succeed in driving it out of the programme. This ballet is a rendering in sound and vision of the peasants' soul, in its gravity, in its deliberate and simple-minded intricacy, in its subtly varied rhythms, in its deep undercurrents of excitement, that will astonish and delight every intelligent man or woman who goes to see it.'

Les Noces was retained in the programme, followed by the

same composer's *Pulcinella*, Auric's *Pastorale* and Karsavina in a revival of *Thamar*, which Eugene considered to be the perfect ballet. Another novelty was *Jack in the Box*. Edwin Evans explained its genesis in his programme note: 'The composer [Satie] always believed he had left the MS in a cab, but he was in the habit of accumulating his discarded suits, of which a large number were found at his death and in the pocket of an old jacket were discovered the long lost dances which have since been orchestrated by Darius Milhaud.'

It was the custom for the orchestra to give the conductor a complimentary dinner at the end of the season, with a celebrity guest list. 'Heaven alone knows what I am doing here with the Russian Ballet,' groaned Jim Thomas who was a Labour MP and General Secretary of the National Union of Railwaymen. 'If it gets known outside, all the morning posters will be shouting "J H Thomas with the Bolsheviks again!"' The *Daily Sketch* gave a full report of his comments and presence at the dinner at the Hotel Cecil on 26th July 1925.

Eugene returned to Barcelona in May 1927 for what was to be his last season with Diaghilev. He invited his parents to Paris for a holiday while he conducted there. 'Just a line before flying out to the "Liceo",' he wrote. 'It's Alfonso's birthday, or something, and we've got to start with the Spanish national anthem, which is unpopular in Catalonia!' Eugene and Annie were too busy to accept. They were in the process of moving from Edith Road to 'Durban', the house they had bought at 576, Finchley High Road, a few minutes away from Marie and her husband Fred.

The pressure of performance in Barcelona proved so great that Eugene backed out of the Paris commitment, deciding that it was essential for him to have a 'breather' before opening in London at the Prince's Theatre.

The British premieres included Berners' *Triumph of Neptune*, Constant Lambert's first ballet *Romeo and Juliet* and Milhaud's *Le Train Bleu*. Considering Eugene's artistic skills – since boyhood his hobby had always been painting and sketching – it is surprising that he comments so little on the visual dimension of the Ballet Russe and Diaghilev's patronage of contemporary artists. He fails to mention in any of his writing his friend Picasso's front curtain depicting two heroically endowed females racing towards la Plage to join Nijinska playing tennis and Dolin performing acrobatics, costumed by Coco Chanel. One misses a pristine view of Matisse's fairy-tale costumes for *Le Chant du Rossignol*, Utrillo's only ballet décor for *Barabau* or Braque's designs for *Zephyr et Floré*.

Rumours circulated that Prokofiev's *Le Pas d'Acier*, with a scenario of machinery and factory workers, was Bolshevik propaganda and would provoke a hostile demonstration in London. On the first night, Diaghilev followed Eugene into the orchestra pit and took a seat next to the first flautist. 'I'm carrying a revolver,' he told him, 'and at the first sign of any demonstration I shall fire it in the air.'

What he hoped to accomplish by this Eugene never discovered. His theory was that a well-timed pistol shot would have brought about the disturbance that Diaghilev was secretly hoping for. No interruption marred the performance at the end of which the audience burst into a stupendous ovation. According to Eugene, 'Diaghilev made his way out of the orchestra, more than ever perplexed by the unpredictable British public.'[5]

The emotional and physical strain of six weeks' nightly performances took its toll following his punishing schedule in America. He regretfully told Diaghilev he would not be able to complete the London season and retired to a nursing home with what was described by a sympathetic press as a nervous breakdown. Thanks to the complete rest, he was able to sail at the end of July for his concerts at the Hollywood Bowl.

Diaghilev had expressed interest in Eugene's ballet *L'Ecole en Crinoline* but failed to produce it, probably because he found the early Victorian scenario excessively stylised. Eugene started work on another ballet for Diaghilev, *The Rake's Progress*, but wrote to his father from Rochester on 18th November 1927: '*The Rake's Progress* is definitely shelved for the time being. I am getting real tired of Diaghilev and his empty promises, consequently I'm now contemplating *Villon* my new opera.' The *Morning Post* had reported on 12th December 1926: 'I hear that Eugene Goossens is collaborating with C H Meltzer in a lyric drama on the subject of François Villon.' Eugene had cherished François Villon as a potential operatic hero but never brought the project to fruition.

At the end of the following Rochester season he was able to

reassure his parents that his health was much improved. 'I'm very well, thank God, and in spite of the most strenuous season I've ever had, I can truthfully say I've never had a day's illness. This is thanks to my cure in the summer and also to the fact that I haven't touched anything stronger than water since last June. In the country of "bootleg" that's a pretty good record! I sleep much better and have put on weight and most important of all, my conducting work doesn't exert the slightest strain on me as it used to do sometimes last year . . . I'm going to take things very easily this summer and don't propose conducting *anything* unless it be a concert. But certainly *no* Russian ballet. Let them find someone else.'[6]

Despite his good intentions, on his return to London Eugene found himself in conflict with another temperamental Russian giant, Feodor Chaliapin. Chaliapin was singing Mephistopheles in Gounod's *Faust*, one of his greatest roles, for the first time in London on 22nd June 1928. Eugene was telephoned the night before by Colonel Blois, General Administrator of Covent Garden, asking him if he would take over the performance owing to the illness of the scheduled French conductor. He reluctantly said yes.

He had already recorded 'Le veau d'or' and Mephistopheles' serenade with Chaliapin as part of a series for Gramophone Red Label in June and July 1923 and a second series in May 1926, including excerpts from *Boris Godunov*. He respected his unique artistry but knew that his French was shaky and that he was notoriously inaccurate in note values. They met for a short piano rehearsal on the morning of the performance which confirmed his worst fears.

Chaliapin's performance was a superb dramatic characterisation but musically cavalier and hair-raising for the conductor. In Act II, scene i, the Kermesse, he missed a lead during the waltz and extemporised with some 'la,la,la's'. He then came down stage and started conducting the orchestra trying to give the impression that Eugene was at fault. But Eugene 'kept on serenely, with undeviating tempo, and paid no attention to him, till he was shortly engulfed by the *corps de ballet*.'[7]

He was woken up at six o'clock the next morning to comment on the front page story in the *Daily Express*: 'Violent altercation between singer and conductor.' The *Daily Mail* devoted an even-handed editorial to the event, headed 'Chaliapiniana':

Greek meets Greek when an operatic singer of the first eminence crosses the path of a brilliantly distinguished conductor. The production the other night at Covent Garden of a hackneyed opera which ordinarily would have stirred only a languid interest, took on a dramatic tenseness. This was not only through the vivid art of a Mephistopheles who made the mortals round about him seem mere puppets, but also through that personage's challenges to the authority of one to whom even the Arch-fiend usually has to bow – namely the orchestral conductor, on this occasion Mr Eugene Goossens.

Mr Goossens is far too well able to look after himself for any condolences to be in place. The Great Man's caprices did indeed lead him a dance – a dance that would have turned into a cropper with a conductor of less exquisite skill. The suggestion has been made that the almighty Chaliapin – his head at length a little turned by so many years of adulation in the two hemispheres – was deliberately not playing the game; but that strikes us as ungenerous.

Rather we prefer to believe that he had acquired such a confidence in the brilliant young Englishman's almost uncanny alertness and flexibility that he felt it safe to give the reins for once to his wildest fantasy. And Mr Goossens, so far from having to be condoled with, probably enjoyed giving this exhibition of jugglery with the baton. It was certainly the most entertaining *Faust* seen at Covent Garden for a generation. All the same, the Great Man may be reminded of the dangers (if there is a Russian equivalent of our idiom) of a swelled head.[8]

His father summed it up in his diary as 'Fencing bout between Zenny and Chaliapin!' Excerpts from a live recording of the performance were eventually issued on record (a rare collector's item). Their relationship remained sufficiently cordial for a recording session on 30th June of Schubert's *Der Doppelgänger* and *Der Tod und das Mädchen* with orchestral accompaniment.

The following season Eugene had far more serious problems at Covent Garden with the production of his one act opera *Judith*, with libretto by Arnold Bennett. He had first met the

famous writer in 1911 as he was a friend of Cedric Sharpe's
father and often came to their house in Putney when the Philharmonic Quartet – Beckwith, Goossens, Jeremy and Sharpe
– were rehearsing. 'In a peremptory high-pitched stammer he
would demand "B-Borodine, p-p-p-please", his favourite composer, and he always got it,' Eugene recalled.[9]

Their friendship flourished and Eugene discovered that
'AB' had read and acquired more knowledge of music than
any other contemporary writer except, of course, Bernard
Shaw. Eugene was looking for a suitable subject for a short
opera and had discussed the project with Shaw, Galsworthy
and Somerset Maugham without managing to persuade any
of those distinguished dramatists to dip his toe into operatic
waters. Lunching with Bennett in March 1924, Eugene picked
up a copy of his play *Judith*. This had been a great success
with Lillah McCarthy as the Biblical heroine at the Kingsway
Theatre in 1919. He suggested it would make an excellent
one act opera and AB agreed to compress the five acts into
a prose libretto of fifty to sixty minutes, his first venture into
the operatic world.

Eugene added a ballet at the suggestion of Diaghilev but
decided to leave out an opening chorus. Progress was slow,
mainly because Beecham's promises of a production at Covent
Garden failed to materialise. Chesters agreed to publish the
score and on 16th June 1928, AB noted in his diary: 'Eugene
Goossens came for dinner. Eugene began to play and sing our
opera *Judith*. He has evidently set out to do something not
too incomprehensible. Better than I had expected. Dramatic,
effective. My libretto seemed quite good.'

Eugene later complained to Chesters about certain phrases.
'The answer to the criticism that the words "dried fish" are
"a little out of the picture" is that they are intended to be a
great deal out of the picture,' explained the aggrieved author.
'Judith is a very beautiful woman of extreme charm, and here
she is likening herself to a dried fish! Obviously her
humility in making this comparison is meant to be ironic to
the point of wilful absurdity. If anybody can suggest to me
a phrase more satisfactory to Mr Goossens, I will pass it if I
possibly can.'[10]

He had also made some helpful comments on the cos-

tumes, which they hoped would be designed by Charles
Ricketts who had designed the stage production. 'In the
play Miss Lillah McCarthy (Lady Keeble) wore as little as
propriety and the censor would allow – that is, after she had
removed her travelling garment. It is to be remembered that
she came prepared to fascinate Holofernes.'[11]

Colonel Blois, Chairman of the Royal Opera Syndicate, had
agreed to risk the premiere of *Judith* for two performances in the
last week of the International Grand Season at the end of June
1929. Eugene returned from America seven weeks beforehand,
anxious to discover how preparations for the production were
progressing. He found to his horror that no rehearsals had so
far been scheduled, the specially designed décor consisted of
two palm trees complete with coconuts and a striped awning
for Holofernes' tent. Costumes were to be from stock and
the title role had been given to a Swedish soprano, Göta
Ljungberg.

Madame Ljungberg was singing at the Charlottenburg Opera
in Berlin and Eugene wired her to say he was arriving in
twenty-four hours to coach her in her part. His worst fears
were justified: 'She hadn't even begun to study her formidable
role and the little she read at sight convinced me that her fine
voice wasn't even suitable for the part. Moreover, worst of all,
her pronunciation of English – of which she hardly knew a word
– was with a thick Swedish accent.'

He stayed in Berlin for two weeks to teach her every
note and every word of her role. By the time of the final
dress rehearsal, the orchestra and singers were well prepared
but the costumes were not ready and there was no lighting
plot. 'The amateurishness and apathy displayed by everyone
in the theatre in connection with my new piece would have
been impossible even at a fourth-rate Italian opera house; it
could only have happened in England. During the scene where
Judith pretends to seduce Holofernes, she gradually removes
her tunic. To everyone's consternation, instead of revealing a
greater degree of epidermis, Ljungberg was seen to be wearing
a sort of sequinned bust bodice.'[12] Eugene stopped the
orchestra and with some heat asked her to remove the offending
garment. He does not record what, if anything, she was wearing underneath.

As is so often the case, the performance went incomparably better than the dress rehearsal. When the curtain fell, Bennett was too shy to join Eugene to acknowledge the ovations. The general criticism was that *Judith* was an opera without a tune and that Eugene was no Puccini.

The most perspicacious assessment of the work came from Ernest Newman in the *Sunday Times*:

There is a superficial resemblance between Strauss' *Salome* and *Judith*. But to say nothing of the fact that at the end of *Salome* the head of Jochanaan is boldly exhibited on a charger, while at the end of *Judith* the head of Holofernes is hastily stuffed into a sack by the handmaid Haggith (at Covent Garden the two women had the air of a couple of shoplifters making a furtive exit from the main counter with the swag under the gimlet eyes of the store detective), the general resemblance between the two operas is of the slightest; while the texture of the two scores is as different as that of *Petrushka* and *Sea Drift*. The harmonic basis of *Salome* is the ordinary diatonic scale with chromatic subtilisations; the harmonic basis of the greater part of *Judith* is something so remote from this that on the comparatively rare occasions when the common chord is insisted on it has a quite astonishing effect.

That *Judith* is not lyrical in the ordinary way goes without saying. It could not and should not be. Mr Arnold Bennett's efficient text is not an operatic libretto; it is a drama told simply and straightforwardly, without any repetition of points for purely musical purposes, any holding up of the action to give the composer a pretext for exploiting a form, or the singers a chance to show us what fine fellows they are. The story of the drama is for the most part told musically in the orchestra, the voices merely making the course of it and the motives of the characters clear.

I find Mr Goossens' score of great interest. Not only is it a marvel of subtlety and of flawless logic (for Mr Goossens handles this recondite language of his with complete ease and certainty), but it seems to me to do successfully what the composer set out to do – to see the action and the characters from a certain individual angle and bathed in a certain atmosphere, and to make the point of view and the atmosphere convincing for the listener. At the same time I can see the matter as the man in the street sees it, and understand why he may not greatly take to the work. He is hustled too rapidly from point to point; he would no doubt have liked more lyrical expansion – something in the nature of a love scene, in fact – when the affair between Holofernes and Judith reaches its climax of voluptuousness.

The vocal parts were mostly so unsatisfactorily done that the opera can hardly be said to have been presented precisely as the composer conceived it. Madame Ljungberg's English is very good indeed for ordinary purposes, but it is not good enough to permit of our abandoning ourselves completely to illusion in the theatre; I was too conscious of the careful management of the linguistic machine. In a German version of the opera she would no doubt be more completely successful. The Germans have the art of delivering non-lyrical phrases in a conversational style. Our English singers lack this art, and are obviously uncomfortable when they are called upon to attempt it. They want to sing their phrases in the grand style and neither time nor the nature of the melodic line permits this.[13]

In contrast, the general obtuseness of the London critics was illustrated by A H Fox-Strangeways in the *Observer*, who bemoaned the lack of a suitable climax to bring down the curtain. 'What was wanted at that moment was a great tune worth singing, and the presence on the stage of the people for whom it would have been worth hearing and perhaps joining in. If there had been such a cantilation as Wagner is supposed to have founded the Meistersinger's theme upon, it would have made every Jew and Jewess in the audience happy.'[14]

The *Daily Telegraph* drew attention to the fact that Eugene could claim the distinction of having the first new opera in English included in the Italian Season at Covent Garden since an opera called *Harvest* had been performed in 1902. The next day a letter appeared from the composer who had been so honoured, Sir Frederic Cowen pointing out that his opera had been called *Harold*!

Eugene conducted the American premiere of *Judith* in December 1929 with the Philadelphia Grand Opera Company. The redeeming features of the evening were the performance of Bianca Saroya in the title role and the superb playing of the Philadelphia Orchestra. The production was abysmal, culminating in a coconut falling from a stage palm tree, narrowly avoiding the premature decapitation of the Russian baritone struggling through the role of Holofernes. *Judith* was to receive an excellent concert performance in Cincinnati at the 1937 May Festival with Elisabeth Rethberg in the title role.

He remained convinced that if only a competent producer could be found the opera would find a place in the repertoire. One act operas are notoriously difficult to place. *Judith* might have fared better if he had written a companion piece, but he decided to embark on a full length work. He enjoyed collaborating with Arnold Bennett and felt that the writer's somewhat staccato style of short precise sentences was ideally suited to his particular musical idiom. Their second opera was to be *Don Juan de Mañara.*

9

The World's Greatest Oboist

Léon Goossens transformed the oboe from a necessary, but often unpleasant, bleating noise in the orchestra to an instrument capable of producing unimagined refinement and beauty of tone. The virtuoso qualities that he revealed, together with his delicacy of phrasing and richness of sound, put the oboe on the map as a twentieth-century solo instrument in the same way that Lionel Tertis transformed the status of the viola and Segovia that of the guitar. Eugene gave him one of his first important London solo engagements in the Queen's Hall in the third of the Goossens Orchestral Concerts on 12th December 1921. The work was Sir Henry Wood's arrangement of Bach's Suite in G for Organ, Oboe and Strings; Léon had missed his solo debut in the 1916 Promenade Concert premiere due to his army enlistment.

As his opportunities for playing the small repertoire of classical and baroque works for solo oboe and orchestra gradually increased, his opinion of them altered. 'I remember so well as a small boy hearing all the important concertos in Liverpool. In those days my pet aversion was the music of Bach and Handel. Why? Simply because the performances of those great composers' works were so pedantic and lacking in virtuosity that the inner meaning and subtlety were almost entirely absent, so far as my ear was concerned. I have since learned that there is as much humour in the works of Bach and Handel, and indeed many other eighteenth-century composers, as there is in some of the present day compositions.'[1]

His solo engagements increased both in London and the provinces but Léon continued to earn his living as an orchestral player, primarily as first oboe in the Queen's Hall Orchestra. The life of an orchestral musician can be tedious and Léon, renowned for his sense of fun, became increasingly more humorous during concerts and rehearsals. Eventually Sir Henry Wood's patience was exhausted and he wrote to him: 'No one appreciates more than I do the buoyancy of your spirits, which I hope you may long keep, but there is a time and a place for everything, and it is certainly not either the band rehearsal or when you are under the eyes of several members of an audience. Probably you do not realise that every little note scribbled, every message passed round, and every little joke is noticed by a number of the audience and found distracting by some.'

The rebuke took Léon by surprise and he wrote back in contrition: 'I am tremendously sorry for the worry and trouble I have caused you and only wish I had been pulled up before.' Their excellent relationship was resumed.

Léon had been engaged as first oboe for the opening concert of the City of Birmingham Orchestra, in an all Elgar programme conducted by the composer on 10th November 1920. He continued to play for the first two seasons and then received solo engagements with the orchestra. In 1924 he joined Marie and Sidonie for opera seasons with the Covent Garden Orchestra and his name continues to appear as first oboe with the Queen's Hall Orchestra as late as the Delius Festival Concerts in October 1929.

He was meanwhile increasing his scope and repertoire as solo recitalist with chamber ensembles. He later described how the Philharmonic Trio came into being: 'It consisted of Albert Fransella, the famous flautist, Francesco Ticciati, composer and pianist and myself. We conceived the idea of each giving individual recitals with our own trio as a background. We felt that the public really wanted a change from string quartets, quintets and sextets and were ripe for any novel ideas. Events proved that we were not mistaken.'[2]

His artistry and unmistakeable individual voice inspired more than a hundred compositions over the length of his career, ranging from works dedicated to him by Bax, Bliss, Boughton, Britten, Elgar and Vaughan Williams, to offerings from unknown musicians who had heard him on the wireless.

The first work of major significance was the Oboe Quintet which Arnold Bax composed in the autumn of 1922, exploiting the liveliness of Léon's playing with a wild Irish jig in the last of three movements. The first performance was delayed until 11th May 1924 in one of the Chamber Concerts organised by Mrs Adela Maddison at the Hyde Park Hotel. Léon later recorded it in March 1927 with the International Quartet led by André Mangeot. Bax never took up the suggestion of converting the work into a concerto for oboe and orchestra. It was somewhat galling for Léon that this eventually took place long after the composer's death when Sir John Barbirolli arranged it for his wife Evelyn Rothwell, Léon's erstwhile pupil. (First performance 21st April 1969, Free Trade Hall, Manchester.)

Another new work Léon premiered was the Fugal Concerto for Flute, Oboe and Strings by Gustav Holst, conducted by the composer at a Promenade Concert on 11th October 1923. The following year, Eugene conducted a performance at a Royal Philharmonic Society Concert on 21st February 1924, Léon's first appearance as a soloist with London's most venerable concert organisation, founded in 1813. It was repeated in the Wigmore Hall a month later in a programme which included the first performance of Eugene's 'Miniature Fantasy for Flute, Oboe and Pianoforte' written for the Philharmonic Trio, and the Mozart Oboe Quartet (K370). 'The best thing by far was Mr Léon Goossens playing in the quartet for oboe,' was the opinion of the *Times*. 'The unique colour of the oboe is a delight in the orchestra, but never having been much cultivated as a solo instrument, it had not as a rule, endured to have greatness thrust upon it for more than a few moments. Mr Goossens has so cultivated it, and we must confess to having waited for his entry with breathless interest. His whole range of two and a half octaves, is perfectly capable and uniform, and he can do musically just what he likes with any and every note of it.'

Two other names of note on the programme were John (no longer Giovanni) Barbirolli as cellist in the Music Society String Quartet and the soprano Dora Labbette, a favoured protégée of Sir Thomas Beecham. She was one of the singers for whom Léon delighted in playing Bach obligati. He was becoming acknowledged as the supreme exponent in this field, unsurpassed in the rapport between voice and instrument. His playing became a feature of the Bach Choir's annual performance of the *St Matthew Passion* in the Queen's Hall. The

127

Cantatas were still little known, despite the efforts of the Bach Cantata Club under Charles Kennedy Scott. This was bemoaned by *Marcato* reviewing a performance of Bach's Cantata no. 21 at St Margaret's, Westminster as 'a Bach masterpiece. Last night the church was far from full. The soprano of the evening, Miss Dora Labbette, sang the wonderful aria "Sighing, weeping" beautifully. The performance was also remarkable for the surpassing beauty of Mr Léon Goossens' playing.'[3]

Léon was now recommended to singers of international stature when they visited London – in November 1927 with Elisabeth Schumann he recorded 'Es ist vollbracht' from Cantata no. 159. This was a bass aria that Schumann's husband, Carl Alwin had arranged for her. As far as contemporary music was concerned, one of the most important premieres from this period was the Quintet for Oboe and Strings by Arthur Bliss. Léon went to Venice for the first performance on 11th November 1927 with the Venetian Quartet, in a concert arranged by the American philanthropist, Mrs Elizabeth Sprague Coolidge.

On 27th July 1926 Léon ventured into matrimony. His bride was Fay Yeatman, a beautiful blonde soprano whom he had got to know when he was playing in *The Immortal Hour*; she understudied Gwen Frangcon-Davis in the leading role which she sang on a number of occasions. They had first met when she was in the chorus of *Hassan*, but Léon at that time was engaged to Olga Morrison, sister of the pianist Angus Morrison, a great friend of the Goossens brothers and sisters. Sidonie did not think that they were suited to each other and was relieved when Olga married Constant Lambert's brother instead.

Fay had already had a brief, unsuccessful marriage to a fellow singer. Apart from the fact that she was not a Catholic, she seemed an ideal partner for Léon. She had trained at the Royal College of Music, one of her brothers was a successful writer, R J Yeatman, co-author of the best-selling historical spoof *1066 and All That* and the family was comfortably off. The wedding was in the Savoy Chapel. Their first child was a daughter, born on 7th October 1927 and christened Benedicta Eugenie. Léon hoped that Eugene IV was waiting in the wings to perpetuate the family name and musical tradition, but Bene was to be their only child.

He was not terribly pleased when Fay returned to the

stage to sing in Noel Coward's *Bitter Sweet*, but there was little money to finance classical music in the late twenties and despite his growing reputation, solo engagements were still not as plentiful as he would have wished.

At the end of the year he took part in the first of Sir Thomas Beecham's definitive recordings of the music of Delius with the Royal Philharmonic Orchestra, *The Walk to the Paradise Garden* and *On hearing the First Cuckoo in Spring*, followed in 1928 by *Brigg Fair* and *Summer Night on the River*.

Eric Fenby, the young Yorkshireman newly arrived in Grez-sur-Loing to help the aged and crippled composer, was interested to observe his reactions to his music on gramophone records: 'He chose Sir Thomas Beecham's beautiful record of his *On hearing the First Cuckoo in Spring*. Never had the sound of strings nor Goossens' oboe playing seemed so magical. A curious other worldliness possessed him. With his head thrown back, and swaying slightly to the rhythm, he seemed to be seeing with those now wide-open yet unseeing eyes and his spirit ebbed and flowed with the rise and fall of his music.'[4]

Léon had decided to follow Eugene's example and experience the enthusiasm of American audiences. His arrival was anticipated by the *Musical Courier* of 12th January 1928: 'Hailed as the world's greatest oboist, Léon Goossens, who is coming to America this month, promises to raise tremendous interest in this, the most beautiful of all reed instruments.'

Eugene had for some time been planning an oboe concerto, inspired by his brother's virtuosity, for his New York debut but it was not finished to the composer's satisfaction. Instead, he accompanied Léon in his recital at the Guild Theatre on 22nd January 1928, the first time that an oboe had been featured in a solo professional recital in the USA. They were assisted by the Marianne Kneisel Quartet in a programme of the Mozart and Bliss oboe quartets, a group of solos and a new sonata for oboe and piano by David Stanley Smith, a music professor at Harvard. It seemed to Eugene as if all the wind players in New York were at the concert: 'Léon made the New York public and critics rub their eyes at his incontestable artistry.'

He received a superlative press. 'Mr Goossens is clearly a master of his instrument,' decided the *New York Herald*. 'He phrases with taste, his rhythmic sense is vital and precise, he has a wide dynamic range, he is musical in his instincts – an artist as well as a virtuoso.' The formidable Olin Downes was even more generous: 'An admirably clean and precise technique, an exceptional knowledge of ensemble and evident musicianship. His mastery of his instrument is indisputable.' But it was the *Daily Telegraph* that described Léon's playing in the greatest detail: 'The sweet-throated pastoral instrument was its plaintive and whimsical self in a variety of colour patterns, kaleidoscopic and amazing. We think of the oboe among instruments as the "Lass with the Delicate Air". She did not step out of her character, to be sure – she could not be other than herself – yet there was a scope of performance in the hands or at the lips of Léon Goossens which presented a new vista of tonal possibilities. One noted the absence of reed licking, so common with most players of the oboe. And in the difficult passages of his programme, the artist recalled Heifetz. One is tempted to say of Léon Goossens that he is the greatest player of the oboe.'

Léon returned a year later for the re-scheduled official premiere of the concerto in Boston, at the Jordan Hall on 25th February. As the orchestration was still not complete, Eugene accompanied him in a version with piano. 'Mr Goossens, with his brother's art in mind, wrote robuster melodies for the oboe than those usually allotted that gentle pastoral pipe, melodies fitting bagpipes or the melodies in vogue in Handel's time,' the *Boston Herald* reported the next day. The *Boston Globe* added: 'Mr Goossens' concerto for his brother indulges in no far-fetched virtuosities; by concision it avoids tedium; the songful section has intrinsical musical quality, yet is apt for the voice that sings it. Mr Léon Goossens, escaping both dryness and acidity, played it in smooth, rounded, moist and transparent tone, outflowing with technical skill transmuted into felicity and imagination. Here and there potentates from Symphony Hall were to be seen intently listening. As likely as not they suspected that when oboes are in question, their orchestra leaves something to be desired.'

History does not record whether the message was conveyed to Koussevitzky, with any lasting effect on the oboe section of the Boston Symphony Orchestra! Apart from de Busscher in

Los Angeles, the harsher German school of oboe playing was prevalent in American orchestras.

Léon came home trailing clouds of glory from his second successful concert tour in America and found that his status as a soloist in England was greatly enhanced. After a concert in Brighton, disaster struck; his Lorée oboe which he had had since the age of ten was stolen from his car. Police later found his empty despatch case and feared that the thief had thrown the instrument into the sea. Two years later Léon received a phone call saying that his beloved and irreplaceable oboe was on sale in a pawn shop in South East London, labelled as a clarinet. He recovered it safely for only £1 more than his father had paid for it in 1907 and no questions were asked.

Although the volume of his solo engagements had increased, they were still not sufficient to support a wife and family. He was therefore delighted when he was approached by the BBC in connection with the formation of the BBC Symphony Orchestra. 'I was led to believe that I was going to be First Oboe,' he recalled many years later. 'Adrian Boult and the Orchestral Manager took me out to lunch; the Orchestral Manager, whom I couldn't stand, started buttering me up. "Of course we ought to mention at this juncture that it is for the Cor Anglais that we principally want you as we have already appointed our First Oboe." I got up from my seat and said: "No thank you. Good afternoon, gentlemen," and walked out. Adrian wrote me a letter to apologise.' The First Oboe was in fact Alec Whittaker who had been poached from the Hallé.[5]

Léon did however play as soloist with the orchestra in the Promenade Season. Because of his American commitments, Eugene was not available to conduct the first performance of the Oboe Concerto with orchestra. This formed part of the last British Composers' Night of the Promenade Concert on 2nd October 1930, conducted by Sir Henry Wood; the programme also included the premiere of John Ireland's Piano Concerto. At Léon's suggestion, Eugene had added further pyrotechnics for the cadenza demonstrating the full range of his phenomenal virtuosity and technique. The brothers used to joke that the cadenza was based on Léon's warm-up exercises! Richard Temple Savage, bass clarinet player, remembers Léon complaining to Eugene at a later performance that the concerto was too difficult: ' "I only wrote down what you practised, the twiddles," he replied, rather like the story of Strauss' father complaining about the Horn Concerto.'[6]

The concerto is one of Eugene's most successful and attractive compositions and received unanimous approbation from the British press:

> Exquisite craftsmanship and a cunning sense of orchestral values marked the Oboe Concerto written for the composer's brother Léon who was soloist. It is a short, somewhat rhapsodic work in one movement, clearly designed to exploit the instrument's technical possibilities. The composer, knowing well its emotional limitations, cut his coat, so to speak, according to his cloth, and the result was a compact, tidy, elegant, well-fitting little work.
>
> The oboe has never been better played in our time than by Léon Goossens, and as in this he played a virtuoso's part, he was heartily applauded at the close.[7]

Ernest Newman found Eugene's concerto 'brilliantly played by his accomplished brother, Léon. The general bent of the work is rhapsodical with a good deal of the arabesque and the colour that we Westerns are accustomed to call oriental. [Produced by the choice of percussion instruments: the cadenza is accompanied by the sustained sound of a tam-tam.] There is a slimness and grace about it that is very charming, and the concerto should prove popular.'

Eugene did not conduct the work until the following year, in a Sunday Orchestral Concert with the BBC Orchestra on 24th May 1931. It became so much of a standard repertoire piece for the two brothers' joint appearances that Eugene began to resent its popularity, especially with the BBC. Sadly they never recorded their performance; Léon recorded it when he was still at the height of his powers, with Walter Susskind and the Philharmonia Orchestra for EMI in 1949. Although he promised Léon a sequel, Eugene never found the time to write one, only a 'Concert Piece' for Marie, Sidonie and Léon in 1957.

The repertoire for solo oboe remained limited. Typical of the chamber music recitals that Léon enjoyed playing was one that he gave on 1st February 1932 with violinist, May Harrison: Bach Concerto in C minor for Violin and Oboe; Marcello Concerto for Oboe; Handel Sonata for Oboe and Violin. The string accompaniment was in the distinguished hands of Jean Pougnet, Harry Berly, Eugene Pini, Lauri Kennedy and Eugene Cruft.

Léon was also beginning to be invited to give solo recitals in London and the provinces. One of his favourite accompanists was Ivor Newton who on one occasion when they were playing in Dublin, took Léon to meet Count John McCormack. 'I've heard all about you,' the great Irish tenor said. 'You're the man who never breathes when you play. They say the same about me that I never breathe when I sing. But I bet you're just like me, breathing all over the place and taking darned good care that no one ever sees or hears you doing it!'[8]

Léon acquired his superb breath control, as so much else of his basic technique, from his first teacher, Charles Reynolds. Reynolds had perfected the art of breathing in through the nose while sustaining the sound of his instrument and always said he had learnt this 'double breathing' from a glass-blower who lived near him at St Helens.

There was however one idiosyncratic feature of Reynolds' teaching which Léon did not pass on to his own pupils: 'My master used to have a silver weight with an elastic band which he attached to my finger. It was like having a trotting horse with heavy plates on his feet instead of ordinary light shoes. It makes them have much more action in the movement of their feet, so that they overcompensate when it comes to the race. I never used it with my pupils, partly because I have never seen the attachment. Reynolds probably designed it himself.'[9]

Léon began his teaching career in 1924 when he was appointed a Professor to both the Royal Academy of Music and the Royal College. His name remained on the prospectus of the RAM until 1935 and on 9th June 1932 he was elected an Honorary Member of the RAM. One of his early pupils there was Helen Gaskill, first of the group of well brought up young ladies who took the revolutionary step of becoming professional instrumentalists and playing the oboe in London orchestras.

I was bulldozed into playing the oboe by Gussie Holst when I was fifteen or sixteen. He was Director of Music at St Paul's Girls School. 'We don't need string players or flutes in school,' he said, 'we need oboes. Go and see Estelle White who lives at No. 6 Brook Green.' She was learning with Léon and took me to tea with him just a few minutes away across the Hammersmith Road. It was 1923 or 24 and he was still living at the family house before he was married. He was very friendly, a bit intimidating but very nice and never aggressive. I didn't learn with him until about a year later when I went to the Academy. He sat at the piano and played and said: 'Fit a scale to this.' Once in a while he produced Gillet studies but I wasn't very good at them. For him the most important thing was the quality of sound you produced. If he was coaching me for any particular piece he was very careful about phrasing. The way he used phrasing was lovely and his use of tonguing was very, very subtle.

I don't think he knew much about teaching and he wasn't really very interested. If I wanted to play anything I would take it to him and he was most helpful but as far as technique was concerned I was very lazy and I didn't really want to be bothered.

I learnt much more in the orchestra from two to five on Tuesdays and Fridays. The professors played together with the students in the orchestra which was conducted by Sir Henry Wood. I sat between Léon and Old Man McDonagh* who played the Cor Anglais. When I improved we'd change parts. He taught me things he wanted me to know, like the oboe part in *The Immortal Hour* so that I could then deputise for him. I was a student for a very long time. I had a scholarship for five years which I didn't really need financially. I got to know his other pupils Evelyn Rothwell, Joy Boughton and Natalie Caine and we became fast friends.[10]

Evelyn Rothwell (Lady Barbirolli) was one of his favourite pupils. She looks back on their relationship with respect and affection: 'He really changed the oboe sound. He made people realise that the oboe could be a beautiful instrument and a solo instrument. His was always a beautiful sound with a lovely long musical line. He broke completely new ground and a lot of composers wrote works for him.'[11]

Evelyn started studying with him at the RCM in the late

*James McDonagh, father of the distinguished oboe player Terence McDonagh.

twenties. 'Let me give him enormous credit: he made a school of his own, based on what he'd learnt from Reynolds and de Busscher. He was marvellous musically, he had a natural talent but to be frank he was not a teacher. He didn't want to be at the College and the Academy at the same time. He was terribly naughty! He had little books that he put dots in for lessons. I remember one term when he came on the first day and put little dots for the rest of the term although he didn't come to any more lessons.' Léon remained on the books of the RCM until 1942, but as the pace of his professional career increased it became progressively more difficult for him to fulfil his teaching commitments.

Evelyn continues:

He used to take us to play with him in amateur orchestras and theatres so that we learnt by precept. He had enormous charm. We all adored him and had great crushes on him. Sometimes instead of having a lesson at the College, we'd have a lesson at his flat in Gloucester Road. His first wife Fay was very attractive. I always got the impression she didn't like it when he had pupils! I remember one occasion when he asked Natalie and me to tea there on a Sunday afternoon. Their little daughter Bene was there. There was an atmosphere between them that you could cut with a knife but we didn't know how to deal with it!

He never taught us anything about making reeds. He had a marvellous reed maker called Tommy Brearley from Liverpool who used to make reeds for Louis in Chelsea and had an enormous selection. But if you had a reed which he liked, he used to say: 'That's too hard for you. I'll have that one!'

He always wanted to be the centre of attention and he was jealous of his pupils if he felt they were a threat. Gordon Jacob was writing an oboe concerto for me to play at the Patrons' Fund concert at the College. Gordon used to ask me 'Is this practical to play?' and I used to take the manuscript to my lessons with Léon. It was a good work and he was rather taken with it.

The next thing I knew was Léon had told Gordon that if he took the dedication away from me, he would play it with Beecham and the RPO. Léon played the first performance and had the dedication; I played it many times subsequently. I quite understand why Gordon agreed but his wife said he regretted doing so until the end of his life.

Evelyn's best friend was Natalie Caine (Natalie James). She had originally gone to the RCM as a pianist. After hearing Sylvia Spencer play with John Francis and Millicent Silver, she fell in love with the oboe and marched in to Léon Goossens saying she wanted to study with him.

> He was a young professor of thirty-four; he said straight away he'd get me an oboe. He didn't teach scientifically, he taught by example. I used to watch his fingers. One learnt through watching and listening. Evelyn and I used to go to the Thursday morning rehearsals of the Royal Philharmonic to hear him play. Even from a distance you could hear the magic sound of the oboe. Only Goossens pupils could make a sound like that and we knew that if we learnt to play like him, one day we would be able to produce that magic sound too.
>
> I had only been playing for two terms when I was rung up in the middle of the night and asked if I would go down to Brighton and play as second to Léon Goossens with a very good amateur orchestra, the Brighton Symphonic Players, conducted by Herbert Menges. The Eroica was very frightening but he looked after me and took me out to tea with some friends of his. I remember his saying 'This girl's only been learning for two terms!'
>
> He wouldn't hang his hat in the Band Room; he went into the Conductor's Room! He liked to be made a fuss of and he was worthy of it. He made the oboe respectable; he made orchestral players respectable so that we were considered fit to stay in people's houses overnight!
>
> Evelyn and I shared a flat in Hornton Street until I got married. He was very fatherly and as we got busy and started earning money, he would always advise us how to accept engagements and whether to refuse them or not. I had a letter asking me to tour with the 'Ladies Viennese Orchestra'. He didn't want me to be away from College for so long so he said: 'You can't accept that. Write and tell them that you're neither Viennese nor a lady!'
>
> He used to give us a little homily, words of advice which he called 'from Pro to Pupe: never accept a fee that's too low. Take into account whether you will have to buy an evening dress. Remember if it's a wet night you'll have to take a taxi. You've got to keep the fee up for the rest of us!' If we played a *St Matthew Passion* together I would get £3.3 and he would have got £10.10. [12]

Evelyn's memories were less charitable. 'If Natalie and I were doing a *St Matthew* together, we'd ask him what a suitable fee

would be and the next thing we heard from the Choral Society
was that Mr Goossens was willing to do it for less! He
was very peculiar in that sort of way. He was terribly jealous
but he needn't have worried.'

His jealousy of Evelyn Rothwell when she was beginning to
make her name was confirmed by Margaret Eliot, who studied
with him a few years later.

I think he got a little bit jealous if someone was enjoying a
lot of success, like Evelyn, but while you were with him he
couldn't have been more encouraging. The way he taught varied
enormously from lesson to lesson. Sometimes you just stood there
and played, at other times he would go through your piece note by
note. I know we were all rather wicked. He rarely set us anything
specific to do, like 'prepare this Bach aria for next week'. We all
had one particular study which we played rather well so we would
play it at one lesson and he never remembered from week to week
what we had played, so we could repeat it the next time as well.
I suppose it all sank in though because we all learnt an enormous
amount from him.

He quite liked the person coming next to arrive fifteen minutes
early for their lesson so that we could play duets. Sometimes we
used to run errands for him but there was no feeling of 'I'm the
great man, you're the student', no demand for recognition and
status as he made outside. I think he rather liked students. He
preferred people who were no threat to him.

He had enormous charm but I don't think he was a womaniser.
All his female pupils rather hoped he was. One girl used to go out
after her lesson and wait the rest of the afternoon by his car, hoping
for a lift.[13]

In the 1930s all theatres had live music in the entr'actes
provided by a trio or quartet, ranging up to a full orchestra if it was a show with music. Léon and other renowned
players would be given five or six theatres each, known as
'shops' for which they provided the musicians, including their
advanced students. Two operettas in which Léon was involved
were Lehár's *The Land of Smiles* with Richard Tauber at the
Theatre Royal, Drury Lane and Millöcker's *The Du Barry* at
His Majesty's which ran for a year before the lovely leading
lady Annie Ahlers committed suicide.

'Poor Annie Ahlers!' Natalie Caine recalled. 'Some

character in the show took a pinch of snuff and said "Rot her merry lungs!" It put a kind of curse on her; her lover deserted her and she felt she couldn't continue living. Léon played first oboe and Helen [Gaskill] second, with Evelyn and me as deputies. As time went on, if I played with Léon he would shut the score and make me play from memory which was terrifying!'

Franz Lehár conducted the opening performances of *The Land of Smiles* in 1931 before handing over to Ernest Irving. The orchestra included many well-known instrumentalists. Sixty years ago far fewer symphony concerts took place and the only orchestra which offered players a regular contract was the newly formed BBC Symphony Orchestra. Otherwise instrumentalists were paid per performance and relied on theatre orchestras as a valuable source of income with no loss of professional status. Irving accepted Evelyn as second oboe to Léon or Helen on condition that she must never play first as she lacked the necessary experience.

One night fate intervened.

Léon was playing a solo date and Helen's father had died very suddenly, so I had to play first, although I was still only a student on the fringes of the profession and there were a lot of prominent solos written for Léon. Peter Barbirolli was playing viola in the orchestra and knew that his brother was looking for an oboe player for the Covent Garden touring orchestra. 'You'd better hear that girl,' he told him. 'She sounds like Goossens.'

He sent me a note to College asking me to audition at the Crush Bar. I took it to Léon and we both tried to decipher the signature which looked like 'Barkworth'. It was only when I arrived at the auditorium that I realised it was Barbirolli. I got the job of second oboe and that was the beginning of my acquaintanceship with John, all thanks to Léon.

Sir Henry Wood helped Helen Gaskill in her career.

He engaged me in the Proms for a ten week season. I felt I was resented at first by all those men in the orchestra but I was accepted quite soon. Without Lee [Léon] I would never have succeeded. He got me into the Musicians' Union.

I wasn't the first woman to play the oboe professionally. There was an old lady called Angela Bull, daughter of a Canon of Hereford

Cathedral, playing long before I was born. Apparently she was absolutely terrible! Old Alexander Mackenzie used to say: 'Oh Miss Bull, can't you do something with it. Pull the reed out, or push it in or something!'

There was another female who appeared in theatre orchestras, then came a flush of us, all pupils of Léon. It never occurred to us that anyone could not like us.

When Helen Gaskill joined the BBC Symphony Orchestra in 1933 she established a firm friendship with Sidonie. For many years harpists had been the only female members of an orchestra but the number of women string players was increasing, especially in the BBC Symphony Orchestra. Léon's 'pupes' were now becoming a familiar sight in the woodwind section. There was no feeling of militancy among these polite young ladies invading a male stronghold. In the world of professional musicians the sex of a player is irrelevant. The sole criterion for their engagement is how well they can play, but pretty faces can be distracting.

Natalie Caine found it terrifying to be the only woman in the orchestra. 'I remember going with the orchestra to play at Christ's Hospital. Nobody showed me where the loo was and I was too shy to ask. Nowadays I'd come straight out with it! We were hell bent on playing well. We didn't flirt with anyone. Most of the time we were sight reading all the well-known symphonies and it was all we could do to play the part. A horn player once paid me a compliment by saying there was never any question of Evelyn and me causing any upset with the men. It was a question of innocence I suppose. Providing you had been brought up properly, there weren't any naughty men in those days!' (Natalie married Cecil James, second bassoon in the LSO and Helen Gaskill married Paul Marinari who led the cellos for Sir Henry Wood in the Queen's Hall Orchestra.)

Fritz Busch paid another compliment to Léon and his pupils when the first season of Glyndebourne Festival Opera was started in 1934. He strongly disliked the sound of the oboes in the London Symphony Orchestra and insisted on engaging Evelyn and Natalie instead. 'The LSO players produced an old-fashioned sound,' Evelyn explained, 'very efficient, very steely, edgy, hard and unsweet. A sound that cut through everything. Léon's sound was much more expressive, because of his use of vibrato. It sounded like the violin.'

'Léon was the first to make a beautiful sound,' added Natalie, 'although some people said it was too individualistic. Nowadays you can hear the most exquisite sounds from all oboe players and that is his legacy.' When Léon was creating his legendary performances with Beecham and the RPO, if an orchestra suddenly wanted a deputy oboe, unless a Goossens pupil was available, according to Cecil James, 'they were faced with somebody who made a noise like treading on an egg.'[14]

Margaret Eliot emphasised how helpful Léon had been when she started her professional career. 'He advised me if I was playing first oboe, particularly with an ad hoc orchestra, to tune on the sharp side as the pitch of the players would drop during performance. If you were playing second and he first he was always very helpful, making suggestions as to the best way to play and how you could make things easier.'

But the avuncular bonhomie never clouded his total professionalism and dedication to the highest standards of performance which he expected his students to share, as Margaret Eliot recalls. 'I remember his taking me to play with him at a rehearsal at the Wigmore Hall. "Do you know what you're doing?" he reprimanded me. "You're wishing your life away! You're bored and wishing you were somewhere else instead of giving your best at this rehearsal!" '

Perhaps it was Léon's conception of the oboe's femininity which led to his special rapport with his female students. He always stressed that the oboe was very much the lady of the orchestra who had changed very little in character since the boxwood instrument on which the works of Bach and Handel had originally been played.

My conception of the modern lady is much the same as a lady of the eighteenth century. If we lose her feminine qualities we neutralise the sound which thousands of years of history have sought to sustain and beautify. Strauss invariably uses the oboe as soon as there is any romance in the orchestra, as does Wagner in *Tristan*. For Delius it is the essential voice of Nature, always depicting something outdoors.

My instrument, unlike most others, is very light in weight. If you want to stand up and give a recital of two hours you cannot have much more weight resting on the thumb of your right hand. For me the instrument is like an extension of my vocal chords.

I've had distinguished singers like Dorothy Silk and Elsie Suddaby come to me to help them sing Bach because they had trouble with their breathing. They were too intense and couldn't relax enough. The secret for both instrumentalist and singer is to learn to relax in your intensity. It's a question of diaphragm control so that you can use the minutest amount of breath and conserve it. The whole front of you expands and it is so important to stand well.

Mothers come to me saying that their daughter is so worried because she doesn't feel that she can sustain a phrase. When I see the daughter play the problem is the natural difficulty that many girls have, they stand cramped. They are afraid of being noticed at the age when their figure is developing. In order to play any wind instrument you must stand upright, you cannot hold your elbows to your side. Be rather proud of yourself so that you have ease of movement and no pressure against your lungs.

The great fear when you first start to play is that you won't be heard. As long as you know how to project your tone it will go through the orchestra. It's the quality of sound that matters and the reed gives the quality of sound that travels. The conductor will be the first one to let you know if you're not coming through![15]

'People often ask me about my personal approach to the oboe. As my development has been natural rather than philosophical, I can only say that what the violinist gets out of the violin with *legato* I try to get in the same way out of the oboe. Hence the importance I attach to purity of outline and phrasing, though not forgetting the tonal possibilities of the instrument and what the Americans like to call "dynamics".' Léon analysed 'the unique melodic quality of the oboe as a solo instrument' for an article in *The Listener* on 19th January 1938. By this stage in his career not only was he hailed as 'the world's greatest oboist', he was also recognised as the founder of an English school of oboe playing.

10

Welcome to Cincinnati

Cincinnati, the 'Queen City' on the Ohio river, has a long and distinguished musical heritage. A Philharmonic Society was founded as early as 1856 by German immigrants, anxious to form 'a large and permanent orchestra for the performance of compositions of the great masters'. The city owed much of its prosperity to the pork-packing industry, hence its disparaging nickname of 'Porkopolis', but Theodore Thomas, on his first orchestral tour in 1869, was favourably impressed: 'Cincinnati not only possesses wealth and culture, but sincere and capable musicians who by their influence as teachers developed a genuine love and understanding of music in that community. I found excellent choral societies there and an orchestra superior to any city west of New York.'

In 1894 the Cincinnati Orchestra was put on a proper financial basis by a group of energetic ladies who contributed $15,000 for three series of three concerts. Mrs William Howard Taft, wife of the future President of the United States, was first President of the sponsoring association. She was succeeded by Eugene's friend, Mrs Bettie Holmes. In 1929, the orchestra was reincorporated and became the major project of the Cincinnati Institute of Fine Arts, endowed by Mr and Mrs Charles Phelps Taft and other wealthy benefactors.

By 1930 the Cincinnati Orchestra ranked amongst the six best in America with Boston, Chicago, Cleveland, New York and Philadelphia. The city enjoyed an international musical reputation through its May Festival; next to the Worcester Music Festival started in 1858 it is the oldest in America. In 1873 Theodore Thomas had held the first National American Festival of Choral and Symphonic Music in Cincinnati. The festival was such a popular success that it became a biennial event with a specially constructed Music Hall opened in 1878. Until 1904 Thomas continued to conduct the festivals, with his Chicago Orchestra augmented by local players.

He was succeeded by the American-born conductor, Frank van der Stucken, who persuaded Elgar to conduct four of his own works at the 1906 Festival for a fee of £1,500, reflecting Cincinnati's wealth and prestige. 'My feelings are dead against coming here but my pocket gapes aloud,' Elgar had complained.[1]

When Eugene took over, the musical directorship of the festival and the orchestra were again united. He was following a distinguished roster of conductors, including Stokowski, Ysaÿe and Fritz Reiner. Reiner's precipitous divorce and remarriage had shocked the provincial morality of many in the community; ticket sales had fallen and his contract had not been renewed. Reiner was an excellent musician who had transformed the orchestra but he was a strict disciplinarian with a somewhat harsh temperament. Eugene's considerate, even-tempered approach to conducting came as a welcome relief.

The May Festival was not only the biennial apogee of the local cultural and social calendar; it had retained its position over the years as a musical event of national consequence. 'It is a colossal affair involving many amateur singers (610 grown-ups this year, 703 school-children) beside the Cincinnati Symphony and imported soloists,' explained *Time* magazine. 'The performances are meticulously prepared and attended by special pomp corresponding to that which Manhattan and Chicago bestow on their opera. Cincinnati newspapers devote columns to describing the costumes of local dowagers and debutantes. The programmes were for the most part ambitious and substantial. Of the soloists two from England made promising US debuts, tenor Walter Widdop and contralto Muriel Brunskill. Lily Pons, the Metropolitan's new French find, walked away with a programme in which she sang three florid coloratura airs. But the hero for the duration of the five-day festival was conductor Eugene Goossens . . . an important milestone, one which few conductors could put behind them at thirty-eight.'[2]

Obviously local critics hailed their new conductor with the highest praise but it was the opinion of Olin Downes, reviewing

143

Mahler's Eighth Symphony for the *New York Times*, that Eugene valued. 'There is the danger, in a work of such manifold details and mammoth proportions, of conductor and performers becoming absorbed in details and being unable to see the forest for the trees. Mr Goossens had no such limitations. He flung himself at and into the music. He felt and he saw its big lines. He moulded the immense choral masses and the interweaving effects of choral and orchestral tone into one immense fabric of his own shaping. The sheer effect of music and performance was overwhelming.'³

The one disadvantage of Eugene's new responsibilities was that they would leave him with even less time for composition. The previous summer, after a long gap, he had completed a major new chamber work, Sonata for Violin and Piano no. 2, dedicated to Paul Kochanski. It was first performed at the Bradford Music Club on 20th January 1931 by Albert Sammons and William Murdoch and repeated on 5th February at the Wigmore Hall. The critics praised it as a work of new found artistic maturity. 'The violin seems to unlock all the romanticism in Goossens that nothing else does. This new work is big music which builds up coherently into a firm structure more than capable of carrying its rich decoration, its vigorous impulse and some unusual features. Its interest is mainly harmonic. Clashes and negation of tonality are transitory,' was the verdict of the *Times*.⁴ 'Only a musician who was past master of both violin and piano could have written these eloquent, ingenious, well-sounding pages,' added the *Daily Mail*.

The following month it was played at the Music Society's concert at St John's Institute by two other old friends of Eugene's, André Mangeot and his erstwhile neighbour from Edith Road, Yvonne Arnaud. 'Clever woman pianist,' decided critic Richard Capell, 'whose triumphs in musical comedy have nearly but not quite eclipsed her musical renown . . . and Goossens' work is a handful.' Eugene, back in England with Jansi for his annual vacation, was able to hear the sonata at the Ninth Festival of the International Society for Contemporary Music held in Oxford in July. He had conducted a broadcast of his oboe concerto on 24th May with Léon as soloist and Sidonie as Principal Harp; he was astonished by the improvement in the BBC Symphony Orchestra. 'The public will one day wake up to the fact that they now possess a wonderful orchestra. If it was in America, people would go crazy over it.'[5]

His quiet holiday plans to work on his new opera *Don Juan* were shattered by a telephone call from Beecham. Would he take over the British premiere of Rimsky-Korsakov's opera *Sadko* at the Lyceum Theatre? This meant only a piano rehearsal with the Russian principals and none at all with orchestra and chorus. It was a challenge that Eugene could not resist and although he had never even heard the opera, by the performance he had the full score under control. A few nights later he conducted de Falla's *El Amor Brujo* and *Chout* by Prokofiev and revivals of *Petrushka* and *Pulcinella*, all with unfamiliar dancers. 'Only when Chaliapin appeared in an act of Massenet's *Don Quixote* did I recognise a familiar friend.'

The event which had given his father (who never changed his Belgian nationality) the greatest pleasure was Eugene's invitation to conduct at the Ostend Festival on 30th July. He took his parents and Jansi for a brief holiday to Belgium so that they could enjoy his programme of Rachmaninov's E minor Symphony and Frank Bridge's *The Sea*, plus a performance of his *Phantasy Quartet* played by the Pro Arte Quartet.

When Eugene disembarked from the SS *Leviathan* on his return to the USA, he was greeted by the news that the UK had left the Gold Standard. '*Don't hesitate* to let me know,' he told his parents, 'should things in England become financially critical for you at any moment, as I can always wire you money at half an hour's notice. I should be miserable at the thought of you both enduring any hardship due to rising prices without telling me anything about it.' He was always to remain an affectionate and generous son. He constantly invited his parents to come to America but they preferred the quiet routine of life in Finchley, and their increasing age and infirmity frustrated his plans for them to cross the Atlantic.

As he was conductor of the Cincinnati Symphony Orchestra, Eugene and Jansi enjoyed a position of enormous social and cultural significance and were expected to follow an appropriate lifestyle. They always lived in rented property; their first home was one of Cincinnati's historic mansions, surrounded by seven acres of gardens and orchards. They had brought his oldest daughter Anne with them and Jansi wrote glowing reports back to her parents-in-law of Anne's progress in school and her dancing and piano lessons.

The Cincinnati schedule was a heavy one, twenty-four pairs of concerts in a season running from October to the end of April, each concert being given on a Thursday evening and repeated on Friday afternoon. Eugene knew what to expect from the stifling matinée atmosphere of smart hats and mink coats. His opening programme on 15th October was skilfully chosen to cater for his audience's susceptibilities and to display his own and the orchestra's brilliance and versatility: the *Mastersingers* overture, Mozart's *Jupiter* Symphony, Debussy's *Iberia* and Strauss' *Till Eulenspiegel*. The only unfamiliar work was Delius' *The Walk to the Paradise Garden*, the most romantically appealing of all 'modern' compositions. It was guaranteed to dispel rumours that he was about to inflict an unpalatable diet of 'difficult' contemporary works on loyal subscription holders as Reiner had done.

He received a unanimous seal of approval from press and public. 'If any proof were needed of the saying that in times of depression, men seek the profound consolation of music, it could be found in the tense eagerness of the audience that crowded Emery Auditorium to hear a concert of music that, for the most part, Cincinnati knows and loves. Mr Goossens' platform appearance has everything favourable for him. A commanding figure, an action vigorous but without exaggeration, a cordiality which established between him and his audience an immediate understanding. The orchestral beat is accurate but without violence. It permits color and flexibility from the orchestra and promotes a really marvellous legato. The orchestra's playing was superb. It was a different orchestra. It is a playing which conquers and wins, through exquisite discrimination, through exact musicianship. Mr Goossens and his men had a wild ovation.'[6]

He had worked hard to counteract the disadvantages of the Emery Auditorium. It was too small for the orchestra and resulted in a timid and attenuated quality of *pianissimo* playing in the string sections. 'I finally succeeded in coercing the players into a less repressed style by brutally observing that

during certain very quiet passages, many of them ceased playing altogether. I put the culprits through an intensive course
of *cantilena* playing, with the result that an unprecedented
freedom of style prevailed and *pianissimo* took on a more
audible complexion.'

'The orchestra is a magnificent one with practically no
weak spots at all,' he reported to his father. 'Some of the
first desk men are very great artists and I think that I have
the world's finest clarinet and trombone player. Wednesday I
gave my first children's concert to an audience of three thousand young kiddies. Anne had five of her girlfriends from the
school in her box and it would have done you good to hear the
storms of applause that greeted each number. They behaved
marvellously throughout, particularly when I was giving them
short explanations of the music between each item.'[7]

Throughout his conducting career Eugene maintained that it
was not necessary to have a famous soloist to attract an audience
to an orchestral concert; the orchestra and conductor should be
of sufficient interest. Accordingly in the 1931 – 32 season, eight
pairs of concerts had no soloist. Cincinnati was a prestigious
engagement for international artists; those engaged included
violinists Kochanski, Thibaud and Milstein playing concerti
by Szymanowski, Bach and Dvořák; pianists Harold Bauer
(Brahms Second Concerto), Gieseking (Mozart C major Concerto), Moiseiwitsch (one of Eugene's favourite poker-playing
friends who gave an inspired performance of the Schumann
A minor Concerto) and Harriet Cohen (Walton's *Sinfonia Concertante*). Among the singers were Metropolitan Opera stars
Richard Crooks and Grace Moore whose décolletage on this
occasion proved more impressive than her rendition of 'Depuis
le Jour'. As well as the Walton, Eugene introduced works by
Poulenc, Křenek, Kodály, Turina, Prokofiev and the Second
Piano Concerto of Alexander Tansman which was described as
a musical biography of Charlie Chaplin!

As well as works by contemporary American composers,
throughout his tenure in Cincinnati he carried through a con-
certed policy of introducing as many works by modern British
composers as he could. These included Bax, Bliss, Holbrooke,
Moeran, Quilter and Scott as well as Delius, Walton and
Vaughan Williams.

In contrast to these contemporary novelties, Eugene re-introduced a Sunday evening series of 'Pop' Concerts. 'A rich store of lightweight nineteenth-century classics – all the lovely almost forgotten lighter music of our grandfathers' day was steadily lapsing into oblivion. The programmes based very much on Henry Wood's Queen's Hall Sunday afternoon concerts made instantaneous appeal and drew crowded houses. They helped to win over literally hundreds of new subscribers for whom the tariff and atmosphere of the rather exclusive symphony concerts had hitherto held little appeal.'[8]

He had little time left for relaxation but he was able to indulge in one of his passions when he rode in the cab of Locomotive 6616 from Cincinnati's Grand Central Depot to Dayton. He was suitably clad for the hour-long adventure in blue overalls, yellow gauntlets and a navy Belgian beret. 'Goossens thought he would get a hand on the throttle of the big locomotive,' reported the *Dayton Herald*, 'but railroad rules would not permit that. Nor did he get to shovel coal into the boiler as he was aboard an automatic stoking engine. Which led him to remark when he alighted "some day I'm going to get me an engine and run it to suit myself, consequences be hanged!" '[9] Was the famous conductor getting tuned up with the proper rhythm for a 'railroad blues' or another epic like 'Casey Jones', the newspaper men wanted to know? No, he'd just been along for the ride, Goossens told them, but he had discovered that the whistle of the mighty 6616 was pitched in A!

On a more serious note, Eugene conducted a further performance of *Tosca* for the Philadelphia Grand Opera Company in which John Charles Thomas, later to become a stalwart of the Met., sang his first Scarpia. He then gave the American premiere of his new violin sonata with Paul Kochanski, its dedicatee. The occasion was a Musicale given by Mrs Holmes at 1107 Fifth Avenue on 8th January 1932. Kochanski had been a friend since the pre-war soirées of Muriel Draper; his death in January 1934 from cancer of the liver was to come as a great shock.

Eugene also accompanied Jeanne Dusseau in six songs he had written to poems of Mrs Holmes' and five of his James Joyce settings from *Chamber Music* (1907), in many ways his

most successful song cycle. Eugene found an affinity with
Joyce's poetry and had contributed a setting of 'A Memory of
the Players' from *Pomes Penyeach* to *The Joyce Book* (The Sylvan
Press, 1932).*

On 5th May 1932 Eugene made his debut at the Metropolitan Opera House but not conducting opera. It was the last
of a benefit series of five concerts given by a scratch orchestra
of 200 unemployed musicians. The soloists in Bach's Triple
Piano Concerto were Myra Hess, Harold Bauer and Ernest
Schelling. 'I got a lump in my throat every time I faced the
unemployed orchestra. Conditions for musicians are terrible in
New York and heaven only knows when this dreadful slump
throughout America will end.'[11] The following day, Eugene
received an emergency call to conduct the NBC orchestra in a
$5,000 prize competition concert for a new American orchestral
work. He was given twenty-four hours to conduct the five scores
short-listed, one of the occasions on which he demonstrated his
ability to assimilate immediately the most complex orchestral
score, reading it as easily as he would a book.

At the beginning of March he broke the news to his parents
that he and Jansi were looking forward to the arrival of Eugene
IV, or failing him Sidonie II, at the end of May. 'If wishing and
hoping could do it then the long awaited "son and heir" is (DV)
a prospective *fait accompli.*' On 22nd April 1932 his father
wrote in his diary: 'Premature and in a sense disappointing. Yet
good news received from Zenny, a daughter! All well!'
Eugene quickly recovered from his disappointment at failing,
yet again, to provide an heir to grasp the family baton; he and
Jansi were very soon doting parents of their musically gifted
little daughter.

Because of young Sidonie's arrival, Eugene spent a brief
holiday in England with no professional engagements and then
travelled to Munich. With the next Festival in mind he heard
'two or three singers (including the daughter of the American
Consul General in London), a portion of *Siegfried* under a gent

*Herbert Hughes and Arthur Bliss had been distressed to find Joyce living in
poverty in Paris after *Ulysses* was banned. In order to raise money for him, Eugene
was one of thirteen composers they had invited to donate settings to an impressive
limited edition, bound in royal blue handwoven silk, with a line drawing of Joyce
by Augustus John as a frontispiece.[10]

called Knappertsbusch, not so good and saw a bit of the city
– very beautiful.' (July 1932.) After a cure in Marienbad he
returned to America to work on *Don Juan*.

Among the twenty soloists allotted to him for the 1932 – 33
season, only the pianists José Iturbi and Harold Samuel, the
incomparable Bach player, and a return visit from Nathan
Milstein made any impact on his memory. He was disappointed
with Göta Ljungberg when she sang an excerpt from *Judith* (27th
and 28th October).

> Yes, it is a pity that Ljungberg was not in better voice, but like
> many other operatic sopranos, including Jeritza, Lily Pons and
> others, she gets stagefright on a concert platform. Singers are a
> nuisance at symphony concerts anyway, and I shortly intend to
> discontinue using them here.
>
> I think I told you that Koussevitzky was here recently. He
> repeated again what he already hinted at on previous occasions,
> that he was keeping the Boston Orchestra warm for me as a
> successor and requesting that I should not sign any new contract
> here in Cincinnati longer than a period of a further two years. I
> believe that Koussevitzky is quite sincere in all this, and it's nice
> to feel, such being the case, prospects connected with one of the
> three big Eastern orchestras are rosy for the future.
>
> By the way, I notice that Barbirolli is now indulging in splash
> advertising in the American musical papers. Mr B is obviously out
> for an American job, but I am afraid he is doomed to disappoint-
> ment for they simply don't exist. It has taken me ten years to get
> to where I am at the present moment and it is hardly likely that
> an inexperienced chap like Barbirolli could suddenly step into a
> rosy job here.[12]

Events were to prove Eugene wrong in his assessment of
both Koussevitzky and Barbirolli. In 1936, when Toscanini
resigned from the New York Philharmonic, Arthur Judson
arranged a guest engagement for Barbirolli as a result of which
the virtually unknown young man was confirmed as Toscanini's
successor. Judson enjoyed a position of unrivalled power, since
he was both manager of the orchestra and of the leading artists'
agency.

Despite what he confided to his parents, on the surface
the relationship between the two British conductors in leading

American posts was to remain warm and friendly. John thanked Eugene for his congratulations on his New York appointment: 'Your letter gave me so much pleasure especially as regards the wisdom of learning our job in the orchestra. It has brought back many memories of happy hours spent under you and your courtesy and kindness to a young cellist who wanted to play a work of yours. Ethel Bartlett is here and we were talking of the "Rhapsody" the other day.' (One of Eugene's chamber works for cello and piano which the young duo had played twenty years earlier.)

At the beginning of 1933 Eugene had returned to conduct his old orchestra in Rochester. After the second series of concerts, he was suddenly taken ill in New York. 'I accepted an invitation out to dinner with Bettie Holmes and unusually for me, quietly fainted after dinner. Fortunately a doctor was there who diagnosed my complaint as toxic poisoning of the stomach which combined with a certain amount of overwork and nerves knocked me out (no it wasn't bootleg!!!),' he assured his parents. 'I have had to go through a long and trying period of a cure and trying to eradicate the trouble in a New York nursing home. Of course I had to give up some of my Cincinnati concerts, which as you can imagine was harder to endure than illness. Fortunately there were substitutes to take my place and everybody, from the President to the office boy, were towers of strength and sympathy.'[13]

Eugene insisted on returning for the final concerts of the season and to prepare for the May Festival. He tried to minimise the seriousness of his illness both to his parents and his employers. He summoned up the enormous reserves of strength and vitality required for acclaimed Festival performances of Handel's *Samson*, Bach's B minor Mass, with Margarete Matzenauer, Richard Crooks and Ezio Pinza and *Belshazzar's Feast*. The strain was to take a heavy toll on his health for nearly two years. When he arrived in England for his annual holiday at the end of May, he had suffered a complete breakdown and had to retire to a nursing home. He never again enjoyed the energy and vitality of his earlier years. There was a husbanding of resources on the podium, a holding back from the ultimate climax; the performances became more subtle, more skilled but as the years advanced routine replaced

151

spontaneity and the heart was always ruled by the head.

His joint salaries from the orchestra and the May Festival were reputed to make him one of the highest paid conductors in the USA. England could not compete with the remuneration musicians received in America. His emotional home always remained with his parents in England and, as he constantly repeated to them, if only the right post were open to him he would far rather return to England on a permanent basis. 'If England wants me it had better let me know in ample time. The only thing that will induce me to abandon the results of eleven years hard work in this country will be a foolproof contract from England signed, sealed and delivered by at least three responsible people. I have got to a stage now when there is no longer any excuse on my part for taking prolonged holidays until "something turns up".'[14]

As with many artists, Eugene was generous and unworldly. He was totally lacking in financial expertise and, despite the large sums he earned throughout his career, he never owned his own home nor managed to save nor invest. His outgoings in Cincinnati were high for luxurious rented houses and the staff to maintain them, lavish entertainment, an extravagant wife, a succession of nursemaids, chauffeurs, valets and the schooling of his daughters in America and Europe. He also paid his ex-wife Boonie an allowance.

His daughter Donie remembers his saying to her as a child: 'Always pay your bills when they come in. Don't forget to pay them.' 'Why would he have said that to me unless that was a mistake that he had made?' she wonders. 'If he had had a frugal wife, who was a good manager he might have ended up with some money.'[15] A good accountant would have been a valuable investment and obviated the threat by British Inland Revenue to tax him on his American and British earnings. The decision was eventually appealed against and settled in his favour.

On his return to Cincinnati for the 1933 – 34 season, Eugene found to his dismay that because of the need for stringent economies brought about by the continuing Depression, the Symphony Trustees had cut down the concerts to sixteen pairs and reduced the salaries of the conductor and the orchestra by one third. This was a unilateral policy throughout the USA. The largest expenditure was still on internationally famed soloists guaranteed to draw the maximum audience, particularly pianists of the calibre of Schnabel, Gieseking, Hofmann and Horowitz (Toscanini's son-in-law), or a violinist like Heifetz, and singers Elisabeth Rethberg and Richard Crooks. Analysing the list of soloists throughout his tenure in Cincinnati, the choice remains conservative: established pianists, violinists, cellists and singers. Léon always complained that his brother never offered him a date in Cincinnati; an oboist, flautist or viola player would not appeal to the conservative subscription holders of the Midwest.

Eugene's health remained a grave cause for concern. He found the orchestra's touring schedule to Toledo, Louisville, Ann Arbor and Indianapolis increasingly stressful. 'I seem to have lost that old love of railroad travelling which used to be one of my chief characteristics,' he told his parents.[16]

Jansi continually wrote warm and reassuring letters to her parents-in-law. On 31st January 1934 she reported back to them with great joy:

All's well. Gene fine and still gaining weight and strength. I am still acting the policeman as far as *any* outside activities are concerned, so I am adamant and hard-boiled about refusing everything except things connected with the musicians which I can go to and represent the family.

Sidonie is still the most amusing person in the world, tries to sing and dance and conduct all at once.

Anne has grown into such a lovely girl and is gradually fulfilling every promise she has shown of being a rare personality. Also she is getting better looking every day! I love having her here to be with us, Gene especially and only hope that she will be able to spend most of her time over here but these things are so uncertain always.

Eugene always tried to fulfil his responsibilities as a father; he was hampered by Boonie's unreliability and unwillingness to commit herself over plans for her daughters' future. The twins' education fluctuated between boarding schools in Paris and Switzerland, while every time Anne settled down in Cincinnati her mother insisted on her returning to Europe.

He decided to spend the summer recuperating on the shores of Lake Ontario. His doctor and dentist had discovered and removed eight abscessed teeth, diagnosed as the probable source of his health problems. He also had a tonsillectomy. 'Both gave off a ringing D flat as they fell on the operating table.'[17] 'I suppose we all have to go through a certain amount of this sort of thing to make up for our sins in past incarnations. If there is anything in Cyril Scott's theory, then Mendelssohn must have been an out-and-out scoundrel.'[18] (Cyril Scott was convinced that Eugene was the reincarnation of Mendelssohn and Sidonie of his sister Fanny!)

Meanwhile it did not look as if the British musical tide was turning in his favour. 'I had a letter from the Broadcasting Company asking me to do one concert in their studio in June for the same fee as they paid me three years ago. They will have to think of something better than this if they want to lure me back to England again. Let them get Edward Clark to conduct the concert at 3/6 an hour! I have come to the conclusion that the London musical public is the most gullible in the world. They know nothing and care less!'[19]

Perhaps as a result of his illness Eugene wanted to placate his Catholic conscience and arranged for a private ceremony so that his marriage to Jansi could be recognised by the Catholic Church and Sidonie receive a Catholic christening.

Eugene returned in the autumn of 1934 in much better health after his vacation and the omens seemed favourable. He had been awarded the French Legion of Honour in recognition of his services to French music in England and America. He opted for a private ceremony at home rather than a public celebration. He explained his decision to his parents: 'In view of the very strong German element here, I am averse to any kind of pomp and circumstance so far as I am concerned. Had it been a posthumous award for Adolphe's sacrifice in the war (or Léon's share in the fighting) then I should have summoned all the flags and bugles possible.'[20]

The programmes for the new season included Hindemith's *Mathis der Maler*, Holst's *The Planets*, Elgar's two symphonies which had never been programmed in Cincinnati and Ravel's Concerto for the Left Hand, played by its dedicatee Paul Wittgenstein. After his return to Europe, Wittgenstein took the trouble to write to Eugene recommending a specialist in Vienna he might visit for help with the stomach ulcers from which he was now reported to be suffering.[21]

Later in December the Boston Symphony Orchestra returned to Cincinnati with Koussevitzky. After the concert Eugene accompanied him to the special train on which the orchestra travelled. 'He was heart-broken when I announced that I would not take supper with him in the dining car. His affectionate demonstrations towards me were even embarrassing. The sight of two conductors in fur coats embracing in full view of everybody in our new and gorgeous station was too much for the local natives. He still reiterated the assurance that he was keeping the Boston Symphony warm for me and definitely invited me next season (if he still remained the conductor of the orchestra) to conduct for a fortnight during his vacation in January 1936. Nous verrons!'[22]

Eugene was disconcerted by the engagement of Boult to conduct in Boston during Koussevitzky's 1935 vacation but decided that was a quid pro quo for the latter's guest concerts with the BBC Symphony Orchestra. It was not until December 1937 that he was finally disillusioned regarding Koussevitzky's promises. 'It appears that Mrs K lost all her money in the stock market crash of '29, with the result that, not having regained it in subsequent years, K is compelled to remain on with the orchestra and earn his bread by the sweat of his brow until the end of his days or thereabouts. It seems that he has so many dependants in Russia, France, China and elsewhere that he cannot afford to give the job up and retire.'[23]

In the event, Koussevitzky did not relinquish the Boston Orchestra until 1949 by which time Eugene had been in Sydney for two years. The post went to Charles Munch.

Eugene was also somewhat jealous of the success Walton was enjoying. 'Reading one of the criticisms of the Walton Symphony, one would think he were a second Beethoven. Why don't some of these critics maintain a sense of proportion instead of turning the heads of these youngsters? Here is the case of a boy with quite a facility of writing but with no real depth of sentiment – at least he hasn't displayed it in any of his previous works. It is probably a hash of clichés and according to Mr R C [Richard Capell] full of stark tragedy. Of all the untragic lives I know, his is conspicuous.'[24]

His letters to his parents provided an invaluable means of

155

letting off confidential steam, of venting his passing grievances and jealousies of his contemporaries' good fortune. Walton remained a friend whose works he programmed in Cincinnati and whose house he borrowed in London. Walton always said that he only learnt to conduct his own compositions thanks to Eugene's lessons.

Eugene closed the year with a broadcast from Radio City in the Rockefeller Centre, New York, the last of the season of concerts sponsored by the General Motors Corporation. 'I got a great reception from the orchestra which consisted largely of the New York Philharmonic boys [Toscanini's orchestra] who deplore the fact, through their manager, that they did not see me more often.'[25] Eugene had parted company with Arthur Judson over fees. 'For two years we have been fighting on the question of commissions on my Cincinnati engagement which I steadfastly refused to pay after the initial season. But the New York lawyers ruled against me and rather than face a court action I took my lawyer's advice and decided to settle out of court. Nevertheless I was and still am in the right.'[26]

Eugene may have had right on his side morally but from the practical point of view, by antagonising the most powerful manager in America – Judson also had the ruling voice in Columbia Records – he was doing his career a great disservice. It was a mixture of unworldliness and arrogance which convinced him that because he was such a good and successful conductor, he could dispense with a manager and professional promotion and continue to be offered the best engagements without having to pay a commission on his fees. He eventually returned to Judson but never completely trusted him, with some justification as Judson was furthering the career of other conductors such as Barbirolli.

One conductor who impressed him very favourably was the young Rafael Kubelík when he shared a concert in February 1935 with his violinist father. He described him to his parents:

> The young boy is a tall, not unattractive youth of six-foot-three with quite a clear beat and, above all modest and unassuming. I handed over the orchestra to him this morning so that he could try out the orchestra part of his father's concerto (his own composition, the fourth one he has written, quite an effective one too). Kubelík

himself I was quite impressed with. He is fifty-five years old but is remarkably well preserved and a real type of the old time virtuoso with big black sombrero and a shock of stiff long black hair which sticks out almost like straw from his head. His type is supplanted by the slick Heifetz crowd and it was like stepping back into the past to see what we had all considered an extinct type. I reminded him of that far away Sunday sometime in 1900 when you took me to the New Brighton Tower to hear him. Do you remember Dad, the crowd of people and how we were compelled to stand on the stage to hear him? It was my first artistic thrill as far as virtuosity was concerned.[27]

He used to tell his young daughter Sidonie stories of his childhood in Liverpool, of how he and Lee used to eat a tin of condensed milk after school or go train-spotting. 'I always felt the cold,' she remembered, 'but he used to say it was nothing. When he was a little boy at school in Bruges they used to have to break the ice on the water in the basins before they could wash! He wasn't really a story-telling person, he would always much rather draw things for me,' she remembers.

Donie adored her father and her early memories are of a very happy childhood.

He was a very caring father, very loving and very demonstrative. I had a little stove that I used to cook up things like apple sauce and custard. Nanny would go up to his study and say: you've got to come and taste this. He was very tolerant, so he would stop writing music and come down and taste the mush and say it was lovely! It was not until I started learning instruments that he imposed any discipline to do with hours of practice, method of practice, sight-reading etc. But in a much gentler way I would imagine than his father did to him.

During my father's sixteen years in Cincinnati, we lived in thirteen different houses. We always had a different address and someone else's furniture. The only things he retained were his piano, his clothes, my toys, his books and pictures and something to write music on.

Mother was very pretty with beautiful long fingers, she was really quite a good pianist. She always looked fantastic with lovely clothes and jewellery. Half the game in those days was what you wore not what you did. She had a good relationship revolving round his professional activities, the women's committee of the orchestra and the string quartet which she called her quartet. She was not at

157

all domesticated; she used to write out the menus for the week and give them to the cook. She was very good with words. She never did anything on a Sunday until she had finished the crossword puzzle in the Sunday paper. My grandparents used to send her the *Telegraph* crossword puzzles from England. She was very attached to all my father's family.

She didn't really like children. She didn't know what to do with them. Occasionally she bought me clothes but everything else was done by my Nanny, Dorothy Cubitt. She was a real English Nanny with a veil, who'd come when I was a baby, a most wonderful warm and loving human being. Without her I would have been a very deprived human being. My mother never even bathed me.[28]

The young English baritone Keith Falkner became a friend of the family. He sang for the first time in Cincinnati in the 1935 May Festival in Bach's *St Matthew Passion*. The next afternoon he sang Brahms' 'Four Serious Songs' in the orchestral version which he remembers as one of the highlights of his singing life. 'The whole city was involved in the Festival maybe because it was a German city. There were huge placards down Main Street with FALKNER SINGS BRAHMS! I found Gene the most remarkable musician, so casual and so off-hand but absolutely brilliant. He had a wonderful ear and a great sensitivity for performers; he just let you sing; he was always with you.

'I had never sung the Brahms with an orchestra before, but Gene was there looking after everything. "You don't have anything to worry about dear boy." '[29] Falkner received plaudits from press and public alike and was invited back to the Festivals of 1937 and 1939.

The closing concert of 1939 was a marathon, a three and a half hour concert with the whole of *The Creation* in the first half followed by *Alexander's Feast* in the second. I was singing with Flagstad. Two nights before she had sung the closing scene from *Götterdämmerung*. You could hear her voice two or three blocks away and I thought: 'How am I going to sing *The Creation* with that voice?!' But with Gene in charge everything was under control. Flagstad sang like an angel, like Elsie Suddaby or a boy soprano. It was ravishing to take part in.

There was such a friendly atmosphere between conductor,

soloists and orchestra. He was a very genial character and the orchestra was like a club. The social life was very much part of the Festival. His wife was a very good hostess. She astonished us by wearing different coloured shoes: red on one foot and green on the other. 'Smashing, wonderful idea!' was my wife's verdict. Gene was extremely popular with the musicians and with the whole city.

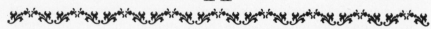

11

Léon, Marie and the LPO

By the beginning of 1932, Léon's marriage to Fay was at an end. He had fallen in love with another beautiful and talented artist, a dancer called Leslie Burrowes whom he had first met at Margaret Morris' Little Theatre in Chelsea.

She was eleven years younger than Léon; her father was a professional soldier and her mother had trained as a violinist at the Paris Conservatoire. Leslie became Margaret Morris' principal dancer and teacher but left in 1929 to further her studies of modern dance with its foremost exponent, Mary Wigman in Dresden. On her return to London she opened her 'Studio of the Dance' to introduce Wigman's experimental and creative work to England. 'She had a suppleness and flexibility which gave to her items a fiery vividness; and especially in one dance called "Primitive Joy" the strongly rhythmical and free movement which is her speciality was most effective.' The *Evening News* review typified the success of her solo recitals.

Léon had moved out of the marital home in Gloucester Road to stay with Sidonie and Bumps. He was tempted to cut the Gordian knot of emotional entanglements and professional insecurity by returning to America. On hearing the news about the marriage breakdown, Eugene wrote an understanding letter to his parents:

> Naturally I am sorry about it all but it is better to take any drastic steps immediately rather than drag on with an unsatisfactory situation. I have been through the same thing myself and know a little bit about it although the circumstances in my case were probably a little different.
>
> Tommy Beecham, whom I had lunch with the day before yesterday in New York, told me he had definitely offered Lee

the first oboe position in the new orchestra and that this position should give him sufficient work and also sufficient leisure to make his economic and artistic future in London assured, without his being compelled to look to America for his salvation. Actually this is no country for a foreigner at the moment unless he has been here for some time. The unemployment and distress is appalling and music has suffered more than any other profession.[1]

Eugene always admired his brother's artistry but he never invited him to Cincinnati to repeat the success he had enjoyed in Rochester, Boston and New York or to play the Oboe Concerto with his orchestra.

Beecham had written to Léon on 30th July from Munich: 'I do not know what transpired at the interview between you and Harold Holt, but I am most anxious that you give your adherence to the new orchestra without too much preliminary. You can take it from me that a satisfactory arrangement for you can be made. The problem in England is to start as I appear to be the only person there who does not suffer chronically from cold feet.' (Harold Holt and Ibbs & Tillett were London's two leading concert agents, a dominance they were to maintain for sixty years.)

On 7th October 1932, Léon took his seat in the Queen's Hall as Principal Oboe of the London Philharmonic Orchestra. For their initial season they were engaged for the Royal Philharmonic Society and Courtauld – Sargent Concerts, the International Opera Season at Covent Garden and a recording contract with HMV.

The LPO was something of a Goossens family affair with Marie as Principal Harp and her husband, Fred Laurence, as Orchestral Manager. Léon was one of a group of brilliant instrumentalists of solo calibre whom Beecham persuaded to join the orchestra as section leaders. It was Léon's unparalleled beauty of phrasing and tone which set the seal on the performance of Delius' *Brigg Fair* in the opening concert; it was to be a distinctive feature of all concerts and recordings until both Léon and Beecham parted company with the orchestra in 1939.

'Sir Thomas Beecham's new orchestra began its operations in the Queen's Hall on Friday evening,' enthused Ernest Newman. 'He began with a performance of Berlioz' *Carnaval*

161

Romain overture that had an air of "You Londoners want to know what an orchestra ought to be like? Well just listen to this." Nothing so electrifying has been heard in a London concert room for years. The tone was magnificent, the precision perfect, the reading a miracle of fire and beauty.'[2] The BBC Symphony Orchestra would have to look to its laurels.

Léon considered the formation of the LPO as the most exciting period of his career: 'We were starting a new chapter in music-making because Beecham was like a breath of fresh air. He had this electrical personality. Others may have had a greater depth of musical understanding. I don't think you can make an absolute choice in that way. He was a very good friend to me. I think we understood each other's shortcomings – and I don't think either of us was without them.'[3] There was the famous occasion when Beecham asked Léon for an A and commented to the orchestra 'Gentlemen, you may take your pick', a hint that Léon sometimes overindulged his vibrato, what he described as 'the soul of the sound'.

Marie found playing for Sir Thomas, 'a wonderful experience. He was a poet – he used to sing (literally) his way through a work; he did not stop very much as there was a certain magic in his beat which conveyed more than words. He did not waste our time and in solos he let us have the reins. If there was anything to say he would call the player into his room after the rehearsal and sing the passage as he wanted it phrased.'[4]

Léon's position in the new orchestra was established from the beginning: 'A sensible combination of players has to realise who is the most important personality as far as wind players are concerned. In the LPO I was considered the one to take command for which one must have courage and confidence.'[5]

For Gwydion Brooke, Joseph Holbrooke's son, who was engaged as second bassoon for the first three years, Léon was, 'the Laurence Olivier, the Bob Hope of the woodwind world; he was streets ahead of everyone else, something you realised as soon as he walked onto the platform. He was always immaculately turned out and had the air of a great artist, even in the orchestra.'[6] Léon and Gwydion were well known for their high spirits. Their inventiveness proved useful when the orchestra was trying to clear Irish Customs travelling from

Dublin to Belfast in March 1933. Léon reminisced: 'We had to cross the border and catch a train for the next concert, but we were held up as the orchestra's baggage was suspected of smuggling arms. As endless instrument cases were unpacked, I think it was myself who suggested to Gwydion that we should establish our bona fides, so we struck up The Keel Row; others soon joined us, and the conductor's personal version of an Irish jig proved a conclusive argument of our harmless insanity and we were rushed through.'[7] No one noticed that The Keel Row hails from Northumberland!

Léon was feeling far happier about his professional career now that he had found emotional security in his relationship with Leslie. Fay had moved to America where she married the publisher Stanley Rhinehart in July 1933 and the following month Léon and Leslie were married. They spent their honeymoon in Austria, where as Léon relates: 'The conductor Furtwängler asked my wife, "Is your husband still playing the oboe?" He was most surprised when he learnt that I was indeed. "Oh most of my players give up when they're thirty-five or forty," he replied. "The strain is too much." With the old-fashioned instrument players had to blow so hard that they damaged their heart and their lungs. There was a myth that oboists go mad because of the pressure on the brain and never live beyond the age of forty-eight. In the past it was often true!'[8] The couple set up home in World's End Studio in Davies Place, Chelsea. Leslie, who was a very strong personality, encouraged Léon in his solo career whilst continuing with her own teaching and recitals.

Eugene approved of Leslie and described her as 'a bright girl' but he had reservations about her career. 'With regard to Leslie's dance recital and the use of our name,' he wrote to his father, 'in that respect she is of course perfectly entitled to use it. Personally I think she will retain her personality as a dancer more by sticking to her maiden name than adopting our name which is so exclusively associated with music. What a pity it is that someone doesn't finance her so that she could open a school under her own name. I am sure she could make a great success of it.'[9]

Jack Brymer, the virtuoso clarinetist, who was to become a

163

friend and colleague of Léon's after the Second World War, stresses the influence that his playing had on the whole range of woodwind players:

> My affection for him started at the age of thirteen when I heard him play Ravel's *Habañéra* in a BBC Morning Recital. In that special moment I became aware of the sounds of the Spanish night, of warmth and mystery and a hint of distant flamenco singing. It was an equal revelation every time thereafter when I heard him perform either on radio or on record.[10] He became my idol and when I went to London University (not to study music) I went to hear him as often as I could. The first time was in an LPO concert in 1933. *Benvenuto Cellini* overture and the Mozart *Sinfonia Concertante* for Oboe, Clarinet, Horn and Bassoon showed off the virtuosity of the woodwind and the majesty of the orchestral balance that Beecham was able to achieve. There was a tremendous crystallisation with Léon right in the middle, the central figure in the orchestra despite other great players like cellist Anthony Pini and Paul Beard who was leading.[11]

(The other soloists in the Mozart on 2nd November 1933 were Reginald Kell, Charles Gregory and John Alexandra. Eugene senior noted in his diary: 'Lee as usual played delightfully.')

When Richard Temple Savage joined the LPO as Bass Clarinet in 1936 he found that Léon was not always the easiest of colleagues.

> He had this little trick if he had a solo, he would punch the reed in to make it slightly sharp so that the sound stood out. I didn't know that. The first opera season I played in opened with *Lohengrin*. In the Second Act Duet between oboe and bass clarinet I knew there was something wrong. Horace Halstead, who was Second Oboe, told me what was going on. I had to have a piece cut off my instrument otherwise I couldn't match Léon's pitch.
>
> They were a very cliquey orchestra in those days; no one spoke to me; then after a couple of weeks Léon turned round and said 'Good morning'. The principal woodwind players were referred to as 'The Royal Family': Léon, Reginald Kell, First Clarinet, John Alexandra, First Bassoon and Geoffrey Gilbert, Flute, who was known as The Boy as when he had joined he had been very young. I used to sit next to Marie in the pit at Covent Garden; she was always a very pleasant person although

The Goossens children, ca. 1901. *From l to r:* Adolphe, Marie, Eugene, Sidonie, Léon.

Eugene Goossens I.

Eugene Goossens II.

Annie (Cook) Goossens.

Aynsley Cook.

Liscard, 1902

The family quintet in the back garden, Liverpool, 1904.

Edith Road, 1913.
Back row, l to r: Thomas Peatfield, Léon, Eugene;
Front row, l to r: Adolphe, John Snowdon, Bunny Warren.

Adolphe, 1914

Muriel Jack's Ladies Orchestra, 1915.
Marie is in the back row wearing the hat.

Eugene, Puma, Philip Heseltine and Hasam Shahid Suhrawardy, Crickley Hill,
Gloucestershire, July 1915.

Léon convalescing in hospital,
Epsom, 1919.

Eugene and Léon, ca. 1920.

Eugene, ca. 1919.

Boonie with Anne, Jane
and Julia, 1923.

Eugene in Hollywood with Lillian Gish, 1925.

Eastman School Conducting Class, Rochester, 1925.

Marie and Sidonie, 1923.

Marie, ca. 1923.

Fred Laurence, 1940.

Sidonie, 1926.

Bumps, ca. 1920.

Léon, 1925.

Léon and Fay's Wedding, 1926.

Eugene relaxing in Rochester, ca. 1927.

Eugene with the twelve-year-old violin prodigy, Yehudi Menuhin, Rochester,, 1927.

Cartoon by Avtori for J W Chesters, 1929.

Premiere of *Judith*, 1929.

'Durban' Finchley, 1930.
From l to r: Fay, Eugene, Annie, Léon, Bene, Tony, Marie and Jansi.

Léon and Leslie's Wedding, 1933.

Eugene being presented with the Legion of Honour, 1934.

Eugene and Sidonie, Wetherby Gardens, 1935.

Bumps, Léon and Eugene, Wetherby Gardens, 1935.

I didn't get to know her well.

The great success of Beecham and the LPO was that Tommy picked his players and they knew what he wanted.[12]

Looking back in *Beecham Remembered*, Léon analysed this special relationship: 'Once you had gained his confidence (and your own), he made you feel you were doing the whole thing yourself, playing as you always had wanted to play. And in performance something always came out that had not shown itself in rehearsal; he always had some trump card up his sleeve – that extra build-up to a climax, or some caress of a cadence: one could tell from his beat beforehand that something was coming up that he had in reserve.'[13]

Beecham's belief that spontaneity was spoilt by too much rehearsal led to the occasional disaster. He did not consider any rehearsal necessary for the orchestra's first performance of Sibelius' Second Symphony; he gave out the parts and Léon discovered he had a lovely languorous solo in the third movement which he took home to practise. He played it that evening with great feeling, delicacy of tone and rubato. The performance was broadcast on long wave by the BBC National Programme and the following day Beecham telephoned Sibelius in Finland to hear how he had enjoyed it. 'Who was the oboist?' the composer asked. 'My young protégé Goossens.' 'Tell him not to be such a gentleman,' Sibelius instructed. 'That solo is supposed to be wild and savage, not soft and beautiful!'[14]

The LPO's style of playing under Beecham with freedom of expression and rubato was not always acceptable to distinguished visiting conductors, particularly of the stricter German school. Temple Savage recalls Bruno Walter at a rehearsal of a Mahler Symphony asking 'Mr Goossens, could you not play in time for once?' and Furtwängler's exasperation at Covent Garden when he found that the orchestra played *Tristan* the Beecham way, regardless of what he conducted.

For Marie, as Principal Harp, the Wagner operas were always the highlight of the LPO's annual engagement at Covent Garden:

> The news came round: 'The Germans have arrived'. I can't tell you how I reacted to those words. Those wonderful singers

brought with them such dignity. They walked through the stalls
in slow procession, great broad-shouldered tall men and women,
the men in square-shouldered long raincoats and the women in
tailored suits. Their work was as perfect as their performance.
They never tired, singing full out at rehearsals and still fresh at
night.

As harpists we had very long waits which made the effect
so much greater when we came to play. During these waits,
it is a well-known fact that I used to lean my forehead on
the harp and have a little sleep, but as my cue came up so I
woke up. This was why I was able to remain fresh and go home
and do many household duties which I would not otherwise have
attended to.[15]

Marie usually managed to balance all the conflicting demands
of wife, mother and professional musician. She had a nurse to
help her with young Anthony and Jean, Freda Giles, cousin
of the cartoonist, and invaluable support from her mother-in-
law and parents. Beecham relied implicitly on Fred's unique
knowledge of the capabilities and whereabouts of every British
orchestral player to keep the LPO functioning efficiently, but
the Orchestral Manager came at the bottom of the salary scale.
In order to supplement the family income, Marie played for
recording and film sessions when the harp was not required
for an LPO concert. 'I used to go to Twickenham to record
music for films; this had to be done at night as the studio was
near the railway and the sound of the trains held up work. As
soon as the last train left we started. We recorded through the
night until a break for refreshment at 4am. We were given
bacon and eggs and sauté potatoes – did ever anything taste
better! After this we were quite fresh and we carried on
till the first train. They sent us home in buses and I remember
being home at dawn just as my babes were about to open their
eyes. I don't remember going to bed but if so it could not have
been for long.'[16]

Eugene was concerned to hear from his parents that Marie's
health had begun to suffer under this punishing regime. He
wrote: 'How I sympathise with poor Mor and I do hope that
all is well at Crewkerne now. She certainly deserves a good
long holiday and I hope she gets it. Tell her not to judge the
quantity of my affection by the number of letters I send her

or she will have a poor opinion of me. But tell her that I send strict orders that she begins to realise the fact that she is after all human and only has one pair of hands.'[17] Eugene was not sympathetically inclined towards his brother-in-law.

At Covent Garden, Fred had his office in a small room under the stage. Richard Temple Savage found his working methods unconventional but generally effective: 'He had a large sheet of paper pinned up on the wall covered with telephone numbers and no names. He only had to look at the number and he knew who the player was. "Don't bother me now" was always his remark when we met. Normally he conducted his business at the "Nag's Head" where there was a long bar with an entrance at both sides. He would stand at one door so that he could make a quick getaway if someone was coming in whom he didn't want to see. If he took it into his head to be difficult he would transfer his custom to the "Sun" and you had to know that. Fred was a great character!'[18]

During the opera season, Beecham often sent a message to Fred that he would be late arriving and Léon would then take charge of the orchestral rehearsal.

The LPO gave regular concerts in the main provincial cities and their Sunday Concerts at the Queen's Hall had become the leading London series with international soloists. Kreisler emphasised that one of his great joys was performing the Brahms Violin Concerto when Léon was playing. 'Whenever we played it together, Kreisler would stand aside at the beginning of the slow movement and half turn towards the audience and then at the end of the movement he would always give me a little bow before he went on with the finale.'[19]

Léon did however confess to 'one of the greatest clangers in the history of recorded sound!'

Piatigorsky was recording the Schumann Cello Concerto and was having an off day as all artists do from time to time. He was finding it terribly difficult to keep up to his usual standard of playing and he could not get the cadenza, which is extremely difficult, right. He tried time and time again and each time I broke out in a bigger sweat as I knew only too well what it was like to experience difficulties in recording. Each time he tried the cadenza, he broke down at the same place. The producer was very understanding. 'Don't worry,' he said, 'we'll take a pause and then just to get your nerve back we'll have a rehearse run before we record.' Piatigorsky played the cadenza perfectly. I was so excited and relieved that I shouted out 'Bravo'. After a moment's silence the producer came into the studio ashen faced. They had recorded it! What were they to do? 'Simple,' said Piatigorsky. 'Put on the label:

CELLO – PIATIGORSKY
BRAVO – GOOSSENS[20]

Considering how well his instrumental tone recorded it is to be regretted that Léon did not record more works during the 1930s, particularly the compositions written for him. Among his favourite recordings with the LPO, which he felt showed his empathy with Beecham to best advantage were Delius' *Brigg Fair* and *La Calinda*, Handel's *The Entry of the Queen of Sheba* and Rossini's overture to *The Silken Ladder*. Lord Harewood describes his playing in the Rossini as being 'like cut glass'.[21]

After Elgar had recorded his *Froissart* overture with the LPO in February 1933, he wrote to Fred Gaisberg of the Gramophone Company who had made the recording: 'Léon G's oboe passages are divine – what an artist!' Léon had become friendly with Sir Edward in the 1920s when he had taught him to drive a motorcar: 'Whether in gratitude for this, or for more serious reasons, must remain one of those enigmas Elgar loved to create for his friends – but in 1931 he actually began to compose a "Suite for Oboe". Now he was ill and only had a year or two more to live. So the sketches he made for the piece never advanced farther than the slow movement. The fly-leaf of the manuscript bore my name in Elgar's hand.'[22]

Elgar wrote to him on 21st January 1931, apologising for his delay: 'Alas! I have been a hostage to sciatica ever since I had the pleasure of seeing you. I have managed to keep one or two engagements but that's all. However I have most of the material available. As soon as I can write decently I shall get to work and let you hear.'[23]

After his death, Elgar's friend W H Reed discovered the unfinished manuscript among his papers and sent it to Léon.

For his seventieth birthday in 1967 he asked Gordon Jacob to orchestrate the one movement entitled 'Soliloquy'; he later recorded it with the Bournemouth Sinfonietta conducted by Norman Del Mar.

Léon also inspired young talent. Benjamin Britten dedicated his Phantasy Quartet op. 2 for Oboe, Violin, Viola and Cello to him. Its first official performance was a broadcast on 6th August 1933 under the maverick patronage of Edward Clark, the BBC's champion of contemporary music. Britten commented: 'Goossens does his part splendidly. The rest, although they are intelligent players, aren't really first class instrumentalists.'[24] He was far happier with the performance at the ISCM Festival in Florence in April the following year, when Léon was joined by three members of the Griller Quartet.

Léon was often invited to play in private houses and enjoyed the opportunity of socialising with the wealthy and well connected. David McKenna's father was financial advisor to the Royal College of Music.

> Léon moved into our family circle primarily for musical evenings after Sir Hugh Allen, Principal of the RCM, had introduced us. I remember the first time he came to stay at my parents' house in the country. It was a hot summer evening and we were sitting on the terrace after dinner, looking out onto a vista of green parkland enclosed by woods. Léon had disappeared. He had got his oboe and sneaked up along the path through the trees. Suddenly a magical sound came from the woods; it came nearer and nearer; it was electrifying – no known composition – it sounded like Pan playing his pipes; it was Léon improvising to give us all a wonderful surprise. It was an unforgettable experience for us. He loved company, he liked the good life and was a marvellous raconteur. The first time I met Leslie was when our second daughter was christened and they came for the weekend. Leslie adored him.[25]

Although Marie enjoyed playing at private engagements she did not share Léon's social aspirations. Lady Astor, Lady Wimborne and Lady Cunard gave the most distinguished musical soirées. Throughout the thirties, Lady Cunard remained Beecham's close companion. Marie recalled one memorable occasion:

> We had been rehearsing all day at Maida Vale Studios for the BBC with Sir Thomas and were due at Lady Cunard's in Mayfair that

evening. Before the guests arrived we had to have a short rehearsal for the Ravel Septet. We discovered the guests of honour were to be the Duchess of Buccleuch and the Prince of Wales. Whilst we rehearsed, already in our evening clothes, Lady Cunard was arranging the flowers.

Then things became rather strained. The Duchess was chatting in a very normal friendly way, when in walked the Prince accompanied by Mrs Simpson. Talk about a cat among the pigeons! The Duchess stayed at our end of the room and ignored the new arrivals. I was very impressed with Mrs Simpson's appearance and bearing. She wore a very simple but dainty dress, which seemed to be a mass of black frills edged with cream lace.

After we had given a good performance of the Septet – we had not found time to worry about it – the Duchess thanked us and found it necessary to catch an earlier train than anticipated. The Prince came up shaking hands and congratulating us, saying to me 'Are you Welsh?' to which I replied 'No, Your Highness.' 'Oh,' he said, 'I've seen them playing harps in Wales with those funny little hats on.' I remembered that he used to visit Wales quite often and had a deep feeling for the miners.[26]

Despite his popularity and success as a performer, Léon was having problems with the hierarchy of the BBC. On 12th January 1935, Julian Herbage, Programme Planner, circulated the following Internal Memorandum to his colleagues in Music Department:

> There have been one or two cases recently where we have wished to engage Léon Goossens for some particular kind of work, where his normal fee as a solo oboe has been rather high. Negotiations have been made rather difficult by the fact that we practically never engage him as a normal soloist in our studio programmes.
>
> Might I suggest that he might be given an engagement at some time in the future with the BBC Orchestra. Apart from the usual repertoire, Léon Goossens has played here the Concerto for Oboe and Strings by Ticciati, which I have heard is a very good work. There is also a concerto for oboe and strings by Gordon Jacob in which Goossens is interested.[27]

Kenneth Wright, Assistant Director of Music, wrote his comment: 'Agreed, both for gollowing and wallowing'; conductor

Aylmer Buesst added 'OK and swallowing'. Wright wrote to Edward Clark: 'Whatever one's personal dislikes of his tone-making, he has a big gollowing and we certainly ought to use an artist of his standing occasionally.' An unknown hand has added: 'I presume this should read "wollowing".' Léon's request to raise his fee from fifteen to twenty guineas was refused.

Many of Léon's broadcasts came from the BBC regions. Dad's diary entry for 5th March 1935 reads: 'Lee playing again as only Lee could play. Handel Concerto and Zenny's Concerto. BBC North Regional from L'pool.' The concert prompted a nostalgic letter from J E Matthews: 'Just a line to say how delighted and pleased I was to hear Léon on Tuesday at the Phil. His playing proved a great joy in every way. Such wonderful artistry. My little wife was quite entranced with his playing. It brought back to us both such happy memories of the days in L'pool and the days when he and poor Adolphe used to come to the OCOS rehearsals and I used to give them their bars of chocolate for playing so well. I often think of those visits to Wallasey for Eugene's lessons.'[28] (James Matthews, deputy leader of the Liverpool Philharmonic, had given Eugene his first violin lessons at the age of five. Adolphe and Léon played for him in the Oxton and Cloughton Orchestral Society which he conducted for many years.)

It was always a relief for Léon to turn from the machinations of the BBC to the consideration Beecham showed towards his soloists. On Sunday 9th February 1936, Dad noted: '3.15pm. Went to Queen's Hall. Beecham's return to England from New York visit. Bumps arranged Marcello Concerto which Lee played with all the artistry and feeling that are in him. Adjourned with Marie, Sid, Bumps to World's End Studio. Mum and I stayed for a meal. 10.30pm Lee kindly drove us back to "Durban".' On those occasions no doubt the Goossens family wished that North Finchley was nearer to SW3!

On 21st August 1936 they welcomed a new member, Jennifer. Eugene wrote: 'Léon's wire announcing arrival of a daughter just arrived. We Goossens certainly stick to tradition – or should I say form – so far as this generation is concerned. Now it's my turn to try again, but this competition is an expensive luxury. So I'll refrain for a while.'[29]

Coming from such a philoprogenitive family, it was galling

to Eugene that he never fathered a son. Léon and Leslie had a second daughter Corinne in 1940; tragically a third pregnancy was of a boy who did not survive. Tony, Marie and Fred's son, remained the only male in the next generation; he and his sister Jean had inherited musical talent from both their parents but neither had time to supervise their children's musical studies. Finchley was thirty years removed from Liverpool and without parental discipline, history could not repeat itself.

Tony has vivid memories of his musical training:

> I was presented with a violin when I was five years old. Grandpa Goossens used to coach me through the week, Mondays to Fridays. I went to his house every night for an hour, five days a week excluding Bank Holidays! Hands had to be scrubbed clean; I had to be there dead on six and at seven o'clock he used to say 'Right-o Anthony, that's it for today.' On Saturdays he would take me on the tram to Mark Saunders who gave me a lesson. I think I became quite proficient but I never really enjoyed it. Everyone was very disappointed when I said I didn't want to play any more.
>
> Then Grandpa started me on the clarinet but that wasn't for me either. I wasn't prepared to practise. I just used to sit down and play the piano when I felt like it. My mother never pushed me; she wasn't that sort of person.
>
> My father used to take me to rehearsals and Beecham sat me on his knee. He always gave my father Havana cigars and my father never told him that he didn't smoke. When I was about eight I tried one in the lavatory. 'You're not smoking, are you, Tony?' 'Oh no, Dad,' I replied, as the smoke curled out under the door. My father was the kindest man and never lost his temper. When the Queen's Hall was bombed it broke his heart.[30]

Both Marie and Léon considered that the LPO's tour of Germany in November 1936 showed the orchestra's concert playing at its height. Beecham's acceptance of an official invitation, although artistically attractive, was politically naïve. In contrast, the BBC Symphony Orchestra had played in Vienna and Budapest in March 1936 but refused German engagements. The Nazis seized on the LPO's tour as a wonderful propaganda exercise to demonstrate official British endorsement of their regime; they believed that Beecham was a leading aristocrat and friend of the King.

Tongue in cheek, Beecham left all the tour arrangements to Dr Bertha Geissmar, now his General Secretary, who was of Jewish birth. She had been Furtwängler's Personal Assistant for fifteen years until she was forced out by the Nazis on racial grounds. In her autobiography *The Baton and the Jackboot*, she describes how the orchestra 'were immensely fêted in every town. The German orchestral players were especially interested in them. Léon Goossens, particularly, probably the finest oboe player in the world, created a great sensation.'[31]

Like most of the orchestra, Marie found the tour full of disturbing experiences.

We gave our first concert in Berlin where Hitler, Goering and Goebbels were in a private box. I had to open the concert with a page of solo harp in the Dvořák Slavonic Rhapsody in A flat no. 3, a nerve-racking experience. After the concert I hurried round to the front entrance to see the Führer make his exit. I managed to get in front of the crowds of people, women in tears trying to touch his coat, as he stalked towards the door, with little Goebbels close by his side, making Hitler look like a giant.

In the concert halls the SS men were placed so that they never lost sight of us nor we of them, be it at the stage door, behind the stage, or at the side of the platform. In Dresden we asked to see the china factory, but they made an excuse. In Cologne we asked to see where the Eau de Cologne was made but, in spite of the fact that the building was a blaze of lights, some excuse was conjured up. We guessed that these places were now munitions factories.

I think our visit to Frankfurt was the most revealing. The town was really shabby, shop windows dirty and neglected looking, whilst the most picturesque part of the town with old houses covered with beautifully painted murals was deserted. We could guess what had happened to the Jews who used to populate this part.

But conditions were different when after the concerts we were invited to sumptuous repasts. The wine flowed and there were speeches.[32]

'I made thirty-nine speeches,' Beecham complained at a dinner at the Savoy Hotel welcoming the Berlin Philharmonic the following June, 'the same number as the articles of the English Church, and every one of them was different. In reply to my orations, a high German official of one designation or another made a similar number of speeches, each of them identical, thus showing the superiority of the Teutonic mind.'[33]

By the time they reached Ludwigshafen, Beecham had tired of the charade and failed to appear at the banquet for six hundred guests after the concert. Fred Laurence was left with the embarrassing task of making excuses for him.

Raymond Cooke, Léon's son-in-law, has another version of the episode: 'Ludwigshafen is the home of IG Farbenindustrie, the biggest chemical conglomerate in the world. They had developed BASF tape and magnetic tape recorders. Beecham had been asked if he would like to try out this unknown new recording process; he was so absorbed in listening to the recording after the concert that he completely forgot the banquet. Léon was playing *On hearing the First Cuckoo*. The recording was of quite remarkable quality despite a lot of residual distortion. The British didn't know anything about magnetic tape recording until after the war.'[34]

Léon's international reputation continued to increase. At the Salzburg Festival of August 1937 he gave the first performance out of England of Rutland Boughton's First Oboe Concerto, with the Boyd Neel Orchestra. Boughton, composer of *The Immortal Hour*, had written the concerto for his daughter Joy, one of Léon's pupils. He wrote to Léon, appreciatively but with tactful criticism, after a broadcast with the Bournemouth Municipal Orchestra the following February: 'I must just send you a word of deep thanks for your beautiful performance yesterday – I especially marvelled at the instinctive rightness of the nuances in the first and third movements. That is the soul of artistry that only comes by the gift of the gods, plus human industry. I believe that another time you might find the slow movement more satisfactory if the beginning and end were less emotional. I have always felt it as a very calm and restrained thing, except for a little self-revelation in the middle, where you were absolutely right. Now I want to hear you do Number 2.'[35] (Boughton dedicated his Second Oboe Concerto to Léon.)

Unlike most of his concerts, when Léon gave the first performance in London of Francesco Ticciati's Concerto in G for Oboe and Strings, it did not receive universal acclaim.[36] Eugene commented to his parents: 'I am sorry Lee was so disappointed with his notices of the Ticciati concerts. I suppose

174

the truth of the matter is that he is really so accustomed to an excess of praise that when some unfortunate critic uses the wrong adjective, he rather resents it. Tell him to be a philosopher like his elder brother who is inured by now to what Americans call "panning" or the gentle process of being "kicked in the pants".'[37]

A more popular addition to the repertoire was Bach's Harpsichord Concerto in A major arranged for Oboe d'amore. He gave the first performance of this on 21st November with the LPO and asked Sir Donald Tovey to reconstruct the concerto for him from the sketchy material that had survived. Tovey, Reid Professor of Music at Edinburgh, was a musicologist of the old school who had mixed feelings as to the value of historical authenticity.

Two weeks before the performance, he wrote:

Here is all the material I can collect without undue delay. What I send is the *absolutely essential* continuo part, as filled out by me. It can be played on the harpsichord to satisfy the consciences of the high-brows. I thoroughly agree both with Philipp Emanuel and with Schweitzer that Bach put up with the harpsichord as an unpunctual nuisance, that does not blend with the strings and that halfway down the hall conveys only a faint impression of chewing the cud. The pianoforte on the other hand, needs a very soft touch. You may remember that when we did the C minor Double Concerto (for Oboe and Violin), I had to oust a first-rate student from the pianoforte and take the continuo myself, because his touch was too hard.

One of my principles is to avoid including ornamentation, which Bach had only because he was rewriting for the harpsichord. You may remember that I restored your part largely on the basis of information furnished by the preface and the appendix of Vol. XVII of the Bach-Gesellschaft. Nobody can quarrel with you for adopting whatever you think fit of the clavier ornamentation. But I am myself convinced that most of it is a concession to the prickliness of the harpsichord and that it would not only dehumanise and delocalise your instrument, but would blur some important outlines of form.[38]

Although they enjoyed their share of the limelight, Marie and Sidonie had no ambitions to develop the solo potential of the harp. Marie always distinguished herself in orchestral

175

works where the harp is featured, ranging from the 'Valse des Fleurs' from Tchaikovsky's *Casse-Noisette* Suite to the second London performance of the Fauré Requiem, conducted by Nadia Boulanger. She played in the trio for two flutes and harp in Berlioz' *L'Enfance du Christ* at the Queen's Hall and Debussy's *Danse Sacrée et Danse Profane* for the ballet *Protée* in the last pre-war season of the de Basil Company at Covent Garden.

But she regarded the greatest honour to be a performance of the Mozart Flute and Harp Concerto with Geoffrey Gilbert for a Royal Philharmonic Society Concert on 1st December 1938. 'This was the first time they had had a harp as a solo instrument. Sir Thomas was so helpful, he cut down the number of players to make more of a chamber orchestra such as Mozart would have had in his day. It was a great success and Sir Thomas put in two more performances, one at Cheltenham and one at Leeds.'[39]

Dad commented in the diary: 'Marnie played delightfully and appeared calm and collected – while *I* felt exceedingly nervous and anxious!'

In the summer of 1938 Léon and Leslie decided to move out of London to Sussex. They converted two condemned Elizabethan cottages, Holter's Green, at Cooksbridge near Lewes. Leslie started to teach modern dance locally and Léon found that riding and farming provided ideal relaxation from the tensions of the concert platform.

By the 1938 – 39 season it was rumoured that the LPO was in financial difficulties from which there appeared little hope of extrication. Léon accepted an invitation to go to New York for two concerts of contemporary British music at the 1939 World Fair. On 9th June he gave the first performance in the USA of his brother's Oboe Concerto with the New York Philharmonic Orchestra conducted by Sir Adrian Boult at Carnegie Hall. The other new works written for the occasion were Bax's Seventh Symphony, *Five variants of 'Dives and Lazarus'* by Vaughan Williams and the Piano Concerto in B flat by Bliss, played by Solomon.

Léon's success was overwhelming. A Walter Kramer reported to his friend Eugene who was in England for the summer:

Just a few lines in my enthusiasm, to tell you that I heard your brother Léon yesterday, at the first of the two British concerts and that I must tell you that I have *never* heard anything like him!

I introduced myself to him at the luncheon we gave Sir Adrian at the Beethoven Association yesterday at which your brother and Bliss were also guests of honour. In the evening I went to the concert, and shouted 'Bravo' with the rest of the big audience. He is *phenomenal*. I have never heard anything like him. I told him that I did not know that what he does could be done on an oboe![40]

Léon returned to London to find the LPO on the verge of bankruptcy and the country poised on the brink of war. He had accepted a secret contract from the BBC together with three other principals of the LPO: Anthony Pini (cello), Frederick Riddle (viola) and Victor Watson (double bass) to form the nucleus of a new BBC orchestra should hostilities break out.

For the first time in the orchestra's existence, the players had been given a paid holiday. On their return, Richard Temple Savage telephoned Fred and asked: 'What's happening now?' 'Nothing's happening,' he said. 'It's all finished.' The LPO was declared bankrupt and reconstituted under an elected committee of players with Thomas Russell as secretary and business manager. On 1st October 1939, seventy players met at Paddington Station for the start of a Welsh tour. To Temple Savage's surprise, there was no Marie and no Fred. Since Léon had defected to the BBC Salon Orchestra at Evesham, neither his sister nor her husband were asked to work for the orchestra again.

12

Sid and Bumps

On 22nd October 1930, Sidonie took her seat as First Harp for the inaugural concert of the BBC Symphony Orchestra in the Queen's Hall conducted by Adrian Boult. Although she had been the BBC's resident harpist since 1923, she was not automatically offered the position when the Symphony Orchestra was formed: 'Adrian said they had to advertise but they only seriously considered a few people. Maria Korchinska thought it would not be right for her to accept as she was a foreigner; John Cockerill wanted to conduct; Jeanne Cheverau was playing for the opera. Adrian wired me to Cap Ferrat where I was on holiday with Bumps to say I had the job.' She was to remain First Harp for fifty years, the longest serving member of the orchestra, and continued to play as a guest until her ninetieth birthday!

> Principals were paid £14 a week, rank and file £11. Jeanne Cheverau was engaged as Second Harp but insisted that she was called Principal Harp No. 2. For many years we were both on part-time contracts; harpists were not considered to be employed full-time in the orchestra!* Out of 110 players, there were about twenty-five women which was breaking new ground. Sir Henry Wood had sixteen women in his orchestra for the Proms; the LSO and the LPO had only one woman player, the harpist. At thirty I was quite old compared with a lot of people who were engaged straight from college but the solo woodwind were older. We had wonderful brass and woodwind; a lot of players had been lured away from the Hallé in Manchester.

Their contracts began at the end of July when they had a week of rehearsals before playing for the Promenade Concerts.

*Sidonie was not given a full-time contract with the BBC until 1944.

We first saw each other at the Central Hall, Westminster; Adrian made a little speech of welcome and we read through Elgar's First Symphony – one of the best performances we ever gave as everyone was on their mettle.

Broadcasting House was being built complete with the Concert Hall designed for 110 players but the architect had miscalculated and had only allowed room for 110 on the platform standing up so we rehearsed in the auditorium and could never use the Concert Hall for a concert with the full orchestra. We worked in a studio under the arches at Waterloo Bridge by the wharves, beautifully curtained and carpeted but we used to see the rats running along the iron girders of the roof.[1]

It was not until 1934 that they were to have a permanent home for rehearsals and broadcasts in Maida Vale Studios, converted from a roller-skating rink. The BBC Symphony Orchestra soon established itself as the best orchestra in Britain; it had the advantage over its older rivals of being the first orchestra to have its players under annual contract with a regular salary and thus free from the notorious deputy system, by which, if a player were engaged for a concert, he might subsequently decide to send a deputy to a rehearsal or to the actual performance.)

Sidonie emphasises Boult's excellence as an orchestral trainer.

He hated losing his temper. Some of the older principals took advantage of him if they had had too much to drink in the interval. He flew at them which he did not like. All the strings were saints! Boult conducted everything better as he got older. He was not an easy conductor to follow; he had a very wide beat but we got used to him. Wood and Sargent both had very clear beats. Wood was very well organised. His main interest was cutting down the playing time. 'We took two minutes off that,' he'd say with great pride.

Players can be very bolshie. Charles Munch got very annoyed with the brass because there was too much talking and walked out. He was persuaded to come back but it spoilt the atmosphere. The way musicians criticise conductors is very unfair; I felt that particularly when Eugene was a guest with the orchestra.[2]

At least one regular salary was coming in to Wetherby Gardens; Bumps was finding it a struggle to establish himself as a conductor in the classical field but other avenues were opening. Sid wrote to her parents on 26th January 1932 suggesting that they should celebrate their wedding anniversary by seeing the new film of *Frankenstein* at the Tivoli followed by a meal, 'unless it is too horrible for Mum! I am not sure if Bumps will be able to meet us as he is more than busy now. I know you will be pleased to hear that Cochran has asked him to conduct his new show at the Palace Theatre *The Cat and the Fiddle*. Isn't it marvellous! To get in with Cochran alone is the ambition of every man and woman in the theatre world. So I think Bumps is very fortunate. It is thanks to Willie Walton's recommendation.'

Bumps always proved himself an accomplished and versatile musician and the contact with Cochran prospered. He moved from the Palace Theatre to the Adelphi to conduct *Words and Music* by Noel Coward, memorable for the song 'Mad Dogs and Englishmen'. The following year, October 1933, he conducted *Nymph Errant* at the Adelphi with music by Cole Porter, starring Gertrude Lawrence. The American cabaret singer Elizabeth Welch, who was making her London debut, stopped the show in the harem scene with 'Solomon had a thousand wives'.

Welch remembers Bumps with affection and admiration:

He gave you so much from the pit; so much support and confidence. He always made you think 'Go on girl, you're wonderful!' All the musicians adored him. I never saw him lose his temper; he could ride any kind of storm. There was a wonderful camaraderie in that show from the top to the bottom. Cocky and Cole came to every rehearsal. They'd take off their coats and sit in their shirt-sleeves and send out for coffee and sandwiches. That was before the days of Equity rules and we would rehearse until two or three in the morning!

Bumps took me to my first pub, the Fitzroy in Bloomsbury with Constant Lambert and Willie Walton. Augustus John was there and all the great writers. I was eyes all agog! I was the only woman and they were saying 'Who the hell is this brown skin person anyway?' 'That's Elizabeth Welch who's one of Cochran's stars,' they whispered. Thank goodness I didn't swell up with too much pride – just enough!

Then Bumps took me home to Wetherby Gardens to meet

Sidonie and we've been friends ever since. She was the rock of the family and he knew that she was always there. She accepted him as a crazy musician. With all his devilment and playing up to the ladies, he adored her! They were both musicians but otherwise they were completely different in every way; like honey and vinegar but they blended. They were a wonderful pair with this genuine rapport, which was real not forced.

When Sidonie was at home she used to give little cocktail parties or dinners. How she did it when she was working I don't know. We'd often be there drinking when she came home after a concert. She'd greet us all then sometimes she'd go to bed on us if she had to be up for a 10am rehearsal. She would always have a hot bath and the steam would come out from under the door. We old tramps would be there until the early hours and then go home and stay in bed all next morning.[3]

Both Sidonie and Bumps were established as glamorous personalities in the public eye; they merited a gossip piece in the *Daily Express* of 23rd September 1933:

Harping at tonight's Promenade Concert is Sidonie Goossens, reputed best harpist in Britain. To meet she is less like a harpist than you'd expect. Kind-hearted, speaks good French. Tans for four weeks in the South of France every year. Now on a slimming diet. Quasi-Titian hair, Goossens nose. Shakes a good cocktail. Fan of Harpo Marx.

She is married to Hyam Greenbaum. He is thirty. Fine theatre conductor, made gramophone history at nineteen by conducting first disc made here of *Rosenkavalier*; has since conducted everything from grand opera to jazz. Favourite food: Delysia's French cook's. Favourite drink: strong ale. Once asked to leave a Pimlico pub for singing madrigals with the late Peter Warlock: 'We've no licence for that sort of thing 'ere Sir!'

Sidonie still regards Warlock/Heseltine as a corrupting influence, responsible for the start of Bumps' excessive drinking. She had been endowed with exceptional qualities of generosity of spirit, resilience, tolerance and love; it was only due to these that Bumps was able to maintain both his career and his marriage in face of his losing battle with alcoholism. 'He was very Jewish, very subject to depression and ups and downs of mood,' Sidonie recalls. 'I never knew when he would let me or himself down. I came home one evening and found he had smashed up the vase of flowers we had on the piano and there was blood all round the walls to the bed. One night he fell out of bed and cut his head on the corner of the bedside table which had bevelled glass. I was a pack of nerves. There was no Alcoholics Anonymous in those days, no one I could turn to for help. I did try putting ipecacuanha in his night-cap but he said there was something wrong with the whisky and he would have to change to brandy! He was so wonderful in other ways, such a genius!'[4]

At the time of *Nymph Errant* he was still making spasmodic efforts to keep his drinking under control. Dad notes in his diary Sidonie's birthday lunch at L'Escargot Bienvenue on 19th October 1933, 'Champagne lunch in company with Hyam. All in happy mood except Hyam (he being bound to Vichy water!).' They always remained a family for celebrating birthdays and anniversaries. It had become a tradition for Sid and Bumps to entertain her parents on Christmas Eve at Wetherby Gardens; the 1933 celebrations included a party for their friends to meet Léon and his new wife Leslie.

After the Cochran show closed, Bumps was out of work again. 'I am sorry to hear that Bumps still has no work,' wrote Eugene from Cincinnati. 'There is absolutely nothing doing over here, but one would think that he would be able to apply his talents to some remunerative job in spite of his shattered ideals.'[5] He was concerned at his parents' report that his sister was in poor health. 'So far as Sidonie's loss of weight is concerned it is altogether too much. It may be due to many causes a) nervous and physical exhaustion after too strenuous a season, b) worry about her husband, c) some source of infection such as has been my lot.'

Sidonie had been working hard and Bumps' problems were imposing an increasing strain on her health. In addition to her orchestral concert, in May 1934 she had played the Dittersdorf Concerto for Harp and Orchestra for the BBC and given the first performance at the Wigmore Hall of two solo works written for her: 'Valse' by Arnold Bax and Estemporale nos. 1 and 2 by Bernard van Dieren. 'They were very difficult works. Van Dieren went through the part with me and wrote big notes on

the score to help me like "DASHINGLY TO HELL and QUIET".'
She dismisses the theory that he was the evil genius behind
Heseltine/Warlock's death. 'He was a wonderful influence on
younger composers, so kind and patient despite the fact he was
often in agony from kidney stones.'[6]

Eugene did not share his sister's admiration for van Dieren.
'I can't understand this ridiculous worship of everything the
man has ever done, by a certain group of overfaithful disci-
ples,' he wrote to his father at the news that a group including
Sid, Bumps and Walton were trying to organise a production
of van Dieren's opera *The Tailor*. 'I don't know two notes of
van Dieren's music which have ever warranted the slightest
attention and if he is this giant that we are asked to believe
in, why doesn't someone let us hear some of this miraculous
music? It is rather on a par with the exaggerated adulation that
is being bestowed on Walton at the present moment.'[7]

Eugene showed even less sympathy for his brother-in-
law's aspirations, although in a more generous mood he had
recommended him for a conducting post in Pittsburgh. He sent
Sidonie a telegram wishing her a happy holiday and on her
return commented to their parents: 'Sid's condition of being
"broke to the winds" is no novelty in this family but it is not
to be wondered at if her better half is out of a job. I am, as you
know, very tolerant minded in most things but in that particular
case I have no sympathy at all. One cannot graduate from a West
End musical comedy to the rostrum of the Queen's Hall and
I do not say this with any superiority. I have every sympathy
with a man's ideals but when it is a case of bread and butter,
to hell with ideals. This sounds very prosaic but "them's my
sentiments".'[8]

Eugene's attitude does seem to be a harsh and unsympathetic
one. Twenty years earlier he had owed his own success to
the opportunities that Beecham had given him to conduct
as a completely unknown quantity with far less experience
than Bumps had had. In September 1935 Beecham called on
Bumps to assist him at Covent Garden but to play continuo
not to conduct. Beecham had been criticised for using a piano
in Mozart recitatives and had decided to bow to authenticity
and use a harpsichord for Rossini's *Barber of Seville*. It was a
family occasion with Bumps joining Léon and Marie in the pit.

Beecham had no quarrel with Bumps' musicality but decided that despite the purists he disliked the harpsichord. 'It sounds like two skeletons copulating on a tin tray,' was his dry comment.

Despite all its vicissitudes, Sidonie and Bumps' relationship, as far as their marriage and their careers were concerned, remained essentially one of unquestioning loyalty between equal partners. But when Sidonie was asked to write an article for the *Radio Times* entitled 'Can women create great art?' her conclusion was: 'No, but they have always been its chief inspiration.' She confined herself to creativity in the first degree as composition not interpretation. One wonders what Dame Ethel Smyth must have thought of Sidonie's failure to find a single woman who had created anything of real artistic merit compared with brothers, husbands or lovers. 'One might say that if there never was a woman who could produce music from her own soul, composers themselves have told us that without the help of woman they never could have produced those works by which we know them today.'

Despite the fact that she was an intelligent, articulate and gifted woman and had earned her living from the age of eighteen on equal professional terms in what was essentially a man's world, Sidonie saw her role as that of traditional help-mate and provider of feminine inspiration. Van Dieren helped her with the article and she quotes the example of the wives of Elgar, Busoni and Delius. 'Could there be a prouder task for any woman than that of enabling a man of talent to reveal his soul to the world? Let us confess that this alone is the higher achievement than the production of works that do not reach the highest levels of creative power.'9 Sidonie, for all her sophistication, remained far closer to her mother's Victorian concept of woman's fulfilment in marriage; she never thought of herself as a liberated New Woman.

Sidonie took particular pride in the fact that the BBC Symphony Orchestra's first visit abroad should be to the native land of her father and grandfather, Belgium. At their concert in the Grande Salle du Palais des Beaux-Arts in Brussels on 12th March 1935 the orchestra was acclaimed: 'Superb in its ensemble, colour and shading.' (*Indépendance Belge.*) Sidonie, as always, excelled in Ravel's *Daphnis and Chloe* Suite no. 2, established as a showpiece in their repertoire since their opening concert. She became a favourite of Toscanini with her handling of Ravel's virtuoso demands and her ability to fit in the harp glissandi with the other instruments without disturbing the flow of the music. 'He had me sitting right beside him for the *Prometheus* ballet music, the only Beethoven work which has a harp part. "Molto intelligente," he said as he walked off the platform after the performance and whacked me on the head with his baton which got caught in my hair! He said we were the finest orchestra he had ever heard.'[10]

She has less happy memories of Hermann Scherchen although she enjoyed the challenge of the repertoire he conducted including Berg's *Der Wein* and Webern's *Das Augenlicht*: 'He was quite terrifying; he wore a white doctor's coat and little metal-rimmed glasses as if he was going to operate on us!'[11]

Bumps found a new outlet for his versatility in film music, again thanks to William Walton. Through a young film director friend, Dallas Bower, Walton had been commissioned to write the music for *Escape me Never* starring Elisabeth Bergner and directed by her husband Dr Paul Czinner at Elstree Studios. Bumps did most of Walton's orchestration and after meeting Czinner and Bower, his assistant, on set found himself engaged to conduct the music. Dad notes seeing the film with credit for the orchestration to Hyam Greenbaum on 11th April 1935.

One of Walton's most endearing qualities was the help he always extended to his friends. He had now moved on from the Sitwells in Carlyle Square to a new relationship with Lady Alice Wimborne. In 1932 he persuaded her to start the Quartet Society, a series of private subscription concerts of chamber music in the candlelit ballroom of Wimborne House, the magnificent Palladian mansion designed by William Kent at 22, Arlington Street, Piccadilly.

The atmosphere of those concerts is captured in a painting by Sir John Lavery entitled 'Chamber Music at Wimborne House', which was exhibited at the Royal Academy in the summer of 1937. Sidonie who was playing the Dittersdorf Harp Concerto, is the focal point of the picture in an emerald green dress. In the foreground to the right are Lady Wimborne and Lord Drogheda and to the left Walton and Lord Wimborne, the latter somewhat imaginatively portrayed as he never attended the concerts. Also

identifiable are the Sitwells and Anthony Asquith who used
to introduce each programme with a short talk; this was an
expediency by which the evenings qualified as 'educational'
and avoided Entertainment Tax.[12]

Sidonie recalls the Lavery painting: 'He was so taken
with the green of the dress against the gold of the harp
that he made me look like a giantess. I had to go for an
extra sitting at his studio by which time I had dyed the
original dress brown, so I had to have another one specially
made. Willie wanted to make an arrangement for me with
Lord Wimborne: "Just spend the weekend with him in Paris
and he'll pay your income tax!" They all seemed very
surprised when I declined but quite apart from being faithful
to one's husband, he was very old and dithery!'[13]

Sidonie found it essential after a taxing season with the
Symphony Orchestra to escape to the sun for a month with a
female friend, nicknamed 'Rufus'. She was the wife of Philip
Jordan, a feature writer for the *News Chronicle*.

> If Bumps came he ruined my holiday because he started drinking
> and then became jealous of anyone who danced with me. Rufus
> had discovered a lovely little hotel at Tossa del Mar on the Costa
> Brava which was then totally unspoilt. I went there again in July
> 1936 by myself. When the Spanish Civil War broke out, Bumps
> came to rescue me. I remember going to meet him at Gerona;
> all he had brought with him was a little case with six pocket
> handkerchiefs. The station was surrounded by men with machine
> guns to defend it against the Nationalists; Catalonia was fiercely
> Republican.
>
> Because I worked for the BBC I was advised to leave as
> soon as possible. The Foreign Office got a message through to a
> British destroyer, HMS *Gallant* which was sailing from Barcelona
> to Marseilles; they anchored off Tossa and sent a little boat to the
> beach for us. The ship was crowded with over fifty British refugees
> and we were given blankets to sleep on deck. It was a wonderful
> journey at thirty-eight knots, cutting through the breakers with
> a bright moon shining and for breakfast the sailors brought us
> steaming bowls of tea with a large shot of navy rum.[14]

Despite her adventure, Dad noted after they visited her on
27th July: 'She looks and feels wonderfully well. Now fair hair
and darkest skin.'

Eugene had been concerned about his sister's safety and wrote from San Francisco: 'From the reports in papers over here it would seem that there are very few people left alive in Spain and naturally I was a bit anxious as to whether she had actually got out of Barcelona safely before the real trouble started. It is almost impossible over here to get accurate news about the whole European situation. It all seems so garbled and inaccurate one does not know whether Europe has gone Communist or whether these ridiculous stories of France helping the Reds in Spain and these wholesale massacres of priests and nuns are based on fact.[15]

By 17th August Sidonie had become an international personality: 'By the way,' Eugene wrote, 'the Associated Press has been bombarding me for photos of "Sid" to illustrate the story of her rescue from the Spanish Revolution. One paper asked whether I had a picture of her in a bathing costume. That adjective "beauteous" seems to have travelled round the world![16]

Eugene found the whole episode rather embarrassing, particularly when it became known that Sid's sympathies were with the Republicans whom he persisted in identifying as Reds or Communists. When Sid wrote to him he found her letter 'so full of peculiar political sentiments that I felt bound to point out that I did not quite agree with them. I am getting very pugnacious in my old age.'[17]

Sid and Bumps had visited Finchley on 3rd December and discussed Bumps' plans to volunteer for the International Brigade which did not materialise. Eugene wrote to his father: 'Your account of the Communist meeting at Durban gave me a bad attack of hiccoughs. The thought of Bumps arriving at Madrid with gun is too touching to bear contemplating. I am afraid however that the gun would be in someone else's hands and resting comfortably between Bumps' sixth and seventh ribs before he had been there two minutes. Besides, who knows, were he to arrive in Madrid, it is conceivable that General Franco might get wind of his presence in the country and radio him an offer to head the television department of the Rebel armies. This Bumps would doubtless accept, irrespective of politics.'[18]

Sidonie found her brother's cynicism in bad taste considering the strength of her husband's political ideals.

> Eugene agreed with us in the end and changed his mind about Franco. We knew from the very beginning that Franco was backed by Hitler, who was using the Spanish Civil War as a dress rehearsal for his own Nazi offensive but we were never Communists.
>
> I wanted to adopt a little orphan girl from Galicia but the British authorities wouldn't allow it. We had a refugee couple staying in the flat until they moved on to America; then we were friendly with a Spanish anarchist group and stored their leaflets in our attic. Jessie Hinchcliffe and I used to collect money for Spanish babies from the orchestra; people used to give a few pence just to please us although many of them thought that we were just fools.[19]

Jessie, a violinist and founder member, remained Sidonie's closest friend in the orchestra. She was married to Alan Rawsthorne, one of the group of composers who relied on Bumps for help with their scores.

When the BBC Television Service was started in 1936, Bumps had applied for the post of Musical Director and Dad was delighted to provide a character reference. It finally looked as if he would achieve recognition and scope for his musical talents in an artistically congenial position. According to Sidonie: 'Adrian [Boult] had given Bumps the TV job. He said he was the only man he knew who could do it.' For the opening transmission on 2nd November 1936, relayed first on the Baird and then on the EMI system, Bumps conducted the BBC Television Orchestra in a programme including music from the film *Things to Come* by Bliss and Vaughan Williams' *Folk Song Suite*.

Lionel Salter, later to become Assistant Controller of Music for the BBC, was a young music graduate recently down from Cambridge. He found himself as Station Accompanist and Musical Assistant to Bumps.

> He was a most remarkable man and an extraordinarily versatile conductor. You had to be if you were in TV in those days. It was nothing to conduct tea-time cabaret in the afternoon and opera in the evening, all live of course. He was extremely erudite and knowledgeable about contemporary composers. The orchestra adored him.

188

Unfortunately his big weakness was the bottle. There were forty-four bars at Alexandra Palace and one of my functions was to find out which was his current favourite and get him out of it half an hour before we went on air. On one occasion I found him sitting on the floor, discoursing learnedly on the String Quartets of Karol Rathaus to a totally empty bar![20]

Dallas Bower who had been appointed joint Producer/Director for Drama emphasises that however much Bumps had imbibed, his professionalism as a conductor remained unimpaired. 'Once on the podium his beat was rock steady and one hundred per cent reliable. One of the highlights from my point of view was the Second Act of *Tristan* which he conducted with a hand-picked orchestra, including twelve horns. It was performed as a mime, with choreography by Anthony Tudor.'[21] The two principal singers were Walter Widdop and Isobel Baillie: the Scottish light soprano lacked the voice and temperament to sing Isolde in the opera house but was particularly keen to try the role. *Tristan* was the thirteenth opera presented on the new medium.

When Bower directed *The Tempest* with Peggy Ashcroft as Miranda and George Devine as Caliban, Bumps conducted the Sibelius incidental music, heard for the first time in its theatrical context. (It had been commissioned by Gordon Craig for a performance in Copenhagen which had never taken place.) Bower recalled:

> The great problem was the storm which was scored for a Wagnerian orchestra. Bumps said he'd have a go at reducing it. Cecil Gray took the result to Sibelius in Finland and the composer said 'I cannot imagine why I didn't score it like that in the first place!'
>
> Greenbaum had this amazing virtuosity. We soon found out he was just as at home with a music hall programme as with an operatic score. Our programmes were very mixed as we were trying to appeal to as wide an audience as possible. When I went to see George Robey in his dressing-room he said to me 'Well my boy, I'm told you're something of a Wagnerian. Well so am I! But this evening I'm afraid there's going to be no *Tristan*, no *Meistersinger*. I'm going to sing you a little number called "Safety First".' He produced a frightful set of tattered old band parts which I took out to Greenbaum, and afterwards Robey said, 'My goodness me! What an orchestra and what a conductor!' The pièce

de la résistance was Piatigorsky playing a Haydn Cello Concerto, all on the same programme. Piatigorsky said it was the best performance of the Haydn he had ever done, all thanks to Bumps.

Bower was taken home on many convivial occasions to Wetherby Gardens and was enchanted by Sid. 'She played Ravel's *Introduction and Allegro* for me in a concert for TV. When I made a film in 1937 of the achievements of the first six months of television I featured Sid playing some wonderful Spanish music by Granados. The only problem was I had to place her on a rostrum six foot in the air as we didn't have a "high hat" camera stand. She was absolutely terrified that the harp would overbalance and always reminds me of the experience when we meet.' The TV Survey Film, made at the Stoll Film Studio in Cricklewood, was used to demonstrate television sets and Sid could be seen plucking the strings with great allure, every morning in Selfridges and Harrods.

In the Spring of 1937 she also accompanied Margot Fonteyn in Debussy's *Clair de Lune* which Bumps arranged for the harp and was featured in 'Fugue for Four Cameras' in an after supper revue on TV. For this she was requested to wear a special light coloured evening gown and raised the question of the extra expense involved in its purchase. The BBC eventually agreed to pay her an extra £2.2.0 in addition to her fee of £8.8.0 which included transport of harp.

The Goossens family had been very much in the public eye and ear throughout the Coronation Season of 1937, with Eugene's opera *Don Juan de Mañara* at Covent Garden. Sidonie played stage harp and at the First Night of the Proms on 7th August 1937 she gave the British premiere of Germaine Tailleferre's Concertino for Harp and Orchestra.

Eugene had no compunction in asking his sister to use her influence to help him with any problems that arose concerning BBC engagements. Despite the recognition that Bumps was now gaining as a conductor in his TV post, Eugene retained reservations about helping him in his career. He wrote to his parents in April 1938:

> I had a cable from Sid asking me to cable immediately to a certain gentleman in Glasgow, strongly urging him to engage Bumps as conductor of the Scottish orchestra next season. This cable came

as a surprise to me for several reasons a) I had only just received a letter from Ibbs & Tillett, telling me that Szell has been engaged as a permanent conductor for this orchestra next season, b) I don't know the gentleman to whom I was asked to address the cable and c) I have never seen Bumps conduct a symphony orchestra. Loyalty to one's family is all very well in its way, but there are certain ethics which have to be observed in the matter of recommending people for posts of responsibility. However I sent a cable stressing the fact that Bumps was a fine musician, and saying that I thought he would fit the post.[22]

Bumps' younger brother and sister, Bernard and Kyla Greenbaum have very positive memories of the hospitality and sympathetic guidance they received at Wetherby Gardens. Bernard wanted to be a commercial artist: 'Sidonie has a rare gift for making teenagers feel that all decisions concerning their future are theirs alone. Many grandiose ideas were floated when my future was being discussed; she went out and did the practical things and arranged contacts for me in Fleet Street who then commissioned my work.'[23] Kyla, who was twenty years younger than Bumps, had also inherited outstanding musical talent; she was to excel as a pianist specialising in the most complex of contemporary works. She recalls:

The sad thing about Bumps is that he was before his time. Schoenberg, Webern and Busoni, he knew all about them but no one was interested in performing them. He did manage to put on the first staged performance in England of Busoni's opera *Arlecchino* which he conducted for TV.

I was the youngest of the family and didn't really get to know him or Sid until I was a music student at the Academy and started staying with them at Wetherby Gardens. They were a very elegant couple. Sid has a legendary persona which was accentuated in that Gertie Lawrence generation of glamour and perfume and furs.

You never knew who was going to turn up at their parties in their huge attic room. The walls were painted shiny black and seemed to vanish into infinity except for the Paul Nash paintings. It was like a stage set with the gold of the harp, the ivory and black of the grand piano and very large settees covered in old gold set off by a cherry red carpet. Lambert was there constantly for help

191

with his orchestrations. I remember Walton coming to ask Bumps what he thought of his Violin Concerto and Bumps saying that it wasn't up to much because he hadn't got the beginning right and Walton saying 'I'll come back again tomorrow and we'll go into it further,' just like a student.[24]

Bumps' friend Cecil Gray explained why Walton, Lambert and Rawsthorne came to him with their scores: 'Not merely for advice on technical matters but also for constructive aesthetic criticism in the process of composition. He had a deep understanding of, and insight into, all the problems of artistic creation.'[25]

In January 1939 Sidonie once more displayed her theatrical and vocal talents as leading lady of the BBC's Amateur Dramatic Society's Revue. *I'm no Angle* ran for three nights at the Fortune Theatre; Sidonie learnt tap-dancing from Buddy Bradley to lead the Typing Typtoes in their song and dance routines and rivalled Mae West as a Nordic nautch-girl. Mum and Dad celebrated their forty-seventh wedding anniversary by going to the second night and 'feasting our eyes on our darling Sidonie, an ideal Principal Boy and alluring Leading Lady.'[26] Sidonie certainly followed in the family tradition; Annie decided that she had inherited her excellent legs from Aynsley Cook's youngest sister, 'Sporty Aunty Al'.

Musical life in 1939 was overshadowed by the uncertainty of the European situation and the growing threat of Fascism. The BBC had already made contingency plans for the outbreak of war. Sidonie remembers that first Sunday in September 1939 as the end of an era. 'As soon as the announcement was made we were told to pack our bags and go to Bristol. Bumps took me to Paddington for the three o'clock train which was crowded with evacuees and took five hours. After a few weeks Bumps joined me, as conductor of the Variety Orchestra, consisting of most of his players from TV. All he was allowed to do was to provide chords on for comedians which broke his spirit entirely.'[27]

The Symphony Orchestra resumed public concerts from the beginning of November in the Colston Hall. Sid and Bumps teamed up with Jessie and Alan Rawsthorne; they moved into the Clifton Arts Club on the corner of Park Street and Charlotte Street and the two women found themselves providing a focal centre for the orchestra and visiting celebrities. Sid remembers the somewhat unreal atmosphere of the first year of the war:

> We rented the huge studio which was the entertainment room of the club complete with curtained off stage where Bumps and I slept. It was an old Victorian building which had a ghost: the Little Lady in Grey who was well known to everyone including the local policeman. We got quite used to her.
>
> That first year we lived off the fat of the land. I sent to Tiptrees for a 7lb stone jar of marmalade; a farmer came in from the country with a basket of eggs every week; the butcher gave us everything we wanted and nobody took any notice of the 2oz butter ration. Then in June 1940 the air-raids started and life became progressively more difficult. We used to record in the day and walk home in our tin helmets so that we could all be back in our billets by the blackout. We only lost one member of the orchestra, Albert Cockerill the double bass player and his wife who were killed in their flat. Paul Beard, our leader, was blown off his bicycle by bomb blast but was not seriously hurt.
>
> Making music was our job so we just got on with it. On one occasion I was playing some light music solos including Carlos Salzedo's *Whirlwind* which I hadn't had time to practise and I remember wishing that there would be an air-raid so that I didn't have to play. Just before we were due to go on the air, the siren sounded and my prayers were answered![28]

On the night of 24th November 1940 Bristol was subjected to its heaviest raid.

> It was a Sunday. Bumps and I had been copying out music for the Variety Orchestra. He had been very ill with sclerosis of the liver and it was really the beginning of the end for him. We could hear the incendiaries clattering down in the street and then the people from upstairs came and told us the house was on fire. We grabbed a few silly things like an umbrella, hair-cutting scissors and a blanket and went across the road to the pub on the corner by the ice rink. W W Thompson, the manager of the orchestra, was there and Constant [Lambert] who had been conducting a concert that weekend. Constant had found one of those little hoses that you use to wash glasses and was playing it against the wall of the furniture repository next door which was blazing away.

You seem to have no fear in a crisis like that. Every time we heard a shell coming down we lay flat on the floor. Then came the whistling of a bomb and the eerie silence as we waited for the explosion. Three came down and got wedged in the ice rink, which was a miracle otherwise none of us would have survived.

In the morning we walked through the ruins to our favourite pub, the Llandoger Trow opposite the Theatre Royal. They managed to give us breakfast as they had oil lamps. There was no gas or electricity and the whole of Park Street was flooded. Our house was completely flattened.[29]

For the next few months Sid and Bumps moved out of Bristol and enjoyed the tranquillity of a hospitable farm near Nailsea on the road to Weston-super-Mare. In April 1941 the Variety Orchestra was sent to Bangor and at the end of July the Symphony Orchestra moved to Bedford where they were to remain until September 1945. Sid and Jessie found a little furnished flat where they were able to provide the same warm hospitality as in Bristol. 'Bumps hated Bangor and he hated variety work. Away from me he was tempted to drink more and more. He lived in a pub and once set his bed on fire there.'

In November 1941, thanks to Boult's insistence, he was at last given the opportunity of conducting the Symphony Orchestra: a programme at the Arts Theatre in Cambridge including the Busoni Violin Concerto on 19th November and the following day a studio concert in Bedford which featured Bartók's *Divertimento* for Strings. 'All the orchestra said he was marvellous but it was the last work he was able to do. He went into a nursing home in London where the doctor gave him four months to live. Then I had him with me in Bedford with a nurse to look after him until he died.'[30]

Bumps died on 13th May 1942 at the tragically premature age of forty-one. He was buried at the Jewish Cemetery in Brighton. His brother Bernard remembers standing on the railway station platform afterwards with Cecil Gray and Eugene senior. 'Sid's father was such a kind man; he just put his hand on my shoulder and I could feel all his sympathy without his saying anything.'[31]

Cecil Gray wrote a passionate obituary for his friend in the *Music Review* of August 1942, mourning him as 'the best conductor of his generation in this country. For Greenbaum orchestral players had a love, a respect, a veneration almost, which had to be seen and heard to be believed. They recognised in him a leader who knew exactly what he wanted, and who knew exactly how to get it – one of themselves, but their master.'

He castigated the BBC for refusing to recognise Bumps' talents until it was too late. 'Nothing is more sickening than the sanctimonious, hypocritical tributes to him that one hears on all sides now that he is safely out of the way. They remind one a little too forcibly of the lavish floral tributes paid by Chicago gangsters to the rivals they had successfully bumped off. It is one of the tragedies of life that an exceptional talent automatically, fatally, inevitably raises up against itself a formidable, almost impersonal opposition, which can only be overcome by a fortunate combination of circumstances, which in this particular case did not occur. There is no more tragic figure than the great interpretative artist who has never been given the chance to reveal his powers. Such was Hyam Greenbaum.'

Bumps' unquiet spirit was laid to rest but for Sidonie life had to go on.

13

Don Juan de Mañara

Eugene and Arnold Bennett were not discouraged by the mixed reception which *Judith* had received at Covent Garden. They discussed a number of different projects before deciding on a suitable subject for their next collaboration. 'The Samuel 2 idea is abandoned,' wrote the author to Eugene on 25th July 1929. 'I read the story again and abandoned the idea before I got your letter. The Aztec idea remains. A story would have to be invented; but I daresay that I could invent one. Would you prefer it to end happily or not? Either ending could be made to seem true. Have you ever read my play *Don Juan de Mañara*? Sixteenth-century Spain.* It is the other – and a quite different – version of the Don Juan story and in my opinion the better one. It would mean four acts!'

The play, written in 1913, had been privately printed in 1923 but never performed. Its origin was a dramatised version by Alexandre Dumas (père) of a short story by Prosper Mérimée, appropriately entitled 'Souls in Torment' (*Les Ames de Purgatoire*). They all owed their inspiration to a real life libertine: Miguel de Mañara Vincentelo de Leca who led a life of criminal debauchery considered excessive even in the lax climate of seventeenth-century Seville. He finally repented of his profligacy and took the vows of the Brotherhood of Charity. The Hospital de la Caridad which he endowed, still stands today in Seville as a monument to his contrition.

Although the same man inspired Tirso de Molina's drama *Burlador de Sevilla* written in 1630 from which da Ponte shaped his libretto for Mozart's *Don Giovanni*, the version Bennett uses

*Although Bennett refers to 'sixteenth-century Spain', Goossens, in his Foreword to the published score, describes their hero as 'born in the seventeenth century'.

196

tells a very different story. His Don is a profligate and a murderer who drives women to murder and suicide; he devotes his life and his fortune to the quest for the ideal woman and so remains for author and composer a sympathetic hero. 'He is not a sensualist; he is an idealist. He is passionately hungry for perfection and with him, the end justifies the means. As for his more startling deeds, it is to be noted that he did not transgress the codes of his age.'[1]

Don Juan provided a colourful setting and a rich profusion of dramatic incident. Eugene never comments on the psychological implications of the story and the hero's profligacy; it must have salved his Catholic conscience that Don Juan's soul is finally saved through the sacrifice of a pure woman. As with *Judith*, he considered the music as subsidiary to the text. He stressed that his objects were to prove that opera could be sung intelligently in English, even to the accompaniment of a large orchestra and that it was not necessary for an opera to have 'opportunities for vocal exhibition (arias, scenas etc.) without which its musical and dramatic appeal and its capacity for evoking "audience enthusiasm" cease to exist.'

Eugene was on holiday at Strete in Devon, Bennett in Cornwall; from adjacent counties they kept up a daily correspondence. Every second day the postman would bring Eugene the latest instalment of words which he would return with suggestions for alterations when necessary. He had learnt from the experience of *Judith* and wanted in the new work to develop character and situation without holding up the dramatic flow of the action. He found Bennett very responsive to his ideas.

Everything was done by letter; Eugene returned to America in August 1929 and Bennett, who was by this time seriously ill wrote to him there: 'I now enclose the final form of Act One. There has been some delay, but I have been much put about, especially by dental troubles. I fully understand that in the libretto of an opera a certain amount of literary elegance and subtlety must be sacrificed to musical elegance and interest, so that is quite all right. I have embodied practically all your suggestions.'[2]

Bennett tried to use his influence with Colonel Blois to secure a revival of *Judith* at Covent Garden and a production for the new opera. John Barbirolli, now appointed chief conductor to the reformed Covent Garden Opera Company, was not kindly disposed towards the Goossens family. He was no longer employing Eugene II as a touring conductor and considered Eugene III, with his superior experience and credentials, as a potential threat to his own status. Bennett died at the beginning of 1931, disappointed that there was no production in view for his finished libretto. *Don Juan* had to wait until the Coronation Season of 1937 when Beecham was once more in control.

Eugene chronicles the gestation of the opera in his draft for a second volume of memoirs, which gives valuable insight into his creative processes. He resumed work on the score after his first vacation from Cincinnati in the summer of 1932. After a rest cure in Marienbad and a brief three weeks in London, he completed the third act in six weeks, spent in a wooden summer house on Nantucket Island.

> The atmosphere of gaming, duels, seduction and poison of this act was in sharp contrast to that of the clean wind-swept shores of Nantucket. So, contrary to my custom of writing always in the clear light of morning, I composed mostly at night to the accompaniment of waves and gale, of distant murmur of surf, with the oil lamp casting its shadows on the log walls of my room. I am infinitely susceptible to environment, being incapable of immediate adjustment to the atmosphere of new surroundings – pleasant or otherwise; for this reason the world has probably been spared some excessively tedious music. Confronted by powerful literary images, such as those of Bennett's third act, I became oblivious of environment, and sixteenth-century Spain took possession of a New England world.[3]

In February 1933 Eugene was taken seriously ill and despite three months' recuperation on the shores of Lake Ontario, near to the familiar sights of Rochester, found himself unable to continue with composition. 'The disturbing, disquieting inability to summon up a musical conception equal to Bennett's dramatic finale intensified a nervous disorder which I realised could only be cured by an expert. So I called him from Chicago in the shape of Percival Bailey, a neurologist of repute. He achieved in a month what others had failed to bring about in the course of over a year, and I forthwith embarked on an era of renewed mental vigour and physical recuperation.'

By the end of January 1935 he was able to write: 'Act IV of *Don Juan* is being photostated. It is now just as I want it. My relief at the realisation that I was not after all doomed to a lifetime of non-creativeness can be imagined. Despairing of regaining any creative energy, I had actually sought another hand – unsuccessfully, fortunately – to undertake the writing of the last act. I fervently thanked God for having regained my powers; three weeks intensive labour sufficed to put down the thoughts that had eluded me: Don Juan went to his mysterious fate in the Cathedral to the chanting of Carmelite nuns whose words echoed my own deepest thoughts.'

He rented his friend William Murdoch's house in St John's Wood and spent a quiet summer in London, correcting the final proofs of *Don Juan*, which was to be published by Chesters. 'Proof correcting, whether musical or literary, can be recommended as an absorbing rest cure. The quiet sense of satisfaction derived from grooming one's brainchild for its first public appearance is only equalled by the sense of permanence – spurious or otherwise – at the sight of usually undecipherable MS transferred to cold black print.'

It was not until two years later in 1937 that the production was finally under way at Covent Garden.

With bitter memories of the ill-prepared *Judith* I arrived expecting to find history repeating itself in the case of my bigger and better opera. With five weeks still to go before the premiere, I was pleasantly surprised to find a large cast, headed by Lawrence Tibbett, already note-perfect in its work, due largely to the expert playing and coaching of the repetiteur George Reeves. I was impressed by the galvanic influence of Tibbett on his fellow artists. A perfectionist in his own work, he had insisted on equal precision in the supporting cast. His dynamic virility was also a good corrective to the sound but somnolent direction of André, the Stockholm Opera House producer, who had been imported for the occasion and tended to convey a somewhat patriarchal character to the proceedings.

Aubrey Hammond, jovial and sensitive artist, had designed scenes for the four acts which easily put in the shade every previous scenic illusion at Covent Garden. The church interior of the last act was the epitome of all gloomy Spanish cathedrals. When the first night audience saw an interminable nave apparently stretching beyond the back wall of the great stage and into the street, it gasped

199

with wonderment. Other things stirred as well – the handsome Don Juan wooing, duelling and seducing his way through Bennett's adaptation of Dumas' play as though profligacy and murder were everyday matters of no moment whatsoever to him.

The huge cast and perfectly functioning orchestra contributing their expertness to make my subtlest musical expression sound better than I ever hope to hear it again. There were enthusiastic and prolonged ovations at the close – one particularly telling 'Bravo' I recall emanating from my proud father, who had attended almost every rehearsal and out of the fund of his own past experience in the world of operatic conducting had given many a helpful suggestion to better the final product.

The Goossens family was there in force: Marie and Léon in the orchestra, Sidonie in the wings playing the harp for Don Juan's Serenade, Annie in the audience seated with Jansi and Leslie. Eugene's one regret was that Bennett had not lived to enjoy the occasion. Beecham, who was enthusiastic about the work, had grudged nothing that could ensure a smooth premiere. 'Once again he had fearlessly championed my cause, as in those far away days of 1916, when – a youth of twenty-two – I had walked from a seat in the Queen's Hall orchestra right into a conductor's post with his company.'

The press was sharply divided next morning into a group headed by Newman and Capell who, with some reservations, praised the work and those who had been antagonised by Bennett's treatment of the subject.

Newman warned his readers:

Of set tunes there are not many but of fine music always apt to the dramatic occasion and rich in appeal to the musical ear, there is any amount. Goossens' object was not to foist standard lyrical forms on a drama that could under no circumstances take them, but to heighten that drama by musical means. Goossens' musical idiom looks more complex on paper than it sounds in performance; the thinking is orchestral not pianistic, and heard with the orchestra with each note in its proper wash of colour and its proper perspective, the music presents no difficulty whatever, even I should imagine, to the ordinary listener. *Don Juan* seems to me the best thing that English opera has so far produced – the best in itself, musically, and the most dramatic and stageworthy; the third act in particular is as good as anything known to me in the opera of recent years.[4]

Constant Lambert, who wrote for *The Referee*, admitted that he was being called a 'Cad Critic' but did not let his friendship with Eugene influence his professional judgement.

> Goossens' opera *Don Juan de Mañara* has one quality which distinguishes it from any other opera – you can hear every word. Considering that a large modern orchestra is used, the utmost praise is due to the composer for so skilfully preserving the balance between stage and orchestra pit. There is only one thing wrong with this happy state of affairs. None of the words are worth listening to.
>
> Arnold Bennett was on the face of it just the wrong calibre of writer to employ as a librettist. Either you want a writer whose words have poetic and musical value in themselves like Maeterlinck, Yeats or Synge, or else you want a good old hack who can turn out words of a suitable quality to order. Words which you can cut, repeat, rearrange, drown with the brass and generally subordinate to your musical plan. Arnold Bennett was neither. He had little or no appreciation of the music of words, and he was too eminent to be a hack.
>
> It is bad enough in an opera like *Pelléas* to feel that the composer is holding himself in leash all the while so that the libretto may come over, but the lines we hear are at least worth listening to as such. It is far more irritating in *Don Juan* to hear the composer breaking off some promising Spanish tune in order to let us hear Bennett's workmanlike but pedestrian dialogue.

Lambert dismisses Eugene as having written 'highly skilled and elegant background music'.[5]

His colleague on the *Morning Post* was more positive. 'The wonderfully ingenious score is remarkable for its clarity and at its best for a commendable directness and incisiveness not often found in English opera. Personally, I regret the almost continuous subservience of the voices to the orchestra, to which practically everything of musical interest is allotted. There are notable exceptions in Don Juan's serenade and Donna Inez's fan song and these together with the truly beautiful melody associated with Paquita and the charming Intermezzo before the last act were the undoubted successes of the evening.'[6]

There was a general consensus of praise for the sets and the singers, particularly Lawrence Tibbett in the title role. He looked as if he had stepped out of a Velázquez portrait, although *The Stage* found his love-making 'laborious rather than ardent'. Dennis Noble, as the wronged brother Don José, was singled out, together with Marie Burke, stepping up from musical comedy, as Doña Paquita. But if Eugene's aim was to write a contemporary opera which would be a popular success he had failed.

Eugene's strengths and weaknesses as an opera composer were excellently assessed in the *Evening Standard*:

> Mr Eugene Goossens is a composer of such penetrating insight and intellectual alertness that everything he writes has a lucid and vivid distinction which always delights the head if it never troubles the heart. Indeed it is a little melancholy to reflect on the high price we have had to pay for our modern music. We have sacrificed emotion for intellect and given the power to enchant in exchange for the power to astonish.
>
> The new Goossens opera, performed in magnificent style has certainly the power to astonish – by its masterly orchestration, by its urgent movement and the crisp vitalising of words by the inevitable appropriate note. Yet one's chief memory of this score is of a rather sterile brilliance. It has hints now and then of romantic mystery, it has harsh and opulent colouring, and then, notably in Act II, the composer is almost trapped, off his guard into writing a tune.
>
> But is this music of the kind to grapple to one's soul and nourish one's heart on? Does it fire and feed the imagination? Would we care greatly if we never heard a note of it again? This Juan is as brilliant and heartless as the music Mr Goossens has written for him.[7]

Don Juan de Mañara has never been produced on stage since those two performances at Covent Garden. Eugene was so disillusioned by its rejection in London that he decided his spiritual home from now on lay in America.

'Mr Eugene Goossens, now conductor of the Cincinnati Symphony Orchestra, said the other day he would be glad to get back to America,' reported Atticus of the *Sunday Times*. 'In his *Don Juan* he refused to rewrite Wagner, put aside all tendency towards Verdi-Gurdy and would not ape either Puccini or the Russians. When the critics found that there were no tunes to whistle, no arias to hum and no Wagnerian climaxes to recognise, they were angry. "Conductor's music!" they said scornfully, which is the worst thing that can be said about a new composition. "Take me back to where they understand," muttered Goossens. "Take me back to Cincinnati." '8

Eugene hoped that *Don Juan* might establish itself in the repertoire of the Metropolitan Opera House in New York. Much to his disappointment, the new administrator, Edward Johnson, had other ideas as Eugene explained to his father at the beginning of December 1937.

> Johnson's excuse is that the Metropolitan had no money left which is obviously untrue. He also said that it was necessary to perform American works this season in the vernacular. The only two he was able to find were a) a specimen entitled *Amelia goes to the Ball* by a young gentleman born in Italy [Gian Carlo Menotti] and sponsored by Riccordi and b) Walter Damrosch's *The Man without a Country*. Of these two exhibits, the first is so light that I doubt very much whether it will carry across the wide spaces of the Metropolitan and the second is so devastatingly boring that nobody will cross the road to hear it. It therefore follows that even if the Met had to have new scenery made for my work and engage a whole batch of new singers, they couldn't conceivably lose more money over mounting it than they will automatically do in the case of the two so-called American works.
>
> I am afraid it will be a long time before I embark on another opera. One spends two or three years writing them and waits another three to have them performed. The number of performances amounts to two or three at the most. And so what's the good?9

Eugene blamed Johnson's refusal to stage *Don Juan* on 'the feud between Tibbett and Johnson'; Johnson's increasing dissatisfaction with Tibbett had been caused by a deterioration in his performance rather than any personal enmity. Considering Eugene's vast experience as an operatic conductor, it is difficult to justify both Gatti-Casazza's and Johnson's failure to engage him to conduct at the Met. The problem lay in operatic politics and Eugene's unsatisfactory relations with his manager Arthur Judson.10

In 1953 he was to sound out 'Dear friend Webster' as to the possibility of a revival of *Don Juan de Mañara* which he

203

offered to conduct, produce (if necessary) and rehearse for a nominal figure.[11] Webster replied: 'We are in policy committed to producing works by English composers but in interpreting this policy we in fact turn all our attention to new works.' As far as Webster was concerned, the 1937 premiere of *Don Juan de Mañara* counted as two productions at Covent Garden, the first and the last!

If Eugene had accepted the offer of Musical Director at Covent Garden in 1946 no doubt both *Judith* and *Don Juan* would have entered the repertoire. Guaranteed productions might also have provided him with the incentive to explore the operatic medium in partnership with other librettists, using the more extended vocal lines he was to develop in *The Apocalypse*. Amongst his papers at his death was the unfinished score of a comic opera based on Goldoni's play *The Crafty Widow*, a tantalising glimpse of what his operatic development might have been.

14

Inspirational and Talented Guidance (Cincinnati II)

Eugene only conducted once in London during the summer of 1935, a studio concert for the BBC in a refreshingly eclectic programme of Handel, Bruckner, Vaughan Williams, Ravel, Debussy's *En blanc et noir* orchestrated by Goossens and Wagner's *Chorus of the Gibichungs* also transcribed by Goossens. 'At last Zenny conducts again in London,' his father wrote in his diary on 14th June 1935. 'He has developed a very broad beat.' Previously he had always been noted for the precision of his beat; the alteration might well have been due to a recommendation to relax his arm after his crippling attack of neuritis the previous year.

Considering his international reputation, it is surprising that Eugene was not given more BBC engagements during his annual visits to England. The higher echelons of the Corporation were riddled with Machiavellian intrigue; Adrian Boult's suggestion that Eugene should be given a public concert with the Symphony Orchestra the following year was overridden by Roger Eckersley. Kenneth Wright (Assistant Director of Music) reported back to Eckersley (Assistant Controller of Programmes): 'I am afraid that Mr Goossens has refused any studio engagements. Public concerts are the least he will consider. He would probably like a Goossens festival of Goossens music in chronological order, conducted by Goossens with an oboe concerto played by Goossens and a new work for two harps played by the Goossens sisters. This I am afraid is more than we can compete with at present!'[1]

To a younger generation, Goossens was a glamorous and almost legendary figure. Felix Aprahamian was thrilled to be granted his first celebrity interview at the age of seventeen and found him friendly and unpompous. 'Goossens has always been considered a pioneer,' he wrote in the *Musical Times*, 'so it was not surprising to hear him refer disparagingly to the conservatism of our London programmes. If novelties of exceptional merit were becoming scarce, why was so much existing orchestral music being shelved?'[2]

Eugene had already announced to his father his plans to incorporate performances of opera in the next season's programme in Cincinnati as was the pattern in Philadelphia and Cleveland. 'The whole public of America is like a spoiled child crying for something – it knows not what, and so the element of novelty has to be introduced into the make-up of the orchestra seasons. We have a magnificent hall in which to give opera, Music Hall, and a fine orchestra to play it. I think the trustees should be able to recover some of their lost dollars. Experienced and well-known singers would be engaged for the principal roles and a chorus and small parts would be allotted to local singers. Naturally I shall have supreme artistic control over the whole affair.'[3]

One fact he had not discovered in his research for the autobiography on which he was intermittently working; his grandparents, Aynsley and Harriet Cook had sung opera for a week in Cincinnati from 27th November to 2nd December 1871. They appeared at Pike's Opera House on tour with the Parepa–Rosa Company.

Eugene was elated by the success of his opening venture:

Although I shouldn't say so, it is safe to say that probably never in its long history has *Valkyrie* received such an orchestral performance. We had a hundred men in the pit including the Wagner tubas and thanks to their splendid virtuosity not a note dropped by the wayside in either evening. None of the old bubbling horns, scratching strings and bleating woodwinds which one usually associates with operatic performances! The singers were very expert in their parts too; all of them being experienced in the routine of German opera, especially artists like Stückgold and Althouse, the work on the stage was very smooth.

I had one final flare-up with the producer at the dress rehearsal and lost my temper in full view of all the stage, much to the benefit of the lookers-on, and ultimately to Mr Korst himself. He is the type of pig-headed German who tries at times to impose his will on the production, but without any success whatever. It is not that he is incompetent, but that occasionally he has a faculty of rubbing everyone up the wrong way and conveying an illusion of what Tommy Beecham used to call 'simulated activity'. So, after the fire scene had gone badly, I decided to crack down on him once and for all and did so with a vengeance with the result that now he eats out of my hand.

Seventy-six hundred people attended both performances which so astonished the management that they have not yet got over the shock.[4]

His second success was with *Tannhäuser*, the first performance in English in America of the 'Paris version'. It was an appropriate choice since his grandfather had conducted the first English performance of the opera in England in 1892.

> I find in *Tannhäuser* my ideal vehicle. Of course there was a nostalgia of my early youth ever present to serve as inspiration. Thoughts and memories of the countless rehearsals and performances under your baton at which I had assisted in different towns in England with the Rosa Company were ever present and I determined that this performance should atone for all the disabilities and shortcomings under which you had to labour in the old days. In other words it was a tribute to my teacher without whose guidance and unselfishness and hard work none of these things could today have been possible. From all of which you will infer that you Dad, were the inspiration of the performance and I think you would have been proud of the results.[5]

There were equally memorable performances of *Tristan* and *Mastersingers*, justifying Eugene's choice of an inaugural season of Wagner for a city where fifty per cent of the population were of German origin. German churches and German beer cellars flourish in the downtown area around Music Hall which is still called 'Over the Rhine'. The following season he widened the repertoire to introduce *Carmen*, *Tosca*, *Figaro* and *Salome*. Despite their popularity, the Trustees decided that opera was too expensive and that the money was better spent on an annual visit of Colonel de Basil's Ballet Russe. Although Eugene's role as operatic supremo had brought him greater artistic fulfilment, he enjoyed reviving memories of the Diaghilev days with Danilova, Toumanova, Massine and Lichine. An extra bonus for Eugene and Jansi was watching their adored daughter, Donie, make her stage debut as the little girl in *La Boutique Fantasque* in April 1937.

His relationship with his eldest daughter Anne had deteriorated during a further year that she had spent in Cincinnati. In the spring of 1936 he wrote a dispassionate analysis to Boonie of their daughter's problems and character, telling her of his decision that she should return to Europe to complete her education:

As you know, Anne is of the three eldest girls my favourite and I have every sympathy with the strange workings of her mind and body brought about by, alas, a too unsettled childhood. In spite of the fact that she has just turned fifteen, she has the physical and mental development of a girl of at least eighteen. She is, as you know, at one of the two really smart and 'social' schools in the city, nevertheless she complains that the work is too hard for her and the type of girl with whom she mixes too unsympathetic to bring her the happiness in her environment she desires. I am the last person to be swayed by the desires and whims of mere children. But I do not want it held against me in future years that my obstinacy in keeping her in an uncongenial environment was the means of souring and generally adversely affecting her disposition. Anne does not conceal her feelings easily and after a long day rehearsing, I am in no mood when I return to the house to cope with the aftermath of Anne's unpleasant episodes at school, or otherwise continued dissatisfaction. She has a very snobbish attitude towards Bohemians and musical people generally, which is due largely to the fact that she does not speak their language, musically or in any other way. So all in all, I think you will agree with me it is wiser that she return to England and finish her education at a school in London. Anne is now definitely a young woman and needs girls considerably older than herself as her associates. Any other situation will ruin both her character and her disposition.

She is a grand character and a beautiful girl with a real capacity for loyalty and affection and naturally I shall miss her dreadfully when it comes to returning to America without her. She has many natural gifts, chief of which is her talent for graceful movement and dramatic expression and, in my opinion, her future will lie in the theatre. She is ultra-sophisticated and for her age, has tremendous poise and strength of character. Jansi has been marvellous with her and she and Anne get on well together. At the same time, Anne is apt to think that because of Jansi's comparative youth (in spite of the fact that she is after all her stepmother and a woman of the world) Anne is entitled to a measure of the freedom that Jansi enjoys as my wife.

Boonie, who had enjoyed a similar freedom when she had been married to Eugene, would understand his tolerant attitude towards his wife's friendships with other men and the reciprocal latitude he expected to enjoy. The situation must have been very confusing to a precocious fifteen-year-old, trying to find a way through the moral maze of the adult world.

In the summer of 1936 Eugene returned to the Hollywood Bowl for the first time in seven years. He hated to disappoint his parents by curtailing his stay in England but he explained to them 'the necessity of rebuilding some of the bridges which my illness of three years ago had burned behind me. There still seems to prevail a slight idea in certain circles over here that my long stay in Cincinnati is an enforced one, due to my inability to accept other engagements on the grounds either of health or of contract. I have been too long buried here in the eyes of the rest of America and an engagement such as the Bowl is the best means of counteracting any propaganda which my enemies may have been encouraging. My associates will be worthy ones, people like Klemperer and Monteux.'[6]

His decision was certainly vindicated by the success of his concerts both in Hollywood and San Francisco. Critic Carl Bronson hailed him as 'the great English-American conductor. A very large audience greeted an old friend and favourite director in Eugene Goossens and the orchestra stood up and flourished its trumpets.'[7] 'Goossens has changed his baton technique,' commented the critic Isabel Morse Jones, 'relaxed his stick tension somewhat and conducts now with a broader stroke, often ending his beat close to the floor. His indications seem easy for the orchestra to follow and there is an emotional quality in his playing that reaches an audience at once.' (It is interesting to note that at this stage in his career there is no suggestion of his beat being too broad to follow or his interpretations lacking in emotional warmth.)

Donie and Nanny had joined them in Santa Monica in a luxurious rented house complete with automobile, cook and chauffeur. Donie remembers as a four-year-old the excitement of going to a rehearsal at the Hollywood Bowl. 'The acoustics were marvellous; you could hear everything that was happening on stage from the very back of the auditorium but someone told me there were rattle snakes out there which made me frightened. When I was taken to my first concert I got up and ran down the aisle and said "That's my daddy!" I hope he didn't hear.'[8]

Eugene looked forward to a quiet family holiday in the Californian sunshine. He told his parents he planned 'to flop and take life easy for a while. It isn't the concerts that are tiring, it's the incidentals – rehearsals, parties, travelling etc. Jansi is invaluable on these trips and does all the packing, valeting, changing and what not herself. I'd be lost without her.'[9] To his parents he still presented his marriage to Jansi as an ideal relationship and she continued to add affectionate postscripts to his letters.

The only blot on the landscape was that Tom Hill, his bootmaker in Knightsbridge, had sent his new white suede shoes to Cincinnati instead of to the Hollywood Hotel. Nevertheless the snapshots he sent home must have been appropriate to his celebrity status. 'I am glad to think that I look like a millionaire Mum darling; I wish I felt like one. It is amazing what a panama hat will do.'[10]

There were however penalties to fame:

It is becoming increasingly difficult to fight off the importunities of people who are beginning to discover that we are still in California. Certain people cannot be ignored but the majority of them can and are. Next week we shall probably be lunching or dining with Charlie Chaplin. Sidonie had an appointment to visit Shirley Temple yesterday, but at the last minute Shirley was unable to see her owing to having caught a cold. Sidonie being a philosopher was not disappointed. I am going to take her on Monday to see Mickey Mouse's films being made at the Walt Disney Studio.[11]

We've already seen a lot of the new film stars and spent a short time with Mamoulian at United Artists Studio watching him direct a film featuring Ida Lupino, who is the daughter of the celebrated Stanley Lupino, the English comedian. The amount of money wasted in these studios is something fantastic. Everybody gets fabulous fees and nobody seems to care how much money is wasted.[12]

(Rouben Mamoulian, his old colleague from Rochester, was now a successful film director and producer.)

Eugene was not seduced by the reputed fortunes that musicians could earn in the movie world. 'Rumour has it that last week Alf Brain, by dint of playing night and day, made $850 in salary for his week's work in a movie studio. This is equivalent to £175. He was up all night most nights. The fees paid here in the studios are preposterous and it's a case of get-rich-quick while you can. Brain is only here for his holidays as he plays regularly at Cleveland.'[13]

He had long arguments about the future of the films with another English instrumentalist resident in Hollywood, Warwick Evans who had been the cellist of the London String Quartet. Their friendship dated back to 1912 when they had first played together in the Queen's Hall Orchestra.

Arguing with Warwick Evans resembles trying to shout down a fog-horn. He like all other musicians employed in the studios is a believer in recording symphonies on the films with the orchestra filmed at the same time and he maintains that eventually music will come to this with a minimum of flesh-and-blood musicians and flesh-and-blood concerts for the audiences of the world to patronise. In other words, symphony music is ultimately going to be absorbed by the films. Unfortunately, one or two so-called conductors in this country are lending a certain truth to this illusion by connecting their names with the different film studios and threatening to make 'sound' films. All this proves what an isolated point of view people are apt to acquire when they live within this part of the country, thousands of miles from anywhere and surrounded by all the glamour of movie-making.[14]

(Eugene was to have the opportunity of pursuing this argument publicly in Cincinnati when he was asked to review the film of *Fantasia* of which he did not approve.)

He was trying to finish the scoring of *Don Juan* and did not find the physical or intellectual climate of California conducive to musical inspiration. 'It's still raw West. Imagine Schoenberg – of all people – making a home here and waiting for pupils! Driven out of his own country and for long the leader of contemporary thought in Europe. What can he hope to find here in the way of culture and a livelihood?? I saw him recently and a short conversation with him made me realise how utterly out of place he is here! This place has

211

only its superb climate to recommend it. The rest is a mixture of fake Spanish houses, movie stars – and froth. The Los Angeles Philharmonic hasn't even raised sufficient money for its coming season. Klemperer is somewhat perturbed (another Hitler victim!). In comparison to LA, Cincinnati is a cultural centre comparable with London or Paris!!'[15]

Thanks to the success of the opera and ballet performances in Cincinnati, the popularity of the orchestra had increased and the number of subscribers to their concert series had risen. Eugene had been able to persuade the President of the Fine Arts Association to transfer all the concerts back to the orchestra's legitimate home, from the autumn of 1936. Music Hall, which had superb acoustics and a beautiful interior, was large enough to hold Shreiner's three-ring circus.

An old friend engaged as a soloist for the 1936 – 37 season was Percy Grainger, who played Saint-Saëns' Concerto no. 2 in G minor and the Delius Piano Concerto. The programme also included Grainger's *Passacaglia* on an old English folk tune 'Green Bushes' (March 1937).

Eugene admired Percy's 'vigorous yet sensitive piano-playing' and invited him back to Cincinnati, with his statuesque Swedish wife Ella, in November 1940. The second half of the concert was devoted entirely to Grainger's own compositions. His orchestral suite *In a Nutshell* required an unusual range of percussion instruments: 'The Wooden Marimba, Steel Marimba (Vibraphone or Vibraharp) Xylophone and Glockenspiel parts are not awkward for the symphony percussionists to play,' explained Percy to Eugene. 'But the Staff Bells part is, and I have made up my mind to always let Ella play it (she knows it by heart, so it is easy for her to make the distance between the big bells as she is not looking at music at the same time), or to leave out the Staff Bells altogether. If there is Union objection, neither she nor I will mind in the least leaving them out!'[16]

Eugene could not persuade the Union to give Ella permission to play until the work was repeated on the Graingers' third visit in November 1942. 'Where's Ella?' Eugene asked when he went to the station to meet them. Percy replied, glancing down the platform, 'She's coming right along with the Staff Bells.' 'And there she was,' recalled Eugene, 'with the weighty impedimenta in a sack slung over her shoulder.'[17]

One of the most memorable concerts Eugene conducted in Cincinnati was with another pianist composer. At the end of October 1937, Rachmaninov returned to the platform of Music Hall for the first time since 1910. Eugene reported: 'Rachmaninov was in great form and played the first Beethoven Concerto as though it had been written yesterday; in other words, he recreated it anew in an entirely wonderful manner. Needless to say the orchestra reacted to his work and accompanied him beautifully. He had never played this concerto before and was consequently somewhat tense about it; he even kept a copy on the piano in case he should suffer a lapse of memory, which fortunately he didn't. He was so delighted with the way it went that when the time came to play his Paganini Variations, he rollicked through these at such a fantastic pace that it was as much as we could do to keep pace with him. It is said there were 3,700 people at each performance.'[18]

Eugene was now growing increasingly anxious about the political situation in Europe. As well as its large German population, Cincinnati has a well-established Jewish community. The friction between them and Nazi sympathisers was evident when Hitler annexed Austria. Ironically both factions were catered for in the concert programme for that day which included Bloch's *Schelomo*, Rhapsody for Cello and Orchestra on Hebrew themes with Felix Salmond as soloist and Strauss' Teutonic folk hero *Till Eulenspiegel*.

'All the Jews in the orchestra played *Schelomo* as though it were their swan-song, the Germans meantime preserving rather glum set looks. But when it came to *Till*, the Germans let go with a vengeance and gave a virtuoso performance such as probably has never been equalled by any orchestra. Both numbers were received with proportionate enthusiasm by a very mixed audience. Both scored an ovation, but one could easily tell that in both cases it arose from rather racial sources.'[19]

After seven years in Cincinnati Eugene felt that he had to make a determined effort to improve his status. He had renegotiated his contract to allow him to accept autumn engagements in England and a greater number of guest engagements during the 1937 – 38 season in America. In April, he broke the news to his parents that the annual summer holiday he so much enjoyed in England would be interrupted.

> You will be surprised to hear that I have been offered engagements in Philadelphia, Chicago, Portland and the Hollywood Bowl from the period of the middle of July to the middle of August. This offer came from Judson, my manager in New York. Quite frankly I am in no position to refuse this available series of dates. The publicity value is something which cannot be overestimated. The psychological moment has arrived when I have got to take every worthwhile and dignified engagement possible over here in order to build towards a possible change in 1939 for another city.
>   With the glut of alien conductors flooding this country, particularly the Jews, not even the conductor of a big permanent symphony orchestra is in a position to turn down summer engagements.[20]

He was still convinced that Boston would grow tired of Koussevitzky and that the summons would at last come for him to replace him.

He realised that he also had to keep his name before the public in England but was not very sanguine as to the opportunities open to him. The news that Beecham was increasingly incapacitated through rheumatism or gout caused him to reflect to his father: 'With TB out of the picture, the BBC will automatically absorb all musical activity in England and leave it an arid desert so far as new personalities are concerned. It seems unlikely Boult would impair his position by inviting any serious prima donna conductor to head his orchestra except, of course, the inevitable Toscanini. Outside the BBC there are no musical powers which can seriously affect the situation in England for the better, for Wood has a limited public and Harty is, it seems, out of the running. Where would I fit into this picture, unless the directors of the Philharmonic, in Beecham's absence, elected to hand me that particular orchestra with full powers to do as I pleased with it? Short of this, nothing would induce me to change my professional place of residence.'[21]

He was offered a Philharmonic Society concert but was disconcerted by the programme they required. He expressed his views in no uncertain terms to his agents Ibbs & Tillett:

> I can't quite frankly see the point of the Royal Philharmonic Society

being so anxious to have me conduct after an absence of fifteen years a programme the main feature of which is Tchaikovsky's *Pathétique* Symphony. London has been surfeited with performances and the versions which other conductors have given at the Queen's Hall probably met with the approval of the London public to a far greater extent than the version devoid of sentimentality and showmanship which *I'd* be likely to give.

It is virtually understood that a program conducted by a certain conductor represents the favourite choice of that conductor. The London public would therefore be justified in expressing some astonishment that I, who have been associated for so long with the unhackneyed in music, should choose to make my reappearance with the one work which is most calculated to make an appeal to the gallery. It also seems to me that much though I enjoy having my brother Léon on the same platform in the capacity of soloist, my oboe concerto has been done to death in London.[22]

The eventual compromise did include the oboe concerto but also Debussy's *La Mer* and Ravel's orchestration of Mussorgsky's *Pictures at an Exhibition*. Ernest Newman was favourably impressed: 'Eugene Goossens treated us to some conducting that was completely without fuss or showmanship but that always got to the root of the matter in hand. The result was that we could sit back and give ourselves up delightedly to what, after all, ought to be the main business of the listener at a concert – seeing the workings of the composer's mind and hearing him speak for himself. Léon Goossens lived up to the full height of his reputation in his playing of the solo part in his brother's charmingly exotic oboe concerto of 1929.'[23]

The only opera his agents could arrange for him was *Madam Butterfly* with the Covent Garden English Opera Company and a studio performance of *Judith* for the BBC. There were concerts in Oxford, Liverpool, Manchester and Leeds where Léon played the concerto written for him by Francesco Ticciati. He at last conducted the BBC Symphony Orchestra in public, in the Queen's Hall on 9th November. Stravinsky's *Rite of Spring* was the highlight of the programme as it always was when he conducted it. Richard Capell asked in the *Daily Telegraph*: 'Has the famous *Rite* been better played? Never, we should say.'[24]

The *Times* welcomed him after his many years absence in America: 'The catholicity of his taste, the serious purpose behind his unsensational interpretations, the clarity of the performance he obtained from the orchestra indicate the measure of Cincinnati's gain and London's loss.'[25]

Two other musical events gave him much nostalgic pleasure: conducting the hundredth concert on 10th May 1938 of the Chelsea Music Club which he had helped to found in 1923 and the end of term concert on 10th June at the Royal College of Music which brought back memories of his conducting debut there in 1912.

As always when Eugene and Jansi visited England there were many family parties and reunions. They introduced Mum and Dad to the delights of poker and laughed loudly and boisterously when they went to the pictures to see the Marx Brothers. L'Escargot Bienvenue was now the favourite Soho restaurant for birthday lunches or suppers. Here they celebrated Zenny's 45th birthday. 'Enjoyed Filet saignant *and glasses* of burgundy,' noted Dad. 'Lee revelled in his dozen escargots. Jansi chose Aqua pura while Mum and Leslie joined me in the stronger beverages. Poor Zen, as usual, little to eat and nothing to drink.' He was still observing his strict no smoking, no drinking regime and as a result was enjoying much better health.

They again stayed in Walton's house in South Eaton Place for five guineas a week. He sent them a picture postcard from Ravello where he was staying with Alice Wimborne at the Villa Cimbrone, trying to finish the Violin Concerto. 'The only snag about letting you the house is that I don't see you, but there it is – one can't have everything!'

The Goossens family presented a very glamorous image to the world, an image that Eugene's eldest daughter Anne was finding it increasingly difficult to live up to. 'The main topic of conversation between the Goossens was music; they created a world of their own and a language of their own. I didn't feel left out of it, I felt totally overawed by it. I felt very humble, a person of no consequence. I could never be as beautiful or as talented as they were. They were people who lived on Mount Olympus and I was just an ordinary mortal right down at the bottom. Many children of great artists have the same problem of becoming a person in their own right.'[26]

Eugene thought that Anne had talent as an actress and

dancer. He was delighted when she was accepted at RADA for the autumn of 1937 and arranged for her to live with Viola Tree.

> My father came to see our final performance. I played Portia and he was very pleased. He tried to help me by sending me to see his friends. I went to see Richard Tauber for a film interview who made me raise my skirts well above my knee. Then he arranged for me to see Basil Dean. I went in my best dress with my heart in my mouth. He sat me down in a low chair with a spotlight on my face and asked me to read a script. I was paralysed. A great artist who is asked to see the child of a fellow artist, what is he going to say? It doesn't work like that.
>
> I was awed by my father, I was frightened of behaving like an idiot. I could never match my outward behaviour with my inner feelings. The theatre was a growing-up period for me. It wasn't my place; my voice was not strong enough; I wasn't extrovert enough.[27]

The annual visits to England were a great excitement for Anne's half sister Donie, so called to distinguish her from her adored Aunt Sidonie. 'I would go and stay with Nanny's people in Cobham in Surrey while my parents stayed in London. I always enjoyed visiting my grandparents in Finchley; they were wonderful people. Grandma was very big and Grandpa was very small.'[28]

Donie was also a favourite with her other grandparents in Rochester. Her proud father reported on his return to the USA: 'Donie is in Rochester and made her radio debut there by singing two short songs during a local 'Children's Hour' in aid of a charity. She made a sensation apparently and I had a telegram from my old manager of the orchestra offering to engage her for the regular symphony concerts to sing dramatic soprano roles!'[29] On a more serious level he was delighted by her musical talent. She had perfect pitch and had been learning the piano from the age of four; she took great delight in the two Piano Pieces her father wrote for her in 1938, 'Pikki's Lament' and 'Bonzo's Dance'. As soon as her hands were large enough, she would start harp lessons with Vojmir Attl, the orchestra's principal harpist.

The Goossens family reunion in the summer of 1939 was

overshadowed by the threat of war. Eugene tried later to recall the atmosphere of that fateful Sunday in September for the second volume of his autobiography:

At my father's house in North London, we listened to Mr Chamberlain sadly eating the words of his optimistic peace message of the previous year and announcing a state of war between England and Germany. The chill wailing of an air-raid siren broke the Sunday morning peace. With set features Father remarked grimly: 'They haven't wasted much time.' My mother, in her jocund manner reminiscent of the 1914 – 18 air-raids, said 'We'll play rummy.' There was a quiet heroism about this scene duplicated in so many English homes: the familiar room with the windows criss-crossed by bomb blast adhesive and draped by blackout curtains; the alert occupants, outwardly calm but inwardly cursing the bully responsible for coming horrors; the desultory conversation; an increasing tension of waiting and finally the anti-climax of the all clear.

Eugene's Promenade Concert at the Queen's Hall on 4th September was cancelled. Despite his concern for his parents whom he had been trying to persuade, unsuccessfully as ever, to seek safety across the Atlantic, he decided on an immediate return to America. The British immigration officer at Southampton stamped his passport and said: 'You're no earthly use to us over here. You're over military age, unfit for active service and you'd only be one more stay at home Londoner to feed. So you would probably be of much more use to America in your present job.'[30]

They sailed back on the *Aquitania*, the boat on which Eugene had first crossed the Atlantic in 1923. It was a traumatic voyage although children like Donie were too young to understand why: 'The ship was all blacked out. We all had to go on deck to be given gas masks. There was a hassle because there were not enough to go round so mothers grabbed them for their children. I had this thing pushed over my face. I still suffer from claustrophobia but was it because of the gas mask or would I have suffered from it anyway?'[31]

Back in Cincinnati at the opening orchestral rehearsal on 2nd October, Eugene announced that he had applied for his first American citizenship papers. 'I believe that at a time like this with all the world seemingly tumbling about our ears, a man owes his allegiance to the country to which he owes his livelihood, his safety and his happiness. I love the country of my birth but after sixteen years of an uninterrupted artistic career in America I cannot but admit that my heart and sympathies are always in this country.'[32]

He found it more difficult to justify his action to his father: 'I hope you will approve of the step I have taken. Disloyalty has nothing to do with it. It is a matter partly of necessity and partly of choice. However sorry I shall be to relinquish my British citizenship, I shall have few regrets from the professional point of view, for England has certainly not shown itself overanxious to retain my services for its own benefit. As for my English colleagues, they may be good friends in theory, but when they are put to the test, their friendship certainly does not extend to me professionally.'[33]

There was a five year interval between the first and the final papers. By April 1941, with America still refusing to come to the aid of Britain in her darkest hour, his British patriotism had overcome his professional pique. He told his parents: 'I have been compelled by the Union to take out my first papers as an American citizen, but I shall *never* take out my second.'[34] Despite reports to the contrary, he retained his British nationality; he was not a Belgian by birth and never completed his American naturalisation.

As the news from Europe grew more menacing, Eugene found the situation in neutral America increasingly disturbing. 'In a city so predominantly German as Cincinnati, signs of sympathy for Britain and the Allied cause were hard to come by. Not only was there a spirit of isolationism, typified by the "America First" buttons in so many coat lapels, but antagonism and hostility were to be met with on every hand. The orchestra contained many active Nazis, members of the German-American "Bund" who after Pearl Harbour engaged the special attention of the FBI. Their joy at every German victory was evident and unconfined. I was therefore impelled to announce to the orchestra that I expected backstage at Music Hall to be treated as strictly neutral ground.'[35]

Throughout the war, the first part of Eugene's long letters would be detailed analyses of American political developments and attitudes towards European hostilities, followed by the regular account of his musical successes and family news. In November 1939 one of his favourite artists played in Cincinnati for the first time in twenty years. 'Kreisler was terribly glad to see me again. He had his usual colossal success and played like a god. His performance of the slow movement of the Viotti concerto was the most moving thing I can recall for many years. He is the last, or almost the last of the Great Ones, for he has a dignity and a personality and a nobility of artistic vision which make him tower over everyone. On the Saturday night he had one of his sinus headaches, which steadily got worse as the evening progressed and he said as he got off the platform after the Paganini concerto that had the work lasted four minutes longer he would have collapsed with pain.'[36]

In December Eugene sent Jansi to Cleveland to hear their friend Heifetz give the world premiere of Walton's long awaited Violin Concerto. Walton wrote to thank her for her cable, letter and cuttings about the work's success and gave a depressing account of music in England being 'distinctly on the downgrade. The war is just too boring for words, so we won't talk about it anymore. Incidentally I am not driving an ambulance in France as the American press seem to think. They will be giving me a VC next! I am driving an ambulance somewhere in the Midlands.'[37]

On 12th April 1940 came the premiere of Eugene's First Symphony which he dedicated to the Cincinnati Symphony Orchestra. He explained in the programme notes why, having composed music in most recognisable forms, he had delayed so long before 'inflicting a symphony on a musically jaded world.'

Perhaps it was in my twenty-five years career as a conductor I had encountered a surfeit of immature pomposities labelled symphonies from the pens of youthful composers with a message. Perhaps it was also because until a very few years ago I felt little urge to project my sparse ideas through the medium of a form which for its successful manipulation calls for a cunning hand and real artistic maturity.

It has no 'message'. Neither is there any literary or other significance in it. Nor does it purport to illustrate any particular incidents of my life or times. It deals with the old abstractions, or what my master Stanford rather portentously used to refer to as 'The Eternal Verities'.

The orchestra showed their appreciation by presenting him with an embarrassingly heavy bronze plaque with which he staggered off the platform at the end of the evening. 'This evidence of deep loyalty and devotion is presented to Eugene Goossens under whose inspirational and talented guidance the world premiere of his Symphony no. 1 was rendered by the members of the Cincinnati Symphony Orchestra.' The symphony is a very attractive and approachable work and was a great success with the audience both in Boston and New York the following spring. (Barbirolli conducted it in New York and Eugene as a guest in Boston.) He resented press criticism that it was old-fashioned and lacked a distinctive signature of the composer: 'They would have liked me to have written something ultra-modern and full of modern clichés which would have enabled them to write that I was writing music which didn't come naturally to me.'[38]

The one positive outcome of his isolation from England was that he could spend the summers concentrating on composing. Their friends the Danas lent them a cottage in Bideford Pool, Maine where Eugene completed his Second String Quartet for Mrs Coolidge. He found it difficult to return to the medium of chamber music – it was sixteen years since he had composed the Second Violin Sonata – but he was pleased with the result. Many consider it to be his finest chamber work.

The four movements are closely interrelated by their thematic material producing a 'disciplined romanticism' and 'admirable contrast of moods'. (Robin Hull's retrospective assessment in 1954.) The slow movement bears an inscription from *Fears in Solitude* by Samuel Taylor Coleridge: 'There lives nor form nor feeling in my soul/Unborrowed from my country', expressing Eugene's helplessness in the face of Nazi tyranny and fears for his family's safety during the Blitz. The emotions are reflected by a poignant fantasy on 'Searching for Lambs'. For Eugene this folk song always brought back memories of his picaresque adventures with Philip Heseltine through a lost idyllic English countryside.

The work was first performed by the Coolidge Quartet in the Founder's Day Concert in the Library of Congress on 30th October 1940 and shared its success with a new quartet by Darius Milhaud. Neither composer was able to attend.

Eugene found the news from England increasingly worrying
and never gave up his efforts to get his parents to America.
Anne had remained in London to make her living in the
theatre throughout the war. He also offered hospitality to
either Léon or Marie's children. He was more callous about
Boonie's daughters, Jane and Julia, who were reported to be
in a chateau with her somewhere in France. They would be
two females too many in his household. He also drew the line
at Bumps' sister Kyla, a talented young pianist: 'There's no
sign of her arrival and you need have no fear that in the event
of her turning up we would even consider taking her in,' he
wrote to his parents. 'Don't forget that in America there are
very strong lines of demarcation between Jews and Gentiles
(not to mention Communists!!!). In Cincinnati all the Jews
live in their own quarter, however rich or poor they may be,
and I should be socially ostracised were I to attempt to introduce a strange Jewess into my own particular circle, relation or
no relation.'[39]
Like most musicians Eugene could claim, with justification,
that 'many of his best friends were Jews': Heifetz, Rubinstein,
Milhaud, Moiseiwitsch etc. He had no problems in giving and
receiving hospitality from the influential Jewish patrons of the
orchestra. When it came to the potential inconvenience of being
responsible for a young woman who was neither rich nor famous,
racial prejudice seems a poor excuse.
To everyone's surprise, on 16th August 1940 Jansi presented
Eugene with another daughter, Renée. He explained to his
parents that the pregnancy had been undetected as the doctors
had diagnosed a fibroid tumour!
As the months went by, Eugene found it increasingly difficult to concentrate on his saga of musical triumphs while his
family endured the horror of the Blitz:

The press censorship is permitting the publication of bombed
churches and streets. One of the first shocks I got was to see a
photo of my beloved Our Lady of Victories in Kensington a mere
shell. This used to be the church where I went every Sunday. And
so each day there followed one well-known place after another: the
Middle Temple, Burlington Arcade; St Giles', Cripplegate etc. etc.

Nothing could be more calculated to work me into a condition bordering on complete frenzy than these photographs. The more damage is done to London and the more these barbaric raids are prolonged, the more I feel it my duty to leave this country and be with you. Yet what would be the good of it? I could hardly bring you any solace and would probably bring you added anxiety, as my nervous system would not react any too well to the constant strain of bombardment to which you are being subjected. So I suppose I must indulge in a series of heroics through these letters in place of being put to the test like all you poor darlings are at present.

Jansi echoed his sentiments: 'As your son has told you we find it hard to write a letter these days, for any remarks of ours on the present trials and tribulations you are going through seem inadequate to the point of impudence and stupidity!'[40]

Nothing could bridge the gap between Cincinnati and Finchley but Eugene's letters brought a semblance of normality and were an essential means of preserving contact with his parents. 'America is an unhappy, restless country of strikes and factory sabotage thanks to the fine activities of the 5th column.'[41] He described the visit of his old friend Stravinsky to Cincinnati to conduct the whole concert in November including his new symphony:

I can't say that I relish this very much, because his conducting hasn't improved at all. His new symphony is in parts unnecessarily complicated. Conductors simply cannot afford in these days of more restricted rehearsal to lavish endless time on a needlessly difficult piece of music lasting four minutes (the scherzo). It has taken the composer himself five rehearsals to get the orchestra used to the devilish sequence of time measures. Quite frankly even after this result has been achieved, the effect on the listener is by no means convincing. It is a pity because the three other movements of the symphony are very beautiful and quite the best thing he has done up to date.

He has remarried and is a much happier man today than he was in the old days when I first knew him. Our relations remain as cordial as ever and there is really a strong bond of affection between us for we feel music and the attitude to music very similarly. He is unquestionably the most important figure in contemporary music.

He next reported Heifetz's performance of Walton's Violin
Concerto which had received its world premiere in Cleveland
the previous December. 'Willy's concerto is really an amazing
piece of work. I know no contemporary concerto which could
approach it for technical complexity and well-knit structure. It
also has great lyric beauty and Heifetz played it for all it's worth.
It is one of the hardest things I have ever had to accompany and
Jascha and I rehearsed it for five hours at a stretch. Willy is
to be congratulated on a real "tour de force", and I think it
proves him to be at all odds the most important figure in contemporary "Young England music".'

He was also trying to further the career of another young
English composer, Benjamin Britten. He had programmed *Variations on a Theme of Frank Bridge* in the previous concert season
on 4th March 1939 and described to the Cincinnati audience
the talent the young man displayed in the fugue as 'diabolical'.
Britten and Peter Pears drove up to Maine to see Eugene in
September 1940. 'He may be doing some things of mine next
season,' Britten wrote to another friend, Wulf Scherchen, 'and
I've got to be nice to him. Luckily he's a very pleasant person.'[42]

Bideford Pool was something of an intellectual holiday
colony. Eugene, Jansi and their two English visitors went to an
impromptu after dinner party at the house of a young American composer John Hauserman. Britten played his Diversions
for Piano (left-hand) and Orchestra which confirmed Eugene's
opinion that he was 'the outstanding young man in the world
of creative music today.'[43] Jansi, with her striking good looks
and amusing extrovert personality was, as always, the centre
of attention and established an immediate rapport with the
two young English musicians. She became their 'devoted old
Mumsie'.

As soon as she returned to Cincinnati she sent them photos
from the party with suggested titles such as 'The Boy Benjamin
ascends to Valhalla' and 'Mother Carey and her Chickens'. 'On
gazing round our town we are more than ever convinced that
it needs the addition of a) Britain's Boy-composer and b) the
singer-wot-knows the music and plays the piano (old Indian
name). So you had better turn your noble vehicle west and
come out and invade Ohio. And you know you need a mother's
care, duckies!'[44]

She wrote to them again in reply to their Christmas letter, repeating her invitation to Cincinnati:

One of our wishes for the New Year is that you Brooklyn Boys may find your way out here to see us. For we have SUCH a house – it is huge, rambling, shabby, standing in its Own Grounds, and altogether on the palatial side – and a room for Mummie's Boys at any time. Gene's workroom looks like the drawing room of a suite at the old Langham – all gold brocade walls and elegant clocks that don't work. So come out and see us while this unusual dignity and elegance surrounds us.

Gene is up to here in work, already getting ready for the May Festival and now he has three Sundays with the Ford Hour and I am practically a widow as the dear boy is seldom to be found under the roof tree. But I manage to keep going and of late, the social scene locally has been only too active and rather tiresome.

I believe Rae and Ethel are due here with the orchestra one of these days – it will be fun to be with them again. And maybe we will hear your little tune for them – who knows?

Gene and I are coming to New York for a few minutes in March – about the 20th I think – as Barbirolli is to do his Symphony then. We will be here almost all the time except for the weekend (23rd) when Beecham conducts here and Gene and I go to Detroit for his last concert with the Ford lads.

News from England hasn't been too good. Sid and Bumps got thoroughly bombed out at Bristol but we have had amazingly cheery letters from them and Gene's father was badly hurt by an RAF guy on a motorbike during a blackout – but he seems to be getting over it nicely. And we are surrounded by a pretty group of isolationists who are sure there really isn't a war at all and another group of hysterical dames who see Nazi spies under every bed. I don't know which is the more trying. Luckily we manage to keep busy enough not to worry unduly nor argue overmuch. But it's not very bright.[45]

Eugene conducted the first performance of *Scottish Ballad* for Two Pianos and Orchestra, Britten's piece for Ethel Bartlett and Rae Robertson, in Cincinnati on 28th November 1941. At their last meeting in New York before 'Mummie's Boys' returned to England, Britten found Gene 'very white and puffy, she amusing'.[46]

Eugene's championship of contemporary composers still did not meet with universal approval but he felt his policy was justified: 'Time was, in most cities – including Cincinnati – when any *new* piece of music earned an apathetic and sometimes hostile reception. Today with our live audiences of nearly 7,000 people a week, the absence of a novelty from my programmes would be looked upon with genuine concern.

'Quite frankly, the conductor of a major orchestra who hesitates to program regularly important contemporary novelties is failing in his duty to his audience, his orchestra and his art.'[47]

15

A Rather Nice Person In Many Ways (Cincinnati III)

It was not until the end of 1941 that Eugene and Jansi were able to hear on short wave the BBC's tribute to the Goossens family originally broadcast on 19th January:

There, through a great deal of crackling and static interference, we heard Big Ben, followed by 'Rule Britannia', and later the usual BBC announcer saying they were broadcasting a half hour of 'The Goossens Family' for America's benefit. Quite frankly as soon as we heard the beloved voices of Sid, Mor and Lee we could do nothing but bawl! With tears streaming down our cheeks we listened in silence and with mixed feelings to the very cleverly put together half hour. I thought it extremely good, but my one regret was that *you* did not choose to speak, Dad. Bumps did a splendid job with my works, the arrangement of the 'Hurdy-Gurdy' particularly intrigued me, and Lee's playing of the oboe concerto was, as always, a breathtaking miracle. The broadcast came to an end and we slumped back to Cincinnati and everyday hum-drum realities.[1]

He was at least able to 'keep the flag of English music flying in America'[2] by recording the Walton Violin Concerto with Heifetz and Vaughan Williams' *London Symphony* for a series of RCA Victor records which show both Goossens and the Cincinnati Symphony Orchestra at the height of their powers. Subsequent records were Stravinsky's *Le Chant du Rossignol*, Strauss' *Rosenkavalier* Suite, Tchaikovsky's Symphony no. 2 *The Little Russian*, Schumann's Symphony no 4, Respighi's *The Pines of Rome* and Grieg's *Peer Gynt* Suite no. 1.

Eugene and his orchestra even featured in a murder mystery, *Clue in Two Flats* by R L F McCombs, better known for his programme notes. The crime is committed back stage at Music Hall and solved by a rank and file violinist. The denouement takes place in the Green Room where the hero reveals to Mr and Mrs Goossens that the murderer was a demented, deformed, half-Jewish German refugee composer, who strangled the charlatan pianist, who had been exploiting his genius, with a cello string.[3]

In January 1941 a reminder of home arrived in the shape of Sir Thomas Beecham and Lady Cunard, after a controversial tour of Australia. 'I had a killing time in Australia, a truly extraordinary country, intellectually on another planet,' was his summary of the experience. Owing to the illness of the Rumanian conductor/violinist Enescu, Beecham was engaged for a pair of concerts in Cincinnati. 'My beautifully disciplined orchestra found him very much of a puzzle and yet appreciated his sense of humour, but his lack of control at rehearsals is very disconcerting to some of them. But all unite in calling him a magnificent musician and a very fine conductor. Personally, I am glad that TB is getting out at the end of the week, otherwise his laxity might have a demoralising effect on the routine of the orchestra. On arrival here, one of the first things he asked me to do was to secure him a slight advance of $100 from the symphony office! Evidently Lady C keeps him strictly rationed. . .'[4] By the following year, Eugene was surprised to find that Lady Cunard had been displaced by the pianist, Betty Humby.

The Goossens always entertained visiting musical celebrities at home and Donie was taught to call them all 'Aunt' and 'Uncle':

> You wind up with all these Aunts and Uncles you don't particularly like but some of them I liked very much, like Uncle José Iturbi. When he came to Cincinnati he promptly hired an aeroplane and took my mother and me up over our house and my school. Whenever people were around she was quite fun but when they had gone she never even spoke to me. It was weird. I was ugly. She felt far more maternal towards Renée. She was very pretty, a decorative asset, far more the kind of child that people took to.
>
> Soloists are always nice to all the children of the conductor! Some were particular friends of the family like Arthur Rubinstein, Heifetz, Stravinsky and Darius Milhaud who was a very fat lumbering sort of man. I don't think I'd ever seen such a gentle giant who wrote such lovely music.[5]

Much though he enjoyed the visits of his old friends, Eugene was not uncritical of their performances. Milhaud was a sick man for his concert at the end of December 1941. 'It was only the ingenuousness of his music which made a success of his portion of the program. His conducting and piano playing are both amateurish and unimpressive. So that when I came along with my Tchaikovsky 4th I pulled the whole audience immediately out of a rather torpid, though respectful condition.'[6]

Now that the horrors of the Blitz had abated, Eugene had less fears for his parents' safety although he constantly tried to persuade them to leave London to stay near Sid in Bedford or Léon in the Cotswolds. Marie held a lunch party to celebrate Eugene and Annie's golden wedding on 18th January 1942 but because of the exigencies of war, she was the only one of the Goossens children who could be present. It did not seem that the family's musical tradition would be carried on by the next generation. Anthony, Marie and Fred's son, had rebelled against daily violin practice but their daughter Jean was making good progress on the harp. When she was asked to play at the golden wedding party, a well-meaning family friend commented 'You'll have to play well to do your mother justice!' The child felt that she could not live up to the family's reputation and refused to continue with the harp.[7]

Both Léon and Eugene loved and respected their sisters but they shared serious reservations about their husbands. They resented the fact that Fred Laurence had earned so little as an orchestral manager (until he parted company with the RPO), leaving Marie to run the house, look after two children and two step-children as well as being the main bread winner of the family. In April Eugene commented: 'Mor seems to be as perky as ever. She bemoans the fact that Fred can't get any work to do and so I suppose is quite resigned to having to cater for the whole family.'[8]

Bumps had been suffering from the long-term effects of alcoholism and Eugene could not understand why Sid was still nursing him at home instead of putting him in a hospital: 'As far as Sid is concerned, there is a limit to the amount of suffering and strain one endures on behalf of those who are close and dear to one. As Léon said in his letter, he had it coming to him – which of course doesn't alter the fact that one so brilliant and gifted as he formerly was, should through his own weakness, succumb to such a condition.'[9]

Fred died suddenly on 3rd May and Bumps on 13th May. Eugene offered financial help, but his comments were unemotional to the point of callousness:

> We never expected that both Mor and Sid would be left alone virtually within the same week. By the time this letter gets to you they will have adjusted themselves to the pain of a new existence. We can only guess, of course, as to how and to what degree the girls will readjust themselves to circumstances. I imagine that both of them, being what they are, resourceful and stoical, this process will not take much effort or much time. Marie at any rate has the children and providing she is not saddled by too great a burden of 'in-laws', she will be able to cope with the situation. Sidonie, I imagine, has breathed a long sigh of relief. I refuse to believe that however fond she was of Bumps, she will persist in looking on her bereavement as anything but a God-send.[10]

He was also concerned about Léon's future when he heard that he was leaving the Salon Orchestra and resigning from the BBC: 'I am surprised and yet not sorry. How badly he is needed in America and what a wonderful field there would be for him at the present time. I know of course his patriotic duties come first, but if it can be humanly managed, it seems a pity that the world's greatest artist should not benefit America by his outstanding work. His name over here is increasingly mentioned and throughout the country is synonymous with the greatest manifestation of oboe playing that has ever been. His records are well known. What a pity. . .'[11]

Eugene's relationship with Barbirolli continued to be an ambivalent one. He had always felt that the younger man was overparted as the successor to Toscanini with the New York Philharmonic and was jealous of his relative success with the orchestra. Barbirolli was not yet rated a Maestro conductor whereas Goossens had enjoyed that accolade for a dozen years. He was one of the ten guest conductors engaged to celebrate the centenary of the New York Philharmonic Orchestra: in order of performance they were Stokowski, Bruno Walter, Mitropoulos, Fritz Busch, Koussevitzky, Rodzinski,

Goossens, Damrosch and Toscanini, with Barbirolli filling in between.

When Eugene took up the baton at the beginning of February 1942 he found 'a jaded, rather sullen and utterly worn out Philharmonic.'

> Not that my sympathies weren't very much with them, when one considers what they have actually been going through. Since the beginning of the season they have experienced the ministrations of seven conductors – with two more to come. They have been shifted about in position according to the whim of each conductor – they have been bullied and stormed at, entreated, cajoled, by all of us and they are heartily sick of it. They behaved rather better for me than they did for some of the others, but used as I am to the perfect discipline of my orchestra, I found it a little hard to get used to the lethargy and talkativeness of the New Yorkers.
>
> The actual concerts were all of them a great success. We played the Weinberger *Lincoln Symphony* and Heifetz, the Brahms Concerto. Two notices will give you an idea of the venomous mood of the NY critics. Downes' attack on Heifetz, who was quite sick from influenza that evening, is characteristic of the cruelty which some critics don't scruple to employ when they feel they can do a big artist harm.[12]

Olin Downes' criticism was as follows: 'From personal experience we have not heard Mr Heifetz play the Brahms Concerto as badly as he did last night. Even technically the performance was far from smooth and there were moments when intonation was more than suspect. His performance was not poised. The tempi in the first movement particularly were hurried and the tone forced. We preferred Mr Goossens' treatment of the concerto before the violin enters to the soloist's, although like an experienced and expert conductor, Mr Goossens followed suit as Mr Heifetz went along. Conceding that Mr Heifetz was not completely himself in this performance, we concede that Brahms is not himself when treated in that way.'[13]

Downes was more complimentary about Menuhin as soloist in the second pair of concerts, although he found Dvořák's Violin Concerto 'weak music'. He gave tempered praise to Eugene's 'Phantasy for Strings' in one movement, based on his sextet of 1923. 'It is written with great facility and considerable colour. The ear welcomes the tang of the counterpoint, the English lilt of the first section, the colour and the poetical sentiment of the middle part, the brilliancy of the final fugato. But it is diffuse and rather conventional writing albeit by a composer who scores skilfully.'[14]

In Eugene's absence, Barbirolli had been conducting the Cincinnati Orchestra. 'I got a great reception from my orchestra. It was the old story of intense relief at the return of the man who apparently seems to understand his orchestra and get more out of it both in performance and in sympathy than any other conductor. It is a nice comforting feeling to realise, that as the years go by, so the bonds between us grow stronger. The reaction of my orchestra to its guest conductor was by no means a cordial one! They objected primarily to his "phoney" showmanship and his attitude of striving to achieve something which didn't come naturally to him.'[15]

The orchestral players could hardly say anything else to their conductor for the past eleven years. Fred Yeiser, critic of the *Cincinnati Enquirer*, dared to be positive about the visitor, despite his personal friendship with Eugene: 'There is nothing like a change of diet. It works in music, too, with conductors. John Barbirolli, having swapped pulpits for a concert or two with Eugene Goossens, had an invigorating effect on the atmosphere in Music Hall yesterday. Both the members of the Cincinnati Symphony Orchestra and the public reacted to Mr Barbirolli's direction like a tonic. . . He creates the illusion of playing on the orchestra as though it were an instrument, instead of merely leading it.'

Whatever his private reservations, publicly the friendship flourished; Eugene and Jansi had thrown a lavish party for John and Evelyn Barbirolli on the last night of their visit to Cincinnati.

Barbirolli was far more single-minded in his ambitions and far more adept in using the system to further his career – a skill that Eugene never tried to master. He was initially scathing when he heard of Barbirolli's plan to return to war-torn England in the spring of 1942 to conduct concerts in aid of English orchestral musicians: 'This all strikes me as rather funny for he doesn't seem to have taken into account the lukewarm reception he might possibly receive from the British public and musicians. Had he left England with a big reputation, it would have been otherwise, but as he was none too great a favourite when he left, it can hardly be said that the orchestras and the public, not to mention his colleagues, will cheer themselves hoarse when he appears on the horizon. I believe, however, that he is perfectly honest in his desire to – as he thinks – help the musicians through the concerts that he will direct.'[16]

On the positive side, Eugene praised the performance that Barbirolli had given of his First Symphony in New York. Barbirolli had reacted effusively to the symphony from his first sight of the score. 'I can't tell you how happy it has made me to see such a fine piece of music. Finely and largely conceived and so beautifully carried out. It restores one's faith that it is still possible to write Music but to want to write it is not enough; you, my dear friend, were born for this. Bravo!'

Eugene's acid remarks seem somewhat churlish in the context of such enthusiastic support. Understandably he expressed a preference for Barbirolli to conduct the British premiere of the symphony rather than Basil Cameron who, he felt, would not insist on sufficient rehearsal time nor show adequate regard for detail.

Much to his surprise, not only did Barbirolli manage to arrange his passage to England and back in 1942 – something that Eugene was to fail in all his efforts to achieve until 1946 – but his concerts, broadcasts and lectures in England were all a great success. 'It is obvious he is paving his way for a glorious return to England at the end of the war as the highest ranking English conductor. He will then decide to stay in England, probably at the head of either the Philharmonic or the BBC and should anyone question his right to do so, he can always point to his magnanimous gesture and his pluck (?) in returning to England during the war.'[17] Eugene much appreciated Barbirolli making the trek out to Finchley to give his parents a first-hand account of the health and happiness of their much missed eldest child.

In the event, Barbirolli returned to England permanently in 1943 as conductor of the Hallé Orchestra. Eugene would have been flattered to have been offered his post with the New York Philharmonic. It did not materialise and by the end of 1942 he had decided that he was much better off remaining in Cincinnati. 'Changes in the American orchestras are imminent,' he wrote to his father on 29th December 1942:

> Stock, the conductor of the Chicago orchestra, died recently and someone will have to be found for that place. This morning it was announced that Rodzinski of Cleveland was to be made permanent conductor of the NY Philharmonic – Bruno Walter to act as guest conductor for about two months of that time. This finally puts Barbirolli out of New York and he will doubtless either receive that worst of all orchestras, the Los Angeles Philharmonic, or spend his time guest conducting.
>
> I don't envy Rodzinski his new post, nor do I envy the men who have to play under him. Both are tough and hard-boiled and I imagine there will be scenes as soon as operations begin next season. Rumours that Koussevitzky is finally giving up Boston are going the rounds, but as this rumour is ten years old I don't put much stock in it. Personally I have come to the conclusion that it's much better to be connected with one of the good orchestras in the middle west (like mine) where one has one's own way and a constant public. The salary may not be so great, but the strain on one's shoulders is considerably less, so far as work is concerned, than if one is connected with one of the 'big three' [Boston, New York, Philadelphia].

Eugene had reached a crucial point in his career. Because of his health problems he had to husband his physical resources; he had lost the dynamic energy and emotional resilience of his youth. As he approached his fiftieth birthday, he no longer sought out orchestral challenges. He preferred the security of Cincinnati and his acknowledged position in the community as musical supremo. He realised the advantages of an orchestra which he had moulded, during the twelve years of his tenure, into a reliable and responsive musical entity.

He also valued the time and emotional freedom to concentrate on composing. Deprived of his annual visits to England, he had rediscovered his creativity as a composer during the restful summer vacations in New England. His works after 1940 show a new maturity, a new voice. His Second String Quartet had been well received at its British premiere on 17th October 1942 at the Wigmore Hall, played by the Stratton Quartet. He had completed a Piano Fantasy for Iturbi and a Second Symphony. He had now embarked on an ambition which had been fired long ago by Sir Edward Elgar to write a large scale choral work as a reaffirmation of his Catholic faith: *The Apocalypse.*

One effect of America's increasing involvement in the war was the replacement at the beginning of the 1942 season of eleven members of the Cincinnati Orchestra who had been drafted into the armed services. Eugene reluctantly accepted two female violinists. As 'a stirring and significant contribution to the war effort' he asked a large number of American composers to write short fanfares with patriotic titles to be played at each of the season's concerts, similar to the fanfares he had featured in his Queen's Hall Concerts in 1921. Twenty-three composers responded including Aaron Copland, Paul Creston, Morton Gould, Roy Harris, Walter Piston, Roger Sessions, William Grant Still and Virgil Thomson. Eugene's own contribution was entitled 'Fanfare for the Merchant Marine'.

He also volunteered to write for nothing the score for an American propaganda film entitled *Cowboy*, issued by the Office of War Information, to be shown in the British Empire. It was mostly of ranching scenes in Texas, depicting the Wild West as furnishing the major portion of the nation's food supply, thanks to its hard-working farmers. The score provides continuous background music, conducted by the composer and illustrates his theory that by amplifying a few selected instruments, the effect could be obtained of a full symphony orchestra. He hoped the twenty-two minute documentary would lead to a major film for the OWI or something in Hollywood but neither project materialised.[18]

One long-standing promise that was fulfilled in February 1943 was the visit to Cincinnati of Toscanini. Eugene's letter to his parents of 14th February 1943 is reminiscent of his enthusiastic account of their first meeting in 1926.

> I need hardly tell you that it was my personal letter to Toscanini that did the trick. I told him that the orchestra was going through one of its annual financial scares and that this time, owing to war conditions, the scare was a real one. I also told him that he would find a fairly good orchestra here and to have seen his face last night after the concert was sufficient reward for my years of training of this orchestra. Outside of changing the position of the second

violins he had no fault to find with it. He refused to accept any fee as he said he was doing it out of friendship for me and in these days, the survival of the big American orchestras was very important.

He takes absolutely no care of himself and though he arrived with his wife and son, they seem incapable of persuading him even to take ordinary precautions. He goes about without a hat and in a thin coat and caught his cold in New York recently by going out to post a letter in the snow without a hat, overcoat or galoshes. He then got lost and was missing for ten to fifteen minutes before he could find his house again. Last night we gave him a nice supper after the concert and he consumed enormous quantities of minestrone, champagne cocktails, red wine and entrecôte à la minute.

He is really a lovely man and in many ways reminds me of you, Dad darling (except, as Jansi rightly observes, in his tempo for the *Mastersingers* overture which he took at a pace which shocked all the staid Cincinnatians and left the orchestra panting!). Obviously he is determined to counteract the effect of his years by speeding up his tempi – and he gave the Prelude and Liebestod much faster than I ever heard it. I was proud of my boys and they really gave him a swell show.

When I sat in the box last night I had an awful moment of nostalgia for those old days when I used to sit in the stalls and listen to *your Tristan*. It led me on to a train of thought which ended by my concluding that were the public not so sensation-seeking and were it able to perceive the subtleties of a fine musician as well as the more obvious exhibitionist musical tendencies, *you* would come into your own today, were you to resume your career.

If Toscanini was still conducting at seventy-seven, why not his father who was the same age?

Eugene still continued his policy of mixing the old with the new in his concert programmes, faced with the difficult task of catering for all tastes in times of war and economic stringency. The 1942–43 season included performances of Symphonies no. 5 and 7 by Shostakovich, a Gershwin Evening with Oscar Levant as soloist, Virgil Thomson conducting his Second Symphony, Rubinstein playing the Khachaturian Piano Concerto, and Vaughan Williams' Pastoral Symphony, in honour of the composer's seventieth birthday.

David Ewen in *Dictators of the Baton*, a critical survey of

American orchestral directors, described Eugene's performances with the Cincinnati Orchestra as having 'classic objectivity, high polish, grace, refinement' given by 'an artist in the
finest meaning of the term; fastidiously he carves each line and
phrase with the discernment of a sculptor moulding clay.'[19] The
only qualification in his praise was of a certain lack of dynamism
and 'burning fire', something that was becoming more manifest
as Eugene settled into middle-age.

As a composer, Eugene was described as 'one of the most
gifted men of the Bliss-Howells-Moeran generation' when the
First Symphony received its British premiere at a BBC Promenade Concert on 6th July 1943, with the LPO conducted by Basil
Cameron. But, the critics were non-plussed and disappointed.
Ralph Hill in the *Sunday Times* imagined that 'as Goossens is one
of the most able composers of our time and therefore possesses
all the necessary technical equipment and experience to write a
symphony, he would, as a mature composer, turn out something
outstanding in craftsmanship and original in conception. Not at
all; the result is a long and laboured and rather pretentious piece
of writing.'

The *Times* described him as 'musician rather than composer,
for the symphony like his previous music is a matter of skill
rather than imagination. Goossens is a musician to his finger
tips, whether the fingers hold a bow, a baton or a pen. And
the design of this symphony attests the intellectual resource of
its author. All four movements are based on two mottoes, one
abrupt, the other more smooth spoken. Such a scheme would be
extremely interesting if one could find an initial interest in the
themes themselves, or if the composer impressed them upon us
in a personal idiom of his own. In a word the music is dry.'

Scott Goddard assessed the work and its composer the
most accurately: 'Goossens remains one of the most nimble
musical minds produced in this country between the two wars.
But the nature of a symphony which is a mixture of profound
and consecutive thought demands more than even Goossens'
great technical ability. The impression that remained from a
first hearing of this work was that the ideas embedded in it
were less significant than the treatment they received.'

The health of both Goossens parents had been giving cause

for concern; the symphony's premiere had been a rare outing for Annie who was now eighty-three. Marie had taken her parents to the Albert Hall and back by taxi. Annie wrote to her eldest son on 18th August 1943, still in a firm copperplate hand telling him how much she had enjoyed every note of the work and congratulating him on the success of the concerts he had been conducting in Mexico.

We have Sidonie with us for the last few Sundays while they have been at the Proms and last Sunday week we had Léon also. Of course we see Marie nearly every day. She is looking a bit better but she works very hard, poor girl. I am pleased to say that Dad is much better but still looks a bit delicate.

We never go out, at least I don't. Dad does all the shopping. I stay at home and look after the house and the cooking. There is nothing to take me out.

I wonder when we shall all meet again dear. I am simply longing to see you. I hope it will not be another four years. Anyway the time has passed very quickly, that is one consolation. I don't know if it has passed quickly with you?

With fondest love to Janet and the children and all my best love to you 'My Darling Boy' from your ever loving and devoted Mother.

Eugene answered his mother's letter in late September from Spring Lake, New Jersey, by the Atlantic Ocean:

If you knew the joy that last lovely letter gave me, Mum darling – to see your handwriting as of old, and to read all your news. That you're both well is wonderful news, for your wellbeing is my first and only concern – especially in these awful days of separation. Though definitely the news is better; but I'm afraid we're up against the really tough period of the war beginning right now in Italy.

You'll wonder at my address. I slipped down here for a few days' sea air and rest after too long a time spent in New York looking for new music and new musicians. I've lost my former French horn, First trombone and tuba; the first to the NY Philharmonic and the last two to the army. All the good young players are in the army. It's disturbing to have the personnel and consequently the quality of one's orchestra disturbed. New music too isn't any too plentiful but one can always get along without novelties, for there's so much good music still unperformed.

I've entirely rebuilt my second symphony; the results I think are

238

pretty good and the work is much nearer my original conception.

My Jansi is well and flourishing and I miss her here. But occasionally it does one good to have a few days isolation, quite apart from the difficulty of travelling and securing accommodation which makes peregrinations of two people twice as difficult than if one's alone!

I wish I were with you darlings; sometimes the acute realisation of the time and distance that separates us becomes too intolerable to bear. From my window here I see the ships in convoy going home (though this'll probably annoy the censor, I still have to tell it you to give an idea of how homesick I get at the sight).[20]

The 1943–44 season in Cincinnati evoked nostalgic memories for Eugene. He conducted Carmen Amaya in da Falla's *Ritual Fire Dance* and remembered when Diaghilev had discovered her fiery dancing as a gypsy child of five years old in Barcelona. He always conducted some performances for the annual visit of the ballet company starring Alicia Markova and Anton Dolin, another reminder of the Ballet Russe. Muriel Draper's son Paul, in a light-hearted duo programme with Larry Adler, took him back even further, to London before the First World War and 'Music at Midnight'.

When Eugene's Second Quartet was played in Town Hall, New York on 17th January 1944 in a programme sponsored by Boosey & Hawkes, including Britten's First Quartet and Copland's Sonata for Violin and Piano, Olin Downes accused all the composers involved as having their 'eyes turned to the past'. He was dismayed by their 'persistence of a rearward vision, and the absence of any consciousness of a new age or a new order.'[21]

Eugene vigorously countered his old friend's criticism: 'Does he seriously expect that at these times of world cataclysm, hardened old sinners like myself should forsake at the drop of a hat their personal idiomatic form of speech, built up over thirty years or more, in favour of a demagogic or revolutionary box of tricks just to "épater les bourgeois" and the critics? Composition, unlike journalism and the graphic arts, is a reflective, retrospective, ruminative process and does not immediately adjust itself to vivid contemporaneous happenings, particularly catastrophic ones like this war.'[22]

239

In contrast, when Iturbi finally gave the long-awaited premiere of Eugene's Phantasy Concerto on 25th February 1944, Howard W Hess in the Cincinnati *Times Star* described it as 'right up to the minute, standing on its tip-toes looking into the future.'[23]

The composer explained the genesis of the piece in his habitually lucid and informative programme notes:

> Discussing with me four years ago the paucity of new works for piano and orchestra, Mr Iturbi suggested that I write something fairly short and original for him, as a contrast to the usual lengthy concerto form. I decided upon a piece in which the piano and orchestra were to be allotted almost equally important roles; something 'conversational', and consequently, different from the accepted form of virtuoso piece with orchestral accompaniment.
>
> A 'Phantasy' is a work based entirely on a short initial motto theme. Such were the 'fancies' of the old madrigalists of Elizabethan England, pieces woven into a complex structure founded entirely on an introductory key figure. A wealthy amateur, W W Cobbett, revived the vogue for this form about 1905 by offering prizes to English composers in chamber music based on the sixteenth-century pattern. He christened them 'Phantasies' and they usually consisted of works in one long movement, subdivided into shorter movements, each movement being based on the preliminary MOTTO.
>
> The concerto is based on a four note motto heard at the outset in the trumpets.

Irene Kohler gave the British premiere on 1st November 1944 with the BBC Symphony Orchestra, conducted by Sir Adrian Boult, from the Corn Exchange in Bedford. Edwin Evans, whose friendship with Eugene went back thirty years, broadcast the interval talk: 'Well now at last we are to hear the most recent work of one of our most eminent composers who has been virtually lost to us for the last twenty years, simply because the present boom in orchestral music was then a dream of the future and we could not offer him, as a conductor, the opportunities which awaited him across the Atlantic.'

The Piano Phantasy was well received but criticised for over complexity. It certainly would never rival the oboe concerto in popularity. Eugene wrote to his parents on 12th June 1944: 'I do wish Lee would do something about having my oboe concerto recorded. I am only fearful that one day it may be too late to do so. There is much demand over here for all his records and in particular *that one*. Doesn't HMV realise what an enormous record public Léon has over here and how he's looked up to as the God of all the young oboe players of this generation? Don't they realise that my concerto is the one virtuoso work which is looked upon as Lee's proper vehicle for display, and that everybody is astonished that no record exists of it?!!'

At the end of the concert season in Cincinnati Eugene was involved in an acrimonious and widely publicised dispute with the Cincinnati Musicians' Union. Traditionally all members of the orchestra were engaged for the May Festival but because of a renewed financial crisis, the orchestra had a deficit of $20,000. Eugene and a committee of five from the orchestra endeavoured to economise by reducing the number of players for the 1944 Festival by ten. They were accused by the Union of 'unwarranted attempts to defeat efforts of the association to obtain wage increases and/or advocating loss of engagements for their colleagues in order that they themselves might continue to be employed.'

Eugene and the five others denied the charges and labelled them as 'unfair'.[24] They were found guilty, fined and suspended from Union membership for three months. Eugene had to pay $1,250 and could not conduct during that time. They appealed against the decision and the Union eventually repaid the fines in July 1945.

The Union dispute crystallised criticism from those who felt that despite his undoubted achievements, Eugene had wielded the baton in Cincinnati for long enough and that orchestra and public would benefit from a new figure on the podium. Because of the power of the Union he was forced to keep on players whom he did not consider to be of a sufficiently high standard. Philip Dreyfuss, who joined the First Violins in 1942, had become a close friend. He felt that orchestral discipline had suffered: 'Gene was too kind and considerate, too English to reprimand players who were being disruptive and disrespectful towards him. Some people criticised his baton technique and his interpretations for lacking warmth. For me his beat was always beautifully clear and from my seat so near

241

him I could see the expression on his face and how deeply he felt the music that he was conducting.'[25]

The American composer Gunther Schuller, who had joined the orchestra as First Horn in 1943, recalled: 'He was sometimes given to circular beating – where a lazy musician could not tell where the beat was. It never bothered me, but others complained of it. I was a great admirer of Gene's – for a lot of reasons including his superb programming and his interest and support of me as a fledgling composer. He gave me my twin debut as composer/horn soloist in my own First Horn Concerto.'[26]

Opinions differed as to how well he knew the scores he conducted; whether his renowned facility for coping with the complexities of new works, if necessary at a few hours notice, mitigated against deeper study and a heart-felt interpretation. He appeared to be cold and aloof as a personality and always preserved the public formality of a hat and coat even on the beach. The players in the orchestra who became his friends agreed that beneath the reserved English exterior was, in the words of Emil Schmachtenberg (bass clarinettist); 'a rather nice person in many ways'.

In February 1944 Eugene suddenly broke the upsetting news to his parents that he and Jansi were parting and that she was taking the children to live in New York. On 20th May she was granted a divorce on the charge of neglect; the day after he wrote his version of events:

The lawyer who handled the case did so very cleverly and with a minimum of 'gory' detail, in fact the whole thing was granted on the grounds that I had been so immersed in my work over the past years that I hadn't had time for my home life and in consequence had been pretty neglectful of it. In point of fact, this is to a large extent true, for I find that the older I get and the more my professional responsibilities grow, the less time I have for the things which are looked upon as so important in America and which to me are so really comparatively insignificant. It all boils down to the fact that I'm really a poor specimen of a 'family man' and much more prone to spend an extra hour or two over some detail of my work than spend it on the company of my family.

Certainly we parted in no spirit of enmity, but only one of great sorrow that a life together which promised so well at the beginning had not fulfilled itself. While there are many reasons one would have expected her to elect to remain with me, yet there are many others which warranted her choosing a new life for herself, rather than remaining in an invidious and anomalous position as my wife. When I tell you that my own happiness counted very much in her own part of the decision, you'll perhaps believe that her share in the proceedings wasn't entirely as selfish as it appears at first sight. I really do beg of you to leave the door open just a little bit longer so that you won't entirely shut out from your affections one who is still in certain respects very dear to me.[27]

Obviously Eugene was not going to give his parents the full picture of a marriage that had deteriorated into an unsatisfactory relationship for both partners. Jansi overindulged in food and alcohol; her name had been linked with various men. Eugene remained a sophisticated Bohemian, a Don Juan at heart. As in his first marriage to Boonie, he had shown a remarkable degree of tolerance over the years to his wife's liaisons and expected reciprocal acceptance of his own adventures. Gunther Schuller found that their conductor's complaisant attitude towards adultery was common gossip. 'We all knew and constantly heard in those mid-forties years that Gene's private life was in turmoil and that too many women were involved. I can well imagine that in those years the strait-laced Boards and Trustees of the major symphony orchestras in the US would not have wanted anything to do with a "rake" like Eugene.'[28]

Philip Dreyfuss commented: 'People found him too formal, and austere but he was a very kind man, a very sincere and unworldly man who was used and abused. He had no sense of money and always lived beyond his means. Jansi was an opportunist who had no love left for him. He was very English and charming; he was hounded by women who were crazy for him and threw themselves at him. He was a man without much sentiment who wasn't aware of the fact. I don't think he was ever in love with any of his wives!'[29]

Eugene and Jansi had remained together, preserving a front of conventional respectability for the sake of his public position – Eugene's predecessor in Cincinnati, Fritz Reiner, had been

243

forced to resign following his divorce – and to provide a stable home background for Donie and Renée. Jansi was given custody of the children and moved to New York, with the faithful Nanny Dorothy Cubitt to look after the children. Eugene hoped that she would find satisfaction in a literary job with either the *New York Times* or *Tribune*. She eventually worked in the publicity office of the Columbia Concerts Corporation in charge of artists' releases.

'Donie has been amazing through all this readjustment,' Eugene explained proudly to his parents. 'So philosophic is she indeed and so calm and level-headed about the whole business, that it is as though she were a woman of twenty-two instead of twelve. We shall always find a common bond in our darling child as there is nothing we wouldn't do for her happiness for we both idolise her and would make any sacrifice for her.' The reality was to prove sadly different. 'She is a *real* Goossens,' he continues, 'with all the best traits of the family and none of its variable ones (if indeed it contains any of the latter). I heard her play last week at her Convent concert and she did a remarkable job. She has a perfect finger technique – strong, well-shaped hands and fingers like steel. A very fine style too, and playing with real inborn musical feeling.'[30]

Eugene, as on many occasions, proved to be out of touch with the harsh realities of life. Neither parent was able to give Donie and Renée the love and security they needed. Donie wrote a sad little letter to her London grandparents in October: 'I miss Cincinnati and Daddy terribly. New York is such a big noisy city and the cost of living is so much higher here. I am studying piano at school and am soon going to resume the harp which I like very much. I miss going to Daddie's concerts.'[31]

The following year, she joined the 1,800 students at the High School of Music and Art and went to Carlos Salzedo for harp lessons. 'I had to relearn everything. He had revolutionised harp playing and made it into a solo instrument. He had me in tears. I still wasn't sure whether I really wanted to play the harp or whether it was because my father wanted me to do it. I used to feel very guilty that I had failed to live up to the name Sidonie and the family image but think how much worse it would have been if I had been a boy and had had the responsibility of being Eugene IV!'[32]

Meanwhile Eugene officially resumed a bachelor's existence. In November 1944 he returned to the Chicago Civic Opera house to conduct *Pelléas and Mélisande*. It was difficult to efface the memory of its last performance there in 1931 with Mary Garden in the role she had created for Debussy, but Eugene was praised for his conducting of 'the great web of the score subtly and richly, understanding its iridescent textures of music drama.'[33] An understanding which unfortunately many of the audience lacked. 'Much of the continuity of the music was disturbed by the disposition of the audience to applaud whenever the curtain fell. Mr Goossens turned round, shook a violently disapproving head or held up his left hand but all was in vain.'[34]

'I always enjoy trips to the "Windy City",' Eugene wrote to his parents, 'which after the rather sedate pomposity of Cincinnati strikes me as stimulating and virile. Young Leonard Bernstein, a gifted New Yorker who is enjoying a vogue something similar to the one I enjoyed in the early twenties, took over the Cincinnati orchestra for a week.'[35]

Bernstein had been engaged as conductor and pianist and wrote effusively to Eugene on his return to New York: 'I want to send you my warmest thanks for the privilege of conducting your fine orchestra. The men were wonderful to work with. It was a great pleasure to get to know you better and I can't tell you what a pleasure it was to know a conductor who carries out that often heard, but seldom executed, promise of playing contemporary music.'[36]

1944–45 was the Golden Jubilee season of the Cincinnati Orchestra. As part of the celebrations, Eugene had invited ten American composers to contribute 'Variations on an original Theme'; the Finale was Eugene's triumphant recapitulation of the theme with which he had introduced the work. The first performance was enthusiastically received on 23rd March 1945; the other composers included Paul Creston, Aaron Copland, William Schumann, Walter Piston and Ernest Bloch. The black composer William Grant Still won the orchestra's $1,000 prize for a festival overture, a further celebratory scheme suggested by Eugene.

When he wrote about the success of the Variations 'hailed

already as the most important contribution to contemporary musical literature of the past fifteen years', he also mentioned to his parents for the first time the possibility of his returning to London as Musical Director of Covent Garden.[37] Eugene senior noted in his diary: 'Important news re. CG.' The only other offer Eugene had so far received was from Walter Legge to conduct twenty-five ENSA concerts for factory workers.[38] Legge seemed oblivious of the fact that Eugene could not break his contract in Cincinnati mid-season even if the engagements had been sufficiently prestigious to tempt him to find deputies.

In America he was held in far higher esteem and was invited to conduct one of the four gala concerts in San Francisco for the delegates to the United Nations Security Conference in May 1945. His programme included Vaughan Williams' *London Symphony* and Prokofiev's *Classical Symphony*. Eugene's first appearance with the San Francisco Symphony Orchestra since 1936 was described as 'the most refreshing event of the season. He gave us really big music-making, big in thought, in execution and in warm-hearted result.'[39]

Now that the war in Europe had ended, he redoubled his efforts to return home to see his parents. Barbirolli and Beecham knew how to use the system; Eugene singularly failed. In desperation he telegraphed his parents on 27th July: 'If Boult could cable me an immediate invitation to conduct a BBC concert late August or early September it might immensely facilitate securing quick permit for London visit. Restrictions almost insurmountable and negotiations interminable. Suggest Sidonie contact Boult. Haste essential.'

Sidonie acted immediately but Eugene had forgotten the Proms and the BBC's concept of forward planning. Five days later he cabled again: 'Deeply appreciate Sidonie's efforts. British Embassy here unable guarantee return transportation from England even eight months from now without official Government invitation such as BBC. So have reluctantly abandoned hope. However return to England definite next May and possibly permanent. Am resigned but inconsolable. Courage till next year.'[40]

Eugene did not confide in his parents that he was planning to marry for a third time. He hoped that it would be third time lucky with Majorie Foulkrod, a beautiful and glamorous divorcée, twenty years younger than himself. Born Marjorie Fetter on 20th March 1912 in Alinde, Pennsylvania, she was a talented pianist and graduate of the Juilliard School of Music whom he had met when she was working for RCA Victor. Donie remembered her coming up to stay with them one summer at Bideford Pool: 'She was quite delightful. I wasn't used to adults apart from Nanny paying any attention to us. Then we saw her in New York. After the divorce we lived in the same house as she did on 93rd Street. She lived upstairs and we lived downstairs. When Daddy came up to New York, on a Sunday afternoon we'd go round the Docks to look at the boats and we would pile into Marjorie's tiny car which was called "Francesca". She was far better organised than he was and made him voice his opinions as to what he wanted from his career. My mother had no skills in that direction.'[41]

They married secretly on 18th April 1946; the news was not made public in Cincinnati until after the May Festival. Eugene and Marjorie boarded the *Queen Mary* for a brief honeymoon in London, to be followed by a leap into the unknown, a guest tour of Australia.

16

Covent Garden:
The Lost Opportunity

Early in 1945 Eugene had at last been offered the opportunity to re-establish himself on a permanent basis in London that he had been waiting for. During the war the Royal Opera House had been used as a dance hall. Boosey & Hawkes had taken over the lease of the building and a charitable trust under the chairmanship of Lord Keynes was setting up an opera company which would receive public subsidy. David Webster had been appointed General Administrator; Keynes and Ralph Hawkes came to America to look for a musical director. They were considering Szell, Walter and Goossens and the most likely candidate seemed to be Goossens.[1] On 30th March 1945 Eugene had for the first time mentioned the negotiations in a letter to his parents.

> I have been asked to consider a scheme in connection with Covent Garden (*please, please* don't breathe a word of it to anyone, not even to our immediate family, as the essence of its successful negotiation depends a great deal on the secrecy which can be maintained about my prospective return until the very moment of that return), a scheme which would involve my accepting a position of great responsibility there for the future. Its nature would be of the highest importance, both to me personally and the cause of opera in general and would mean a commanding position. Naturally I'm not going to burn my bridges behind in America until I have everything in black and white. Yet it seems that, providing the conditions I would impose are all met (and somehow I think they will be met), this is the psychological time and offer which for the past few years I have been waiting for with some anxiety as with confident anticipation.
>
> The more I speculate on the outcome – and I can do little else but speculate until further precise details come from the

CG authorities, or until they give me definite answers to certain questions my NY agent has formulated – the more I am convinced that somehow or other, I shall accept the offer when I know more of its details.

A strong proviso is of course that I shall have the fullest outlet for *symphony* conducting *in London* and the provinces outside of my operatic responsibilities. Naturally I could not contemplate a retirement to nothing but opera for the rest of my career when that career has lain so long in the track of the concert hall and virtuoso conducting!

If I do come back home to accept it, I'll be returning in the most dignified and important role I could possibly return to: something which I think would make you very proud of me – at last!

One wonders at the emphasis on secrecy and the cloak and dagger aspect of the operation, also that even at this stage in his career Eugene indulged in the fantasy that his professional achievements had previously failed to merit his parents' praise.

In June he sent a progress report, or rather the lack of it.

Well as yet the promised letter from Hawkes hasn't arrived. Twice he has cabled, just to say that some legal difficulties about the status of CG have only just been settled and secondly to say, in answer to a cable I sent him, that he was fully aware of the need for quick decisions and the letter would leave immediately (in reply to the one I sent him many, many weeks ago in which I asked for more detailed particulars about his offer to me).

Hawkes blows hot and cold, and although I don't question his integrity or sincerity, I think he's afflicted with the common complaint of the English businessman, when he starts handling any artistic venture such as this one – indecision and procrastination. It all starts off with a great burst of optimism and a 'that'll-be-alright-old-man' attitude which later gives way to a slow-down caution when the real difficulties of the scheme begin to be apparent. There may be a greater number of complications than we can ever guess at. So I'll possess my soul in patience for a week or so longer and see what happens.[2]

Eugene grew increasingly irritated by the triumvirate's failure to specify exactly what they were offering him and in the interim accepted a guest contract from the Australian Broadcasting Corporation. Negotiations dragged on until March 1946 when Hawkes cabled to Webster from New York: 'We shall lose Goossens unless we can come to brass tacks immediately. After consultation with Keynes who has spoken to Goossens on telephone I am therefore offering him definite engagement for two years from July at five thousand pounds per annum. He cannot cancel Australian engagement thus arrival London earlier than July impossible. Most important reach provisional conclusions with him about operatic repertoire before he leaves for Australia. Am meeting Goossens Cincinnati Saturday night.'[3]

Meanwhile Eugene had at last received a letter from David Webster giving him more precise details of the plans for the opera company and his role in it. 'Anything that we do by way of opera has more or less to be from scratch. Not that England is entirely devoid of good singers but there are naturally few of them and these few, for obvious reasons, are not well schooled in opera. We must give every encouragement to the British artist and consider him first and not at long last as used to be the case in the Grand Season. We also intend giving every encouragement to the British Composer.'

They anticipated alternating nights of opera and ballet, and a resident season of not less than six months to perform all operas in English in order to justify their subsidy. Webster continues:

> Frankly opera has never really prospered anywhere unless given in the language of the audience attending the performance. Lambert, as you know, has been associated with Sadler's Wells for a long time, and is here now and would be available. Other conductors we might use would be Sargent, Barbirolli, a newcomer here, a Czech named Suskind, and one or two others.
>
> The general set-up would be that the general direction of the company would be in the hands of yourself and the principal producer, with myself in the Chair and for the purpose of single productions this trio might be joined by whoever was taking the conducting or producing.
>
> From all this you will realise that the job we would like you to do is no sinecure nor can it offer you the immediate glamour of the Grand Season. It is indeed a building job which ought to prove exciting and we would like you here with us.[4]

Eugene found Webster's letter bitterly disappointing and wrote immediately to Hawkes in New York with his reactions and decision:

Unless those few [singers] 'not well schooled' in opera prove susceptible to training and coaching and turning into the finished article within a reasonable amount of time, either their places must be taken by the foreign artist (with imperfect English diction) thus defeating the main idea of the project – or else the whole idea of opera in English must be abandoned. It is the prospect of shouldering the responsibility of making bricks without straw that alarms me a great deal. There is always the answer that one can fall back on the 'old guard' if the new ones don't make good showing. I know the 'old guard' and worked with it for many years, but with all respect to their brilliant past records, they are no longer vocally in their 'prime'! The British public, as you well know, knows singing as well (if not better than) any other, and I personally wouldn't shoulder the responsibility of presenting it with anything but the very best quality of singing artistry.

I am one of the foremost champions of opera in English, but I can't agree with Mr Webster's statement. The Metropolitan Opera in New York plays all its operas in their original language, with the exception of about three productions per season given (excruciatingly) in an English translation. I certainly think that we should all aim to keep up the good work of Rosa, Quinlen, Beecham et al, but my memories of Covent Garden recall really packed houses chiefly on the glamorous nights of the 'Grand Season' (with big singers) rather than during performances of the Beecham Opera Company and the BNOC. (Sadlers Wells and the Old Vic are rather exceptions to this – for obvious reasons.)

With regard to the directorial set-up, I am a little inclined to view with misgiving any divided authority. Blame for the shortcomings of a production as well as credit for its good points should fall on the shoulders of a single individual – the artistic director. Differences of opinion between conductor and producer, can of course be ironed out, nine times out of ten, yet when the conception of a producer might differ diametrically from that of a musical director, and radically hamper the smooth working of the performance, there is only one court of appeal – the artistic director. In his absence, one of the two individuals should have a deciding voice. Mr Webster copes with this situation by acting as chairman of a triumvirate; either with a power of ruling or else of throwing his added vote against one or other of his associates. This is not satisfactory.

When the project was first mentioned to me it appealed to me and still does – as much from sentimental considerations as from any other. The thought of returning to my country and guiding

251

the artistic and musical destinies of what was once my operatic
home was almost irresistible. Quite frankly, it was only when I
realised – as the months went by and the real difficulties of the
London situation began to reveal themselves – that I had built
up too rosy a picture of what I might hope to find there, that I
began to have misgivings. Yet, even today, when Webster's letter
removed the last illusion concerning the conditions with which I
would be confronted in England, I had continued optimistic about
the artistic resources I would have had at my disposal.

Webster's letter has finally made me realise that I cannot safely
undertake the responsibility for a project the artistic outcome of
which I cannot foresee and consequently take full musical responsibility for.

As Webster says, what I am being called upon to do is neither
a sinecure nor glamorous, but just rather an exciting building job.
Were I a younger man, with more years of a career facing me than
are at present left me, the last feature would be sufficient to attract
me; and the sinecure and glamour would both automatically follow.
But now that the full aspects of the venture have been set before
me in black and white, I realise they fall short of the possibilities
for personal artistic expression I had ventured to visualise. In other
words, after more than a score of years spent over here in a constant
series of exciting artistic experiences, sampled through the medium
of highly skilled orchestras and a large receptive public following,
I can't suddenly reconcile myself to taking up the rather grim role
of operatic pioneer with its chances of failure.[5]

Eugene did not however wish to close irrevocably the door of
the Royal Opera House. He suggested that he could be available for three months later that year between his engagements
in Australia and Cincinnati and from April 1947 he could be
entirely at their disposal.

Keynes' reaction to Eugene's reply was predictable. He
wrote to Hawkes:

This is very disappointing. If Goossens lacks these sympathies
or these hopes and optimisms (namely to build up an English
opera that has its own traditions and standards), and is in fact a
little too much a man of the older tradition, even though not so
old in years, then perhaps he is not the man for us.

His final conclusion seems to be a half attempt to undo what
he has said in the first part, subject to his gaining a certain amount
of time and coming in late. I suppose the advantage from his point
of view would be that he would not have to burn his boats until

he had the opportunity of sniffing around and seeing whether we were likely to make good. But meanwhile someone else would have been pioneering and doing all the difficult work of founding the new organisation. I do not see why we should hold out any expectations to Goossens that if this individual, whose name we do not yet know, has made sufficiently good in the first six months we shall get rid of him and let Goossens take his job.[6]

In the event Eugene's prognosis proved correct. Apart from some notable successes such as *The Faery Queen* and *Peter Grimes*, the rigid concept of 'English' opera could not be reconciled with the establishment of Covent Garden as a leading international opera house. The absurdity of the concept was illustrated by Hans Hotter and Kirsten Flagstad having to relearn Wotan and Brünnhilde for an English version of *The Ring*.

Eugene commented privately in 1958:

> I felt, as I have always felt, that the position of Intendant of any great opera house is synonymous with its musical direction and that a sound artistic policy can only be achieved by a Director who is at once responsible, not only for the musical efficiency and smooth running of the operas, but also for the choice of repertory and singers who will be featured in those operas.
>
> I felt justified in seeking this condition, not only because of my own considerable operatic experience and something of a hereditary aptitude, but also because I felt disinclined to abandon the fruit of years of symphonic work just to conduct a few performances per annum at Covent Garden and be blamed for their shortcomings.
>
> As a result, Ralph Hawkes appointed Rankl, who merely conducted a few operas and auditioned endless singers, as I predicted would be the case.[7]

Goossens, the man whom they had wished to make Musical Director, was never to be offered a single guest performance of an opera with the new company. In September 1954 the Board of Directors offered him the post of Musical Director for the Ballet.[8] He declined with thanks.[9]

If Keynes, Hawkes and Webster had been able to negotiate a compromise, the post-war development of the Royal Opera House might have been very different. Eugene's personal and professional life would have taken another course entirely. Covent Garden's loss was to be Australia's gain.

253

17

Britain Can Take It!

Léon spent the first years of the war in Evesham, one of a group of top instrumentalists led by Jean Pougnet, whom the BBC had recruited for the Salon Orchestra. 'The formation of this orchestra from among the finest players in the country gave the impression and hope that music of a parallel quality would be offered to its listeners,' commented Thomas Russell, struggling to continue public concerts with the LPO. 'Almost the entire playing time of these unfortunate musicians was given over to the performance of music of barely third-rate importance and quality. The fact that this poor stuff was delightfully performed stressed rather than eased the blunder.'[1]

Leslie Bridgewater, the conductor of the Salon orchestra, wrote to its members on 16th June 1942 informing them that the BBC no longer required their services. Some joined the Armed Forces, Reginald Kell moved to America, while Léon and a few of his colleagues formed the nucleus of the Liverpool Philharmonic Orchestra. Léon's continuing contribution to the War Effort ranged from entertaining the Royal Navy on Scapa Flow to the famous series of Pub Concerts which were a valuable boost for civilian morale throughout the darkest hours of the Blitz.

Meanwhile his recordings with the Liverpool Philharmonic Orchestra included Handel's Concerto Grosso in G minor, Arthur Benjamin's arrangement of a Cimarosa Concerto for Oboe and Strings and a piece that was always particularly associated with him, the Sinfonia from Bach's *Easter Oratorio*. In Liverpool he also gave the first performance of Vaughan Williams' Oboe Concerto, conducted by Sir Malcolm Sargent on 30th September 1944.

Vaughan Williams had dedicated the work to Léon and

wrote to him: 'I hear from the BBC that they have asked you to play my new concerto at the Proms. I need hardly say I am much pleased at the prospect, if you are also pleased – you had better see it before you make up your mind! I hope to send you the oboe part and a pianoforte reduction of the score in about a fortnight. Of course, I shall welcome any suggestions from you as to making the part more "oboistic".'[2]

'Unfortunately my first attempts to play Vaughan Williams' Concerto in 1944 were thwarted by the attacks of buzz-bombs, which closed down the Henry Wood Promenade Concerts for that year,' Léon explained. 'This work showed the oboe in all its guises from piping shepherd to brilliant virtuoso. The rehearsal presents a vivid picture in my mind of Vaughan Williams sitting on the platform as solid as a statue, holding an old-fashioned ear-trumpet, for all the world like a reincarnation of Beethoven.'[3] (Léon's description presumably refers to the first London performance given on 4th May 1945 by the Bromley and Chislehurst Orchestra, conducted by Marjorie Whyte.)

As well as the hardships of war, Marie and Sidonie had had to cope with the tragic loss of their husbands, both within the same month of May 1942. A lifetime's discipline of keeping to orchestral schedules, of putting professional commitments before personal concerns provided them with an essential framework to face the desolation of life continuing without their partner. 'I had experienced indeed a terrible shock,' Marie recollected, 'but I could not sit back; there were two children to think about and educate, and my step-children Geoffrey and Kathleen. Fortunately an LSO tour came very soon after and I was advised to go with the orchestra. I went but can honestly say that I don't recollect any of the tour, my mind was constantly being dimmed and the shock seemed to become greater as time went on.'[4]

She had first been invited to play with the LSO in the autumn of 1939 when their Principal Harpist, John Cockerill joined the BBC Salon Orchestra. She played the harp cadenza in the 'Valse des Fleurs' from the *Nutcracker* Suite with such brilliance that she was asked to become a permanent member of the orchestra and stayed with them for nineteen years. The LSO was traditionally an all male orchestra and was to remain so until 1980, but once she had devised her scheme for changing behind the harp, Marie found no problems in being the only female member. She did not approve of women who achieved musical eminence through other talents.

'The first recording that I did as a member of the LSO was the Liszt *Mephisto Waltz* with Felix Weingartner. My impression of him was that of a very tall, stately figure who beat time like a metronome, but he got the results – no fuss, no unnecessary remarks. With him was a tall, very good-looking young woman, dressed very plainly but smartly and before long he handed the baton over to her. They said she was his wife but also a pupil. Strange are the things that great men can do!'[5] Marie gives no indication as to how well the lady conducted.

Marie remained in London throughout the war; she exemplified the courage and unruffled fortitude with which professional musicians continued to provide public concerts despite the discomfort and dangers involved. As the BBC Symphony Orchestra was in Bristol, the LSO was engaged for the 1940 Promenade Concerts at the Queen's Hall. She gives a graphic account of what was to be the last season in their historic home:

> On 26th August the Blitz started with an all-night raid. Neither orchestra nor audience could leave the building as everything in the way of transport had been stopped – even the underground closed down with thousands of people sleeping on the platforms and in the corridors. So we used to sing and play to keep ourselves occupied and the audience amused, though some just lay on the floor and slept.
>
> As nights such as these continued we became organised, bringing with us music such as solos, duets, trios etc. We worried little about the outside world, never dreaming that we could be hit at any moment. Finally the 'all-clear' and we went home. We were always back for a ten o'clock rehearsal the next morning. But it was all becoming too much so the last Prom at the Queen's Hall was on 7th September.[6]

The Queen's Hall was totally gutted by enemy action on 10th May 1941, during the terrible night which destroyed the House of Commons Chamber and damaged Westminster Abbey, the British Museum, the Law Courts, the Mansion House and the Tower. A Promenade Concert Season was held that year nevertheless, in the Albert Hall which was to become their new permanent home. Whenever there was an air-raid warning a red light would go on but the performance continued regardless until the light went off signalling the all-clear. At the traditional Last Night of the Proms on 23rd August, Marie played one of her favourite harp solos in the 'Faery Song' from *The Immortal Hour*.

She had featured as soloist in the Debussy *Danse Sacrée et Danse Profane* on tour with the short-lived Oxford Philharmonic Orchestra, organised by Sidney Beer. She was also broadcasting with the Lyra Quartet, drawn from principals of the LSO: Gordon Walker (flute), George Stratton (who led the orchestra) and Max Gilbert (viola). She joined an ensemble of flute (Gareth Morris), viola (Zygmunt Jarecki) and harp with whom she played the Debussy Sonata (1915) at the Wigmore Hall on 25th June 1942. Jarecki had studied the work with Debussy so Marie was able to add some of the composer's personal directions to her score.

On the lighter side, she took part in a Variety Entertainment, given for the Royal Family at Windsor Castle. It was organised by Louis Levy, Director of Music for Gaumont British Films, who had been in charge of the Windsor Home Guard. The artists included Max Miller, whose repertoire might have been considered a little racy for Royal ears.

I had quite a conversation with the King about the similarity of a harp to a piano and as a grand piano was at hand we crossed over to it and examined the harp-like structure of the mechanism. I had a little chat with Princess Margaret, then a young girl, regretting that her sister Elizabeth was unable to be present, owing to the fact that she was christening a ship somewhere up North.

I shall never forget Margaret's shoes. I'm quite sure they didn't belong to her. They were obviously for a grown-up as they had pointed toes and Louis heels. I expect she thought her own girl's shoes were too childlike for such an occasion and I could just imagine her insisting, bearing in mind my own sister who would not wear anything she did not like.[7]

Sidonie had been resident in Bedford with the BBC Symphony Orchestra from July 1941. 'We gave live concerts in the Corn Exchange and the Great Hall of Bedford School and travelled

257

round playing at British and American Air Force camps. Jessie Hinchcliffe and I had found a lovely top flat overlooking the river which became a centre for visiting artists. "Go to Sid and Jessie's. You'll have some food there," they were told. Charles Munch, when he first came back to England from France, hadn't had any proper food for months. He let me off the end of the rehearsal: "Go cook beef steak!" he said. We managed to give him a nice lunch.'[8]

Sir Adrian Boult was always a close friend. He had written to Eugene in June 1942: 'I want to tell you your sisters are *marvellous*. I was away when Sidonie's blow fell and she came back two or three days later, just her serene and balanced self with that grand poise and dignity. Marie comes down to Bedford fairly often when we need two harps and it is so nice to see them together.'[9]

Sidonie recalls: 'Adrian was always hungry so we gave him our chocolate rations. We used to leave a big slab on his score and then he was happy. He had a large frame and I don't think he was well fed at home.'[10]

Sidonie had few opportunities for solo work; on 24th March 1943, Boult arranged for her to play the Mozart Concerto for Flute and Harp (K299) with Gerald Jackson, First Flute. C B Rees provided enthusiastic Programme Notes:

> Tonight two magnificent artists whom we always hear as members of the orchestra come before us as soloists. Sidonie – 'Sid' to her friends – is one of the best-known instrumentalists in the country. It is not necessary to remind any concert audience that to her rare musical skill she allies great personal charm: an artist that (whether they should or not!) people go to *see* as well as hear!
>
> Not until she was nine could Sidonie reach the harp strings, and she remembers vividly how she would stand on tiptoes working the pedals and stretching with her small hand to find the low C string, trying at the same time to preserve the balance of the harp!

Shortly before the concert she had written to ask if she could receive a fee of fifteen guineas for solo work: 'I appear to have received eight guineas since 1924. I don't think I should be asking too much of the Corporation to raise my fee to a higher rate after so many years.'[11] She was offered ten guineas. The BBC continued to exploit its monopolistic position as far as the broadcasting of classical music was concerned. As late as 1965, young artists selected for recital work after rigorous auditions were still offered a starting fee of twelve guineas.

Sidonie was still on a part-time contract but in December 1943 the question was raised of a change over to a full-time contract at a weekly salary of £13.10, plus £1.10 additional payment. W W Thompson, Concerts Manager for the BBC SO, added a note of caution to his superiors in Music Department: 'We should, I feel, go out of our way to avoid giving the impression that it is only necessary for our musicians to obtain offers from outside sources in order to secure better terms of service from us.' The disadvantage of being on full-time contract was that she now had to obtain permission for outside engagements. In April 1944, Thompson refused to allow her to play in the film of *Caesar and Cleopatra*.

As often as she could, Sidonie snatched a few days in London to visit her elderly parents. They had steadfastly refused to move during the new terror of the 'Doodlebugs'. Annie Goossens, aged eighty-four, would stand outside shaking her formidable fist at the V2 Bombers and warning them off: 'Not in my vegetable garden!' Her tactics were successful and both 'Durban' and 'Crewkerne' survived unscathed.

By the autumn of 1945, Sidonie was able to move back to London to a flat in Ormonde Terrace, Regent's Park and was promptly burgled of her jewellery and furs replaced after the Bristol Blitz. On 19th December 1945 she remarried. Her second husband was Major Norman Millar, a handsome Scotsman from Dundee serving in the Black Watch. 'I couldn't have lived by myself. I like to have a man to look after me and for me to look after him,' she explains.[12] It was to prove a very happy union. They celebrated in traditional family style by taking her parents to lunch on New Year's Eve at L'Escargot, which had happily survived the Blitz.

Anne, Eugene's eldest daughter, had also introduced her husband to the family: Dr Edgar Obermer, an American physician only a couple of years younger than her father.

'Sid's wedding news came as a great surprise,' Eugene wrote to his parents from Cincinnati, 'and I'm glad you approve of her man. How glad I am for her sake that she's got someone to look after her. As for Anne's husband, I am afraid he "puzzles"

259

you because Anne (perhaps like her father!) has always seemed to attract "puzzling" people. Obviously a man of his age is not going to be easily summed up and I imagine that he's a combination of maturity (or sophistication) and a certain intellectual depth.'[13]

Edgar Obermer was to remain something of a mystery man to the family and in the summer of 1946 took Anne to live in an isolated house he owned near Lake Como in Italy. She had been able to meet up with her mother and twin sisters in Switzerland for the first time since the beginning of the war. Boonie and her third husband bought a house next door to the Obermers where they were to remain for many years. Both Anne's daughters were born in Italy.

Eugene was looking forward to a long summer reunion at last with his parents and was relieved to see from snapshots how well they seemed to have survived the trauma of the past six years.

> Mum darling, you seem hardly to have changed at all (taking after your eldest son in all the usual particulars!) and I was thrilled and proud of you and could have hugged you forever! You too, Dad darling, look superbly well, and I must say you look younger than ever. It seems incredible that over six years have passed since I saw your dear face – it's almost as if time has stood still, judging by your appearance. (How I wish it had!) The morning was completed when Mor's picture – taken outside the Albert Hall – arrived and she is miraculously young looking. More like a girl of eighteen than a middle-aged lady of fifty! What a family – now all I need are recent snaps of Sid and Lee to complete the family group.[14]

At the end of February he informed them of a change of plan: instead of spending the whole summer in England, he had accepted an invitation for a ten-week tour of Australia, received via the American State Department.

> The purpose of these concerts seems to be to present to the Australian audiences a conductor of a big American orchestra (the first to appear there since the war) who best seems fitted by the State Department to appear to Australia the type most representative of the cultured Anglo-American musician. There seems to be an element of propaganda in the whole thing which puts the invitation in a rather more delicate and unusual light

than were the State Department to send over the average sample of long-haired, temperamental, undiplomatic type of symphony conductor who apparently in the past seems to have created no great impression on the sensitive Australians.

Judson [his New York manager] pointed out rather forcibly the tremendous publicity value to me of the visit in relation to my comparative professional inactivity during the past six years. I have lost a certain amount of the international character I used to enjoy as a conductor and Cincinnati isn't New York or Boston! So the Australian thing would provide that 'shot in the arm' that my professional existence needs at the moment.[15]

Eugene was still not prepared to take his parents fully into his confidence. It was not until 30th April that he confided to them the effusive details of his third marriage in a letter marked STRICTLY CONFIDENTIAL:

For well over the past three years, a very wonderful person has brought a new light into my life. By her understanding, sympathy and completely unselfish and devoted love for me, she has brought a new emotional and inspirational force into my existence which seemed to me devoid of the steadfast elements of loyal love and companionship I have always craved. When I first met her, close on four years ago, a first acquaintance and eventual friendship soon ripened into something much deeper. We fell deeply and inalterably in love with each other and *are more so than ever today*.

Though we have always been separated by long distance, we have shared each other's activities and interests by voluminous correspondence. Only during the summer months in the remote countryside were we able to be together for any time; and at such times my life was completely happy. She combines a personality of unusual charm and distinction with a simplicity and domestic ability which are her greatest and most conspicuous qualities. With it all, too, she is my intellectual equal as our interests are common.

This long stretch of coming summer months – now that certain obstacles to marriage have been removed [Marjorie's divorce] – were inconceivable without each other's companionship especially in foreign lands; so we resolved some time back to take the irrevocable step. We motored two weeks ago into the heart of Kentucky and were married by the local judge at the court house 'after hours'. (A religious – Catholic – ceremony will follow in due course, as soon as certain rigorous formalities in connection with my former marriage are completed and those ties nullified.)

261

I insisted all along on the ceremony being completely secret as my remarriage would have created a great deal of embarrassing publicity at a time when all publicity should be concentrated on purely musical matters connected solely with the orchestra and the May Festival.

Marjorie is, curiously enough, on quite friendly terms with Janet, and Donie *adores* her. Renée and Nanny both are very fond of her as they have all known her for some considerable time. This had provided a very harmonious and dignified situation all round.

She has a fine cultural and musical sensibility – a good pianist (amateur strictly!) and a sharp critical faculty where music and orchestras are concerned. (She is a Philadelphia girl of proud Pennsylvania lineage, a 'thoroughbred'.) She is, in my eyes, very beautiful and a superbly poised woman of the world – a 'lady' as we would say in England.

Above all, she is someone who inspires me to work, who understands me and who has lifted the pall of loneliness which threatened to cloud the rest of my life. She longs to see you both, darlings, and will be very proud when you consent to take her to your hearts, as I have to mine.[16]

Eugene and Marjorie sailed for England on the *Queen Mary* and stayed at the Savoy from 19th to 23rd May. The Goossens turned out in force to welcome them at Waterloo Station and enjoyed a family supper at the Savoy. Eugene proudly paraded Marjorie to his parents, Sid, Marie, Léon and Leslie and their children. Léon's daughter Jennie remembers the wonderfully kind, sweet uncle who suddenly appeared from America and opened up a case full of Hershey chocolate bars and all the goodies that little English children had forgotten during the war.

The time was far too short for the family to form more than a superficial impression of Marjorie before the newly-weds departed for Australia. Eugene sent his parents detailed letters of his success, news of his mother's Cook cousins who had welcomed him in Sydney and of many members of the Carl Rosa Opera Company who sent their warmest greetings and memories of working with Eugene I and II and Grandpa Cook. 'Other old stagers who have turned up here [Melbourne] to greet me like shades of the past have been Gertrude Johnson who sang the Queen of the Night with me in BNOC, Browning

Mummery, Fred Collier and Horace Stevens, whose names will all be familiar to you, Dad darling. Apparently they're all doing a roaring business as "Singing Teachers". So it seems that in Australia like in America, "there's a sucker born every minute" as the Yanks say!'[17] (Gertrude Johnson merited more serious appraisal; a prize pupil of Melba's she had become a teacher of some distinction and success.)

He sent his mother warmest wishes for her eighty-sixth birthday and details of a gift parcel of the one commodity he found in plentiful supply: woollen underwear. He was providing combinations, vests, pants, socks and scarves to keep his parents, Léon, Marie, Sid and Norman all warm throughout the winter. They were to prove a lifesaver through the appalling British winter of 1946–47.

Eugene and Marjorie were not able to return from Australia until 2nd September. They missed the BBC Symphony Orchestra's first concert at the Proms on 24th August at which Sidonie was the soloist in the British premiere of Paul Creston's *Poem* for Harp and Orchestra. The evening is engraved on her memory. 'During the first half my mother was taken ill. I could hear the announcement over the tannoy in the interval asking if there was a doctor in the house. I had no idea who it was for; I was opening the second half and they didn't want to worry me. Afterwards we got her home as quickly as possible. I had on an evening dress with an enormous skirt of pre-war Parisian black net. It kept getting in the way as I was trying to undress my mother and get her into bed. I kept ripping off yards of the stuff in my hurry.'[18]

Marie was enjoying a well-earned family holiday in Folkestone but offered to come home immediately if their mother's condition deteriorated. Despite their concern, Léon and Sidonie had to continue with their professional engagements. They gave an impeccable Sunday afternoon concert for the BBC the following day, a rare opportunity to play the interesting but limited twentieth-century repertoire for oboe and harp. They were joined by Joseph Szigeti and Gerald Moore for a programme including William Alwyn's Suite for Oboe and Harp, Satie's *Gymnopédie* no. 2 arranged for Oboe and Harp, André Caplet's *Divertissement à la française* for

263

Harp and Poulenc's *Mouvements perpétueles* for Oboe and Harp, arranged by Heifetz.

Annie Goossens died peacefully at home on 15th September 1946, fortified by her unswerving Catholic faith. One of the expressions of condolence the family most appreciated was from Lady Jessie Wood: 'In grateful Remembrance knowing with what pleasure and comfort Henry treasured his life-long association with the Goossens family and always expressed thankfulness in their utter sincerity to the music they all served infallibly.'

It had been a long and happy marriage. Eugene suggested that his father might like to return with him to the United States but he decided that at seventy-nine he was too old for travelling; he preferred to remain in his familiar home, cherishing his chrysanthemums, his geraniums and his tomato plants. Fortunately he had the health and resilience of spirit to continue enjoying both his independence and the companionship of his children and grandchildren. He was to survive his wife until 1958.

18

Challenging Australia

If history had worked out differently Eugene Goossens might have followed in his father's footsteps as guest conductor in Australia. In February 1922 Eugene Goossens senior had received a letter from The Agent-General for New South Wales enquiring whether he would 'entertain a proposal to conduct fifty orchestral concerts in Australia over a period of four months, beginning on the 1st May next for the sum of £1000 and travelling expenses. You are doubtless aware that there is a most excellent orchestra in Sydney under the conductorship of Mr Henri Verbrugghen, Director of the State Conservatorium of Music, Sydney.'

Goossens senior expressed interest in accepting the appointment while Verbrugghen, a fellow Belgian, was conducting in Minneapolis and was disappointed when three weeks later he received a second letter informing him that the position had been filled. He was somewhat mollified to read in a press cutting from Sydney that he had headed the three candidates whose names had been sent to the Advisory Board. 'Goossens senior, by the way, is the father of the famous ultra-modernist, Eugene Goossens.' The board however decided a bird in the hand was worth two in the bush and asked the Polish pianist, André Skalski (already *in situ*) to take up the baton 'until such time as Mr Verbrugghen returns.' He never did and a year later the NSW Orchestra was disbanded.

When the Australian Broadcasting Commission was set up in 1932 they established a studio orchestra in Sydney of twenty-five players augmented to fifty in 1934 for a short season of four concerts conducted by Sir Hamilton Harty, the first conductor of international rank to be invited to Australia by the ABC. When Bernard Heinze, Ormond Professor and Director of the Melbourne Conservatorium, was appointed Musical Advisor to the ABC, he advocated one national professional orchestra based on the Melbourne Symphony Orchestra, which he conducted. Despite his advice, the Commission decided to establish professional orchestras in each of the six states to provide broadcast music and live concerts, but the main thrust remained in Sydney; the orchestra was enlarged to seventy for an annual season of eight public concerts with distinguished musicians from overseas.

One of the names Heinze put forward in 1936 as a visiting conductor was Eugene Goossens junior. He was conducting at the Hollywood Bowl when he received a telegram from his agent, Harold Holt on 17th September.[1] 'Would you entertain visiting Australia for conducting tour next summer about two months there if so please cable terms?' His reply had been: 'Much regret other dates prevent visit.' They included the premiere of *Don Juan de Mañara* for the Coronation Season at Covent Garden. He wrote to his father on 20th September from Santa Monica: 'The enclosed telegram will amuse you. My answer I hope you'll agree with. As well be buried than pack off to Australia for five months!!'[2]

In musical terms, Australia was still on the other side of the world, an undiscovered continent separated from the international circuit by a long sea voyage from San Francisco and an even longer one from Southampton. Those who were willing to overcome the tyranny of distance included Sargent, Szell and Beecham with Rubinstein, Schnabel, Tauber and Lotte Lehmann among the soloists.

The war imposed cultural isolation on Australia and further consolidated the position of Bernard Heinze as the ABC's Chief Conductor for the duration but change was in the air. Dr Edgar Bainton was about to retire as Director of the NSW Conservatorium of Music and Robert Heffron, Minister of Education for New South Wales, suggested appointing a distinguished international conductor to the joint posts of Director of the Conservatorium and Musical Director of an enlarged and fully professional Sydney Symphony Orchestra.

There were high hopes for the orchestra when it was first heard in its new form on 23rd January 1946. Neville Cardus, then music critic of the *Sydney Morning Herald*, was less san-guine. 'It sounded much as usual, no better, no worse. The tone was reasonably good, though the strings became frequently obscure or thin in short bowed passages; the woodwinds, secure in parts, now and again disagreed in the whole. The brass had moments of power and some dignity . . . at other times it was brass to the point of hardware and the metal trade.' Such material would certainly present a challenge to a guest conductor!

Cardus had written for the *Manchester Guardian* since 1916 and was equally authoritative on his twin loves of music and cricket. He had come out originally to report on his friend Sir Thomas Beecham's tour in the summer of 1940 and although he found the Australian cricketers of a far higher standard than their musicians, he stayed on to write for the *Sydney Morning Herald* until 1947.

Despite the influence of European Jewish refugees on the musical life of Sydney and Melbourne, Australia remained a WASP culture. Charles Moses, the General Manager of the ABC, who had emigrated from England in 1922, was convinced that the orchestra and the Australian public needed a British conductor. Eugene seemed to fit the bill as Moses explained in an ABC interview after his retirement: 'We had heard about Goossens – he was British, thoroughly so; why despite his years in the United States, he still pronounced schedule the way British people do.' Not perhaps the most accurate gauge of a conductor's competence!

After fifteen years in Cincinnati, Eugene was considering the possibility of moving on. The ABC's offer of a three-month tour of twenty-two concerts arrived at an opportune moment. Perhaps Australia might provide the creative stimu-lus he was seeking; the new horizons of a young challenging country to match the glamour and excitement of his new wife.

Eugene and Marjorie arrived in Brisbane at the end of May 1946. The journey took three days in a converted Lancaster bomber, equipped with sleeping berths. The first of Eugene's concerts for the ABC was in Brisbane but everyone was waiting for his debut in Sydney in a programme including Brahms' First Symphony and Stravinsky's *Firebird*. Audience and critics alike were overwhelmed by the spectacular display of tone, colour and dramatic excitement he was able to summon up from the orchestra's undisciplined players.

The one critic in Australia whose judgement and knowledge Eugene valued was Cardus: 'It was a symphony concert in the truest sense,' he wrote, 'there were no tricks or appeals to non-musical susceptibilities. . . His manner is serious, economical, but strong; the sweeping downbeat, which carries the baton behind his back, is very impressive in its suggestion of command. He is absolutely free of that consciousness of audience which marks the contemporary second-rater.'

Eugene wrote to his father: 'You'll remember Neville Cardus, formerly of the *Manchester Guardian* and Sydney's most caustic and most feared critic. He obviously had a good time and came to dinner the other night and talked with real veneration of you and the Carl Rosa Opera Company, saying how he learnt everything at your feet and how much he owed to you for his early training in music and opera. Sydney is full of your old admirers, people who remember your performances as though they had happened yesterday. Their veneration of the name Goossens is almost fanatical!'[3]

The orchestra presented a stimulating challenge and by the end of the tour Eugene felt they had made so much progress that he could entrust them with a performance of his favourite showpiece, *Le Sacre du Printemps*, on only three three-hour rehearsals. Violinist Patricia (Bambi) Tuckwell (Lady Harewood) remembers him describing it to the players as 'the yardstick of the modern orchestra'.[4] Despite their unfamiliarity with the style, he compared their performance favourably with the London concert premiere of the work he had conducted a quarter of a century earlier. The programme also included his own Concertino for Double String Orchestra. Cardus commented of it: 'Interesting to hear again, not only for the beautiful and ingenious part writing . . . but because this work, composed in 1928, will hold its own in fine astringent musical thinking with anything done recently by Britten or Bax.'

Eugene was keen to promote Australian music and asked for scores from contemporary composers. John Antill, then an ABC control engineer, was too self-effacing to offer his ballet

Corroboree for consideration. Sargent had turned it down in 1945 and the music had lain forgotten on a studio shelf until the ABC moved to King's Cross, Sydney's equivalent of Soho. Eventually Antill was persuaded to take it to Goossens. 'He danced around the table,' the composer recalled. 'He said "I'll take this page and this page and that section, and make a suite of it." This suite was what he played in the Town Hall a week later.' It received an eight minute ovation. For the first time the public realised that music belonging to the twentieth century was being written in Australia.

Eugene also made a publicity film of himself conducting Tchaikovsky's *Pathétique* Symphony so that he could demonstrate the excellence of the orchestra abroad. Extracts from the film were widely screened in Australian cinemas.

Helen Bainton, playing amongst the violins, remembers the feeling of security they all experienced from 'his authoritative direction, his patience and experience of the recording technique. When the session ended many members of the orchestra stepped up to the rostrum to wish him goodbye with a genuine feeling of regret, so when the news of his appointment came we all rejoiced, feeling it augured well for the future development of the SSO.'[5] Like Sir Hamilton Harty twelve years earlier, Eugene felt that the sincerity of the Australian musicians made up for what they lacked in mere technical proficiency.

The love affair between Eugene and Australia was mutual. He was entranced by the wild beauty of its coasts, the mysterious excitement of untrammelled space which made up the interior, and, as a painter, by the special quality of its light. He loved the beauty of Sydney Harbour, its great wide sweeps of water, its network of secluded bays and wooded coves. His romantic fascination with ships of all shapes and sizes had remained since his early days in Liverpool. The *coup de grâce* was the view from the Director's office at the Conservatorium. He looked out over the lush green Botanic Gardens and the calm blue waters of Farm Cove towards the Heads, where the First Fleet had sailed towards a safe harbour after their historic journey from England in 1788.

Australia presented a revitalising challenge to a middle-aged man: the opportunity to build up an orchestra, to educate a public and create a musical tradition in a country which idolised the cricket bat and the tennis racket rather than the writer's pen or the violinist's bow. He expressed his conviction that there was a national craving for beauty hidden beneath a veneer of indifference. 'You Australians are exposed all the time to physical beauty. Deep down you cannot help loving too, the beautiful things of the spirit.' Before he left, Moses offered Eugene a three-year contract as permanent conductor of the SSO and Director of the Conservatorium. He had to be convinced that a resident position in Australia would not interfere with his conducting engagements in Europe and that financially it would be worth his while to leave Cincinnati. The eventual salary Moses was able to offer him, funded by the ABC, the Sydney City Council and the Government of New South Wales made up a combined package of over £7,000 a year. The Prime Minister of Australia, Ben Chiffley, was being paid only £5,000.

Moses was totally committed to the engagement of Eugene. The two men had quickly become friends and although Eugene was not always the best judge of character, on this occasion the instinctive empathy he felt was justified. Moses was to remain his loyal friend and supporter to the bitter end. Charles Moses was typical of the amateur who often attained a position of great authority in the pioneering days of broadcasting. He was an English Army Officer who initially failed in Australia, first as a fruit-grower and then as a car salesman. But he was blessed with an imposing presence, a handsome physique and the right accent. He joined the infant ABC and quickly rose from a Company announcer to General Manager, a post he was to hold from 1935 to 1964.

He was not a musician but a passionate music-lover who often repeated his aim 'to provide fine music to enrich our broadcast programs.'[6] He was a man whose integrity was never questioned, unlike his predecessor, Major J C W Conder. Bernard Heinze, exploiting his role of King Maker, had put forward Conder, a former Governor of Pentridge Prison. After less than two years Conder resigned, just before the accountants caught up with him. A vast financial scandal was exposed, including his lucrative sideline of private commissions when engaging artists for the ABC. He became in quick succession a circus owner, a bankrupt and for a brief time a prisoner in the jail where he had once been governor.

Eugene had time to consider Moses' offer during his autumn engagements in England. These included a well received performance of *Corroboree* with the London Symphony Orchestra at the Albert Hall on 20th October and the premiere of his own Second Symphony with the BBC Symphony Orchestra at the People's Palace on 2nd November. He had begun the work in Maine in 1943 and described its introspective main themes as being permeated by the grim background of the war years. He dedicated it to Marjorie.

His old friend Richard Capell commented in the *Daily Telegraph*: 'What was above all striking in these four movements was the mastery of the orchestration which abounded in ingenious inventions and piquant effects. The central feature of the slow movement is the old English folk tune 'The Turtle Dove' which finds itself transplanted into a world of curious dissonances.'[7] Ralph Hill in the *Daily Mail* summed it up as 'the work of an alert and ingenious mind.'[8] The general critical assessment was that it was a clever and overcomplex work, more interesting for its orchestral effects than its emotional content.

Eugene was welcomed back, after seven years, as a distinguished guest conductor. 'His style made for performances that were flowing, elegant and full of life,' was Capell's verdict.[9] 'Grand to watch Goossens playing himself in with sweeping baton beat; swaying the London Philharmonic Orchestra as Hammond sways the crowd when he is hitting sixes,' enthused Roy Johnson in the *Daily Express* after praising the collaborative *American Variations* written for the Cincinnati Jubilee.[10] But there did not seem to be any permanent orchestral position open to him: Boult was ensconced at the BBC; Barbirolli at the Hallé and Sargent at the LPO; a suggestion that Eugene might take over Basil Cameron's share of the 1946 Promenade Concerts had not materialised.[11] According to Sir Charles Mackerras, Walter Legge who founded the Philharmonia Orchestra was not interested in British conductors.[12] War-ravaged London, suffering from food rationing and a fuel shortage, compared unfavourably with the sunshine and cornucopial profusion he had enjoyed in Sydney.

Eugene and Marjorie returned to the USA on the *Queen Elizabeth*. 'Everything was chi-chi,' announced the tall willowy 'brownette' to the waiting reporters in Cincinnati. 'Glamour was as thick as the London fog, what with the Duke and Duchess of Windsor, the Goldwyn Girls and British mannequins aboard.'[13] The main news was that Eugene would be stepping down from the Cincinnati podium at the close of the season to take up his dual position in Australia.

The parting was by mutual consent. 'One cannot conduct an orchestra as long as I have and [not] hate to sever connections,' commented Eugene. 'But after sixteen years both sides felt they might benefit from a change.'[14] Although the Orchestral Board in Cincinnati realised they would be hard put to find a musician of equal calibre they were not willing to match the money he was being offered in Australia. His appointment was announced in the British and Australian press on 18th November 1946 at a fee of £5,000 a year for the Sydney orchestral appointment.

He wrote to his father explaining his decision: 'One can stay too long in one place, though frankly I look back on the fifteen years spent here as years of considerable artistic development and mutual benefit for Cincinnati and myself. The field to which I shall go next season is an enormous one, a fresh country and one in which I can build up a lasting tradition and create new things and organisations in my own way, instead of merely perpetuating an old tradition.'[15]

He further opened his heart in a letter to Moses at the ABC:

It seems hard to believe that the remote slender prospect of my Australian permanence has actually become a concrete thing. Accomplished with a minimum of complexity (no animosity here and our own negotiations of the most pleasurable and friendly kind), it seems as though there was an inevitability about the whole thing which augurs well for the future.

It'll be a good thing to be back in our future home. The thought of belonging to such a friendly community and helping to mould its musical destinies is enormously exciting. The thought too of enjoying the long loyal friendship of Charles Moses and his family is a grand one.[16]

Eugene undertook to transform the Sydney Symphony Orchestra into one of the sixth greatest in the world in two years. In return he wanted uninterrupted control of the orchestra and a guarantee that only conductors resident in Australia would conduct it in his absence. Was this an insecure man trying to ensure that no illustrious competitors could be engaged to steal his thunder?

William G James, Federal Controller of Music for the ABC, analysed Goossens' strengths and weaknesses in a letter to Moses from New York. 'He is a great musician and fine conductor and all musicians here who count congratulate the ABC on being able to secure his services. I believe he will eventually build the Sydney Orchestra up to a very high standard but, as you know, he is not spectacular and must become an acquired taste if he is to sustain public interest. I therefore do not think he should be available day in and day out to the public but rather reserved for the important concerts and festivals.' Bill James was a successful pianist and composer. He was best known for his Australian Christmas Carols which dispensed with items irrelevant to the Southern Hemisphere like holly, ivy and snow. He was to become a good friend of Eugene's as well as a respected colleague.

Moses had agreed that no other overseas conductor would be engaged for Sydney until the end of June 1948, except Rafael Kubelík. Eugene explained his beliefs as to the relative status of conductor and orchestra to Moses:

The public should be made to realize that a symphony concert *without* soloists every now and then is not necessarily incomplete or deficient. They should be taught, as Koussevitzky has taught the Boston audience and as I have been trying to teach the Cincinnati audience, that the main attraction of a symphony concert is the orchestra and its conductor.

As you know, I have no spark of the prima donna about me, but I know the psychology of audiences and I know full well that unless the new incumbent of an important post, such as the one in Sydney, is 'built up' properly into the figure of importance he undoubtedly *is* in the musical community, he will automatically lapse into the matter-of-fact everyday figure that many conductors who occupy permanent posts have become. Please don't get the idea that I am against soloists for the orchestra, quite the contrary, but please let me have an occasional concert without a soloist and, above all, let me have my first concert alone.[17]

He proved his point at the special orchestral concert, on 17th July 1947, to mark his debut as the SSO's resident conductor, in the presence of the Governor General and the Premier of New South Wales. The programme established what had always been his policy, of mixing popular favourites like Beethoven's Fifth Symphony with works unfamiliar to his audience, in this case the first Australian performance of Delius' *Dance Rhapsody* no. 1 and Ravel's *Daphnis and Chloe* Suite no. 1. Eugene repeated his determination to put the orchestra in two years amongst the six greatest in the world. It is interesting to see which orchestras he considered were the greatest in the world. He listed them, though not in order of excellence, as: the Boston Symphony, Philadelphia Symphony, New York Philharmonic, Toscanini's NBC Orchestra and Beecham's Royal Philharmonic in London.

The orchestra's commitment to Eugene's ideal had been underlined by Deputy Conductor, Joseph Post at their own welcome reception in the orchestral studio above Woolworths in King's Cross.

Eugene quickly announced two further ambitions: to improve standards at the Conservatorium so that it would no longer be necessary for gifted young musicians to train abroad and the foundation of an Australian opera and ballet company in its own auditorium. He suggested that an opera house would be a suitable memorial to servicemen and women of World War II, an idea enthusiastically taken up by Sydney's Lord Mayor, Alderman Bartley: 'The City Council would co-operate in any memorial like this, but it could not undertake the cost. An opera house would cost more than £1,000,000.'[18]

Eugene reiterated this theme in a Personality Profile in the *Sydney Daily Telegraph*: 'One of my biggest castles-in-the-air is an opera house for Sydney. There should be one in a city of this size for opera, ballet, theatre and concerts. A home for music is of vital concern to me, because a community should be kept in touch with contemporary thought and feeling in music.'

The interviewer continues:

He says he is not a 'hot air person', that he doesn't make promises unless he thinks he has a good chance of fulfilling them and you feel after talking to him that he will succeed. . .

Goossens is a British citizen, not an American as some people believe. He is a big, pink man with large ears, a long, pointed nose, alert eyes, a bulging forehead and long side-burns turning grey at the ends. He moves slowly, speaks softly, with an accent that has a faint flavour of the English North Country about it; but you are conscious all the time of tremendous latent force in the man, of controlled and directed power.

In photographs he looks unemotional, almost cold, but he is one proof that the camera can lie. He is warm, friendly, direct, with immense personal charm and manners which would make the average Australian executive type look like an oaf beside him.[19]

Even the *Sunday Sun*, not usually known for its championship of the Arts, commented: 'To have such a world figure as Mr Goossens directing our musical education is significant and important. The encouragement of culture in a young nation is just as vital as the encouragement of agriculture.'[20]

As for the Women's Page, Carol Bertie of the *Sydney Sun* decided that Mrs Goossens would probably be the personality of 1947. She summed her up as 'delightful but firm, clever but not pernickety'. It is difficult to decide how far Ms Bertie's tongue was in her cheek when she continued: 'Asked in that frank, humble way Australians have, for ten good reasons why Goossens and she came here, she settled for two good ones: "We sat on the beach at Manly in the sun on a week day. It was so long and white."' The second reason was more to the point: that conducting the Cincinnati Symphony Orchestra had become routine after sixteen years.[21]

Eugene, as a cosmopolitan musician of international repute, a friend of Heifetz, Copland and Rubinstein, was enthusiastically welcomed by Sydney's influential group of emigré music critics. Walter Wagner gave him authoritative support in *The Canon*, the monthly magazine he had recently founded as the Australian Journal of Music.

Curt Prerauer in *Tempo*, the Australian Musical News Magazine, warned him of some dangers ahead: 'You'll find a more or less musical community which is more or less ready to accept

275

unquestioningly your leadership. You'll find much hypocrisy too. There are many people who TALK progress. Amongst them there may be a few who really MEAN it and you'll find others who TALK progress better to prevent it.'[22]

As during his career in the USA, the most revealing indication of Eugene's ambitions and triumphs in Australia are to be found in the regular progress reports he wrote to his father. He commented after his first orchestral rehearsal:

> I think by the time I've weeded out some dead wood it'll be a very fine orchestra indeed. After which I'll work it up gradually to top virtuoso rank. The spirit behind it is fine, as their relief at having a permanent conductor – especially one of my own calibre – is terrific after all they've been through at the hands of visiting 'maestri'!! My hardest work will actually be putting the Conservatorium to right. It's a picturesque building overlooking the harbour (you've no idea how beautiful the view is; I'll send you some photos of it later) and some of the professors are also picturesque, but in the wrong way. Anno domini and incompetence have both had full sway here and there's lots of Clearing Out to be done. But I anticipated that.
>
> I'm starting an 'opera house' and a 'concert hall' movement. The Town Hall in a city of one and a half million is quite inadequate, though it possesses probably the finest organ in the world. It holds about 2,500 and I want a hall holding 3,600 at least. The spirit and enthusiasm behind this public is immense but it needs constant kindling.
>
> My darling is being as always of tremendous help and encouragement to me. She has done a lot of work arranging my rooms at the conservatory.
>
> Rejoice that your oldest and tallest, as Director of the NSW conservatory, a state institution has finally joined the ranks of civil servants, hence the envelopes marked OHMS![23]

Once he and Marjorie were settled, he had hoped to persuade his father to join them in Sydney: 'It'll be hard to relinquish Durban and the company of Mor and Sid but in exchange you'll have us with you, plus a lovely new country, superb climate and an utterly new environment which should give you a new lease of life. Also you'll be with me while I'm building up something very important (your watchful help and advice during the new opera house building and organisation would be always invaluable) and we'll have finally what we've always longed for, a life together, in beautiful surroundings away from the grimness of London.'[24]

The scheme, like his constant plans to bring his parents to the USA, did not materialise. After forty years of operatic touring, in his old age his father preferred the comfort of his own home to sharing the glamour of his son's international career.

The Sydney Symphony Orchestra concerts were run as a subscription series. Eugene's appointment proved so popular with the public that the number of subscribers increased from 3,663 to 5,302 for the major 1947 series, plus nearly two thousand subscribers under twenty-five for Youth Concerts. By the 1950s there were four separate subscription series each of ten concerts. Hundreds of concert-goers, unable to get into the packed Town Hall had the music relayed to them outside. Isaac Stern was astonished by the warmth of audience appreciation he received on his first visit to Sydney to play the Prokofiev First Violin Concerto. He commented that in the USA, it would be impossible to play six concerts in one city as he did in Sydney.

The SSO was in obvious need of a larger auditorium than the Town Hall, until Goossens' dream of a purpose-built arts centre could be realised. The solution seemed to lie in the temporary use of the Capitol Theatre; this was on short-term lease as a cinema, showing mainly horror films. Charles Moses asked the City Council to make the theatre available to the ABC for orchestral and choral concerts, opera, ballet and theatre. 'Its acoustic properties, seating capacity and "presentation" facilities are immeasurably superior to the Town Hall,' wrote Eugene. It had 600 more seats. The State Minister for Housing, Mr Evatt also sent a letter supporting the proposal.

The City Council unanimously turned them down and renewed the cinema lease. 'The ABC has not stated whether it is prepared to pay for the use of the Capitol Theatre,' added Alderman Shannon. 'We are already contributing £10,000 a year towards the orchestra.' He strongly resented the pressure tactics used by the orchestra's supporters. 'The Labour Council [of NSW], nearly half of whose members are Communist [*sic*] should attend to its own work instead of trying to tell the City Council how to go about its business. Ninety-nine per cent of those people who have written to the Press supporting the orchestra's claims on the theatre live outside the city and so do not contribute to the city's rates.'[25]

Eugene had had his first taste of Australian philistinism: 'If our authorities were far-sighted enough to appoint a conductor of world standards as leader of our musical life, they should not retrace their steps by preferring Frankenstein to Mozart,' wrote Curt Prerauer to the editor of the *Sydney Morning Herald*.

Eugene was undismayed.

> I am an incurable optimist. The council's decision is disappointing, but I feel that there must be some eleventh hour solution – that some group of citizens with a love of music and an understanding of its importance in the community will find something that we can do. I want a big hall, a hall with a large seating capacity, good acoustics, and a stage large enough for the sort of choral festival I have in mind, with at least 450 singers and an orchestra of about 150.
>
> I also want a hall that will be the home for the orchestra, where we can rehearse regularly, instead of having, as at present, to remake all our efforts in one single rehearsal on the morning of the concert, because earlier rehearsals have been held in another place where the tonal balance and sonority are completely different.
>
> Frankly I do not know how the problem is going to be solved. But do not forget, I am an optimist.[26]

Over the next nine years even Eugene's optimism was to become dented by the refusal of politicians at City and State level to implement the improvements he sought for both the orchestra and the Conservatorium. The principle was always approved of, the problem was finding the funds. No one in power was willing to endanger popular support by committing his mouth to his voters' pocket. Despite Australia's strong choral tradition and flourishing choral societies, he never realised his dreams of establishing a Sydney Music Festival on the lines of the May Festival in Cincinnati.

Eugene was far more successful in inspiring the orchestra to achieve his aims for them. He imposed a rigorous and disciplined rehearsal schedule to which they were unaccustomed. 'Watch my beat,' he would say, 'it never varies.' One anecdote of his martinet tendencies found its way into the gossip columns, adding variety to the descriptions of Mrs Goossens' stylish gowns and tasteful jewellery with which they were regularly filled. 'When Eugene Goossens rehearses the orchestra he really makes them rehearse. At about four minutes to one, when they're all thinking of lunch, he invariably says "Well now, I think we've just got time to go over that piece once more." They were all astonished the other day when he didn't say it. "No," he said, "I think we can leave off now." And with a crash the electric clock fell down off the wall.'

He developed a special rapport with a group of attractive and talented young musicians in the orchestra, including Bambi Tuckwell who played in the first violins during that first season.

> We were an awfully ignorant lot, not capable of saying what his standards were like except that he was brilliant at conducting difficult pieces by taking the work apart, having sectional rehearsals and putting it together again. He was very musicianly, not a bully but we'd never had to work so hard in our lives!
>
> We all found him very English with his cultured voice and seemingly aloof manner, mixed with very un-English traits like his habit of walking around with his jacket over his shoulders like a terribly dashing cloak. He was much more fun than he looked; he looked very forbidding but he was enormously charming. I knew him a bit socially and he gave me away at my first wedding, a very informal occasion in a Melbourne hotel.'[27]

Her brother Barry, leading the horns, sums him up retrospectively as 'a cold fish but a wonderful musician, a great innovator. He had to contend with the lotus-eating attitude of some of the players – it's a nice day, so let's go to the beach and have a barbie – which gets in the way of excellence!'[28]

Despite his ambitions for the orchestra, he did not have a possessive attitude towards brilliant young players like Barry Tuckwell, Charles Mackerras, violinist Brenton Langbein and oboist Ian Wilson destined for international careers. His advice was always 'You should go abroad, dear boy', not 'You must stay here and play in my orchestra.'

Sir Charles Mackerras was First Oboe in the SSO:

> I was very keen to get as many contacts from Goossens as I could, so I went for him hammer and tongs. I learnt his oboe concerto to try and impress him. He was very nice to me; he sympathised with my ambitions and gave me lots of introductions, to his brother Léon, to Constant Lambert and Sir Adrian Boult.

He had this withdrawn, rather lofty manner which a lot of Australians found rather stuck up. I, who had been brought up to regard everything British as much better than everything Australian, rather admired that but a lot of the Aussies didn't like it at all. The orchestra found him Pommie but they realised he was by far the best conductor they were likely to get on a permanent basis. A lot of players grew to worship him and he became very keen on the orchestra. He revelled in the first Australian performances of *The Rite of Spring* and *Daphnis and Chloe* even though he had to do them without a bass flute. The only bass flute in Australia belonged to someone in the Melbourne Orchestra. He excelled in that repertoire of colourful twentieth-century music.[29]

Eugene had a guaranteed minimum of fifteen concerts a year outside New South Wales. When he was conducting in Adelaide he discovered that the post of Director of the Elder Conservatorium was vacant so on 21st October 1947 he wrote to his old friend Percy Grainger telling him that he had put his name forward: 'With Heinze and myself at the head of the schools at Melbourne and Sydney respectively, to have you at the head of the only important other Conservatorium in the country, would be a tremendous thing for Australian music. The list of applicants which I happened to see consisted of the usual nonentities from England, all with FRCO after their names, denoting that they are organists. This breed has no contact with the actualities of the musical profession and would, in my opinion, set music back in Adelaide, rather than advance it.'

Percy wrote to Eugene thanking him for the offer:

But it is truly out of the question for me. I am far too old [sixty-five]. And I have far too many unfinished compositions to finish and other kindred artistic jobs to finish. So I couldn't face a life with administrative work in it. I am much more worn out than other men of my age (although bodily spry perhaps) because for over forty years I have always sacrificed *everything* to money-making and *always* suppressed all my musical impulses, opinions and interests, which is very hard for a man of my temperament. So I am determined that the tail end of my life shall be reserved for things *I want* to do, at last!

Why do they not offer the Adelaide post to H Balfour Gardiner? He is very unforeknowable, has had some set-backs in his heart-stirs lately and it is conceivable *he might relish a change to a new scene.*

Is he not the kind of man you favour – a creative and practical musician, with roots in live music and remote from the College of organists?[30]

Eugene accepted his friend's decision with regret. Although Grainger's prestige as Australia's first pianist and composer of international renown would have lent lustre to an academic institution, his eccentric lifestyle, undisguised racial prejudices and secret addiction to flagellation were not ideal recommendations for the post. It went to a distinguished educationalist, John Bishop, who later founded the Adelaide Festival and the Australian Youth Orchestra.

19

Music is the Birthright
of the People

Eugene was a skilful publicist. Despite his seeming aloofness and English reserve, he had a down to earth realisation of the necessity of increasing popular support for classical music. The orchestra spent much of its time on tour in remote areas of New South Wales. When they arrived in Newcastle in December 1947 to celebrate the town's 150th anniversary, to the consternation of the welcoming committee of civic dignitaries, the distinguished conductor descended from the footplate of the Newcastle Flier grimy faced, in overalls and cloth cap at a raffish angle, with an oil-stained rag in his hand. Rumour had it that he had driven the express all the way from Sydney. Driver Guilfoyle maintained a discreet silence regarding the distance for which Eugene had actually been at the controls. He always compared the exhilaration he obtained from driving a locomotive with conducting an orchestra: something hugely powerful controlled by a sensitive and alert hand.

The evening's concert which included The Prelude and Liebestod from *Tristan and Isolde*, Liszt's *Hungarian Fantasy* for Piano and Orchestra with the young Australian pianist Valda Aveling and Brahms' Second Symphony, was sold out, with people sitting on the gallery stairs or standing at the back of the stalls. Before the encores, Eugene told the audience: 'To judge from the response to this concert, Newcastle is starved for symphonic music. The need for a permanent orchestra in this city is paramount.' He emphasised this to a meeting of the Businessmen's Clubs plus the desirability of opening a branch of the Sydney Conservatorium in Newcastle. He undertook to obtain plans of leading concert halls in the United States as a blueprint for a new auditorium.[1]

In March 1948 he wrote a guest column in *Labor News* headed 'Music is the birthright of the people' and expounded this credo with great fervour. 'The great composers whose music is timeless have a message for all who will hear it. Music is not the property of a small group of initiates or a privileged few to whom its secrets are alone vouchsafed. It exists for our enjoyment, physically, mentally and spiritually and whether the orchestra is playing Stravinsky or Bach, its message is a universal one. I want to see the day come in this country when the great orchestras will travel from town to town and play full-sized programmes of the greatest music, in halls seating 3,000 to 4,000 people, to all who will come and hear its message. Among these audiences, the workers of this country will preponderate.'

A noble dream which still has not been fulfilled!

The reality of country touring was far more prosaic. Eugene often told the orchestra how much better touring conditions were in the USA, where a special train was provided for the Cincinnati Symphony Orchestra with a first-class restaurant car and a private drawing-room plus a comfortable Pullman sleeping car for the personal use of the conductor. He found it difficult to accept the less formal atmosphere of touring. Violinist Brenton Langbein remembers incurring his disapproval. 'Everybody drank like mad on those trips. We had been drinking quite heavily one morning waiting for a train at a country station. Len Dommett, who later became leader of the Melbourne Orchestra, and I had straw hats from horse-riding the day before. We sat on our suitcases, put the hats on the ground in front of us and started playing hillbilly music. An interstate train pulled up and people were leaning out of the windows throwing money into our hats. Suddenly Goossens appeared in his immaculate suit and elegant hat. He just looked, didn't say a word and walked on. I never felt so small in all my life.'[2]

Rex Ellis was the ABC's assistant Concert Manager for New South Wales and remembers an occasion when Eugene was conducting a concert in Armidale, a small town in the north west of the state. The venue was an old cinema and the guest artist was one of Australia's best-loved singers, Peter Dawson, then approaching the end of his long career. 'In the first aria he had a bit of difficulty, took his handkerchief out of his pocket, coughed and muttered to Goossens: "They're gone, Eugene, they're gone!" He'd got rid of his false teeth. "There they were Rex," he told me in the interval, "rattling around in my mouth like peas in a can!" But Goossens didn't quite appreciate the joke!'[3]

The only time he showed his annoyance with Ellis was when he managed to leave one of the s's out of his name for a Sunday concert at Sydney Town Hall. 'I do not mind if you leave my name out of the programme altogether,' he remonstrated in his august, austere English tones, 'but if you do put it in, at least spell it correctly!'

Ellis continues: 'He had a burning desire to convince the Australian public that they should respect and appreciate THEIR orchestra. He always felt that Australians were not as supportive of cultural aspects as they were of sporting idols. They didn't realise that amongst the orchestra were players of world standard like Neville Amadio, First Flute. He tried to illustrate the point by describing Amadio as "the Bradman of the Flute", one comparison which he felt Australians might understand.'[4]

When any player fell sick, after one week the ABC ceased to pay his salary. Eugene, remembering the insecurity of his early days as a violinist with the Queen's Hall Orchestra, instigated the setting up of a pension fund. He and the orchestra gave their services free at an annual benefit concert to raise money for the fund.

He was always gratified when his pioneering work in Australia was recognised by visiting international celebrities. In 1947 one of his old friends, Sir Laurence Olivier toured Australia with the Old Vic company; he later described in his autobiography Eugene's instinctive sympathy towards his emotional needs and the solace he found in his music.

We were overtired before the Antipodean tour was halfway through. I soon began to dread *Richard III*, particularly the double dose on matinée days. One day my friend Eugene Goossens saw that I was feeling the strain and said 'How would you like to hear some music – might do you a bit of good. Come to the rehearsal tomorrow, I've got a wonderful artist playing.'

Ginette Neveu must have been one of the most astonishing violinists in the history of instrumentalists. Eugene was conducting his Sydney Symphony Orchestra and Ginette was playing Sibelius op. 47. I was lifted from my wretched state as if by an archangel. As I sat putting on my make-up for the matinée that afternoon, I felt inspired and blessed.[5]

He was horrified to learn only a few months later, of Neveu's death in a plane crash.

Whether they liked it or not, Eugene was determined to remedy the deficiencies in the musical experience of Sydney's concert-going public by presenting them with as wide a range of orchestral repertoire as possible. During his first two seasons he conducted the Australian premieres of works as diverse as Bloch's *Schelomo*, Strauss' *Don Quixote*, Ravel's *Valses Nobles et Sentimentales*, Khachaturian's Symphony no. 2, Roy Harris' Third Symphony and Vaughan Williams' Fifth Symphony to mark the latter's seventy-fifth birthday. The list also included standard repertoire which had surprisingly never been played in Australia, such as Mahler's Symphony no. 1 and Tchaikovsky's *Manfred*.

He was determined to sharpen his audiences' musical appreciation regardless of their protests. 'Some people like old music and some new,' he declared to his audience in the Town Hall, waving a letter which criticised him for his Youth Concert programmes in 1948. 'I like both and while I conduct this orchestra I shall play what I think best.' He was also criticised for failure in communication: 'Mr Goossens seldom addresses more than a few rather tentative sentences to his young audiences, although much of the music he provides calls for explanation.'[6]

He found the ingrained prejudices of the Subscription Concert audiences even more difficult to overcome. The situation came to a head in July 1951 after Ravel's *Daphnis and Chloe*, described by visiting organist Dr George Thalben-Ball as the finest performance that he had heard anywhere. The Saturday night audience was in the habit of straggling out before the concert was over, grabbing their coats and programmes before the last bars had died away, leaving only a handful of people to pay a meagre tribute to the orchestra and its conductor.

Eugene described the audience's paltry recognition of the orchestra's achievement as a deliberate affront. Ernest Llewellyn as Concert Master voiced the opinion of the orchestra: 'We are disgusted. What's the use of slaving to perform difficult works if we get no response from the audience?'[7]

The most socially prestigious and oldest concert series was known as the First Red. No matter how stirring the performance, the applause from the audience was always minimal. The majority of society ladies in the audience (and there were always more women than men), still wore long white gloves and kept them on throughout the evening. One old lady known as 'the Battleship' sat in the sixth row of the stalls and ostentatiously put her fingers in her ears and kept them there throughout any piece of modern music. Still, audience appreciation had improved: the ladies no longer brought their knitting!

John Moses in the *Sunday Herald* suggested a radical change of policy: 'At the moment subscribers can renew their seats year after year and thus a kind of hereditary nobility of concert-goers has been formed. The obvious solution is to throw the bookings open to everybody. The really enthusiastic music-lovers would then have the chance to attend concerts which so many others regard, not as a satisfying experience, but as something to go to because they happen to have tickets.'[8] But the ABC preferred to solve the problem by doubling the number of series and by 1956 the subscribers had increased to nearly ten thousand. Until 1953 all the tickets for each concert were still written out by hand.

Eugene could not be accused of favouring his own compositions. Helen Bainton remembers his Symphony no. 1 as 'the work of a highly intellectual craftsman, but certainly not the sort of music which sent you home singing!'[9] It called forth a distinctive eulogy from critic Lindsey Browne: 'It is an eminently approachable work, which gleefully seized its own early pages of dark and wistful reflection, smothered them with colouristic kerosene and sent them blazing sky-high in the prodigious fanfaronade of brass and organ and shriller demons in the coda of the finale.'[10] Australian audiences had to wait until November 1950 to hear his Symphony no. 2.

Some of his chamber works had been featured by The Music Viva Society at a concert on 20th October 1947 at the Conservatorium Hall: the Violin Sonata no. 2. played by Robert Pikler and Maureen Jones (she was later to give the Australian premiere of Eugene's Piano Concerto), two miniatures *By the*

Tarn and *Jack o'Lantern* in the original string quartet version and two of the Three Songs, op. 26, 'Melancholy' and 'The Appeal' for baritone and string quartet. The concert came as a timely reminder of Eugene's stature among contemporary British composers. Another work, *Three Pictures* for Flute, Strings and Percussion – an evocative tone painting of the perspective from Bruges, Bredon and Montparnasse – had been premiered with great acclaim at a Promenade Concert in London on 26th August 1947.

Eugene was finding the Australian ambiance conducive to composition; he announced in Melbourne in July 1948 that he had completed the Violin Concerto promised to his friend Jascha Heifetz fifteen years earlier. He described the work as a 'phantasy-concerto' of four main movements, linked together without interruption and based on two motto themes. 'I have become very self-critical in my old age,' he explained, 'that's why this piece has taken so long. Anyway it's finished and the last laugh is mine. I'm sure Jascha will get the shock of his life when he gets it.'[11]

The shock that Heifetz experienced was not exactly what Eugene had expected. Heifetz did not like the work and eventually broke the news to his friend that he was not willing to play it. It was not premiered until after Eugene had returned to London, when the young British violinist Tessa Robbins played it in a revised version on the BBC Third Programme. This was followed by a Promenade Concert on 7th September 1960, on both occasions with the BBC Symphony Orchestra conducted by the composer.

Though he had expressed his total commitment to improving standards of musical training in Australia, Eugene was to find his position as Director of the Conservatorium increasingly frustrating. The New South Wales Conservatorium of Music is still picturesquely, but totally inadequately, housed in Governor Macquarie's castellated stables built in 1817–19. Eugene discovered little had changed since Verbrugghen was installed as the first Director in 1915. The building had been converted on the cheap, with little thought as to how harness rooms and grooms' sleeping quarters could best be transformed into music studios. There were no Common

Rooms for staff or students and the library was in a corridor.

A concert hall had been constructed in the old exercise yard; by 1947 the original upholstery had worn so thin that it had disappeared completely from many of the 950 seats. The front entrance was boarded up and the smell of the lavatories was appalling. Accommodation originally intended for 250 students had to cope with more than two thousand plus a staff of sixty. There was also a High School for musically gifted children which had a hundred pupils enrolled.[12]

Eugene saw the situation as utterly impossible; the only solution was a completely new building. 'I am anxious to enlarge the Conservatorium and bring it up to the standard of the best Continental and American music academies,' he had told the *Sydney Daily Telegraph* shortly after his arrival. Despite their encouraging noises, he found the Education Department completely intransigent on the matter of extra funding, let alone rebuilding.

On the positive side, because of his appointment at the Conservatorium, the Education Department provided him with a full-time private secretary, Phyllis Williams who was to prove one of his most loyal and devoted aides. Phyllis never married and thirty years after his death, is still an attractive, wonderfully warm and friendly woman who maintains her discretion and protective devotion towards Eugene. She had the ideal background to work for him, as she had been a singing student at the Conservatorium under Ruth Ladd, herself a pupil of Melba's. She remembers being very nervous at her first interview and how Eugene had immediately impressed her as a kindly soul who put her at her ease by saying 'I believe you're coming up to give me a hand!'

'Marjorie was there to look me over and immediately saw I was no competition. He wasn't a good administrator, he hadn't the patience or the interest. One of his weaknesses was that he hated saying "no". People were always pestering him, particularly singers. Eventually he said to me about one singer "Phyl, I don't want to hear that damn woman again," so I always had to find some excuse to fob her off.'

Eugene had an impossibly heavy workload and there were many ways in which Phyllis Williams felt she could have done more to help him and simplify the administrative chores but 'a mere secretary did not have the authority to take over certain matters. During the last couple of years the situation was improved when Neville Salmon was appointed Assistant to the Director to take over a lot of the administration and particularly the liaison between the Director and staff.'[13]

Once Eugene started the unpleasant but essential task of weeding out incompetent teaching staff, he upset a number of long established vested interests among Sydney's musical community. This laid the foundations of enmity against him, leading inevitably to cabal and intrigue.

In the spring of 1947, an old friend from Cincinnati, journalist Douglas M Allen Jnr. visited Eugene Goossens in Sydney on the eve of his fifty-fifth birthday. He found him sunburnt, healthier and happier than he had ever known him in the USA. 'He still strolls about humming unidentifiable melodies to himself, but a smile has replaced his old serious expression.' Allen attributed his contentment partially to his success in his new position but more significantly to the happiness of his third marriage. Marjorie was 'gracious, beautiful and superbly dressed. She is one of the most popular women in Sydney. Dozens of Australians have told me they consider her the United States' greatest asset here.'[14]

The Goossens brought an air of glamorous sophistication to Sydney's provincial social life. The press featured them as their favourite couple, handsome and adoring at a Symphony Concert interval or cuddling a koala together at Taronga Park Zoo. Marjorie took care to emphasise that the recipe for a successful marriage was a wife sharing her husband's interests: in their case not only good food and wine and reading anything from whodunnits to philosophy but a life-long interest in music. 'I have studied music for many years, so I can and do discuss things with my husband and I am as keen about his work as he is himself. One last word,' she added in the *ABC Weekly* magazine of 1st November 1947, 'my husband has always known where he is going and has always put his music before all else. That singleness of purpose he has carried into everything he does.'

Marjorie proved herself to be a wonderful organiser. Phyllis Williams commented that Goossens obviously loved her dearly and relied on her musical criticism. 'In the early days, she went to all his orchestral rehearsals. He would ask her to move about to check the acoustics for him when they shifted from the rehearsal studio to the Town Hall.'[15] She realised the importance of socialising and tried hard to disguise the fact that she was something of an intellectual snob who did not suffer fools gladly. She found it difficult to go through the more tedious motions expected of her as Conductor's Consort. Making small talk at receptions organised by the Ladies' Committee before each concert was an unwelcome chore if the guests failed to be amusing, rich or influential. Eugene also had difficulty in talking to people on these occasions unless they were interested in music, books or painting. He often gave the impression of being aloof but unlike Marjorie, his real problem was shyness.

Described as 'one of Sydney's smartest frockers', she was admired for her classical good looks and elegant wardrobe and was constantly quoted in the press as an arbiter of fashion. Charles Buttrose, who has somewhat jaundiced memories of the Goossens era, criticises Marjorie for insincere flattery of the Australians in the service of manipulative public relations. 'Australia's Average Woman Leader of Fashion World' ran the banner headline when she returned after four months in Europe and the USA.[16] 'In her opinion "the average Australian woman is the only woman in the world to approach her American counterpart's high standards of dress."' In contrast, Buttrose found Australian women incredibly badly dressed when he came back from New York.

Eugene had always been saddened at his failure to provide his children with the warmth and stability of family life he had experienced as a child. Marjorie appeared to get on very well with his two youngest daughters and had promised to make a home for them once he was established in Australia. In the summer of 1948 she sailed from San Francisco to Sydney in a Swedish cargo liner, the *Mangarella*, with Sidonie aged sixteen and Renée aged seven. Donie, who had always idolised her father, still remembers her immense excitement when the pilot boat appeared on the wintery waters of Sydney Harbour. Up the swaying ladder with the pilot and the Health Officer clambered her father in his big fur coat. 'That was the only time I knew him to break the law, but he hadn't seen us for eighteen months!'[17] She found her father in far better health and spirits than when he was in the USA. 'He adored everything to do with Sydney Harbour; he used to stand outside and watch the boats and breathe in the fresh air and get a little colour in his face. He knew the tonnage and sailing date of every boat just as he told me he had done when he was a boy in Liverpool.'

He found renewed pleasure in the family's artistic skills which his daughter had inherited. 'When we went on picnics, as well as the paints he would always take two sketch books; then he'd say "I'm going to draw this boat, you draw that one." Ultimately I wound up with his paint box and best brush which set me off on my happiest hours. He would draw on anything; table cloths, napkins, menus, maybe on music I don't know. It was compulsive. If anything happened he would draw it rather than talk about it.'

The one thing they were not allowed to talk about was his health, specifically his heart condition; no management would employ a conductor who was not entirely well. 'He had to take digitalis every day and Nembutal. If he ran out he was in a panic. "Where are my blinks?" he'd ask.'[18] The fact that he was overweight and a slow mover could have been exacerbated by the long term prescribed use of drugs. It was, without doubt, a contributory factor towards the lack of overt emotionalism in his conducting, a certain coolness particularly in classical as compared with twentieth-century repertoire that some listeners criticised. According to Marjorie he had been warned that if he became overexcited or lost his temper he could die. He also suffered from diabetes, a contributory cause of poor circulation, so the famous fur coat so often mentioned as an affectation in Sydney's mild climate was an essential to someone who felt the cold as keenly as he did.

Marjorie was very protective, trying to provide Eugene with an ordered routine and settled environment. When he was working the girls were told not to disturb him by making a noise and visitors would be asked to go away. 'In Sydney, Father had the same foibles of losing things, of being totally useless round the house as in Cincinnati. Both mothers used to say "your father's a genius!"' As a teenager, Donie found his attitude towards Catholicism puzzling. Why was he allowed to eat meat on a Friday when she had to eat fish? 'Ah,' he used to say. 'I'm travelling!' Although he did not go regularly

291

to Mass or Confession, the Pope's picture and a crucifix were always on his desk and he had many friends among the Catholic clergy. When asked to comment on her father's Catholicism, she now emphasises: 'Going into churches regularly is no measure of "Goodness". One's interpretation of one's relationship with God, one's fellow man and one's own conscience is a purely private matter. And that was the situation with my father.'[19]

Although Marjorie initially tried hard to prove herself a good mother to Donie and Renée, she had no perception of the running of a normal household and no experience of a normal relationship between mother and daughter. Emotionally she was scarred by the death of her beautiful sister when she was very young and by the fact that her mother wished the situation had been reversed and that Marjorie had been the one to die. In face of her mother's rejection, Marjorie's estimation of herself had been seriously undermined. She never thought of herself as being beautiful although she had matured into an intelligent, attractive and exquisitely groomed woman. She needed constant male admiration to reaffirm her desirability. Her spiritual quest for reassurance led her from Presbyterianism to Christian Science and eventually Catholicism.

On the boat from San Francisco, Marjorie had befriended the Second Mate, Albert Wargren, a tall blond Swede, blessed with the rare combination of exceptional good looks, intelligence and warmth of heart. Recently divorced and lonely for his own children, Albert started to read *Winnie-the-Pooh* to Renée and laid the foundations of an invaluable friendship with the Goossens family. 'They invited me to dinner in Sydney and asked me what plans I had. I had none and realised that my English was not good enough. I started to work for them in September 1948. I was called EG's Secretary but really I was a General Factotum. My duties extended from looking after the garden to cooking the food and seeing that the bills were paid. EG gave the impression of being a helpless human being which was quite smart because he wasn't expected to do anything about the house. He was a musician first, second and last.'[20]

Albert took over the role of personal valet. He became one of the family and was perhaps the person who got to know Eugene best during those Australian years. In many ways the older man regarded him as the son he had never had. He said at Wargren's wedding in April 1955: 'If I'd had a son, I'd have liked to have one like Albert!'

Albert remembers him with great affection.

> You couldn't help being fond of EG. He liked to stroll through town; he always walked slowly and he would always give a coin to a street musician even if he had to cross the road to do it. 'Albert, never forget,' he would say, 'there but for the Grace of God, go I!'
>
> He spoke most beautiful English and took endless pains to give me a thorough knowledge of the language. He was always trying to explain the difference between s and z as in 'because'. He would remind me that Caruso used to say '*because* is the most beautiful word in the English language' which didn't make it any easier for me to pronounce!

Albert reveals a basic dichotomy in Eugene's character. He builds up a picture of a very laid-back and easy-going man, someone who never lost his temper, whom nothing could phase; but someone who controlled and disciplined himself to the nth degree and seemed to believe that showing emotion and behaving like a human being were the equivalent of sinning. 'He had a great sense of suppressed religion and a guilt complex because he had not remained an observant Catholic.'[21]

Like all professional musicians, he was very self-engrossed and adhered to a rigid schedule when he was conducting. 'He would always have a sleep in the afternoon and before a concert he would always eat two soft-boiled eggs which had to be cooked for three minutes, no more and no less. After the concert he was very hyped up and it took him hours to unwind. He ate like a horse; he loved liverwurst and mustard pickles. When people came back for supper, he insisted on eating English mustard with everything I cooked, even an omelette and when I protested that it ruined the taste, he would protest "Can't you humour my whims?"'[22]

Donie remembers his fondness for old-fashioned English puddings like his mother used to make in Liverpool. As they were very much alike in temperament, Donie's memories of her adored father are tolerant and affectionate ones. Renée, however, feels that their family life was a failure and that they were unable to make contact with each other on a realistic level. 'Marjorie was an overpowering personality. My father was unaware of what was going on around him and didn't even know what to talk about at the breakfast table. He went through the motions of a father-daughter relationship, asking me whether I had done my homework or my violin practice but basically he had a total inability to communicate.'[23]

20

Boomerang and Fire Sticks

By the beginning of his second season, Eugene had reached certain decisions as to the strengths and weaknesses of his orchestra's personnel. He had reduced the high proportion of women players, a left-over effect of the war, from thirty-two to fifteen. He realised that he would have to compensate for talented players leaving to further their careers overseas by attracting British musicians to improve the standards of the SSO. Among the players he brought in were Charles Gray from the Boyd Neel Orchestra to lead the double basses, Horace (Jimmy) Green, a pupil of Léon's, to replace Charles Mackerras as First Oboe and Charles Gregory to replace Barry Tuckwell.

In 1949 he appointed John Kennedy as Principal Cello, a brilliant musician who made his solo debut with the orchestra in the Elgar concerto. His parents Lauri and Dorothy Kennedy were originally from England and had made distinguished careers in Australia as a cello and piano duo. They were among the Goossens' closest friends. John Kennedy was a flamboyant and unpredictable character who sometimes 'did a whirly' with his cello during a performance but played so well that he was never reprimanded. He resigned after two years explaining to Eugene that 'the strain of attempting to combine with my orchestral duties any serious efforts at solo work, chamber music or teaching, is beginning to impair my health.' After two years as Principal Cello at Covent Garden he returned to Australia. Sadly, because of an alcohol problem, he never played in public again. His son, the violinist Nigel Kennedy, has inherited his flamboyance and his virtuosity.

Kennedy was succeeded by Hans George. Both he and Robert Pikler, who led the Musica Viva Quartet, were Hungarian Jews who had been interned by the Japanese in Java during the war, eventually arriving in Australia. When the quartet broke up through lack of funds in 1952, Goossens persuaded Pikler to lead the violas in the SSO.

Goossens' policy of importing musicians from the UK and employing New Australian 'reffos', provoked opposition from the Returned Servicemen's League, who felt that the position of ex-servicemen was threatened and from the Musicians' Union, who were suffering from acute xenophobia. In January 1949 the Union, fearing an influx of musicians from overseas 'migrating in large numbers to Australia, lured by good conditions, including food and other considerations', imposed a membership ban on all aliens. They allowed a membership of only ten per cent to British musicians who had lived in Australia for ten years.

The Union's secretary, Mr F Kitson, justified the policy by saying 'until there's sufficient work available for Australian musicians, employers must be prevented from engaging aliens here. There are many Australian musicians who are just as fine artists as imported celebrities. Our people should get first priority for all musical engagements.'[1] Eugene accused them of slamming 'the country's gates in the faces of those who could make all the difference to orchestral standards.' He saw his hard won achievements with the SSO, together with his planned expansion for the training of Australia's new generation of professional musicians, totally undermined by the Union's bigoted intransigence.

He retaliated by writing an article in the *Sydney Morning Herald* lambasting the Union's pig-headedness and complacency. He exposed 'certain unpalatable, but inescapable facts regarding the general symphonic situation throughout the country.' These included 'the incontestable and absolute dearth of first-class Australian symphonic material, measured by international standards – the fine Sydney and Melbourne orchestras alone excepted; a past heritage of mediocre teaching of stringed, woodwind and brass instruments which has produced, with a few notable exceptions, a generation of players lacking in style and technical brilliance; the inability of many players, particularly strings, to pass even the most elementary sight-reading and aural tests at auditions. No conductor, however skilled or patient, can ever convert an orchestra of technically inadequate players into a first-class organisation.'[2]

He was equally damning on the effect that the ban would have on teaching standards and the conservatoria that Brisbane and Perth were hoping to build: 'Where are these much needed high-grade professors to train young students into first-class players? If not in our cities they must come from abroad. No first-class solo orchestral performer is too good to hold a post at the local conservatorium; conversely the fallacy that any unqualified antiquarian is good enough to teach must be exploded and is being exploded rapidly.'

In an editorial the following day headed 'Another Blow to our Cultural Progress', the *Sydney Morning Herald* came out strongly in support of Eugene against the Union's closed-shop policy, with an indictment of Australia's cultural philistinism: 'Unhappily, this ill-considered move towards musical isolation has had equivalents in other cultural spheres . . . the scandalous crudity of a system by which wholly unqualified persons in petty official positions are entitled to censor the literary fare of Australian citizens. Such practices as these are part of the national immaturity, from which long since we should have begun to emerge.'[3] These were to prove ominously prophetic words as far as Eugene was concerned.

In the 1990s, with a multi-ethnic population of sixteen million and the official recognition that Australia is geographically part of South East Asia, it is difficult to appreciate the degree of rabid racial prejudice prevalent forty years ago. Although the post-war Labour Government realised that Australia's most urgent need was to increase its population of 7.4 million, throughout the 1940s they maintained a 'White Australia Policy'. '£10 Poms' were infinitely preferable to Southern Europeans, who smelt of garlic and had dubious morals. In July 1947 Arthur Calwell, Labour Minister of Immigration, had signed an agreement for an unlimited number of Displaced Persons from the camps in Europe to become New Australians. The need was for labourers and factory workers; the 'reffos', whatever their qualifications, were supposed to work where they were directed for a minimum of two years, involving much hardship for doctors, engineers and musicians forced onto building sites and assembly lines.

The closed-shop policy of the Musicians' Union was in line with the attitude of other unions towards the influx of competitive labour: 'European immigrants have made Australia what it is today and now is no time to ban them. The more we can get the right type the better, otherwise we will not have much chance of keeping out the Japanese, Indonesians, or other Asiatics,' was the assessment of the General Secretary of the Australian Workers' Union. The Miners' Federation welcomed British immigrants but applied 'certain restrictions on Balts, Poles and other Europeans mainly because of the fear that racial settlements might be established.'[4]

This was the prejudice within Australian society with which Eugene had locked horns. One of the allegations Kitson made was that he had engaged a foreigner who could speak no English at all. Pointing out that he had since learnt English, Eugene countered: 'This gentleman was the only applicant for a string position who satisfactorily met the standard of sight-reading and performance I demanded of applicants for our orchestra. So on the principle of better an inarticulate virtuoso than a garrulous third-rater, he was engaged.'[5]

The 'inarticulate virtuoso' was Dr Michael Bialoguski, later to gain notoriety as a double agent in the Petrov spy scandal of 1954. He had escaped from Poland to Australia in 1941 and later qualified as a doctor. He originally went to Eugene to ask for conducting lessons. By 1955, when he published his somewhat unreliable memoirs, his feelings towards him had soured. 'I found Goossens a tall, ascetic-looking man in his fifties with a bloodless parchment-like skin. His manner was somewhat pompous, and he appeared to enjoy his maestro part as much offstage as on. "There is no short cut to conducting, doctor," he said. "I quite believe on your showing here that you would make an excellent conductor, given a chance. But how can I give you the chance? Unless of course, you would agree to join the Sydney Symphony Orchestra as a violinist. I could then give you private tuition concurrently."'[6]

Bialoguski remained with the orchestra until 1952 when he was sacked, according to him, because of the ten per cent quota of foreign-born musicians imposed by the Musicians' Union on the ABC. Despite his persistent efforts he had never received any private tuition from Eugene. 'It may be that I became a dispensable foreigner because I was so ardent in my pursuit of tuition in conductorship, or perhaps my radical associations overshadowed my musicianship.'[7] Had someone warned Eugene about the suspected activities of the Good Doctor? Whatever the sub text, Bialoguski was extremely resentful and continued to harbour a grudge against him.

Eugene did not neglect talented young Australian musicians. He raised the standard of the Diploma Class at the Conservatorium to provide a forcing ground for the best instrumentalists who then joined the orchestra on graduation. Conductor Richard Bonynge, who had trained as a pianist, analysed the Goossens effect: 'He was a real shock to the place after the relatively easy reign of Bainton, because for the first couple of years of his directorship Goossens failed almost everyone in the diploma course. In 1950 I was the only person to pass. I took up my scholarship at the Royal College of Music and I can tell you standards there were much lower than they were in Sydney. That was all Goossens' doing. He attracted better instrumental teachers and opened up our ears to new repertoire.'[8]

He also toured the country auditioning potential recruits. In Adelaide he discovered Brenton Langbein, a twenty-year-old violinist who was to become a close friend of the family.

My parents had booked my passage to England thinking it was time for me to have further study abroad for a solo career but Goossens persuaded me to come to Sydney as second desk in the orchestra. Those years with Goossens were a Golden Age for music in Australia. He had an aura about him; we were all in awe of him with his grand English manner. He was a great musician and he had arrived at just the right moment in Sydney, to introduce us to the European culture for which we all hungered. Everything gelled; the atmosphere in the orchestra was incredible and in the audience as well. Everyone felt that they were contributing, no matter what instrument they played or what background they came from.

He had the elegance of an Edwardian gentleman. His conducting was very economical, nothing Central European getting very passionate with hair hanging everywhere! The organ gallery in the Old Town Hall was always full of young people, whistling and cheering after a Bruckner Symphony like at a football match. There was the same enthusiasm for all the great Romantic symphonies, the Impressionists, Stravinsky; he built up a fabulous repertoire and we all, orchestra and audience alike, learnt a tremendous amount.[9]

At the end of 1948 Eugene had been seriously ill with pleurisy. He had been forced to postpone a visit to England, his first in three years, to conduct the BBC Symphony Orchestra, until the summer of 1949. Returning from a sea voyage of convalescence with Marjorie, he learnt that Otto Klemperer had been engaged to conduct his Sydney Symphony Orchestra. This prompted an irate letter to Charles Moses:

> Since our tacit agreement of 1947 that I should be consulted in a friendly way about foreign conductors for my orchestra seems to have fallen by the wayside, I feel no hesitation in writing you these lines, which are for your private eye. Negotiations to secure Klemperer, whose engagement for eighteen concerts is announced in the *ABC Weekly*, have seemingly been in prospect for some little time. Don't wince if I tell you frankly that I consider this catastrophic.
>
> K. is a notorious mental case. *He has been shut up in mental homes for long periods on at least three occasions.* Having been in America for the last twenty-five years *I happen to know these things* and have met at least three women who have had to barricade themselves in their hotel rooms to avoid his violent and insane attentions. These are not stories; they have appeared in print. Two years ago he was picked up in the gutter in downtown Los Angeles, battered by toughs who resented his goings on with their women. This got wide publicity, but it was long prior to that that American orchestras fought shy of him owing to his unreliability and insane actions on the platform.
>
> His ungovernable temper is made worse by his lunatic ravings at rehearsal. When I left Vancouver in '47 to come here (the last orchestra in America to try engaging him again), the orchestra president had to send him packing after only one of three announced concerts had taken place. K's attention to the president's daughter (not to mention his moronic activities in the town) made this necessary.
>
> I have never written or spoken ill of a colleague in my life, but not only because of his damaging impact (artistically and otherwise) on my orchestra here, plus what I consider may prove a dangerous presence in the community, I feel it my duty to tell you all this. Musical circles abroad, when they read of this six-foot-four imbecile let loose on the Australian community, will eye us with apprehension and some considerable pity. Thank heavens I won't be here, not to mention my wife and daughter. . .
>
> I shall of course breathe *no word* of the above to anyone else.[10]

300

Moses scribbled a note on the letter to his secretary 'Put this away safely' while he cogitated on a soothing reply.

The popular press played up Klemperer's reputation as an ogre; the *Sunday Sun* referred to him as 'an intellectual Boris Karloff'. On one occasion when he was trying to get the orchestra to agree to an extra rehearsal, he brandished a gun at a terrified William James and asked 'Do you think this will persuade them?'[11] Nevertheless his visit was an overwhelming artistic success and he gave due praise to Eugene's work in transforming the orchestra.

Klemperer's success with Mahler's Resurrection Symphony was to prompt Eugene to one of the high points of his Australian career: Mahler's mammoth Symphony no. 8 which he conducted in October 1951. It was not performed in Sydney again until 1988.

While Klemperer was conducting the SSO, Eugene was conducting the Berlin Philharmonic Orchestra in three concerts in the 1949 Edinburgh Festival (25th and 26th August, afternoon and evening). He was delighted to renew his acquaintance with twenty of the players whom he had met in 1922, as the first British conductor with the orchestra after the First World War. He and Barbirolli were now the first British conductors to work with the orchestra since the Second World War. Inevitable comparisons were made between the emotional depth of Barbirolli's performances contrasted with Goossens' mixture of flamboyance and cool intellectualism.

The *Times* praised Goossens' imaginative programming, including Mahler's First Symphony, Dukas' *La Péri*, Hindemith's *Symphonic Metamorphosis* of themes by Weber and Elgar's *Cockaigne* Overture in 'a programme more worthy of a festival than any that have been offered so far. . . Maybe he is too nonchalant, but to have the orchestra discoursing music in an easy, civilised way without frantic effort or emotional lather was, in itself, refreshing.'[12] Was this the same Mr Goossens who 'gives the impression of almost frightening efficiency', leading in the Mahler to 'a highly controlled performance of great precision . . . an outstanding exhibition of orchestral technique'?[13]

Eugene's unquestioned expertise in contemporary music was displayed in his second programme which included Roy Harris' Third Symphony and the Ballet Suite from *Corroboree*.

Antill's music received an ovation although the audience had waited in vain for: 'much usage of boomerang, spear and fire sticks' described in the programme notes. His own Oboe Concerto, played by Léon, was the climax of the evening. 'Brother Eugene handed all the bouquets to brother Léon, who was indeed the lion of the occasion.'[14] The concerto was to be repeated with equal success at the Albert Hall in February 1950 with the London Symphony Orchestra. It was widely reported as 'A Family Affair' as both Marie and Sidonie were featured in the prominent harp parts of *Daphnis and Chloe*.

Unfortunately for Eugene's career, the Germans had preferred Barbirolli and invited him as guest conductor to Berlin the following April, the beginning of a long and fruitful relationship with the Berlin Philharmonic which Eugene would dearly have loved to have had.

Before starting rehearsals in Edinburgh, he had conducted the BBC Symphony Orchestra in another two of his compositions at a Promenade Concert in the Albert Hall on 15th August: the *Sinfonietta* and the Piano Concerto with Irene Kohler, who had given the first English performance in Bedford in 1943. It had been rumoured in the Australian press that Goossens had 'accepted the position of musical director of the BBC' in succession to Sir Adrian Boult and would not be returning from London. He strenuously denied this, pointing out that his Australian contract had another eighteen months to run and adding 'I have settled in Australia. This is my home.'[15]

Eugene was never officially approached as to whether he would be interested in becoming Chief Conductor of the BBC Symphony Orchestra when Boult, its founder conductor, was unwillingly forced into retirement at the age of sixty. The post was originally offered to Barbirolli, then to Rafael Kubelík and finally given to Sir Malcolm Sargent. Eugene provided one of the letters of tribute in the presentation book on Boult's retirement and Sidonie proposed the guests' health at the dinner given by the orchestra at the Savoy to mark his actual sixtieth birthday.

Although Eugene was warmly welcomed by both press and public on his return to the British concert platform, he was not accorded the status of one of the world's leading

conductors. He had been away for too long and lacked powerful patrons to further his cause. There were no more overtures
from Covent Garden. His only appearance there was a concert
with the Philharmonia Orchestra on 25th September, featuring
Martinů's Double Concerto written in 1938. This ended a gru-
elling provincial tour with the orchestra of eight cities in nine
days.

The four-year-old Philharmonia Orchestra was acknowledged
as second to none in the country; their Beethoven programme
was judged in Birmingham to be of dazzling brilliance and
Eugene a conductor with an amazingly incisive and no-nonsense
beat. The attendance at the same programme in Leeds Town
Hall had been deplorably low and one saddened concert-goer
wondered whether the cause for this was that Goossens' name
was not 'unfortunately, in this country at least, surrounded by
a halo of myth and legend.'[16]

As always, the family parties and reunions were what
gave Eugene the greatest pleasure on his visits to England
and above all, the opportunity to spend time with his father.
Marjorie did not develop the same rapport as Jansi had done.
Sidonie felt she never got to know his third wife. 'Eugene had
a strange artificial attitude towards her: "Isn't she marvellous?"
he would say, showing her off like some prized possession.'[17]

Eugene returned to Australia with an invitation for the SSO
to participate in the Edinburgh Festival of 1950. This failed
to come to fruition, neither did a scheme for an exchange
visit of the orchestra with the Hallé suggested by Barbirolli
in 1951. Despite Barbirolli's tribute to Eugene's achievement
that 'the orchestra, if sent to Europe, would give everybody
a pleasant surprise', Sydney City Council and the New South
Wales Government on both occasions refused to provide the
necessary funding. The orchestra had to wait until 1965 for its
first overseas tour.

Eugene at last had an ideal concert master in Ernest
Llewellyn, someone whose musicianship and authority he
respected on a professional level and whom on a personal level
he could regard as a friend. He brought him in as leader after
having heard him play the Walton Violin Concerto conducted
by Kletzki. Llewellyn's posthumous tribute to his friend Gene
provides some clues to the real person beneath the ambivalent

303

exterior he presented to the world. Llewellyn summed him up as 'a musician in world class of his day, an unequivocal leader of men and musicians, and a close and sincere friend. His reputation was built up on his interpretation, the acuteness of his orchestral ear for balance of tone and colour, stick technique and panache – panache which drove *con slancia* through stylistic vagaries and human fallibilities to show the wholeness and fullness of the human spirit in the major musical art forms. He had many acquaintances but few friends. My wife and I had the honour and privilege to be included among his close friends. I know this because of confidences we shared together.'[18]

Looking back more than forty years, his widow Ruth Llewellyn questions the closeness of that friendship.

> They travelled together everywhere on tour by car and shared the same Green Room but he was very reserved and never talked very much. Ernie didn't feel that he knew Goossens. He was like a hoarding hiding the real person. 'Goosey's kinky!' he told me once. As resident conductor he had hire and fire power but he got Ernie to do his dirty work of sacking players. He was very jealous of other conductors and very possessive of Ernie. When he played the Walton Concerto in Melbourne for the Coronation Concert, Goossens wouldn't let him have any extra time off from the orchestra for rehearsal.
>
> Goossens didn't like me or rather he didn't have any interest in me as I wasn't a pretty woman and I wasn't important or influential. But he valued my husband.[19]

Eva Wagner, the widow of music critic Walter Wagner, editor of *The Canon*, felt similarly slighted by Eugene's failure to value her as an individual, much though he respected her husband's opinions.[20]

A major milestone of the spring season in late 1949 was Eugene conducting Sydney's first open-air free symphony concert in the Botanic Gardens, something that he had been advocating since his arrival. An audience of 20,000 for a programme including Dvořák's Symphony *From the New World* proved how popular the idea was in what is essentially an open-air city. Eugene, with his experience of over a hundred open-air concerts in America, was delighted but he soon discovered the shortcomings of the Botanic Gardens compared with the Hollywood Bowl. From the orchestra's point of view, playing a concert at three o'clock in the afternoon was a potential disaster as the hot sun threatened to melt the glue of the stringed instruments. Yet by the following April (Australia's autumn), Eugene was writing to Moses complaining about the cold. 'Yesterday's concert in the Gardens again forcibly emphasised the necessity of a *closed season* for open-air concerts. There was a steady and cold wind blowing, which chilled us all and gave me a sore throat as a result of my perspiring freely after the first number. The music blew all over the place, the children were again undisciplined and the ubiquitous speed boat distracted us in the neighbouring cove. Some of the violinists complained of the wood of their instruments warping and opening because of the cold.'[21]

At Christmas Eugene joined Marjorie and his two youngest daughters for a well-earned vacation. After the Edinburgh Festival, Marjorie had rented the 'Villa Namouna' at his old haunt of St Jean Cap Ferrat on the Côte d'Azur. Donie went to a course for foreign students and Renée learnt French at the village school. Eugene enjoyed the company of his old friend Willie (Somerset) Maugham who was their next-door neighbour. Donie remembers her father sitting for hours totally absorbed in listening to the radio. 'If you were very clever, on a clear day you could pick up North Africa. He used to jot down all the Arabic rhythms. We thought it was ghastly, totally repetitive but he was fascinated.'[22]

Eugene went on to fulfil engagements in Italy where Keith Falkner was now Music Officer for the British Council. Sir Keith remembered a marvellous few days with Eugene in Naples when Willie Walton and his wife came over to join them. Eugene was always loyal to his friends and was now in a position to reciprocate by inviting Falkner to Australia. A distinguished colleague from England would have provided welcome support in his battle against faculty intrigue and intransigence at the Conservatorium. 'In 1950 I got the sack as the British Council had no more money. Eugene offered me the job as Head of the Voice Faculty in Sydney. Boult had told me it was quite possible he could find me a job in the BBC and Cornell University had asked me if I would like to open up their Voice Department. When Bruce Boyce told me that the Cornell golf course was only two hundred yards away from the music building I decided to go to the USA instead of the BBC or Australia.'[23]

A perennial problem for performing artists is how to react to criticism, gratifying when positive and best, when negative, ignored and dismissed, as the personal prejudice of the ill-informed or ill-natured. Eugene always remained sensitive to press opinion and on his return to Sydney to open the 1950 season was questioned as to the hostile reviews he had received for concerts in Rome. These had described him as 'superficial and negligent, lacking in warmth and abandon'. 'Compared with what Italian music critics said about two of my titled British colleagues [Beecham and Sargent],' he countered, 'the basting I got sounded more like a glorious paean of praise. The sort of quiet restrained objectivity about British music quite baffles the effervescent Italian temperament.'[24]

If Eugene had been more positively received in Europe he would have had less concern about his future in Australia. He had previously threatened to resign in face of a refusal to pay his return fare for engagements abroad. He now wrote a confidential letter to Moses asking for a meeting to discuss a new agreement which he hoped would ensure his economic position and end tensions between himself and Marjorie.

> The urgency for this talk lies in the fact that my professional future in Australia is inextricably bound up with my domestic happiness, also the fact that Marjorie will only consent to join me permanently here if the conditions on which that future is based are clearly defined and agreed upon within the next two or three weeks. Marjorie waits to hear from me before definitely putting down passage money to come here with the family. The necessity for introducing at least *one* concretely attractive improvement to our new contract is *essential* if the outcome of our talk is to successfully persuade and convince my very realistic and very dear wife that she can undertake this serious and expensive step with confidence in what the future holds. I'll only add it is essential for my work and happiness that she should.[25]

On the strength of the new contract Marjorie not only agreed to return to Australia but to purchase a house in the desirable suburb of Wahroonga, the first time that Eugene and any of his wives had owned a permanent home. Externally 28 Burns Road has changed little, a pleasant one-storey detached house with its own tennis court in a quiet tree-lined road about eight miles from the centre of Sydney. Eugene painted one of the reception rooms with a mural eight foot high evoking their memories of the Mediterranean. Here Marjorie, thanks to Albert's catering, would hold large formal parties for the people they had to cultivate and dinner parties for visiting celebrities who were Eugene's old friends. There were more relaxed intimate occasions for the select group of people in Sydney whose company they most enjoyed: painters and designers like Loudon Sainthill or Bill Constable and his wife, Tana, Editor of the *Sydney Morning Herald*, Eric Kennedy and his wife Gwen, chosen musicians from the orchestra such as flautist Neville Amadio, cellist John Kennedy, violinist Brenton Langbein, pianist Maureen Jones and a few professors from the Conservatorium, including opera coach and singing teacher Leo Demant and his wife.

Brenton had become friendly with Marjorie and Donie when they came to orchestral rehearsals and had been invited back to the house to play sonatas with Marjorie, whom he found quite a good pianist. 'She was a very attractive woman and very much in love with Gene. At home he was a delightful host and enjoyed the company of young friends of his daughter. He would join in and tell us stories of his youth when he was the friend of Casella and Honegger and other famous people whom we knew about. It was quite frightening for me to be taken into the household of the great master I'd come to work with and I remained completely overawed by the whole experience. Donie was a good harpist and started to play as a deputy in her father's orchestra but she always thought of herself as an ugly duckling. Perhaps she was disappointed that our relationship didn't develop.'[26]

Donie maintains that Brenton was her parents' friend not hers. 'Marjorie didn't encourage me to talk when their friends were there. She didn't like me making stupid teenage conversation so I was usually in the kitchen helping Albert with the washing up. My father liked visitors but when he felt they had stayed long enough he would get up and wind the cuckoo clock with a great whirring of chains. People would look up and say "Is that the time?" and he'd ask if they wanted him to call them a hired car. He wanted to go to bed or go to his room and get on with scoring.'[27]

307

Eugene was enjoying greater personal happiness and professional fulfilment than he had known for many years. 1951 brought him literary recognition too when his autobiography *Overture and Beginners* was at last published. He had only gone as far as 1931 and his appointment in Cincinnati, leaving the rest for a second volume, which sadly he never completed. 'It would be hard to imagine a more engaging musical figure for biography than Eugene Goossens,' decided the *Manchester Guardian.* 'These pages are not of a mere gossipy kind. They are full of frank and witty remarks about eminent musical personalities and about many of the world's best orchestras.'

Australian critic, Lindsey Browne complained that the book 'was remarkably reticent about the things that must be regarded as the vital productive facts of any artist's life – his art, his reflections upon it, his reasons, his problems, his excuses, his code of ethics and aesthetics, the quality and direction of his introspection.' That was not what Eugene had intended to write. Like its writer the book is sophisticated, urbane and amusing but resolutely gives nothing away about the man himself. The wives and the children are strictly one-liners! The reader looks in vain for emotional insights or intellectual analysis. As always, Eugene was obdurately protecting his heart from the public gaze.

21

So Dignified and Aloof

Perhaps Eugene's most popular claim to fame is that he discovered Joan Sutherland. She sang the title role in his one act opera *Judith* at the Conservatorium in June 1951. He recognised the outstanding vocal potential of the gawky, unsophisticated secretary from the Sydney suburbs; forty years later she still retains bemused memories of her stage debut.

> I wasn't even a student at the Con. He'd heard me in the Concerto and Vocal competition run by the ABC and asked me to sing in his opera. I was so surprised and so excited. I had never been on stage before. He was very kindly but he seemed very reserved and very proper, almost a forbidding figure and nobody would have thought of calling him Gene! When I went to England he gave me a marvellous letter of introduction to his own agent Wilfrid Van Wyck and to Sir David Webster at Covent Garden. [1]
>
> 'The bearer of this letter has a magnificent dramatic soprano voice, and has done excellent work here in concert and operatic performances. Her voice is in the true Austral tradition and she made quite a sensation here recently in her creation of Judith in my opera of that name. Her departure for Europe will be a great loss to Australia for such grand natural voices as hers are all too rare nowadays.'

Walter Wagner, the Editor of *The Canon* analysed Goossens' musical style for the opera as 'mid-way between the emotional song-speech of *Pelléas and Mélisande* and the rational manner in which Benjamin Britten makes his protagonists converse. Joan Sutherland sang Judith exceedingly well. Her rich dramatic soprano and her ringing high tones compensated fully for her somewhat stiff and too conventional acting.'

Both the opera and singer suffered from the shortcomings of the production. Martin Long of the *Sydney Sun* found: 'Joan

309

Sutherland, as Judith, used her voice well, but not well enough to compensate for her undeveloped acting. Very little thought seemed to have been given to the generalities or the details of production; in some instances the actual stage directions of the printed score were disregarded even though the composer held the baton.'[2] He also castigated Ronald Dowd, later to make a distinguished career as leading tenor at Sadler's Wells, for misinterpreting the role of the crafty eunuch, Bagoas.

Brenton Langbein, one of the group of musicians who were Joan's friends, recalls sitting together at the dress rehearsal with Marjorie and Donie. 'It was so funny seeing Joanie trying to be seductive. I can remember this glorious voice but crying tears at the way she was acting: making love to Holofernes and then cutting off his head! I still think it's a marvellous opera.'[3]

The second half of the bill, *Gianni Schicchi* was more favourably received. The Renée Goossens listed in the cast was not the conductor's youngest daughter but, by a remarkable coincidence, another Renée Goossens whose father, also called Eugene, had emigrated from Belgium to Australia. He had been the first professor of singing to be appointed to the Conservatorium.[4] Eugene had to rebut the charge of nepotism when he engaged the other Renée Goossens to teach singing there.

Until he could fulfil his ambition of a professional opera house for Sydney, Eugene concentrated on improving the standard of public performances given by the Opera School at the Conservatorium. His twin aims were to give experience to young singers and provide the public with a more challenging operatic diet than the invariable *White Horse Inn* and Gilbert and Sullivan provided by visiting companies and local groups. Productions in the first five years of his tenure included *Louise*, *Pelléas and Mélisande*, *Falstaff*, *Otello*, *Mastersingers* and *Boris Godunov*. Two of the young musicians to whom he gave invaluable experience as repetiteurs were Geoffrey Parsons, whom he called on to sight-read the first scene of *Falstaff* and Richard Bonynge, who was rehearsal pianist for *The Marriage of Figaro*.

His policy met criticism, typified by Lindsey Browne who had succeeded Cardus as chief music critic of the *Sydney Morning Herald*. (Eugene's successor with the Sydney Symphony Orchestra Nikolai Malko was to say that the initials LB stood for

Lousy Bastard!) 'Various orchestral and chamber music activities among the students, which used to be an important part of the Conservatorium's practical work, have largely gone by the board. So many professional musicians are brought into the opera productions and so little use is made of bona fide Conservatorium students, that the opera school no longer performs its original function.'[5] Conversely he criticised the production of *Pelléas and Mélisande* for not coming up to professional standards. 'If the Conservatorium production had no richer value, it did show that Debussy's twilit masterpiece cannot even begin to exist unless its singers are supremely sensitive actors, directed by a regisseur who is artist, poet, practical technician all in one. None of these demands was met.'

Goossens was quick to take up the cudgels in print:

> Your critic not only applies super Covent Garden standards to a student production but revives the old accusation that Conservatorium opera is a tawdry, ill-sung, inexpert bungle. The serious musician invites and welcomes fair criticism, but somehow there is a gratuitous arrogance about the critical reception of hitherto unperformed works in Sydney; all of which prompts one to confine future offerings to performances of *The Student Prince* and *Blossom Time*.
>
> Shortcomings yes; but surely three-quarters of a fresh loaf in Sydney's empty operatic larder is better than no bread at all.

Goossens was gratified by the warmth of public support in his defence. 'No one expects Conservatorium performances to reach the standard of Covent Garden or the Paris opera,' wrote *Opera Lover* to the Editor of the *Sydney Morning Herald*, 'but surely it is better for music lovers to become acquainted with these masterpieces, whatever the imperfections may be, than for them to remain unheard and unknown.'

One production that gave Eugene particular pleasure was Gounod's *Romeo and Juliet*. His daughter Donie was playing the harp in the orchestra and had recently become engaged to a young baritone, John Young, who was singing Friar Lawrence. Eugene Goossens III explained to the company that this was family history repeating itself; not only had his father conducted the opera but his grandfather as well, with his father playing in the orchestra and his mother singing on stage as the Nurse.

311

'The orchestral parts had been sent out from London,' Donie remembers, 'and one of the players had done a caricature of my grandfather. Talk about genetics! That was one of the most thrilling things that ever happened to me.'[6]

Obviously there were many operas which the Conservatorium could not tackle, even with professional stiffening. In order to build up public interest and demand for professional opera, Eugene provided concert performances with the Sydney Symphony Orchestra of excerpts from *The Ring* and other works which required large expert forces such as *Elektra*. The cast for *Salome* in 1951 'was led by one of Australia's most distinguished international opera singers, Marjorie Lawrence'. Salomé and Brünnhilde had been among her acclaimed roles at the Met. until she was stricken with polio in 1941. She resumed her career in 1943, singing concert performances from a wheelchair.

For Geoffrey Parsons, *Salomé* epitomised Eugene's success in convincing the Sydney public that they could at last be active participants in European musical life. At the Conservatorium he inspired hero worship among a brilliant group of students in his Diploma Class including Parsons, Malcolm Williamson (now Master of the Queen's Music), Richard Bonynge and pianist, Roger Woodward. For Bonynge he was like a god 'partly, I suppose, because he was so dignified and aloof.'[7]

Parsons emphasises:

He was a tremendous inspiration to me. There was a large number of 'Rehabs' [ex-Servicemen who came as Rehabilitation Students after the war]; they were much more mature and he was able to identify with them and they with him. In contrast, I was seventeen, very young and very naïve and from a strict non-conformist background, which meant very strait-laced. He brought in all kinds of sweeping reforms to the age old curriculum, abolishing chamber music classes for example, because he wanted to encourage us all to think of ourselves as mainstream soloists.

One of the ways in which he tried to broaden our horizons and introduce us to European culture was to invite a German friend of his, Alfons Silbermann to give a course in Aesthetics. He couched everything in most luxuriant language which seemed impressive at the time but subsequently proved highly suspect.[8]

Pianist Raymond Fisher (Fischer), another member of the Diploma Class, was more favourably impressed. 'He gave extremely fine lectures; his one on Bruckner was the best I have ever heard. But he was a poseur; very suave, elegant and impeccably dressed.[9]

Silbermann had introduced the hamburger to Sydney in a chain of restaurants called 'The Silver Grill'. He was reported to be writing Eugene's biography and Donie remembers his lending the family his house at Woollahra one summer. After his return to Europe he became Professor of Philosophy at Cologne University. In 1955 he published *Introduction à une Sociologie de la Musique*, much of which is a detailed and laudatory critique of Eugene's contribution to twentieth century music.[10]

Puritan Sydney had been alternately shocked and titillated by rumours of Silbermann's sexual deviance and decadent parties. It is surprising the degree of distaste that his name still arouses among the musicians who knew him in Sydney in their youth such as Langbein, Mackerras and the Tuckwells. Langbein felt that he exerted an evil influence over Eugene.

Eugene did not officially teach conducting or composition at the Conservatorium. He concentrated the limited time at his disposal on the biennial productions of the Opera School and on the Diploma Class which took place every Monday afternoon.

Clarinetist Anne Menzies was Class Secretary and had more opportunity of getting to know the austere figure who would stride through the corridors of the Con. in his large woollen coat with the astrakhan collar, parting the respectful students like the waves of the sea.

> I had to see him every week to organise the programme. In contrast to his public image, I found him such a genial, warm-hearted, fatherly character and most helpful in every way possible. The class took the form of a performance, every student having to play as a soloist twice a term. He would then give a criticism in front of the whole class. He was very astute and had a very good idea of what was required from every instrument. We all valued his advice a great deal but it was quite terrifying when you had to front up because you knew he held your future in his hands. He was always one of the examiners at the final concerto performance and there were so few opportunities for orchestral jobs. I did my first audition for the SSO for him and although it was a terrifying occasion, he made it quite a palatable one.[11]

Anne is married to Donald Hazelwood who was appointed

313

joint leader of the SSO in 1965 on the retirement of Ernest Llewellyn. He studied at the Con. from 1948 to 1951.

> Goossens connected the role of the Chief Conductor with that of the Director of the Conservatorium. He insisted that students were aware of the orchestra and our ambition was to join it. I played for a year in the back desk of the Second Violins as a seasonal engagement and then in 1953 was taken on on a more permanent basis. It was difficult for young players like Anne and myself to assess Goossens as a conductor. Our critical faculties were still being formed and we didn't have the means of comparison that we have now. He was the Great Man who stood in front of the orchestra and made all these wonderful things happen![12]

One of Eugene's ambitions for the SSO was that it should be recognised as a major recording orchestra. The first step towards this was the recording of the Ballet Suite from *Corroboree* by HMV on 5th December 1950, followed by a series of transcriptions by the ABC for the BBC to broadcast on Australia Day. These included excerpts from Turina's *Sinfonía Sevillana*, Berlioz' *Romeo and Juliet*, the Prelude to Act III of *Siegfried*, and Ravel's *La Valse*. Eugene eagerly awaited his father's verdict on the Ravel. Despite the acclaim of international critics, as he approached his sixtieth year it was still his father's opinion that was the most important to him.

When Charles Moses and William James visited London the following year, they had no difficulty in persuading EMI (now the parent company of HMV) to take on a joint project with the ABC. 'Putting music on record is a relentless undertaking,' emphasised Arthur Clarke, the senior recording engineer, when he travelled to Australia to supervise ten sessions in the Great Hall of Sydney University. Clarke had been with HMV since 1907 and had recorded Caruso, Gigli and Elgar.[13]

Three works were released in September 1952 on the HMV Red Label series: Beethoven Symphony no. 2; Turina *Sinfonía Sevillana* and Saint-Saëns *Danse Macabre*. The recordings, despite certain technical imperfections, were hailed as an historic event and a sign to the world of Australia's musical maturity.

Meanwhile, Eugene did not slacken in his campaign for a Sydney Opera House. In April 1949 he set out his ideas in the *Sunday Herald*, illustrated by his friend William Constable, for an auditorium with adjustable interior walls, which would allow the same auditorium to be used as an opera house, concert hall or theatre. 'We have frequently explored the site which I consider from every angle to be the most suitable: Fort Macquarie which at present shelters some of our more decorative trams.'[14] Their inspiration was the War Memorial Opera House in San Francisco, but they did not face the main disadvantage of a multi-purpose auditorium, that it can be used for only one purpose at a time.

Ever the optimist, Eugene wrote: 'The Australian public is a generous one and the mere prospect of the world spotlight being focused on Sydney will stimulate an irresistible rally of civic-minded music lovers to the cause. For once the Government will find itself called upon to contribute only a fraction of the construction costs, so generous and immediate will be the response of our citizens.' His faith in the generosity of Sydney's citizens was to prove sadly misplaced. Despite the publicly voiced support of Mr R J Heffron, Minister of Education, who linked the project with the urgently needed enlargement and modernisation of the Conservatorium, there were no moves towards the realisation of the scheme.

Before Eugene returned from Europe in March 1950, the headline was: 'An Opera House or no Goossens.'[15] On his arrival he told a press conference that he would be recommending to the State Government and Civic Authorities that the site for the Opera House should be on Bennelong Point where the tram shed stood in the shadow of Fort Macquarie. 'I can visualise there by the harbour a building which will be an architectural triumph and an asset to the city.'

In view of Eugene's subsequent removal from the scene and the chequered history of the Opera House, it is essential to emphasise that the original concept for the building on that site was his and that he conceived it as an opera house which would be a cultural centre for 'the second city of the British Empire' and also provide a home for the Sydney Symphony Orchestra. Phyllis Williams, Eugene's secretary, remembers his taking her for lunch-time walks to the tram shed at Bennelong Point and saying: 'This is where the Opera House is to be!'[16]

Perhaps he should have taken heed of the landmark's tragic origin. Bennelong was a young aborigine captured and befriended in 1789 by Captain Arthur Phillip, who took him

315

to London to meet George III. Despite the King's gift of a gold braided coat, on his return, Bennelong found that he had forfeited his tribal status and tribal wife. He lived out a wretched existence in a hut by the water where he eventually died of drink and despair. In 1817, Governor Macquarie built a fort on the site, designed by Francis Greenway, the convict architect responsible for Sydney's best Georgian architecture, including St James's Church.

Eugene's choice of site and indeed the whole project continued to be highly controversial. The Maritime Services Board had earmarked the site for an International Shipping Terminal. There was also a suggestion that it might be used for a luxury hotel. The *Sydney Sun* thought the priorities were wrong: 'Music is a fine thing and Mr Goossens has had a wonderful cultural effect on Sydney but I can't help thinking that it is more important at the moment to build some hospitals to hold 3,500 people [the estimated capacity of the Opera House] or maybe some houses. There's precious little music about some of the hovels Australian families are forced to live in.'

The Opera House had become an *idée fixe* as far as Eugene was concerned and he was becoming increasingly frustrated and impatient at its lack of progress. His scathing attacks in the press on New South Wales' Labour Premier Mr J McGirr and other politicians as 'philistines' embarrassed Charles Moses as General Manager of the ABC, and the Governors of the Conservatorium. He was biting the hands that gave them the subsidies. In general, Labour politicians were more favourably inclined towards subsidising the Arts; as Moses explained, having survived the Depression, 'they didn't know much about classical music but they liked the idea of their children attending symphony concerts.'[17]

After the New South Wales elections of 1952, Moses arranged for Eugene to meet the new State Premier, J J (Joe) Cahill and the two struck up an unlikely friendship. Cahill committed his Government's support for the scheme and presided over a conference of persons and organisations interested in the establishment of an opera house in Sydney.

The three favoured locations were over Wynyard Station, a site near St Mary's Cathedral, which caused consternation to the Sydney Bowling Club as it threatened their hallowed green, and

316

Bennelong Point. Eugene spoke out strongly in favour of the third option but was not in favour of the Conservatorium being housed in the same building, on the grounds that teaching and entertainment did not mix. 'Nowhere in the world will you find a teaching body having its headquarters in an opera house.' Not a multi-faceted teaching academy perhaps, but in view of his commitment to opera and to the furthering of young singers, Eugene might have been the first administrator with the vision to suggest an Opera Studio attached to the Opera House. His duties at the Conservatorium were becoming an increasingly unwelcome burden. He viewed them as an encroachment on his schedule, necessitating a sacrifice of the limited time available for conducting and composing.

Cahill estimated that the costs would be between £1–1½ million. By the time it was completed twenty years later it had cost £51 million. In November 1954 he appointed a five man committee of Eugene, Charles Moses, the Dean of the Faculty of Architecture of Sydney University and the Town Clerk, chaired by the Under Secretary of Public Works. 'Sydney's Opera House will be the first in Australia,' Cahill explained. 'This country just cannot go on without proper facilities for the expression of talent and the staging of the highest forms of artistic entertainment.'[18] Because of his prestige and influence, Eugene was able to circumvent the opposition of the Maritime Board and assorted property developers. It was agreed that the new International Shipping Terminal would be sited on the opposite side of Sydney Cove and that in three years the trams would be replaced by buses with a depot in Ultimo.

On 17th May 1955, the State Cabinet announced that the State Opera House would be built at Bennelong Point, described as 'a setting unique in the world for a building of such a monumental character.' There were to be two halls: the opera auditorium seating 3,500 people would also be used for ballet, choral and orchestral performances and a smaller hall, seating 1,200 for theatre. The press were united in their praise of Eugene for his vision and pertinacity in guiding the opera house idea through to its fulfilment. 'Completion of an Opera House such as Mr Cahill visualises would be an historic accomplishment for the present government. But as no doubt Mr Cahill would gladly admit, the main hero of the Opera

317

House site choice is Mr Eugene Goossens. His artist's eye picked out the site within a year of his coming here in 1947. For six years Mr Goossens worked to rally public opinion and force official action. So Australian music owes yet another debt to the distinguished conductor of the Sydney Symphony Orchestra and director of the Conservatorium.'[19]

'Magnificent, absolutely superb,' commented visiting conductor Sir John Barbirolli, wholeheartedly endorsing his friend Gene's foresight when he was taken to visit Bennelong Point. 'I can imagine no better site in the world for a music centre. The new building should be an inspiration to your architects. I hope they don't erect a blot on the landscape like the Festival Hall in London.'[20]

There were of course dissenting voices raising practical as well as philistine objections. *Truth* condemned the plan as 'preposterous and unreal. Why steal a beauty spot that belongs to everyone for the benefit of a mere handful in the community. In view of the Government's frequent announcements that insufficient money is available for important public works, the public is not likely to stand for large expenditure on a State Opera House.'[21]

When an international competition to design the Opera House was announced, Eugene volunteered on his coming visit to Europe to report on the opera houses of Hamburg and Vienna (both destroyed during the war), as a guideline for judging the entries. They formed a useful contrast: the State Opera House in Vienna was reopened in November 1955, rebuilt as a replica of the 1869 building, but benefiting from all the most modern developments in technical equipment; in Hamburg the decision had been made to construct a totally new building.

Eugene wrote to Charles Moses on 17th February 1956 from the Colonnade Hotel, Maida Vale, which vied with the Savage Club as his favourite London base: 'I am going next week to Vienna and Hamburg to get first-hand impressions and information about the two most modern houses. I hope the best features of both theatres, the big stage and elaborate machinery of Vienna and the effectively laid out auditorium of Hamburg will both characterise the winning design for the Sydney Opera House.'

22

Playing From the Heart

After the Second World War, Léon had decided to hold no more orchestral posts but to devote himself to his solo career. A major work with which his name now became identified was the Strauss Oboe Concerto. He gave the first British performance on 17th August 1946 in a Promenade Concert conducted by Sir Adrian Boult. It was only two nights after his mother had died and his father wrote touchingly in his diary: 'Listened to Lee's broadcast from Albert Hall. Playing beautifully. I finished up with tears in my eyes. Darling Mum I am sure listened in and sent down her blessings on him for Lee's success.'

Strauss had written the work for the Swiss oboist Marcel Saillet who had given the premiere in Zurich a few months earlier in February 1946. He preferred Léon's interpretation and was delighted that he was to make the first recording in 1947 with the Philharmonia String Orchestra. The *Times* later described his playing of the concerto as 'a thing to marvel at. It made time stand still and as a technical feat it was astonishing that so fine a line of tone could be drawn out of so stubborn an instrument without it ceasing to speak.'[1] It remained for Léon 'a very beautiful and satisfying work. Strauss seems to bring into it all the musical happenings of his lifetime. It's as if he's sitting back passing the time when he's too old to do anything new.'[2]

In 1948 he also gave the premiere of the Oboe Concerto that Cyril Scott had written for him, in a Promenade Concert on 13th September conducted by Stanford Robinson.

Leslie was encouraging him to develop his career as a recitalist. Ivor Newton, one of his major accompanists, described Léon's working methods in preparation for a recital programme:

'He instinctively feels the music and doesn't have to study it or work it over to any great extent. He looks at the music and knows immediately every possibility about it and expects the accompanist, his collaborator at the piano to know it equally well. He is not addicted to too much rehearsal which he feels spoils the spontaneity of the performance.'[3]

He had the distinction in the autumn of 1946 of giving the first ever oboe recital in Vienna. His British Council host, Richard Rickett, recalled 'the critics were dumbfounded and I remember one of them opining that "Goossens extracts tones from his instrument which do not exist in ordinary oboes." No wonder he had his reed stolen from the Artists' Room in Graz!'[4]

Ten years later he was one of eight English musicians sponsored by the British Council for their first official concert tour of the Soviet Union: the conductor Clarence Raybould, the violinist Campoli, soprano Jennifer Vyvyan, and duo pianists Cyril Smith and Phyllis Sellick, led by Master of the Queen's Music, Sir Arthur Bliss. Sir Arthur kept a diary of the three weeks' tour and noted on 25th April:

> At our opening concert (in Leningrad) Goossens introduced the new concerto written for him by Gordon Jacob; the parts had luckily just arrived in time. This work proved a distinguished addition to our repertoire.
>
> Two oboists came all the way from Tallinn (two hundred miles away in Estonia) to see Goossens play, after having heard him on the radio, and to learn next morning at his hotel how he managed certain technical difficulties. They couldn't believe it possible that a man could produce that tone. He gave them reeds and showed them how he played.

Jennie Goossens remembers her father's visit to Russia: 'He used to phone us practically every day to use up his roubles, explaining that he wouldn't be able to bring any of the money out. There was nothing to spend it on, only a couple of pieces of jewellery and fur hats!'[5]

The BBC, with its newly founded Third Programme, often seemed to prefer music from the head to Léon's music from the heart. Lionel Salter typified the more academic approach. Although he admired Léon as a musician, he found him 'wonderfully old-fashioned in some ways. I was asked to write new editions of early music for the Third Programme, including Handel's oboe sonatas, putting in embellishments of the time. Lee was to have played these. He looked at them over his half glasses with considerable astonishment and said "I've always prided myself as having played Handel exactly as he was written and I'm certainly not going to change now!"'[6]

'I've never been able to acclimatise myself to these ideas,' Léon later explained to Edwin Roxburgh. 'I think these tunes are so beautiful the way they're written. Obviously there is some latitude in filling up the gaps, in making them sound interesting. In some instances I add a trill on a long note where I feel it needs one. My general principle in Handel and Bach is to make the ornamentation as unobtrusive as possible.'

Jack Brymer, who had joined the last orchestra Beecham was to form, the resurrected Royal Philharmonic, had no reservations about Léon's playing.

> I was particularly delighted to work with him for the first time in 1951, in a BBC Thursday Concert where we played the Milhaud for oboe, clarinet and strings. Just before we went on he said 'You know Jack, they say we don't get nervous but feel this' and he put his hand in mine and it was like a frog it was so cold! That was a great revelation to me. Like everyone else he had to have the adrenalin, the spur. He played with absolute majesty and complete dedication.
>
> In 1954 he played with the RPO for a couple of months when Terence McDonagh was unwell. I very much treasure the recordings in which he took part of Russian music. Some were conducted by Artur Rodzinski from New York who was particularly delighted when he found that Léon was coming back to the orchestra.
>
> Léon was incredibly adaptable; it's difficult for some players to readjust to orchestral playing after a solo career, but he had no problems. He was never a pompous individual; he never threw his weight about as a colleague. He was always willing to discuss rather than override anyone's opinion. He was very well tempered and humorous. He wouldn't hesitate to pull people's legs and see the funny side of characters, especially conductors.[7]

Lionel Salter retains a less charitable impression of Léon's personality: 'Although he was always extremely courteous, he occasionally lost his temper about small things when conductors niggled him in some way. He was always a little aloof from the rest of the orchestra and chamber players. He was a cut above the majority of musicians socially, or so he felt. He regarded musical people and social people in separate groups.'[8]

Léon enjoyed the company of the famous and titled but was never such a blatant runner after royalty as Sir Malcolm Sargent. On one occasion Sargent asked him to stay behind after an Albert Hall concert to meet a special friend. The Green Room eventually cleared except for one tall distinguished gentleman. 'Your Majesty,' said Sargent with due deference, 'I would like to present my friend and colleague Léon Goossens. Lee, may I introduce you to the King of Norway.' There was a slight pause before the distinguished gentleman proffered his hand and muttered apologetically: 'Denmark . . . Denmark!'[9]

Léon was no stranger to the British Royal Family. In 1940 he had been one of a small group of musicians invited to play for the Queen at Windsor Castle while Gerald Kelly continued with another of his innumerable sittings for Her Majesty's state portrait in Coronation robes. At the end of June he received a letter from the Queen's Acting Private Secretary, Sir Arthur Penn: 'I am now sending you the pair of links which accompany this letter and am to express the hope that they will serve to recall a day to which Her Majesty looks back with very genuine pleasure.'[10]

In 1950 Léon had been the first of the family to receive a British honour for their services to music, the CBE. The letter of congratulation which brought him the most pleasure was from his father: 'Darling Lee, I would be among the first of your innumerable admirers to congratulate and applaud you on your nomination as confirmed in today's New Year's Honours List, this last enhanced by the mention of your name, nobly upheld in your service to art and by excellence of your own! What can I say more except that I wish you ever increasing Renown, Happiness and Prosperity.'[11]

At last Léon felt that he had surpassed his elder brother in achievement and merited his father's unqualified respect. His supremacy was cut short in 1955 when Eugene was awarded his knighthood. Sidonie received the MBE followed, with Marie, by the OBE for their contribution to British orchestral playing. Marie at the LSO and Sidonie with the BBC Symphony Orchestra enjoyed unrivalled supremacy as Queens of the Harp.

In 1948 the London Symphony Orchestra was reorganised but Marie retained her position as Principal Harp. She found some conductors more stimulating than others. 'Josef Krips brought fresh blood to the orchestra. He was a conductor with a soul. I especially remember his Strauss' *Don Juan* – at one point in rehearsing he would look across at me with those piercing grey eyes and say "Sing Mary, sing", little knowing that it does not take much to encourage me to do this vocally, leave alone mentally. His Strauss waltzes were really wonderful; he always smiled which is very refreshing. An orchestra sits hour after hour concentrating, it is a very serious profession and a little light-heartedness helps one to relax.'[12]

In contrast Stokowski was 'rather frightening as he appeared so stern, wanting everything his own way. Twice at recordings I have known him to change the orchestration as far as the harp part was concerned. Once at EMI Studios he changed the microphone round – this nearly caused a strike. Another time they were playing the soundtrack back to us and two of the violinists left their seats to go out for a smoke. They were not allowed back to us for this session or for the remaining session. He acted in the same manner when I had retired and was called in to deputise for the LSO. By that time he was a nonagenarian and had to be almost carried on but his brain seemed to be as alert as ever.'[13]

Sidonie discovered Stokowski was similarly dictatorial when he conducted Britten's *Young Person's Guide to the Orchestra*. 'There are two different harp versions according to whether the work is being performed with or without a narrator. He insisted I was playing the wrong one so I said if that was the way he wanted it I would play it that way although I knew he was wrong. It sounded terrible in the performance. I had lunch with him in a party once and he never took his gloves off; he only took them off when he conducted!'[14]

Marie had played the harp solo in the premiere of the Britten, which proved to be more complicated than she had anticipated. 'Nobody had seen the parts beforehand and we recorded it in three hours. This record was used as a background to a film for schools. We appeared in the film miming to our own playing. We had to appear looking the same each day. My hair was done in the Edwardian style which keeps very tidy, but I still had to sleep on four pillows and remain half-conscious all night; then I only had to comb up the sides and back and it was ready for the filming.'15

The repertoire for solo harp and orchestra is limited so the sisters were always gratified with the occasional solo dates that came their way. In the Promenade season of 1953 Marie played in the *Petite Symphonie Concertante* by Frank Martin, written for harp, harpsichord, piano and strings, the first concert performance in its original form; her fellow soloists were Charles Spinks and Joseph Weingarten. Sidonie played it the following year on 3rd November with the BBC SO conducted by Jean Martinon. She also gave the premiere of the Harp Concerto written for her by William Alwyn, subtitled 'Lyra Angelica'. 'I hope it won't vanish from the repertoire like the Creston work,' was her comment on confirming the engagement for 27th July 1954. She played a second performance conducted by Barbirolli on 2nd January 1955.

Sidonie had resisted temptations to leave the BBC Symphony Orchestra during the difficult period it experienced after the war. Standards had deteriorated and new orchestras such as the Philharmonia and the Royal Philharmonic Orchestra increased the competition for good players, offering better pay and working conditions. Sidonie was Secretary of the BBC Symphony Orchestra Committee, fighting a hard battle to obtain pensions for players when they retired. 'Although we were members of staff, the BBC would not consider us eligible for staff pensions. Eventually in the 50s, when they agreed to give us back-dated pensions, they were only back-dated from 1949 which meant original members of the orchestra lost twenty years. Ernest Hall [Principal Trumpet, 1929–53] and Eugene Cruft [Principal Double Bass, 1926–49] got a mere pittance of six shillings a week!'16

Sargent, who was to be appointed Chief Conductor after Boult's unwilling retirement in 1950, did not increase his popularity with the orchestra by his known opposition to a pension scheme. 'As soon as a man thinks he is in his orchestral job for life, with a pension waiting for him at the end of it, he tends to lose something of his supreme fire,' he had stated in 1935.

Apart from this basic difference of principle Sidonie relates:

'I got on very well with him personally. He was very, very efficient; safe but not inspired. He was at his best conducting choral works. I had to tell him the tempo of the Brabançon – the Belgian National Anthem – when we played at the Brussels Exhibition in 1958, he was playing it terribly slowly. He forgot everything at the concert because Royalty were there – the King of the Belgians and Duke of Edinburgh – he couldn't take his eyes off their box. He went quite gaga when Royalty were present – a most odd thing about him.'[17]

Marie also took part in the Exhibition with the LSO. 'Conditions had changed so much since 1910 when we visited our first Exhibition with our parents. I remember going to Laeken to see an old aunt of my father's who was the widow of a Flemish painter called Cornelius van Leemputten. Her flat overlooked a beautiful park, unrecognisable now as the site of the 1958 Exhibition!'[18]

Sidonie has inherited a collection of oil paintings by Van Leemputten; sunless Flemish landscapes, far removed from her own sparkling personality. They hang on the walls of the seventeenth-century farmhouse near Reigate to which she and Norman moved in 1949. Although she found Léon in some ways the least sympathetic of her siblings, they shared a love of country pursuits. Sidonie, long blessed with a delight in domesticity, now developed a new personality as a farmer's wife.

We had five acres of land which we ran as a small holding. We started off with two little wee pigs that Beecham gave us when he lived at Ringmer. We fattened them up and when they were ready to be killed, because meat was still rationed, we were allowed half and the butcher half. I was faced with half a pig's head in a basket, not a pretty sight. But I pulled myself together, looked in all the cookery books and made brawn.

We used to breed chickens, North Holland Blues which lay lovely dark brown eggs. I took them up to the orchestra and everyone would crowd round me asking 'Got any eggs Sid?' At Christmas we bred capons. Norman gave them their injections and they used to start growing wonderfully; then they would lose their crow which was quite comic. I used to take them up to the orchestra at Christmas time, at least a dozen. Norman killed them and I would do the trussing on the kitchen table.

It was hard work but it was all a matter of organisation. We would get up at 5.30am, light the oil lamps, feed the chickens, exercise the dog and get the 8.40am train up to London. I only had concerts once a week and apart from that, it was daytime studio work.[19]

Sidonie flourished on this exacting schedule until she was in her mid-sixties; they then decided to give up farming because Norman had badly broken his leg for the second time. Although he had no professional musical background, Norman Millar had fitted into the family very well. He found his métier in Arts Administration and followed the Goossens tradition of working for Beecham.

Norman had applied for the post of BBC Artists Booking Manager. The job went to a viola player in our orchestra, but Sir Steuart Wilson, Head of Music, recommended him to Beecham who was looking for someone to take over the management of the Royal Philharmonic Orchestra. Norman talked to Daddy and me and we all shook our heads: 'Oh dear! working for Beecham!' He was warned that the orchestra was already in the red but he wouldn't take advice from any of us. Beecham and Lady Beecham were both in evening dress when he went to see them saying that his visit made it a special evening. Only at the end when Beecham offered him the job did Norman mention that his wife was Sidonie Goossens. That evidently knocked them flat but Tommy still said he'd like him to start straight away as Administrator.

Norman found they were in a terrible mess at the office in Maddox Street; all the staff were living off Tommy, travelling to concerts First Class, staying at the best hotels. The only thing to do was to give them all notice; he got them out of the red in a year but he was very much disliked. The orchestral managers were hopeless and would bring all their friends in to play. Norman was very unpopular when he tried to enforce any discipline for the players.

He had a very good woman secretary, Miss Valentine who stayed on until she left to marry Gerald Jackson, the Principal Flautist. Her replacement was Shirley Hudson who had started in the office when she was seventeen. After Betty Humby died she suddenly became Lady Beecham. After that Norman decided to leave; he became General Manager of the Old Vic.[20]

(Beecham married Shirley Hudson as his third wife in Zurich on 10th August 1959; she was twenty-seven and he was eighty.)

Marie never remarried. Without a husband and farm to

occupy her surplus energies she was involved in an enormously wide range of musical activities besides classical concerts with the LSO. She played for innumerable films, from *Tom Jones*, *Those Magnificent Men in their Flying Machines* and the incomparable Margaret Rutherford as Miss Marple to the Vaughan Williams scores for *Scott of the Antarctic* and *The 49th Parallel*. She was to be seen in period costume in the film of *Le Moulin Rouge* and the masque of *Comus*, for which she arranged the music. She also made an arrangement for voices and harp from Mendelssohn's incidental music for a production of *A Midsummer Night's Dream* at the Open-Air Theatre in Regent's Park. She played the harp for the famous record on which Gracie Fields bemoans 'I took my harp to a party and nobody asked me to play!' 'When I appeared as a guest on Pete Murray's "Open House" for the BBC, Pete said jokingly "I took my Harp to a Party". I said immediately "Yes, I made that!" He could hardly believe it and roared with laughter.'[21]

Marie, completely unpretentious and of unfailing good humour, was one of the best-known and loved figures in the musical profession. Her original role of Little Mother to her brothers and sister was perpetuated in the entertainment world. She often found herself acting as unofficial chaperone to a child star: the young Jean Simmons filming at Denham Studios; seven-year-old Petula Clark making her debut in a Charity Concert at the Albert Hall; Julie Andrews singing on the Vic Oliver Show with a remarkably mature voice for a twelve-year-old. They all remembered the motherly little lady who brought them their orangeade in the meal break or interval. Marie was delighted when her own daughter Jean married Maurice John Meek, a viola player with the LSO.

Like all the Goossens family, Marie lacked business acumen and never reaped the financial rewards her talents deserved. 'In 1948 the BBC engaged me to play a Signature Tune to go before a new serial that was to be broadcast. When I arrived I found I had to compose something myself. After a while I hit on a sort of formula which they liked. So I worked on it and made it sound presentable. Then they wanted a similar ending; I more or less put the tune upside down and that was done. It turned out to be the introduction to *Mrs Dale's Diary* and as everyone knows, the series went on for many years. Unfortunately I did not make a fortune out of it as I had nothing written down. If I had the same chance again I would be a good deal wiser.'[22]

She still lived at 'Crewkerne', able to keep an eye on her father a few doors away. Her step-son Geoffrey started married life in the house, soon to be followed by Anthony and Pam. Grandfather Eugene recorded in his diary on 21st June 1947: 'I witnessed and attended at Anthony's wedding today but with no gladness in my heart, no joyous thought in my mind. What does the future hold for these two young people? Alone HE knows. I dare not think!!' Not that he disapproved of Pam, his pretty young granddaughter-in-law, but he feared for the young couple's future; Anthony was only nineteen and still in the Royal Signals. He was not going to carry on the Goossens tradition into the fourth generation; he had inherited talent from both sides of the family but he was not willing to accept the discipline necessary to develop it as a professional classical musician.

Tony, with his relaxed personality and happy-go-lucky attitude ruefully describes himself as 'the black sheep of the family. I didn't go about things in a conventional manner. I became a jazz pianist, playing by ear in nightclubs and bands, all the old evergreens. I play that sort of music because I like it. As long as I can give people pleasure I'm happy.' Despite his grandfather's initial disappointment, their relationship was a mutually enjoyable one: 'In 1949 I bought a black Buick convertible and I used to take Grandpa Goossens out for a spin. He loved that and always wanted me to go faster. I can remember him sitting down and listening to a couple of jazz records to find out what sort of music meant so much to me.'[23]

Tony's wife Pam remembers him as a delightful old gentleman who rolled his own cigarettes and never lost his Belgian accent or gave up his Belgian nationality. 'He loved England though and when it was the Queen's Coronation he insisted on clambering up onto a ladder so that he could put both the British and Belgian flags over the porch. He was such a little man and he was eighty-six years old!'[24]

The previous year the BBC had celebrated his eighty-fifth birthday by recording a 'Celebrity Quintet' of Eugene Senior and his four famous children, including Eugene III over from Australia.[25] They were subsequently invited to tea in the Drawing Room of Broadcasting House to listen to a playback. There had been an actual birthday celebratory lunch on 28th January 1952 at L'Escargot, still the favourite rendezvous for family celebrations. Although Léon and his sisters enjoyed their frequent meetings on 'business' occasions, with Léon and Sidonie living out of London their private lives had grown further apart. Léon was determined that his children's upbringing should be very different from his own childhood.

After the war Léon had looked forward to a reunion with his oldest daughter Bene who had been brought up by her mother in the United States. Jennie and Corinne were suddenly confronted with an older sister without any prior knowledge of her existence. Leslie found it difficult to explain to them that their father had been married before. 'Oh Mum, I can't think of Dad belonging to anyone else but us,' was Jennie's reaction. 'Sometimes people don't get on together, darling.' 'Well she must have been nice to start off with otherwise Daddy wouldn't have married her!' was the little girl's reply.[26] The experiment of Bene coming to stay was not a success. Leslie resented any reminder of her predecessor; Jennie and Corinne were discouraged from having contact with their half sister and Léon was forced to meet her clandestinely in London.[27] For many years, Leslie excised any mention of Léon's first marriage and oldest daughter from biographical information such as in *Who's Who*.

Away from the concert platform Léon enjoyed the life of a country gentleman and the masculine pursuits of riding, shooting, driving fast cars and above all his great passion of sailing. In 1950 he and Leslie had moved from Holter's Green to North Hall, a Victorian house a few miles away at East Chiltington. His youngest daughter Corinne remembers it as 'a big, big house with a gorgeous red flagged stone hall, a minstrels' gallery and solid elm steps. It had outbuildings and twenty-one acres of land. Dad used to plough with a little tractor and grow wheat, oats and barley. We'd all join in the harvest and put up the stooks together. It took Mum and Dad some time to be accepted in local society; people weren't used to the idea of a musician and a dancer in their midst. We were always accumulating horses which were either too old or couldn't be ridden. "Give them to the Goossens, they've got a paddock," people would say. Dad taught us all we knew about horses from when he'd been in the Cavalry in the First World War.'[28]

'He never spoke about those war experiences,' Jennie explains. 'They were too horrific. He had a large scar on his left breast where the bullet had been. On our first family holiday in Cornwall after the Second World War, he developed an abscess on the scar which turned into a carbuncle. A piece of material started coming out, a piece of his vest which had been embedded in the wound since November 1918!'[29]

Both Jennie and Corinne remember him as a wonderful father. Jennie is more analytical than her sister.

> There was a definite reaction against the very rigid strictures of his own childhood. He was away a lot when we were children, on tour or abroad or playing to Music Clubs in far-flung corners of Britain, but when he was at home he was great for doing all the childhood things that he had never had time or money to do when he was a child, like having steam engines and ponies.
>
> There was very little talk of music as such in the house, nor did we hear an enormous amount, which always amazes people. 'It must have been very difficult having to keep quiet while your father practised,' other musicians' children say to me, and I say, 'what do you mean practise, he never did practise at home.'[30]

Corinne recalls her father coming downstairs 'smelling of Pears soap, never aftershave and extemporising at the piano just to limber up the fingers.'

> He could have made a career as a concert pianist. I can't remember when I was first aware that he had another life outside our home and was somebody special. I suppose I asked 'Where's Dad going' and the answer was 'to Russia, or Czechoslovakia or Australia'. I do remember the tremendous feeling of pride when he came on the platform at the Albert Hall, the glow of belonging to him. 'Is he smiling at me; does he know we're here?' And the thrill of going round afterwards. Tommy [Beecham] would make a fuss of us, and Sargent. A lot of people around you, trying to find a space . . . Dad laughing and joking . . . the embarrassment of

330

his anecdotes . . . he's not going to tell that one is he!'[31]

Jennie's embarrassment was when people discovered that her name was Goossens.

> They would recognise the name and a light of fervour would come into their eyes. 'And what do you play?' they'd ask. If I played anything at all it was lamentably badly. I just dreaded that moment and wished that my name was Smith! I hated being pushed into the limelight as a child, like when I had to stand in the wings holding Myra Hess' hot water bottle at the Dome in Brighton; she always suffered from cold hands. I had to turn pages once at the piano when Dad was trying out a new work written by Franz Reizenstein. It was all black notes, I was petrified! I think if we had shown any real musical talent it would have been different. We were encouraged but never with any degree of intensity. My father came once a week to give me an oboe lesson when I was at boarding school but that was because it gave him an extra opportunity for seeing me not because he thought I could follow in his footsteps.
>
> I remember Kathleen Ferrier who was a dear friend of Dad's coming to tea when she was singing Orfeo. I wanted to be an opera singer and longed to be one even more when I had a temporary job as an assistant telephone operator at Glyndebourne. I grew out of being ashamed of being called Goossens; I met so many fascinating people there as soon as they heard my name. I also realised I hadn't sufficient voice to be a singer and decided to be an actress instead.[32]

Both daughters displayed dramatic rather than musical gifts. Jennie trained at the Central School of Music and Drama and married a fellow actor Brian Spink when she was working with the Old Vic Company. Corinne remained content to bathe in reflected glory.

> When Dad was doing a lot of film work, he often took me to the studios with him. I loved meeting the people, seeing the stars. I'm still a child in that way and I've ended up as a film extra, doing walk-ons. I don't think anyone could have had a happier childhood than we did. It was very loving with great hugs and kisses and Dad reading us *Swallows and Amazons* in the bath. He and Mum were quite volatile but they had a wonderful relationship and couldn't live without each other. We

had closer links with mother's than father's family. Her brother was in the Army, stationed in Germany and we used to have a family Christmas with them in Osnabrück.

But I was well aware that I was a Goossens. I used to love family get-togethers: best frock time and the fact that all these people had come to see Dad. Uncle Zen had this lovely French 'r' in the back of the throat. He was always beautifully dressed and very attractive to women. I could feel that even as a little girl.[33]

Jennie commented on the relationship between the brothers and sisters as being very fond and full of laughter. 'Dad admired Uncle Zen's works and we always went to hear him conduct when he was over from Australia. They were not a family for birthday cards, they couldn't even remember when their birthdays were. When they met on the concert platform or the recording studio it was as if they had never been apart. It's difficult now to realise what a dedicated life they led, it was all schedules and timetables. They only had a holiday if they had a gap and some spare money.'[34]

It was primarily Léon who had loosened the bonds and forgot the wider family birthdays and anniversaries. His parents meticulously observed all birthdays and wedding anniversaries of their children, their husbands and wives and the grandchildren with cards and presents.

Jennie remembers her grandparents' visits to Holter's Green in June 1946:

Grandpa sitting with his blue beret. He was very little but quite gruff and stern. We hardly ever saw him laugh but his eyes used to twinkle a lot. Grandma was twice as big as he was and Dad told us that she used to rule the roost when they were children and his father was away on tour. Mother was very fond of them but quite in awe as we all were.

After Grandma died we used to have to go up occasionally and have tea with Grandpa in Finchley. He would always do a full Northern high tea with jelly, cakes, cold meat and fish. He used to get quite upset when we couldn't eat it all. 'What's wrong? Don't they like it? I've got all this prepared!' He was a darling.[35]

In the autumn of 1955, Léon's career gained a new dimension

when he was invited to join the Sinfonia of London. This was a break away group from the LSO, organised by his old friend the flautist Gordon Walker, which concentrated on film music under the baton of Muir Mattheson. James Brown, who had once cycled fifteen miles in the dark to hear Léon play a recital, found himself playing second oboe to his idol.

He was wonderful to work with. It was a revelation to me how he phrased. I'd always admired his flow of sound, the way he made the instrument sing. His rubato sounded quite right and natural when he did it and quite wrong when anyone else did. On the technical side he had a wonderful facility to double tongue, i.e. interrupt the air stream by closing the throat momentarily as a flute player does, a knack that you discover for yourself.

He was always good humoured and had a fantastic wit but he considered one or two things beneath him as an artist. One of the 'Carry On' Films we made was *Raising the Wind*, about a Music College with James Robertson Justice as the Principal. We had to play for the passing out exam of the conductors, with Leslie Phillips as the goodie and Kenneth Williams the baddie. Léon refused to be seen so I was on camera while his was the sound that was heard.

He didn't pull rank although he had been at the top of the profession for so long. He was having such fun playing with that orchestra three or four days a week; we never knew what was going to turn up, the ink was still wet on the page. He found it an ideal combination with his solo work.

I was always aware of the strong family bonds. He was terribly fond of Marie and Sidonie and his father; he was concerned that his father was living by himself and getting so elderly. He thought very highly of his brother's works, particularly the Oboe Concerto. He became a father figure for me as well as a colleague; he was very concerned about people and used to give me advice on my marital problems. The only fault he had was a lack of generosity towards his former pupils; having got them into the position where they could be self-sufficient he rather resented the fact that they were doing all right thank you. I enjoyed playing second oboe so there was never any sense of rivalry. He would look through the paper and see that Evelyn Rothwell or Joy Boughton of whom he was very fond were playing a concerto that had been written for them and make some acerbic remark. The only oboist of whom he spoke favourably was Jaap Stotyn, First Oboe of the Concertgebouw

333

whom he had met when he had played in Holland before the war with Beecham. But Lee wouldn't play Graham Whettham's Concertino for oboe because Graham had written it for Jaap and he had played it first.

The only time our relationship was threatened was when an innocent remark of mine was misinterpreted. The principals of the Sinfonia played as the Virtuoso Ensemble; they relied on their expertise to knock their programmes into shape with the minimum of rehearsal. I commented after a broadcast that the balance was not right and that Léon was far too loud. 'When you're as good as he is, you can criticise,' was the reaction of Eddie [Gordon] Walker the Manager and he told Léon what I had said.

I felt I had to explain myself to him as I admired and respected him far too much to risk losing his friendship or jeopardising our professional relationship. 'I've gone so long without anyone making any comment that I would welcome criticism,' was his reaction. When I explained that I wasn't criticising him, Lee said 'Even if you were, I wouldn't have minded.'[36]

In 1958 Léon and Leslie decided to move back to London. Leslie had felt starved of artistic friends in the country; they took a short lease on a house in 7, St Peter's Square, Hammersmith, where Sir Alec Guinness had previously lived, and found a congenial community of artists, actors and musicians. They resumed contact with their old friends of the Chelsea days: Yvonne Arnaud, Susie Hughes (Spike's mother), Phyllis Calvert, the blacksmith's daughter whom Leslie had taught to dance, Bernard Miles, Margaretta Scott, Edward Halliday, the artist of the Bovril advertisements. Léon rejoined the Garrick Club.

Although he was now in his sixties, an age at which most oboists have retired, Léon's mastery of his instrument and its effortless stream of beautiful tone seemed to be the product of a perennial youth. Only a handful of records preserve the full glory of his mature art: the Mozart Oboe Concerto with the Sinfonia of London conducted by Colin Davis, three Handel Concerti for Oboe and Strings, the Vivaldi Concerto in B minor with Yehudi Menuhin and the Bath Festival Chamber Orchestra and the Bach Double Concerto for Violin and Oboe with Menuhin, conducted by Colin Davis. Age and experience had their advantages. 'Perhaps because I'm an older person, conductors and other soloists usually defer to me,' he reflected. 'In the Bach double concerto there is sometimes a problem where the oboe has to double the violin but with Yehudi he and I were in perfect accord, even on the vexed question as to the ending of the shake before the trill.'

In 1956 the legendary Joe Batten, who had recorded Léon throughout his career from the days of Edison Bell in the 1920s, wrote: 'In chamber music or as a soloist he stands alone, a master of his instrument. Batten, Beecham or Barbirolli, it would be just the same to Léon, loyally giving of his best, a prince of good fellows, a gleam of sunshine in any studio, no matter how dull the day.' Fred Gaisberg, of equal significance in the recording world, described Léon as 'the recording angel'.

It is difficult to understand the neglect of his talents by the major companies in the late fifties at a time when improvements in recording techniques clearly demanded the remake of all his major repertoire. At EMI, Barbirolli used his influence to ensure that preferential treatment for the oboe repertoire was given to Evelyn Rothwell (Lady Barbirolli) to the detriment of Léon Goossens.

23

Apocalypse

Eugene considered his dramatic cantata *The Apocalypse* to be the apogee of his composing career. It received its world premiere in Sydney Town Hall on 22nd November 1954. It had taken him more than ten years to complete his setting of the last book of the New Testament, The Revelation of St John the Divine with its cataclysmic vision of the end of the world and the redemption of the New Jerusalem, on the grandiose orchestral and choral scale of Berlioz' *Damnation of Faust* or Mahler's *Symphony of a Thousand*. He had been deeply troubled by his isolation in Cincinnati from the war in Europe; he had seen in Hitler's hideous victories an equivalent to 'The Fall of Babylon'. He asked his friend, the distinguished Episcopalian Biblical scholar, the Reverend Frank Moore, to condense the Biblical text for him.

The Apocalypse became the summation of his own spiritual credo, that despite all the sins that a man commits following the temptation of Satan, he will be forgiven and redeemed through God's holy love. His first musical sketches were made in 1943 but it was not until 1949 in Sydney that he started composing in earnest. Both Rex Ellis and Ernest Llewellyn recalled him oblivious to his surroundings on tour with the orchestra, snatching every spare moment to finish the score. He completed the 300th page in London in 1953.

Its two performances on 22nd and 23rd November 1954 made an enormous impact on the audience in Sydney and on listeners who heard it broadcast throughout Australia. His overwhelming musical depiction of apocalyptic horsemen, earthquakes, cataclysms and radiant visionary scenes of heaven and hell, demanded an orchestra of ninety, extra brass players on stage, a consort of recorders, the massive organ of the Town Hall, mixed choirs of four hundred voices, five soloists and innovatory special effects with echo for The Voice of God. This last provided endless problems for the Chief Technical Officer, Dene Barnett. Eventually the voice of bass Stewart Harvey boomed through the Town Hall ceiling at the right intensity to satisfy the composer: 'Fear not, I am Alpha and Omega, the First and the Last.'

'We removed several panels from the ceiling of the hall,' explained Barnett at the time, 'and put in two high power amplifiers wired back to the electrician's box, diffusing the sound throughout the hall. For the first time, the Voice of God will be available through me!'[1]

After the final rehearsal Harvey was asked what mental approach he felt appropriate to his formidable task. 'I try in my humble way,' he replied quietly, 'to convey the sense of monumental calmness and serenity one would expect and to cope with the technical difficulties. There are so many filters and gadgets in the control room that it won't sound like my voice at all.'[2]

It had taken five months to prepare the performance and Eugene became increasingly exasperated with the difficulties that Sydney's amateur choral societies found with their parts. 'Musical accuracy and flexibility rather than size should be the principal characteristics of the two choirs,' he stipulates in his foreword but these were the qualities that were lacking in performance. 'The iridescent glories of the big choruses seem to fade,' commented Franz Holford in *The Canon*, 'and often the spontaneous element was completely absent. The choral writing is stamped with the superb assurance of maturity, even so, on one or two occasions, the vocal line overstepped the limits of any but super virtuoso choirs. The music is adventurous and challenging but it is music that can be dismantled by vocal insecurity. The orchestral score is not so perilous yet reaches considerable heights of eloquence and undeniable virtuosity.'[3]

There was uniform praise for the final chorus with its Handelian echoes of *The Messiah*: 'Alleluia, for the Lord God omnipotent reigneth forever and ever.' 'I doubt if Australia has ever heard such a shattering musical climax as comes at the end of the final double chorus,' was the summing up of the composer Dorian le Gallienne in the *Melbourne Argus*.[4] He makes a comparison with Gustav Mahler, described as 'an Australian, not so well known outside musical circles' and obviously completely unknown to Melbourne typographers!

Eugene continued to have a problematic relationship with Lindsey Browne the senior music critic of the *Sydney Morning Herald*. He scribbled a note on the review that he sent home to his father: 'Our local know-all who dislikes me!' But even L.B. gave discriminating praise to *The Apocalypse*: 'Magnificent pages where imagination and invention are at white heat to match the white hot text. The orchestra brilliantly gave Goossens everything he asked of it.'[5] His basic criticism remained that Eugene was not a late nineteenth-century Romantic composer but one who preferred the language of extreme chromaticism, bordering on atonality. Because of this he made little attempt 'to leap upon picturesque parts of the text as excuses for extravagant splashing of orchestral oils in sumptuous Romantic style; Goossens prefers a music of etched outlines, of quick hints and suggestions and dry ellipsis. . . Perhaps the considerable values of this difficult music will emerge more clearly when it is sung a good deal more convincingly than it was sung last night.'

Despite the flaws in its performance *The Apocalypse* was received as the work of a master at the zenith of his creative powers. It marked a considerable achievement for music in Australia and was a mutual expression of confidence between Eugene and the ABC. The fact that the world premiere of a work of such complexity and one on which he set so much store should be entrusted to Sydney rather than London, was an acknowledgement of what he had achieved; his ambition to mould the Sydney Symphony into an orchestra of international class though perhaps not yet 'the sixth best in the world'.

Only the verdict of one old friend revisiting Sydney dissented from the general approbation. 'Neville Cardus wrote a spiteful, inaccurate and unfriendly review due, amongst other things, to his lumbago,' Eugene reported to Richard Howgill, Controller, Music at the BBC. 'Our old friendship is now, as a result, discarded.'[6]

Eugene wrote to Moses on 25th November expressing his gratitude:

> I don't have to remind you that had it not been for your courageous vision and bold decision, last week's events would never have come to pass. Despite what must have proved a costly venture, I hope you genuinely feel that the prestige and artistic values of the performances have made it all worthwhile. If I have contributed something to world music – and some people seem to think I have – then the credit for bringing this about is largely yours.
>
> I can only hope that the fine tapes resulting from the performance will not only be a potent publicity asset for the ABC when they are heard in foreign broadcasting stations, but help to show that the standard of Australian cultural levels is of an impressively high calibre and prove what a good country this is for an artist to labour in!

Moses replied immediately saying how proud he was to have been associated with such a magnificent work. 'When you came to us you promised you would build an orchestra worthy to be considered with the best abroad, this has been achieved, but you have given us so much more in your untiring efforts to help in many other ways in the development of music in this country.'[7]

Less than a year and a half later Eugene would have cause to test the quality of Australian gratitude for these achievements. It is tempting to find the seeds of his downfall within the pages of *The Apocalypse*. After 'The Vision of the Ark of the Covenant' comes the satanic rites of 'The Worship of the Beast': 'And I stood upon the sand of the sea, and saw a beast rise up out of the sea, having seven heads and ten horns, and upon his horns ten crowns, and upon his head the name of blasphemy.'

Eugene had always been interested in the occult, an interest which dated, according to his sister Sidonie, from his friendship with Philip Heseltine, but unlike Heseltine, he had not been drawn into the orbit of the sinister Aleister Crowley.[8] Marjorie found his bedside reading on witchcraft and necromancy disturbing. These elements had inspired the magical atmosphere he conjured up in the First Violin Sonata and *Don Juan de Mañara*; an extreme sensuality of sound expressed in constantly changing chromaticism and a shimmering orchestral palette. His was the world of *Faust* and *The Tempest*; his search was for the secret formula that would enable him to reconcile his Catholic conflict between desire and conscience and engender perfect harmony between body and mind.

There were few practitioners of the secret arts in the conventional, repressive and Puritanical climate of Sydney in the 1950s. Anyone who managed to enjoy a Bohemian lifestyle was built up into a monster of depravity by the popular press. Rosaleen Norton, known as 'The Witch of King's Cross', had the field almost to herself. One day in the Notanda Gallery on Rowe Street, just off St Martin's Place which was then a centre of artists' studios, Eugene discovered a book called *The Art of Rosaleen Norton*. He wrote to the artist saying how much he enjoyed the book and was invited to tea in her studio at 179, Brougham Street.

The orchestra's rehearsal studio was above Woolworth's in William Street, King's Cross, the 'Soho of Sydney'. Brougham Street was only a few minutes walk away. Eugene got into the habit of dropping in to visit 'Roie' Norton and her homosexual lover Gavin Greenlees after rehearsals. He had always enjoyed a wide circle of unconventional friendships but there was a strange incongruity in the distinguished maestro, immaculate in Saville Row suit and Homburg hat, disappearing into the dubious recesses of the rundown three-storey house tenanted by vagrants and beatniks. He descended the basement steps to the converted laundry. 'Welcome to the house of ghosts, goblins, werewolves, vampires, witches, wizards and poltergeists,' proclaimed a placard on the door. Inside, amid a squalor of animal skulls, forgotten coffee cups and empty cigarette cartons, Norton and Greenlees indulged their fantasies.

Norton described herself as a daughter of Pan and a trance artist. Under the influence of self-hypnosis and hallucinogenic drugs she portrayed a wide range of supernatural beings in her paintings and drawings. Her specialities were naked hermaphrodites, mythical beings endowed with giant phalluses transmuting into serpents and nubile females in the passionate embrace of black panthers. Her work was compared with that of Norman Lindsay, one of Australia's most distinguished painters, but as she herself said, Lindsay's erotic drawings were creatures of the day and had frivolous happy natures, whereas her compositions showed figures of the night, phantasms from the darker recesses of the soul.

An attempt to prosecute her in 1949 for exhibiting lewd paintings in Melbourne had failed. Early in February 1953 *The Art of Rosaleen Norton*, with poems by Greenlees, was judged to have two illustrations which were 'obscene and an offence to chastity and delicacy'. Wally Glover, the publisher, was fined £5 and ordered to black out the offending pages. He sent copies of the book to Edith Sitwell, T S Eliot, Carl Jung and Albert Einstein; Norton wrote to C S Lewis, comparing her Gnostic and Kabbalistic cosmology with his Christian one. It is not known whether any of the recipients replied.

Over the next three years Roie Norton became notorious in King's Cross with her pointed ears and Satanic eyebrows. Certain coffee-houses, in particular the Apollyon and the Kashmir, were reputed to be the haunt of her 'Devil's Cult'. Eugene found her a useful source of material for the Satanic scenes in *The Apocalypse*; she was often to be seen on guest tickets at his concerts in the Town Hall. It was rumoured that she held orgiastic Black Masses in Brougham Street and that Eugene was among Sydney's prominent respectable citizens who attended. They must have formed an intriguing contrast to the receptions of the Ladies' Concert Committee at the Town Hall! After the success of *The Apocalypse*, Eugene was reputedly continuing to explore the darker recesses of occult experience with the couple for an operatic version of Edgar Allan Poe's *The Fall of the House of Usher*. This was to have a libretto by Greenlees and sets and design by Norton. When he died, sketches of the work were found among his papers but as a ballet not an opera.

It is difficult to determine whether he was oblivious to the couple's unsavoury reputation and the fact that the police were beginning to take an interest in their gatherings, or whether he was driven by a growing arrogance and disregard of the petty conventions of sexual mores which restricted the behaviour of lesser mortals.

Marjorie later told Brenton Langbein that she had been very deeply in love with Eugene. 'She adored him. She might have had her little flings but didn't treat them seriously. When she found out that something was wrong with their marriage it was devastating to her. She found photographs that were more or less pornographic with another woman in the picture [Norton]. Her great love had been thrown in her face and she couldn't cope. She returned to Europe and made contact with a great friend who was a Dominican nun and eventually converted to Catholicism.'9

Renée Goossens' version of events is less charitable. 'In 1954 Marjorie persuaded my father that I should go to a convent school in France. She left me there and went off with a Polish Count whom she had met when she was helping immigrants in Australia. We only found out where she was when I had appendicitis and had to have her permission for an operation. Interpol traced them to Spain. Marjorie was an overpowering personality and failed to give my father the love and stability he needed. He was the victim of his emotional life. Once he was left for long periods without her in Australia, his loneliness led him to despair.'10

Despite the increasing divergence of their lives, when Marjorie returned to Australia they kept up appearances as a devoted couple, although they slept in different wings of the house. Eugene's aura of a Magus was enhanced by the baroque atmosphere of his bedroom and study. Bill Coldstream had designed its theatrical colour scheme of dark painted walls, highlighted by red and gold pelmets. Above the bed was a plain wooden crucifix and on the desk, two of his most prized possessions, a head of Nefertiti and a wind-up toy of a monkey playing the cymbals. Those dark walls made an impression on everyone who came to the house, usually described as black or dark blue. According to Albert Wargren who painted them, the colour was ox blood red! 'To go to the loo, you had to go through a totally black room!' was Felix Aprahamian's memory from 1953 when he renewed his acquaintance with Eugene.

I had leave of absence from the *Sunday Times* to go to Australia for eleven weeks as amanuensis to André Marchal, the blind organist. We were invited to dinner, the house was very well appointed and it was a very happy party. Gene was elderly and as affable as ever. He was married to a young American wife, very glamorous and hard as nails. He behaved punctiliously towards her with no overt intimacy but there hardly ever is at a dinner party. I would think myself that he was not getting what he had hoped for from the marriage and probably had his own sex life. There was an extraordinarily handsome young man dancing attendance on Marjorie; Scandinavian, blond. I couldn't make up my mind where he fitted in the household.

I heard Gene conduct three concerts in Sydney Town Hall with stunning performances of *The Rite of Spring*, Hindemith's *Symphonie Metamorphosis* and *Joseph's Legend* by Strauss. I don't suppose the Sydney Symphony Orchestra has ever been as good before or since. When I came back I said it justified the orchestra coming with Goossens to the Edinburgh Festival. He was working day in and out with an orchestra that knew him but that does not mean to say that a strange orchestra would be able to adapt so well to his idiosyncrasies. Gene was a big man and his beat was very wide and very expansive. His stick technique was loose but it got results. I never thought of him as a master of orchestral technique but I was used to the cataclysms that Beecham got with the point of his stick or the flick of his beard![11]

Eugene regarded Felix as a detached critic, someone who was on his side although not a close friend. The concert tour that he instigated for his brother Léon in June and July 1954 provided a more intimate companionship. Although they respected each other as musicians a certain sibling rivalry haunted their adult lives, a nagging reminder to Léon that his brother remained their father's favourite. 'The Goossens family are to music what the Sitwells are to literature and the Barrymores to the theatre,' was the comment in *People*. 'Pink cheeked, humorous, well-built Léon has a persuasive voice and manner and the habit of striking graceful, almost actorish attitudes.'[12] Léon was welcomed as the most famous oboe player in the world who almost single-handed had raised the status of the instrument from 'the mating call of the duck' to a solo instrument with a repertoire of twenty-five concerti. Eugene retained his amazement at his brother's technique: 'He puffs himself up like a great ox and then he produces this endless stream of the most beautiful tone. He doesn't seem to breathe again for hours!'

The highlight of the tour was the Goossens Oboe Concerto with the SSO in Sydney Town Hall, winning unstinted praise: 'With the composer in charge of the baton, the collaboration between soloist and orchestra was superb. Not only is the work most brilliantly written for the instrument, but the orchestration is subtly evolved and blended to highlight every aspect of tonal beauty that Léon Goossens commands to an amazing degree.'[13]

When a Pacific tour was first mooted Léon had written to Benjamin Britten asking: 'Is there a remote chance of your writing a work for me to take to Australia and New Zealand? I do so want to take something that is up to the minute and it will help my tour of twenty-eight concerts tremendously.'[14] But Britten, with regret, was not able to provide a successor for the Phantasy Quartet he had dedicated to him in 1933.

Eugene had renewed his friendship with Britten on his annual visits to England. Britten's admiration for Eugene as an interpreter of his music culminated in his asking him to conduct three definitive recordings for Decca: Peter Pears singing *Les Illuminations* (the first time the work had been recorded), the Serenade for Tenor, Horn and Strings with Pears and Denis Brain and the Simple Symphony.

Eugene always returned to Australia for the opening of the first Subscription Concerts in March. By 1955 his health was giving him more and more cause for anxiety and during the first Australian performance of the Bartók Violin Concerto with Max Rostal as soloist, he collapsed on the rostrum. Both orchestra and audience were thrown into confusion. Two Sydney doctors ran forward from the auditorium, leapt on the stage and helped to carry him to the artists' room. Ernest Llewellyn then asked the audience to go home, saying 'Mr Goossens is very seriously ill.' Stunned and anxious, they filed slowly out of the hall, some people openly in tears, as an ambulance rushed him to hospital.

Although it was never publicly acknowledged, it seems likely that he had had a slight stroke. Members of the orchestra had noticed that during the opening Haydn Symphony he was unable to use his left hand to turn the pages of the score. Max Rostal felt from the start of the performance that all was not well. 'By the time the second movement was reached, I knew there was something desperately wrong. I played on in the solo music, but the orchestral part simply wasn't there any more.'

Two years earlier Eugene had fallen backwards from an unrailed stairway in Lismore. The damage to his back was compounded by a subsequent fall from the rostrum when the conductor's stool tipped backwards during a rehearsal for the final concert of the Concerto and Vocal Competitions.

He had always shown indomitable courage in face of a lifetime of ill health; a week after the Bartók incident he was back on the rostrum conducting a concert for Flood Relief. 'All this talk about heart attacks is rubbish,' he told reporters. 'My illness was a slight recurrence of something I thought I had got rid of twenty years ago.' Both Ruth Llewellyn and Eva Wagner believe that the problem was epilepsy; when Ernest Llewellyn visited him in hospital he apologised for what had happened, saying that he had forgotten to take his preventative medicine.

Two months later Sir John Barbirolli arrived for a concert tour and found him looking pasty and puffy and walking with a stick. Eugene had always given Lady Barbirolli the impression of being a weak and conceited man and although they were on superficially friendly terms, he certainly did not confide his state of health to them. 'When John asked him why he walked with a stick but didn't lean on it he said: "Well you know old boy, I rather like it".'[15]

Eugene understandably had mixed feelings towards the acclaim Barbirolli received for his concerts with the SSO. Raymond Fisher, who played the Grieg Piano Concerto on tour with Eugene feels that despite his competence as a conductor, his greatest achievement was as an orchestral trainer. 'Because of his training the orchestra gave superb concerts under Barbirolli, Klemperer and Malcolm Sargent. They never played quite as well in performance for Gene. Despite his great intellectual and musical gifts, there was always an inhibition, an inability to convey emotion, to speak from his heart to the heart of his audience.'[16] This was a very different Goossens from the young genius who had dazzled London in 1921 with the vigour and electric excitement of *The Rite of Spring* or bowled over New York in 1929 with the 'splendid strength and beauty' of his Brahms Fourth Symphony. The passion of youth had matured into the routine of middle-age; always in the background was the shadow of ill health, the necessity of husbanding his physical strength and emotional resources.

To the press and public he was at the height of his

fame and popularity. He was a glamorous idol, the ultimate in European sophistication for impressionable teenage maidens who crowded the gallery and queued at stage doors for his autograph. At the parties after provincial concerts his bonhomie would continue, making the committee ladies' hearts beat a little faster, despite their husbands in tow. It was always the public mask of the private man. Not everyone in the orchestra regarded him as a hero. Cliff Goodchild played the tuba with the Sydney Symphony Orchestra from 1951–1987. Brass players are notorious for their lack of finesse and his interpretation of the Bartók incident was that Eugene could not cope with the complexities of Hungarian rhythms and had staged a faint to distract attention from his shortcomings. He feels that by 1955 Eugene's popularity was wearing rather thin. 'Before a performance, he always walked up from the back of the Town Hall with his big fur coat on. We used to be warming up on stage and Frank Lock, who played Second Trombone, would say "Here comes the stately bag of bullshit!" Goossens had once put him out of a concert for being drunk on the job! We used to imitate the way Goossens put glycerine on his fingers to help him turn the pages of difficult scores. He had done nine years with us and I think the ABC were getting to a stage where they might have been looking for a replacement after a year or two.'[17]

It is easy to be wise after the event. Goodchild's assessment smacks of the Tall Poppy Syndrome, the Australian mistrust of exceptional talent as being elitist and therefore something which has to be cut down to size. No murmur of criticism was heard at the time, especially in June 1955 when Eugene was knighted for his services to music in Australia. 'It puts me on a plane with my fellow knights,' Eugene told the orchestra, referring to Barbirolli, Beecham, Boult and Sargent with well-deserved pride. Marjorie celebrated the event in Paris.

'The news of Sir Eugene's knighthood was greeted with spontaneous delight and approval throughout Australia,' commented *Radio-Active*. 'It is of historic significance that this honour has been conferred on a musician of world status while resident in this country, where for the past eight years he has pursued

Eugene with Anne and Donie, Cincinnati, 1936.

Léon with members of the LPO, Germany, 1936.

The set design for Act IV of *Don Juan de Mañara*, 1937.

Photo courtesy of the Royal Opera House, Covent Garden.

Sidonie as Principal Boy in a BBC Amateur Dramatic Society Revue, 1939.

Eugene with Efrem Kurz and Marina Franca,
Cincinnati, 1939.

Eugene, Benjamin Britten and Peter Pears in Bideford Pool, Maine, 1940.

Photo courtesy of Boosey & Hawkes.

Eugene and Jansi with Mr and Mrs Stravinsky, Cincinnati, 1940.

Eugene and Jansi with Toscanini, Cincinnati, 1943.

Sidonie and Norman's Wedding, 1945.

Sidonie and the BBC Symphony
Orchestra, 1942.

Sidonie, Eugene, Marie and Léon at the Albert Hall, 1946.

Eugene, William Constable and John Antill, Sydney, 1946.

Eugene meeting Marjorie, Donie and Renée on their arrival in Sydney, 1948.

Eugene conducting the Berlin Philharmonic at the 1949 Edinburgh Festival.

Eugene with Arthur Benjamin and Alfred Hill, Sydney, 1950.

Eugene II, Marie, Tony and his first son Chris, 1951.

The Goossens family at Woodstock Farm, 1952. *From l to r:* Marie, Renée, Donie, Eugene II, Eugene III, Sidonie, Norman, Jane, Catherine (Jane's daughter).

Clarence Raybould, Sir Arthur Bliss, Léon,
Jennifer Vyvyan and Lady Bliss in Moscow, 1956.

Eugene II's ninetieth birthday at L'Escargot, 1957. *From l to r:* Norman, Leslie,
Eugene III, Eugene II, Marie, Léon (standing) and Sidonie.

Eugene with Pamela Main, Oxford, 1958.

Cyril Scott, Eugene and Percy Grainger, 1958.

Sidonie working with Stravinsky, Maida Vale Studios, 1958.

Léon and Yehudi Menuhin, BBC Television, 1961.

Léon demonstrating the oboe to students, Belfast Music Week, 1965.

Seventieth birthday portrait of Léon by Edward Halliday, 1967.

Sidonie with Sir Adrian Boult, 1968.

Marie's eightieth birthday, 1974.

Sidonie and Marie on the picket line outside Broadcasting House protesting against the BBC's axing of five house orchestras, July 1980.

Sidonie receiving her Fellowship of the Royal College of Music from Her Majesty the Queen Mother, 1981.

Sidonie's official retirement from the BBC Symphony Orchestra at the First Night of the Proms, 1981.

Sidonie, Léon and Marie at the tenth anniversary celebration of the Sydney Opera House, New South Wales House, London, 1983.

Marie in the Courtyard of Buckingham Palace with
her son Tony and daughter Jean, after being
presented with the OBE, March 1984.

Marie, Sidonie and Dame Eva Turner at Léon's ninetieth birthday concert, Wigmore
Hall, June, 1987.

Photo courtesy of James Brown

his cosmopolitan career in a grand crescendo.'

To the connoisseur, whether in London or New York, Paris or Sydney, Sir Eugene's name connotes virtuosity, superlative musicianship, impeccable style. During four decades he has combined the roles of conductor and composer with a distinction and consistency almost unique in our time. Sir Eugene has identified himself completely with the musical aspirations of this country and has shown a general's capacity for organising and directing, together with a diplomat's skill in compassing his main objectives. A born leader in all the main branches of music, he is also a splendid propagandist for his art and a tremendous cultural force in the community at large.

The future historian of Australian music will assuredly devote one of his finest chapters to the achievements of the mid-twentieth century and written large in those pages will be the name of Sir Eugene Goossens.[18]

Alas, the irony of prophesy!

'To find the name of Eugene Goossens (pictured here) among those knighted in the birthday honours list must surely have given joyful satisfaction to thousands of music lovers,' echoed the Adelaide paper, *News*. They showed a picture of Léon instead of Eugene, doubly unfortunate as although Léon had received the CBE in 1950, the knighthood he so richly deserved was never bestowed on him.[19]

In October 1955 Eugene left for London at the beginning of a five-month European tour. He was met at the airport by his father, aged eighty-eight, Marjorie, back from a visit to her parents in Pennsylvania and an emissary of the Royal Philharmonic Orchestra, asking him to take Beecham's place at a concert the following week.

As always he sent regular progress reports of his success back to Charles Moses. He described 'the vortex of BBC concerts' into which he had been plunged marking the Silver Jubilee of the Symphony Orchestra: four studio concerts including the Bloch Violin Concerto played by Ruggiero Ricci, Peter Racine Fricker's Symphony no. 2 and Enescu's Symphonie Concertante with William Pleeth as soloist and a Royal Festival Hall concert on 26th October with a programme of excerpts from Berlioz' *Romeo and Juliet*, Debussy's *Iberia* and

Rolf Liebermann's Concerto for Jazz Band and Orchestra.

The most satisfying event was the British premiere of *The Apocalypse*. The ABC recording had been condemned by Maurice Johnstone, Head of Music Programmes. 'This gargantuan and expensive monstrosity lasting one hour forty minutes must be very impressive to *look* at in performance. As heard by record it is tedious and to a great extent deafening. The musical texture is monotonously thick, harmonic colour without design or notable phrase. The emotions and images of the words are reflected in an obvious way with a deal of slightly out-of-date dissonance, but Goossens' craft and thought are far from equal to his lofty subject, before which I think Beethoven, Berlioz and Verdi combined would have hesitated.'[20]

Fortunately Richard Howgill, Controller Music, had far more sympathy for Eugene's compositions and invited him to conduct a studio performance for the Third Programme on 28th October. Eugene, as always, deeply resented any adverse criticism and he wrote to Moses on 5th November: 'I am exasperated at the *Times* and *Telegraph* reviews of *The Apocalypse*. The broadcast took place in Maida Vale Studio and these men ignorantly judged the performance without "listening in" to the balance. Naturally they received a distorted version of it and they delighted in judging it by that. (I understand the *Times* critic was a young man in his early twenties.) Vaughan Williams and Bliss both sent me enthusiastic letters and the entire BBC beamed with delight at the performances and their finish. The small 150 piece choir was a *miracle* of accuracy.'

His last letter to Moses in his inimitable effusive style was dated 3rd March, from the Savage Club, just before his departure for Australia.

My dear Carlos,

A line to say how much I'm looking forward to seeing you on my return on the 9th (I leave here on Tuesday 3rd, by the new 'Connoisseur' Service – *no night stops*!!) It will be good to get back to all my friends – chief of whom I count *you*.

It'll also be good to see the sun!!

Affectionately as ever,
Gene.

P.S. I am in fine fettle (just back from Vienna and Hamburg) though life here is a little hectic. Marjorie sends her love – she'll be out with Renée later, by ship.

Marjorie was in the process of converting to Catholicism and would be spending a short retreat at the Couvent de l'Epiphanie at Soisy-sur-Seine, outside Paris before rejoining Eugene in Sydney. Meanwhile they were both staying at the Colonnade Hotel where Sidonie visited them on Eugene's last evening in London. Although Eugene was, as always, delighted to see his favourite sister, he seemed to be even more preoccupied than usual with his own private world.

24

❧❧❧❧❧❧❧❧❧❧❧❧❧❧❧❧❧❧❧

Fall of a Titan

'**W**orld famous musician held by Vice Squad at Airport' screamed news bulletins and headlines around the world.

Sir Eugene Goossens had landed at Sydney's Mascot Airport at 8am on 9th March 1956 after a long and tiring flight from London via Darwin. Usually when he returned from abroad he was ushered straight through the baggage clearance room to the press and reception committee waiting outside. To his astonishment, on this occasion he was stopped by the Senior Customs Investigator, Nat Craig and taken to a small annexe known as the search room where Detectives A H Trevenar and J Kilpatrick of the Vice Squad were waiting to interview him. After forty-five minutes he emerged to tell reporters that he had been airsick on the journey and felt dizzy. 'I'm sorry I did not see you before, but I've been lying down inside.'[1]

If he had telephoned Charles Moses at this stage and refused to answer any questions except in the presence of Mervyn Finlay, his solicitor, the course of music in Australia and the finale of Eugene's own career might have been very different. Whether through arrogance or failure to appreciate the potential gravity of the situation, he made no attempt to get help or advice and left with the detectives for another building where the contents of his briefcase and six bags were examined. After the arrival of the Chief of the Vice Squad, Detective Inspector Walden, the detectives departed with seven parcels wrapped in brown paper including envelopes labelled 'Brahms', 'Beethoven' etc. According to a police statement issued later that day, instead of musical scores, these contained films, between 1,000 and 1,100 photographs, literature and several rubber masks.

350

Just before midday, Sir Eugene agreed to accompany the officers in a police car to the Criminal Investigation Branch. He remained there for a further three hours while 'a number of photos and a quantity of 9mm film' were examined. He was eventually allowed to leave the CIB at 3pm. His urbanity had not deserted him and he calmly faced up to the waiting battery of photographers and reporters. According to the *Daily Mirror*, 'when asked whether he planned to carry out his musical schedule, he replied "Of course, of course".' Asked whether any police action was likely to develop as a result of the day's interview, he replied: 'There is no charge against me. What could I be charged with?' He then murmured: 'I must go home now . . . they'll be waiting for me.' Asked if he wanted a taxi home, he said: 'No, no, I am enjoying my little walk down this way' and wandered towards the railway, en route for Wahroonga.[2]

After seven hours of questioning, Sir Eugene may have been too punch-drunk to appreciate the gravity of the situation or that there could be any threat to him, aloof on his pinnacle of cultural supremacy. He had been knighted by the Queen for his services to Australian music, his friends included the Prime Minister Bob Menzies and the Premier of New South Wales, Joe Cahill. There is no way of knowing whether he had brought prohibited material into the country on previous occasions, but it would seem foolhardy to have introduced 1,166 pornographic photographs into a moral climate of almost Victorian repression and prurience. As late as 1970 a Sydney bookshop owner was arrested for displaying a poster of Michaelangelo's David!

The CIB switchboard was jammed with international calls from VIPs demanding to know what was happening. It was later announced that Vice Squad enquiries had been going on in Sydney for six months and that a report was being prepared for the Commissioner of Police, C J Delaney.

By the time Eugene reached his home at 28, Burns Road the nightmare had started. The press were already at the door and were to continue their day and night siege for the next six weeks. When he awoke in the morning in despair he asked his daughter Donie 'Are they still there?' Donie had the unenviable task of answering the door to importunate reporters, stonewalling with: 'My father has nothing to say; he is not well and is confined to bed on doctor's orders.' Marjorie telephoned Albert Wargren from the Convent at Soisy-sur-Seine, alarmed by the news and its possible effect on her husband's health. She was told not to join him.

Eugene may well have been trying to shield her from the full glare of the tabloid press. If their relationship had been closer she might have disregarded the advice and taken the first available flight. She could have been of great comfort and support to him as his ordeal intensified and his isolation increased, particularly after Donie and her husband John Young had to return to Melbourne where they were performing in *Kismet*.

The press rumours intensified daily. On 11th March the *Sunday Telegraph* reported: 'Big Names in Devil Rite Probe. Police investigations have disclosed that "black masses" and other devil worship ceremonies have taken place in luxurious homes on the North Shore. A banker, a lawyer, and one or two radio artists are said to be among those involved. Police disclosures followed an intensive Sydney wide check on practising of Satanic rites. The extent of devil worship in Sydney amazed police. They are expected to make shock disclosures soon.'

They never did. Eugene was to suffer rapid and devastating disillusionment, not only on the probity of the police but over the loyalty of those he had considered his friends and the gratitude of the Australian establishment for his much lauded achievements.

On 12th March he issued a statement requesting to be relieved temporarily of duties with the State Conservatorium and as Conductor of the Sydney Symphony Orchestra 'owing to ill health'. It was announced that Joseph Post would conduct the Sydney Symphony Orchestra in the first series of orchestral subscription concerts and that the official 'Welcome Home' reception was cancelled.

The brunt of advising and persuading Eugene on what course of action he should take seems to have fallen to the Assistant General Manager of the ABC, A N (Huck) Finlay. 'It has been a tough few days,' he wrote to his boss Charles Moses on 12th March. 'This morning Gene signed the attached statement which was approved by Heffron [Minister of Education],

Wurth [Chairman of the Public Service Board], Adams and the Chairman. I feel it is the only possible course for him to have taken and on our behalf we are protected. Mervyn [Mervyn Finlay, Eugene's solicitor and Huck's brother] saw Gene last night and again this morning with me. He has briefed Jack Shand as Counsel.'

The original version of '*We have* briefed Jack Shand' had been crossed out. It had taken Eugene's employers only three days to decide on his fate and to persuade him, before any charges were laid against him, to take the first step towards resignation.

The following day, the posse of press men besieging Burns Road was rewarded with some action. Two customs officers arrived to serve a personal summons returnable before the Court of Petty Sessions at 10am the next morning: 'At Sydney on 9th March Eugene Goossens, of 28 Burns Road Wahroonga, did unlawfully have in his possession prohibited imports, to wit indecent works and articles, namely a number of prints, a number of photographs and a quantity of film.' The prosecution was brought under Section 233(1) (d) of the Customs Act, 1901–1954, which provided a maximum penalty of £100 to 'any person who unlawfully conveys or has in his possession any smuggled goods or prohibited imports or exports'.

Eugene ran the press gauntlet to be driven by car to his heart specialist in Macquarie Street and was certified as being too ill to attend the next day's Court hearing. His solicitor, Mervyn Finlay requested an adjournment to allow him time to prepare the case with senior counsel Mr J W Shand QC. But he asked for the hearing to be at the earliest date convenient to the Court: 'My client has naturally been distressed by these proceedings and is anxious that they be heard as soon as possible. It is such a matter of importance and he is such a public figure.' Senior Magistrate Mr M J McCauley agreed to adjourn the case until 2pm, Thursday 21st March.

The tabloid press worked hard to keep public interest at boiling point nationwide. On 17th March Melbourne *Truth* claimed: 'People of culture, wealth, education and social standing have utterly debased themselves in orgiastic ritual gatherings. Much of their behaviour is described as "plain filth". Police have been making long term enquiries in utmost secrecy. The report which Commissioner Delaney received on Monday is believed to name persons other than Sir Eugene. It is also believed to refer to investigations at a luxury Blue Mountain home near Katoomba. The report, which is the result of six months investigation by Vice Squad detectives, is also understood to contain statements, letters and references to several people well known in Sydney, including artists.'

Further disclosures to titillate the Puritan burghers of Sydney were offered by their edition of *Truth* the following day, 18th March. 'Participants in Black Mass sex orgies in Sydney have been blackmailed over their activities. This allegation was made in a statement given to the police. Police are certain that at least one cultist was bled by a blackmailer in possession of incriminating evidence against the cult member. The basis of the blackmailer's hold on victims is said to be the fact that cult members take part in gross exhibitions of normal sexual functions. Police believe that the blackmailer has photographs of their participation in disgusting rituals. Although the police are reasonably sure of the blackmailer's identity, it is doubtful whether any prosecutions will result because of victims' natural reluctance to give evidence.'

Eugene's health further deteriorated under the strain of the impending Court hearing. Donie constantly repeated to the clamouring press that he was confined to bed on doctor's orders and was too ill to be interviewed. He was still too ill to attend the Court of Petty Sessions on 21st March. A medical certificate was produced saying that he was 'in a state of physical and mental collapse'. He pleaded guilty to the charge under Section 233.

Outlining the Crown's case, Mr J D Holmes QC emphasised that the nature and number of obscene photographs found in Sir Eugene Goossens' luggage at Mascot airport on 9th March 'make it difficult to imagine a worse case.' The first item of the defendant's luggage to be searched was the briefcase he was carrying which contained two canisters of film. When asked by the senior investigator of the Customs Department Mr Craig where they had been obtained, he had replied 'I bought them at a shop in Leicester Square in London about three months ago. The film cost £1.' The defendant made no reply when Mr Craig continued, 'I am going to seize this film because I think it is obscene.' Another container of film had been found amongst his luggage of six cases and two prints from this were tendered in court.[3]

> Mr Craig found a number of large envelopes in the cases. Inside the envelopes were smaller envelopes stuck to the inside of the larger envelopes. The smaller envelopes contained obscene pictures. Sir Eugene told Mr Craig that the photographs had been bought at the same shop in Leicester Square. Some of the larger envelopes had markings on them which would indicate that they contained either sheets of music or material relating to well-known composers. The defendant said that he knew the photographs were there, that they had been fixed up in this way by a personal servant whom he had engaged on this visit and previous visits. He also said they were for a private collection. The Crown had selected some of the photographs to show the types of pornography involved. Also in the baggage there was a collection of prints mentioned in the summons. These prints demonstrated a particular form of aberration.
>
> The photographs total 1,166 and of these at least 844 are obviously covered by the charge. We do not think any useful purpose would be served in stating degrees of obscenity or making distinctions. The photographs were carried in a manner likely to deceive a customs officer.
>
> Despite what no doubt will be said for the defendant, there are, we submit, no mitigating circumstances. Throughout the interview with Mr Craig, the defendant made it clear that he realised the significance of his act. He was fully conscious of the character of the exhibits, and apart from his assertion that they were for a private collection, he made no claim that they were not obscene.[4]

Obviously his Defence Counsel Jack Shand QC could not deny the existence of those 1,166 photographs and the manner in which his illustrious client had brought them into Australia. He offered as explanation and mitigation the argument that the defendant was a weak and timid man who was acting under duress. To this effect he called only one witness, his executive employer and closest friend in Australia, Charles Moses.

Moses emphasised Eugene's contribution to Australian music: 'I would say that the engagement of Sir Eugene Goossens from a musical point of view was one of the most fortunate things that could have happened for this country. When he came he said he would make the Sydney Symphony

355

Orchestra one of the world's best six. Well it is certainly among the world's best ten and possibly the best six.'

'Would you call him a worldly man?' led Shand.

'No, I would say he is just the opposite,' answered Moses. 'In the field of music I would say he has positive opinions and is not afraid of expressing them, but in other matters I would say he is not a practical man. He is a very timid man, a very nervous man. I would say he was one of the most timid men among the artists we bring to this country every year. I meet them all and get to know them. He is very diffident about anything affecting himself. He has never approached me since 1951 about altering the terms of his contract, although the cost of living has gone up considerably.'

'What has been his reputation up to the time of this incident?'

'Of the very highest. There has never been a whisper to his discredit from anywhere. It doesn't take very long for rumours about artists who come out here to reach my ears. No artist who has come out here has had a higher reputation. I find it impossible to associate him with extremely pornographic literature,' concluded Moses.

Now came the most sensational assertions from Shand in Eugene's defence.

One finds it almost impossible to reconcile the life of the defendant, which has been lived for a long time on a high aesthetic plane, with these very bad types of pornographic and salacious pictures which are exhibited in this case. Now there are two factors which my friend called attention to: that those photographs were in double envelopes and double sealed. The other factor is the tremendous number – over 1,000.

Now it may be considered whether there is not an indication that these photographs and the literature were brought out as part of a trade from England to Australia – a trade with which no one in this community would associate the defendant as being a willing accessory.

It will be revealed that these photographs were brought out as a result of threats, the nature of which will become apparent in later days – very soon I hope. The matter I can say is now under investigation, and whether the aim of those whom I suggest are responsible for these most pornographic exhibits coming to Australia are persons who hope to have them brought out here, feeling that the name of the person in the position of the defendant would not receive the keenest scrutiny, or whether this was constituted as an attempt to destroy a world figure, it is hoped these investigations will reveal.

In the circumstances which existed, the defendant could not reveal to the authorities matters which, as soon as his legal advisers tell him he can and should, he will reveal, and he will at that time seek police aid.

Shand made no attempt to use these claims as mitigation. 'Nothing of what I have said,' he concluded, 'would obviate the fact that a very grave offence has taken place in breach of the Customs Act, and we do not suggest that your Worship should impose anything less than the maximum penalty.'[5]

Sir Eugene Goossens was convicted *in absentia* and fined £100.

Despite the character assassination to which he had been subjected in Court, Eugene, somewhat unrealistically, hoped he would be able to ride out the storm. As soon as Jack Shand gave the go ahead he would be able to reveal the full circumstances behind his actions. There would then be no obstacle to his fulfilling his contract as conductor of the Sydney Symphony Orchestra.

His position as Director of the Conservatorium was more vulnerable since he was technically responsible for the morals of the children in the High School as well as the older students in tertiary education. He realised that in many ways he would find it a relief to relinquish his administrative duties at the Conservatorium, which he had neither adequate time nor interest to fulfil. It might well be possible for him to retain the two spheres he did enjoy: the Diploma Class and the Opera School.

He was encouraged by the announcement that the Attorney General and Minister of Justice, Mr R R Downing had instructed the Commissioner of Police to take no further action against him on the grounds that the evidence did not disclose any criminal offence with which he could be charged. Premier Cahill, when questioned as to his future, emphasised that he had been fined under a Federal Act. The Crown law authorities had examined the police report of the case and decided to take no further action against him.

The harsh reality of the situation was rapidly brought home

to him and his optimism shattered. His employers would not defend his reputation. He had been publicly disgraced and the penalty exacted by Australian Puritan morality was immediate resignation from both his positions. Technically he was still under contract and the ABC had no grounds to dismiss him but Eugene was too much of an English gentleman, too unaggressive in temperament and too broken in physical and psychological health to force an issue. He was still utterly bewildered by the total unexpectedness of his fall from grace, embarrassed rather than ashamed.

He sent two letters of resignation dated 26th March, finding the one to Charles Moses particularly painful to write:

> I cannot tell you how upset I am that I have caused embarrassment to the Commission and have prejudiced the work of the past nine years during which we have striven together to develop the musical life of this State. I have as you know devoted myself to the maximum of my ability to the task of establishing the Sydney Symphony Orchestra as an orchestra which would receive recognition as being of world standing, and I deplore the sudden cessation of my efforts in this respect.
>
> If, after consideration, the Commission should wish me to continue with the orchestra, I would gladly do so. In this event may I suggest that the appropriate place and date for resumption would be in Sydney at the third series of subscription concerts which begin on 29th May. This would afford me a six week period of recuperation essential to me because of the past fortnight's events.
>
> I feel I should make it clear that whatever decision the Commission makes in this matter, I have definitely decided that I could not continue as Director of the Conservatorium. Prior to my recent visit to Europe I had already been finding that my joint responsibilities with the orchestra and with the Conservatorium were making too great demands upon me.
>
> Finally, I should like to say again that I hope the Commission and yourself will understand my very deep regret about the circumstances that have led me to write this letter. My own personal distress, keen though it is, is less important to me than the knowledge that I have prejudiced the work which has meant so much to me and in which I have had such generous encouragement from the Commission as well as from the music-loving public of my adopted country.

'He did not want to go,' remembered a distressed Sir Charles

Moses, thirty years later. 'I persuaded him he had to and I was supposed to be his friend. I told him he could come back (as Chief Conductor of the SSO). I thought he could, when all the fuss had died down.'[6] Moses and Goossens seemed to have shared an ostrich complex as far as the consequences of the situation were concerned. Their naïve optimism was soon disabused.

When the Australian Broadcasting Commission met on 11th April, the members resolved: to accept the immediate resignation of Sir Eugene Goossens from the position of Conductor of the Sydney Symphony Orchestra; that an immediate press statement to this effect should be issued by the Chairman without any comment and that 'in the event of any proposal being made by the Sydney Symphony Orchestra Subscribers' Committee or any other body officially associated with the ABC to arrange a public farewell for Sir Eugene, the Commission records its view that it could not agree to any proposal of this type.'

As far as the ABC was concerned, Sir Eugene Goossens was professionally disgraced and as good as dead and buried. He would remain a non-person for the next twenty years. The strength of grass roots public opinion against him had been typified by an editorial in the *Sun Herald* on 1st April: 'The ABC has a deep responsibility to the concert-going and radio-listening public. Offence would be given to a large body of opinion if Sir Eugene Goossens were permitted to reoccupy his place on the podium, whatever more tolerant or indulgent sections might think.'

Immediately his resignation was announced, Mr E J Ward (Labour NSW) raised the issue in the House of Representatives as to whether he should be stripped of his knighthood on the grounds that he had rendered himself unworthy of the honour by his conviction and fine on a customs offence. The *Sydney Morning Herald* responded with a mature and balanced assessment of the rise and fall of Sir Eugene Goossens. 'With the possible exception of Mr Ward, whose question yesterday was a disgrace to the Federal Parliament, everyone in New South Wales will read of Sir Eugene Goossens' resignation with profound sadness. The end of his career has been pitiful beyond measure, yet it will be some consolation to him to know that, long after the nature of his offence has been forgotten, he will be remembered as the man who recreated the Sydney Symphony Orchestra and, with the help of the ABC, brought great music to millions for the first time in Australia. Sydney, which has so long heard "his voice in all her music", will not forget its debt.'[7]

Eugene found himself isolated in limbo, the whole professional and private world he had built up over the past nine years in Australia tumbling around him in ruins. The press still kept constant watch on the house and very few of his erstwhile friends and colleagues ran the gauntlet. Sydney society rapidly ostracised him. 'As far as the Concert Committee was concerned, there was a veil over proceedings,' Mrs Ritchie, then its organising secretary, recalls. 'It was quite extraordinary. I felt very sorry for him but didn't feel that I knew him well enough to offer any kind of help.'[8]

Many of the musicians with whom he had established a rapport and who would have offered loyal support and continuing friendship, were out of the country. Ernest Llewellyn was studying teaching methods at the Juilliard in New York; the group of brilliant young artists he had inspired including Charles Mackerras, Brenton Langbein, the Tuckwells, Maureen Jones, Richard Bonynge, Joan Sutherland and Malcolm Williamson were following his advice and seeking their musical fortunes in Europe.

In general, members of the orchestra felt too inhibited to try and see him. They hesitated because they felt they did not know him well enough to offer sympathy in his misfortune; as employees of the ABC they might jeopardise their own positions. Apart from a few close friends like Neville Amadio, the only orchestra member who did have the courage to go and see him was Ron Smart, a young trombone player who followed his conscience as a fundamentalist Christian and cycled out to Wahroonga. 'I made the effort to see him because I wanted to thank him for putting me on my career path. Most people ostracised him because they were frightened.'[9]

'What could one do or say?' queried Anne Menzies (clarinetist with the SSO). 'He wasn't really close to members of the orchestra. I'm sure if he had asked for help, or consolation, everyone would have thronged to his side.'[10] One of the few musicians who did make a positive offer of help was Raymond Fisher. Eugene had recently appointed him to teach piano at the NSW Conservatorium in place of Lotte Dehrn, who had been dismissed for falsifying her pupils' examination successes. He wrote offering Eugene accommodation in the family home in Hornsby to escape the intolerable press encampment. He received a letter of thanks from Phyllis Williams, declining and saying that he hoped to see his friends again soon.

According to Cliff Goodchild, as Goossens' popularity with the orchestra had already worn thin, the only person to regret his departure was the orchestra's devoted manager, Ken Lawson. Certain hardened old-timers were definitely glad to see him go. 'The orchestra never saw Goossens again after what happened at the airport. We were on tour in Mori right in the north of NSW when he left. He had done a lot for Australian music. He knew how to write for orchestras and he was a great musician. But he was not a great conductor; he tended to stand apart from the music.'[11]

Phyllis Williams, Eugene's devoted secretary, came up to the house every few days with correspondence. There was an immediate telegram of support and friendship from Percy and Ella Grainger, working on his personal museum in Melbourne, but there was no communication from the Ormond Professor of Music. 'Every time he would ask me: "Has Bernie rung?"' she recalled. 'He had always regarded Sir Bernard Heinze as one of his close friends and was particularly hurt by the fact that he received no word from him at all. Neville Salmon, the Deputy Director at the Con, asked Sir Bernard why he hadn't contacted him and he assured him he had written a letter but it wasn't true.'[12]

According to his official biographer, Thérèse Radic, Heinze was jealous of Eugene's success and coveted his dual appointment in Sydney. It has been suggested that he was the prime mover in a plot against Eugene. Although he stood most to gain from his rival's disgrace, Dr Radic is convinced that he did not engineer it. On the other hand, he always enjoyed the role of puppet master, pulling strings behind the scenes and used a network of lady friends in strategic positions with whom he was in regular correspondence. 'Poor silly Gene' had been his comment when the Goossens scandal broke.[13]

By the beginning of May, Heinze was already manoeuvering with Moses to be appointed Eugene's successor with the orchestra and the Conservatorium. Moses wrote unofficially to him on 8th May: 'I had my talk with Wallace Wurth this afternoon. What he is going to propose to the NSW Government is that he should be empowered to offer you the Directorship of the Conservatorium at a salary of £2,750. As you gathered last Saturday, Mr Wurth is most anxious that you should have some official connection with the Sydney SO after we have engaged Barbirolli (assuming we do) – as Associate Conductor or some similar association.'

As far as the Australian press was concerned, Eugene was already yesterday's man. No more was heard of the sensational revelations Jack Shand had promised in Court as to blackmail and coercion. No more was heard of the Vice Squad's six month investigation into Satanic practices. Eugene had always been a secretive man and did not confide in his daughter and son-in-law. 'He had never asked me where I was going and I would never have asked him about his friends or activities,'[14] Donie emphasised. There were a few hints, never any facts. Immediately after the Customs debacle, he had told Albert Wargren whom he regarded almost as an adopted son: 'It's weirder than even Edgar Wallace would have thought of!' But he never revealed the details.[15]

Two days before his departure Eugene was persuaded to issue the following statement to the press:

> I regretfully bid farewell to Australia, where I have spent so many happy years in making my modest contribution to its musical development. I shall always look back with pride to my association with the Sydney Symphony Orchestra and the NSW Conservatorium of Music, and hope that both will continue to grow in artistic achievement.
>
> It is my misfortune that I allowed myself to be used to bring prohibited matter into this country as a result of persistent menaces involving others.

The ABC eventually agreed to pay his air fare to London and he left under the name of Mr E Gray on a KLM flight for Rome on 26th May. 'Exit Sir Eugene with a change of tune,' was the small item on an inside page of the *Telegraph*. 'Sir Eugene yesterday looked thinner than he did at any time

362

during his brilliant musical career in Sydney in the past nine years. When he reached the top of the stairs at the aircraft door, he half turned quickly and raised his right arm shoulder high in a farewell wave.'[16] The previous day, the Prime Minister, Robert Menzies had finally answered Mr Ward's question of 11th April and announced that he would not be recommending the cancellation of Sir Eugene Goossens' knighthood. The day before the announcement, he had invited his friend Gene to lunch, to set his mind at rest.

The Puritans were on the warpath and many people were running scared. Percy Grainger hastily gathered up his porno-graphic books on flagellism, caught a tram to the Melbourne Public Library and deposited them under plain cover with the Chief Librarian. Included with such titles as *The History of the Rod* and *Sadism and Masochism* was *The Lure of the Rod* by Sir Robert Bruce Lockhart, which turned out to be a disappoint-ingly respectable manual on fishing.[17]

Eugene left Australia still hoping that he would be able to return to conduct what he always continued to think of as 'his' orchestra. If his friends were hoping to be taken into his confidence they were disappointed. Instead, they received a Roneoed letter which formed a bizarre and totally inadequate explanation of events:

> As you can well imagine, only threats of a really dangerous nature were responsible for compelling my action. Unfortunately I am still unable to identify those persons who, telephonically over a period of months, menacingly forced me to eventually comply with their demands. They remained anonymous throughout, merely stating that I would be 'contacted' on returning to Sydney. My reception there by press and officials on landing might indicate that I had been deliberately victimised, or that my mysterious callers had themselves been exposed.
>
> In addition to this, a matter mischievously distorted by a section of the press into sheer sensationalism was my operatic collaboration with two members of a local group and some carnival masks I had brought from Vienna for my daughter were given a sinister signifi-cance. In short, no invention was too ludicrous to use against me.
>
> I realise what a strain has been imposed on your friendship by my enforced silence. Sound health and resilience of spirit have enabled me to endure my ordeal. Fortunately, too, my artistic enthusiasm remains always unimpaired.[18]

363

He concluded this strange missive with the hope that further discussion – certainly in the press – should cease, but he had done nothing to dissipate the rumours surrounding the affair which continued to flourish. Eugene had been 'shopped' or, as the Australians say 'dobbed in', by someone in the know as to the incriminating contents of his suitcases. Moses, in a series of interviews taped for the Sydney Opera House Archives long after the event, states that he had received an anonymous phone call on 8th March telling him to 'get in touch with Goossens and warn him there might be trouble at the airport.' He had dismissed the caller as a crank.

Various scenarios have been suggested as to motives for Eugene's disgrace. At the height of the McCarthy era, the CIA saw Reds under many Australian beds. John Pilger claims that the CIA were implicated in the notorious Petrov Affair which had ruined Menzies' chief political opponent, Labour leader 'Red Doc Evatt'.[19] Although Menzies was a personal friend, according to Albert Wargren, Eugene had made no secret of his opposition to the anti-Communist legislation he sought to bring in. One of the most persistent rumours is that Eugene was destroyed in order to discredit Joe Cahill, the Labour Premier of New South Wales. Cahill was backing Eugene's scheme for the opera house on Bennelong Point. Property developers trying to exploit the site commercially were anxious for the political demise of both Eugene and Cahill but in the event the opera house lumbered on to its eventual completion, impervious to the removal of the two prime instigators from the scene. (Cahill died in Office in October 1959.) Renée Goossens is convinced that her father was a Secret Agent for the British bringing in information for the ASIO (Australian Secret Intelligence Service), including secret codes within his music scores![20]

The Sydney Police in the 1950s were mainly working-class Catholics of Irish extraction. Many were ignorant, corrupt and zealous in stamping out vice in any shape or form which contravened their intolerant moral code. They also had close connections with the tabloid press. The Vice Squad had had their eye on Eugene, who had never concealed his involvement with Rosaleen Norton and her lover Gavin Greenlees. Since the performances of *The Apocalypse*, interest in the occult had become far more widespread amongst the fashionable circles of

Sydney's prominent citizens. A little indulgence in Pantheism with sexual overtones made a welcome contrast to barbecued ribs on the North Shore or cocktails in Katoomba. Whether this amounted to the 'gross exhibitions of normal functions' claimed by *Truth* is difficult to ascertain. The participants in these rituals have always been understandably reticent to reveal their identity and details of their activities have been left to the lurid imagination of the uninitiated.

In June 1955 a film had been made in Brougham Street showing Norton and Greenlees ceremonially garbed, performing 'an unnatural sexual act' in a ritual dedicated to Pan. The negative was stolen by two men, Francis Honer and Raymond Ager who allegedly offered obscene photographs to a variety of Sydney newspapers.[21] They had all declined them as being too hot to handle. The Editor of the *Sun* turned the two men over to the Vice Squad who used the photos as an excuse to raid Brougham Street. In return, Detectives Trevenar and Kilpatrick allowed Joe Morris, a crime reporter from the *Sun* to accompany them on the raid.

Tucked behind a sofa, Morris found a bundle of letters to Norton signed 'Eugene' or 'Gene'. These were later identified as having been written to her by Eugene Goossens and detailed rituals of 'Sex Magic' which they had practised together. He was convinced that this was an invaluable source of inspiration and aid to his creative powers. Eugene had already left for Europe. The only criminal offence with which he might be charged was that of Scandalous Conduct defined as behaviour offensive to public morality but the letters were dynamite in the hands of a blackmailer and were to bring about his downfall.

Trevenar, an upright Anglican and a Mason, did a deal with Morris: that in return for using the paper's contacts to keep tabs on Eugene in England, Morris would get the scoop when he returned to Australia. At the beginning of March, Morris telephoned Trevenar with details of Eugene's arrival and the news that he would be carrying a large quantity of pornographic material. This would constitute a Federal rather than a State offence and Trevenar alerted Nat Craig in Customs.

Eugene could have refused to accompany the Vice Squad detectives to CIB headquarters as they had no warrant for his arrest and were not charging him with any criminal offence.

He identified the photographs and letters in police possession and gave details of the oral sex involved in the rituals of 'Sex Magic'. He had explained the large quantity of pornographic photographs in his luggage as being 'to replace a private collection which had been destroyed.'[22]

There seem to have been no further investigations as to the ownership of this collection or whether the pictures were intended for sale. Questioned in 1992 by David Salter of ABC Television, Trevenar claimed Eugene stated the photographs were not for 'a' collection but for 'his' collection. 'So the police and the press had successfully despatched a once celebrated musician,' boasted 'Bondi' Bill Jenkings, Crime Reporter of the *Mirror*.

Jack Shand QC never made his promised revelations public. The can of worms was too putrid to open. If he revealed who was blackmailing Eugene, the reputations of too many of the Great and the Good in Australia might be destroyed. Once their involvement with Norton and Greenlees was made public, the scandal would be of mindboggling proportions. Coincidentally, Shand had been Defence Counsel when *The Art of Rosaleen Norton* had been judged obscene in November 1952 and press baron Frank Packer, also a friend of Eugene's, had paid the legal expenses of her publisher.[23]

The only way to protect so many prominent reputations was by a conspiracy of silence. Eugene had committed the cardinal sin of being found out. When the chips were down he was an outsider and he was expendable. If he were sacrificed, they would all be saved. 'Goossens was fingered by one of the group to buy themselves out of trouble,' was the verdict of Ron Best, retired State Crown Solicitor who listed Mervyn Finlay and Charles Moses amongst the cultists but not among the suspects.[24] 'I am more sinned against than sinning' still stands in the police report of Eugene's interrogators; they failed to realise he was quoting from *King Lear*.

For the majority of participants, the ritual worship of Pan had provided sexual excitement that was both exotic and illicit. But for Eugene it was something much more, a search for the mystical truth that was the fount of artistic inspiration and enlightenment. He felt that he had betrayed both his Catholic conscience and the Great Horned God. They had brought about his downfall and they were to haunt him for the remainder of his days.

25

Aftermath

On 19th April 1956, Eugene's agent Wilfrid Van Wyck wrote to the BBC's Controller of Music Richard Howgill informing him that his client was 'busy clearing up his affairs in Australia and preparing to return to this country for good some time next month. He would be grateful for any work that could be put his way from June onwards. I think I need say no more.'

The matter was considered of sufficient gravity to be decided by the Director-General of the BBC at a meeting of the Board of Governors. To his credit his report was a positive one: 'It was proposed that the BBC's attitude toward him should follow precedent: after a suitable interval there should be no ban on his use as a conductor by the BBC. The Board Agreed.'[1]

The family had been totally overwhelmed by the news of the scandal. Despite their closeness and affection, Eugene never confided in his father, Sidonie, Marie or Léon; it was a subject which was never discussed and remains as mystifying now as it was at the time. Sidonie comments: 'My brother remains an enigma; he would always be in a world of his own, thinking about his music, never really listening to what you were saying.'[2]

Léon was equally in the dark. Jimmy Brown remembers his reaction when the news of the customs charge broke: 'We were giving a concert with the Virtuoso Ensemble at Reading University. Lee was also agitated because there were thirteen of us playing. He and I went out of the back door afterwards in case there were any press around. He thought his brother had been set up by someone who had an axe to grind, but he didn't seem to know very much about it and didn't want to talk about it. He found it extremely upsetting.'[3]

Whatever faults Marjorie may have shown in the past, she
was of invaluable help to Eugene immediately after the debacle.
The international press were waiting for him at London Airport.
He slipped off the plane unnoticed at Rome where Marjorie had
come to meet him. She drove him to the South of France to the
Couvent Dominicain des Tourelles, near Montpellier. Here,
within the Dominican Community, he was able to recuperate
both physically and spiritually.

By July they were in England and he had recovered sufficient
resilience to face his old friends and contemplate the future.
He wrote from the Savage Club to Richard Howgill: 'A line to
tell you I'm back from France and have taken a house on the
Downs near Alfriston, where I'm writing music and finishing
a book. Marjorie and our youngest daughter are with me and
very occasionally I go up to town. One day, perhaps, we'll have
a quiet lunch together, in the not too distant future. I will then
make things clearer to you than I can now.'[4]

Mabel Lovering, a near neighbour of Léon and Leslie
in Sussex, remembered Léon bringing his brother over to
meet her when he was staying with them at Holter's Green.
'He asked me to play him the Preludes by Frank Martin; he
spoke about them very knowledgeably; I don't think there
was much music he didn't know about. He was very nice,
but worried and disturbed – somewhat subdued. They were
very brotherly together and obviously got on extremely well.
Eugene didn't look well. He was very pale, a little puffy, not
at his best. Unlike Léon he looked his age. Léon always looked
in excellent health and was very particular about watching his
diet and keeping fit.'

A few days later Leslie told her that Beecham had telephoned
to tell Eugene that he was recommending him for some concerts in Germany. '"Who's going to worry in Germany about
what happened in Australia!" Eugene was absolutely
delighted: he was quite sure that Tommy could have done
the concerts himself but he had always been very fond of
Eugene.'[5]

At the end of August Eugene wrote to his close friends
Bill and Tana Constable in Sydney, a relaxed and cheerful
letter still from the 'delicious small house bang on top of the
Sussex Downs. Bookings here and there are coming in apace;

so far up to February. But I will miss my work in Australia. I conduct Malcuzynski at the Albert Hall in October and other concerts follow immediately, but I am absorbed in composing at present.'

When he returned to London in September, other friends and colleagues made a point of rallying round, of going out of their way to show that their affection and respect for him were unchanged. Ursula Vaughan Williams remembers that she and her husband immediately invited him to lunch.[6]

Stephen Spender and his wife, the pianist Natasha Litvinov who had become friendly with Eugene and Marjorie during a concert tour of Australia, were reassured by the remarkably good-humoured stoicism he displayed, combined with the Goossens discipline of getting on with one's work. Lord Harewood, then married to Marion Stein, comments: 'We invited him to one or two parties at Orme Square and once or twice to dinner. He was very agreeable and urbane but I had the impression of a very much wounded person. People are tremendously mealy-mouthed about those who have suffered public disgrace.'[7]

Brenton Langbein and Maureen Jones, two of his protégés from Australia, now launched on successful European careers, had been so disturbed by the events that they decided to come to London from Switzerland. They had tea with Eugene while Marjorie was confined to bed with 'flu. Langbein found him a broken man.

> All the tautness had gone; the energy had gone out of his whole demeanour. He said that all that had happened was very distressing but that perhaps one day it would come out into the open about the way in which he had been set up. Marjorie was trying to get to the bottom of the theory that many people in very high places had been involved. She later told me that when she was having dinner with close friends from Australia and asking questions, they suddenly said 'Marjorie, drop it' and she realised that she was up against a brick wall.
>
> Marjorie's love had not changed but after several months in London it became obvious that Eugene had shut himself off from her entirely and that she could not get back to him in any way.[8]

In the autumn of 1956 Eugene had written to a young pianist friend from Adelaide, Pamela Main asking her to come to

England and sending her money towards her fare. He could not promise what the future would hold and would quite understand if she decided to remain in Australia. Pam arrived in London just before Christmas and began to play an increasingly important role in his life. Her status was never clarified to the Goossens family; Eugene, ever secretive about his personal life, told his sister Sidonie that 'some friends from Australia had arrived, Mrs Main and her daughter' who were to housekeep for him.[9] (Mrs Main never arrived.)

Marjorie left London at the end of January 1957 and returned to the USA to take a higher degree in Gregorian Chant at Bloomington, Indiana. She later came back to Europe and qualified as a Jungian music therapist in Zurich where she felt able to confide in Brenton Langbein her problematic relationship with Eugene.

It was an unfortunate coincidence that the first recording contract Eugene was offered by HMV with the RPO after his return was Mussorgsky's *Pictures at an Exhibition*! The current Green Room story was that Sir Malcolm Sargent had also been stopped at customs and asked to open his suitcase. It was found to contain 1,000 photographs . . . all of himself. (Sir Malcolm's vanity was well known.) The general consensus amongst professional musicians in England was that the events in Australia, though mystifying, were an irrelevance as far as Eugene's career was concerned.

At the end of August 1957, he took the lease of a large ground-floor flat at 76 Hamilton Terrace, St John's Wood. The forty foot drawing room provided an impressive studio where he could rehearse, entertain and teach. Malcolm Williamson, to whom he had taught composition in Sydney, eagerly returned to him for lessons. His main conducting students included two other gifted musicians who had made their reputations in Australia: Ron Grainer and Hans Hubert Schönzler and a Canadian, Gaspar Chiarelli. His life-long encouragement of contemporary music made him a focal centre for younger composers such as Wilfred Josephs, Graham Whettham and Stephen Dodgson.

Eugene was in a difficult position. No one could deny his competence and experience but the musical establishment no longer considered him to be in the front rank of conductors. Although he was only sixty-three when he returned to London, he looked much more than his years. His health was a constant problem with his congenital heart condition, recurring bouts of bronchitis and a deteriorating back condition for which he had to wear a steel corset. No conducting appointment was forthcoming in England. In order to earn a living he was compelled to do far more touring abroad than ever previously in his career; whereas in the twenties it had been prestigious events in Paris and Berlin, now it was the less attractive and less lucrative engagements behind the Iron Curtain in Leipzig, Prague and Budapest.

Wherever he could he performed contemporary British music, particularly Britten, to whom he wrote: 'It may interest you to hear that, at my recent concerts in Czechoslovakia, I programmed 'Sea Pieces' from *Peter Grimes* and your Purcell Variations, the former in Prague and the latter with the fine orchestra I found at Brno. Needless to say they literally brought the house down and their impact on the music-loving Czechs in both cities was electrifying.'[10]

Sir Eugene Goossens has gone down in legend with the Pest Philharmonic Orchestra as the conductor who, when asked in the concert interval if he wanted anything to eat or drink, requested pure alcohol. 'But it was to wash his hands in!' they told another British guest conductor Howard Williams in 1990. Eugene, who like many conductors sweated profusely during a performance, always rubbed himself down with alcohol before changing his clothes.[11]

Yet the strain of travelling by himself and his deteriorating health was affecting the standard of his performances. His agent Wilfrid Van Wyck told Sidonie in the spring of 1958 that he was not receiving good reports of the concerts in Budapest. He looked drawn and gaunt in the photographs of his first visit to South America in May 1957 for six concerts with the State Radio Symphony Orchestra in Buenos Aires. There were tours of Scandinavia, including a performance of the oboe concerto with Léon in Helsinki. He even conducted at Catania in Sicily.

As far as North America was concerned, he was to spend February 1959 in Toronto, conducting the CBC Symphony Orchestra. His programmes were his usual skilled mixture of classical and contemporary music and he was delighted with their reception. Two years later he made a long delayed debut in Montreal, conducting the Montreal Symphony Orchestra in what was hailed as 'a definitive performance' of Haydn's *Creation* with Nicolai Gedda, Donald Gramm and Pierrette Alarie as soloists.[12]

Australia remained painfully at the back of his mind. He kept in touch with Sir Charles Moses who congratulated him on his continuing conducting successes in London and asked his advice on appointing his successor. 'As long as I am here your work will not be forgotten,' promised Moses but the assurance had a somewhat hollow ring.[13] In June 1958, Eugene wrote to Frank Hutchens on the Staff of the Conservatorium thanking him for a letter and enquiry about a possible return:

> The scars of my ordeal – and its impact on all of you – of two years ago are still too unhealed and too recent in my mind to risk the effects of a premature return, both on me, as well as on that still loyal section of Australian music lovers you hint at. You ask me to say that I have some wish to see you all again, the answer, 'Yes – very definitely so'. (One of my worst trials has been the complete severance of personal contacts and ties with my many good friends, professional and otherwise.)
>
> Only if and when an overwhelming majority of the Australian public clamoured for my return might I consider so doing. As this is a most improbable occurrence, we must leave it to time to bridge the gap of years which must form before we next meet in Sydney.[14]

He expressed no grudge against those who had failed to stand by him. Writing to L J Keegan, Registrar of the Conservatorium, in April 1961, he sent his best regards to his successor there, Sir Bernard Heinze: 'I often try to picture him in the setting of the room which I grew to love. The view of the harbour from the garden always remains in my memory.'[15]

He was always delighted to see friends and ex-students from Australia. Charles Mackerras visiting him at Hamilton Terrace was surprised by his equanimity: 'He talked with very great love and fond remembrances of Australia. "You remember what that house was like in Wahroonga? You remember old so-and-so? I wonder how he is these days."'[16] Geoffrey Parsons came when his piano teacher Winifred Burston was in London and was distressed to find him 'a broken old man.'[17]

Joan Sutherland and Richard Bonynge were also disturbed by the change they saw in the man who had had such a large effect on both their lives. Sutherland recalls: 'He was thin and haggard, a shadow of himself; he'd always been very upright, he seemed to cave in. We didn't know what to say or do.'[18]

He had also been a musical hero to Raymond Fischer who arrived from Australia at the beginning of 1960.

> He invited me to tea and was very pleasant, talking about the musical scene in general terms and asking me about my plans. He had one leg propped up on a chair and didn't get up at all during my visit. He played me the recording of *Firebird* which he had just made with the LSO and then Pamela brought in the tea. It was obvious that their relationship was a close one but she appeared in the role of trusted housekeeper. I'm not sure whether because of my Australian connections he would have preferred not to see me. I left with a feeling of distance between us which could no longer be bridged, of regret and sadness because I did like and respect him very much.[19]

Barry Tuckwell recalls meeting him in July 1960 at the Wigmore Hall at the oboe and piano recital given by Ian Wilson and Gabor Reeves. '"I've come to hear my boys play," he told me with such pride.'[20] He wrote to Ian who had played for him in the Sydney Orchestra and was to become First Oboe in the Philharmonia:

'I want to tell you how impressed and delighted I was by your very fine performance. You have developed into a still finer artist than you were in the old days, and I enormously enjoyed your beautiful sense of phrasing and tone quality.'[21] He was gratified by his inclusion of *Pastorale and Harlequinade* (written for Léon in 1924) in recital programmes and also his performance of the Oboe Concerto in Finland. Ian's widow, Irene remembers Sir Eugene coming to dinner and being 'charming but very grand and expecting to be the centre of attention. I always thought he had the most sensual lips I'd ever seen!'[22]

One of the compensations of being back in London was the amount of time Eugene could spend with his father.

He spoke to him on the telephone every day if only for a couple of minutes and visited him in Finchley every week. To celebrate his ninetieth birthday on 28th January 1957, Douglas Glass took a studio portrait for the *Sunday Times* of the proud patriarch surrounded by his four distinguished children. 'The small man with the fine veined hands, high forehead, white beard parted in the centre, invited us into a flower-filled dining room in Finchley. 'Fancy', he said, 'anyone remembering me – even if I am ninety today. The public have such a knack of forgetting. . . Don't see much of my children. They're too busy these days. I miss them.' The *Sunday Times* asked the man who gave up conducting in 1930 for a word on 1957 composers: 'Don't like the new composers. Television's not suited to opera either.' Rock 'n roll? The old eyes widened in horror. 'Terrible, terrible. I'd rather listen to cannibals in the jungle.'

Eugene would go down to Woodstock Farm to stay with Sidonie and Norman or visit Léon and Leslie in St Peter's Square. He felt most at ease with Marie whom he took on the occasional jaunt abroad – to Bruges for the Holy Blood Procession and to Esjberg in Denmark.

He dedicated his last chamber work, Concert Piece for Two Harps, Oboe and English Horn to Marie, Sidonie and Léon. The suggestion had originally come from their old friend Hubert Foster Clark, who used his wealth, derived from the manufacture of custard powder, to the good purpose of financing his Chelsea Chamber Orchestra. The premiere in Chelsea Town Hall on 3rd February 1958 was very much a family occasion. 'A work composed and conducted by one member of the family with three others of its members playing the solo parts must surely be unique,' stated the *Musical Times*. 'More especially so since their 91-year-old father was present to hear them. Not having the powers of a Lytton Strachey with the elderly Queen Victoria, I cannot say what was passing through his mind. Unadulterated pride would be pardonable. The last movement contained quotations from the symphonic repertory to depict the various orchestral backgrounds of the Goossens. It was encored and Sir Eugene observed that they were all touched that we wanted it again. The work and the family should appear at the Proms.'

They did on 16th August 1958 with equal success but their father was sadly no longer there to share a family triumph. He had died after a short illness on 31st July. Eugene expressed to Richard Howgill at the BBC their feelings, bereft after so many years of the begetter of their musical lives. 'You, who knew Papa and our love for him, can well imagine how deep is our sense of utter loss at his passing.'[23]

As a composer, Eugene found himself marginalised, regarded by the establishment as an unfashionable relic of the twenties. Howgill's booking of a studio performance of *Don Juan de Mañara* for early April 1959 came as a pleasant surprise. Vivien Dixon who had recently joined the First Violins of the BBC Symphony Orchestra, found him disappointing: 'He seemed old and very wooden and pompous as a conductor. He was totally humourless and the orchestra did not behave well, particularly when he started to rehearse a new act at 5.25pm, five minutes before the end of the session.'[24]

Eugene was gratified however by the response to the broadcast of fellow composers, like Franz Reizenstein, a comparative stranger. 'I feel impelled to write and extend my most sincere congratulations to you on your wonderful opera *Don Juan de Mañara*. I was enthralled by it from beginning to end and came to the conclusion that it is the best English opera ever written that I have ever heard. Your opera has tremendous dramatic power, most persuasive music right through and most exquisite variety of orchestration.'[25]

His old friend John Ireland was equally enthusiastic: 'I must write at once and tell you how profoundly moved and impressed I am by your *Don Juan* masterpiece. For a truly great masterpiece it is in every way, and a unique one. Even over the wireless every moment of it held me spellbound and its structure is such a complete whole, musically and psychologically. No other composer could have produced anything like it. It has the quality of true greatness.'[26] (Eugene had written to the Prime Minister the previous year recommending Ireland, who was nearly eighty, for the Order of Merit.)

Another pleasure of being back in England was the opportunity of renewing old friendships and reminiscing over shared triumphs. When Percy and Ella Grainger had come on a visit from the USA, they spent a day in Eastbourne with Cyril Scott.

Aftermath

The three elderly composers had their photograph taken and Eugene, the youngest, jokingly referred to himself as 'a rose between two thorns'! Grainger's visit coincided with one of the large cocktail parties Eugene gave at least once a year 'just so my friends can see each other' – a useful Public Relations exercise to demonstrate his status in the musical world. *Music and Musicians* reported the event with photographs of Grainger, Sir Arthur Bliss, Hephzibah Menuhin, Rafael Kubelík and Robert Cassadesus amongst the guests.[27]

Eugene had always found it difficult to maintain a close relationship with his daughters. At the beginning of 1958 he had been delighted by a visit from Australia of his daughter Donie and her husband en route for an African safari. He had been worried by strains in the marital relationship and was not surprised when they parted the following year. The first marriage of his youngest daughter Renée to a French-Swiss boy also ended stormily. His eldest daughter Anne was now a widow, Edgar Obermer having died in January 1958, and she decided to return to England in 1959 with her two young daughters, thinking that her father might need her care.

After a few months at Hamilton Terrace she moved into a flat of her own and took a secretarial job. Eugene wrote to an old friend of Cincinnati days: 'Anne and her family live in the next street to me and it does me much good to be with my two grandchildren.'[28] Both Anne and Donie found their father's relationship with Pamela Main difficult to understand; she was so unlike his previous wives and women friends who had always been beautiful, elegant and sophisticated. But she offered him total, selfless, uncritical love and devotion; she was content to remain a shadowy figure in the background of his life, to nurse and cosset him, to bring in the tea-tray for visitors and lace up his shoes.

Eugene was anxious to supplement his precarious income from freelance conducting by obtaining lucrative composing commissions. In May 1958 he approached his old friend Sir Laurence Olivier, reminding him of his experience and past success in writing stage and screen music:

377

I am interested in exploring the more contemporary and original avenues of dramatic music, in contrast to the drab clichés and timeworn conventions of much of so-called incidental music one hears nowadays. Precision in timing and historical accuracy are things which also concern me greatly.

Forty years' experience in the recording world have helped me to devise an economical procedure in the recording studio, in contrast to the vast amount of time and money thrown away on indecisive, hesitant and inexperienced handling of expensive orchestral material.

It would be like old times and afford me enormous pleasure if we could collaborate together in any future projects – great or small – you may have in view.

P.S. My operatic years naturally gave me a preference for setting music to highly dramatic and exciting subjects.[29]

Olivier was planning to film *Macbeth* and wrote to him on 1st July 1958: 'If *Macbeth* comes off, as I desperately hope it will, I have already committed myself to William Walton, who, as you know, did the music for my three other Shakespeare films.' He tried to soften the blow by adding: 'It was so very nice to hear from you, and very heart-warming to think that a musician of your calibre should want to take a serious interest in the cinema' and signed himself: 'affectionately Larry O.'

The response from Robert Graves, embarking on the uncharted waters of a Broadway musical *Solomon and Sheba*, was equally friendly:

Tyrone Guthrie and I agreed and impressed on the producer Alexander A Cohen, that we didn't need anyone *schmaltzy*; and nice Willie Walton had told my daughter Jenny Nicholson at Rome that he was tired of writing symphonies and wanted to write a musical, we naturally jumped and sent WW the book.

We are still waiting for an answer but he's only had it for a couple of days – if indeed it has yet reached him at Ischia. If he can and will work according to schedule and limit himself to twenty-four instruments – or whatever the number is – then that's that. If he can't, we will need to go around among musicians of stature, because this is a very difficult job musically. So of course I'll joyfully tell Cohen and Guthrie of your offer and see what their reaction is and hope it matches mine. Me, I can't do anything on my own responsibility. I think this is plain, frank and grateful enough.

P.P.S. Excuse me – I don't know your honorific prefixes

or affixes, but your NAME is what counts. Me, I keep mine bare.[30]

Eugene had to content himself with writing the music for a feature film called *The Day* directed by the Australian actor, Peter Finch.

He had also kept in contact with his friend from Rochester and Hollywood, Rouben Mamoulian, to whom he made his most unrealistic and grandiose proposition:

> I was immensely interested to hear about your forthcoming *Cleopatra*. I have spent some years studying post-dynastic Egyptian music, likewise that of the Graeco-Roman period, roughly contemporary with the lifetime of Cleopatra. If you need any advisory help in this matter I'll certainly put it at your disposal.
>
> There will undoubtedly be spectacular crowd scenes in *Cleopatra* which would appeal very much to my sense of large-scale musical design, in contrast to the subtly dramatic 'mood music' of which there will probably be a lot in your film. My music would use every contemporary harmonic and rhythmic device, yet would be subjugated to 'period authenticity'. I work quickly and co-operatively and I would not need large orchestral forces. Colour and sonority are what matters; volume comes automatically with amplification.
>
> I tell you all this, not to take advantage of our friendship, but just to let you know that in the event of your not having so far made a decision regarding your musical collaborator, my services and long experience are at your disposal. Moreover, I can think of nothing that would give me greater pleasure, or inspiration, than our collaboration.
>
> I am relieved to know that you are in charge of this film. I tremble to think what tonal vulgarities might be perpetrated were the picture in less fastidious hands than yours![31]

The irony of the situation was that apart from his claim of omniscience as to music of the first century BC, Eugene had all the inventiveness, facility and speed required to write excellent film music. If only he had used his powerful contacts from Walter Wanger of United Artists downwards when he was conducting in the Hollywood Bowl to obtain the occasional commission for a lucrative film score, he would not have been eking out his last years in London in straitened financial circumstances.

It was Beecham who held out a generous helping hand. He was to record *Messiah* for RCA with the Royal Philharmonic Orchestra and Chorus; he commissioned Eugene to reorchestrate Handel, reminding him that forty years before he had commissioned him to reorchestrate Bach: his Suite in G as ballet music for *Phoebus and Pan* at the Aldwych Theatre in 1917.

Beecham paid for Eugene to travel to Nice to discuss the project with him and wrote to him on 19th May 1959: 'I hear that work on *Messiah* is proceeding very satisfactorily. You will not forget, I am sure, that 'Hallelujah' (that is the first three bars of it) must lead off with the most glorious and crashing noise, everybody going all out – hell for leather!' Eugene used cymbals for a good big bang. 'And why not?' he asked. 'Aren't we exhorted in the Bible to "praise the Lord with the sound of cymbals?"'[32]

He used 400 large sheets of twenty-eight stave manuscript paper; as he finished each set of a few sheets, messengers from the RPO office collected them from Hamilton Terrace and a team of five copyists wrote out the individual parts. There were often telephone demands from Beecham for more speed.

Eugene's approach was pragmatic: rescoring music of the past for modern performance was a question of aesthetics not ethics. 'The only justification for changing anything is in the effectiveness of the result, as long as the composer's original intention is not distorted,' he explained in an interview for *Records and Recordings* in April 1960. 'If the original results in a puny sound from the orchestra in comparison with the voices, then you must build up the orchestra to balance. All my life I've been obsessed with this matter of "balance" of sound; and that is what I have aimed at in this new orchestration.'

Beecham conducted the first public performance of the new version in September 1959 at the Lucerne Festival, with the Philharmonia Orchestra and Chorus. Charles Reid, Beecham's biographer, described the effect: 'As rescored by Goossens ("at my instigation" Beecham insisted), Handel's music glowed, boomed and tinkled unprecedentedly. "What are the purists going to say about all this?" Reid asked. "My dear boy," he answered. "I never think about the purists. They are a breed that has sprung up recently. The most important thing about *Messiah* is that it is one of the *grand* scores."'[33]

Eugene had given *Messiah* a suitably *grand* orchestration in compliance with Beecham's wishes and his own convictions.

The record was to prove a bestseller but by the time it was issued on compact disc in 1992, the publicity from Music Discount Centre claimed: 'Sir Eugene Goossens was commissioned to arrange *Messiah* so that it would come as a surprise, but the result was not to Beecham's liking. *Dis-arranged* was one term he used to describe it, so he reorchestrated it himself.' Andrew Porter, distinguished music critic of the *Observer*, described the recording as 'grand, graceful, ever stirring. The orchestration, credited to Goossens, is really, we are told, mainly Beecham's own.'[32] The score has never been published. According to Norman Millar, present at the recording sessions as manager of the Royal Philharmonic Orchestra, Beecham decided at the last minute that he wanted a small section normally cut from performance to be included; this was rescored by the RPO's Librarian George Brownfoot. Apart from this minor addition, the entire recording was of Goossens' orchestration as commissioned and approved by Beecham.

Eugene had regretted the retirement of Richard Howgill from the BBC in February 1959, feeling that he had lost 'a friend at Court'. After his successor as Controller of Music, William Glock, had expressed an interest in Eugene's last completed orchestral work *Divertissement*, he felt that he could confide in him his dissatisfaction and frustration with the treatment that he was receiving from orchestral managements and the BBC:

I suppose that after over thirty years as resident conductor abroad, the daily routine of making and conducting lively, worthwhile, big-scale programmes covering all schools and periods – particularly contemporary – became too ingrained a habit for me to resign myself to my present regime of a scattered handful of hackneyed concerts per year, plus some sporadic and uncommissioned composing.

While all this is really no concern of yours, you'll readily understand why it is that my mental, artistic and physical energies crave for greater outlet. In this connection you will realise that the thought of ten months or more having gone by without my having been invited to conduct the BBC orchestra – formerly quite frequent and satisfying occasions for all concerned – saddens me a little.

Sensing your quality of sympathetic understanding, I know you won't resent this perhaps unethical, and I hope not too embarrassing *cri de coeur* of mine. Frankly I am not reconciled to a premature retirement from the conducting scene of action when there remains so much activity in the fields of interpretation and pioneering. The nauseating hack programmes which cater to Festival Hall audiences, after a long spell of conducting the full orchestral repertoire from A to Z, make no appeal to me. But if long experience and authority in the past count for anything these days, I still want to put their fruits to good use whenever I can.[35]

Glock was to prove a sympathetic friend and staunch supporter. He responded to Eugene's predicament by offering him two Promenade Concerts, including *The Rite of Spring* and Debussy's *La Mer*, plus the first public performance of his Violin Concerto, previously heard in a Third Programme studio broadcast.

The concerts met with a mixed critical reception: 'Sir Eugene Goossens' early and enduring championship of Stravinsky made him a particularly suitable choice as conductor of *The Rite of Spring*. This was nevertheless a curious performance from one who was in at the birth of a tradition. When it is Sir Eugene who takes many of the slow passages so fast and some of the fast ones so slow, one listens with respect but reserves the opinion that the work's dynamic stress is seriously imperilled. The baroque contours of Sir Eugene's beat seemed often to leave an embarrassing width of choice open to the London Symphony Orchestra's players both here and in *La Mer*'.[36]

The *Times* found his interpretation of the Stravinsky 'straightforward rather than subtle' and looked for 'greater flexibility of rhythm and phrasing' in *La Mer*.

Martin Cooper had assessed the Violin Concerto on its premiere as: 'one of the key documents of the era which ended with the last war. The four movements are dramatic and highly coloured character pieces. They derive their main interest from the virtuosity of the solo part – played with great fire and brilliance by Tessa Robbins – and the skilful, though overelaborate orchestral writing, an uneasy alliance of Strauss and Stravinsky. The composer's dominant impulse is always to dazzle and to decorate . . . sheer presentation had less chance to conceal the emotional emptiness of the music.'

The *Times* dismissed the Violin Concerto as 'eclectic and

extremely diffuse'.[37] Eugene was bitterly hurt by the reception the work received at the Prom on 7th September 1960. He sent the *Daily Mail* review, headed 'Prom Audience Walks Out Of Goossens Concerto' to Glock. 'The conduct of the departing audience and the little impact the work made on the jaded press, especially those who delighted in the opportunity of slinging mud, must be blamed on the Concerto being placed at the very end of a 100 minute all-Tchaikovsky programme. I knew exactly what would happen, but kept silent before the concert, as there is nothing more tiresome than the plaintive voice of the conductor-composer being heard in the land!'[38]

Eugene resented his patronising dismissal by the Young Turks of the critical establishment as an anachronism, both as a conductor and a composer. His steadfast champion remained Neville Cardus; in November 1960 when Eugene went to Austria to conduct Delius' *Mass of Life* in Linz, Cardus commented in the *Guardian*: 'It is strange that Linz is eager to hear Delius and that he is, as far as most of the London critics go, definitely "out". As curious is the fact that Sir Eugene nowadays conducts mostly abroad and gets few chances here. Yet apart from Sir Thomas, no British conductor equals Goossens in experience and comprehensive musicianship.'

In the summer of 1960 he was approached concerning an operatic project which would have brought the Goossens family history to full circle: to take up the musical and artistic directorship of a resuscitated Carl Rosa Company. Charles Wilson, Chairman of the Board of Directors, planned to open a season in Bournemouth in under four weeks. Eugene analysed the scheme and diplomatically made the following points:

a) The inauguration of a revived Carl Rosa season (even with my name in an 'advisory' capacity) will command such national and critical attention that any falling below even Sadler's Wells standards would court disaster for the future.
b) How could we hope to attain even these standards in three or four weeks time with no principals, chorus, orchestra or producer engaged and probably scenery and costumes needing extensive refurbishing!
c) The association of my name with the Company would naturally lead to the assumptions that the original pre-war I standards would be resumed: I would only be interested in such a resumption. (I

write this with deep admiration for those who have kept the flag
flying during many recent difficult years.)

d) I would and will be interested if given fairly adequate time,
I can decide on the full artistic personnel and the standard of
production in which they will appear.

Unfortunately Charles Wilson was unable to satisfy Eugene's
very reasonable requirements; without his strong hand the Carl
Rosa Company embarked on its disastrous final performances.

Eugene was meanwhile enjoying an Indian summer in the
recording studios; both HMV and Everest recognised his value
as an authoritative interpreter of Debussy, Ravel and Stravinsky
and the inheritor of the mantle of Nikisch and Koussevitzky for
the romantic nineteenth-century repertoire. 'I am delighted to
see Sir Eugene Goossens getting more and more recording
opportunities,' affirmed the reviewer of his Everest recording
of Berlioz' *Symphonie Fantastique*. 'He is one of the most urbane
and sensitive conductors we have; he is also a superb craftsman
of his art, the possessor of a keen, innate musical intelligence.
All these qualities combine to make of Goossens' recording
of the *Symphonie Fantastique* a really memorable experience.
He is inside the music but he is able to keep his emotional
involvement from running away with itself.'[39]

Eugene took exception to an adverse criticism in *Records and
Recordings* of his *Petrushka* recording, pointing out that he took
part in the original performances of the ballet at Drury Lane
before the First World War. He refused to admit the possible
fallibility of his memory on every authentic detail over a period
of fifty years!

Although he had spent twenty-four years in the USA, after
leaving in 1947 he did not return there until July 1961. He
conducted two concerts in up-state New York, at the Empire
State Musical Festival, at Bear Mountain, an enjoyable but
somewhat incongruous engagement for an international conductor of the eminence of Sir Eugene Goossens. While he
was in New York he had what he described as 'a grand old
day together with Marjorie at Landsburg'. She was shocked
at how frail he looked.

On his return he conducted a Promenade Concert on 11th
August 1961 including the first British performance of his
orchestration of Ravel's 'Le Gibet' (from the piano suite *Gaspard*

de la Nuit). He was incensed by Donald Mitchell's criticism in the *Daily Telegraph* of his performance of Roussel's Third Symphony: 'Unbalanced textures, disorganised tempi and unpolished orchestral playing made this a most disagreeable experience.'[40]

He sent to William Glock for his approval a suggested reply to the *Telegraph*. The second paragraph read: 'As authorities on "texture and tempi", your younger reviewers should modify their generalisations and give chapter and verse for their strictures. The composer's own textures and tempi, plus those of the commissioner of the symphony, Koussevitzky, and his successor Munch, to all of which I have attentively listened over the years, constituted the basis of what I believe was in essence – after adequate and patient rehearsals – a fairly representative performance of a great work.' He added to Glock: 'I am getting used to being insulted in my own country but it's just a question of how much longer I can take it before retiring permanently to USA, where I had a wonderful fortnight in NY two weeks ago, with fine orchestral audiences.'[41]

He had to content himself with the acclaim he received when he was called in to conduct the LPO at the Festival Hall on 3rd October 1961 replacing an indisposed Josef Krips. The programme was a challenging one to take over at the last minute including the first performance of Franz Reizenstein's second piano concerto, Walton's *Scapino* overture and Bruckner's Fourth Symphony. The Bruckner, not a composer with whom Eugene was usually associated, drew forth the highest praise from Neville Cardus. 'This was conducting of unusual – these days! – experience and quiet authority. Sir Eugene has no spectacular egoistical and unnecessary gestures, no passionate pressings of the hand over his heart. It is a commentary on our musical situation just now that a conductor of Sir Eugene's technical and cultural equipment should appear but seldom in the London concert scene at the present time.'[42]

His renowned ability to handle complex scores was often exploited by the BBC, as when he received a contract to conduct an opera called *Yerma* by Denis ApIvor. He wrote to Glock complaining, with justification, 'that it would have been more courteous if someone had written asking whether I would care to undertake these performances of a work unknown to me, by a presumably contemporary Welshman, instead of issuing a summons to conduct the work as if I were a staff conductor. If I take umbrage at this rather cavalier approach it is less because I am being asked to take charge of what will probably turn out to be an "ungrateful" new opera, but rather because opportunities to conduct the BBC Orchestra in worthwhile symphonic works, come to me so infrequently.'[43]

Glock, with his tact and charm, managed to assuage Eugene's *amour-propre*. *Yerma*, a setting of the Lorca play, had originally been commissioned by Sadler's Wells and then shelved as being too difficult. He convinced Eugene that it was a worthwhile project for him to undertake, particularly as the title role was to be sung by the Antipodean soprano, Joan Hammond. 'To watch Gene working with us all, day after day, when he was already a very sick man, was inspiring,' she later recounted. 'What a musical genius he was! Scrupulously thorough and with the patience of Job, few conductors could equal him.' Because of the technical difficulties of the opera for the orchestra, Eugene decided to record the last act first, a difficult feat for Hammond demanding intense concentration. 'I had to gear myself up to believing that the story was working up to the final bloodthirsty tragedy. I had to die, forget about it and begin Act I alive and vibrant. *Yerma* was the last opera this impeccable musician conducted.'[44]

She wrote to thank him for an evening at Hamilton Terrace and a Chinese meal cooked by two of his conducting pupils. 'Pam is unique and it is grand to see someone loving the life she had chosen – that is true happiness. Take care of yourself for all our sakes – we need you in this topsy-turvy music world of today.'[43]

Eugene had eventually committed himself to marrying Pamela Main and Marjorie had agreed to a divorce. Despite a further deterioration in his health, Eugene looked forward to 1962 with unquenchable optimism. His championship of the works of contemporary composers had been marked by his election as Chairman of the Composers Guild of Great Britain for the coming year. His engagements abroad included concerts in Holland, Canada and America.

He was taken seriously ill with pleurisy at the beginning of January, forcing him to cancel four concerts with the Radio

Filharmonisch Orkest in Holland. He underwent a successful operation to drain fluid from his lungs and suspected cancer was not proven. Against his doctor's orders, he conducted the LSO at the Festival Hall on 30th March 1962 in a strenuous programme including the first performance of Robert Still's Third Symphony and Léon playing both the Strauss and Goossens Oboe Concertos. Hardly able to walk, he conducted sitting down and remained seated between items. John Warrack commented in the *Sunday Telegraph*: 'Is there another composer who has done so much to perform his contemporaries?'

It was to be his last London concert; he recorded the Still Symphony for Decca on 9th May. Shortly afterwards he and Pam travelled to Geneva to visit his daughters Jane and Julia and to see his first wife Boonie who was living in Berne. After a week he collapsed; he was flown home and taken by ambulance to Hillingdon hospital where he died on 13th June 1962 at the age of sixty-nine. All Anne was handed as next of kin were his glasses, his false teeth and his surgical corset.

To the surprise of the Goossens family, Eugene had made a new will in Geneva on 2nd June, leaving 'the whole residue of my assets, copyright and royalties to my faithful companion and assistant, Miss Pamela Main'. He had appointed Sidonie his executrix and left her his printed music which included the historic opera scores from which he, his father and his grandfather had all conducted.

He had obviously wished to recompense Pam for the years she had selflessly devoted to him. As he had no money to leave her, he hoped his royalties would provide her with an income. There was no mention of the rest of the family. The will had been witnessed only by the landlady in Geneva, but according to Swiss law, a will does not even need one witness as long as it is written in the person's own hand. It was.

Sidonie relates that Cyril Scott telephoned her as soon as he heard the news of his old friend's death: 'It's all right. Eugene's with Percy Grainger on the other side and they've already formed their own orchestra!' Marie and Sidonie arranged for a Requiem Mass at the Church of Our Lady of Victories in Kensington Church Street where Eugene had attended Holy Mass as a student at the Royal College of Music. Marjorie, living in Zurich, was not able to attend but came later to the Cemetery at East Finchley to lay flowers on the grave, with its inscription of Eugene's favourite quotation from Shakespeare:

Music when soft voices die,
Vibrates in the memory.

26

Survivor

For Léon, 1962 was to prove a disastrous year. His daughter Corinne's marriage to John Spence, son of the architect Sir Basil Spence, had lasted less than twelve months, leaving Léon and Leslie with the financial responsibility for their grandson, Dominic. They were in Malta, enjoying a much needed holiday, when on 13th June came the shock of Eugene's death. Léon flew back alone and after the funeral, because of professional commitments, decided to stay in England.

On Sunday, 24th June he spent the day with the composer Elizabeth Poston and her mother at their home in Stevenage, Hertfordshire. In order to avoid heavy home-going traffic at the end of a summer weekend, he delayed his departure until 11.15pm. Cutting through North West London on his way back to Hammersmith, he was suddenly aware of a car approaching him at top speed on the wrong side of the road. He braked violently and felt a sickening impact. Between waves of unconsciousness and excruciating pain, seeing so much blood he thought he had damaged his hands; he remained unaware of the seriousness of the injuries he had sustained until he finally regained consciousness in Willesden General Hospital. 'It was a head on collision. Everything was thrown in at me. The steering wheel was in my chest, breaking ribs and cracking my sternum. The horn ring on the steering wheel broke off and lashed across my mouth, tearing all my teeth out.'[1]

'I was dumbfounded, I couldn't believe it,' was Yehudi Menuhin's reaction on learning of the catastrophe. That Monday morning they had been scheduled to record final pages of ensemble for the Bach Double Concerto. 'Nothing is as sudden or ugly as an accident, especially following the dedicated search

389

for beauty he and I pursued together. I was appalled by the hideous futility and idiocy of human fate, as I was supremely grateful to have been allowed to live and work and play with so dear a colleague.'[2]

The duty house surgeon had been incorrectly informed that the seriously injured casualty was Léon Goossens, 'a famous Hollywood producer'. It was not until Marie arrived that he was told he had the life and career of the world's most famous oboe player in his hands. By the time Jennie and her fiancé Brian reached the hospital the young surgeon was working through the night, inserting 150 stitches and doing all he could to repair the mouth and shattered jaw. Thanks to his skill, without the help of micro-surgery, Léon was eventually able to resume his career.

He had lost all his lower incisor teeth and had no sensation in his lower lip. 'With the oboe,' he later explained, 'the whole sound is made by the mouth and the muscles around it. If you have no control of your mouth you can never get the instrument in tune. I used to play by putting the reed in the centre of my mouth, but the muscles are gone and the nerves are quite dead so I have no means of keeping my lips pressed up to the reed.'[3]

The lawyers, trying to assess his claim for damages, sought the professional opinion of Sir Arthur Bliss, Master of the Queen's Music. 'To a great player like Mr Goossens, the embouchure is all important, as important indeed as vocal chords to a singer. Mr Goossens received injuries which affected his lips and I am of the opinion that they cannot be patched up or repaired so as to enable him to produce the same continuity of phrasing as was possible before the accident. Mr Goossens lost many teeth in the accident and, again, I feel that this materially affected his powers of control and makes it virtually impossible for him to perform all the great works that have been written for and dedicated to him.'[4]

'For about a year after the accident,' Leslie recalled, 'he had a feeling of being useless. He could very well have sat back and thought he was finished. It was so painful for us to see him sitting there, lost and aimless.'[5] Before that he had always shared his sisters' equanimity of temperament and unquenchable optimism.

At the age of sixty-five Léon might have accepted the inevitable, that his distinguished career was at an end. But with Leslie always there to encourage and support him, he decided that he had to devise a new technique to enable him to play again. It was a slow, laborious and dispiriting process. He started off by returning to small Music Clubs with Mabel Lovering, who had been a close family friend and one of his accompanists for many years, talking about his career and gradually building up his confidence by playing a little more on each occasion.

Two years after the accident, Jack Brymer arrived at Denham Film Studios at nine o'clock in the morning and to his amazement found Léon there for a session. 'He was standing in a corner facing the wall, trying to get the old Goossens sound out of a new and modified reed. I thought "Léon, you'll never make it." An hour later he was in the orchestra, playing with absolute control. The sound was a little smaller but equally fine.'[6] The therapeutic effect of rejoining his old friends and colleagues from the Sinfonia of London gave a considerable boost to Léon's morale. 'The little body of players applauded me and I was terribly moved.'

He explained how he had circumvented his injuries. 'I now have to bunch up the side muscles so that they push in this way and get behind my lip and force it up to the reed. At the same time, I hug it a bit with the upper lip so that there is pressure all round the reed which produces quite a difference in sound from the old technique.'[7] The remaining hurdle was whether he had the stamina to sustain a solo concerto. He was persuaded by an American conductor, Gene Forell, whom he had got to know through film sessions, to accept a concert of baroque music in New York, playing at the Town Hall on 25th April 1966 with Forell's Master Virtuosi Ensemble.

The *New York Times* was enraptured.

Instead of the delicate, slender figure we expected, in came the deep-chested, powerful Mr Goossens to take possession of the hall and its audience. Seeing him stride on stage, like an erect, well-exercised Board Chairman of fifty-five or so, it seems incredible that Mr Goossens has been playing the oboe for more than fifty years. But the record shows that he will be sixty-nine in June and that he has been playing since 1913.

391

Before he played a note, it was obvious that he was a man who had come to enjoy himself and in the charming Concerto in G major, arranged from five keyboard sonatas of Domenico Scarlatti, the objective and its fulfilment were shared with his splendid colleagues and by their fortunate listeners. In the Albinoni B flat Concerto (op. 7, no. 3), the instrument was not merely played, it fairly sang. Trills and ornaments were executed with such an air of spontaneity that they served only to embellish the pleasure of the music, not to call attention to the difficulties that, for Mr Goossens, apparently never existed.[8]

Meeting Jack Brymer after the concert, he brushed aside his congratulations on his incredible achievement. 'My dear boy, I went onto the platform not knowing whether I would be able to get a sound out of the thing!'

The one remaining hurdle was to demonstrate to the world of British music that he was restored to complete musical and physical health. The *Daily Telegraph* confirmed this on 16th May 1966 with a review headed 'Léon Goossens at his best'.

It was well-known that a few years ago Léon Goossens, the supreme oboe player, severely damaged his mouth in a motoring accident. Although he lost all feeling in his lower lip, he would not accept defeat and began practising again in an attempt to recover his old mastery.

His recital at Macclesfield yesterday afternoon convinced the audience that his perseverance had been richly rewarded. The tone seemed as seductive, the control as effortless, the phrasing as immaculate, as ever. The astonishing crescendos in Bach's Adagio seemed to materialise out of space at no given point in time, and grow and grow until they filled the hall. The last note of his encore, high and perfectly controlled, lingers in the memory.

No false sympathy was required. The miracle had been accomplished.

After the accident, Léon and Leslie moved to a smaller house, 7a Ravenscourt Square. Léon built a studio in the garden where he had his piano, his memorabilia and library of music, including the scores of over one hundred works which had been written for him. He would lavish as much care in a recital on a piece dedicated to him by a forgotten minor composer like Walter Stanton or John Somers-Cocks, as Malcolm Arnold's *Sonatina* or a Schumann 'Romance'. Like

Beecham, he could cherish a trivial piece and make it sound masterly.

As he grew older he increased the number of lecture recitals he gave all over the country, entitled 'Highlights from my Career'. Despite his international reputation, Brian Spink feels his then father-in-law was 'almost naïvely straightforward and unpretentious with no artistic affectation and no sense of his commercial value.'

If they paid his fee which was very slight he would go anywhere. Leslie used to compare the fees of Segovia or Casals with what Léon received and point out that he was acknowledged to be as great on his instrument as they were on theirs. She always complained about the agents for not getting him a better fee. But he would go to any school, any private house, it was just work.

His stage presence was very impressive indeed. It was second nature; where he got it from I do not know. Maybe it was a tradition from Victorian or Edwardian times, a certain way you comported yourself as a soloist. He was never self-conscious in any way but he used to get very nervous, another endearing trait. I sometimes saw him trembling before a concert, yet as soon as he got onto the platform, he was so calm, in complete control of the audience.

He would come on, the audience would clap politely and he'd acknowledge them. He'd pause for quite a time then he'd take up his pose on the platform; he'd lean back on his left foot with his right foot forward and his back absolutely straight, so that he was very statuesque. He would fiddle with the instrument for a little while, then he would start to talk, very quietly to the audience so that they had to listen. He never raised his voice so some would be bending forward in order to hear him. He'd start to talk about the piece he was going to play and the composer whoever he might be, when it was written, when it was presented to him. Halfway through, he'd pick up the instrument to play and put it down again and tell another little anecdote. By this time the audience was fascinated with the story, never mind the music. Then he'd tell a little joke. If you read the joke on paper you'd say that's not very funny but by the time he'd gone through this process of talking to the audience they thought it was hysterical and the whole house was in an uproar of delighted laughter. When he'd really won them over to him, he'd put the instrument into his mouth and start to play and he played like an angel.[9]

His story of the Cup Tie Match was a typical favourite:

> I was playing a recital up in, I think it was Blackburn. It was on
> a Saturday evening and it was a day on which they were having a
> Cup Tie Match in the football ground. The only way I could do it
> was to sit up all night in the train after the concert because I had a
> rehearsal with Beecham the following morning in London. I went
> straight to the station after the concert and made my way to the
> refreshment room which was a glorious place. It was an absolute
> oasis that night, although I thought I was never going to get in,
> it was so packed with all these footballers. I'd changed naturally
> because I had to sit up all night, so I put on this famous blue
> jersey, grey flannels and a thick coat and a cap, and I had my
> bag with me.
>
> As I walked into the refreshment room the blonde lady who
> was serving the drinks and pulling the beer saw me and her face
> lit up as much as to say 'I know this man' and she made people
> make way for me to come in. I had to fight my way in, the smoke
> was terrible. I got up to the bar and she looked at me and said
> 'What'll you drink, love?' I said 'That's very kind of you. I'd like
> a pint of bitter – I've got to go the night in the train. I'm going
> to have a pint of bitter and a sandwich.' 'And so you shall,' she
> said, in her lovely Lancashire. While she was pulling the beer
> she was looking at me. 'Have you been playing?' she asked. I
> thought, well here's fame at last, so I said 'As a matter of fact
> you're quite right, I have!' 'I thought so,' she said. 'And
> did you win?'[10]

In later years many of his recitals were dedicated to the raising
of money for the restoration of ancient churches. Jennie quotes
her mother as saying that Léon 'as a Roman Catholic put more
roofs on Anglican churches than anyone else!'

In 1972, when he celebrated his seventy-fifth birthday, he
was still enjoying a busy schedule of performances including
the Vaughan Williams Concerto for the composer's centenary
and the Mozart Oboe Concerto at the first Saturday of the
Proms. Listening to a tribute from Ivor Newton on the radio
introducing Léon's contribution to the Kreisler recording of the
Brahms Violin Concerto, Jennie impulsively wrote to her father:
'I have to say this here and now – I have such intense pride
in being your daughter. We so rarely let our feelings really be
known, or I don't and it has to be done when emotion runs

high. The longer I live, the more I hear you play and the more people I meet to whom you've given pleasure and who honour you, the more I love and honour you as my father and the greatest artist I'll ever know.' As an actress Jennie found some of her most satisfying performances were of music and poetry programmes with her father. When he was asked whether any younger members of his family were taking up a musical career, Léon countered: 'We've had three generations – and I don't think one should go on plugging the name for too long.'

Another letter in 1972 which gave him great pleasure brought back memories of student days at the RCM. It came from his old friend Herbert Howells, after he had been made a Companion of Honour. 'When CH came my way in June I had (and I was all the happier) the feeling that it was retrospectively for those of us who were a group of students, marvellously together in learning our jobs, under three or four devoted teachers. Gene was so much in my thoughts, and you and Bengy [Arthur Benjamin] of blessed memory, and Gurney and Bunny Warren and gentle Adolphe. And I've been everlastingly grateful to have been one of the group. I like to think that any such Honours as have come to you and Gene and me are in a real sense for men like Parry and Stanford, who gave us whatever values seemed to them to be the most worthwhile.'[11]

Léon accepted no regular teaching commitments. He continued to extend his influence by lecturing and judging competitions, particularly the International Competition in Munich, and through his admirable book on the oboe, written in collaboration with Edwin Roxburgh for the Menuhin Music Guides. His criticism of the new generation of players was always constructive, stressing the necessity for technique to be at the service of interpretation. 'One girl at Munich with red hair of about twenty-two or three played the Mozart Concerto so fast that everything was stripped from it. She had a wonderful facility with her tongue but it was as if the performance had been wound up and put on the wrong speed of recording. She had never got down to considering tone quality. I explained how you can make a tune sound beautiful by playing it a little slower; then you can make use of the extra quality obtained by perfection of technique.'[12]

Raymond Cooke recalled going to a Verdi *Requiem* with him at the Albert Hall where he scrutinised the oboist through binoculars and commented: '"He's flat!"' 'He was unstinting of praise for musicians who turned in a good performance. When he was over eighty he rose to his feet to applaud John Lill's performance of Rachmaninov's Third Piano Concerto. He said he hadn't heard it played as well as that since Rachmaninov himself had played it.'[13]

Every Easter Leslie drove him up to Haddo House in Aberdeenshire. Canon Patrick Shannon described Haddo as 'a musical phenomenon in a remote corner of the North of Scotland, which owes its origin and continued existence to June, Marchioness of Aberdeen. She created from nothing a Choral Society which has tackled with distinction all the major works in the repertory.'[14]

'I was such a bad conductor when I started off with the *St Matthew Passion* in 1950, that I needed help from my leading players,' Lady Aberdeen confesses with disarming frankness.[15] She was delighted when the formidable Emmie Tillett, who controlled the careers of all players and singers in the world of oratorio, offered her Léon Goossens through Ibbs & Tillett Ltd.

He thought he was coming to the depths of the Arctic Circle. He was a wonderful help to the other players, this great artist in the midst of locals, and to me. I relied on his special nod of the head for my entries. He taught me how to conduct. He had wonderful breath control which went on forever but he always had a tussle with Elsie Suddaby in the aria 'Jesu Saviour, I am yours'. She would pull out the phrases despite the fact that Léon did not want it to be as slow. She usually won because she was the singer!

When we were doing the *St John Passion* with Peter Pears and Benjamin Britten, Pears went on in full fig morning dress. Ben, who was playing continuo, said 'I'm not going to dress up. If someone as great as Léon Gossens doesn't, why should I!' Everyone always wore dark suits.

Then there was his dreadful accident. Haddo was one of the first places he played at after he learnt to replay the instrument; I couldn't manage without him. I stopped in the middle of the tenor aria with oboe obligato as I didn't want to tire him. I heard this desperate voice from the middle of the orchestra saying 'Let me play it. I must know whether I can!' I realised how agonising the accident had been and how brave he was to play again.

He and Leslie always used to come up early and stay on with me after every one else had left. Sometimes they brought their grandson Dominic up for a holiday in the summer. Léon was a great favourite of the Queen Mother's; she loved his music. He loved a title in the nicest possible way. He wasn't a snob in that he wouldn't talk to people without titles but he enjoyed the situation of being able to say 'My friend, the Marchioness of Aberdeen.'

There's never been an oboe tone like his and there never will be. It really was playing from the heart.[16]

In 1954 Léon had been awarded the Cobbett Medal, but he richly deserved a knighthood for his unique and unstinting lifetime of service to British music. Preserved amongst his correspondence are letters from Harold Wilson, Edward Heath, Jeremy Thorpe, James Callaghan and Margaret Thatcher, thanking him for his congratulations on their appointment as Prime Minister or election to leadership of their party. Perhaps a residual prejudice existed against the vulgarity of wind players; although actors, conductors and singers seemed to receive a knighthood as a matter of course, it was an honour sadly denied to the greatest British instrumentalist of the twentieth century.

In 1977 there was a series of celebrations for his eightieth birthday: at Haddo House, at John Dankworth and Cleo Laine's home and at the Royal College of Music to open the Goossens Room. Recordings issued included 'The Art of Léon Goossens' and Léon, Marie and Sidonie combining in a little trio written for them by Michael Krein. The BBC devoted 'Collector's Corner' to fifty years of recordings made by the family, ranging from *I Pagliacci* conducted by Eugene senior in 1927 to Gaspar Chiarelli's recent recording of Eugene's last work *Divertissement*. Léon's book on the oboe was launched on the Martini Terrace of New Zealand House and family and friends applauded the presentation of a life-sized portrait by June Mendoza.

Léon was devasted when Leslie was diagnosed as suffering from mylo fibrosis, a disease akin to leukaemia. She was ill for nine or ten years but contrived to drive Léon all round the country to his engagements. Brian Spink recalls: 'Towards the end it was a very stressful time. Jennie was with the Royal Shakespeare Company; they wanted her to go on tour, she wanted to look after her mother; our marriage was breaking up. Leslie was very angry and rebellious at what was happening and that she could no longer devote herself to Léon as she had done for so many years. It was dreadful to see her suffer although she bore her illness with the greatest fortitude.'[17]

After fifty-two years of marriage, Léon never really recovered from her death in August 1985 at the age of seventy-seven. He suffered a stroke ten days after the funeral and later moved to Dulas Court, the Musicians' Benevolent Fund Home near Hereford. He spent two years there in a comfortable room surrounded by his favourite paintings and pieces of furniture. Many of his old friends and pupils who visited him commented on how peaceful he seemed. Only Evelyn Rothwell was unable to see him there, as the first Mrs Barbirolli was in the room next door.

He was not well enough to attend the concert in the Wigmore Hall to celebrate his ninetieth birthday on 12th June 1987. It was organised by Nicholas Daniel, the outstanding young oboist who had been the BBC's Musician of the Year in 1980, with pianist Julius Drake. The music 'inspired by the artistry of Léon Goossens', included sonatas for oboe and piano by his friends York Bowen and Herbert Howells and musical tributes from a distinguished array of other contemporary composers: Wilfrid Josephs, Arnold Cooke, Alan Ridout, Edwin Roxburgh, Elizabeth Maconchy and Alan Bush. Amongst the audience were three sprightly ladies whose looks belied their years – Marie and Sidonie sitting with their father's operatic protégée, Dame Eva Turner.

Léon died in hospital in Tunbridge Wells on 13th February 1988. There was to be a Memorial Service at Westminister Abbey on 16th May with an eloquent and moving address by Jack Brymer on Léon's life and his unique influence on English music and musicians. First came a simple family funeral with an appreciation by Canon Patrick Shannon. He spoke for all those who had loved Léon and his music in his concluding hope that 'when I die, if I am fortunate enough to get to heaven, what will greet me will not be the trumpets of the Archangels, but the sound of Léon's oboe.'

At tea after the funeral, the hospital sister who had been with Léon during his last hours told Mabel Lovering: 'At the end people's breathing changes, but with Mr Goossens it never did. When he breathed in, he might have inhaled a little quicker but when he exhaled it went on and on and on so steadily that the doctor who was there was amazed. He went out of the room and came back with a stopwatch. It was quite incredible. Every breath that he exhaled was perfectly even and steady. His breathing didn't vary right to the very last breath.'[18]

27

Queens of the Harp

I959 marked Marie's official retirement after nineteen years with the London Symphony Orchestra at the age of sixty-five. She sold 'Crewkerne' and moved into a flat in Finchley. 'I could now sit in a deckchair in the garden and enjoy life but did not feel that way inclined.'[1]

Instead she was busier than ever. She continued to teach the harp at the Royal College of Music until she was seventy. She was a popular and respected Professor; Edwin Roxburgh recalls her as a revered colleague:

> I sat on examining boards with her for the Diploma of the RCM and much admired her approach towards assessing candidates. She always combined criticism with encouragement; she was meticulous in putting things absolutely right for students so that they should feel that they had a goal and understand the way in which they could fulfil their potential. She had the great gift of making comments which were incredibly apposite and analytical, yet always considerate and encouraging. Whenever she met you it was as if you were a life-long friend. She took great joy and pleasure in people and loved talking to them. They all did – Marie, Sid and Léon – which says a lot for their old Dad and Mother![2]

In 1965 she was invited to teach a class of harpists for the first time as tutor for the National Youth Orchestra of Wales. The Welsh visit became an annual assignment which gave her much pleasure: 'The Welsh are born musicians and seem to take to their national instrument quite naturally.'[3]

She continued to teach privately. Apart from Sioned Williams who was to succeed Sidonie at the BBC SO, three of her best and most successful pupils were men: John Marson who followed her in the LSO; David Snell who played at the Royal Opera House and then became one of the few successful jazz harpists, before turning to composition and conducting and Michael Jefferies who went to the Western Australia Symphony Orchestra in Perth. In 1964 Michael Jefferies and John Marson founded the United Kingdom Harpists Association in which both Marie and Sidonie were to play a very active part.

As far as Marie was concerned there were only good musicians and bad. She never made any distinction between a soloist and an orchestral player. 'She was a solo recording artist in the twenties,' John Marson pointed out, 'but it suited her warm and vigorous personality to sit in the hurly-burly of the orchestral world where her acute ear, quick perception, musicality and unrivalled richness of tone assured her success.'[4]

In addition to her classical career, Marie had always enjoyed light music. 'Although today it is accepted that musicians work in all fields without prejudice,' she was to explain in 1981, 'this was not always so. Indeed I can remember a violinist who was so ashamed to be playing at a theatre, that he kept his dress suit there, travelling in his ordinary clothes so that if his son should see him he would not know his father's secret.'

There were no such problems with Marie's son, Tony, since he was a jazz musician: 'My mother's always been very broadminded musically. She likes lush music.' Marie revelled in the variety offered to her as the most sought after harpist for film and recording sessions. 'By the early 1960s there was an uneasy anxiety that recordings and studio performances would put an end to live concerts. For me this was not a threat; as new studios opened up from week to week I found myself busier than ever.' She often recorded in four different studios a day, ending up with an advertising jingle for commercial television recorded from 11pm to midnight.[5]

She played for all the well-known names in light music between 1950 and 1980. 'Among those on whose records I played were Ray Martin, Cyril Ornadel, Geoff Love, Peter Knight, Sidney Torch, Stanley Black, Ted Heath, Mantovani and George Melachrino. James Moody arranged the record called 'Life of Reillie' in which he, Tommy Reillie and I play Irish Music.'[6]

She played in Robert Farnon's earlier recordings including a harp solo which he wrote for her called 'Intermezzo'. She also played solo harp on the famous 'Ebb Tide' record, the first time she worked with conductor Frank Chacksfield at Decca.

Filming had changed since the leisurely pre-war days when she had played the music for *Henry VIII*. 'The lighting was very strong, so Charles Laughton kept his dark glasses on. It amused me to see him take them off at the very last second and drop them into his tankard. He then picked up his piece of chicken and ate ravenously.'[7]

Now, working for composer Phil Green, she found that he wrote the film score so quickly that she had no time to look round to see who she was playing with in the orchestra, let alone rehearse. 'One time he wrote some of what I called "toothache music" – it was a sort of murmuring sound at the top of the harp to imitate the sound of gas being administered to the poor man in the dentist's chair. I had to pile all my harp covers on my chair to make it higher so that I was above rather than below the strings. This was to go on for twenty-four bars – I was able to keep going and longer if necessary.'[8] Sydney Saxe, king of the session 'fixers', knew that she would never let him down however bizarre the musical combination or the pyrotechnics demanded of the harp.

Another uncomfortable experience was playing for Cliff Richard in a television show when the harp accompaniment for his song had to come from the clouds. Marie by this time was well over seventy. 'The producer was very kind and asked if I minded very much climbing a ladder up to a platform on which was placed my harp and a stool. Never having seen the music I insisted on having a music-stand. The harp could be visible but neither the player nor the stand must be seen, so a stagehand held the music so far away from me that it was impossible for me to see the notes. However, suitably draped in gossamer in case my arm showed, I just about managed to play. I then had to be hauled down the ladder very carefully as there wasn't time to have me insured!'[9]

Two highlights of Marie's remarkable career were playing for Tony Bennett at The Talk of the Town and with Count Basie at the Odeon, Hammersmith, 'the only woman instrumentalist ever to appear in his band', according to her son, Tony. This was an exhilarating contrast to recording for pop singers and groups: 'Such sessions are very impersonal as we do not know whom we are accompanying. The music is put in

front of us and most times we follow a click track which beats
"one, two, three, four" and we are in. I am often shut in a
little room with headphones and have to work by myself from
there. Some of the names I have found out later, like The
Moody Blues, Cat Stevens or the latest David Soul which
reached the top ten, I believe. There is no real music in this
kind of work as we don't hear more than the rhythm and
accompaniment so there is nothing to take away with us.'[10]
She far preferred lush arrangements of evergreens for LPs.

Almost the only time Marie appeared on the concert platform during these years was for the Last Night of the Proms,
1960–62 where she joined Sidonie to play a special arrangement of 'Home, Sweet Home'. They also worked together
when two harps were required for sessions such as the music
for the cartoon film of *Watership Down*. 'That was very difficult
music,' Sidonie remembered, 'we just had the parts put in front
of us to read with no time to practise and no opportunity of
taking them home to work out. "That's the nest," I was told
for flute and harp alone – very nasty, very quick with lots of
pedal changes. I was very scared about that but we did it all
right. Some of those sessions were very nerve-racking.'[11]

Marie was always very tolerant towards her son and her
grandsons growing up in a world far removed from her own
Victorian, Catholic childhood. Although Tony had refused to
accept the discipline of a classical musical career, he gave his
five sons every encouragement to develop their musical talents.
Two of them have become professional double bass players:
Christopher the eldest plays mainly with the Academy of St
Martin-in-the-Fields but, following in his father's footsteps,
often ends the day playing jazz at Ronnie Scott's; Patrick,
the youngest, is with Marie's last orchestra the LSO and Vice
Chairman of their Board of Directors, elected from orchestral
members.

Christopher looks back fondly on the afternoon sessions
they used to have in Finchley.

Dad would have a few guys from work so we'd have piano,
bass, vibraphone, saxophone, drums, all in the front room. We'd
all be there and Grandma would be loving every minute, sitting
with her eyes closed. She wasn't actually asleep; she always said
she was concentrating. She encouraged us all to go to music

college. I went to the Royal College every Saturday morning as a Junior Exhibitioner, dragging my bass all the way on the bus. We all started off on the piano, then we branched out onto clarinet, French Horn, cello and bass. We weren't pressurised, we were left to get on with it. We were surrounded by a wide variety of music and we played because we wanted to. My other three brothers still enjoy music but they don't play professionally any more. Patrick was at the RCM, Peter graduated from Trinity [College of Music] on the French Horn and I was at the Guildhall [School of Music and Drama].

Christopher would often find himself working with Marie.

On one occasion we were recording at CTS by Wembley Stadium and I leaned across and said 'Give us an A, Grandma'. 'You can't call that lady "Grandma",' someone said in a shocked voice, 'she's Marie Goossens!' 'As a matter of fact she is my Grandma!' I said.

I don't usually tell people about the Goossens, who my grandmother was and my great uncles and my great aunt, although of course I'm very proud of them. Obviously there's a thread that goes along from one generation to the next but I'm me. Their achievements in the past don't actually make any difference to the kind of person I have become. I'm a Laurence but I'm well aware of my Goossens heritage.[12]

His younger brother Andrew has fond memories of Marie's infinite patience and kindness. 'She lived with us for a time in Essex; with five boys there would be lots of rows and bad language but she just used to sit there and hum to herself and shuffle papers about on the table. She never had a bad word for anyone. She was one of life's givers; her greatest pleasure was sharing anything she had.'[13]

Apart from the occasional family celebration, Sidonie had very little time left over from the Symphony Orchestra, her life with Norman and the farm, to meet Marie's grandchildren. 'The official retiring age for the BBC Symphony Orchestra was sixty. Ernest Hall stayed on until he was seventy. Jeanne Chevreau was older than I was. It was Sargent who said: "She's got to go, she's old, she's sixty-five!" I was only fifty-five and by the time I had reached sixty in October 1959, Sargent had left and they said they were not taking any notice of my birthday.

As far as I was concerned, it was my job and I was doing it well.'[14]

There was no one else who could replace Sidonie, no one else who could cope with the complexities of contemporary music in which she excelled. 'She is a harpist, the others are only harpers,' Guido Cantelli had said after she had stepped in at the last moment for a performance of Bartók's Concerto for Orchestra with the Philharmonia Orchestra. Certainly William Glock, who had been appointed Controller of Music for the BBC in 1959, realised her value in implementing his policy of introducing into British musical life the most adventurous developments of contemporary European music.

When asked to analyse her affinity with complex scores, Sidonie modestly dismisses the suggestion:

It just came along with the job. If I had had to play Johann Strauss, I would have felt an affinity with Viennese Waltzes. From the very beginning of the orchestra we had had contemporary concerts, once a month or so. We played all the Webern and Berg in the early 30s. The avant-garde became part of my repertoire in the same way as French and German music.

Avant-garde composers often use the harp much more percussively. Heinz Holliger's wife is a harpist but I think the music he has written for her is very ungrateful to play. Berio hits the strings with knitting needles.

Schoenberg wrote very difficult things for the harp with massive arpeggios and lots of footwork. His earlier works like *Pelléas* and *Gurrelieder* are very harpistic, with lots of notes but playable. *Moses and Aaron* is horrible. When you have to record these works you have to make sure that you do them properly. You're very exposed with your individual microphone; you can be heard when you breathe let alone play a wrong note.

When you first read through a work in rehearsal you can fake it, but then you have to bring it home and study it. I would spend hours learning something new and working out my footwork. Norman would sit here by the fire and say it sounds like a child picking out her notes. I like a little bit of intellectual challenge, that you get from new works; but the most difficult piece in the whole of the repertoire remains Wagner's 'Fire Music' – purely chromatic, the most atrocious piece of harp writing![15]

Sidonie considers her work with the orchestra under Boulez as the best years of her career. Pierre Boulez first conducted the BBC Symphony Orchestra in 1964 and formed a close affinity with Sidonie on a musical and personal level. She was amazed at the profound understanding he showed of the complexities of her instrument: 'In fact, you could have said that he played the harp. He would tell us how to play a phrase and how to move the pedals. If we played an A flat instead of a G sharp to adjust the pedals, he would say "No, no, that won't do, because it will clash." But he was most understanding of technical difficulties.'[16] She has great admiration for him both as composer and conductor; in many ways he symbolised for her what her own son might have achieved had he lived.

In July 1992 Boulez paid tribute to a remarkable personality:

> Sidonie was, certainly, during all those years past in Maida Vale I, a superb harpist; but she was no less a marvellous personality, of the kind that inspires you to make music and who makes you realise that age has in no way whatever diminished her curiosity, her generosity, her capacity for work, her enthusiasm, her constant willingness to encompass new horizons. Whether it is in the stand-ard repertoire which she negotiates in complete security and with the greatest ease, whether it is in new works where she dedicates herself to the task not only with her accustomed professional conscientiousness, but with a commitment, an outstanding will to succeed, Sidonie has always been a model. She is also a model of kindness, charm and good humour. I must stop! Or you will reach a stage of disbelief in the hyberbole of my praise! But I can say that Sidonie has been the great happiness of my musical life in London.[17]

When Vivien Dixon, who was to become co-leader, joined the BBC Symphony Orchestra in 1958, she asked if there were any rules about clothes; the Orchestral Manager told her 'You'll have to ask Miss Goossens about that.' Vivien recalls:

> She was always extremely elegantly dressed herself, both on and off the platform, and took a very professional view as to what people looked like. She disapproved of off-the-shoulder dresses, large handbags on stage and players wearing colours for the Last Night of the Proms.
>
> If she was sitting at the harp, every conductor knew that everything would be all right in that department. I have never known any conductor to have a moment's criticism of her playing;

she got on with them all which is an amazing achievement.

She was dearly loved and highly regarded by us all and we were never conscious of the age gap. She was extremely hospitable in her lovely Surrey farmhouse with its beautifully tended gardens. We would all help her with her luggage on tour; there was one exceptionally heavy bag which contained the bottles of everyone's favourite drinks which she would invite us to consume in her hotel room. [18]

Sidonie always enjoyed touring, particularly the 1965 tour of the USA with Boulez and Dorati and the Russian tour in 1967 with Boulez and Barbirolli. 'I went to Japan with the orchestra when I was seventy-five. When I was over eighty, we were due to go to China. I had arthritis in my knees and couldn't cope with those terrible lavatories, just holes in the ground. I said to the Concerts Manager that I didn't think I ought to go; he said "I don't think you ought either, in fact perhaps you should be thinking of retiring."'[19]

Sidonie officially retired on 17th July, the First Night of the Proms, in 1981, shortly before her eighty-second birthday. Until she was ninety, she continued to teach at the Guildhall School of Music twice a week and play with the BBC Symphony Orchestra. She was still essential for Boulez's *Pli selon Pli* which required three harpists playing five instruments all differently tuned.

She found that standards had inevitably changed in seventy years since her first symphony concert at the Queen's Hall in 1921. 'A lot of young orchestral players asked me to decipher the hieroglyphics of contemporary scores. They have wonderful technique, but no phrasing and no discipline. They saunter in late to rehearsal with paper cups of coffee. I was always at rehearsal fifteen minutes early to tune the harp; everyone had to be in their places five minutes before a 10am rehearsal was due to begin. Toscanini insisted on absolute silence when he came into the hall.'[20]

On 14th September 1991, she was invited back as soloist for the Last Night of the Proms. Superbly poised in a glamorous cerise dress, she played 'The Last Rose of Summer' for Dame Gwyneth Jones. It was difficult to believe that she was ninety-one and the oldest soloist to have been engaged for the series by the BBC.

Marie's last professional recording was the music for the film *Spiderman* in 1981. She then reluctantly retired after a suspected cardiac arrest and moved to sheltered housing in an Abbeyfield House in Hampstead Garden Suburb. Her grandsons persuaded her to write her memoirs *Life on a Harp String*; she donated all the proceeds to a prize for young harpists. She continued to teach the small Clarsach harp. 'I wish Marie were my Grandma,' her young pupils used to say.

Both Marie and Sidonie were gifted teachers who passed on their technical mastery, their interpretive insight and their professionalism to new generations of harpists. In 1981 they were both appointed Fellows of the Royal College of Music, an honour Léon had received in 1962 and Eugene as early as 1924.

'Music is something that you have to make yourself,' Sidonie has always emphasised. 'You have to put your own interpretation into what you play.' Alison Martin with the English National Opera, Janice Beven with the London Philharmonic Orchestra and Isobel Frayling-Cork with the Festival Ballet are amongst her distinguished pupils. 'I never dominate my pupils. If they are good musicians they will feel the music themselves.'

Marie in her nineties still kept her concert clothes hanging in the wardrobe 'in case they're needed'. She attributed her longevity to the exercise involved in playing the harp. 'You have to move every muscle in your body, from your eyes and your neck right down to your ankles and your toes. Music is something in the body and in the mind, the way you think, the way you look. You can find music in everything.'[21] She retained her amazing vitality, her infectious giggle, her pleasure in her family and her delight in all God's gifts. Sadly her conviction that she would live to be a hundred was not fulfilled. She died at the age of ninety-seven on 18th December 1991.

Sidonie is the sole survivor. Her husband Norman died in April 1991 and she is content to live alone with her cat Libby and friends within call. She has four harp pupils including an ex-policeman; she corresponds with colleagues and ex-students all over the world and entertains a constant stream of friends and family with legendary hospitality. It is only in her dreams that she is haunted by the past, of the disasters that never occurred during her exemplary professional career. 'I have nightmares about arriving at a concert and finding all my strings broken or my harp isn't there. Only the other night I dreamt it had been balanced on a pile of sand and kept toppling over. My waking life has always been wonderful.'[22]

Through the wrong end of the telescope Sidonie glimpses the five Goossens children, picnicking on the sands with their mother at Liscard or striving to please their father at the Sunday soirées in Liverpool. 'The saddest thing is that at my time of life, I still want to have my mother and father. You miss them more when you're older. There are no more male Goossens now. We've done it all; we've finished!'[23]

The Goossens have completed their musical century, but their legacy to the world of music lives on.

28

Epilogue

It took twenty-five years for Eugene's dream of a Sydney Opera House on Bennelong Point to come to fruition. Jørn Utzon's original prize-winning design was beset with endless difficulties before the Queen officially opened the complex on 20th October 1973. The interior remains a subject of acrimonious controversy. The exterior has made it one of the best known and aesthetically satisfying buildings created in the twentieth century; it seems to float on the blue waters of Sydney Harbour beneath the sails of the First Fleet or the folding wings of the graceful white ibis.

Eugene had envisaged a multifunctional auditorium for opera, concerts and ballet with a smaller drama theatre. This had been the brief of the winning Danish architect Utzon in 1957. Six years into construction the Opera House had become a political hot potato, a long-running saga of escalating costs and allegations of pay-offs and constructional blunders. In 1965 the Labour Party in New South Wales was ousted by the Liberal-Country Party and Sir Charles Moses retired as General Manager of the ABC. The main support for the Goossens/Utzon vision was removed. The ABC Chairman, Dr James Darling insisted that the function of the main hall was to be a concert hall for the Sydney Symphony Orchestra seating its 3,000 subscribers. Utzon resigned, to be replaced by a team of Australian architects. The orchestra pit and stage machinery were torn out of the half-finished auditorium and opera relegated to the drama theatre seating 1,100. Perhaps it was the unquiet spirit of poor benighted Bennelong that cursed the infant Australian Opera with the wrong acoustics, insufficient space for stage machinery and an orchestra pit too small for Strauss or Wagner.

In July 1962 Donie Goossens had received a letter from

the Department of Local Government assuring her that in the completed Opera House her father's name 'would be commemorated in an appropriate manner'. But eleven years later, when Queen Elizabeth II officially opened the building,[1] there was no mention of Eugene, no plaque or even a brick dedicated to him in the building. In protest, a Goossens Memorial Concert was organised at the Conservatorium the previous evening by the Director Rex Hobcroft and musicians who wished to acknowledge their personal debt to Goossens. The programme was drawn from his chamber music written between 1914 and 1942 and included Carl Pini playing the Second Violin Sonata and Neville Amadio (still First Flute with the SSO) in *Pastorale and Harlequinade* for Flute, Oboe and Piano.

In his opening address, Rex Hobcroft suggested that the most fitting tribute to Eugene would be to name the main hall of the Opera House the Goossens Hall. The idea was immediately championed in the Press: 'After all without Goossens, the Sydney Symphony Orchestra would not be what it is today, Australian composers would not have the recognition and status they enjoy today and there would be no opera house on Bennelong Point. The cruel irony of it all is that, had he not left Australia when he did, the Sydney Opera House would not be the unfunctional mess that it is.'[2]

Ernest Llewellyn, who had left the SSO to become Director of the Music School in Canberra, vented his strong views on the wrong done to his friend Gene: 'At last somebody has found the courage after all these years to come out into the open and honour this man. I thought it lamentable that, so far as I know, the ABC has done nothing to perpetuate his memory, to show respect and gratitude for the immeasurable, boundless contributions he made to Sydney's music.'[3]

The first attempt at a Goossens Memorial Concert at the Conservatorium, scheduled for 6th April 1963 by the Bartók Society of Australia, had been postponed indefinitely 'due to unexpected alteration of concert dates'. (Eugene had remained a patron of the Bartók Society until his death the previous year.) As Martin Long commented in the *Daily Telegraph*: 'The Conservatorium is under the administration of the Department of Education, and pending a change of heart of Government, there will not be any Goossens tributes there. What is more, if

411

the concert does take place somewhere else members of the Conservatorium will not be visibly engaged in the running of it – if they know what is good for them.'[4]

Even after seven years there was still political pressure to veto any reminder of Sydney's disgraced musical hero. Pamela Main had returned to Australia to work in the Music Department of the ABC in Sydney, bringing the score of *Divertissement* for orchestra, his last completed orchestral work which had never been performed. Despite opposition, as a tribute to his friend Gene, Sir Charles Moses insisted that the Sydney Symphony Orchestra include the work in its Subscription Concerts. The premiere was conducted by Joseph Post on 22nd and 24th June 1963.

Two years later, on 6th March 1965, Eva Kelly and John Painter who had both played under Goossens in the SSO, finally succeeded in organising their Memorial Concert at the Conservatorium, under the patronage of its Director, Sir Bernard and Lady Heinze. Heinze no longer considered it politically dangerous to acknowledge the existence of his predecessor. The door had been cracked open but Australia was not yet willing to let Goossens out of its closet. As late as 1966 Donie, working in a record store in Canberra, recommended a recording conducted by her father, to be met by the customer's retort: 'I'm not buying anything of that dirty old man!' He was nonplussed when she replied: 'I'm his daughter.'[5]

The pornography scandal remained far more deeply rooted in the collective consciousness than Eugene's invaluable contribution to Australian music but the details were becoming blurred. 'The Memorial Concert was attended by several persons notorious for their vilification of the good but unfortunate Goossens at the time of his unfortunate brush with the Australian customs department on a little matter of "pornographic" films,' stated Peter Crowe in *Nation Review*.[6]

It took another nine years for a memorial to Eugene to be placed in the Opera House, a striking bronze and black granite bust by the Sydney sculptor, Peter Latona. The prime mover behind the scheme was George Fleischer who was in charge of the ABC's 630 Youth Concerts (held at 6.30pm). Within six months the Subscribers' Committee had raised more than $4,000, with the support of staunch Goossens

412

friends such as Dame Joan Sutherland, Richard Bonynge and
Sir Charles Moses. Latona produced a powerful evocation of
a great musician but he had to work from photographs and a
few details are strangely inaccurate. Donie was disappointed
that her father, whose dress was always immaculate and who
spent hours getting his collar and bow tie correct is portrayed
with a wrinkled collar and a drooping eyelid over the wrong
eye!

The bust was presented to the Opera House Trust on 13th
November 1982 during the second of two performances of *The
Apocalypse* which formed part of the 50th Anniversary celebrations of the ABC. Myer Fredman, another English musician
resident for many years in Australia, conducted the SSO,
with soloists including two international opera singers who
had started their careers with Goossens in Australia: Lauris
Elms and Ronald Dowd and extensive choral forces, among
them the appropriately named 'Special Apocalyptic Choir'.

During the performance, Fredman lost his baton at a moment
of intense involvement and excitement. Donie, sitting in the
audience, was reminded of a similar incident when her father
was premiering the work. His baton hit the music-stand and
broke. She sent the pieces to Fredman. Werner Baer quoted
the story when the ABC issued the recording of the work.
'Like Siegmund's sword, the broken pieces of Sir Eugene's
baton were symbolic of the rebirth of the mighty work under
a younger, also English conductor, who realised the intentions
of the late, much reversed and lamented composer.'

It was not until 4th September 1990 that the Conservatorium paid their official tribute. They launched the 'Eugene
Goossens Conducting Fellowship' with a concert given by
the Conservatorium Symphony Orchestra including Eugene's
Fantasy (1924) for nine wind instruments, *By the Tarn* in the
version for string orchestra and clarinet and the orchestral
setting of *Cadet Rousselle*. The first recipient was a young Polish
conductor Henryk Pisarek, already working as assistant to John
Hopkins, the Director of the Conservatorium. The award was
made possible by the generosity of two anonymous donors as a
tribute to Goossens' work in Australia; its officially stated aim
was that it 'will help to establish already proven young orchestral
conductors in the professional world.' It is the kind of practical

memorial of which Eugene would surely have approved but no information was provided as to how the candidates were to be selected or what the future of the fellowship would be after Pisarek's tenure.

The concert elicited a tribute from Fred Blanks in the *Sydney Morning Herald*, on behalf of all those who, like himself, had 'matured musically in the Goossens Generation. I often burn an imaginary candle to his memory before his bust in the Opera House Concert Hall foyer. Under his direction of the Sydney Symphony Orchestra and Conservatorium from 1947 to 1956, we experienced a unique musical awakening. For Sydney music it was the decade of the century. But Sydney repaid him miserably, not only with respect to his abrupt departure, but by not naming anything significant after him.'[7]

The ABC at last acknowledged their debt to Eugene in 1991 by dedicating the Goossens Hall, in their new purpose-built ultra-modern headquarters at Ultimo. It serves as the Sydney Symphony Orchestra's main rehearsal studio; its tasteful blond wood and grey upholstery are far removed from the dingy makeshift hall above Woolworth's where Eugene strove to inspire the orchestra in his relentless search for perfection. He is commemorated by a large portrait photo and outline of his life on the wall outside, together with a showcase of scores personally dedicated to him by some of the distinguished composers who were his friends. These include Stravinsky, Walton and Vaughan Williams. Pride of place is given to Elgar's *Introduction and Allegro for Strings*, inscribed: 'To my friend and guardian angel. With affectionate good wishes.' It is dated 1905 when Eugene would have been all of twelve years old! Nor was Elgar on sufficiently friendly terms with grandfather Eugene I, despite his excellent choir, to explain the dedication. On closer perusal the dedicatee appears to be Griffiths rather than Goossens! Arthur Troyte Griffith was an architect in Malvern and a close friend of Elgar's of many years standing.

In the 1960s the authorised version of Eugene's career avoided any embarrassment of what happened in 1956 by stating that he had left Australia in 1957, repeated both in the ABC's promotional booklet and Helen Bainton's history of the SSO. By the sixtieth anniversary of the SSO in 1992,

Eugene had been rehabilitated. In many circles he is now unstintingly praised: for transforming the Sydney Symphony Orchestra from a provincial band into a world-class orchestra; for his innovative programming which broadened the horizons of an ultra-conservative audience; for inspiring a generation of talented musicians who have achieved international fame and for being the founding father of the Sydney Opera House on Bennelong Point.

In the last instance, his resuscitation seems to have been somewhat specious in that he provides an ideal whipping boy for the ABC's disastrous policy of converting the Opera House into a concert hall. 'Goossens wanted a permanent home for the SSO' runs the apologia which is somewhat economical with the truth.

On 17th April 1949 he had written in the *Sunday Herald*:

Two years ago – and on countless occasions since – I urged the vital need for an auditorium which would provide both a permanent home for the Sydney Symphony Orchestra and accommodation for opera, ballet, choral performances and drama. Since the concert-shell in which the orchestra will perform is a removable unit, there will be no undue interference with scenery and properties which might be currently in use by an opera company or ballet group.

We must have a theatre dedicated night and day to the performance of the masterpieces of orchestral, operatic, ballet and choral literature, a proud symbol of Australian culture and a home for the elite of Australian performers.

Ironically the article was headed 'How long before our Opera House dream comes true?'

Eugene had emphasised Sydney's need for an opera house to merit recognition as a national and eventually international centre for the performing arts. He might have welcomed the Queen as artistic supremo of an enviable empire: Artistic Director and Chief Conductor of The Australian Opera and Ballet Company as well as the Sydney Symphony Orchestra. But events conspired to rob him of this dream.

In the last ten years, Sydney has enjoyed a velvet revolution as far as morality is concerned. This is typified by the contrast between the treatment of Eugene in 1956 and Stuart Challender, Chief Conductor of the SSO from 1987.

Challender, only the second Australian-born musician to hold the post, died of AIDS in December 1991 and has been widely eulogised for his honesty and bravery in facing the disease. The ABC gave full publicity to his death and its cause.

King's Cross in the 1990s outbids Soho or Greenwich Village with the exuberance of its alternative lifestyle. Some old-fashioned Sydneysiders still utter muffled complaints at the wilder excesses of Gay Mardi Gras but in cultural circles there is a laid-back, total acceptance of sexual non-conformity. Eugene remains an embarrassment; he was disgraced for attempting to smuggle into the country the kind of pornographic material that is now freely available on magazine racks and bookstalls. The actual content of his films and photos has never been publicly revealed but in today's liberal climate, no one would take exception to a harmless little private indulgence. This version may salve Sydney's artistic conscience but it does little to right the wrongs done to him or explain the mystery surrounding them.

The full story may never be known yet it continues to feed many fertile imaginations. A drama documentary commissioned for Australian TV claims that Eugene was being blackmailed for homosexuality. Renée Goossens is convinced that her biography of her father *Facing the Music*, in which she claims that he was working for the Secret Service, was stymied by an agent disguised as a British naval officer, who mysteriously left the country. 'People think that you are mad when you start mentioning suitors who may have been Secret Service men,' she explained. 'They think you are trying to make excuses. I wish I knew what did happen.'[8]

The centenary of Sir Eugene Goossens' birth in 1993 has received far more attention in Australia than in the land of his birth. The ABC organised a lecture series and extensive commemorative broadcasts, culminating in 'A Goossens Tribute' scheduled for 19th November, a public concert in the Opera House Concert Hall given by the Sydney Symphony Orchestra conducted by the British conductor, Vernon Handley.

In England, he is dimly remembered as a conductor but sadly, as a composer, most of his music no longer vibrates in the public memory. Sidonie, writing to ask Simon Rattle, Music Director of the City of Birmingham Symphony Orchestra and outstanding conductor of his generation, whether he planned to programme any of her brother's works for his centenary was told by Rattle that he knew of Goossens as a conductor but was unaware that he had been a composer as well.

Ironically in London it was only at Australia House that a Centenary Concert of his compositions was given.

NOTES

OB   *Overture and Beginners*, Autobiography of Eugene Goossens, Methuen 1951.

LHS   *Life on a Harp String*, Autobiography of Marie Goossens, Thorne Printing & Publishing Co Ltd, 1987.

GA   Goossens Archives.

EGII   Eugene Goossens II.

EGIII   Eugene Goossens III.

Heritage

1. Interview with Marie Goossens, 27th February 1989.
2. Euphrosyne Parepa-Rosa (1836 – 1874). Scottish soprano of Wallachian descent.
3. OB, p.6.
4. EGII to Jansi Goossens, 15th January 1941.
5. 'Memories of Mummers and the Old Standard Theatre', Albert Douglass, *The Era*, London 1924. The Douglass family ran the Standard Theatre, Shoreditch for forty years.
6. *My Theatrical and Musical Recollections*, Emily Soldene, Downey & Co, London 1897.
7. Letter quoted by kind permission of Mrs Rhonda Hammond.
8. Charles Dickens to John Forster, 11th January 1838.
9. OB, p.22.
10. ibid, p.17.

Liverpool

1. *Come Listen to my Song*, Roland Foster, Collins, 1949, p.29.
2. Unidentified press review, 18th May 1895. Prospectus of 'The Goossens Choir' for 1896 – 97.
3. Letters from Edward Elgar, 20th and 26th March 1902. Facsimile OB.
4. LHS, p.4.
5. Interview with Marie Goossens, 24th February 1987.
6. OB, p.61.
7. Interview with Sidonie Goossens, 25th February 1987.
8. *Music in the Wind*, Barry Wynne, Souvenir Press, 1967, p.51.
9. Interview with Sidonie Goossens, 25th February 1987.
10. Interview with Marie Goossens, 24th February 1987.

The Goossens

11. OB, pp.42 – 3.
12. Interview with Sidonie Goossens, 25th February 1987.
13. OB, p.43.
14. Interview with Sidonie Goossens, 25th February 1987.
15. ibid.
16. Interview with Marie Goossens, 24th February 1987.
17. Charles Reynolds to EGII, 4th September 1908.
18. ibid, 7th October 1908 and 25th June 1909.
19. LHS, p.14.
20. OB, p.55.
21. LHS, p.18.
22. OB, p.59.
23. Two undated letters headed '125, Chatham Street, Liverpool. Thursday evening' and 'Sunday'.
24. Like the Goossens children, the four Harrison sisters, Beatrice, May, Monica and Margaret were all outstandingly musically gifted; May and Margaret as violinists, Monica as a singer. Beatrice (1892 – 1965), the cellist, became the most famous as a favourite performer of Elgar and Delius and for her pioneer BBC broadcast on 19th May 1924 when she charmed the nightingales to sing with her cello.
25. Interview with Marie Goossens, 24th February 1987.
26. Interview with Jennie Goossens, 16th June 1987.

London

1. OB, p.62.
2. ibid, p.63.
3. ibid, p.81.
4. 'Some Aspects of the Present Musical Situation', lecture given by Sir Arthur Bliss to the Musical Association, 1923, *Bliss on Music*, OUP 1991, p.41.
5. OB, p.88.
6. *Times*, 21st June 1912.
7. Letter from Charles Reynolds, 4th May 1912.
8. LHS, p.32.
9. *Adrian Boult*, Michael Kennedy, Hamish Hamilton 1987, p.57. (LHS, p.35.)
10. LHS, p.33.
11. Interview with Sidonie Goossens, 20th October 1992.
12. LHS, p.106.
13. Léon Goossens in conversation with Edwin Roxburgh, 1975, in preparation for the Menuhin Music Guide.
14. Léon Goossens', BBC Television, 1st May 1966.
15. Interview with Sidonie Goossens, 2nd December 1991.
16. OB, p.95.
17. *Music at Midnight*, Muriel Draper, Harper & Bros 1929, p.33.

Notes

18. ibid, p.151.
19. ibid, p.76.
20. ibid, p.75.
21. ibid, p.73.
22. Edward, Viscount Grey of Falloden, 3rd August 1914.

The Great War

1. Interview with Eva Turner, *Manchester Evening News*, 19th June 1929.
2. LHS, p.40.
3. ibid.
4. ibid, p.44.
5. Interview with Sidonie Goossens, 2nd February 1991.
6. *Sir John Barbirolli*, Charles Rigby, John Sherratt & Son, 1948, p.21.
7. EGIII to Philip Heseltine, undated.
8. *Delius: A Life in Letters*, Lionel Carley, Scolar Press, 1988, p.163.
9. Delius to Heseltine, 27th May 1917.
10. Delius to C W Orr, 10th April 1917.
11. *The Music Student*, November 1916.
12. Heseltine to EGIII, 12th September 1916.
13. Heseltine to Colin Taylor, 12th November 1915.
14. LHS, p.36.
15. Léon Goossens in conversation with Edwin Roxburgh, 1975.
16. OB, p.109.
17. ibid, p.115.
18. ibid, p.118.
19. ibid, p.120.
20. Interview with Marie Goossens, 24th February 1987.
21. OB, p.121.
22. ibid, p.122.
23. ibid.
24. *A Mingled Chime*, Thomas Beecham, Bart., Hutchinson & Co Ltd, 1944, p.143.
25. OB, p.128.
26. Léon gave a detailed account of his war experiences and his escape from death to Barry Wynne.
27. Interview with Marie Goossens, 24th February 1987.

My Heart Loosens When I Listen To Goossens

1. *Cadet Rousselle*: Eugene later orchestrated the work and the new version was used as an interlude in the Carmargo Society's Ballet Season in 1932.
2. *Telegraph*, 24th March 1919.
3. *Globe*, 25th May 1919.
4. Interview with Sidonie Goossens, 2nd December 1991.

5. *London Has A Garden*, Autobiography of Clemence Dane, Michael Joseph, 1964.
6. OB, p.142.
7. *New Witness*, 12th November 1919.
8. OB, p.146.
9. J D Fergusson, innovative Scottish painter, husband of the dancer, Margaret Morris, qv.
10. Interview with Horace Johnson, *Musical Courier*, 20th August 1932, quoted in *The Instrumental Chamber Music of Sir Eugene Goossens*, Judith Smith, University of Cincinnati, 1987, p.9.
11. 'Reflections on Three Works of Eugene Goossens', Arthur Bliss, *Musical News and Herald*, 4th June 1921.
12. Malcolm Rudland, Secretary of Peter Warlock Society, to Carole Rosen, 12th October 1992.
13. *George Eastman*, Carl W Ackerman, Constable & Co, 1930, pp.143 & 237.
14. OB, p.139.
15. *The Art of J D Fergusson*, Margaret Morris, Blackie, 1974, p.135.
16. OB, p.137.
17. *Arnold Bax: A Composer and his Times*, Lewis Foreman, Scolar Press 1983.
18. OB, pp.161 – 3.
19. Aurelie Révy-Chapman to EGII, 16th February 1922.
20. Tyrone Guthrie to EGII, 11th March 1922.
21. OB, p.40.
22. ibid, p.193.
23. *Musical Times*, April 1922.
24. OB, p.208.
    (Margaret Morris also describes the Summer School at Antibes in *My Life in Movement*, Peter Owen, 1969.)
25. EGIII to EGII written from Gloucester Cottage, Collingham Road, London SW7, August 1923.
26. Jelka Delius to Adine O'Neill, 20th January 1926.
27. 'Memories of *Hassan*'. Basil Dean, *Radio Times*, 31st October 1952.
28. Delius to Universal Edition, 28th September 1923.
29. Interview with Sidonie Goossens, 10th December 1992.

Sisters

1. Interview with Marie Goossens, 27th October 1987.
2. Interview with Sidonie Goossens, 28th October 1987.
3. ibid.
4. LHS, p.68.
5. Interview with Sidonie Goossens, 22nd February 1989.
6. 'Two Lady Harpists', unidentified press cutting, September 1922. EGII Diaries.

Notes

7. LHS, p.49.
8. 'Here We Are Again', article, W Crawford Snowden, source unknown.
9. Interview with Marie Goossens, 27th October 1987.
10. Marie Goossens to her parents, Crown & Anchor Hotel, Ipswich, 22nd April 1923.
11. *Musical News and Herald*, 7th February 1925.
12. Interview with Sidonie Goossens, 28th October 1987.
13. Harold Holt of Messrs Lionel Powell & Holt (later Harold Holt Ltd).
14. Interview with Sidonie Goossens, 10th December 1992.
15. ibid, 22nd February 1989.
16. *The Gramophone*, September 1927.
17. *Morning Post*, 28th January 1925.
18. *Musical News and Herald*, 21st February 1925.
19. Frederick Laurence to EGII, 1st November 1925.
20. Interview with Marie Goossens, 27th October 1987 and LHS, p.53.
21. ibid.
22. LHS, p.51.
23. Talk given by Sidonie Goossens to the Delius Society, 23rd September 1992.
24. Interview with Sidonie Goossens, 22nd February 1989.
25. Rex Workman to Mr and Mrs Goossens, June 1921.
26. Interview with Sidonie Goossens, 2nd December 1991.
27. ibid.
28. ibid, 10th December 1992.
29. ibid.
30. ibid.
31. ibid.
32. ibid.

Rochester

1. *Utopia Limited*, Act I.
2. *New York Times*, 21st March 1920.
3. OB, p.215.
4. *New York Times*, 18th October 1923.
5. OB, p.219.
6. *Mrs Coolidge and her British Connections*, Stephen Banfield, American Music 1986, p.66.
7. *Adrian Boult*, Michael Kennedy, Hamish Hamilton, 1987.
8. *My Own Trumpet*, Sir Adrian Boult, Hamish Hamilton, 1973, p.56.
9. *Musical Times*, 1st April 1924.
10. *Musical News and Herald*, 20th September 1924.
11. 'Eugene Goossens discusses conducting', *Musical America*, 19th November 1927.
12. EGIII to parents, 9th October 1925.
13. ibid.
14. ibid, 25th March 1926.

The Goossens

15. Interview with Anne Goossens Obermer, 17th June 1987.
16. OB, p.239.
17. *Encounters with Stravinsky*, Paul Horgan, Bodley Head, 1972, p.32.
18. Paul Horgan to EGIII, 9th December 1933.
19. *New York Times*, 6th September 1929.
20. Ralph Holmes, *Detroit Evening Times*, 30th November 1928.
21. OB, p.264.
22. Interview with Anne Goossens Obermer, 3rd July 1991.
23. *Musical Courier*, 6th December 1930.

Diaghilev, Chaliapin and Arnold Benett

1. Catalogue of Costumes and Curtains from Diaghilev and de Basil ballets, Sotheby & Co, 17th July 1968. Introduction by Richard Buckle.
2. OB, p.230.
3. LHS, p.48.
4. Interview with Dame Ninette de Valois, 22nd April 1991.
5. OB, p.247.
6. EGIII to parents, 19th March 1928.
7. OB, p.256.
8. *Daily Mail*, 23rd June 1928.
9. OB, p.97.
10. Arnold Bennett to Messrs J & W Chester, 4th March 1929.
11. ibid, 3rd January 1929.
12. OB, p.270.
13. *Sunday Times*, 30th June 1929.
14. *Observer*, 30th June 1929.

The World's Greatest Oboist

1. Programme in BBC *Creation of Music* Series, Far Eastern Service 2nd June 1949.
2. *The Listener*, 19th January 1938.
3. *Marcato*, October 1931.
4. *Delius As I Knew Him*, Eric Fenby, G Bell & Sons, 1936, p.23.
5. Léon Goossens interview with James Brown, April 1983.
6. Interview with Richard Temple Savage, 28th February 1993.
7. *Daily Telegraph*, 4th October 1930.
8. 'Léon Goossens', BBC Television, 1st May 1966.
9. Léon Goossens in conversation with Edwin Roxburgh, 1975.
10. Interview with Helen Gaskill, 26th February 1991.
11. Interview with Evelyn Rothwell (Lady Barbirolli), 19th February 1991.
12. Interview with Natalie Caine (Mrs James), 27th February 1991.
13. Interview with Margaret Eliot (Mrs Asher), 25th January 1991.
14. Interview with Cecil James, 27th February 1991.
15. Léon Goossens in conversation with Edwin Roxburgh, 1975.

Notes

Welcome To Cincinnati

1. *Edward Elgar: A Creative Life*, Jerrold Northrop Moore, OUP, 1984, pp.496 – 8.
2. *Time* Magazine, 18th May 1931.
3. *New York Times*, 7th May 1931.
4. The *Times*, 6th February 1931.
5. The *Star*, 25th May 1931.
6. *Cincinnati Times Star*, 16th October 1931.
7. EGIII to parents, 23rd October 1931.
8. EGIII, unpublished memoirs. (Volume II.)
9. *Dayton Herald*, 8th December 1931.
10. *Bax: A Composer and his Times*, Lewis Foreman, Scolar Press 1983.
11. EGIII to parents, 5th May 1932.
12. ibid, 21st November 1932.
13. ibid, 23rd March 1933.
14. ibid, 17th April 1934.
15. Interview with Sidonie Goossens Scott, 8th February 1992.
16. EGIII to parents, 14th November 1933.
17. ibid, 7th June 1934.
18. ibid, 11th July 1934.
19. ibid, 3rd May 1934.
20. ibid, 17th October 1934.
21. Paul Wittgenstein to EGIII, 17th December 1934.
22. EGIII to parents, 18th December 1934.
23. ibid, 13th December 1937.
24. ibid, 18th December 1934.
25. ibid, 2nd January 1935.
26. ibid, 18th January 1935.
27. ibid, 13th February 1935.
28. Interview with Sidonie Goossens Scott, 8th February 1992.
29. Interview with Sir Keith Falkner, 7th May 1991.

Léon, Marie and the LPO

1. EGIII to parents, 24th March 1932.
2. Ernest Newman, *Sunday Times*, 9th October 1932.
3. Léon Goossens in conversation with Alan Blyth, The *Times*, 14th June 1972.
4. LHS, p.58.
5. Léon Goossens in conversation with Edwin Roxburgh, 1975.
6. Interview with Gwydion Brooke, 3rd December 1991.
7. *Beecham Remembered*, Humphrey Proctor-Gregg, Duckworth 1966, p.66.
8. Léon Goossens in conversation with Edwin Roxburgh, 1975.
9. EGIII to EGII, 13th November 1934.
10. Jack Brymer, Address at Memorial Service for Léon Goossens, Westminster Abbey, 16th May 1988.

425

11. Interview with Jack Brymer, 18th March 1991.
12. Interview with Richard Temple Savage, 28th February 1993.
13. op. cit., Humphrey Proctor-Gregg, p.65.
14. Interview with Raymond Cooke OBE, 17th July 1991.
15. LHS, p.72.
16. ibid, p.64.
17. EGIII to parents, 11th July 1934.
18. Interview with Richard Temple Savage, 28th February 1993.
19. 'Léon Goossens', BBC Television, 1st May 1966.
20. Léon Goossens interview with James Brown for Royal College of Music Magazine, Centenary Number, vol.79, no.1, spring 1983.
21. Interview with Lord Harewood, 30th May 1991.
22. Yehudi Menuhin Music Guides OBOE, Léon Goossens and Edwin Roxburgh, Macdonald and Jane's, 1977.
23. Facsimile of Elgar's letter reproduced in Menuhin Music Guide, 21st January 1931.
24. Britten's diary, 6th August 1933, Britten – Pears Library.
25. Interview with David McKenna, 19th March 1991.
26. LHS, p.67.
27. BBC Written Archives Centre, Caversham.
28. J E Matthews to EGII, 10th March 1935.
29. EGIII to parents, 22nd August 1936.
30. Interview with Tony Laurence, 1st April 1987.
31. *The Baton and the Jackboot*, Dr Bertha Geissmar, Hamish Hamilton, 1944.
32. LHS, pp.59 – 60.
33. Speech of Welcome to the Berlin Philharmonic, Sir Thomas Beecham, Savoy Hotel, June 1937.
34. Interview with Raymond Cooke, 17th July 1991.
35. Rutland Boughton to Léon Goossens, 18th February 1938.
36. First London performance, 11th October 1936.
37. EGIII to parents, 26th October 1936.
38. Sir Donald Tovey to Léon Goossens, 8th November 1937.
39. LHS, p.59.
40. A Walter Kramer to EGIII, 10th June 1939.

Sid and Bumps

1. Interview with Sidonie Goossens, 20th October 1992.
2. ibid.
3. Interview with Elizabeth Welch, 10th September 1991.
4. Interview with Sidonie Goossens, 20th October 1992.
5. EGIII to parents, 11th July 1934.
6. Interview with Sidonie Goossens, 20th October 1992.
7. EGIII to parents, 14th November 1935.
8. ibid, 10th August 1934.

Notes

9. *Radio Times*, 23rd November 1934.
10. Interview with Sidonie Goossens, 20th October 1992.
11. ibid.
12. Programme notes from concert series presented in 1981 by Eagle Star at 22, Arlington Street (now William Kent House).
13. Interview with Sidonie Goossens, 10th March 1993.
14. ibid, 20th October 1992.
15. EGIII to parents, 3rd August 1936.
16. ibid, 17th August 1936.
17. ibid, 6th September 1936.
18. ibid, 13th December 1936.
19. Interview with Sidonie Goossens, 20th October 1992.
20. Interview with Lionel Salter, 17th October 1990.
21. Interview with Dallas Bower, 15th October 1991.
22. EGIII to parents, 10th April 1938.
23. Bernard Greenbaum to Carole Rosen, 26th December 1991.
24. Interview with Kyla Greenbaum, 30th May 1991.
25. Hyam Greenbaum (1901–1942), Cecil Gray Music Review, August 1942.
26. EGII Diary, 18th January 1939.
27. Interview with Sidonie Goossens, 20th October 1992.
28. ibid.
29. ibid.
30. ibid.
31. Bernard Greenbaum to Carole Rosen, 26th December 1991.

Don Juan de Mañara

1. Composer's Foreword to published score.
2. Arnold Bennett to EGIII, 30th September 1930.
3. Excerpts from the unpublished memoirs describing the genesis of *Don Juan de Mañara*, were published in *Composer*, Winter 1967 – 68.
4. Ernest Newman, *Sunday Times*, 11th July 1937.
5. Constant Lambert, *Referee*, 11th July 1937.
6. *Morning Post*, 25th June 1937.
7. *Evening Standard*, 25th June 1937.
8. *Sunday Times*, 25th June 1937.
9. EGIII to parents, 6th December 1937.
10. EGIII to David Webster, 29th June 1953.
11. ibid.

Inspirational and Talented Guidance

1. BBC Internal Memorandum, 31st March 1936, BBC Written Archives, Caversham.
2. *Musical Times*, August 1935.

3. EGIII to parents, 6th March 1935.
4. ibid, 14th November 1935.
5. ibid, 16th December 1935.
6. ibid, 30th April 1936.
7. *Los Angeles Evening Herald*, 22nd July 1936.
8. Interview with Sidonie Goossens Scott, 9th February 1992.
9. EGIII to parents, 10th August 1936.
10. ibid, 6th September 1936.
11. ibid, 14th September 1936.
12. ibid, 27th July 1936.
13. ibid, 22nd August 1936.
14. ibid, 6th September 1936.
15. ibid, 17th August 1936.
16. Percy Grainger to EGIII, 4th April 1940.
17. Obituary for Percy Grainger, EGIII, *Music and Musicians*, April 1961.
18. EGIII to parents, 1st November 1937.
19. ibid, 12th March 1938.
20. ibid, 24th April 1938.
21. ibid, 3rd April 1938.
22. EGIII to Ibbs & Tillett, 10th April 1938.
23. Ernest Newman, *Sunday Times*, 6th November 1938.
24. *Daily Telegraph*, 10th November 1938.
25. The *Times*, 10th November 1938.
26. Interview with Anne Goossens Obermer, 17th June 1987.
27. ibid.
28. Interview with Sidonie Goossens Scott, 9th February 1992.
29. EGIII to parents, 18th November 1938.
30. Unpublished memoirs.
31. Interview with Sidonie Goossens Scott, 9th February 1992.
32. EGIII to *Musical Courier*, 1st November 1939.
33. EGIII to parents, 8th October 1939.
34. ibid, 11th April 1941.
35. Unpublished memoirs.
36. EGIII to parents, 8th November 1939.
37. William Walton to Janet Goossens, 8th January 1940.
38. EGIII to parents, 11th April 1941.
39. ibid, 15th August 1940.
40. ibid, 3rd October 1940.
41. ibid, 18th November 1940.
42. Benjamin Britten to Wulf Scherchen, 10th September 1940.
43. EGIII to Hans Heinsheimer, 27th September 1940.
44. Janet Goossens to Benjamin Britten and Peter Pears, 24th September 1940.
45. ibid, 6th January 1941.
46. Benjamin Britten to Antonio and Peggy Brosa, 10th March 1943.

Notes

A Rather Nice Person in Many Ways

1. EGIII to parents, 19th December 1941.
2. ibid, 27th February 1941.
3. *Clue in Two Flats*, R L F McCombs, Mystery House, New York, 1940.
4. EGIII to parents, 21st January 1941.
5. Interview with Sidonie Goossens Scott, 9th February 1992.
6. EGIII to parents, 6th January 1942.
7. Interview with Marie Goossens, 24th February 1987.
8. EGIII to parents, 16th April 1942.
9. ibid.
10. ibid, 16th May 1942.
11. ibid, 13th July 1942.
12. ibid, 19th February 1942.
13. *New York Times*, 2nd March 1942.
14. ibid, 6th March 1942.
15. EGIII to parents, 19th February 1942.
16. ibid, 12th March 1942.
17. ibid, 13th July 1942.
18. ibid, 30th May 1942.
19. Book Review, *Cincinnati Post*, 1st February 1942.
20. EGIII to parents, 23rd September 1943.
21. *New York Times*, 23rd January 1944.
22. EGIII letter published in the *New York Times*, 30th January 1944.
23. *Cincinnati Times-Star*, 26th February 1944.
24. Report, *New York Times*, 28th April 1944.
25. Philip Dreyfuss interview with Judith Smith, Cincinnati, 13th December 1982. Interview with Philip Dreyfuss (by telephone), 29th October 1992.
26. Gunther Schuller to Carole Rosen, 11th December 1991.
27. EGIII to parents, 21st May 1944.
28. Gunther Schuller to Carole Rosen, 11th December 1991.
29. Interview with Philip Dreyfuss (by telephone) 29th October 1992.
30. EGIII to parents, 21st May 1944.
31. Donie Goossens to EGII and Annie Goossens, 16th October 1944.
32. Interview with Sidonie Goossens Scott, 9th February 1992.
33. *Chicago Daily Tribune*, 9th November 1944.
34. *Chicago Sun*, 9th November 1944.
35. EGIII to parents, 5th November 1944.
36. Leonard Bernstein to EGIII, 21st November 1944.
37. EGIII to parents, 30th March 1945.
38. ibid, 9th October 1944.
39. *San Francisco Chronicle*, 5th May 1945.
40. EGIII cable to parents, 3rd August 1945.
41. Interview with Sidonie Goossens Scott, 9th February 1992.

Covent Garden: The Lost Opportunity

1. Ralph Hawkes to David Webster, 11th January 1945.
2. EGIII to parents, 10th June 1945.
3. Ralph Hawkes to David Webster, 4th March 1946.
4. David Webster to EGIII, 26th February 1946.
5. EGIII to Ralph Hawkes, 12th March 1946.
6. Lord Keynes to Ralph Hawkes, 12th March 1946.
7. EGIII to unnamed recipient, 23rd May 1958, GA.
8. Minutes of Meeting of Ballet Sub-Committee, Royal Opera House, Covent Garden, 20th September 1954.
9. Minutes of Meeting of Board of Directors, Royal Opera House, Covent Garden, Ltd, 21st December 1954.

Britain Can Take It

1. *Philharmonic Decade*, Thomas Russell, Hutchinson, 1944.
2. Ralph Vaughan Williams to Léon Goossens, 23rd May 1944.
3. Menuhin Music Guides.
4. LHS, p.91.
5. ibid, p.84.
6. ibid.
7. ibid, p.124.
8. Interview with Sidonie Goossens, 20th October 1992.
9. Sir Adrian Boult to EGIII, 2nd June 1942.
10. Interview with Sidonie Goossens, 20th October 1992.
11. Sidonie Goossens to W W Thompson, Concerts Manager, 26th January 1943.
12. Interview with Sidonie Goossens, 25th February 1987.
13. EGIII to parents, 26th January 1946.
14. ibid, 12th December 1945.
15. ibid, 27th February 1946.
16. ibid, 30th April 1946.
17. ibid, 28th July 1946.
18. Interview with Sidonie Goossens, 10th March 1993.

Challenging Australia

1. Harold Holt to EGIII, 17th September 1936.
2. EGIII to EGII, 20th September 1936.
3. EGIII to parents, 10th June 1946.
4. Interview with Lady Harewood (Patricia Tuckwell), 30th May 1991.
5. *Facing the Music: An Orchestral Player's Notebook*, Helen Bainton, Currawong Publishing Co Ltd, 1967, p.48.
6. *Bernard Heinze*, Thérèse Radic, Macmillan 1986, p.62.
7. *Daily Telegraph*, 4th November 1946.

8. *Daily Mail*, 4th November 1946.
9. *Daily Telegraph*, 18th October 1946.
10. *Daily Express*, 18th October 1946.
11. *The Henry Wood Proms*, David Cox, BBC 1980.
12. Interview with Sir Charles Mackerras, 20th May 1991.
13. *Cincinnati Times-Star*, 18th November 1946.
14. *Cincinnati Enquirer*, 19th November 1946.
15. EGIII to EGII, 24th November 1946.
16. EGIII to Charles Moses, undated.
17. ibid, 26th February 1947.
18. *Sydney Telegraph*, 15th July 1947.
19. *Sydney Daily Telegraph*, 2nd August 1947.
20. *Sunday Sun*, 20th July 1947.
21. *Sydney Sun*, 6th July 1947.
22. *Tempo*, July 1947.
23. EGIII to EGII, 13th July 1947.
24. ibid, 18th March 1947.
25. *Sydney Morning Herald*, 17th November 1947.
26. ibid.
27. Interview with Lady Harewood (Patricia Tuckwell), 30th May 1991.
28. Interview with Barry Tuckwell, 2nd June 1991.
29. Interview with Sir Charles Mackerras, 20th May 1991.
30. Percy Grainger to EGIII, 16th November 1947.

Music is the Birthright of the People

1. *Newcastle Morning Herald*, 20th December 1947.
2. Interview with Brenton Langbein, 6th September 1991.
3. Interview with Rex Ellis, 9th February 1992.
4. ibid.
5. *Confessions of an Actor*, Sir Laurence Olivier, Weidenfeld & Nicolson, 1982.
6. 13th July 1949, A.L. Kelly.
7. *Sunday Herald*, 21st July 1951.
8. ibid.
9. *Facing the Music: An Orchestral Player's Notebook*, Helen Bainton, Currawong Publishing Co Ltd, 1967, p.61.
10. ibid.
11. *Sydney Morning Herald*, 6th July 1948.
12. *Bernard Heinze*, Thérèse Radic, Macmillan, 1986, pp.179 – 80.
13. Interview with Phyllis Williams, 6th February 1992.
14. Douglas M Allen, *Cincinnati Times-Star*, date unknown.
15. Interview with Phyllis Williams, 6th February 1992.
16. *Playing for Australia*, Charles Buttrose, Macmillan Melbourne, 1982, p.60.
17. Interview with Sidonie Goossens Scott, 9th February 1992.

The Goossens

18. ibid.
19. Sidonie Goossens Scott to Carole Rosen, 29th March 1992.
20. Interview with Albert Wargren, 11th February 1992.
21. ibid.
22. ibid.
23. Interview with Renée Goossens, 12th February 1992.

Boomerang and Fire Sticks

1. *Sydney Morning Herald*, 17th January 1949.
2. EGIII to *Sydney Morning Herald*, 17th January 1949.
3. *Sydney Morning Herald*, 18th January 1949.
4. *Sydney Daily Telegraph*, 18th January 1949.
5. EGIII, 17th January 1949.
6. *The Petrov Story*, Michael Bialoguski, Heinemann, 1955, p.47.
7. ibid.
8. *Play On!*, Phillip Sametz, Australian Broadcasting Corporation, 1992, p.176.
9. Interview with Brenton Langbein, 6th September 1991.
10. EGIII to Charles Moses, 23rd March 1949.
11. op. cit., Phillip Sametz, p.158.
12. The *Times*, 27th August 1949.
13. The *Scotsman*, 26th August 1949.
14. *Scottish Daily Mail*, 27th August 1949.
15. *Newcastle Sun*, 29th May 1949.
16. R Graham Taylor (236, Broadway, Horsforth, Leeds) to the Editor, unknown publication, 19th September 1949.
17. Interview with Sidonie Goossens, 2nd December 1991.
18. Address given by Ernest Llewellyn at the NSW Conservatorium Goossens Memorial Concert, 19th October 1973.
19. Interview with Ruth Llewellyn, 30th January 1992.
20. Interview with Eva Wagner, 30th January 1992.
21. EGIII to Charles Moses, 24th April 1950.
22. Interview with Sidonie Goossens Scott, 9th February 1992.
23. Interview with Keith Falkner, 7th May 1991.
24. *Daily Mirror*, 4th March 1950.
25. EGIII to Charles Moses, 16th March 1950.
26. Interview with Brenton Langbein, 6th September 1991.
27. Interview with Sidonie Goossens Scott, 9th February 1992.

So Dignified and Aloof

1. Interview with Dame Joan Sutherland, 21st March 1991.
2. *Sydney Sun*, 9th August 1951.
3. Interview with Brenton Langbein, 6th September 1991.
4. *Age*, 23rd October 1951.

432

5. *Sydney Morning Herald* (assessing Goossens' first five years of tenure), 12th July 1952.
6. Interview with Sidonie Goossens Scott, 9th February 1992.
7. Interview (by telephone) with Richard Bonynge, 30th April 1991.
8. Interview with Geoffrey Parsons, 5th May 1989.
9. Interview with Raymond Fisher (Fischer)*, 9th July 1992.
10. *Introduction à une Sociologie de la Musique*, Alfons Silbermann, Presses Universitaires de France, 1955.
11. Interview with Anne Menzies, 11th February 1992.
12. Interview with Donald Hazelwood, 11th February 1992.
13. *ABC Weekly*, 19th April 1952.
14. *Sunday Herald*, 17th April 1949.
15. *Sunday Telegraph*, 19th February 1950.
16. Interview with Phyllis Williams, 6th February 1992.
17. *The Strange Case of Eugene Goossens and Other Tales from the Opera House*, Ava Hubble, Collins, 1988, p.57.
18. *Sydney Morning Herald*, 31st November 1954.
19. *Daily Telegraph*, 18th May 1955.
20. ibid, 20th May 1955.
21. *Truth*, 22nd May 1955.

Playing From the Heart

1. The *Times*, 25th March 1958.
2. Léon Goossens interview with Alan Blyth, the *Times*, 14th June 1972.
3. 'Léon Goossens', BBC Television, 1st May 1966.
4. Sir Keith Falkner Tribute, Haddo House Chapel, May 1988.
5. Interview with Jennie Goossens, 17th July 1991.
6. Interview with Lionel Salter, 17th October 1990.
7. Interview with Jack Brymer, 18th March 1991.
8. Interview with Lionel Salter, 17th October 1990.
9. Mentioned by both Lionel Salter and Felix Aprahamian when interviewed.
10. Sir Arthur Penn to Léon Goossens, 28th June 1940.
11. EGII to Léon Goossens, 2nd January 1950.
12. LHS, p.92.
13. ibid, p.93.
14. Sidonie Goossens talk given to the Delius Society, 23rd September 1992.
15. LHS, p.124.
16. Interview with Sidonie Goossens, 10th March 1993.
17. ibid.
18. LHS, p.98.

*now reverted to the original spelling of the family name.

19. Interview with Sidonie Goossens, 10th March 1993.
20. ibid.
21. LHS, p.107.
22. ibid, p.129.
23. Interview with Tony Goossens, 1st April 1987.
24. Interview with Pam Goossens, 1st April 1987.
25. BBC General Overseas Service, 18th February 1952.
26. Interview with Mabel Lovering, 24th June 1991. (Lovering was Léon Goossens' accompanist and a family friend.)
27. Interview with Benedicta Cooksey (Goossens), 11th June 1991.
28. Interview with Corinne Lopez (Goossens), 3rd December 1991.
29. Interview with Jennie Goossens, 12th July 1991.
30. ibid, 16th June 1987.
31. Interview with Corinne Lopez (Goossens), 3rd December 1991.
32. Interview with Jennie Goossens, 16th June 1987.
33. Interview with Corinne Lopez (Goossens), 3rd December 1991.
34. Interview with Jennie Goossens, 16th June 1987.
35. ibid, 17th July 1991.
36. Interview with James (Jimmy) Brown, 8th July 1991.

Apocalypse

1. Dene Barnett, *Sydney Morning Herald*, 23rd November 1954.
2. ibid, Steward Harvey.
3. *The Canon*, January 1954.
4. *Melbourne Argus*, 23rd November 1954.
5. *Sydney Morning Herald*, 23rd November 1954.
6. EGIII to Richard Howgill, 11th March 1955.
7. Charles Moses to EGIII, 29th November 1954.
8. Aleister Crowley (1875 – 1947). Known as 'The Beast'; a self-styled magician, widely accused of being a seducer of youth and promoter of the Black Arts.
9. Interview with Brenton Langbein, 6th September 1991.
10. Interview with Renée Goossens, 12th February 1992.
11. Interview with Felix Aprahamian, 15th November 1991.
12. *People*, 16th June 1954.
13. Critic Eunice Garner.
14. Léon Goossens to Benjamin Britten, 29th November 1951.
15. Interview with Lady Barbirolli, 19th February 1991.
16. Interview with Raymond Fisher (Fischer), 9th July 1992.
17. Interview with Clifford Goodchild, 10th February 1992.
18. *Radio – Active*, 25th July 1955.
19. *News*, 13th June 1955.
20. BBC Confidential Memorandum, 12th January 1955.

Notes

Fall of a Titan

1. *Sydney Daily Mirror*, 9th March 1956.
2. ibid.
3. *Sydney Morning Herald*, 22nd March 1956.
4. ibid.
5. ibid.
6. op. cit., Ava Hubble, p.62.
7. *Sydney Morning Herald*, 12th April 1956.
8. Interview with Mrs Ritchie, 13th February 1992.
9. Interview with Dr Ronald Smart, Director, NSW State Conservatorium (1993), 12th February 1992.
10. Interview with Anne Menzies, 11th February 1992.
11. Interview with Clifford Goodchild, 10th February 1992.
12. Interview with Phyllis Williams, 6th February 1992.
13. Interview with Dr Thérèse Radic, 15th February 1992.
14. Interview with Sidonie Goossens Scott, 9th February 1992.
15. Interview with Albert Wargren, 11th February 1992.
16. *Sydney Telegraph*, 27th May 1956.
17. *Bernard Heinze*, Thérèse Radic, Macmillan 1986, pp.174 & 241.
18. op. cit., Ava Hubble, p.69.
19. *A Secret Country*, John Pilger, Jonathan Cape, 1989, p.162.
20. Interview with Renée Gossens, 12th February 1992.
21. Report of preliminary hearing in Sydney Central Court of Rosaleen Norton 'on a charge of committing an unnatural offence with her young lover', *Truth*, 3rd June 1956.
22. Interview with David Salter, Producer ABC TV, 8th September 1992.
23. *Pan's Daughter*, Nevill Drury, Collins, 1988, p.66.
24. Interview (by telephone) with Ron Best, 6th February 1992.

Aftermath

1. Minutes of Meeting of BBC Board of Governors, 26th April 1956.
2. Interview with Sidonie Goossens, 10th March 1993.
3. Interview with James (Jimmy) Brown, 8th July 1991.
4. EGIII, 14th July 1956.
5. Interview with Mabel Lovering, 24th June 1991.
6. Interview with Ursula Vaughan Williams, 30th April 1991.
7. Interview with Lord Harewood, 30th May 1991.
8. Interview with Brenton Langbein, 6th September 1991.
9. Interview with Sidonie Goossens, 10th March 1993.
10. EGIII to Benjamin Britten, 22nd March 1957.
11. Interview with Howard Williams, 13th June 1993.
12. *Montreal Gazette*, 9th March 1961.
13. Charles Moses to EGIII, 30th October 1956.
14. EGIII to Frank Hutchens, 28th June 1958.

15. EGIII to L J Keegan, Registrar, NSW State Conservatorium of Music, 16th April 1961.
16. Interview with Sir Charles Mackerras, 20th May 1991.
17. Interview with Geoffrey Parsons, 5th May 1989.
18. Interview (by telephone) with Dame Joan Sutherland, 21st March 1991.
19. Interview with Raymond Fisher (Fischer), 9th July 1992.
20. Interview (by telephone) with Barry Tuckwell, 2nd June 1991.
21. EGIII to Ian Wilson, 16th July 1960.
22. Interview with Irene Wilson, 20th July 1991.
23. EGIII to Richard Howgill, 12th August 1958.
24. Interview with Vivien Dixon, 17th March 1993.
25. Franz Reizenstein to EGIII, 13th April 1959.
26. John Ireland to EGIII, 21st April 1959.
27. *Music and Musicians*, June 1958.
28. EGIII to Mrs Roger K Rogan, 16th August 1960.
29. EGIII to Sir Laurence Olivier, 23rd May 1958.
30. Robert Graves to EGIII, 2nd May 1959.
31. EGIII to Rouben Mamoulian, 17th June 1960.
32. Interview *Records and Recordings*, April 1960.
33. *Thomas Beecham*, an Independent Biography, Charles Reid, Gollancz 1962, p.241.
34. *Observer*, 11th October 1992.
35. EGIII to William Glock, 28th January 1960.
36. John Warrack, *Sunday Telegraph*, 29th July 1960.
37. The *Times*, 8th September 1960.
38. EGIII to William Glock, 14th September 1960.
39. *Hi Fi/Stereo* review, April 1960.
40. *Daily Telegraph*, 12th August 1961.
41. EGIII to William Glock, 13th August 1961.
42. *Manchester Guardian*, 4th October 1960.
43. EGIII to William Glock, 15th February 1961.
44. Interview with Dame Joan Hammond, 14th February 1992.
    A Voice, a Life, Autobiography of Joan Hammond, Gollancz, 1970.
45. Dame Joan Hammond to EGIII, 5th December 1961.

Survivor

1. 'Léon Goossens', BBC Television, 1st May 1966.
2. *Music in the Wind*, Barry Wynne, Souvenir Press, 1967, p.1.
3. 'Léon Goossens', BBC Television, 1st May 1966.
4. op. cit., Barry Wynne, p.85.
5. 'Léon Goossens', BBC Television, 1st May 1966.
6. Interview with Jack Brymer, 18th March 1991.
7. 'Léon Goossens', BBC Television, 1st May 1966.
8. *New York Times*, 26th April 1965.

Notes

9. Interview with Brian Spink, 12th May 1993.
10. Léon Goossens interview with Roy Plomley, *Desert Island Discs*, 15th February 1960.
11. Herbert Howells to Léon Goossens, 16th August 1972.
12. Léon Goossens interview with Jimmy Brown, spring 1983.
13. Interview with Raymond Cooke, 17th July 1991.
14. Address at Léon Goossens' Funeral Service, Tunbridge Wells, 23rd February 1988.
15. Interview with Lady Aberdeen, 19th June 1992.
16. ibid.
17. Interview with Brian Spink, 12th May 1993.
18. Interview with Mabel Lovering, 24th June 1991.

Queens of the Harp

1. LHS, p.101.
2. Interview with Edwin Roxburgh, 25th November 1991.
3. LHS, p.115.
4. Obituary of Marie Goossens, the *Guardian*, 21st December 1991.
5. LHS, p.102.
6. ibid.
7. ibid, p.104.
8. ibid, p.105.
9. ibid, p.107.
10. ibid, p.105.
11. Interview with Sidonie Goossens, 10th March 1993.
12. Interview with Christopher Laurence, 22nd May 1987.
13. Interview with Andrew Laurence, 7th June 1993.
14. Interview with Sidonie Goossens, 10th March 1993.
15. ibid.
16. Sidonie Goossens BBC Radio 3 Tribute to Pierre Boulez, 3rd January 1993.
17. Pierre Boulez Tribute to Sidonie Goossens, 10th July 1992.
18. Interview with Vivien Dixon, 17th March 1993.
19. Interview with Sidonie Goossens, 10th March 1993.
20. Interview with Sidonie Goossens, 25th February 1987.
21. Interview with Marie Goossens, 24th February 1987.
22. Interview with Sidonie Goossens on her official retirement from the BBC SO, *Ariel*, 29th July 1981.
23. Interview with Sidonie Goossens, 24th February 1987.

Epilogue

1. 20th October 1973.
2. John Sinclair, *Melbourne Herald*, 20th October 1973.
3. Ernest Llewellyn, 19th October 1973.
4. *Sydney Daily Telegraph*, 6th March 1963.

5.   Interview with Sidonie Goossens Scott, 9th February 1992.
6.   *Nation Review*, 1st November 1973.
7.   *Sydney Morning Herald*, 8th September 1990.
8.   *The Strange Case of Eugene Goossens and Other Tales from the Opera House*, Ava Hubble, Collins 1988, p.71.

Select Bibliography

Bacharach, A L (ed.), *British Music of our Time*, Pelican Books, 1946.

Bainton, Helen, *Facing the Music: An Orchestral Player's Notebook*, Currawong Publishing Co Ltd, 1967.

Barany, Inez, *Pagan*, Collins/Angus & Robertson, Australia, 1990.

Beecham, Sir Thomas Bart., *A Mingled Chime*, Hutchinson & Co Ltd, 1944.

Bialoguski, Michael, *The Petrov Story*, Heinemann, Australia, 1955.

Bird, John, *Percy Grainger*, Sun Books, Melbourne, 1977.

Bliss, Arthur, *As I Remember*, Faber & Faber, 1970.

  Bliss on Music: Selected Writings (1920 – 1975), ed. Gregory Roscow, OUP, 1991.

Borovsky, Victor, *Chaliapin*, Hamish Hamilton, 1988.

Boult, Adrian, *My Own Trumpet*, Hamish Hamilton, 1973.

Buckle, Richard, *Diaghilev*, Hamish Hamilton, 1986.

Buttrose, Charles, *Playing for Australia*, Macmillan, Melbourne, 1982.

Cardus, Neville, *Autobiography*, Collins, 1949.

Carley, Lionel, *Delius – A Life in Letters*, Scolar Press, 1988.

Cohen, Harriet, *A Bundle of Time*, Faber & Faber, 1969.

Covell, Roger, *Australia's Music: Themes of a New Society*, Sun Books, Melbourne, 1967.

Cox, David, *The Henry Wood Proms*, BBC, 1980.

Craven, Robert (ed.), *Orchestras of the United States*, Greenwood Press, 1986.

Dane, Clemence, *London Has a Garden*, autobiography, Michael Joseph, 1964.

Demuth, Norman, *Musical Trends in the Twentieth Century*, Rockliff, 1952.

De Valois, Ninette, *Come Dance With Me*, Hamish Hamilton, 1957.

Drury, Nevill, *Pan's Daughter*, Collins, Australia, 1988.

Elkin, Robert, *Royal Philharmonic*, Rider & Company, 1946.

Fenby, Eric, *Delius As I Knew Him*, Faber & Faber, 1981.

Foreman, Lewis, *Arnold Bax*, Scolar Press, 1983.

Foster, Roland, *Come Listen to my Song*, Collins, 1949.

Geissmar, Berta, *The Baton and the Jackboot*, Hamish Hamilton, 1944.

Goossens, Eugene, *Overture and Beginners*, Methuen, 1951.

Goossens, Léon and Roxburgh, Edwin, *Oboe*, Yehudi Menuhin Music Guides, Macdonald and Jane's, 1977.
Goossens, Marie, *Life on a Harp String*, Thorne Printing & Publishing Co Ltd, 1987.
Gray, Cecil, *A Survey of Contemporary Music*, OUP, 1924.
Musical Chairs, Home & Van Thal, 1948.
Hammond, Joan, *A Voice, a Life*, Victor Gollancz, 1970.
Harrison, Beatrice, *The Cello and the Nightingales*, John Murray, 1985.
Holbrooke, Joseph, *Contemporary British Composers*, Cecil Palmer, 1925.
Horgan, Paul, *Encounters with Stravinsky*, Bodley Head, 1972.
Hubble, Ava, *The Strange Case of Eugene Goossens and Other Tales from the Opera House*, Collins, Australia, 1988.
Hughes, Spike, *Opening Bars*, Pilot Press 1946.
Second Movement, Museum Press, 1952.
Jenkings, Bill, *As Crime Goes By*, Ironbark Press, Sydney, 1992.
Kennedy, Michael, *Adrian Boult*, Hamish Hamilton, 1987.
Barbirolli, Macgibbon & Kee, 1971.
Kenyon, Nicholas, *The BBC Symphony Orchestra (1930 – 1980)*, BBC, 1981.
Klein, Herman, *The Golden Age of Opera*, Routledge, 1933.
Kobbe, Gustav, *The Complete Opera Book*, Putnam, 1922.
Kolodin, Irving, *The Metropolitan Opera (1883 – 1939)*, OUP, 1940.
Lambert, Constant, *Music Ho! A Study of Music in Decline*, Faber & Faber, 1934.
Lewis, William Lloyd, *The Book of Harlech*, Barracuda Books Ltd, 1987.
Lutyens, Elisabeth, *A Goldfish Bowl*, Cassell, 1972.
McCombs, R L F, *Clue in Two Flats*, Mystery House, New York, 1940.
Maine, Basil, *Basil Maine on Music*, John Westhouse, 1945.
Moore, Jerrold Northrop, *Edward Elgar: A Creative Life*, OUP 1984.
Morris, Margaret, *The Art of J D Fergusson*, Blackie, 1974.
My Life in Movement, Peter Owen, 1969.
Olivier, Laurence, *Confessions of an Actor*, Weidenfeld & Nicolson, 1982.
Oxford Companion to the Theatre, OUP, 1951.
Pilger, John, *A Secret Country*, Jonathan Cape, 1989.
Pound, Reginald, *Arnold Bennett*, Heinemann, 1952.
Proctor-Gregg, Humphrey, *Beecham Remembered*, Duckworth, 1966.
Radic, Thérèse, *Bernard Heinze*, Macmillan, Australia, 1986.
Melba: The Voice of Australia, Macmillan, Australia, 1986.
Reid, Charles, *John Barbirolli*, Hamish Hamilton, 1971.
Thomas Beecham: An Independent Biography, Victor Gollancz, 1962.
Malcolm Sargent, Hamish Hamilton, 1968.
Russell, Thomas, *Philharmonic*, Hutchinson, 1942.
Philharmonic Decade, 1944.
Salazar, Adolfo, *Music in our Time*, Bodley Head, 1948.
Sametz, Phillip, *Play On!*, Australian Broadcasting Corporation, 1992.
Savage, Richard Temple, *A Voice from the Pit*, David & Charles, 1988.
Shanet, Howard, *Philharmonic: The History of New York's Orchestra*, Doubleday, 1975.

Select Bibliography

Shead, Richard, *Constant Lambert*, Simon Publications, 1973.

Silbermann, Alfons, *Introduction à une Sociologie de la Musique*, Presses Universitaires de France, 1955.

Smith, Judith, *The Instrumental Chamber Music of Sir Eugene Goossens*, University of Cincinnati, 1985.

Soldene, Emily, *My Theatrical and Musical Recollections*, Downey & Co, 1897.

Walker, Katherine Sorley, *Ninette de Valois*, Hamish Hamilton, 1987.

Wilson, Colin, *The Occult*, Hodder & Stoughton, 1971.

Wood, Henry, *My Life in Music*, Victor Gollancz, 1938.

Wynne, Barry, *Music in the Wind*, Souvenir Press 1967.

Wynne Hughes, Oliver, *Every Day was Summer*, Gomer Press, 1989.

LIST OF COMPOSITIONS

Sir Eugene Goossens
(1893–1962)

A list of works compiled by Andrew Guyatt in collaboration with Pamela Main.

(Copyright © 1993 P M Main)

Note: The Opus numbers were changed by Goossens at least once, thus creating some anomalies.

KEY TO PUBLISHERS:

B & H	— Boosey & Hawkes Ltd.
Leduc	— Alphonse Leduc
Chester	— J & W Chester
Comp	— Composer's Copyright
Mills	— Belwin—Mills Music Ltd.
Fischer	— Carl Fischer (UK Agent Boosey & Hawkes)
Lengnick	— Lengnick (Alfred) & Co. Ltd.
OUP	— Oxford University Press

Date of Composition	Opus No.	Title	Publisher	Dedicatee
1911–12	1	Variations on a Chinese Theme orchestra	B & H	
1911	2	Miniature Fantasy string orchestra	B & H	Sir Henry Wood
1911	(3)	Phantasy Octet flute, clarinet, horn, harp and string quartet	Comp	
1912	4 (no.1)	Old Chinese Folk Song violin or cello and piano	B & H	Achille Rivarde
1912	4 (no.2)	Serenade (lost) flute and piano		
1912–14		Perseus (Kingsley 'The Heroes') orchestra	B & H	
1913		Four Sketches flute, violin and piano 1. Legend, 2. Serenade, 3. Romance, 4. Humoresque.	Chester	

443

1914	10	Concert Study piano	Chester	Winifred Christie
1914	7	Five Impressions of a Holiday flute or violin, cello and piano 1. In the hills, 2. By the rivers, 3. The water-wheel, 4. The village church, 5. At the fair.	Chester	
1914	17	Spanish Nocturne cello and piano	B & H	Cedric Sharpe
1914	6	Suite flute, violin and harp 1. Impromptu, 2. Serenade, 3. Divertissement	Chester	Miriam Timothy
1914	9	Deux Melodies (de Musset) 1. Chanson de Fortunio, 2. Chanson de Barberine	Chester	Bertram Binyon
1915	3	Symphonic Prelude 'Ossian' orchestra	Comp	
1915	12	Phantasy String Quartet	Chester	London String Quartet
1915	14	String Quartet no. 1	Chester	Philhar- monic String Quartet
1916	8 (16)	Deux Proses Lyriques (Edwin Evans) voice and piano 1. Hier, dans le jardin ensoleillé, 2. Mon chemin s'était assombri	Chester	
1916	13	Rhapsody cello and piano	Chester	Warwick Evans
1916	15	Two Sketches string quartet 1. By the Tarn (also arranged for string orchestra and clarinet), 2. Jack o'Lantern.	Chester	
1917	19	Three Songs 1. Afternoon (G. Jean-Aubry), 2. Epigram (Edwin Evans), 3. Tea Time (G. Jean-Aubry).	Chester	Adolfo Salazar Madame Alvar
1917	18	Kaleidescope 12 pieces for piano 1920—33 transcribed for orchestra (4 versions)	Chester	Miss d'Erlanger
1917— 18	16 (17a)	Tam O'Shanter scherzo for orchestra	Chester	

1917	20	Four Conceits piano 1. The Gargoyle, 2. Dance Memories, 3. A Walking Tune, 4. The Marionette Show. 1918 orchestra 1932 military band	Chester	William Murdoch
1918	11 (17)	Persian Idylls (Edwin Evans) voice and piano 1. The Breath of Ney, 2. Heart of Kalyan.	Chester	Maurice d'Oisly
1918	22	Phillip II (Verhaeren) small orchestra Prelude (surviving item from incidental music).	Chester	
1918	21	Sonata no. 1 violin and piano	Chester	Albert Sammons
1918	22 (no. 1)	The Cowl (H R Barbor) recitation with piano (lost)		
1918	22 (no. 2)	The Curse (H R Barbor) voice and piano	Chester	Pedro Morales
1918	32	Two Old Scotch Folk Songs voice and piano 1. Behave yourself before folk, 2. I'm owre young to marry yet.	Chester	
1918		Variations on Cadet Rousselle voice and piano (collaboration) 1930 small orchestra	Chester	Edwin Evans
1919		Lotusland (Cyril Scott) voice and piano	B & H	Astra Desmond
1919	35	Lyric Poem violin and orchestra 1920 violin and piano	Chester	André Mangeot
1919	25	Nature Poems piano 1. Awakening, 2. Pastoral, 3. Bacchanal.	Chester	Benno Moiseivitch
	52	1937–38 orchestra	Chester	
1919	23	Quintet piano and string quartet	Chester	George Davison
1920	28	Hommage à Debussy piano	Chester	
1920	30	Rhythmic Dance two pianos 1920 pianola roll 1927 orchestra 1932 military band	B & H	Maier and Pattison

1920	5	The Eternal Rhythm orchestra	Chester	
1920– 21	26	Three Songs piano or string quartet	Chester	
		1. The Appeal (Sir Thomas Wyatt)		Mignon Nevada
		2. Melancholy (John Fletcher)		Bertram Binyon
		3. Philomel (Richard Barnefield).		Napier Miles
1921– 22	29	L'Ecole en Crinoline Ballet orchestra	Chester	
1921	48	1. Fanfare for a Ceremony brass 1930 2. Fanfare for Artists brass	Chester	
1922	33	East of Suez incidental music arranged for piano	Chester	
1922	31	Silence (Walter de la Mare) A Choral Fragment chorus and orchestra	Chester	
1922	32	Two Songs of William Blake (lost)		
1922– 23	34	Sinfonietta orchestra	Chester	Bettie Holmes
1923	36	Fantasy for nine Wind Instruments	Leduc	
1923		The Strange Case of Mr X Collaborative Suite for Chamber Orchestra, 'Captions, being Five Glimpses of an Anonymous Theme.' (lost)		
1923	37	Sextet for Strings (Phantasy Sextet) 1942 Phantasy for Strings arranged for string orchestra	Chester	Mrs Elizabeth Sprague Coolidge
1923	38 (39)	Two Studies piano 1. Folk Tune 2. Scherzo	Chester	Margaret Bannerman Tomford Harris
1924	41	Pastorale and Harlequinade flute, oboe and piano	Leduc	Léon Goossens
1924	42	Ships piano 1. The Tug, 2. The Tramp, 3. The Liner	B & H	

Compositions

1924	38	Two Ballades harp	Leduc	1. Sidonie 2. Marie
1926	47	Concertino string octet 1929 double string orchestra	Chester	André Mangeot
1926	43	The Constant Nymph (Margaret Kennedy) incidental music 1933 revised for film 1926 'When thou art dead' voice and piano	Comp Lengnick	
1926	44	Three Greek Dances small orchestra	B & H	Margaret Morris
1926–29	46	Judith opera in one act (libretto by Arnold Bennett)	Chester	Boonie (Dorothy Millar)
1927	45	Oboe Concerto	Leduc	Léon Goossens
1929	51	Chamber Music (James Joyce) six songs voice and piano 1. Now, O Now	Lengnick	Ursula Greville
		2. Gentle lady, do not sing sad songs		John Coates
		3. Dear heart, why will you use me so		Maurice d'Oisly
		4. O cool is the valley now		Gertrude Erhardt
		5. All day I hear the noise of waters		Anne Thursfield
		6. I hear an army		Bernard Ferguson
1930	49 (no. 1)	A Memory of the Players (James Joyce)	James Joyce Book OUP	James Joyce
1930	50	Sonata no. 2 violin and piano	Chester	Paul Kochanski
1930–35	54	Don Juan de Mañara opera in four acts (libretto by Arnold Bennett)	Chester	
	57	1937 Romance violin and piano	Chester	Jascha Heifetz
1931		Autumn Crocus incidental music to play by C L Anthony	Comp	
1931	49 (2)	Searching for Lambs (Old English folk tune) voice and piano	Chester	Fay Compton
1931	53	Four Songs (Bettie F Holmes) voice and piano 1. Threshold, 2. A Winter Night Idyll, 3. A Woodland Dell, 4. Seascape.	Chester	

447

1935	55	Three Pictures flute, string orchestra and percussion 1. From the Belfry of Bruges, 2. From Bredon in the Cotswolds, 3. From a Balcony in Montparnasse.	Chester	Ary Van Leeuwen
1938	56	Two Piano Pieces 1. Pikki's Lament, 2. Bonzo's Dance	Fischer/ B & H	My Daughter Sidonie
1939 −40	58	Symphony no. 1	B & H	My Colleagues of the Cincinnati Symphony Orchestra
1940	59	String Quartet no. 2	B & H	Mrs Elizabeth Sprague Coolidge
1942		'Pastorale 1942' (Second Movement) arranged for string orchestra		
1941		A British Children's Prayer (Merrick Fifield McCarthy)	B & H	Merrick Fifield McCarthy
1941		Hommage to Paderewski piano	B & H	
1941 −43	60	Phantasy Concerto piano and orchestra	Chester	José Iturbi
1943	61	Cowboy Phantasy small orchestra from film score	B & H	
1942		Fanfare for the Merchant Marine brass	B & H	
1944 −45	62	Symphony no. 2	B & H	
1945		Variations of an Original Theme orchestra (collaboration) Theme and Finale	B & H	
1945		Victory Jubilee Fanfare and British National Anthem orchestra, organ and bugles	B & H	
1946 −48	63	Phantasy Concerto violin and orchestra revised 1958	Chester	Tessa Robbins
1951 −54	64	The Apocalypse chorus, soli and orchestra	B & H	'Marjorie'

Compositions

1953		Coronation Fanfare orchestra	B & H	
1956 −60	66	Divertissement orchestra 1. Dance Prelude, 2. Scherzo and Folk Tune, 3. Ballet Flamenco.	Chester	
1957	65	Concert Piece oboe/English horn, two harps and orchestra	Mills	Marie, Sidonie and Léon Goossens
1958		The Day film score	B & H	
1959		Capriccio piano based on Kaleidescope No 3) the Hurdy- Gurdy Man for Chester's Centenary Album	Chester	
1960		Forlane and Toccata clavichord	B & H	Michael Thomas
1962 (publish- ed)		Islamite Dance oboe and piano	Leduc	
1962 (publish- ed)		Scherzo Fantasque flute and piano	Leduc	
1962 (publish- ed)		Veille chanson à boire bassoon and piano	Leduc	

ARRANGEMENTS OF WORKS BY OTHER COMPOSERS

Date of arrangement	Composer	Title	Publisher
1915	Ketèlby	In a Monastery Garden Silver Cloud violin and piano	
1917	J S Bach	Suite in G ballet divertissement for Beecham's production of *Phoebus and Pan*	Chester
1917	Debussy	Clair de lune orchestra	
1922−23	Mussorgsky	*Boris Godunov* Coronation Scene Scene I orchestra	Chester

1930	Wagner	*Tristan und Isolde* selected orchestrations	
1932	J S Bach	Andante Brandenburg Concerto no. 2 piano for 'A Bach Book for Harriet Cohen'	OUP
1935	Bantock	Easter Hymn orchestra	
1935	Wagner	*Götterdämmerung* Chorus of the Gibichungs orchestra	
1936	Wagner	*Die Walküre* Prelude to Act I, Prelude to Act II orchestra	
1938	Wagner	*Siegfried* 1. Prelude to Act III, 2. Ascent of the Rock.	
1941	Mozart	Minuet from Divertimento no. 2 in D K131 orchestra	
1942	Arensky	Carillon of Karkov orchestra	
1942	Debussy	Blanc et noir orchestra	
1942	Ravel	Le Gibet orchestra	B & H
1942	Wagner	*Parsifal* 1. Prelude, 2. Good Friday Music, 3. Finale. orchestra	
1947	Scarlatti	The Good Humoured Ladies Suite for orchestra	
1948	J S Bach	Chorale 'Come God Creator' orchestra	
1949	Albeniz	Iberia Suite 3 movements arranged for orchestra 1. Eritana, 2. El Puerto, 3. Rondena	B & H
1958	Rachmaninov	Two Preludes, op. 23 & 32 orchestra	
1959	Handel	The Messiah arranged for large orchestra	
Undated	J P Sousa	Star Spangled Banner orchestra	B & H

Goossens Family Discographies

by Raymond E Cooke

(Copyright © 1993 Raymond E Cooke)

The Goossens family made a prodigious contribution to record catalogues during a period of more than half a century. Each member can be said to have enhanced the style, precision and artistry of orchestral playing both in the concert hall and in the recording studio.

Researching these discographies has been a labour of love in which I have been greatly helped by others. I am particularly indebted to Malcolm Walker of *Gramophone*, Ruth Edge and Sarah Hobbs of EMI's Music Archive, Ken Jagger of EMI Music, Yvonne Lakeran – Decca's Archivist, and the late Andrew Guyatt whose alphabetical list of Sir Eugene Goossens' records has been a valuable aid. Ronald Taylor of *Collector's Room* has given me much assistance and advice – likewise Anthony Griffith, who remains a mine of information acquired during his years with EMI.

No discography covering such a long period can be complete and fault-free. During the early years of recording, few firms paid attention to archival considerations. As time goes by, hopefully more information will become available to enhance these lists.

ABBREVIATIONS

The following commercial record labels appear in the various discographies, abbreviated as shown.

Allegro	ALL	Cameo Classics	CAC
ARC	ARC	Capitol (USA)	CAP
Art Union Corporation	AUC	CBS (Columbia USA)	CBS
Beecham Trust	BEE	CDC	CDC
British Broadcasting Corporation	BBC	Chandos Records	CHA
		Claremont	CLA
British Brunswick	BB	Classics Club	CC
Camden (RCA)	CAM	Classics for Pleasure	CFP

Columbia (EMI) UK	COL	Pearl Records	PEA
Decca	DEC	Phase 4	PH4
Deutsche Grammophon Gesellschaft	DGG	Philips	PHI
		Pickwick	PIC
Dutton Laboratories	DUT	Polydor	POL
Edison Bell	EDB	Pye	PYE
Electrical & Musical Industries	EMI	RCA (UK)	RCA
Electrocord	ECD	RCA Victor (USA)	VRI
Electrola	ELA	Record Society	RS
Elgar Society	ELG	Redbridge	RED
Everest Records	EVT	Saga	SAG
Festival	FES	Seraphim	SER
Fidelity	FID	Starecord	STA
Golden Sound	GS	Testament	TES
Hallmark	HAL	Top Rank	TR
His Master's Voice	HMV	Transatlantic	TRA
Invicta	INV	Unicorn	UNI
Kapp	KAP	United Artists	UA
Lyrita	LYR	Veritas	VER
Melodiya	MEL	Victor	VIC
Music for Pleasure	MFP	Vocalion	VOC
National Gramophonic Society	NGS	World Record Club	WRC

RECORD FORMATS

78	78 rpm disc	45m	extended play 45 rpm disc – mono
A78	78 rpm set in auto-couplings		
78a	78 rpm acoustic disc	45s	extended play 45 rpm disc – stereo
80a	80 rpm acoustic disc		
LPm	long playing 33⅓ rpm disc – mono	TCm	tape cassette – mono
		TCs	tape cassette – stereo
LPs	long playing 33⅓ rpm disc – stereo	CD	compact disc

Eugene Goossens II (1867–1958) – Conductor

Eugene Goossens II took enormous pains to produce rigorously precise, yet refined renderings of the light music such as the Edward German pieces which he committed to record. He often made himself unpopular with musicians for insisting on near-perfection during a period when rather slap-dash performances were generally accepted. Save his magnificent achievement with *I Pagliacci*, all his other records were made in the acoustic era when symphonic music suffered from the cramped conditions and unsuitable ambience of the tiny studios which were necessary for the process.

1923 London	Berlioz: *Carnival Romain* – Overture Royal Symphony Orchestra	EDB 78a	VF702
1923 London X 1675A X 1676G	Beethoven: Overture – *Leonora No. 3* Royal Symphony Orchestra	EDB 78a	VF706
1924 2 July London	Verdi: *Aida* Selection New Queens Hall Light Orchestra	COL 78a	L1439
1924 9 July London	Wormser: *L'Enfant Prodigue*, Parts 1 & 2 New Queens Hall Light Orchestra	COL 78a	1647
1924 10 July London	Wormser: *L'Enfant Prodigue*, Part 3 New Queens Hall Light Orchestra	COL 78a	L1648
1924 10 July London	Massenet: *Thaïs* – Meditation New Queens Hall Light Orchestra with Bernard Reillie, solo violin	COL 78a	L1647
1924 16 July London	Edward German: *Nell Gwyn Dances*, Parts I & II New Queens Hall Light Orchestra	COL 78a	L1410
1924 16 July London	*Nell Gwyn Dances*, Part III New Queens Hall Light Orchestra	COL 78a	L1411

453

1924	Leoncavallo: *I Pagliacci* – Prologue	COL 78a	486
27 August	Gounod: *Faust* – Even Bravest Hearts		
London	May Swell		
	Thorpe Bates, baritone with orchestra		
1927	Leoncavallo: *I Pagliacci*	COL 78	4347–
8, 9, 11 March	Complete Opera in English		4358
London	Recorded in the Scala Theatre by the		GSH 4
WRA 5007, 4999	Principals, Chorus and Orchestra of the		
5000, 5045	British National Opera Company		
5062, 5009			
5010, 5048			
5027, 5001			
5002, 5030			
5049, 5029			
5026, 5003			
5044, 5066			
5068, 5064			
5063, 5069			
5065, 5067			

Sir Eugene Goossens KBE
(1893–1962)

Sir Eugene Goossens was very active in recording studios throughout his professional life. He brought a wide repertoire of popular classics to the turntable and recorded over 240 works as conductor, in addition to his role of violinist in the Philharmonic String Quartet. His last recordings for Everest in 1959–60 demonstrate the enormous panache and dynamism which he brought to the rostrum.

SIR EUGENE GOOSSENS KBE (1893–1962) — CONDUCTOR

1916 Hayes HO 1918ac	Haydn: *Creation* – Rolling in Foaming Billows Robert Radford Symphony Orchestra	HMV 78a	D 519
1920 London	Lecoq: *Madame Angot* London Symphony Orchestra	COL 78a	L 1382
1921 London	Bizet: *Carmen* – Toreador's Song Norman Williams Symphony Orchestra	EDB 78a	VF 530
1921 London	Gounod: *Faust* – Even bravest heart (aria) Norman Williams Symphony Orchestra	EDB 78a	VF 530
1921 London 7310A	Liadov: Eight Russian Folk Songs – No. 6 & 8 Goossens Orchestra	EDB 78a	VF 1040
1921 London	Mendelssohn: *Midsummer Night's Dream* Overture Goossens Orchestra	EDB 78a	VF 527
1921 London 7210A	Mussorgsky: *Sorochinsky Fair* – Gopak Goossens Orchestra	EDB 78a	VF 1040
1921 London	Mozart: *Magic Flute* – Within these Sacred Bowers Norman Williams Symphony Orchestra	EDB 78a	VF 526

1921 London	Saint-Saëns: *Dance Macabre* Goossens Orchestra	EDB 78a	VF 521
1921 London X1163G X1164B	Wagner: *Mastersingers* — Overture Goossens Orchestra	EDB 78a	VF 523
1921 London	Wagner: *Tannhäuser* — Overture Goossens Orchestra	EDB 78a	VF 535
1921 London	Wagner: *Tristan and Isolde* — Prelude & Liebestod Goossens Orchestra	EDB 78a	VF 539
1921 London	Wagner: *Tannhäuser* — 'O Star of Eve' Norman Williams Symphony Orchestra	EDB 78a	VF 526
1921 London	Puccini: *La Bohème* — Che Gelida Manina John Perry, tenor Symphony Orchestra	EDB 78a	VF 531
1921 London	Wagner: *Mastersingers* — Prize Song John Perry, tenor Symphony Orchestra	EDB 78a	VF 531
1922 4 & 27 April CC 1182/89 CC 1190/91	Beethoven: Concerto for Piano & Orchestra No. 5 'Emperor' Frederic Lamond, piano Royal Albert Hall Orchestra	HMV 78a	D625/9
1922 15 May London CC 1328	Rimsky-Korsakov: *Dubinushka* Op. 62 Royal Albert Hall Orchestra	HMV 78a	D 623
1922 15 May London CC 1329 CC 1330	Smetana; *The Bartered Bride* — Overture Royal Albert Hall Orchestra	HMV 78a	D 643
1922 15 May London CC 1331	Scriabin: *Rêverie* Royal Albert Hall Orchestra	HMV 78a	D 623
1922 31 Aug London CC 1777	Goossens: *Tam O'Shanter* — Scherzo Royal Albert Hall Orchestra	HMV 78a	D 694
1922 31 Aug London CC 1778/79	Rimsky-Korsakov: *La Nuit de Noël*, Parts I & 2 Royal Albert Hall Orchestra	HMV 78a	D 656

1922 18 Sept London CC 1840	Wagner: *Die Walküre* – Act I A sword my Father foretold me Tudor Davies, tenor Symphony Orchestra	HMV 78a	D 678
1922 18 Sept London CC 1841	Wagner: *Die Walküre* – Act I, Finale Tudor Davies, tenor Symphony Orchestra	HMV 78a	D 679
1922 20 Sept CC 1863/64	Gluck: *Alceste* – O Ma Lyre Immortelle – Ye Powers that dwell below	HMV 78a	Unpub
1922 20 Sept CC 1865	Gluck: *L'Anneau d'Argent*	HMV 78a	Unpub
1922 5 Oct CC 1935/37	Bach: Brandenburg Concerto No. 3 in G – Parts I to III Royal Albert Hall Orchestra	HMV 78a HMV 78a	D 683 D 684
1922 27 Nov CC 2214–4/ –6	Wagner: *Lohengrin* – Bridal Procession to the Cathedral Royal Albert Hall Orchestra	HMV 78a	Unpub
1922 27 Nov CC 2215	Bach: Air on the G string Royal Albert Hall Orchestra	HMV 78a	D 684
1922 11 Dec London CC 2254	Wagner: *Die Walküre* – Wotan warns Brünnhilde not to disobey Symphony Orchestra	HMV 78a	D 680
1922 11 Dec CC 2255	Wagner: *Die Walküre* – Brünnhilde implores protection of fire Florence Austral, soprano; Robert Radford, bass Symphony Orchestra	HMV 78a	D 682
1922 London CC 3166–1	Bizet: *Carmen* – Flower Song Tudor Davies & Symphony Orchestra	HMV 78a HMV LPm	D 739 RLS 707
1922 London CC 4017/19	Delius: *Brigg Fair* Royal Albert Hall Orchestra	HMV 78a	D 799/800
1922 London CR 4081–1	Delius: *On Hearing the First Cuckoo in* *Spring* Royal Albert Hall Orchestra	HMV 78a	D 800
1922 London	Grainger: *Molly on the Shore* Royal Albert Hall Orchestra	HMV 78a	D 694

1922 Hayes HO 4121 af	Handel: *The Messiah* – Why Do the Nations Robert Radford Symphony Orchestra	HMV 78a	D 519
1922 CC 1842	Wagner: *Die Meistersinger* – Introduction to Act III Royal Albert Hall Orchestra	HMV 78a	
1923 17 Jan CC 2395–4 CC 2396–2	Verdi: *Aida* – Fu la Sorte dell'Armi Florence Austral and Edna Thornton	HMV 78	D 776
1923 12 March Hayes CC 2685	Elgar: *King Olaf* – And King Olaf Heard the Cry Tudor Davies, tenor Symphony Orchestra	HMV 78a ELG LPm	D 723 ELP 001
1923 12 March London CC 2689	Puccini: *Tosca* – When the Stars were Brightly Shining Tudor Davies, tenor Symphony Orchestra	HMV 78a	D 707
1923 London 16 April CC 2841–2	Wagner: *The Ring of the Nibelungs* – Siegfried Act II 'Mime's treachery to Siegfried' Tudor Davies, Sydney Russell, Florence Austral Symphony Orchestra	HMV 78a	D 700
1923 London 16 April CC 2842	Wagner: *Götterdämmerung* – Prelude Act III 'Rhine Maidens Scene' Symphony Orchestra	HMV 78a	D 705
1923 26 June Hayes CC 3153–2	Mussorgsky: *Boris Godunov* – Boris' Monologue Act II Theodore Chaliapin, bass Symphony Orchestra	HMV 78a VIC 78a MEL LPm	2-022021 88669 M10 45415 004
1923 26 June Hayes CC 3155–2	Rachmaninov: *Aleko* – The moon is high in the sky unnamed orchestra	HMV 78a	DB 691
1923 2 July Hayes CC 3197–1	Mussorgsky: *Boris Godunov* – Death of Boris Act IV Theodore Chaliapin, bass Symphony Orchestra & Chorus	HMV 78a HMV 78a	2-022020 DB 100
1923 London 11 July CC 2253–2/ 54–2	Wagner: *Die Walküre* Act II 'Wotan warns Brünnhilde not to disobey' Robert Radford, Florence Austral Symphony Orchestra	HMV 78a	D 680

1923 11 July London CC 2255–2	Wagner: *Die Walküre* Act III 'Brünnhilde implores the protection of fire' Florence Austral, Robert Radford Symphony Orchestra	HMV 78a	D 682
1923 3 Oct London CC 1928/29	Puccini: *Madam Butterfly* – Part 1 & 2 Royal Albert Hall Orchestra	HMV 78a	D 659
1923 21 Dec London 4013-16	Stravinsky: *Petrushka* – original version Parts 1, 2, 6 & 7 Royal Albert Hall Orchestra	HMV 78a VIC 78a	D 853/6 55245-8
1923 Dec London CC 2689-1	Puccini: *Tosca* – Strange Harmony of Contrasts Tudor Davies, tenor Symphony Orchestra	HMV 78	E 389
1923 London CC 2687-1	Beethoven: *Adelaide* (song) Tudor Davies, tenor with orchestra	HMV 78a	D 696
1923 London CC 2688-2	Coleridge-Taylor: *Eleanore* (song) Tudor Davies	HMV 78	D 696
1923 London	Delibes: *Coppélia* – Entr'acte & Valse, Prelude & Mazurka London Symphony Orchestra	COL 78	901
1923 London	Delibes: *Le Roi l'a Dit* London Symphony Orchestra	COL 78	923
1923 London CC 3165-1	Gounod: *Faust* – All Hail, thou dwelling pure (aria) Tudor Davies, tenor Orchestra	HMV 78a	D 739
1923 London CC 3167–1/ 68–1	Handel: *The Messiah* – Every Valley & Comfort Ye Tudor Davies, tenor Symphony Orchestra	HMV 78a	D 777
1923 London CC 3167-1/ 68-1	Handel: *Samson* – Return O God of Hosts Edna Thornton, contralto Symphony Orchestra	HMV 78a GS CD	D 781 GSH 21
1923 London CC 3214	Handel: *Saul* – O Lord Whose Mercies Numberless Edna Thornton, contralto Symphony Orchestra	HMV 78a GS CD	D 789 GSH 21

1923 London CC 3215	Mendelssohn: *St Paul* − But the Lord is Mindful of His Own Edna Thornton, contralto Symphony Orchestra	HMV 78a GS CD	D 765 GSH 21
1923 London	Puccini: *Madam Butterfly* − Opera in English Rosina Buckman, Tudor Davies, Nellie Walker, Ranalow, Coltham, Halland, Peel & Symphony Orchestra	HMV 78a HMV CLA LPm	D 893/906 895,7 & 898 SV2.501
1923 London	Puccini: *Tosca* − selection arr. E Tavan Royal Albert Hall Orchestra	HMV 78a	D 913
1923 London	Sibelius: *Festivo* London Symphony Orchestra	COL 78a	908
1923 London	Wolf-Ferrari: *The Jewels of the Madonna* − Introduction Act II, Intermezzo Act III London Symphony Orchestra	COL 78a	914
1923 London	Wolf-Ferrari: *Susanna's Secret* − Overture London Symphony Orchestra	COL 78a	908

1924
15 Jan
London
  4077/79
  4014
  4080
	Stravinsky: *Petrushka* − Parts 3, 4, 5 & 8
	Royal Albert Hall Orchestra
		HMV 78a	D 853/6

1924 23 June London Bb 4762-2	Puccini: *La Bohème* − Quando m'en vo Rosina Buckman, soprano Symphony Orchestra	HMV 78a	E 352
1924 14 July Hayes CC 4891-1	Glinka: *A Life for the Tsar* − Now I am Alone Chaliapin, bass Symphony Orchestra	HMV 78a PEA LPm PEA CD	DB 758 GEMM 170 GEMM CDS 9920
1924 14 July Hayes Bb 4484-3	Koenemann: *Down the Peterskaya* (song) arr. Chaliapin Chaliapin, bass Symphony Orchestra	HMV 78a HMV 78a PEA LPm MEL LPM	7-22021 DA 621 GEMM 170 MIO 45417 009
1924 29 & 30 Dec London	Bruch: Violin Concerto No. 1 Fritz Kreisler, violin Royal Albert Hall Orchestra	PEA LPm	GEMM 250/ 1H
1924 Royal Opera House Covent Garden CR 576-1	Berlioz: *Damnation of Faust* − Hungarian March Royal Opera House, Covent Garden Orchestra	HMV 78a	C 1279

460

1924 Royal Opera House Covent Garden CR 571-1 CR 572-1A	Bizet: *L'Arlésienne* Suite Royal Opera House, Covent Garden Orchestra	HMV 78a VIC 78a	C 1319/20 9112/3
1924 London	Boïeldieu: *The Caliph of Baghdad* — Overture London Symphony Orchestra	COL 78a	921
1924 London	Chabrier: *Habañera* London Symphony Orchestra	COL 78a	921
1924 Royal Opera House Covent Garden CR 561/64	Rimsky-Korsakov: *Scheherazade* Royal Opera House, Covent Garden Orchestra	HMV 78a	C 1287/8
1924 Royal Opera House Covent Garden CR 577-1	Schubert: *Marche Militaire* Royal Opera House, Covent Garden Orchestra	HMV 78a	C 1279
1924 Royal Opera House Covent Garden CR 584/89	Schubert: Symphony No. 6 'Unfinished' Royal Opera House, Covent Garden Orchestra	HMV 78a HMV 78a	C 1294/6 C 7247/9
1924 Royal Opera House Covent Garden CR 578-1	Tchaikovsky: *Eugene Onegin* — Waltz Royal Opera House, Covent Garden Orchestra	HMV 78a VIC 78a	C 1281 9027
1924 Royal Opera House Covent Garden CR 573/75	Tchaikovsky: 1812 Overture Royal Opera House, Covent Garden Orchestra	HMV 78a VIC 78a	C 1280/1 9025/7
1925 3 July 6289 6290	Respighi: *La Boutique Fantasque* — Ballet Suite Royal Albert Hall Orchestra	HMV 78a	D 1018

461

1925 Los Angeles	Balakirev: *Islamey* (orchestrated by Casella) Hollywood Bowl Orchestra	VIC 78a	6870
1926 20 May Hayes CC 8416-1A	Glinka: *Midnight Review* Theodore Chaliapin, bass Symphony Orchestra	HMV 78 PEA LPm PEA CD	DB 933 GEMM 170 GEMM CDS 9920
1926 20 May Hayes CC 8414-2	Mussorgsky: *Boris Godunov* – The Song of the Flea Theodore Chaliapin, bass	HMV 78 PEA LPm PEA CD	DB 932 GEMM 232 GEMM CDS 9920
1926 20 May Hayes CC 8412-1A	Rossini: *The Barber of Seville* – La Calunnia e un Venticello Theodore Chaliapin Symphony Orchestra	HMV 78 PEA LPm PEA CD BBC CD	DB 932 GEMM 152 GEMM CD 9314 CD 715
1926 20 May Hayes CC 8413-2A	Schumann: *The Two Grenadiers* (song) Theodore Chaliapin Symphony Orchestra	HMV 78 PEA LPm	DB 933 GEMM 170
1926 21 & 27 May London CR 371-1 CR 374-4	Mussorgsky: *Boris Godunov* – Farewell my Son & Death of Boris Theodore Chaliapin, bass Symphony Orchestra	HMV 78 PEA LPm COL LPm	DB 934 GEMM 152 GOLH 100
1926 27 May London CR 378-2A	Mussorgsky: *Boris Godunov* – Coronation Scene Part 2	HMV 78 PEA CD	unpub GEMM CD 9920
1926 July London CC 6326-2	Wagner: *Mastersingers* – Sach's Panegyric on German Art Robert Radford, bass Symphony Orchestra and Chorus	HMV 78	D 1021
1926 July London CC 6325-3	Wagner: *Mastersingers* – Prize Song Tudor Davies, tenor Symphony Orchestra	HMV 78	D 1021
1926 London	Wagner: *Parsifal* – Herzeleide Göta Ljungberg Symphony Orchestra	HMV 78 HMV 78	D 1651/2 DB 862
1927 Los Angeles	Berlioz: *Symphonie Fantastique* (4th movement only) Hollywood Bowl Orchestra	VIC 78 VIC 78	6869 M-40
1927 Los Angeles	Dvořák: *Carnival* Overture Hollywood Bowl Orchestra	VIC 78	6868

1927 Los Angeles	Falla: *El Amor Brujo* – Ritual Fire Dance Hollywood Bowl Orchestra	VIC 78	6869
1927 London CR 565/68	Grieg: *Peer Gynt*, Suite No. 1 Royal Opera House Orchestra, Covent Garden	HMV 78	C 1298/9
1927 Hayes Bb 2570-2/71- 2	Handel: *The Messiah* – But Who May Abide and Thus Saith the Lord Robert Radford Symphony Orchestra	HMV 78	E 277
1927 Hayes Bb 2572-2/ 73-2	Handel: *The Messiah* – For Behold Darkness and The People that Walked Robert Radford Symphony Orchestra	HMV 78	E 304
1927 London	Offenbach: *La Périchole* – selection London Symphony Orchestra	COL 78	959
1927 London	Planquette: *Paul Jones* – selection London Symphony Orchestra	COL 78	916
1928 17 May CR 2017-2 CR 2018-1a CR 2019-1a	Bax: *Tintagel* New Symphony Orchestra	HMV 78	C 1619/20
1928 21 May London CR 2024-2 CR 2028-2 CR 2029-2	Granados: *Spanish Dances* Nos. 1–3 New Light Symphony Orchestra	HMV 78	C 1553/4
1928 23 May London CR 2026-2	Albeniz: (Triana only) New Light Symphony Orchestra	HMV 78	C 1554
1928 23 May CR 2025-2	Bax: *Mediterranean* New Symphony Orchestra	HMV 78	C 1620
1928 23 May CR 2027-2	Massenet: *Hérodiade* – Les Phéniciennes New Symphony Orchestra	HMV 78	C 2349
1928 7 June London CR 2073-1A CR 2074-2 CR 2075-2 CR 2076-1A	Massenet: *Le Cid* – Ballet Music New Symphony Orchestra	HMV 78	C 1638/9

1928	Grieg: *Peer Gynt*, Suite No. 2	HMV 78	C 1571/2
8 June	New Light Symphony Orchestra		
London			
CR 2081-2a			
CR 2082-1a			
CR 2083-1a			
CR 2084-1			

1928	Gounod: *Faust* – Selections from Opera	HMV LPm	RLS 742
22 June	Act I (complete)	HMV 78	DB 1189
Royal Opera	Act II 'Allons, amis, point de vaines	HMV LPm	RLS 710
House	alarmes!' to 'Le Veau d'Or' and 'Nous	(Part only)	
Covent	nous retrouverons mes amis' to 'Le		
Garden	Brise' – Waltz Scene		
CR 2097/CR	Act III *'Salut demeure, chaste et pure'*		
2109-1	'Il était temps' – (Invocation)		
	Act IV 'Qu'attendez vous encore to 'vous		
	qui faites' – Serenade		
	Royal Opera House Orchestra, with full		
	cast		

1928	Malashkin: *O Could I In Song Tell my*	HMV 78	DA 993
30 June	*Sorrow*	PEA LPm	GEMM 152
London	Theodore Chaliapin, bass		
Bb 13899-2	Symphony Orchestra		

1928	Schubert: *Death & the Maiden*, (song)	HMV 78	DB 1184
30 June	Theodore Chaliapin	PEA LPm	GEMM 152
London	Symphony Orchestra		
CC 13898-1			

1928	Schubert: *The Wraith* (Der	HMV 78	DB 1184
30 June	Doppelgänger) (song)		
London	Theodore Chaliapin		
CC 13897-1	Symphony Orchestra		

1929	Glazunov: Scenes de Ballet	HMV 78	C 1752/4
3, 5 & 6 June	New Symphony Orchestra	HMV A78	C 7231/3
London			
CC 16650-3			
CC 16657-3			
CC 16656-3			
CC 16654-2			
CC 16658-1			
CC 16655-1			

1919	Turina: *Danzas Fantasticas*	HMV 78	C 1747/8
3 & 5 June	New Symphony Orchestra		
London			
CC 16653-3A			
CC 16651-2			
CC 16652-3A			
CC 16649-3			

1929 6 June London CC 16659-2 CC 16660-2	Albeniz: *Iberia* – Fête Dieu à Seville – Parts 1 & 2 New Symphony Orchestra	HMV 78	C 1751
1929 London CC 16661-2 CC 16662-3A	Goossens: *Judith* – Ballet Music, Parts 1 & 2 Arthur Fear, bass and orchestra	HMV 78	C1706
1929 Los Angeles A 46451 A 46455T1 A 46456/57	Tchaikovsky: *Sleeping Beauty* Suite Hollywood Bowl Orchestra	HMV 78	D 1718/9
1930 21 May Royal Opera House Covent Garden CC 18784-2	Chabrier: *Marche Joyeuse* Royal Opera House, Covent Garden Orchestra	HMV 78	C2017
1930 21 May London CC 18785/86	Mendelssohn: *The Hebrides* (Fingal's Cave) Op. 26 London Symphony Orchestra	HMV 78	unpub
1930 23 May Royal Opera House Covent Garden CC 18791-1 CC 18792-2A CC 18793-3A	Franck: *The Accursed Huntsman* Royal Opera House, Covent Garden Orchestra	HMV 78	C 2016/7
1930 26 May London CC 18794-1A CC 18795-2A/ 96-2A	Sibelius: *En Saga* New Symphony Orchestra	HMV 78	C 1994/5
1930 27 May London CC 18797-2/ 98-2	Balakirev: *Islamey* (orchestrated by Casella) New Symphony Orchestra	HMV 78	C 2086
1930 27 May London CC 18799-1	Sibelius: *Valse Triste* New Symphony Orchestra	HMV 78 VIC 78	C 1995 9926

1930 2 June Royal Opera House Covent Garden CC 19618-1 CC 19619-2	Auber: *The Bronze Horse* – Overture	HMV 78	C 1997
1930 2 June Royal Opera House Covent Garden CC 19617-1 CC 19620-2	Resphigi: *La Boutique Fantasque*– Ballet Suite Royal Opera House, Covent Garden Orchestra	HMV 78	C 1996
1930 London	Auber: *Crown Diamonds* – Overture London Symphony Orchestra	COL 78	918
1931 23 Jan Paris MAT 29114-1	Mussorgsky: *Boris Godunov* – Coronation Scene Part 1 Russian Opera Chorus and Orchestra	HMV 78	unpub
1931 24 June London 2B 592-1 2B 593-2 2B 594-1 2B 595-3	Massenet: *Scènes Pittoresques* London Symphony Orchestra	HMV 78	DB 9781 DB 9782
1931 25 June London 2B 598-1	Tchaikovsky: *Eugene Onegin* – Polonaise London Symphony Orchestra	HMV 78	DB 1760
1931 25 June London 2B 597-3 2B 599-1	Tommasini: *The Good Humoured Ladies* – Suite, after Scarlatti London Symphony Orchestra	HMV 78	C 2272
1931 29 June London OB 1405-1 OB 1406-3	Delibes: *Coppélia* – Mazurka & Czardas London Symphony Orchestra	HMV 78 HMV 78	B 3941 DA 4348
1931 29 June London OB 1407-1 OB 1408-2	Delibes: *Le Roi l'a Dit* London Symphony Orchestra	HMV 78	B 3942

1931 4 July London OB 1413-1/-3	Bizet: *The Pearl Fishers* – Mi par di udir ancora (aria) Beniamino Gigli, tenor Symphony Orchestra	HMV 78 HMV LPm	DA 1216 ALP1681
1931 4 July London 2B 1412-1/-2	Gounod: *Faust* – Salve dimor, casta e pura (aria) Beniamino Gigli, tenor Symphony Orchestra	HMV 78 HMV LPm HMV 45m	DB 1538 ALP 1681 7ER 5081
1931 4 July London 2B 1411-1/-2	Puccini: *La Bohème* – Che Gelida Manina Beniamino Gigli, tenor Symphony Orchestra	HMV 78 HMV TCm HMV CD	DB 1538 ALP 1681 CDH 761051-2
1931 2B 599-1 2B 600-1	Bach, arr. Goossens: Suite in G Op. 24 London Symphony Orchestra	HMV 78	C 2273
1936 25 & 29 June London Abbey Road Studio No. 1 2EA 2999-1/-2 2EA 3000-1 2EA 4001-1A 2EA 4001-2 2EA 4002-2A 2EA 4005-2A 2EA 4006-2	Respighi: *La Boutique Fantasque* – Ballet from Rossini, complete London Philharmonic Orchestra	HMV 78 HMV 78	C 2846/8 C 7468/70
1936 29 July London 2EA 4007-1A 2EA 4010-1 2EA 4009-1A 2EA 4008-1	Tommasini: *The Good Humoured Ladies* – Suite after Scarlatti London Symphony Orchestra	HMV 78	C2864/5
1937 15 July London 2EA 1066/71-1	Schumann: *Carnaval* – Ballet Suite London Philharmonic Orchestra	HMV 78 Spanish HMV 78	C 2916/8 DB 4425/7
1937 16 July London 2EA 1072/75-1	Borodin: *Prince Igor* – Polovtsian Dances London Philharmonic Orchestra	HMV 78	C 3048/9
1937 16 July London 2EA 1076/8-1	Grieg: *Peer Gynt*, Suite No. 1 London Philharmonic Orchestra	HMV 78	C 2933/4

1937 2 Sept London 2EA 5310-2 2EA 5311-1A 2EA 5312-1	Grieg: *Peer Gynt*, Suite No. 1 London Philharmonic Orchestra	HMV 78	C 2933/4
1937 2 Sept London 2EA 5311/12-1	Grieg: Two Elegiac Melodies Op. 34 (The Heart Wounds & The Last Spring) London Philharmonic Orchestra	HMV 78	C 2935
1937 2 Sept London 2EA 5308-1A 2EA 5309-2	Handel: Concerto Grosso in B flat Léon Goossens, oboe London Philharmonic Orchestra	HMV 78 VIC 78	C 2993 12605
1937 3 Sept London 2EA 5313/18-1	Tchaikovsky: *Nutcracker* Suite London Philharmonic Orchestra	HMV 78	C 2922/4
1938 9 May London 2EA 6309/10-1 2EA 6311/12-2	Bizet: *L'Arlesienne* Suite London Symphony Orchestra	HMV 78	C 2021/2
1938 9 May London 2EA 6304-2 2EA 6305-1 2EA 6306-2 2EA 6307-1 2EA 6308-1 2EA 6303-3	Rimsky-Korsakov: *The Golden Cockerel* − Suite (Le Coq d'Or) London Symphony Orchestra	HMV 78 HMV A78 HMV 78	C 3013/5 C 7511/3 JOX 7018/20
1941 18 Feb Cincinnati 2A 062500/ 505	Walton: Violin Concerto − original version Jascha Heifetz, violin Cincinnati Symphony Orchestra	HMV 78 HMV A78 VIC 78	DB 5953/5 DB 8911/3 DM 868
1941 19−20 Feb Cincinnati CS 062506/14	Vaughan Williams: Symphony No. 2 'A London Symphony' − original version Cincinnati Symphony Orchestra (under pseudonym 'Cromwell Symphony Orchestra')	VIC 78 VIC 78 CAM (USA) LPm	11-8375/9 DM 916 CAL 186

1941 20 Feb Cincinnati 2A 062515/22-1	Tchaikovsky: Symphony No. 2 'The Little Russian' Cincinnati Symphony Orchestra	HMV 78 HMV A78	DB 5938/41 DB 8890/3
1945 25 Jan Cincinnati D5-RC-682	Chabrier: *Marche Joyeuse* Cincinnati Symphony Orchestra	HMV 78 HMV A78	DB 6382 DB 9339
1945 25 Jan Cincinnati D5-RC-674	Debussy: *En blanc et noir* Cincinnati Symphony Orchestra	RCA 78	unpub
1945 25 Jan Cincinnati D5-RC-665/8	Grieg: *Peer Gynt*, Suite No. 1 Cincinnati Symphony Orchestra	VIC 78 VIC 78 VIC 78 VIC 45m	11-8864/5 11-9452/3 SP 10 WDM 1100
1945 25 Jan Cincinnati D5-RC-675	Ravel, trans. Goossens: *Gaspard de la nuit* – Le Gibet Cincinnati Symphony Orchestra	RCA 78	unpub
1945 25 Jan Cincinnati D5-RC/676/81	Strauss, Richard: *Der Rosenkavalier* – Suite Prelude, Octavian & Marschallin Duo, Presentation, Intrigue, Ochs, Scene, Trio & Duet, Act III Waltzes Cincinnati Symphony Orchestra	VIC 78 VIC 78 CAM LPm	11-8783/5 DM 997 CAL 155
1945 25 Jan Cincinnati D5-RC-669/73	Stravinsky: *The Song of the Nightingale* (Le Chant du Rossignol) Cincinnati Symphony Orchestra	HMV 78 HMV A78 VIC 78	DB 6380/2 DB 9339/41 DM 1041
1946 14 Feb Cincinnati D6-RC-5139/40	Delius: *Village Romeo & Juliet* – Walk to the Paradise Garden Cincinnati Symphony Orchestra	VIC 78 CAM LPm	11-9493 CAL215
1946 14 Feb Cincinnati D6-RC-5143/6	Respighi: *The Fountains of Rome* (Le Fontane di Roma) Cincinnati Symphony Orchestra	RCA 78	unpub
1946 14 Feb Cincinnati D6-RC-5143/50	Respighi: *The Pines of Rome* (I Pini di Roma) Cincinnati Symphony Orchestra	VIC 78 VIC 78	12-0941/2 M-1039

1946 14 Feb Cincinnati D6-RC-5133/ 8	Schumann: Symphony No. 4 Cincinnati Symphony Orchestra	VIC 78	11-9593/5
1946 14 Feb Cincinnati D6-RC-5141	Wagner: *Götterdämmerung* – Chorus of the Gibichungs (trans. Goossens) Cincinnati Symphony Orchestra	RCA 78	unpub
1946 14 Feb Cincinnati D6-RC-5142	Wagner: *Siegfried* – Prelude to Act III Cincinnati Symphony Orchestra	RCA 78	unpub
1950 5 December Sydney	Antill: *Corroboree* – Ballet Suite Sydney Symphony Orchestra	EMI (Aust) 78 EMI (Aust) LPm	ED 1193/4 OALP 7503
1952 5 April Sydney 2EA 16655/7	Butterworth: *A Shropshire Lad* – Rhapsody Sydney Symphony Orchestra	EMI (Aust) LPm HMV A78	OXLP7620/1 DB 9792/3
1952 5 April Sydney 2EA 16654	Trad. arr. Grainger: Irish Tune from County Derry (Londonderry Air) Sydney Symphony Orchestra	HMV 78 EMI (Aust) LPm	DB 9792/3 OXLP7620/1
1952 8 & 10 April Sydney 2EA 16648/51 2EA 16652/3	Turina: *Sinfonia Sevillana* Sydney Symphony Orchestra	EMI (Aust) LPm EMI (Aust) 78	OALP 7503 ED 1210/2
1952 9 April Sydney OXEA 461/62 2EA 16744/51	Mendelssohn: Symphony No. 3 'Scotch' ABC Sydney Symphony Orchestra	HMV LPm	BLP 1045
1952 10 April Sydney 2EA 16887/8	Saint-Saëns: *Danse Macabre* Op. 40 Sydney Symphony Orchestra	HMV 78 HMV 45m EMI (Aust) LPm	DB21617 7P 236 OXLP7620/1
1952 21–22 April Sydney 2EA 16889/95 2XEA 463/64	Beethoven: Symphony No. 2 Sydney Symphony Orchestra (slow movement only)	HMV 78 HMV LPm EMI :Aust) LPm HMV LPm	ED 1206/9 ALP 1134 OXLP7620/1 CLP 1840
1952 5 May Sydney University 2EA 16866/9	Massenet: *Scènes Pittoresques* Sydney Symphony Orchestra	EMI (Aust) LPm HMV 78	OXLP7620/1 DB 9781/2

1953 2–3 Dec London XAX 448/9	Khatchaturian: Violin Concerto Igor Oistrakh, violin Philharmonia Orchestra	COL LPm MFP LPm	33 CX 1141 2050
1954 16 Jan London	Britten: *Les Illuminations* Op. 18 Peter Pears, tenor New Symphony Orchestra	DEC LPm	LXT 2941
1954 25 Jan London	Britten: Serenade for Tenor, Horn & Strings Op. 31 Peter Pears, tenor; Dennis Brain, horn New Symphony Orchestra	DEC LPm DEC LPm DEC LPs	LXT 2941 ECM 507 ECS 507
1954 26 Jan London	Britten: Simple Symphony Op. 4 New Symphony Orchestra	DEC LPm	LW 5163
1954 27 Jan London	Chopin: Prelude and Fugue for 18-piece string orchestra New Symphony Orchestra	DEC LPm	unpub
1954 15 March London	Bridge: Two Old English Folk Songs (Sally in our Alley & Cherry Ripe) New Symphony Orchestra	DEC 45	71071
1954 London	Schumann: Piano Concerto Bela Siki, piano; Pro Arte Orchestra	PYE LPm PYE CD	CCT 31008 PVCD 8371
1956 13-14 Sept London 2XEA 1293/ 94 2XEA 133-7	Lalo: Symphonie Espagnole Op. 21 Yehudi Menuhin, violin Philharmonia Orchestra	HMV LPm HMV LPs HMV LPs CFP LPs SER TC	ALP 1571 ASD 290 SXLP 30277 40364 4XG60370
1956 22, 24 & 26 Oct London OXEA 1073/ 74	Tchaikovsky: Violin Concerto Op. 35 Ida Haendel, violin Royal Philharmonic Orchestra	HMV LPm,	DLP 1190
1956	Auber: *Manon Lescaut* – C'est l'histoire amoureuse Evelyn Scotney, soprano Orchestra incl. in 'Great Australian Singers'	Aust LPm	AO-1
1957 7–8 Feb London 2XEA 940-1N 2YEA 30-4	Rimsky-Korsakov: *The Golden Cockerel* – Suite (Le Coq d'Or) Philharmonia Orchestra	HMV LPm CFP LPs WRC LPm WRC LPm HMV LP	ALP 1490 126 TC240 T548 ASD 262

1957 8 Feb London 2XEA 939-2N 2YEA 29-4	Balakirev: *Islamey* (orchestrated by Casella) Philharmonia Orchestra	HMV LPm WRC LPm WRC TCm CFP LPs HMV LP	ALP 1490 T 548 TC 240 CFP 128 ASD 262
1957 13 Feb London 2XEA 939-2N 2YEA 29-4	Rimsky-Korsakov: Russian Easter Festival Overture Philharmonia Orchestra	HMV LPm CFP LPs WRC LPm WRC LPm HMV LP	ALP1490 126 TE 246 T 548 ASD 262
1957 13–14 Feb London 2XEA 938	Scriabin: *Poèm of Ecstasy* (Poème de l'èxtase) Op. 54 Philharmonia Orchestra	HMV LPm	ALP 1470
1957 14–15 Feb London 2XEA 937	Albeniz: *Iberia* (orchestrated by Arbos) Philharmonia Orchestra	HMV LPm HMV TCm	ALP 1470 SAT 1019M
1957 14–15 Feb London	Scriabin: *Rêverie* Philharmonia Orchestra	HMV LPm HMV TCs	ALP 1470 SAT 1013
1957 18 Sept London 2XEA 1390	Ravel: *Alborada del Gracioso* Royal Philharmonic Orchestra	HMV LPm	ALP 1706
1957 18 Sept London	Ravel: *Boléro* Royal Philharmonic Orchestra	HMV LPm	ALP 1627
1957 19 Sept London 2XEA 1678 2YEA 241	Respighi: *The Fountains of Rome* (Le Fontane di Roma) Philharmonia Orchestra	HMV LPm HMV LPs HMV LPm HMV LPs HMV LPs CFP LPs	ALP 1785 ASD 366 XLP 30068 SXLP 30068 SXLP 30046 40204
1957 20 Sept 2XEA 1390	Ravel: *Rhapsodie Espagnole* Royal Philharmonic Orchestra	HMV LPm	ALP 1706
1957 23 Sept 2XEA 1391	Debussy: *Iberia* Royal Philharmonic Orchestra	HMV LPm	ALP 1706
1957 23 Sept 2XEA 1391	Dukas: *The Sorcerer's Apprentice* Royal Philharmonic Orchestra	HMV LPm HMV LPm HMV LPs	ALP 1706 XLP 30046 SXLP 30046

1957	Respighi: *La Boutique Fantasque*	HMV LPm	BLP 1104
24 & 26 Sept	— Ballet from Rossini, complete	HMP LPs	BSD 752
London	Royal Philharmonic Orchestra	HMV LPs	SXLP 30046
OXEA 1418/9		HMV LPs	CFP 40204
OYEA 69-3			(Parts only)
OYEA 70-9			
1957	Mussorgsky, orch. Ravel: *Pictures at an*	HMV LPm	ALP 1627
26 & 28 Sept	*Exhibition*	HMV LPs	SXLP 30068
2XEA 1388/	Royal Philharmonic Orchestra		
89			
1957	Mendelssohn: Overture — *The Hebrides*	HMV LP	unpub
28 Sept	(Fingal's Cave) Op. 26		
	Royal Philharmonic Orchestra		
1957	Chopin: Concerto No. 1 in E minor	HMV LPm	ALP 1580
1—3 Oct	Op. 11	MFP LPm	2048
London	Chopin: Concerto No. 2 in F minor		
2XEA 1347/	Op. 21		
48	Abbey Simon, piano		
	Royal Philharmonic Orchestra		
1957	Fauré: Fantaisie for Piano & Orchestra	HMV LPm	CLP 1255
14—15 Oct	Grant Johannessen, piano	HMV LPs	SXLP 30033
London	London Symphony Orchestra		
2XEA 1356			
1957	d'Indy: Symphony on a French	HMV LPm	CLP 1255
14—15 Oct	Mountain Air		
London	Grant Johannessen, piano		
2XEA 1355	London Symphony Orchestra		
1957	Wheeler: *Green Waters*	EMI (Aust)	OALP 7511
	Sydney Symphony Orchestra	LPm	
1958	Antheil: Symphony No. 4	EVT LPs	3013
London	London Symphony Orchestra	EVT LPm	6013
1958	Antill: *Corroboree* — Ballet Suite	EVT LPs	3013
London	London Symphony Orchestra	EVT LPm	6013
		WRC LPm	TC 327
1958	Franck: Symphonic Variations	EVT LPs	3036
London	Peter Katin, piano	TR LPm	35 056
	London Symphony Orchestra	WRC LPm	TP 71
1958	Franck: Symphonic Variations	PYE CD	PVCD 8371
London	Bela Siki, piano		
	Pro Arte Orchestra		
1958	Hindemith: Violin Concerto	EVT LPs	3040
London	Joseph Fuchs, violin		
	London Symphony Orchestra		
1958	Lalo: *Symphonie Espagnole* Op. 21	HMV LPm	ALP 1571
2XEA 1293/	Yehudi Menuhin, violin	HMV LP	ASD 290
94	Philharmonia Orchestra	SER TC	4XG-60370
2YEA 133-2			

1958	Mozart: Violin Concerto No. 3 K216 Joseph Fuchs, violin London Symphony Orchestra	EVT LPs	3040
1958 London	Rachmaninov: Symphonic Dances London Symphony Orchestra	EVT LPs EVT LPs TR LPm WRC LPm EVT TCa	3051 & 3151 SDBR 3004 BUY-002 T 277 3004
1958 London	Stravinsky: Symphony in Three Movements London Symphony Orchestra	EVT LPs EVT LP PHI CD	3009 BR 6009 422 303-2
1959 7 Jan London 2XEA 1678 2YEA 241	Glinka: *Jota Aragonesa* Philharmonia Orchestra	HMV LPm HMV LPs	ALP 1785 ASD 366
1959 7 Jan London 2XEA 1677 2YEA 240	Smetana: *The Bartered Bride* − Overture, Furiant & Dance Philharmonia Orchestra	HMV LPm HMV LPs	ALP 1785 ASD 366
1959 7 Jan London 2XEA 1678 2YEA 241	Weinberger: *Schwanda the Bagpiper* − Polka & Fugue Philharmonia Orchestra	JMV LPm HMV LPs	ALP 1785 ASD 366
1959 March London	Prokofiev: Symphony No. 1 'Classical' Pro Arte Orchestra	PYE LPm	CEC 23032
1959 14 Sept London 2YEA 134-1	Saint-Saëns: *Havanaise* Yehudi Menuhin, violin Philharmonia Orchestra	HMV LPm HMV LPm SER TCs HMV LPs CFP TCs CFP CD	ALP 1571 ASD 290 4XG 60370 SXLP 30277 CFP 40364 MOM 118
1959 14 Sept London 2YEA 134-1	Saint-Saëns: Introduction & Rondo Capriccioso Yehudi Menuhin, violin Philharmonia Orchestra	HMV LPm HMV LPm HMV LPs SER TCs CFP TCs CFP CD	ALP 1571 ASD 290 SXLP 30277 4XG 60370 CFP 40364 MOM 118
1959 London	Ginastera: *Estancia* − Ballet Suite London Symphony Orchestra	EVT LPs EVT LPm EVT LPs	3013 LPBR 6041 3041
1959 London	Ginastera: *Panambi* − Ballet Suite London Symphony Orchestra	EVT LPs EVT LPm EVT LPs	3003 LPBR 6041 3041

1959	Khatchaturian: Cello Concerto Orlov, cello Romanian Philharmonic Orchestra	ECD	
1959 Vienna	Prokofiev: *Peter and the Wolf* José Ferrer, narrator Vienna State Opera Orchestra	KAP LPs	KDC 6002
1959 Vienna	Rachmaninov: Piano Concert No. 3 Ann Schein, piano Vienna State Opera Orchestra	KAP LPs	KDC 6000
1959 London	Rimsky-Korsakov: *Scheherazade* London Symphony Orchestra	EVT LPm EVT LPs WRC LPm HAL LPs PIC CD ALL LPs WRC TCa	SDBR 3026 6026 TP 148 HM 512 DTD 10031 STAE 2005 TTP 148
1959 London	Schumann: Piano Concerto Peter Katin, piano London Symphony Orchestra	EVT LPs TR LPm WRC LPm	3036 35 036 TP 71
1959 London	Stravinsky: *Petrushka* − original version London Symphony Orchestra	EVT LPm EVT LPs WRC LPm WRC LPs TR LPm TR (Aust) LPs TR CD EVT TCs	6033 3033 CM 23 SCM 23 BUY 007 STRC 601T SMBCD 1001 3033
1959 London	Stravinsky: *The Rite of Spring* London Symphony Orchestra	WRC LPs HAL LPm EVT LPs EVT LPm	T159 HM 542 3047 LPBR 6047
1959 London	Tchaikovsky: Manfred Symphony London Symphony Orchestra	EVT LPs EVT LPs WRC LPm	SDBR 3035 BR 3035 T 209
1959 London	Villa-Lobos: *Bachianas Brasilieras* No. 2 − The Little Train of the Caipira (Toccata) London Symphony Orchestra	EVT LPm EVT LPs WRC LPs TRA LPs	BR 6041 3041 TP 164 TRA SAM 24
1960 5−6 & 16−17 May 2YEA 479 2YEA 480 7TEA 1757/ 58 7TYEA 384/ 85	Grieg: Piano Concerto − 3rd movement Mendelssohn: Piano Concerto No. 1 − 2nd movement Rachmaninov: Piano Concerto No. 2 − 1st movement Saint-Saëns: Piano Concerto No. 2 − 2nd movement Schumann: Piano Concerto − 1st movement	HMV LPm HMV LPs HMV 45m HMV 45s	CLP 1461 CSD 1373 7EP 7131 PES 5284

	Tchaikovsky: Piano Concerto No. 1 – 3rd movement Benno Moiseiwitsch, piano Royal Philharmonic Orchestra		
1960 13 May London	Wieniawski: Violin Concerto No. 3 Michael Rabin, violin Philharmonia Orchestra	CAP LPm CAP LPs ELA LPs	P 8534 SP 9534 IC 037-82.112
1960 14 May London	Paganini: Violin Concerto No. 1 Michael Rabin, violin Philharmonia Orchestra	CAP LPm CAP LPs ELA LPs	P 8534 SP 8534 IC 037.82 112
1960 London	Berlioz: *Symphonie Fantastique* London Symphony Orchestra	EVT LPs PIC LPs WRC LPs	3037 SODA 314 T93
1960	Chopin: Piano Concerto No. 2 Ann Schein, piano Vienna State Opera Orchestra	KAP LPs	KDC 6001
1960 London	Respighi: *Roman Festivals* (Feste Romane) London Symphony Orchestra	EVT LPs EVT LPs TR LPm WRC LPm	3150 SDBR 3004 25 019 T 277
1961 June London	Mendelssohn: Symphony No. 4 'Italian' London Philharmonic Orchestra	SAG LPs ARC LPm CC LPm CC Da Vinci LPm	XID 5056 FDX 2061 X 512 61
1961 June London	Mendelssohn: Symphony No. 5 'Reformation' London Philharmonic Orchestra (Andante only)	SAG LPs ARC LPm CC LPm CC Da Vinci LPm FID LPm CC Van Gogh LPm	XID 5056 FDX 2060 X 512 504 FID 2060 1000
1961 London	Bach: Concerto for Two Violins & Orchestra (BWV 1043) David & Igor Oistrakh, violins Royal Philharmonic Orchestra	DGG LPs DGG LPs DGG LPs DGG CD	138820 2726 008 2535 176 419 855-2
1961 London	Beethoven: Romances for Violin & Orchestra No. 1 in G & No. 2 in F David Oistrakh, violin Royal Philharmonic Orchestra	DGG LPs DGG LPs DGG LPs DGG TCs DGG TCs DGG CD	135039 2563 765 3318 006 3335 109 413 844-4 427 192-2
1961 Vienna	Khatchaturian: *Masquerade* – Suite Vienna State Opera Orchestra	KAP LPs	KDC 6002

| 1962
March
London | Still: Symphony No. 3
London Symphony Orchestra | SAG LPm/s
LYR LPs | XID 5256
SRCS 56 |

SIR EUGENE GOOSSENS KBE (1893–1962) — PIANIST

| 1926
London | Goossens: Sonata No. 1 for Violin &
Piano — Molto Adagio only
André Mangeot, violin | NGS 78a | 29/30 |

SIR EUGENE GOOSSENS KBE (1893–1962) — VIOLINIST

Recordings made by the Philharmonic Quartet with Eugene Goossens III playing second violin.

> Arthur Beckwith — first violin
> Raymond Jeremy — viola
> Cedric Sharpe — cello

Recordings by this quartet were issued as single sided pressings with four-digit catalogue numbers sided with D and E catalogue numbers.

1915 12 July London Ho 1671 ab	Boccherini: Quintette Op. 14 No. 3 — Minuet	HMV 78a	8101 E157
1915 12 July London Ho 1674 aB	Tchaikovsky: Quartet No. 1 in D Op. 11 – Andante Cantabile		9104 E157
1916 17 Feb London Ho 2478 ab	Mendelssohn: Quartette No. 1 Op. 12 — Conzonetta in E flat	HMV 78a	8112 E153
1916 27 March London Ho 2671 ae	Mendelssohn: Spring Song in A Op. 62 No. 6	HMV 78a	8121 E156
1916 27 March London Ho 2672 ae	Thomas: Mignon — Gavotte	HMV 78a	8130 E156
1918 23 March London Ho 4036 ae	Traditional, arr. Frank Bridge Cherry Ripe	HMV 78a	8202 E1
1918 25 March London Ho 4037 ae	Schubert: Marche Militaire, Op. 51	HMV 78a	8203 E1

1918 March	Arr. Frank Bridge Londonderry Air/Sally in Our Alley	HMV 78a	D14
1918 March	Frank Bridge: Three Idylls − Nos. 1 and 3	HMV 78a	D479
1918 March	Schumann: Quartet Op. 41 No. 3 (Excerpts)	HMV 78a	D13
1920 9 Jan London	Glazounov: Noveletes for String Quartet, Op. 15 – No. 2 Orientale	HMV 78a	8262 E199
1920 1 June London	Mozart: Minuet in D minor	HMV 78a	8263 E199

Léon Goossens CBE (1897–1988) – Oboist

Léon Goossens made superlative recordings of many works for the oboe including Mozart's Quartet K370 and Quintet K452, the Bax Quintet, Vaughan Williams' Concerto and the first recording of Strauss' Concerto in its original version.

He played in several dance bands during the 1920s and 1930s. This discography contains several examples of recordings in which he is known to have taken part.

Much of his orchestral recording work was done as Principal Oboist in Beecham's London Philharmonic Orchestra. Although unnamed on labels his presence is clearly evident by his distinctive tone. The following list includes works where his unique playing is clearly heard.

Collections of oboe solos issued in the stereo LP era show his wide-ranging style and superb interpretative abilities.

1923 10565K	de Falla: *The Three-Cornered Hat* – Danse des Voisins Russian Ballet Orchestra cond. M Defosse	EDB 78	0150
1923 10566F	de Falla: *The Three-Cornered Hat* – Danse du Meunier Russian Ballet Orchestra cond. M Defosse	EDB 78	0150
1923 X 1147 E	Pierné: *Pastorale* London Wind Quintette Robert Murchie, flute; Haydn Draper, clarinet; Léon Goossens, oboe; W James, bassoon; S Salkeld, horn	EDB 78a	VF 515
1923 X 1148 J	Scarlatti: Andante & Allegro London Wind Quintette Robert Murchie, flute; Haydn Draper, clarinet; Léon Goossens, oboe; W James, bassoon; S Salkeld, horn	EDB 78a	VF 515

The Goossens

1926 Jan/Feb London Q+ R+ S+ Q− R− S−	Mozart: Oboe Quartet in F, K370 Bach: Cantata No. 156 – Arioso Members of the Spencer Dyke Quartet Spencer Dyke and Edwin Quaife, violins; Ernest Tomlinson, viola; P Patterson Parker, cello	NGS 78	Q, R & S
1927 March London 71ex, 72ex 73e, 74e	Bax: Quintet for Oboe and Strings International Quartet André Mangeot and Boris Pecker, violins; Frank Howerd, viola; Herbert Withers, cello	NGS 78	76 77
1927 CC 12007-1	Bach: Cantata No. 159 Es ist Vollbracht sung by Elisabeth Schumann, soprano obbligato by Léon Goossens	HMV 78	D 1410
1928 7 August London Z 564-1	*Dance, Little Lady* Ciro's Club Dance Band dir. Debroy Somers	VOC 78	282A
1929 2 Jan London Bb 15317-3 Bb 15318-2	*There's a Blue Ridge Round My Heart* Virginia Mistakes New Mayfair (Dance) Orchestra dir. Carroll Gibbons	HMV 78	B5588
1929 19 Sept London WAX 4067-1/ 69-1 WAX 4070-1 WAX 4071-1/ 72-1	Mozart: Quintet for Piano and Wind in E flat K452 Kathleen Long, piano; Frederick Thurston, cello; Aubrey Brain, horn; John Alexandra, bassoon	NGS 78	121 122 123
1931 Jan Petit France London WA 11100	Bach: Sinfonia from Cantata No. 156 The Columbia History of Music by Ear and Eye Vol. IV Part 14 Strings of the Bach Cantata Club London cond. Scott	COL 78 HMV LPm	DB 506 HQM 1087
1931 21 Jan Petit France London WA 11081-2	Bach: *Jesus, Joy of Man's Desiring* The Columbia History of Music by Ear and Eye Vol. II Part 15 Bach Cantata Club, London dir. Kennedy Scott	COL 78 DB 507	
1931 10 March London WA 11313-2	Thomé: *Simple Aveu* Clarence Raybould, piano	COL 78	DB 600

480

1931 10 March London WA 11312-2 WA 11314-1	Kreisler: *Leibesleid* Rameau: Gavotte Clarence Raybould, piano	COL 78	DB 768
1931 15 June London WA 11310-4	Saint Saëns: *Le Cygne* *Clarence Raybould, piano*	*COL 78*	*DB 600* *DB 691*
1931 *15 June* *London* *WA 11311-4* *CA 11719-1*	*Londonderry Air* Fauré: *Pièce* Clarence Raybould, piano	COL 78	DB 691
1931 20 Oct Small Queen's Hall, London 2B1176-3/77-3	*Cavalcade* – Part 1 – Prologue *Cavalcade* – Part 2 – Epilogue Noël Coward and New Mayfair Orchestra dir. Ray Noble	HMV 78	C2289
1932 6 Jan London 2B 2089-2 2B 2090-1 OB 2091-1	*Bow Bells* – Selection, Part 1 *Bow Bells* – Selection, Part 2 *The Punter's Lament* HMV 4085 New Mayfair Orchestra dir. Ray Noble	HMV 78 HMV 78 VIC 78	C2342 4085 24022
1932 6 Jan London OB 2091-1	*The Punter's Lament* New Mayfair Orchestra dir. Ray Noble	HMV 78	4085
1932 9 Feb London OB 2177 1-2-3 OB 2178 1-2	*You came into my heart* *I whistle under your window* New Mayfair Orchestra dir. Ray Noble	HMV 78 HMV 78 HMV 78 VIC 78	rejected rejected 6146 24173
1932 9 Feb London OB 2179-2	*Goodnight, little girl, goodnight* New Mayfair Orchestra dir. Ray Noble	HMV 78 HMV 78 HMV 78 VIC 78	rejected rejected 6146 24173
1933 6 May London CAX 6836/37	Rossini: *The Silken Ladder* – Overture Handel: *Solomon* – The Arrival of the Queen of Sheba London Philharmonic Orchestra cond. Beecham	COL 78	LX 255
1933 London CAX 6738/39 CAX 6740/41 7 TEA 1911/12	Mozart: Oboe Quartet in F major, K370 J Lener, violin; S Roth, viola; I Hartman, cello	COL 78 COL 45m WRC LPm	LX 256-7 7ER 5232 SH 318

481

1934 9 April Abbey Road Studio No. 1 CAX 7120-1, 2 CAX 7121-1, 2, 3, 4, 5 CAX 7122-1, 2 CAX 7123-1, 2 CAX 7124-1, 2 CAX 7125-1, 2 2XEA 5723	Delius: *Paris* London Philharmonic Orchestra cond. Beecham	COL 78 WRC LPm BEE CD	SDX1-3 SH 321 BEECHAM 2
1934 13 April London OB 5974-2 2B 6865-1 2B 6866-2	*Three Sisters* − Selection, Part 1 *Three Sisters* − Selection, Part 2 *In a Shelter from a Shower* New Mayfair Orchestra	HMV 78 HMV 78	C2661 B6478
1934 6 July London CA 14581-1 CA 14584-1	Van Phillips: *Nicolette* Elgar, arr. V Phillips: Salut d'amour Van Phillips and his All-star Orchestra Van Phillips Quartet (3 oboes & cor anglais)	COL 78	DB 1440
1934 6 July London CA 14582-1/83- 1	*It's All Forgotten Now* The Breeze Van Phillips and his All-Star Orchestra	COL 78 CB 774	
1936 2EA 2986-92 2EA 2997-98	Brahms: Concerto in D, Op. 77 for violin and orchestra London Philharmonic Orchestra Fritz Kreisler, violin cond. Barbirolli	HMV	DB 2915-8 DBS 2919
1937 1 Feb London CAX 7922-1 CAX 7923-1 CAX 7924-2 CAX 7925-1	Bax: *Nonet* Frederick Thurston, clarinet; J Slater, flute; Victor Watson, double-bass; Korchinska, harp; Griller Quartet	COL 78	ROX 182/4
1937 2 Sept 2EA 5308-9	Handel: Concerto Grosso in B flat major Op. 6 No. 7 London Philharmonic Orchestra cond. E Goossens III	HMV 78	C2993
1937 26 Nov 2EA 5917-24	Bizet: Symphony No. 1 in C London Philharmonic Orchestra cond. Goehr	HMV 78	C2986-89

1938 11 Feb Abbey Road Studio No. 1 CAX 8189-1, 1a CAX 8189-2, 2a 2XEA 5726	Delius, arr. Fenby: *Koanga* – La Calinda London Philharmonic Orchestra cond. Beecham	COL 78 COL LPm WRC LPm BEE CD	SDX 21 SEL 1700 SH 322 BEECHAM 3
1939 23 May & 28 June Abbey Road Studio No. 3 CAX 8579-2 CAX 8580-1/ 81-1 CAX 8593	Schumann: *Three Romances* Op. 94 No. 1 in A minor No. 2 in A major No. 3 in A minor Gerald Moore, piano	COL 78 COL 78 HMV LPm TES CD	DX 936 DX 937 HQM 1087 SBT 1023
1939 23 May London CAX 8582-1/ 82-2	Purcell: (a) Air, (b) Hornpipe Gerald Moore, piano	COL 78	unpub
1939 28 June Abbey Road CAX 8593-1/ 93-2	César Franck: *Pièce* Gerald Moore, piano	COL 78	DX 937
1943 25 Oct Liverpool CAX 9122-1/ 24-1	Cimarosa-Benjamin: Concerto for Oboe and Strings Royal Liverpool Philharmonic Orchestra cond. Sargent	COL 78 COL 78 HMV LPm	DX 1137 DX 1138 HQM 1087
1943 25 Oct Liverpool CAX 9125-1	Bach-Whittaker: Sinfonia from the Easter Oratorio Liverpool Philharmonic Orchestra cond. Sargent	COL 78	DX 1138
1943 20 Dec Liverpool CAX 9134-2 CAX 9135	Handel: Concerto Grosso in G minor Op. 3, No. 10 Liverpool Philharmonic Orchestra cond. Cameron	COL 78	DX 1144
1943 21 Dec Liverpool CAX 9145-1/ 46-1	Marcello: Concerto in C minor Liverpool Philharmonic Orchestra cond. Cameron	COL 78	unpub

1947	Marcello: Concerto in C minor	COL 78	DX 1389
22 April	Philharmonia String Orchestra	COL 78	DX 1390
London	cond. Susskind	HMV LPm	HQM 1087
CAX 9867-1			
CAX 9868-2			
CAX 9869-1			
1947	Scarlatti, (arr. Bryan): Concerto No. 1 in	COL 78	DX 8347/8
23 April	G major	HMV LPm	CLP 1698
London	Philharmonia String Orchestra		
CAX 9878-1	cond. Susskind		
CAX 9870-3			
CAX 9880-3			
1947	Fiocco, arr. Bent and O'Neill: *Arioso*	COL 78	DX 1390
16 June	Gerald Moore, piano		
Abbey Road			
Studio No. 2			
CAX 9973-1			
1947	Pierné: *Aubade*	COL 78	DX 8347
16 June	with Gerald Moore, piano		
Abbey Road			
Studio No.2			
CAX 9973/4			
1947	Strauss: Oboe Concerto in D major	COL 78	DX 1444-6
15 & 23 Sept	Philharmonia String Orchestra	HMV LPm	CLP 1698
Kingsway Hall	cond. Galliera	WRC LPm	SH 243
CAX 10030-3		TES CD	SBT 1009
to			
CAX 10037-8			
2XE 2457			
1948	Bach: Cantata No. 82 — Ich habe genug	COL 78	unpub
15 April	Philharmonia Orchestra		
Kingsway Hall	Hans Hotter, baritone		
CAX 10221-1/	Dr Thalben-Ball, organ		
22-1			
1948	Goossens: Oboe Concerto, Op. 45	COL 78	DCX 84/5
26 April	Philharmonia Orchestra		DX 1578/9
Abbey Road	cond. Susskind	UNI LPm	RHS 348
Studio No. 1			
CAX 10240-1			
CAX 10241-1			
CAX 10242			
CAX 10243-1			
1949	Bach (arr. Tovey): Concerto in A major	HMV LP	CLP 1656
1 & 3 June	Léon Goossens, oboe d'amore	HMV LPm	HQM 1087
Abbey Road	Philharmonia Orchestra	WRC LPm	SH 243
Studio No. 1	cond. Susskind		
2XEA 2315			

1949 1 June London CAX 10530-1 CAX 10531-2 CAX 10532-1	Vivaldi: Oboe Concerto in D minor, Op. 8 No. 9 Philharmonia Orchestra cond. Susskind	COL 78	DX 8367 DX 8368
1950 27 March London Abbey Road CAX 10774-1/- 2 CAX 10779-1/- 2	Albinoni (arr. Paumgartner): Concerto in D Op. 7 No. 6 Philharmonia Orchestra cond. Susskind	COL 78	DX 1753
1950 27 March London Abbey Road CAX 10780-1/- 2	Albinoni: Concerto in B flat, Op. 7 No. 3 Philharmonia Orchestra cond. Susskind	COL 78	DX 8367
1950 27 March Abbey Road Studio No. 3 2EA 14560-2A 2EA 14569-2A 2EA 14561-1A 2EA 14586-2 2EA 14587-1 2EA 14585-6A	Warlock: *The Curlew* René Soames, tenor; Geoffrey Gilbon, flute; Aeolian Quartet	HMV	C 7934/6
1952 4 June & 1 Sept Abbey Road & Kingsway Hall 2XEA 2316	Vaughan Williams: Concerto for Oboe and Strings Philharmonia Orchestra cond. Susskind	HMV LPs HMV LPs WRC LPm	CLP 1656 HQM 1087 SH 243
1960 29 March Walthamstow	Mozart: Concerto for Oboe & Orchestra in C, K314 Sinfonia of London cond. Colin Davis	WRC LPs	T 59
1961 London 7TEA 1547-15	Bach, arr. Thalben-Ball; *Jesu, joy of man's* *desiring* Dr G Thalben-Ball, organ and the Temple Church Choir Handel, arr. Thalben-Ball: *Where's you walk* Dr G Thalben-Ball, organ Edward Walker and George Crozier, flutes	HMV 45m	7ER 5205

7TEA 1548-15 Handel: *Largo*
Dr G Thalben-Ball, organ
and Renata Scheffel-Stein, harp
Bach: *Sheep may safely graze*
Dr G Thalben-Ball, organ
Edward Walker and George Crozier, flutes

1961 London	The Art of Léon Goossens Bach, arr. Whittaker: Sinfonia from the Easter Oratoria Fiocco, arr. Bent and O'Neill: *Arioso* Pierné: *Aubade* Franck, arr. Doney: Andantino (Piece V) Trad, arr. Hughes: *Irish Song* Templeton: *Scherzo Caprice* Senaillé, arr. Moffat: *Entrée et Cotillon* Bach, arr. Whittaker: Sinfonia from Cantata No. 156 Alan Richardson: *Roundelay* Barthé: *Couvre feu* Templeton: *Siciliano* Morgan Nicholas: *Melody* Kelly: *Jig* (from Serenade No. 7)	HMV LPs	CSD 1419
1962 19-20 April London	Bach: Concerto in D minor for Violin and Oboe BWV 1060 Bath Festival Chamber Orchestra with Yehudi Menuhin, violin	HMV LPm HMV LPs HMV TCs	ALP 1949 ASD 500 XLP 30294
1962 19—20 April London	Handel: Three Concerti for Oboe and Strings No. 1 in B flat major No. 2 in B flat major No. 3 in G minor Bath Festival Chamber Orchestra cond. Menuhin	HMV LPm HMV LPs HMV TCs	ALP 1949 ASK 500 XLP 30294
1962 19—20 April London	Vivaldi: Concerto in B minor Op. 3 No. 10 Bath Festival Chamber Orchestra cond. Yehudi Menuhin	HMV LPm HMV LPs HMV TCs	ALP 1949 ASK 500 XLP 30294
1964 1 Oct Abbey Road Studio No. 1 7TEA 2021-15 7TEA 2022-15	Solo Instruments of the Orchestra No. 8 Léon Goossens, oboe and cor anglais with Gerald Moore, pinao Field, arr. Evelyn Rothwell: Nocturne W K Stanton: *Aubade* Handel, arr. Elizabeth Poston for cor anglais: *Semele* – Somnus's aria, Sleep Michael Head: Presto		
1965 London 7TEA 2021-15	Field, arr. Evelyn Rothwell; *Nocturne* Gerald Moore, piano W K Stanton: *Aubade*	HMV 45m	7EP 7185

7TEA 2022-15	Gerald Moore, piano Handel, arr. Elizabeth Poston for Cor Anglais; *Semele* − Sommus's aria, Sleep Michael Head: Presto		
1969 London	A Tribute to Gerald Moore Bach, trans Donald C Powell: Cantata No. 29 *Siciliano* Gerald Moore, piano	HMV LPs	SAN 255
1976 July Guildhall Southampton	Elgar: Suite for Oboe and Orchestra − Soliliquy Bournemouth Sinfonietta cond. Del Mar with nine other short works by Elgar	RCA LPs CHA LPs CHA CD	LRL1 5133 CHAN 8371
1977 27 & 28 July St John's Smith Square London	Bach: Concerto for Violin, Oboe & Orchestra in D minor BWV 1060 Takayoshi Wanami, violin and the London Mozart Players cond. Harry Blech	RCA LPs AUC CD	RL 25153 ART 3011
1977 London	The Art of Léon Goossens	RCA LPs	RL 25142

Michael Krein: Serenade for Oboe and Two Harps
Marie Goossens and Sidonie Goossens, harps

Morgan Nicholas: *Melody*, arr. Marie Goossens
Marie Goossens, harp

Somers-Cocks: Three Sketches Op. 1
Stanton: *Chanson pastorale* (Two Pieces)
Richardson: *Scherzino*
Henschel: *Shepherd's Lament*
Pitfield: *Rondo lirico*
Hughes: *Bard of Armagh*
Dunhill: Three Short Pieces Op. 81 −
Romance
Boyce: *Matelotte*
David Lloyd, piano

Bach: Easter Oratorio − Sinfonia
Finzi: Interlude Op. 21
Saunders: *A Cotswold Pastoral*
Fitzwilliam String Quartet

1977 London	Eugene Goossens: *Islamite Dance* Two songs −*Searching for lambs*, Op. 49 *When thou art dead*, Op. 43 Old Chinese Folk-song, Op. 4 David Lloyd, piano	UNI LPs	RHS 348

487

Concerto for Oboe, Op. 45
Philharmonia Orchestra
cond. Walter Susskind

1979   Vaughan-Williams: Fantasia on *Greensleeves*   UNI LPs   MS 1000
London   arr. Chiarelli
              Sidonie Goossens, harp; John Cargo, flute;
              City of London Junior Chamber Orchestra
              dir. Malcolm Henderson

Marie Goossens OBE (1894–1991)
– Harpist

Marie Goossens' exceptionally long career was characterised by great versatility and a spirit of adventure which remained undiminished throughout her working life. The following list includes some early solo work and a selection of recordings from her periods as Principal Harpist of the London Philharmonic Orchestra and the London Symphony Orchestra in which she can be clearly heard.

She entered the light music field at the age of 65 where, in addition to radio, film and TV work, she made numerous commercial records in which she took great pleasure. Her composition and playing of the signature tune for BBC's *Mrs Dale's Diary* and her backing to Gracie Fields' 'I Took My Harp to a Party' typify her joyful attitude to music making.

1924 03585X 03586	Goossens: Suite for flute, violin and harp Op. 6, Divertissement Charles Stainer, flute; Charles Woodhouse, violin	VOC 78a	KD-05104
1926 22 feb London WA 4271	J Dubez: *Song Without Words* No. 2	COL 78	1624R
1926 10 June London WA 3409-1	Braga: *Angel's Serenade* Violin, flute and harp trio	COL 78	2169R
1926 18 Oct London WA 4270-1	Hasselmans: *Prayer*	COL 78	2169R
1926 18 Oct London WA 4273-1	Molloy: *Love's old Sweet Song* Violin, cello and harp trio	COL 78	1624R

1933 30 Oct Ob 5153	'I Took My Harp to a Party' Gracie Fields, comedienne; with orchestra cond. Ray Noble	HMV 78	B8065
1934 13 April London OB 6874-1	*The Very Thought of You* New Mayfair Orchestra dir. Ray Noble	RVI 78	24657 20-2950
1935 3 & 17 April 16 July London CAX 7502-4 CAX 7521	Dvořák: Slavonic Rhapsody London Philharmonic Orchestra cond. Beecham	COL 78	LX 402 LX 403
1936 19 June London CAX 7806/07	Offenbach: *Tales of Hoffman –* Barcarolle London Philharmonic Orchestra cond. Beecham	COL 78	LX 530
1936 30 Nov London 2EA 3847-1 2EA 3848-1	Medley: *The Very Thought of You* Part 1 – The Touch of Your Lips; Love is the Sweetest Thing Medley: *Love Locked Out* Part II – What More Can I Ask?; Goodnight, Sweetheart New Mayfair Orchestra dir. Ray Noble	HMV 78 RVI 78	C-2872 36194
1939 13 Feb London CAX 8394-95	Debussy: *Prélude à l'Après* *Midi d'un Faune* London Philharmonic Orchestra cond. Beecham	COL 78	LX 805
1939 30 Nov 19 Dec London CAX 8667-68	Chabrier: *España* London Philharmonic Orchestra	COL 78	LX 880
1948 London	On the Air 60 Years of BBC Theme Music Goossens: *Mrs Dale's Diary*	BBC LPm TCs issued	Ref 454 ZCD 454 1982
1952 21 & 22 Feb AR16785-1/ 89-1 AR16790-1/ 92-1	Sibelius: Symphony No. 1 in E minor Op. 39 London Symphony Orchestra cond. Anthony Collins	DEC LPm	LL 5741 B 19069
1954 2 June London E/AR 19106/9 E/AR 19110/ 18	Holst: *The Planets* London Symphony Orchestra cond. Sargent	DEC LPs	LXT 2871 CEP 544

1955 Nov London 2XEA 799 2XEA 800	Rimsky-Korsakov: *Scheherezade* Philharmonia Orchestra cond. Stokowski	HMV LPm	ALP 1339
1957 3, 6, 13 June London	Tchaikovsky: *Sleeping Beauty* London Symphony Orchestra cond. Monteux	DEC LPs	ECS 575 STS 15179
1959 27 April Z/AR 25999/ 00	Ravel: *Daphnis et Chloé* Complete Ballet London Symphony Orchestra with Chorus of the Royal Opera House, Covent Garden cond. Monteux	DEC LPs	LXT 5536 SXL 2164 To CM 9028 CS 6147 ADD 170 STS 15090
1961 11 & 13 Dec London Z/AR 28836	Debussy: *Prélude à l'Après* *Midi d'un Faune* London Symphony Orchestra cond. Monteux	DEC LPs	LXT 5677 SXL 2312 CM 9317
1963 Dec London Z/AR 31818	Britten: *The Young Person's Guide to the* *Orchestra* London Symphony Orchestra cond. Britten	DEC LPs	LXT 6110 SXL 6110 CM 9398
1964 June London RCRM 6105 RCRM 6106	Living Strings Plus Harp The Melody Lingers On cond. Johnny Douglas	CAM LPm CAM LPs	CAL 847 CAS 847
1967	Goodnight Sweetheart Wally Stott's Orchestra and Chorus with David Snell	RCA LPs for Readers Digest	
1967	Mason: Minuet and Impromptu Mason: Nocturne for harp	STA 45s	St 21
1972 London	Homage to Pavlova Saint Saëns: *Carnival of the Animals* with Jascha Silberstein, cello	DEC LPs	SET 523-4
1972 London Chappell Studio	Music for Pleasure Max Jaffa and his Orchestra with Jean Grayston	INV LPs	103
1972	Music for the Kings and Queens of England *Greensleeves* arr. Longbord	CHA LPs	CBR 1006
1975 London	Birds in Music – The Swan Saint Saëns: *Carnival of the Animals* with Jascha Silberstein, cello	DEC LPs	SPA 367

491

1977 Oct London	Larry Adler Massenet: *Thaïs* – Meditation Debussy: *Clair de Lune* with Larry Adler and Orchestra cond. Douglas Ganly	PH4 LPs	PSS 4429
1977 London	Michael Krein: Serenade for oboe and two harps with Léon Goossens, oboe and Sidonie Goossens, harp	RCA LPs	RL 25142
1977 London	Morgan Nicholas: Melody, arr. Marie Goossens with Léon Goossens, oboe	RCA LPs	RL 25142
1978 London	Those Were the Days The London Concert Orchestra cond. Paul Fenhoulet	UA LPs	UAG 29739

Sidonie Goossens OBE – Harpist

The musical career of Sidonie Goossens is one of great stability and continuity in broadcasting orchestras. In her early career she recorded a few solo works and later on made records as Principal Harpist in the BBC Symphony Orchestra under a variety of conductors. The items selected here are representative of her artistry.

During her freelance days she also recorded under assumed names, Gwynneth Evans and Ena Diss, which is Sidonie, phonetically in reverse.

1923 London WA 3407	Thomas Moore: *Oft in the Stilly Night* Violin, flute and harp trio	COL 80a	1477R
1923 London WA 3410	Francis Thomé: *Simple Aveu* Violin, flute and harp trio	COL 80a	1477R
1923 London WA 2853	Balfe, arr. K A Wright: *Killarney* The Kneale Kelley Quartet Violin, flute, harp and organ	COL 80a	3973
1923 London WA 2854	Greene, arr. K A Wright: *Sing Me to Sleep* The Kneale Kelley Quartet Violin, flute, harp and organ	COL 80a	3973
1926 London CA 11487	Irish Air, arr. Cyril Scott: *Londonderry Air*	COL 78a	DB 565
1926 London CA 11490	Salzedo: *Whirlwind*	COL 78a	DB 565
1926 MB 1245 MB 1247	The Bells of Aberdovey arr. John Thomas *Watching the Wheat* Gwynneth Evans, harp	DEC 78	F1773

493

1927 29 June London WAX 2900- 2912	Tchaikovsky: *Nutcracker* Suite The Wireless Symphony Orchestra cond. Pitt	COL 78	9260 9261 9262
1927 London Bb 3942	Edward Macdowell: *Woodland Sketches* — To a Water-Lily	HMV 78	B1753
1927 London Bb 3943	Hamilton Harty: *Spring Fancies* No. 1	HMV 78	B1753
1927 London WA 8961	Russian Folk Tune, arr. C Salzedo: *Song of the Volga Boatmen*	COL 78	5436
1927 London CAX 7666	Schubert, arr. Wilhelmj: *Ave Marie* with William Primrose, viola	COL 78	DX 720
1927 London CAX 7667	Irish Air, arr. Hughes: *Londonderry Air* with William Primrose, viola	COL 78	DX 720
1927 London Bb 3941-III	Rutland Boughton: *The Immortal Hour* — Faery Song with Harold Farrar, tenor	HMV 78	B1759
1927 WA 8960	Handel, arr. C Salzedo: *Xerxes* — Largo	COL 78	5436
1931 22 April London CA 11488-2	*The Harmonious Blacksmith*	COL 78	Unpub
1931 22 April London CA 11489-1	*Danza Andaluza*	COL 78	Unpub
1932 London BB 144-1	Goossens: Ballad No. 2	BB 78	207
1932 London BB 145-2	Tournier: *Jazz Band*	BB 78	207
1937 24 March Abbey Road Studio No. 1 2EA 4697 2EA 4700	Elgar: *Sospiri* BBC Symphony Orchestra cond. Boult	HMV 78 ELG LPm	DB 3199 ELG 001

1938 15 Oct Abbey Road Studio No. 1 CAX 8367-70	Vaughan-Williams: *Serenade to Music* BBC Symphony Orchestra cond. Wood	COL 78 45m 45m DUT CD	SED 5553 7 TCA 840 7 TCA 841 CDAX 8004
1945 2 & 5 Jan Bedford Corn Exchange ZEA 10348/49 ZEA 10350/59 ZEA 10360	Holst: *The Planets* BBC Symphony Orchestra cond. Boult	HMV 78	DB 6227, 8, 9 6230, 1, 2, 3
1956 27 July	Britten: *The Young Person's Guide to the Orchestra* BBC Symphony Orchestra cond. Sargent	HMV LPs	ALP 1101 SXLP 30114 BSD 754
1956 27 August Kingsway Hall 2 XEA 1119 2 XEA 1120	Sibelius: Symphony No. 1 in E minor Op. 39 BBC Symphony Orchestra cond. Sargent	HMV LPs CD	ALP 1542 ASD 260 MST 2018 CFP 132 CDM 7630 942
1964 7 TEA 1996-15	Solo Instruments of the Orchestra No. 6 Prokofiev: Prelude Op. 12 No. 7 Granados, arr. Bruno – *Andaluza*	EMI 45m	7EP 7183
1964 7 TEA 1996-15	Solo Instruments of the Orchestra No. 6 Goossens: Ballade No. 1 Albeniz, arr. Bruno: *Memories of a Journey –* Malaguena	EMI 45m	7ED 7183
1977 London	Michael Krein: Serenade for Oboe & Two Harps with Léon Goossens, oboe and Marie Goossens, harp	RCA LPs	RL 25142
1979 October Maida Vale Studio No. 1	Tchaikovsky: *Sleeping Beauty* (complete) BBC Symphony Orchestra cond. Rozhdestvensky	BBC LPs TCs CDs LPs	3001 ZC 3001 CD 300 3 ED 300 572- 4
1979 5215-4X 5216-4X	William Alwyn: Concerto for Harp and String Orchestra London Philharmonic Orchestra cond. Alwyn	LYR LPs	SRCS 108
1979	Vaughan-Williams, arr. Chiarelli: Fantasia on *Greensleeves* with Léon Goossens	UNI LPs	MS 1000

INDEX

497

Index

Index

505

Index

515

Index